Personal Privacy in an Information Society

The Report of
The Privacy Protection Study Commission

July 1977

For sale by the Superintendent of Documents, U.S. Government Printing Office
Washington, D.C. 20402
Stock No. 052-003-00395-3

PRIVACY PROTECTION STUDY COMMISSION
2120 L Street, NW.
Washington, D.C. 20506

David F. Linowes, Chairman

Willis H. Ware, Vice Chairman

William O. Bailey
William B. Dickinson
Hon. Barry M. Goldwater, Jr.
Hon. Edward I. Koch
Robert J. Tennessen

Carole W. Parsons
Executive Director

Ronald L. Plesser
General Counsel

July 12, 1977

President Jimmy Carter
The White House
Washington, D.C. 20500

Dear Mr. President:

I am pleased to transmit to you the Final Report of the Privacy Protection Study Commission.

Created by the Privacy Act of 1974, the Commission has devoted the past two years to examining individual privacy rights and record-keeping practices in many environments. Although the private sector has been emphasized in our inquiry, we also attempted to assess the effectiveness of protections for personal privacy in the public sector, including the Privacy Act of 1974 as it applies to the Federal government.

In our efforts, we have sought to examine and balance the interests of individuals, record-keeping institutions, and society as a whole. We believe that this report of findings and recommendations could serve to strengthen this balance, while giving particular attention to the individual's role in controlling information about himself in a democratic society. If adopted, we believe these recommendations which are designed to safeguard a person's right to be fairly treated and to be spared unwarranted intrusion would buttress a vital human right of every American -- his right to personal privacy.

For all of us, participation in the work of the Commission has been a challenging and stimulating opportunity to serve our Nation. We appreciate having this privilege.

Respectfully submitted,

David F. Linowes
Chairman

PRIVACY PROTECTION STUDY COMMISSION
2120 L Street, NW.
Washington, D.C.   20506

David F. Linowes, Chairman

Willis H. Ware, Vice Chairman

William O. Bailey
William B. Dickinson
Hon. Barry M. Goldwater, Jr.
Hon. Edward I. Koch
Robert J. Tennessen

Carole W. Parsons
Executive Director
Ronald L. Plesser
General Counsel

July 12, 1977

The Honorable Walter F. Mondale
President of the Senate
Room S-212
The Capitol
Washington, D.C. 20510

Dear Mr. President:

I am pleased to transmit to you the Final Report of the Privacy
Protection Study Commission.

Created by the Privacy Act of 1974, the Commission has devoted the
past two years to examining individual privacy rights and record-keeping
practices in many environments. Although the private sector has been
emphasized in our inquiry, we also attempted to assess the effectiveness
of protections for personal privacy in the public sector, including the
Privacy Act of 1974 as it applies to the Federal government.

In our efforts, we have sought to examine and balance the interests
of individuals, record-keeping institutions, and society as a whole. We
believe that this report of findings and recommendations could serve to
strengthen this balance, while giving particular attention to the
individual's role in controlling information about himself in a
democratic society. If adopted, we believe these recommendations which
are designed to safeguard a person's right to be fairly treated and to
be spared unwarranted intrusion would buttress a vital human right of
every American--his right to personal privacy.

For all of us, participation in the work of the Commission has
been a challenging and stimulating opportunity to serve our Nation. We
appreciate having this privilege.

Respectfully submitted,

David F. Linowes
Chairman

PRIVACY PROTECTION STUDY COMMISSION
2120 L Street, NW.
Washington, D.C. 20506

David F. Linowes, Chairman

Willis H. Ware, Vice Chairman

William O. Bailey
William B. Dickinson
Hon. Barry M. Goldwater, Jr.
Hon. Edward I. Koch
Robert J. Tennessen

Carole W. Parsons
Executive Director

Ronald L. Plesser
General Counsel

July 12, 1977

The Honorable Thomas P. O'Neill, Jr.
Speaker of the House of Representatives
Room H-202
The Capitol
Washington, D.C. 20515

Dear Mr. Speaker:

I am pleased to transmit to you the Final Report of the Privacy Protection Study Commission.

Created by the Privacy Act of 1974, the Commission has devoted the past two years to examining individual privacy rights and record-keeping practices in many environments. Although the private sector has been emphasized in our inquiry, we also attempted to assess the effectiveness of protections for personal privacy in the public sector, including the Privacy Act of 1974 as it applies to the Federal government.

In our efforts, we have sought to examine and balance the interests of individuals, record-keeping institutions, and society as a whole. We believe that this report of findings and recommendations could serve to strengthen this balance, while giving particular attention to the individual's role in controlling information about himself in a democratic society. If adopted, we believe these recommendations which are designed to safeguard a person's right to be fairly treated and to be spared unwarranted intrusion would buttress a vital human right of every American--his right to personal privacy.

For all of us, participation in the work of the Commission has been a challenging and stimulating opportunity to serve our Nation. We appreciate having this privilege.

Respectfully submitted,

David F. Linowes
Chairman

PRIVACY PROTECTION STUDY COMMISSION

Chairman

David F. Linowes
Certified Public Accountant, New York City, and
Boeschenstein Professor of Political Economy
and Public Policy, University of Illinois

Vice Chairman

Dr. Willis H. Ware
The Rand Corporation
Santa Monica, California

William O. Bailey, President
Aetna Life & Casualty Company
Hartford, Connecticut

William B. Dickinson
Retired Managing Editor,
Philadelphia Evening Bulletin
Philadelphia, Pennsylvania

Congressman Barry M. Goldwater, Jr. of California
Washington, D. C.

Congressman Edward I. Koch of New York
Washington, D. C.

State Senator Robert J. Tennessen, Attorney
Grose, Von Holtum, Von Holtum, Sieben & Schmidt
Minneapolis, Minnesota

PRIVACY PROTECTION STUDY COMMISSION — STAFF

Carole W. Parsons
Executive Director

Ronald L. Plesser
General Counsel

Louis D. Higgs
Deputy Executive Director and Director of Research

Office of the Executive Director

Susan J. Bennett, *Special Assistant*
Arthur A. Bushkin, *Staff Technical Advisor*
Commander Walter E. Conner,[1] *Administrative Officer*
Pamela S. Ellsworth, *Administrative Assistant*
Mark F. Ferber, *Special Consultant to the Executive Director*
Christopher E. Heller, *Senior Research Associate*
Justine V. R. Milliken, *Assistant to the Chairman*
James F. Sasser,[2] *Administrative Officer* (September 1975 to February 1977)
Alan F. Westin, *Special Consultant to the Commission*

Office of the General Counsel

Christopher J. Vizas, II, *Special Staff Counsel*
John A. Turner, Jr., *Assistant General Counsel*
Stephen C. Nichols, *Assistant to the General Counsel*
Shirley A. Lewi, *Administrative Assistant*

Office of Public Information

Mark F. Ferber, *Director*
John F. Barker, *Director* (September 1975 to April 1977)
Eleanor B. High, *Assistant*

Project Management

Lois Alexander,[3] *Research and Statistics*
Susan J. Bennett, *Public Assistance, IRS, Social Security Number*
Arthur A. Bushkin, *Privacy Act Assessment, Technology Assessment*
William H. Foskett, *Education*
Christopher E. Heller, *Credit, Credit-Reporting, and Depository Institutions*
Joan Holloway,[4] *Medical Records*
David M. Klaus, *Investigative Agencies*
Christopher J. Vizas, II, *Government Access*
Jane H. Yurow, *Employment and Personnel*

---

[1] On detail from the Department of Defense.
[2] On detail from the Department of Health, Education, and Welfare (DHEW).
[3] On detail from the Social Security Administration, DHEW.
[4] On detail from the Division of Hospitals and Clinics, U.S. Public Health Service.

Professional Staff and Consultants

Arthur J. Altenberg
Donald Bartlett
Joan Berry
Timothy B. Braithwaite[5]
Joe S. Cecil
Nancy H. Chasen
Claire Dalton
Warren O. Davis[6]
Priscilla DeGasparis
Major William R. Elliott, Jr.[5]
David Galbraith
Timothy Gay
Charles Grezlak
Charles Gustafson
Claudia R. Higgins
Florence B. Isbell
Mary Kay Kane
William R. Klamon
Charles R. Knerr
John Langton, III
Donald Letourneau
Abe Levin
Michael Liethan

Daniel H. Lufkin
Kenneth E. Mannella
Ruth Matthews
Justine V. R. Milliken
Hubert A. Mitchell
William B. McMahon
Margaret A. Neel
David Nierenberg
G. Russell Pipe
Bruce Ransome
Ira Reed
James B. Rule
Francis M. Rush, Jr.[5]
Cynthia E. Schaffhausen
Arden Schell
Harold D. Skipper
Joyce R. Starr
J. Michael Taylor[7]
Patricia Tucker
Rein Turn
Philip Vargas
Alease M. Vaughn
Fred W. Weingarten[8]

Administrative Staff

Phyllis R. Anderson
A. Kristen Austin
Zemphria Raymond Baskin
Mary K. Chin
Alice Cumberland
Louise Goldstein
Debbie J. Graham
Emily Hanis
Lori J. Haselhorst

Jeanne L. Holmberg
Fran Hoyle
Susan Kaslow
Alan C. Luckett
Nancy Mathes
Nina A. Mohay
Joanne Robinson
Mary Scott

Research Assistants

Phyllis R. Anderson
Zemphria Raymond Baskin
Laura Bonn
Vernease Herron
Brenda Reddix

Catherine J. Rodgers
Adrienne Taylor
Roger S. Tilton
Helene Toiv
Michael S. Turchin

[5] On detail from the Department of Defense.
[6] On detail from the Bureau of the Census.
[7] On detail from the Department of Labor.
[8] On detail from the National Science Foundation.

Contents

Preface xv

Chapter

1 Introduction 3

2 The Consumer-Credit Relationship 41

3 The Depository Relationship 101

4 Mailing Lists 125

5 The Insurance Relationship 155

6 The Employment Relationship 223

7 Record Keeping in the Medical-Care Relationship 277

8 Investigative-Reporting Agencies 319

9 Government Access to Personal Records and "Private Papers" ... 345

10 Record Keeping in the Education Relationship 393

11 The Citizen as Beneficiary of Government Assistance 445

12 The State Role in Privacy Protection 487

13 The Relationship Between Citizen and Government:
   The Privacy Act of 1974 497

14 The Relationship Between Citizen and Government:
   The Citizen as Taxpayer 537

15 The Relationship Between Citizen and Government:
   The Citizen as Participant in Research and Statistical Studies 567

16 The Social Security Number 605

Epilogue 619

Appendix: Hearings of the Privacy Protection Study Commission 621

Index 639

Preface

Issues of public policy rarely, if ever, emerge on the political scene fully developed and fully articulated. Rather, they result from gradual changes in the social and economic environment, which are then identified and intensively debated. This has been the pattern with the subject of this report. The relationships between individuals and various record-keeping organizations have been developing over a long period of time. An analysis of these relationships and their consequences for personal privacy lie at the heart of the findings and recommendations in this report.

In seeking to address the privacy issue as it emerges in a variety of settings, the Commission has constantly sought to examine the balance between the legitimate, sometimes competing, interests of the individual, the record-keeping organization, and society in general. Each of these interests has been weighed carefully, and, the Commission believes, given fair and forthright treatment.

While broad principles did emerge as our investigations proceeded, for our report we decided not to center our recommendations on an omnibus approach. We concentrated, instead, on recommendations for the specific record-keeping relationships that characterize each of the areas we studied. It was clear to the Commission that historic development and current realities required each area to be dealt with separately.

The Commission's work, we hope, will contribute to a growing public awareness and increased dialogue about the various dimensions of personal privacy. To the extent that some awareness and dialogue have occurred already as the result of our extensive hearings schedule, we are pleased.

The Privacy Protection Study Commission was directed by the Congress, to make a "study of the data banks, automatic data processing programs, and information systems of governmental, regional, and private organizations, in order to determine the standards and procedures in force for the protection of personal information." On the basis of this study the Commission was also asked to recommend to the President and the Congress the extent, if any, to which the principles and requirements of the Privacy Act of 1974 should be applied to organizations other than agencies of the Federal Executive branch and to make such other legislative recommendations as the Commission deems necessary to protect the privacy of individuals while meeting the legitimate needs of government and society for information. This report is the Commission's response to that mandate.

Our general mandate was supplemented with some specific instructions. We were directed to report to the President and to the Congress on:

•whether a person engaged in interstate commerce who maintains a mailing list should be required to remove the name and address of any individual who does not want to be on it;

•whether the Internal Revenue Service should be prohibited from transferring individually identifiable data to other Federal agencies and to agencies of State governments;

•whether an individual who has been harmed as a consequence of a willful or intentional violation of the Privacy Act of 1974 should be able to sue the Federal government for general damages;

•whether—and, if yes, in what way—the standards for security and confidentiality of records that the Privacy Act requires Federal agencies to adopt should be applied when a record is disclosed to a person other than an agency; and

•whether, and to what extent, governmental and private information systems affect Federal-State relations and the principle of separation of powers.

The first two areas are treated in Chapters 4 and 14, respectively. The question of whether the Privacy Act standard of damages should be expanded to general damages is set forth in Chapter 13. That chapter also discusses the issue of extending the standards for security and confidentiality.

On the complex question of Federal-State relations and the separation of powers, the Commission recognizes that these Constitutional principles are also the basis on which all of our recommendations had to be made. Chapter 12 addresses this subject. It should be noted that each of the recommendations in the other chapters are also framed within our perception of their Constitutional implications. Thus, while many of the recommendations call for Federal action, others are specifically directed to policy makers at the State and local levels of government.

Throughout the two years it has been at work, the Commission has made every effort to assure maximum participation by those most likely to be affected by our recommmedations. Sixty days of hearings and meetings were held, during which over 300 witnesses testified. After the initial adoption of particular recommendations, they were released for public comment. The observations we received were taken into account in making our final recommendations.

In its Privacy Act evaluation, the Commission had extensive communications with Federal agencies and held discussion workshops with them. Also, together with the Domestic Council's Committee on the Right of Privacy, we conducted a conference in which many officials from a number of States came together to discuss the application of the principles and requirements of the Privacy Act of 1974 to State and local governments.

Countless individuals and organizations from the public and private sectors gave generously of their time in order to assist us in our efforts. Space does not permit an individual listing of each of them, but the report is liberally sprinkled with references to many of those to whom we owe our appreciation. I would be remiss, however, if I did not offer special thanks to Messers. Thomas S. McFee, John P. Fanning, and Edward Gleiman of the Department of Health, Education, and Welfare; and to Mr. William T. Cavaney of the Department of Defense. In addition to arranging for several individuals of outstanding quality and dedication to be available to the Commission for periods of time, they also continually evidenced keen interest and encouragement for the Commission's work. We are also in debt to the Chairmen, Members, and staffs of the Senate and House Government Operations Committees who continually supported the Commission in matters concerning its tenure and funding.

No work of this scope could have been completed without the wholehearted day-to-day cooperation of many people. To each of the Commissioners, I extend my deep gratitude for his constant dedication to the demanding schedule of hearings and meetings. Each diligently applied his particular professional expertise to the frequent, and often lengthy, sessions on the varied subject areas we covered.

Our staff performed with unusual devotion in what proved to be a most intensive and difficult effort. Their labor was marked by ongoing, exhaustive searches for all sides of the issues the Commission examined. My sincere appreciation to each of them.

David F. Linowes
Chairman

Personal Privacy in an Information Society

Chapter 1

Introduction

This report is about records and people. It looks toward a national policy to guide the way public and private organizations treat the records they keep about individuals. Its findings reflect the fact that in American society today records mediate relationships between individuals and organizations and thus affect an individual more easily, more broadly, and often more unfairly than was possible in the past. This is true in spite of almost a decade of effort to frame the objectives of a national policy to protect personal privacy in an information-dependent society. It will remain true unless steps are taken soon to strike a proper balance between the individual's personal privacy interests and society's information needs. In this report, the Privacy Protection Study Commission identifies the steps necessary to strike that balance and presents the Commission's specific recommendations for achieving it. This introductory chapter briefly describes the problem and focuses and defines the objectives of a national policy. It also weighs major competing values and interests and explains how the Commission believes its policy recommendations should be implemented.

RECORD KEEPING AND PERSONAL PRIVACY

One need only glance at the dramatic changes in our country during the last hundred years to understand why the relationship between organizational record keeping and personal privacy has become an issue in almost all modern societies. The records of a hundred years ago tell little about the average American, except when he died, perhaps when and where he was born, and if he owned land, how he got his title to it. Three quarters of the adult population worked for themselves on farms or in small towns. Attendance at the village schoolhouse was not compulsory and only a tiny fraction pursued formal education beyond it. No national military service was required, and few programs brought individuals into contact with the Federal government. Local governments to be sure made decisions about individuals, but these mainly had to do with taxation, business promotion and regulation, prevention and prosecution of crime, and in some instances, public relief for the poor or the insane.

Record keeping about individuals was correspondingly limited and local in nature. The most complete record was probably kept by churches, who recorded births, baptisms, marriages, and deaths. Town officials and county courts kept records of similar activities. Merchants and bankers maintained financial accounts for their customers, and when they extended credit, it was on the basis of personal knowledge of the borrower's circumstances. Few individuals had insurance of any kind, and a patient's medical record very likely existed only in the doctor's memory. Records about individuals rarely circulated beyond the place they were made.

The past hundred years, and particularly the last three decades, have changed all that. Three out of four Americans now live in cities or their surrounding suburbs, only one in ten of the individuals in the workforce today is self-employed, and education is compulsory for every child. The yeoman farmer and small-town merchant have given way to the skilled workers and white-collar employees who manage and staff the organizations, both public and private, that keep society functioning.

In addition, most Americans now do at least some of their buying on credit, and most have some form of life, health, property, or liability insurance. Institutionalized medical care is almost universally available. Government social services programs now reach deep into the population along with government licensing of occupations and professions, Federal taxation of individuals, and government regulation of business and labor union affairs. Today, government regulates and supports large areas of economic and social life through some of the nation's largest bureaucratic organizations, many of which deal directly with individuals. In fact, many of the private-sector record-keeping relationships discussed in this report are to varying degrees replicated in programs administered or funded by Federal agencies.

A significant consequence of this marked change in the variety and concentration of institutional relationships with individuals is that record keeping about individuals now covers almost everyone and influences everyone's life, from the business executive applying for a personal loan to the school teacher applying for a national credit card, from the riveter seeking check-guarantee privileges from the local bank to the young married couple trying to finance furniture for its first home. All will have their creditworthiness evaluated on the basis of recorded information in the files of one or more organizations. So also with insurance, medical care, employment, education, and social services. Each of those relationships requires the individual to divulge information about himself, and usually leads to some evaluation of him based on information about him that some other record keeper has compiled.

The substitution of records for face-to-face contact in these relationships is what makes the situation today dramatically different from the way it was even as recently as 30 years ago. It is now commonplace for an individual to be asked to divulge information about himself for use by unseen strangers who make decisions about him that directly affect his everyday life. Furthermore, because so many of the services offered by organizations are, or have come to be considered, necessities, an individual has little choice but to submit to whatever demands for information about him an organization may make. Organizations must have some substitute for personal evaluation in order to distinguish between one individual and the next in the endless stream of otherwise anonymous individuals they deal with, and most organizations have come to rely on records as that substitute.

It is important to note, moreover, that organizations increasingly desire information that will facilitate fine-grained decisions about individuals. A credit-card issuer wants to avoid people who do not pay their bills, but it also strives to identify slow payers and well intentioned people who could easily get into debt beyond their ability to repay. Insurance companies seek to avoid people whose reputation or life style suggest that they may have more than the average number of accidents or other types of losses. Employers look for job applicants who give promise of being healthy, productive members of a work force. Social services agencies must sort individuals according to legally established eligibility criteria, but also try to see that people in need take advantage of all the services available to them. Schools try to take "the whole child" into account in making decisions about his progress, and government authorities make increasingly detailed evaluations of an individual's tax liability.

Each individual plays a dual role in this connection—as an object of information gathering and as a consumer of the benefits and services that depend on it. Public opinion data suggest that most Americans treasure their personal privacy, both in the abstract and in their own daily lives, but individuals are clearly also willing to give information about themselves, or allow others to do so, when they can see a concrete benefit to be gained by it. Most of us are pleased to have the conveniences that fine-grained, record-based decisions about us make possible. It is the rare individual who will forego having a credit card because he knows that if he has one, details about his use of it will accumulate in the card issuer's files.

Often one also hears people assert that nobody minds organizational record-keeping practices "if you have nothing to hide," and many apparently like to think of themselves as having nothing to hide, not realizing that whether an individual does or not can be a matter of opinion. We live, inescapably, in an "information society," and few of us have the option of avoiding relationships with record-keeping organizations. To do so is to forego not only credit but also insurance, employment, medical care, education, and all forms of government services to individuals. This being so, each individual has, or should have, a concern that the records organizations make and keep about him do not lead to unfair decisions about him.

In a larger context, Americans must also be concerned about the long-term effect record-keeping practices can have not only on relationships between individuals and organizations, but also on the balance of power between government and the rest of society. Accumulations of information about individuals tend to enhance authority by making it easier for authority to reach individuals directly. Thus, growth in society's record-keeping capability poses the risk that existing power balances will be upset. Recent events illustrate how easily this can happen, and also how difficult it can be to preserve such balances once they are seriously threatened.

This report concentrates on the delicate balance between various types of organizations' need for information about individuals and each individual's desire to be secure and fairly treated. It also recognizes, however, that government's expanding role as regulator and distributor of largess gives it new ways to intrude, creating new privacy protection problems. By opening more avenues for collecting information and more decision-making forums in which it can employ that information, government has enormously broadened its opportunities both to help and to embarrass, harass, and injure the individual. These new avenues and needs for collecting information, particularly when coupled with modern information technology, multiply the dangers of official abuse against which the Constitution seeks to protect. Recent history reminds us that these are real, not mythical, dangers and that while our efforts to protect ourselves against them must ultimately be fashioned into law, the choices they require are not mere legal choices; they are social and political value choices of the most basic kind.

THE FRAMEWORK FOR A NATIONAL POLICY

The imbalance in the relationship between individuals and record-keeping institutions today is pointedly illustrated by the experiences of Catherine Tarver, a "welfare mother" from the State of Washington, and Mitchell Miller, a businessman from Kathleen, Georgia.

In the late 1960's Mrs. Tarver became ill and was hospitalized. The Juvenile Court, after reviewing a report by her caseworker which contained "assertedly derogatory contents," including an allegation of child neglect, placed her children temporarily in the custody of the Department of Public Assistance. A few months later, the Juvenile Court, after another hearing, exonerated Mrs. Tarver and returned her children to her, but the caseworker's report remained in her file at the Department of Public Assistance.

Although Mrs. Tarver had her children back and was no longer on the welfare rolls, she still wanted to have the caseworker's report removed from her file on the grounds that it was false, misleading, and prejudicial and would be available to other State social services agencies with whom she might subsequently have contact. When she asked for a fair hearing[1] to challenge the report, the Public Assistance Department rejected her request because the grievance was not directly related to eligibility for public assistance. She sued in a State court but lost, the court agreeing with the welfare agency that the fair hearing procedure was not meant to deal with collateral problems. The U.S. Supreme Court refused to review her case and the caseworker's report remained in her file.

Mitchell Miller's difficulties began on December 18, 1972, when a deputy sheriff from Houston County, Georgia, stopped a Pepsico truck purportedly owned by Miller and found it was transporting 150 five-gallon plastic jugs, two 100-pound bags of wheat shorts, cylinders of bottled gas, and a shotgun condenser. Less than a month later, while fighting a warehouse fire, the sheriff and fire department officials found a 7,500 gallon distillery and 175 gallons of untaxed whiskey. An agent from the U. S. Treasury Department's Bureau of Alcohol, Tobacco and Firearms suspect-

---

[1] For a discussion of the fair hearing procedures, see Chapter 11.

ed Miller of direct involvement in both events and two weeks later presented grand jury subpoenas to the two banks where Miller maintained accounts. Without notifying Miller, copies of his checks and bank statements were either shown or given to the Treasury agents as soon as they presented the subpoenas. The subpoenas did not require immediate disclosure, but the bank officers nonetheless responded at once.

After he had been indicted, Miller attempted to persuade the court that the grand jury subpoenas used by the Treasury Department were invalid and, thus, the evidence obtained with them could not be used against him. He pointed out that the subpoenas had not been issued by the grand jury itself, and further, that they were returnable on a day when the grand jury was not in session. Finally, Miller argued that the Bank Secrecy Act's requirement that banks maintain microfilm copies of checks for two years[2] was an unconstitutional invasion of his Fourth Amendment rights. The trial court rejected Miller's arguments and he appealed.

The Fifth Circuit Court of Appeals also rejected Miller's claim that the Bank Secrecy Act was unconstitutional, an issue that had already been resolved by the U.S. Supreme Court in 1974.[3] The Court of Appeals agreed, however, that Miller's rights, as well as the bank's, were threatened and that he should be accorded the right to legal process to challenge the validity of the grand jury subpoenas. The Court of Appeals saw Miller's interest in the bank's records as deriving from the Fourth Amendment protection against unreasonable searches and seizures which protected him against "compulsory production of a man's private papers to establish a criminal charge against him."

On April 21, 1976, a fateful day for personal privacy, the U.S. Supreme Court decided that Mitchell Miller had no legitimate "expectation of privacy" in his bank records and thus no protectible interest for the Court to consider. The Court reasoned that because checks are an independent record of an individual's participation in the flow of commerce, they cannot be considered confidential communications. The account record, moreover, is the property of the bank, not of the individual account holder. Thus, according to the Court, Miller's expectation of privacy was neither legitimate, warranted, nor enforceable.

The *Tarver* and *Miller* decisions[4] are the law of the land, and the Commission takes no issue with their legal correctness. Viewed from one perspective, these cases are very narrow and affect only a minute percentage of the population. *Tarver* might be seen as simply refusing an additional request from a welfare mother who had received the benefits she was entitled to under a program; *Miller* as a decision affecting only the technical procedural rights of a criminal defendant. Perhaps these two cases are not very compelling, but the Commission singles them out because each starkly underscores an individual's present defenselessness with respect to records maintained about him. Who is there to raise such issues if not people in

---

[2] *Bank Secrecy Act*, 12 U.S.C. 1829b, 1953; 12 C.F.R. §103.36.
[3] *California Bankers Association v. Schultz*, 416 U.S. 21 (1975).
[4] *State ex rel. Tarver v. Smith* 78 Wash. 2d 152, 470 P.2d 172, *cert. denied*, 402 U.S. 1001 (1971); *United States v. Miller*, 425 U.S. 435 (1976).

trouble? They are the ones who reach for and test the limits of existing legal protections, and if the protections are not there for them, they will not be there for anyone.

In both cases, institutional policies and the legal system failed individuals in their efforts to limit the impact of records on their lives. The *Tarver* case warns that one may be able to do nothing about a damaging record, not even if it is false, until some adverse action is taken on the basis of it; that one has no way to prevent the damage such an action can do. The *Miller* decision goes even further, making records the property solely of the record keeper, so that the individual cannot assert any interest in them, although his interest would be assertible if he himself held the same records. Even worse, it warns that not only a "revenuer" but anyone, public or private, can gain access to an individual's bank records if the bank agrees to disclose them.

Each case illustrates systemic flaws in the existing means available to any individual who tries to protect himself against the untoward consequences of organizational record keeping. Together they strongly suggest that if Americans still value personal privacy, they must make certain changes in the way records about individuals are made, used, and disclosed.

Since so much of an individual's life is now shaped by his relationships with organizations, his interest in the records organizations keep about him is obvious and compelling. The above cases and the rest of this report show how poorly that interest is protected. If it is to be protected, public policy must focus on five systemic features of personal-data record keeping in America today.

> *First,* while an organization makes and keeps records about individuals to facilitate relationships with them, it also makes and keeps records about individuals for other purposes, such as documenting the record-keeping organization's own actions and making it possible for other organizations—government agencies, for example—to monitor the actions of individuals.

> *Second,* there is an accelerating trend, most obvious in the credit and financial areas, toward the accumulation in records of more and more personal details about an individual.

> *Third,* more and more records about an individual are collected, maintained, and disclosed by organizations with which the individual has no direct relationship but whose records help to shape his life.

> *Fourth,* most record-keeping organizations consult the records of other organizations to verify the information they obtain from an individual and thus pay as much or more attention to what other organizations report about him than they pay to what he reports about himself; and

> *Fifth,* neither law nor technology now gives an individual the tools he needs to protect his legitimate interests in the records organizations keep about him.

The topical chapters that follow document the importance of these five systemic characteristics of personal-data record keeping in America today and present the Commission's recommended approach to solving the problems they create. The Commission believes that by focusing on these five characteristics constructive solutions to most of the record-related privacy protection problems that confront American society today and in the foreseeable future can be found.

The first characteristic—the fact that an organization may use its records about individuals in accounting for its operations to other centers of power and authority in society—has important implications for any policy of record-keeping regulation. It prompts caution in considering prohibitions on the collection of items of information from or about individuals, but at the same time draws attention to the need for special safeguards when requiring an organization to record any information about an individual that it does not need to facilitate its own relationship with him.

The second systemic characteristic—the accumulation in records of more and more personal details—is clearly visible in some of an individual's credit and financial relationships. It will become even more apparent as electronic funds transfer systems mature. This accumulation, moreover, is not the result of more and more people being asked more and more questions, but rather reflects the need and capacity of a particular type of record-keeping organization to monitor and control transactions with its individual customers. As the Commission points out in Chapter 3, it is now perilously easy for such a build-up, however innocently practical the purpose, to crystallize into a personal profile of an individual. The possession of such profiles invites the use of them for marketing, research, and law enforcement, and, in an electronic funds transfer environment, could provide a way of tracking an individual's current movements. The dramatic shift in the balance of power between government and the rest of society that such a development could portend has persuaded the Commission of the compelling need to single it out for special public-policy attention and action.

The third systemic characteristic—the attenuation of an individual's relationships with record-keeping organizations when information generated in a direct relationship is recorded in the files of other organizations that have no direct relationship with him—lies at the core of the recommendations in this report. The Commission finds that most organizations that keep records about individuals fall into one of three categories: (1) the primary record keeper (such as a credit grantor, insurer, or social services agency) that has a direct relationship with the individual; (2) support organizations whose sole sources of information are the primary record keepers they serve; and (3) support organizations (usually of an investigative character) that have independent sources of information. While this typology does not fit all cases—credit bureaus, for example, supplement the information they receive from credit grantors with information they search out from public records— it can serve as a guide in apportioning responsibilities among record-keeping institutions.

The fourth characteristic—that a primary record keeper normally verifies the information about himself an individual provides it, and tends to lean as much or more on the verification information it gets from other organizations than on what the individual divulges about himself—gives rise to some of the most difficult privacy protection issues. As records progessively displace face-to-face acquaintance, individuals are more and more driven to permit information in records about them to be disclosed as a condition of receiving services and benefits. For example, an individual who wants a credit card usually cannot have one unless he is willing to permit information about his credit usage to be disclosed regularly to credit bureaus, and through them to other credit grantors. An individual who applies for life insurance must agree to allow medical information about him to be disclosed to the Medical Information Bureau, and through the Bureau to later inquiring life and health insurers. An individual must now allow information to be disclosed from his medical records for a growing number of purposes even though the medical-care relationship requires him to divulge the most intimate details of his life and undergo the most intimate observation.

The sharing of information among record-keeping organizations also transmits the stigma that goes with some kinds of information. One's own physician, for example, may heartily approve of taking a minor or temporary problem to a psychiatrist, but the potential consequences of disclosing the mere fact that one has had psychiatric treatment are too well known to need description. Equally serious for some individuals are the consequences of disclosing arrest records, military discharge codes, and previous adverse insurance decisions, and the simple fact that a number of credit grantors asked for credit reports on a particular individual during a short span of time can adversely affect an evaluation of his credit worthiness. Such problems stem in part from the tendency of organizations to accept at face value information they get about individuals from other organizations. Questions are seldom asked about the social or bureaucratic processes by which the information came to be in the other organization's records, so that unwarranted assumptions can easily be made about its value. For the individual, of course, such an unwarranted assumption can start a progression of fortuitous events that may permanently deprive him of opportunities he deserves, or make it impossible for him to escape a particular line of inquiry whenever he seeks to establish a relationship with another organization.

The fifth and last characteristic—that neither law nor technology gives an individual the tools he needs to protect himself from the undeserved difficulties a record can create for him—may also leave him helpless to stop damage once it has started. Current law is neither strong enough nor specific enough to solve the problems that now exist. In some cases, changes in record-keeping practice have already made even recent legal protections obsolete. As record-keeping systems come to be used to preclude action by the individual, a recent trend in the credit and financial areas, it is important that the individual also be given preventive protections to supplement the after-the-fact protections he sometimes has today. The fact that Fair Credit Reporting Act procedures will enable him to get errors in the record corrected can be small and bitter comfort to a traveler stranded in a strange city late at night because information about his credit-card account status was inaccurately reported to an independent authorization service. He would undoubtedly prefer a procedure that would enable him to get an error corrected *before* it entered into an adverse decision about him, and so would most everyone if he stopped and thought about it.

The Commission also found numerous examples of situations in which decisions or judgments made on the basis of a record about an individual can matter to the individual very much but in which he has no substantive or procedural protection at all. The law as it now stands simply ignores the strong interest many people have in records about them—applicants to graduate and professional schools, people being considered for jobs or promotions for which they have not formally applied, patients whose records are subpoenaed as evidence in court cases that do not involve them directly, proprietors of small businesses who are the subjects of commercial-credit investigations, and individuals who are the subjects of Federal agency records the agency retrieves and uses by reference to some characteristic of the individual other than his name or an assigned identifying particular.

Paralleling the categories of *individuals* without protection under current law, there are categories of *records* that are subject to existing legal requirements if they are created by one particular type of organization, but not if they are created by any other type of organization, although the record and its purpose may be the same in all cases. For example, an investigative report is subject to restrictions if it was prepared by an investigative agency, but not if it was prepared by an insurance company or employer.

The Commission also found that whether a record is subject to existing law can depend on the *technique* by which it is generated or retrieved. For example, how does the Equal Credit Opportunity Act, a law drawn on the assumption that credit decisions turn on one or two particular items of information about the applicant, apply when a credit grantor uses "point scoring," a new method of evaluating credit applicants which submerges all the particular items of information about the applicant into one overall score?

The prescreening of mailing lists[5] is another record-keeping technique that muddies the assumptions underlying existing legal protections. If a mailing list is to be used by a credit grantor to solicit new customers but is first run through an automated credit bureau where an individual's name is deleted from the list because his credit bureau records are in error as to the promptness with which he pays his bills, has he been subjected to an adverse credit decision? The law is currently unclear.

The role that technique can play in determining whether a particular type of record or record-keeping operation is or is not within the scope of existing legal protections is comparatively new. It arises in the main from automation, which multiplies the uses that can be made of a record about an individual, and will grow in importance as new record-keeping applications of computer and telecommunications technology are developed. Computers

---

[5] See Chapter 4.

and telecommunications serve the interests of institutions and can be best appreciated as extensions of those interests, as subsequent chapters suggest. The failure to recognize that relationship has deflected attention from the essential policy choices the new technologies offer. Nonetheless, without the new technologies, certain record-keeping practices and the organizational activities they support would not be possible.

The broad availability and low cost of computer and telecommunications technologies provides both the *impetus* and the *means* to perform new record-keeping functions. These functions can bring the individual substantial benefits, but there are also disadvantages for the individual. On one hand, they can give him easier access to services that make his life more comfortable or convenient. On the other, they also tempt others to demand, and make it easier for them to get access to, information about him for purposes he does not expect and would not agree to if he were asked.

It is also quite evident that record-keeping organizations exploiting these new technologies to facilitate their own operations now pay little heed to the ways they could use the same technologies to facilitate exercise of the individual's rights and prerogatives in records used to make important decisions about him. It is ironic but true that in a society as dependent as ours on computer and telecommunications technology, an individual may still have to make a personal visit to a credit bureau if he wants access to the information the bureau maintains about him, or to get an erroneous record corrected. Although an error in a record can now be propagated all over the country at the speed of light, many organizations have made no provision to propagate corrections through the same channels, and existing law seldom requires them to do so. As a general proposition, system designers by and large have not fully used their knowledge and capabilities to make record-keeping systems serve individual as well as organizational needs and interests.

This is not to lay the blame on system designers, who are people doing what they are asked to do by the record-keeping organizations that support or pay for their services. The fault lies in the lack of strong incentives for the organization to ask them to do what they know how to do in the individual's interest. One reason for the way systems are designed and have been operated in the past has been their high cost. Instead of costing more, however, increased technological capability is now costing less and less, making it easier than ever for record-keeping organizations to take account of the individual's interests as well as their own, if they have incentives to do so.

One of the most striking of the Commission's several findings with respect to the current state of record-keeping law and practice is how difficult it can be for an individual even to find out how records about him are developed and used. What makes the difficulty the more serious is that the limited rights he now has depend in the main on his taking the initiative to exercise them. The list of records kept about an individual of which he is not likely to be aware seems endless. Even when he knows a record is being compiled, he often does not know what his rights with respect to it are, much less how to exercise them effectively, nor is he likely to be aware at the time he enters a record-keeping relationship of the importance of finding out.

In most cases, the individual can only guess at what types of information or records will be marshaled by those making any particular decision about him; furthermore, the specific sources are likely to be concealed from him. The situation makes it all but impossible for him to identify errors, or if he does, to trace them to their source. It also makes it impossible for him to know whether organizations with which he believes he has a confidential relationship have disclosed records about him to others without his knowledge or consent.

THE OBJECTIVES OF A NATIONAL POLICY

Every member of a modern society acts out the major events and transitions of his life with organizations as attentive partners. Each of his countless transactions with them leaves its mark in the records they maintain about him. The uniqueness of this record-generating pressure cannot be overemphasized. Never before the Twentieth Century have organizations tried or been expected to deal with individuals in such an exacting fashion on such a scale. Never before have so many organizations had the facilities for keeping available the information that makes it possible for them to complete daily a multitude of transactions with a multitude of individuals, and to have the relevant facts on each individual available as a basis for making subsequent decisions about him. Obviously the advent of computing technology has greatly contributed to these changes, but automated record-keeping has grown in concert with many other changes in administrative techniques, and in public attitudes and expectations.

The Commission finds that as records continue to supplant face-to-face encounters in our society, there has been no compensating tendency to give the individual the kind of control over the collection, use, and disclosure of information about him that his face-to-face encounters normally entail.

What two people divulge about themselves when they meet for the first time depends on how much personal revelation they believe the situation warrants and how much confidence each has that the other will not misinterpret or misuse what is said. If they meet again, and particularly if they develop a relationship, their self-revelation may expand both in scope and detail. All the while, however, each is in a position to correct any misperception that may develop, and to judge whether the other is likely to misuse the personal revelations, or pass them on to others without asking permission. Should either suspect that the other has violated the trust on which the candor of their communication depends, he can sever the relationship altogether, or alter its terms, perhaps by refusing thereafter to discuss certain topics or to reveal certain details about himself. Face-to-face encounters of this type, and the human relationships that result from them, are the threads from which the fabric of society is woven. The situations in which they arise are inherently social, not private, in that the disclosure of information about oneself is expected.

An individual's relationship with a record-keeping organization has some of the features of his face-to-face relationships with other individuals. It, too, arises in an inherently social context, depends on the individual's willingness to divulge information about himself or to allow others to do so, and often carries some expectation as to its practical consequences. Beyond that, however, the resemblance quickly fades.

By and large it is the organization's sole prerogative to decide what information the individual shall divulge for its records or allow others to divulge about him, and the pace at which he must divulge it. If the record-keeping organization is a private-sector one, the individual theoretically can take his business elsewhere if he objects to the divulgences required of him. Yet in a society in which time is often at a premium, in which organizations performing similar functions tend to ask similar questions, and in which organizational record-keeping practices and the differences among them are poorly perceived or understood, the individual often has little real opportunity to pick and choose. Moreover, if the record-keeping organization is a public-sector one, the individual may have no alternative but to yield whatever information is demanded of him.

Once an individual establishes a relationship with a record-keeping organization, he has even less practical control over what actually gets into a record about him, and almost none over how the record is subsequently used. In contrast to his face-to-face relationships with other individuals, he can seldom check on the accuracy of the information the organization develops about him, or discover and correct errors and misperceptions, or even find out how the information is used, much less participate in deciding to whom it may be disclosed. Nor, as a practical matter, can he sever or alter the terms of the relationship if he finds its informational demands unacceptable.

A society that increasingly relies on records to mediate relationships between individuals and organizations, and in which an individual's survival increasingly depends on his ability to maintain a variety of such relationships, must concern itself with such a situation. Ours has begun to do so, and the Commission's inquiry showed that the individual's ability to protect himself from obvious record-keeping abuses has improved somewhat in recent years. Nevertheless, most record-keeping relationships are still dangerously one-sided and likely to become even more so unless public policy makers create incentives for organizations to modify their record-keeping practices for the individual's protection, and give individuals rights to participate in record-keeping relationships commensurate with their interest in the records organizations create and keep about them.

Accordingly, the Commission has concluded that an effective privacy protection policy must have three concurrent objectives:

- **to create a proper balance between what an individual is expected to divulge to a record-keeping organization and what he seeks in return** *(to minimize intrusiveness)*;

- **to open up record-keeping operations in ways that will minimize the extent to which recorded information about an individual is** itself a source of unfairness in any decision about him made on the basis of it *(to maximize fairness)*; and

- to create and define obligations with respect to the uses and disclosures that will be made of recorded information about an individual *(to create legitimate, enforceable expectations of confidentiality)*.

These three objectives both subsume and conceptually augment the principles of the Privacy Act of 1974[6] and the five fair information practice principles set forth in the 1973 report of the Department of Health, Education, and Welfare's Secretary's Advisory Committee on Automated Personal Data Systems.[7] The second objective, to maximize fairness, in a sense subsumes all of them, and many of the Commission's specific recommendations articulate them in detail. The Commission has gone about protecting personal privacy largely by giving an individual access to records that pertain to him. Taken together, however, the three proposed objectives go beyond the openness and fairness concerns by specifically recognizing the occasional need for *a priori* determinations prohibiting the use, or collection and use, of certain types of information, and by calling for legal definitions of the individual's interest in controlling the disclosure of certain types of records about him.

Minimizing Intrusiveness

The Commission believes that society may have to cope more adequately in the future with objections to the collection of information about an individual on the grounds that it is "nobody's business but his own." There are only a few instances where the collection, or collection and use, of a particular type of information has been proscribed on grounds of impropriety, i.e., unwarranted intrusiveness. There are a number of examples of the proscription of certain *uses* of particular types of information, such as race, sex and marital status, but the character of these fairness-based proscriptions is not the same as when unwarranted intrusiveness is the rationale. When fairness is the overriding concern, organizations must often continue to collect the information in question in order to demonstrate compliance. For example, how can an employer or credit grantor show that it is not systematically using sex and race to discriminate

---

[6] For an analysis of the Privacy Act principles, see Chapter 13.

[7] U.S. Department of Health, Education and Welfare, Secretary's Advisory Committee on Automated Personal Data Systems, *Records, Computers, and the Rights of Citizens* (Washington, D.C.:1973), p.41. The five fair information principles were: (1) there must be no personal-data record-keeping systems whose very existence is secret; (2) there must be a way for an individual to find out what information about him is in a record and how it is used; (3) there must be a way for an individual to prevent information about him obtained for one purpose from being used or made available for other purposes without his consent; (4) there must be a way for an individual to correct or amend a record of identifiable information about him; and (5) any organization creating, maintaining, using, or disseminating records of identifiable personal data must assure the reliability of the data for their intended use and must take reasonable precautions to prevent misuse of the data.

among applicants unless it records the sex and race of all applicants? When impropriety is the main concern, however, the mere asking of the question must be proscribed. The proscription may also apply to use, but only to make sure that if the proscribed information is already on record, it will not enter into the decision-making process.

The intrusiveness issue is perhaps the most difficult one the Commission addresses. Whether or not the questions an organization asks individuals constitute intrusions on personal privacy is a problem that begins with the lines of inquiry society accepts as proper for an organization to pursue in making decisions about individuals. Thus, so long as society countenances a particular line of inquiry, questions as to how far it may properly go seem largely aesthetic. Indeed, if an individual's only concern is to be fairly treated, he should logically prefer to have recorded as much information as possible about himself as protection against inaccurate evaluation. For the individual there is clearly a trade-off. Does he always want to be evaluated on the basis of information that is, from an objective standpoint, strictly relevant, or does he prefer to be evaluated on the basis of a thoroughgoing inquiry that may give context to his particular situation and allow extenuating but not patently relevant circumstances to be taken into account? Such questions are extremely difficult if not impossible to answer. The Commission, in the chapters that follow, recommends four ways of addressing them.

First, the Commission recommends that individuals be informed more fully than they now are of the information needs and collection practices of a record-keeping organization in advance of committing themselves to a relationship with it. If the individual is to serve as a check on unreasonable demands for information or objectionable methods of acquiring it, he must know what to expect so that he will have a proper basis for deciding whether the trade-off is worthwhile for him.

Second, the Commission also recommends that a few specific types of information not be collected at all. For example, in the employment and personnel area, the Commission will recommend that arrest information not be collected by employers for use in hiring and promotion decisions unless its use for such purposes is required by law.

Third, the Commission proposes certain limitations on the information collection methods used by record-keeping organizations. In general, the Commission believes that if an organization, public or private, has declared at the start its intent to make certain inquiries of third parties, and to use certain sources and techniques in doing so, it should be constrained only from exceeding the scope of its declaration. The Commission also recommends that private-sector record keepers be required to exercise reasonable care in selecting and retaining other organizations to collect information about individuals on their behalf. These "reasonable care" recommendations and the ones that would bar pretext interviews and make acquiring confidential information under false pretenses punishable as a criminal offense, are the Commission's response to testimony showing that some organizations make a business of acquiring confidential records about individuals without their authorization for use by lawyers and insurance claim adjusters.

Finally, in some areas, the Commission supports the idea of having governmental mechanisms both to receive complaints about the propriety of inquiries made of individuals and to bring them to the attention of bodies responsible for establishing public policy. The Commission believes, however, that such complaints require the most delicate public-policy response. Our society is wary of government interference in information flows, and rightly so, even when personal privacy is at stake. It may be warranted in some cases, but only as a last resort. Thus, the Commission prefers to see such concerns addressed to the greatest possible extent by enabling the individual to balance what are essentially competing interests within his own scheme of values.

Maximizing Fairness

A principal objective of the Privacy Act of 1974 is to assure that the records a Federal agency maintains about an individual are as accurate, timely, complete, and relevant as is necessary to assure that they are not the cause of unfairness in any decision about the individual made on the basis of them. Proper management of records about individuals is the key to this objective, and the Privacy Act seeks to enlist the individual's help in achieving it by giving him a right to see, copy, and correct or amend records about himself. The Fair Credit Reporting Act (FCRA) and the Fair Credit Billing Act (FCBA) also focus on fairness in record keeping, though their scope of application and their specific requirements differ from those of the Privacy Act. FCRA requirements apply primarily to the support organizations which verify and supplement the information a credit, insurance, or employment applicant divulges to the primary record keepers in those three areas, but which do not themselves participate in decisions about applicants. The FCBA, however, applies to primary record keepers but only to a particular type—grantors of credit that involves regular billing—and only to a particular aspect of their operations—the settlement of billing disputes.

Other recent legislation centering on fairness in record keeping includes the Family Educational Rights and Privacy Act of 1974 and the several State fair-information-practice statutes. Their scope and specific requirements approximate those of the Privacy Act more closely than do those of any of the fairness-centered statutes that currently apply to the private sector.

All of these efforts to establish fairness protections for records about individuals have been resisted. The arguments against them have ranged from the alleged need to keep secret the identity of third-party sources, even institutional sources, to fear that organizations would be inundated with requests to see, copy, and correct records. These arguments are still heard, despite the fact that wherever such protections have been established, most of the anticipated difficulties have failed to materialize.

The vast majority of the Commission's recommendations relate directly or indirectly to fairness in record keeping. For the individual, necessary fairness protections include a right of access to records about himself for the purpose of reviewing, copying, and correcting or amending them as necessary plus some control over the collection and disclosure of information about him. For organizations, fairness protection includes the responsibility to apprise individuals that records have or will be created about them, and to have reasonable procedures for assuring the necessary accuracy, timeliness, completeness, and relevance of the information in the records they maintain about individuals, including a responsibility to forward corrections to other organizations under specified circumstances. The Commission believes, however, that *achieving the fairness objective will depend on varying the combination of rights for individuals and responsibilities for organizations according to the particular circumstances of each type of record-keeping relationship.*

For example, the Commission will recommend that applicants in several areas of record keeping be apprised of the scope, sources, and methods of inquiry the organization intends to use in verifying application information, but the recommended requirement is not precisely the same in each case. Similarly, the Commission will also recommend a general right of access for individuals to the records about them maintained by insurance institutions and medical-care providers. But because credit and depository institutions typically have procedures for keeping an individual apprised of the content of the records they maintain about him, the Commission there will recommend a more limited right of access for individuals to be triggered by an adverse decision. So also the Commission concluded that the individual's right of access to records about him maintained for research and statistical purposes can safely be limited to situations in which such a record may be used in making a decision about him.

The right to correct or amend a record is essential to fairness in many areas. To be effective, it must usually be coupled with an obligation of the record-keeping organization to forward the correction or amendment to past recipients of inaccurate or incomplete information. The Commission has recommended modifying this blanket obligation somewhat to require that record keepers need forward corrections and amendments only to past recipients designated by the individual and those to which the record-keeping organization regularly discloses the kind of information in question. The Commission believes that this modification has the desirable effect of relieving record-keeping organizations of the obligation to keep an accounting of every disclosure of every record about an individual without materially weakening the individual's protection. Amendments would, of course, still have to be forwarded to *future* recipients and the insurance and employment recommendations call, in addition, for automatic propagation of corrections and amendments to investigative support organizations that were sources of corrected or amended information. All of the correction and amendment recommendations also make provision for disagreements between the individual and a record-keeping organization about the accuracy, timeliness, or completeness of a record.

In regard to fairness in disclosure, the Commission recommends requiring the individual's authorization where it finds that a necessary protection, and specifies what it believes the authorization statement should contain if it is to serve both the information needs of, for example, insurers and employers and the individual's interest in controlling the divulgence of information about himself by record keepers with which he has a confidential relationship. The Commission's recommendations in this regard recognize the *gatekeeping* role that certain types of records play—that is, the role they play in decisions as to whether an individual will be allowed to enter into particular social, economic, or political relationships, and if so, under what circumstances. Where records play such a role, the individual usually has no choice but to allow them to be used in making decisions about him. Since informed consent is valid only if wholly voluntary, it means little in this context. Hence, the Commission finds *authorization* the appropriate pre-condition of disclosure, rather than *informed consent*, and couples it with a *principle of limited disclosure*. This principle is a key concept because it asserts that a disclosure should include no more of the recorded information than the authorized request for disclosure specifies. The Commission recognizes, and indeed emphasizes, that the holder of a record cannot and should not bear the burden of deciding what information to disclose when presented with a valid authorization statement of the type the Commission recommends. The main problem is that some keepers of records that contain intimate personal details routinely disclose much more information about individuals than they are asked for, simply as a matter of convenience and economy. The Commission, therefore, has established the principle of limited disclosure as a general tenet of fair record-keeping practice.

The Commission's fairness recommendations generally call for reasonable procedures to assure accuracy, timeliness, and completeness in records of information about individuals. For example, in the public sector, the Commission recommends that reasonable procedures be an affirmative management obligation, while in the private sector, it relies on the rights it recommends for individuals to assure that organizations adopt reasonable procedures.

The Commission believes that by opening up record-keeping practices and by giving an individual opportunities to interact easily with a record keeper, particularly at crucial points in a record-keeping relationship, both individuals and organizations will benefit. The quality of the information in records will be improved while at the same time the individual and the organization will both be protected from errors or other deficiencies that can have untoward consequences for both.

Legitimizing Expectations of Confidentiality

The third public-policy objective, protecting confidentiality, pertains to the disclosure of information about an individual without his consent. Confidential treatment of recorded information is necessary for the maintenance of many kinds of relationships between individuals and organizations. The medical-care relationship, for example, often demands uninhibited candor from the individual about the most intimate details of his private life. There are also relationships between individuals and organizations that depend on the accumulation of extremely detailed records about the individual's activities, such as those compiled by a bank or by an independent credit-card issuer. The records of these relationships provide a revealing, if often incomplete, portrait of the individual, often touching on his beliefs and interests as well as his actions. While in theory these relationships are voluntary, in reality an individual today has little choice but to establish them as he would be severely, and perhaps insurmountably, disadvantaged if he did not.

There is also the fact that many of the records about individuals which these record keepers now maintain are the kinds of records the individual formerly would have kept in his exclusive possession. The transactional record a checking account creates, for example, would have existed a century ago in the form of receipts or, at most, ledger entries kept by the individual himself at home.

As long as records remained in his possession, both law and societal values recognized his right to control their use and disclosure. Government in particular was restricted in its ability to gain access to them, even to facilitate a criminal prosecution. When organizations began to maintain such records, however, the individual began to lose control over who might see and use them. The balance society had deemed crucial was disrupted.

Although individuals have tended to retain the old value system, expecting certain records to be held in confidence by the organizations that now maintain them, the law has not taken account of that fact. The protections that exist still apply in almost all instances only to records in the individual's exclusive possession. The lack of a legal interest for the individual in the records organizations maintain about him has put him in an extremely vulnerable position. The scale and impersonality of organizational record keeping today allows him little opportunity to influence an organization's own use and disclosure practices, and as the *Miller* case showed, he has no interest whatsoever to assert when government demands access to the records an organization maintains about him. The *Miller* case said, in effect, that government no longer has to operate within the strictures of the Fourth and Fifth Amendments when it wants to acquire financial records pertaining to an individual; that what were once his private papers are now open to government scrutiny. What amounts to mere curiosity will suffice as justification if government agents want to see them.

To help redress the imbalances between individuals and organizations on one hand, and individuals, organizations and government on the other, the Commission recommends in this report that a legally enforceable "expectation of confidentiality" be created in several areas. The concept of a legally enforceable expectation of confidentiality has two distinct, though complementary, elements. The first is an enforceable duty of the record keeper which preserves the record keeper's ability to protect itself from improper actions by the individual, but otherwise restricts its discretion to disclose a record about him voluntarily. The second is a legal interest in the record for the individual which he can assert to protect himself against improper or unreasonable demands for disclosure by government or anyone else. The Commission has concluded that without this combination of duty and assertible interest, the law as it stands now will continue to deprive the individual of any opportunity to participate in decisions of organizations to disclose records kept about him, whether the disclosure is voluntary or in response to an authoritative demand.

The Commission specifies what it considers to be the proper terms of the individual's enforceable expectation in relationships with credit grantors, depository institutions, insurers, medical-care providers, the Internal Revenue Service, and providers of long-distance telephone service. Once again the recommendations are tailored to the particulars of each kind of record-keeping relationship. In each case, the Commission recommends that a protectible legal interest for the individual be created by statute; specifies the voluntary disclosures it believes should be permissible without the individual's consent and the procedures for establishing them; and sets forth the rules for initiating and complying with government demands for access to records. In no instance, however, does the Commission advocate complete, unilateral control by the individual. In every case it has respected the record-keeping organization's legitimate interests when threatened by actions of the individual. In essence, the Commission has said that the individual's interest must be recognized; that there must be procedures to force conflicting claims into the open; and that within this framework established by public policy, value conflicts should be resolved on a case-by-case basis.

COMPETING PUBLIC-POLICY INTERESTS

A major theme of this report is that privacy, both as a societal value and as an individual interest, does not and cannot exist in a vacuum. Indeed, "privacy" is a poor label for many of the issues the Commission addresses because to many people the concept connotes isolation and secrecy, whereas the relationships the Commission is concerned with are inherently social. Because they are, moreover, the privacy protections afforded them must be balanced against other significant societal values and interests. The Commission has identified five such competing societal values that must be taken into account in formulating public policy to protect personal privacy: (1) First Amendment interests; (2) freedom of information interests; (3) the societal interest in law enforcement; (4) cost; and (5) Federal-State relations.

THE FIRST AMENDMENT AND PRIVACY

The legitimate expectation of confidentiality is a concept the Commission endorses for several of the record-keeping relationships examined in this report. The policy objective is that when the relationship is one involving confidentiality of records, the record keeper shall be constrained from disclosing information about an individual without his authorization, either voluntarily or in response to a demand for it. The Commission recognizes that recommending any restriction on the free flow of truthful information raises serious questions in a democratic society, and sought ways to avoid conflict with both the goals of the First Amendment to the Constitution, and with the policy of broad access to public information articulated in statutes like the Freedom of Information Act.

When the Commission recommends rules to govern a record keeper's voluntary disclosure of a record about an individual, it does not attempt to specify, nor does it assign to either government or the individual the responsibility of determining which information in the record may or may not be disclosed. Neither does the Commission recommend any liability for third parties who merely receive information or records generated by a confidential relationship. The Commission's recommendations simply specify *to whom* information may be disclosed without the individual's consent. The role of government in the enforcement of a recommended expectation of confidentiality would be simply to act, through the courts, as referee in disputes between a record keeper and an individual about whether an expectation is legitimate and whether it has been violated. Government would have no independent interest to enforce, and would take no enforcement initiative, except where deception or misrepresentation is used to acquire medical records without the patient's consent. Only the individual would have an enforceable interest.

The Commission takes great care to avoid recommendations that would amount to regulating the content of records collected, maintained, or disclosed by private-sector organizations because of two related considerations, one abstract, the other concrete. The first consideration is that a democratic society must keep governmental intrusion into the flow of information to a minimum; the second is that the First Amendment sharply limits such government intrusion. Of importance here are the recent decisions of the U.S. Supreme Court that have found private commercial information flows as deserving of First Amendment protections as the personal exercise of the right of free speech.

In simplified terms, the First Amendment prohibits the Federal government (and through the Fourteenth Amendment, the States) from enacting any law which would abridge the right to communicate information to others or to receive information from others.[8] Broad as it is, this interpretation of the right to free speech does not mean the right is unlimited. It allows for such familiar strictures on the content of information exchanges as prohibiting slanderous or libelous communications, and, more pertinent to the question here, it allows for certain regulation of the *process* of communication when it occurs in a public forum. In other words, government may properly regulate the flow of information to the extent its regulations apply only to the process of communication in public places.

In addition, the Supreme Court has been willing to accept some government actions which require private organizations to comply with the

---

[8] See, e.g., *Stanley v. Georgia*, 394 U.S. 557 (1969); *Kliendienst v. Mandel*, 408 U.S. 753 (1972); *Cox Broadcasting Corp. v. Cohn*, 420 U.S. 469 (1975).

decision *an individual* has made regarding the communications he does not want to receive. In *Lamont v. Postmaster General*,[9] for example, the issue was the constitutionality of a Federal statute requiring the Postal Service to prevent firms from mailing material to individuals who have indicated that they do not want it because they consider it obscene. Because the statute leaves all determinations about content to the individual and requires the Postal Service only to see that the individual's wishes are respected, the Supreme Court held the statute constitutional. In other words, it is not unconstitutional to give an individual standing to assert his own interest in the flow of communication between private parties.

Individuals and organizations that do not engage in commercial activities have traditionally enjoyed the full range of constitutional free speech protections. For commercial entities, however, First Amendment protections have been virtually nonexistent[10] until a few years ago when the U.S. Supreme Court, in *Virginia State Board of Pharmacy v. Virginia Citizens Consumer Council*,[11] declared that the doctrine denying First Amendment protection to commercial speech had been swept away. In sweeping it away, the Court did, however, indicate that some restrictions on commercial communications are legitimate, though it left the standards for such restriction unclear.

The Court in the Virginia case stressed that the decision did not mean that a regulation prohibiting the advertising of an illegal activity would be unconstitutional. In 1974, in *Pittsburgh Press v. Human Relations Commission*,[12] there was a challenge to a municipal ordinance prohibiting the publication of lists of job openings by sex unless the designations were based on *bona fide* occupational considerations. The Court rejected the First Amendment challenge and sustained the ordinance. The majority opinion described the advertisements as "classic examples of commercial speech" and went on to note that commercial advertising ordinarily enjoys some First Amendment protection. What made this particular advertising susceptible to regulation was the illegitimacy of the activity advertised. In effect, the Court argued that if a commercial activity is illegal, then speech which promotes or assists in effecting such activity may be prohibited.

Such a rationale is not entirely satisfactory. Is the decision of the legislature that a certain commercial activity is illegal enough to deny communication concerning that activity free speech and free press protections? If the illegal activity is in part a result of the mere communication of information or ideas, should First Amendment analyses apply? Or should some other standard be employed to test the propriety of the legislative determination restricting communication? In any case, since the illegal-activity standard of *Pittsburgh Press* applies only to commercial communication, this test appears to establish that commercial speech remains doctrinally outside the mainstream of the First Amendment in some ways.

---

[9] 391 U.S. 301 (1965).
[10] Thomas I. Emerson, *The System of Freedom of Expression* (New York: Vintage, 1970), p. 414.
[11] 425 U.S. 748 (1976).
[12] 413 U.S. 376 (1973).

The Commission believes that the extension of First Amendment protections to commercial communication as defined in these recent Supreme Court cases, which almost exclusively concern advertising, does not pose any obstacle to the establishment of legitimate expectations of confidentiality for individuals in the private sector. The Commission is in no instance recommending an absolute restriction on the communication of information; rather, it recommends that an individual be informed at the beginning of a relationship what information may be disclosed from records about him and for what purposes. Following *Lamont*, it also recommends that an individual be given an opportunity to participate in any change that would materially affect his legitimate expectation.

Protection of privacy against *government* intrusions is a complementary limitation to protection of communications from government interference. Therefore, the Commission further recommends that if the requestor of records is a government agency, such agency bear the burden of notifying the individual, and that laws be enacted to allow the individual standing to assert his interest as defined in the recommended measures. This clearly raises no First Amendment issues.

FREEDOM OF INFORMATION AND PRIVACY

The second competing societal value the Commission identified is freedom of information. In enacting the Freedom of Information Act (FOIA) in 1966,[13] and strengthening it eight years later, the Congress gave expression to society's strong interest in opening the records of Federal government agencies to public inspection. The FOIA, to be sure, allows for exceptions from the general openness rule which an agency may invoke for certain information pertaining to national defense and foreign policy, law enforcement, individuals, internal agency deliberations, trade secrets, and information specifically declared confidential by other statutes. The withholding of exempt records, however, is subject to administrative and judicial review. Most of the States have enacted their own FOIA statutes in one form or another. Other statutes, both Federal and State, open meetings of certain governmental bodies to the public. The legal actions brought to test these statutes have shown the courts to be generally sympathetic to broadening public access to government records and deliberations, and, of course, journalists are natural advocates of full access and disclosure. Altogether, the presumption against secrecy in decision making and record keeping by government agencies is now firmly established.

The Commission has recommended the continuation of restrictions on the disclosure of specific records about individuals maintained by government agencies. While this recommendation may seem to conflict with the principle of freedom of information and openness, the Commission firmly believes that it is compatible with those principles and, indeed, that they are complementary aspects of a coherent public policy concerning public records.

In the Federal government, adjustments between freedom of informa-

---

[13] 5 U.S.C. 552.

tion policy and confidentiality policy are made at two levels. At the first of these levels, the Federal FOIA makes adjustments by incorporating several statutes which, with particularity, direct that specific records be withheld from the public. The Federal FOIA does not require the disclosure of matters that are:

> specifically exempted from disclosure by statute (other than section 552b of this title), provided that such statute (A) requires that the matter be withheld from the public in such a manner as to leave no discretion on the issue, or (B) establishes particular criteria for withholding or refers to particular types of matters to be withheld. *[5 U.S.C. 552(b)(3) (1976)]*

Tax returns and the responses of individual households to Census Bureau inquiries fall into this category. The Commission believes that it is preferable for the Congress to create this sort of explicit confidentiality policy than for government administrators to decide when such records should or should not be disclosed.

The second level at which freedom of information and privacy interests relate becomes apparent when a Federal agency receives a legitimate Freedom of Information Act request for access to a record about an individual and finds that the record is subject to the Privacy Act of 1974. When the two Acts are read together any disclosure of a record about an individual in a system of records as defined by the Privacy Act to any member of the public other than the individual to whom the record pertains is forbidden if the disclosure would constitute a "clearly unwarranted invasion of personal privacy." The reverse obligation also holds: even though a record is about an individual, it cannot be withheld from any member of the public who requests it if the disclosure would *not* constitute a clearly unwarranted invasion of personal privacy. The courts are the final arbiters of which disclosures do or do not meet the unwarranted-invasion test and over the years they have established certain types of recorded information which *must* be disclosed without question. Two examples are Civil Service grades of Federal employees, and the names of persons who have participated in elections supervised by the National Labor Relations Board.

For government, the Commission believes that the policy of combining explicit legislation for particular types of records with a general standard to be applied in all other cases is an appropriate way to balance the freedom of information interests and confidentiality interests. As Chapter 13 explains, the combination does not lead to resolution of difficult cases overnight, but it does create a framework within which the conflicts between the two competing though compatible interests can be resolved.

The general concept of freedom of information has no currency in the private sector. Issuers of regulated securities must publicly disclose particular items of information about the individuals who control or manage companies, but organizations in the private sector by and large have no affirmative obligation to disclose their records about individuals to the public. They may be required to disclose such records to government agencies for a variety of reasons, as described in Chapter 9, but in many cases government is prohibited from subsequently disclosing that information to the public. Thus, in the private sector there is no freedom of information policy to conflict with a confidentiality of records policy.

Indeed, the Commission believes that in most instances the persuasive power of an active press can be relied on to work out a proper adjustment between the right to privacy and the freedom of information principle as it applies to public disclosure of information in records about individuals maintained by private-sector organizations. However, the Commission also believes that the individual needs some limited control over the public disclosure of particular types of information about him. An individual should be able to limit the public disclosure of credit, insurance, medical, employment, and education record information about himself. In these areas, the Commission has recommended for the individual an assertible interest so that he can have a role in determining whether information about him should be publicly released. In fact, as to certain identifying information referred to as *directory information*, the Commission's recommendations recognize the general practice of public disclosure in such areas as employment, medical care, and education. Thus, reporters should be able to continue to find out who is in what hospital, who is employed by what firm, and who is enrolled in what school.

The Commission's recommendations, with one exception, do not limit or affect the ability of the press to request or obtain information. The area of medical records is the one area where the Commission not only recommends a duty on the record keeper to respect an individual's expectation of confidentiality but also suggests that it be made a crime to seek such information through misrepresentation or deception. Specific abuses by persons seeking medical-record information for use in adversary situations have led the Commission to conclude that such a recommendation is necessary. In all other cases, the Commission's recommendations do not limit or affect the ability of the press to request or obtain information. These balances are difficult to strike and the Commission has attempted to establish mechanisms for doing so rather than recommend specific disclosure prohibitions.

LAW ENFORCEMENT AND PRIVACY

The third competing interest the Commission identified is the interest in preventing and prosecuting crime. Organizations do and should have the means of protecting themselves from suspected fraud in insurance claims, fraudulent use of credit cards, multiple welfare applications, and the like. Organizations, both private and public, exchange information among themselves and with law enforcement authorities to protect against such losses and to assist in the prosecution of crime. The Commission has not suggested that this organizational interest be curtailed. Rather, it recommends that individuals be apprised, at the time they establish a relationship involving confidential records that information about them may be disclosed for investigative or enforcement purposes if the record keeper develops evidence that points to criminal behavior on their part.

Government requests or demands for recorded information about individuals for law enforcement purposes pose a special problem. As a result of the *Miller* decision discussed earlier, an individual has no constitutional protections against government demands for access to records third parties maintain about him. There are some statutory protections, such as those for census records, Federal income-tax returns, and records developed in connection with federally funded drug abuse research and treatment programs. The Commission believes, however, that the individual should have an assertible interest in other types of records about him, such as those maintained by financial institutions, insurance companies, medical-care providers, and providers of long-distance telephone service, as a matter of general policy.

Government agencies have testified that to enforce the law, they need full and complete access to records kept about individuals by third parties. They argue that to restrict their access, or more specifically to subject it to the assertion of an individual's interest, would unduly handicap their legitimate law enforcement activities. The Commission seriously considered these arguments and has developed a set of recommendations that allow for continued law enforcement access, but under stricter rules. These rules are in two parts. First, they require law enforcement agencies to use legal process of some form whenever they seek information about an individual from a third-party record keeper. Second, when they seek access to records in which the individual has a legitimate expectation of confidentiality, the Commission recommends that the individual involved be given notice and the legal capacity to contest the action. The Commission has not recommended prohibiting government access, but rather giving the individual an assertible interest in the process of government information gathering about him. The requirement for legal process in all instances has the further advantage that it creates the basis for meaningful accountability mechanisms.

THE COST OF PRIVACY

The fourth competing interest the Commission identified is cost. In maximizing fairness, this is the most compelling competing interest. Whether an organization is public or private, to make changes in record-keeping practices can increase its cost of operation and thus make the product or service it provides either more expensive or less accessible, or both. When this happens, both the record-keeping organization and some if not all of its customers or clients suffer. Adoption of the Commission's recommendations means that a great many organizations will have to make some changes in their record keeping. The costs of compliance will be higher or lower depending on how well an organization's current practices reflect the recommended balance between organizational interests and the individual's interest. The Commission has tried to keep compliance costs to a minimum by not recommending that organizations be required to report periodically to Federal or State government agencies, and also by not recommending inflexible procedural requirements.

The Commission's recommendations are aimed at getting results. Thus, they try to take advantage of the shared interest of individuals and organizations in keeping records accurate, timely, and complete. As previously noted, one reason for giving an individual a right of access to records about him is that doing so affords an organization the free help of an expert—the individual himself—on the accuracy of the information the organization uses to make decisions about him. Organizations, however, need some assurance before they are willing to enlist such help that it will not turn out to be unduly or undeservedly expensive.

To open an insurance company's underwriting files to inspection by applicants and policyholders, for example, gives the company a powerful motive to record only accurate, pertinent information about them and to keep its records as timely and complete as necessary. To encourage applicants and policyholders to look for information in underwriting files that could serve as the basis for defamation actions and windfall recoveries, however, would be contrary to the Commission's cost-minimizing objective and also an impediment to systemic reform. *The Commission wants organizations to invest in improving their record-keeping practices; not to spend their money in costly litigation over past practices and honest mistakes.* Hence the Commission's recommendation is to limit the liability of a record keeper that responds to an individual's request for access to a record it maintains about him.

Organizations in the private sector have a strong interest in keeping their decisions about customers, clients, applicants, or employees free of unreasonable government interference. The Commission's recommendations recognize this interest by concentrating on the quality of the information an organization uses as the basis for making a decision about an individual, rather than on the decision itself. For private-sector organizations the adverse-decision requirements the Commission recommends will expose the records used in arriving at a decision to reject an applicant, but the Commission relies on the incentives of the marketplace to prompt reconsideration of a rejection if it turns out to have been made on the basis of inaccurate or otherwise defective information.

For public-sector organizations, the Commission recommends no affirmative requirement that they reverse an adverse decision made on the basis of faulty information. For educational institutions, where the procedures for correcting or amending records are likely to be divorced from decision-making procedures, and where the individual has no easily invokable due process protections, the Commission proposes an affirmative requirement to *reconsider* but not a requirement to *reverse*. The Commission strongly believes that to mix concern about the outcome of individual decisions with concern about the quality of the information used in arriving at them not only risks undesirable interference with organizational prerogatives but also invites confusion as to the nature and extent of the individual's privacy interest, possibly to its detriment in the long run.

FEDERAL-STATE RELATIONS AND PRIVACY

A major interest that must be weighed in the balance of organizations' needs for information against the individual's interest in having his personal privacy protected is society's interest in maintaining the integrity of the Federal system. The division of responsibility and authority between the Federal government and States is a cornerstone of the American political system and the Commission has been particularly attentive to it in both the methods it recommends for establishing legal requirements and the regulatory mechanisms and sanctions for enforcing such requirements.

In areas of record keeping where the States are prominent record keepers, or where records are generated in carrying out State programs, the Commission pays particular attention to the reserved-powers principle enunciated in the Tenth Amendment to the Constitution, emulating the Supreme Court's care[14] not to interfere with the conduct of essential State government functions. Thus, where Federal regulation seems necessary, the Commission recommends making the requirements a condition of Federal benefits, which leaves the States some degree of choice. The Commission recommends tempering such exercise of Federal spending power by leaving considerable latitude in how the States implement the policies, and by urging them to make the minimum Federal requirements part of their own State legislation and to assume most of the responsibility for enforcing them.

In the areas of private-sector record keeping where the States share regulatory power with the Federal government, the Commission recommends maintaining the current balance. For example, in financial areas where the Federal government now does most of the regulating, the Commission relies heavily on current Federal mechanisms in the implementation of the measures it recommends, with the State playing a supplemental role. In the insurance area, where the States now do most of the regulating, the Commission recognizes a need for some limited Federal intervention in order to provide the necessary uniformity, but relies on the State enforcement mechanisms that now have primary responsibility.

Each of the implementation measures the Commission recommends is designed to avoid disturbance of the current Federal-State political balance of power. Indeed, the structure of the Commission's recommendations as a whole should strengthen the Federal-State partnership and increase the State's role in protecting the interests of the individual.

IMPLEMENTATION PRINCIPLES AND CHOICES

Each policy recommendation in this report is supplemented by an implementation recommendation. Collectively, the Commission's implementation recommendations add up to a consistent strategy for the practical application of the policies and practices the Commission believes should be adopted. The Commission has not tried to draft any of its recommendations in final statutory language. The Commission does, however, suggest how and in what manner its recommendations should be adopted, since the

---

[14] *National League of Cities v. Usery*, 426 U.S. 833 (1976).

impact and significance of policies can be adequately assessed only in light of how they are to be applied.

IMPLEMENTATION PRINCIPLES

The Commission's findings clearly reveal an overwhelming imbalance in the record-keeping relationship between an individual and an organization, and its policy recommendations aim at strengthening the ability of the individual to participate in that relationship. This can be accomplished in three ways: by prohibiting or curtailing unjustifiably intrusive information collection practices; by granting the individual basic rights, such as the right to see, copy and correct records about himself, coupled with obligations or organizations to incorporate protections for personal privacy in their routine record-keeping operations; and by giving the individual control over the disclosure of records about him. In exploring ways to implement its policy recommendations, the Commission was guided by three principles: (1) that incentives for systemic reform should be created; (2) that existing regulatory and enforcement mechanisms should be used insofar as possible; and (3) that unnecessary cost should be avoided.

In accordance with the first of these guiding principles, the recommended measures enable the individual to compel compliance with certain specific requirements even if he has suffered little or no injury. The Commission believes that an individual should be able to go to court to compel the production of records and to require the correction of erroneous information in them, and to hold a record-keeping organization responsible for its disclosure practices. Because enforcement of such rights has in the past depended on a showing of direct financial loss, which is often difficult to demonstrate, most individuals have not been able to assert their interests effectively. The Commission's recommendations should make it easy for an individual to assert his interest, thus making it attractive to organizations to comply voluntarily rather than incur the cost of enforcement through judicial or administrative action.

The Commission believes that because giving an individual a right of access to records about him could lead to a defamation or invasion of privacy action, the liability of a record-keeping organization for such claims resulting from its disclosure to an individual of a record about himself should be limited. An institution, however, should be liable for false information where there has been willful intent to injure the individual.

In accordance with the second guiding principle, that the policy recommendations should be implemented through existing regulatory and enforcement mechanisms insofar as possible, the Commission recognizes that while existing regulation seldom aims explicitly at protecting personal privacy in record keeping, it does, in fact, provide some protection, which the Commission has no wish to negate or duplicate. In the consumer-credit area, for example, Regulation Z of the Federal Reserve Board[15], issued pursuant to the Truth-in-Lending Act, explicitly specifies how an individual is to be informed of the terms and conditions of a particular loan. The

---

[15] 12 C.F.R. §226.

Commission's recommendations would add a further requirement that the individual also be informed of the types and sources of information that will be collected about him and the uses to which the information will be put.

Similarly, the Commission relies on the Fair Credit Reporting Act[16] as the vehicle for implementing many of its private-sector recommendations because it is the statute at the Federal level that deals most explicitly and comprehensively with privacy issues in the private sector. For example, the Commission recommends that the individual's right of access to underwriting and certain claim information about himself maintained by an insurance company be provided by amendment of the FCRA in order to assure nationwide compliance. However, the Commission has used a different approach in implementing notice to applicants and insureds in regard to the types of information that will be collected about them and the sources and techniques that will be used. In this instance, the Commission directs its implementation to the State level, where, as a result of the McCarren-Ferguson Act[17], insurance is otherwise regulated unless there is explicit Federal legislation to the contrary. States use this authority to regulate the form of insurance policies, and, in some cases, applications for insurance, and thus can implement the recommended notification requirements as well.

Existing structures also provide a framework for implementing the Commission's recommendations for medical records. There the Commission considered two types of medical record keepers—the institutional medical-care provider and the individual practitioner. Since most institutional providers qualify under Medicare and Medicaid, the qualification process affords an effective means of assuring the compliance of institutional providers with the recommended medical records requirements. Individual practitioners, however, do not currently have to qualify under Medicare and Medicaid, although they are subject to State licensing authorities, and the Commission, therefore, recommends that States adopt model legislation applying the medical records safeguard requirements to all individual practitioners and to any institutional medical-care providers that are not subject to Medicare or Medicaid qualification requirements.

In accordance with the Commission's third guiding principle, it tried to make sure that the privacy protection safeguards it recommended would not involve unnecessary cost, either to individuals or to record-keeping organizations. The Commission believes that granting an individual rights within existing legal frameworks is far more efficient and significantly less costly than embarking on an ambitious new regulatory approach. As noted above, its recommended policy measures put the main ongoing costs of implementation on organizations that do not comply with the requirements, since it is they who will be subject to judicial or administrative sanctions and related costs. The organization that takes affirmative steps to comply with the recommendations should have little expense beyond the cost of educating its employees, initially revising some of its procedures and forms, and creating appropriate policy guidance. Even these costs can be controlled by allowing a reasonable time for transition. With intent the

---

[16] 15 U.S.C. 1681 *et seq.*
[17] 15 U.S.C. 1012.

Commission does *not* recommend that organizations be required to report regularly to anyone or to obtain anyone's approval prior to revising or establishing its record-keeping systems. Thus, the cost to government and to those who comply will be kept to a minimum.

The Commission's single deviation from these three principles is the approach it recommends to the problem of systematic or repeated violations. The Commission advocates rights for individuals and relies primarily on the individual to exercise and protect those rights with the help of the courts, but as many of the chapters point out, however, giving an individual better ways to protect himself can be an inadequate tool. Thus, when there is evidence of repeated or systematic violations, the measures recommended for particular record-keeping areas assign specific responsibility on behalf of the public for enforcing compliance to appropriate government agencies, such as the Federal Trade Commission or State insurance departments.

The Commission's implementation strategy also considers the question of Federal preemption and the desirability of uniform requirements. National bankers, insurers, retailers, and other industries subject to Federal regulations have strongly urged the Commission to recommend that any mandatory requirements be exclusively Federal so that they and, indeed, their customers, do not have to struggle with 50 separate sets of rules. The Fair Credit Reporting Act addresses this desire for uniformity by permitting a State to supplement but not narrow the Act's requirements. For example, the FCRA specifies that an individual shall be informed on request of the nature and substance of a credit report; California law, without contradicting the FCRA, takes the extra step of requiring that an individual be allowed on request to see such a report. When the Commission recommends Federal legislation, it intends such legislation to establish the reasonable basis upon which organizations may deal with all individuals on whom they maintain information or records, regardless of political jurisdiction. While the Commission believes its recommended measures provide proper protections for personal privacy, particular States may deem it desirable to establish further requirements for their own citizens. They should not be prohibited from doing so as long as their requirements do not conflict with or narrow Federal law. The same is true in the public sector where the Commission has recommended Federal requirements applicable to federally funded State programs; there is no barrier to the States going further if they want to do so.

Experience with the term *agency* as used in the Privacy Act of 1974 illustrates a potential problem, which the Commission hopes to avoid with the term *organization* used in its recommendations. The way an agency defines itself for the purpose of complying with the Privacy Act's requirements makes a significant difference in the disclosures of records it can make and in the degree of its responsibility for establishing operating rules and procedures.[18] It is convenient for an agency to define itself as a unit at the highest possible organizational level. Thus, the Office of the Secretary of Health, Education and Welfare, the Office of Education, the

---

[18] See Chapter 13.

Social Security Administration, the Public Health Service, and a number of other units are all deemed to be one agency—the Department of Health, Education and Welfare (DHEW). As a consequence, any disclosure of information about an individual by one office, administration, or service to another can be considered an internal agency disclosure not subject to the Privacy Act's limitations on third-party disclosures without written consent of the individual. Another result is that the rules for Privacy Act compliance are DHEW rules rather than rules of its components.

The term organization presents similar problems in the private sector. The Commission believes that there should be flexibility allowing organizations to define themselves in various ways. For example, a conglomerate corporation or corporate group may or may not want to define itself as a single organization for the purpose of complying with the measures recommended for a particular record-keeping relationship. Considering the many forms of corporate and administrative control, the Commission believes the choice can be left to the organizations on two conditions.

The first is that at whatever level an organization is defined as a single unit, that must be the level responsible for promulgating and enforcing standard operating procedures at all subordinate levels. For example, if the American Telephone and Telegraph Company considers itself and all of its subsidiaries and affiliated local phone companies to be one organization, AT&T must promulgate, enforce, and be accountable for compliance with the procedures to be followed by all of those entities.

The second condition is that regardless of the level at which an organization is defined as a unit, an individual must be assured that information about him collected and maintained in connection with one record-keeping relationship will not be made available for use in connection with another. For example, information collected by an employer from an employee to process a claim under a group health insurance policy is not to be used for personnel purposes. If two affiliated companies define themselves as a unit but perform two different functions—one extending credit and the other selling insurance, for example—information about customers must not flow between them without adherence to the notice, authorization, and other requirements called for in the Commission's recommendations. Likewise, a corporate affiliate in, say, the retailing business should not rent or lend the names and addresses of its customers to another affiliate to market insurance unless the retailer informs its customers that it intends to do so and gives them an opportunity to indicate that they do not want their names used for that purpose.

IMPLEMENTATION CHOICES

The Commission had three basic alternatives for giving effect to its policy recommendations: (1) voluntary compliance; (2) statutory creation of rights, interests, or responsibilities enforceable through either individual or governmental action; and (3) establishment of ongoing governmental mechanisms to investigate, study, and report on privacy protection issues.

Each of the Commission's policy recommendations specifies the alternative it believes is most appropriate for that particular measure.

In the areas of research and statistical activities, and education, for example, the Commission specifies legislation in the form of amendments to existing Federal statutes to define further the responsibilities and duties of those types of record keepers. In the public assistance and social services area, the Commission specifies Federal action that would make State enactment of the recommended statutory rights and responsibilities a condition of Federal funding.

In the private sector, the Commission specifies voluntary compliance when the present need for the recommended change is not acute enough to justify mandatory legislation, or if the organizations in an industry have shown themselves willing to cooperate voluntarily. In its mailing list recommendations for example, the Commission specifies that when an organization has a practice of renting, lending, or exchanging the names of its customers, members, or donors for use by others in a direct-mail marketing or solicitation, it should inform each of them that it does so and give each an opportunity to veto the practice with respect to his own name. The Commission does not call for legislation to enforce compliance with this recommendation because it has reason to believe the industry is willing to accept these restrictions voluntarily, and there are no legal impediments to stop it from doing so.

The Commission also relies mainly on voluntary compliance in the area of employment and personnel; though there are a few exceptions, the most notable being the recommendation dealing with the creation and use of investigative reports, where implementation by amendment of the Fair Credit Reporting Act is the Commission's choice. In this area, the Commission prefers to rely mainly on voluntary compliance because of the complexity of the relationship between employer and employee, and the difficulty of classifying all the various records different employers maintain about their employees and the way they use these records in employment decision making. For the Commission to recommend otherwise would be to recommend uniformity where variation is not only widespread but inherent in the employee-employer relationship as our society now knows it.

Most of the Commission's recommendations, however, do specify mandatory measures. This is partly because the Commission believes that in most cases voluntary compliance would be too uneven to be dependable; but more importantly, many of the issues the Commission's recommendations address are legal ones and require legal remedies. In the *Miller* case described above, for example, if the bank had wholeheartedly tried to protect Miller's interest, it would have done him little or no good since under existing law, Miller would have no interest in the records to assert. If a Federal agency insists on having an individual's account record today, a bank cannot successfully refuse to make it available.

In some cases, existing law and practice also work against the individual when he seeks access to records about himself. For example, the contracts that consumer-reporting agencies have with their insurer, employer, and credit grantor subscribers specify that the client may not disclose the information they report on an individual. Thus, an organization reaching an adverse decision about an individual on the basis of an investigative report cannot disclose the negative information in the report to him, even if it would otherwise be willing to do so. The Commission's recommendations would void such prohibitions.

In choosing mandatory implementation alternatives for the private sector, the Commission also aimed for consistency in the matter of damages and in the method of enforcement. Where the Commission recognizes an individual's right of access to records that have not entered into a decision adverse to him, as in the insurance recommendations for example, it has recommended that when an individual denied this right substantially prevails in court, he be able to recover the costs of compelling compliance, including attorney fees, but that he not be awarded damages. When the individual's right of access is triggered by an adverse decision and a record keeper fails to perform a duty required of it, or fails to correct or amend a record about him or to propagate a correction or amendment, a court which determines that the denial or failure was willful or intentional would not only allow the individual to recover his cost of compelling compliance, including attorney's fees, but also could award him up to $1,000.

For credit, insurance, and depository records, the Commission adopts the concept of a "legitimate expectation of confidentiality." Since the damage an individual can suffer from an organization's breach of confidentiality often cannot be undone, the Commission recommends that an individual so aggrieved have the right to compensation for any special (i.e., actual) damages resulting from a private-sector organization's violation of his legitimate expectation of confidentiality, and, if a court determines that the organization acted willfully or intentionally, to additional compensation for general damages in the amount of at least $1,000 but no more than $10,000.

The third implementation choice obviously requires a Federal body to oversee, regulate, and enforce compliance with certain of the Commission's recommendations. This alternative is not incompatible with the other two. In fact there are powerful arguments for using it in conjunction with the other two, rather than depending on the first two alone.

The strongest argument for using a combination of alternatives is the dynamic character of personal-data record-keeping practices that will continue to create new privacy concerns, and redirect existing ones. Without a focal point to keep privacy concerns in proper perspective for the public as well as for record-keeping organizations, other issues competing for attention may obscure them.

A primary objective of the Commission's implementation strategy is to make sure that the privacy issues stay in proper focus. This requires continuing attention from a broad public-policy perspective—a need that is not fulfilled today even within the scope of the Privacy Act. A means must be found to provide for continued public awareness of what is clearly a continuing and pivotal concern, and to assure ongoing attention to develop and refine understanding of specific and emerging problems. Notwithstanding the broad scope of this report, a number of tasks remain. Significant record-keeping areas, such as licensing at the State and local level, remain unexplored and several chapters of this report highlight other problem areas that need further analysis, including the issue of unreasonable intrusiveness as evidenced by the amount and type of information an individual is required to reveal about himself in return for a desired or needed service or benefit. As indicated earlier, the propriety question is an extremely delicate one and there is as yet no generally accepted method of arriving at answers to it in different contexts. The Commission's recommendations offer mechanisms to identify those kinds of questions so they can be debated in the context most likely to be constructive in determining public policy.

A further argument for combining all three alternatives is that experience with other public-policy issues of this sort suggests a continuing need to coordinate the policies that have been and will be adopted, and to assist in identifying and resolving real or apparent conflicts between existing, modified, and new statutes and regulations.

There is also the consideration that decentralized enforcement spreads responsibility for enforcement among agencies, organizations and individuals, each of which has numerous other responsibilities, thus increasing the risk that privacy objectives and protections will be obscured. The Commission advocates rights for individuals and reliance primarily on the courts to assure exercise of those rights. As indicated in many chapters of this report, however, improving the capability of the individual to protect himself can be an inadequate tool for resolving major systemic problems. The Commission sees a need for some influential "prodding" structure, some sustained oversight over the actual implementation of the protections it recommends. The Federal agency experience under the Privacy Act described in Chapter 13 attests to the need as it has arisen within the Federal government. The experience of the various Federal regulatory bodies that will have additional responsibilities if the Commission's recommendations are adopted—for example, the Federal Trade Commission, the Federal Reserve Board, and the compliance monitoring units of the Department of Health, Education and Welfare—further underscores it.

Finally, in all areas of the public sector the Commission has studied, the need for a mechanism to interpret both law and policy is clear. The difficulty of deciding which disclosures of records about individuals are routine within the meaning of the Privacy Act often raises conflicts of interest or interpretation between two or more Federal agencies. Similarly, as indicated in Chapter 13, Federal agencies often need an efficient means of arriving at common solutions to their common privacy protection problems, such as establishing procedures for the disposal of records, the propagation of corrections, and the maintenance of accountings of disclosures. State agencies frequently complain about being subjected to multiple, and sometimes incompatible, record-keeping rules as a consequence of participating in programs funded by different Federal agencies or by different components within a single agency. There must also be a way of bringing private-sector recommendations for voluntary action to the attention of all the relevant organizations. Many of these varied needs can best be met by the third implementation alternative.

Therefore the Commission recommends:

That the President and the Congress establish an independent entity within the Federal government charged with the responsibility of performing the following functions:

(a) **To monitor and evaluate the implementation of any statutes and regulations enacted pursuant to the recommendations of the Privacy Protection Study Commission, and have the authority to formally participate in any Federal administrative proceeding or process where the action being considered by another agency would have a material effect on the protection of personal privacy, either as the result of direct government action or as a result of government regulation of others.**

(b) **To continue to research, study, and investigate areas of privacy concern, and in particular, pursuant to the Commission's recommendations, if directed by Congress, to supplement other governmental mechanisms through which citizens could question the propriety of information collected and used by various segments of the public and private sector.**

(c) **To issue interpretative rules that must be followed by Federal agencies in implementing the Privacy Act of 1974 or revisions of this Act as suggested by this Commission. These rules may deal with procedural matters as well as the determination of what information must be available to individuals or the public at large, but in no instance shall it direct or suggest that information about an individual be withheld from individuals.**

(d) **To advise the President and the Congress, government agencies, and, upon request, States, regarding the privacy implications of proposed Federal or State statutes or regulations.**

The entity the Commission recommends may be a Federal Privacy Board or some other independent unit. However, if a new entity is established, the only enforcement authority the Commission would recommend it be given would be in connection with the implementation by Federal agencies of the Privacy Act itself. Its oversight responsibility in all of the other areas covered by the Commission's recommendations would require it only to participate in the proceedings of other agencies when substantive privacy issues are involved. For example, if the Federal Reserve Board were to issue proposals to amend its Regulation Z pursuant to the Truth-in-Lending Act after the Commission's recommendations are adopted, the new entity could participate in the proceedings only to the extent of presenting testimony and other comments from a privacy protection point of view.

PRESENTATION OF THE COMMISSION'S FINDINGS

The strongest argument for the need to keep attention focussed on the issue of personal privacy in record keeping is in the facts of record keeping themselves. The facts and the specific recommendations the Commission makes on the basis of its analysis of them are presented in the chapters that follow.

Chapter 2 examines the record-keeping policies and practices of credit grantors and the organizations whose records they use to establish and control their consumer-credit relationships. Consumer credit is an area in which new services and new record-keeping methods have dramatically changed the primary record-keeping relationship. As the chapter points out, personal interaction in consumer-credit transactions has declined markedly in the last several decades, making recorded information the paramount factor in establishing and maintaining the consumer-credit relationship. Chapter 2 ends with a note on the practices of commercial-reporting firms and the Commission's recommendations with respect to the records they maintain about individuals.

Chapter 3 explains why the record-keeping policies and practices of depository institutions (mainly commercial banks and savings and loan associations) are beginning to pattern themselves on those of credit grantors. Chapter 3 includes the Commission's analysis of the impact of electronic funds transfer systems on personal privacy, an impact with potentially profound significance.

Chapter 4 explores the creation and use of mailing lists. It shows that, contrary to popular belief, names and addresses do not get transferred from one mailing list to another in ways that disclose confidential information about individuals, but that impending changes in the way mailing lists are developed will make it easier for that to happen.

Chapter 5 examines record-keeping in the insurance relationship, an area that has been little explored from a privacy protection standpoint. In contrast to the credit and depository relationships, the insurance relationship may depend in part on information about individuals developed from interviews with neighbors and associates. This difference introduces a special set of privacy protection issues which are also present to some extent in the private-sector employee-employer relationship examined in Chapter 6.

Chapter 7 assesses the growing demand on medical-care providers for information in the records they maintain on individual patients. The use of medical-record information to make nonmedical decisions about individuals is explored in the chapters on insurance and employment, but Chapter 7 is where it is brought into focus. The crux of the problem is that individuals are asked to authorize the disclosure of medical-record information about themselves for a variety of purposes, but usually have no way of finding out what is in their medical records and thus must decide to authorize without a proper basis for estimating the consequences such disclosures may have for them.

Chapter 8 examines investigative-reporting services in the private sector, weaving threads from earlier chapters into an analysis of why the Commission believes sweeping changes are needed in the record-keeping practices of these firms.

Chapter 9 begins the transition from the private to the public sector. It concentrates on threats to personal privacy that stem from two main sources: changes in the way individuals go about their day-to-day business, and the tendency of government in recent years to rewrite the rules of the game without letting the other players know. It argues that to wait on the courts to create adequate protections for the individual is to adopt a policy of uncertain outcome and recommends legislation to right the balance between individual liberty and social order that the increase in government's demands for access to records about individuals has upset.

Chapters 10 and 11 address two areas—education, and public assistance and social services—in which both the Federal government and the States have a policy interest. The past decade has seen important initiatives to safeguard personal privacy from obvious record-keeping abuses in both areas. These two chapters evaluate those initiatives in terms of current conditions and emerging trends. Chapter 12 summarizes the State's role in protecting personal privacy as it emerges from the Commission's recommendations in all of the preceding chapters.

With Chapter 13, the report turns to the record-keeping practices of Federal government agencies. The Commission decided early in its inquiry that it could not recommend whether the principles and requirements of the Privacy Act should be extended to organizations outside the Federal government without first assessing the Privacy Act's effectiveness in the one area where its principles and requirements have been applied. Chapter 13 reports the results of the assessment and suggests a strategy for amending the Privacy Act as it applies to Federal agencies.

Chapter 14 on the Federal taxpayer relationship responds to a directive from the Congress that the Commission examine and make recommendations with respect to Internal Revenue Service disclosures of information about taxpayers. The Commission issued an interim report on the topic in June of 1976, just prior to passage of the 1976 Tax Reform Act. Chapter 14 compares the pertinent provisions of the 1976 legislation with the recommendations the Commission made at that time, and covers several related issues that were not addressed in the interim report.

Chapter 15 contributes to the continuing debate over the level of protection that should be afforded records about individuals that are intended to be used for research and statistics.

Chapter 16 on the Social Security Number and other assigned identifiers punctuates the Commission's findings and recommendations. While its principal conclusion is that the core problem is the lack of policy on the disclosures record-keeping organizations may make of a record about an individual, it recommends that government take no action that would encourage the drift toward using the SSN or anything else as a standard, universal identifier until such policy has been developed and made effective.

Chapter 2

The Consumer-Credit Relationship

Credit is essential for the vast majority of Americans. Since World War II, the amount of consumer credit outstanding in the United States has increased more than tenfold, totalling approximately $182 billion in April 1977.[1] Although this expansion is driven by factors such as increases in discretionary income, urbanization, and changes in the age distribution of the population, it has been greatly facilitated by innovations in the way credit records are kept and used.

Commercial banks, savings and loan associations, finance companies, credit unions, and retailers are the principal grantors of consumer credit today.[2] Chief among the factors that influence their record-keeping practices is the type of credit being extended. For a "closed-end" loan of a specific amount, such as an automobile loan, the records are set up for payments on a fixed schedule; additional records become necessary only if the consumer defaults on the agreed upon terms of the loan. By contrast, the credit-card program of a commercial bank, an "open-end" loan for no predetermined amount, generates a record (in triplicate) each time one of its cards is used, leaving a data trail in the records of the merchant who accepts the card as well as in the records of the card issuer. Grantors of open-end credit also depend on an elaborate authorization system to control customer fraud and overextension.

Personal interaction in consumer credit transactions has declined markedly in the last several decades, and this, too, has influenced credit grantor record-keeping practices. One manifestation of this decline is that recorded information is now the paramount factor in establishing and maintaining credit relationships. Growing reliance on recorded information has led credit grantors to improve their facilities for sharing information, especially through credit bureaus,[3] the traditional vehicle for such interchange. It has also encouraged them to experiment with ways of determin-

---

[1] *Federal Reserve Statistical Release*, "Consumer Installment Credit-April 1977," June 6, 1977. The figure as of April 1977 is not seasonally adjusted, and excludes thirty-day charge credit held by retailers, oil and gas companies, and travel and entertainment companies amounting to over $2,303 million at the end of April.

[2] The National Commission on Consumer Finance, *Consumer Credit in the United States,* 1972, p. 11. The Commission recognizes that savings and loan associations technically do not grant "consumer credit," but in terms of record-keeping consequences considers that an artificial distinction.

[3] Most credit bureaus in the early 1900's began by providing service for a specific trade or industry. By 1906, there were 30 retail credit bureaus reporting primarily on individuals rather

ing credit eligibility based on measurable characteristics of categories of individuals rather than on the unique characteristics of any one credit applicant. Finally, it has made the records generated in the context of the consumer-credit relationship increasingly attractive to other types of users, especially to government agencies.

The first part of this chapter focuses on the record-keeping practices of modern-day credit grantors. How is the eligibility of applicants for credit determined? How do credit-card authorization services work? What changes are being made in billing procedures? What information concerning payment habits is reported to credit bureaus, other credit grantors, and collection agencies? How do credit grantors respond to requests for information on their customers that is not necessary to service the credit relationship, including requests by government agencies?

The second section discusses the record-keeping practices of credit bureaus. As the credit grantor's principal source and repository of consumer credit-history information, the credit bureau plays a gatekeeping role which significantly affects not only credit relationships, but also the relationships an individual has with insurers, employers, landlords, and others who make decisions about him on the basis of information in credit bureau records.

The third section examines consumer-credit relationships in the light of the three policy objectives outlined in Chapter 1: (1) to minimize intrusiveness; (2) to maximize fairness; and (3) to create legitimate, enforceable expectations of confidentiality. This section is organized around a set of problems an individual may encounter in the course of establishing and maintaining credit. Business practices, including those prescribed by law, are evaluated in terms of how they comport with the three policy objectives.

Finally, in the last section, the Commission makes specific recommendations, which, if adopted in the context of existing legal protections and business practices, should bring the consumer-credit relationship in line with the three policy objectives.

CREDIT GRANTORS: THE PRIMARY RECORD KEEPERS

ESTABLISHING THE CREDIT RELATIONSHIP

To obtain any form of credit, an individual must apply for it and be evaluated according to a credit grantor's criteria of credit worthiness. Credit grantors need personal information about the applicant as raw material for this evaluative process. Credit grantors differ with respect to the amount of personal information they ask for, the extent to which they verify and supplement it, and the criteria they use to determine credit worthiness. These variations are influenced by the technological sophistication of the credit grantor, its portion of the credit market, and its motives for extending

---

than on businesses. See written statement of Associated Credit Bureaus, Inc., *Credit Reporting and Payment Authorization Services,* Hearings before the Privacy Protection Study Commission, August 4, 1976, p. 7. (hereinafter cited as "Credit Reporting Hearings.")

credit. For example, a credit grantor with highly reliable methods of predicting responsible credit use, and a system that minimizes irresponsible use, might not need reports from a credit bureau.

An applicant typically starts the credit decision process by divulging some information about himself to the credit grantor, usually by filling out an application. The credit grantor then typically verifies and supplements this information. This may involve an inquiry to a credit bureau, or to other sources, such as another credit grantor or the applicant's employer. It is important to recognize that the applicant seldom provides all the information used in making the credit decision. Moreover, credit applications rarely indicate the full extent of the additional inquiries the credit grantor will conduct.

Verifying information provided by the applicant has been considered until recently an essential step in deciding whether to grant credit. The need for an independent source of information about the applicant was a common theme in the testimony credit grantors presented to the Commission. J. C. Penney Company, Inc., put the matter bluntly:

> Let us not overlook a significant fact . . . people tend to state their case most favorably when they know that the information they supply will be the basis of their having their application granted . . . . It is essential that we be permitted to verify the information presented to us by the applicant through credit bureaus and others . . . .[4]

Historically, evaluating a credit application involved a great deal of judgment, albeit according to general standards of credit worthiness. Today, however, the increasing number of applicants has driven many credit grantors, particularly the larger ones, to experiment with methods that promise to be both less costly and more reliable.[5]

Many are experimenting with a technique called "point scoring." This technique scores an applicant's credit worthiness on the basis of a small cluster of personal characteristics which statistics show to be a reliable measure of ability and willingness to pay. For example, there is statistical evidence that people in some occupations are more likely to repay credit obligations than people in other occupations, and a numerical value can be assigned to the difference. The same is true of people who own their homes as compared to those who rent. How long a person has lived at the same address is another such factor. A credit grantor using this system rates its applicants as credit risks according to the total number of points they score on the characteristics it considers predictive. The characteristics in a particular point-scoring cluster and the numerical value assigned to each may vary from credit grantor to credit grantor and from one geographic area to another, and a credit grantor may revise its formula from time to time to

---

[4] Written statement of J. C. Penney Co., Inc., *Credit-Card Issuers and Reservations Systems*, Hearings before the Privacy Protection Study Commission, February 12, 1976, pp. 18-19. (hereinafter cited as "Credit-Card Issuers Hearings.")

[5] Roland E. Brandel, "New Dangers Arise In Point Scoring, But You Can't Afford To Be Without It," *Banking*, March 1977, pp. 86-94.

take account of its experience with customers and of changing economic conditions. An advantage of point scoring is that it may eliminate the need for a credit report. As Anthony Nicholas, Citibank Vice President for Master Charge operations told the Commission:

> Our new credit scoring procedures are expected to allow us to grant or deny credit on the basis of the application in about 20 percent of the cases; formerly, credit reports would have been required to confirm the credit histories of these applicants.[6]

On the other hand, point scoring effectively eliminates the individual's opportunity to challenge the basis for a credit decision. The spread of point scoring and other credit policies predicated entirely on group behavior is diminishing individuality as a factor in granting credit, and threatens to push it out of the credit relationship altogether. The Equal Credit Opportunity Act,[7] which now permits a rejected applicant to request the reasons for an adverse credit decision, relies on the theory that an adverse decision can be explained in terms of one or more particular characteristics of the individual. Point scoring, however, submerges particular characteristics in an overall score. All the characteristics included in a formula contribute to the score, so that a decision is the result of a combination of factors weighted in a particular way. A change in the credit grantor's weighting of any one of the factors could alter the decision. Thus, legal protections do not appear to be keeping pace with credit evaluation practices.

CREDIT-CARD AUTHORIZATION SERVICES

It is doubtful that any other innovation in the history of consumer credit has had a more profound impact than the credit card. The credit card has virtually transformed the consumer-credit relationship, and a whole new record-keeping industry has grown up around it. A credit-card program cannot operate safely unless the credit grantor can monitor credit-card transactions and deny credit when it sees fit.

The type of authorization system used depends primarily on the size of the card issuer's operations. Large card issuers such as Sears, Roebuck and American Express operate their own authorization systems. Banks that offer Master Charge and BankAmericard belong to service organizations that supplement their own authorization systems to provide worldwide coverage.[8] Finally, airlines, hotels, and restaurants often use independent authorization services that provide information obtained from American Express, banks, and other card issuers.

The core of any authorization system is a file showing which accounts

---

[6] Statement of First National City Bank (Citibank), Credit-Card Issuers Hearings, February 11, 1976, p. 4.

[7] 15 U.S.C. 1691 et seq.

[8] Written statement of National BankAmericard, Inc., Credit-Card Issuers Hearings, February 11, 1976, pp. 3-9; Statement of Interbank Card Association, Credit-Card Issuers Hearings, February 11, 1976, pp. 4-8.

have been cancelled or are overextended, and which cards have been lost or stolen. An authorization system protects merchants by providing a central list of the card numbers identifying accounts in trouble. A merchant can check this list before accepting a credit card in payment for a purchase. The card issuer guarantees payment to the merchant as long as the card is not on the list. A merchant who accepts a listed card must absorb any loss that results.

An authorization system also protects the credit grantor by limiting its risk. For credit grantors that specify in advance the total amount that may be charged to an account during a billing period, the system stops the card holder from exceeding his limit. For those that do not establish a credit limit in advance, the system triggers intervention when the balance owed on an account reaches sizable proportions. Trained authorizers then decide whether to approve a new charge on the account. In making the decision, the authorizer may use criteria other than available credit. At American Express, the authorizer may review the card holder's original application, for example, to see if the income originally declared makes it likely that the card holder will be able to pay for the purchase in question.[9] Such *ad hoc* decisions, however, are the exception rather than the rule.

Most authorization systems also monitor credit-card accounts for unusual activity indicating fraud. Most major card issuers are developing systems that allow them to authorize every transaction, no matter how small the amount. This means that instead of relying on files which can show only that a card holder has abused his credit, the card issuer can get instantly a complete, up-to-the-minute status report on any card holder's account.

Card issuers disclose the negative information in their files to independent authorization services which in turn report it to their own subscribers on demand.[10] The main subscribers to these independent services are airlines, hotels, and restaurants, which use them as a supplement to the card issuers' own authorization systems. Although the independent services are functionally similar to the card issuers' authorization systems, they represent yet another source of information that may affect the card holder. It is doubtful, moreover, that many of the card holders on whom an independent service reports derogatory information, card holders with whom the service has no credit relationship, know that it exists. Consequently, a card holder who asks a card issuer to correct inaccurate information in its records about him has no way of knowing if an independent service also has the information in question, much less whether its records will also be corrected.

The adverse impact of billing errors and the growing reliance on independent authorization services underscore the importance of prompt correction of inaccuracies in the records maintained by a credit grantor as well as those maintained outside of its immediate control. Indeed, the harm

---

[9] Written statement of American Express Company, Credit-Card Issuers Hearings, February 11, 1976, p. 4.

[10] Submission of TRW Validata, "Background Information on TRW Validata," *Depository and Lending Institutions,* Hearings before the Privacy Protection Study Commission, April 21, 1976. (hereinafter cited as "Depository and Lending Institutions Hearings.")

that can be done by errors in the files of a credit-card authorization service makes the point sharply. Discovering that "it was all a mistake" can be small and bitter comfort to a traveler stranded in a strange city late at night because information about his credit-card account has been inaccurately reported to an independent authorization service.

BILLING

The traditional forms of closed-end credit need involve no monthly bill because the contract between the credit grantor and its customer specifies at the outset how much will be paid and when. With open-end credit plans, however, the monthly bill is often the principal means of communication between credit grantor and individual. This gives the credit grantor's billing practices great significance for the individual.

Most credit-card issuers initially used the so-called "country club" billing system which supplies the individual with two copies of every charge voucher, one from the merchant at the time of purchase, the other from the card issuer with the monthly statement. To reduce paperwork, many card issuers, and particularly the nationwide bank-card systems, have been switching to "descriptive" billing. Under this new system, the individual still gets a voucher from the merchant at the time of purchase, but the monthly statement includes a brief description of each purchase instead of a copy of the voucher.

In September 1975, the Board of Governors of the Federal Reserve System amended its Regulation Z *[12 C.F.R. 277.7(b)(ii)(B)]* to require credit grantors to furnish enough information on or with their periodic statements of open-end credit-card accounts to enable their customers to identify the transactions for which they are being billed.[11] As a consequence, credit-card issuers must now capture and store more information on individual transactions than they would otherwise record. For example, a retailer's statement must identify the goods or services it covers, while the statements of banks, American Express, and other independent card issuers must show the name of the merchant, and the city and State in which the transaction took place.

The card issuers' move to descriptive billing and the Federal Reserve Board's response to it represent something of a trade-off for a card holder. On the one hand, he is given enough information to tell him whether or not he made each purchase, but on the other, more information than before about how he uses his credit privilege goes into the card issuer's records about him. Moreover, new billing practices are generating special problems in reporting disputes over billing to credit bureaus. These problems are discussed in some detail below; here it is enough to note that the impact of computerization is great, both as it affects the incidence and propagation of record-keeping errors, and as it affects an innocent victim's power to mitigate the adverse consequences of such errors in situations where it is not always assumed that the customer knows best.

---

[11] Board of Governors of the Federal Reserve System, *Annual Report to Congress on Truth-In-Lending for the Year 1975,* January 3, 1976.

DISCLOSURES TO CREDIT BUREAUS AND TO OTHER CREDIT GRANTORS

Cooperation among credit grantors is a basic tenet of the credit-granting business. Its most visible manifestation is the way credit grantors have traditionally used credit bureaus to exchange information about their customers.

Most credit grantors do not inform an applicant that information about him will be reported to credit bureaus. As recently as November 1976, Citibank of New York inserted the following clause in its Master Charge card-holder agreement:

> Your performance of this agreement may be reported to credit reporting agencies. No one else will be given such information without proper legal process or your prior written approval. We will try to notify you by phone or by mail of a court order in order to give you an opportunity to object to it.[12]

Although this notice does not say whether there will actually be a disclosure, nor to which credit bureau a disclosure may be made, nor where the information will go from there, it represents a step forward from the general practice of no notice at all.

What information is disclosed to credit bureaus? Most of the credit grantors with computer-based record-keeping systems provide the following information to one or more credit bureaus every 30 days: customer account number, customer name, spouse's name (if account is a joint account), street address, city, State, ZIP code, account type, date of last activity, scheduled payment date (if an installment plan account), date account opened (month and year), highest credit accumulated, amount owing, amount past due, the credit grantor's rating of the account, which is typically reported under the heading "usual manner of payment," and an indicator as to any outstanding billing dispute (as required by the Fair Credit Billing Act[13]). This information may be reported to automated credit bureaus directly, and to manual bureaus through a microfiche service offered by Associated Credit Bureaus, Inc., the credit bureau trade association.[14]

Of these items regularly disclosed to credit bureaus, "usual manner of payment" and "amount owing," deserve particular attention. As to the former, credit grantors rate an individual (or individuals in a joint account) as illustrated below.[15]

0   Too new to rate; approved but not used
1   Pays (or paid) within 30 days of billing; pays accounts as agreed

---

[12] Submission of Citibank, Credit-Card Issuers Hearings, February 11, 1976.

[13] 15 U.S.C. 1601, 1601 note, 1610, 1631, 1632, 1637, 1666, *et seq.*

[14] Known as the "Trade Verification Service," this microfiche service was developed so that small manual bureaus could continue to receive information from large automated credit grantors. The service routes information to credit bureaus on the basis of ZIP codes.

[15] Submission of Associated Credit Bureaus, Inc., "The Common Language of the Consumer Credit Industry," Credit Reporting Hearings, August 4, 1976.

2   Pays (or paid) in more than 30 days, but not more than 60 days, or not more than one payment past due
3   Pays (or paid) in more than 60 days, but not more than 90 days, or two payments past due
4   Pays (or paid) in more than 90 days, but not more than 120 days, or three or more payments past due
5   Account is at least 120 days overdue but is not yet rated "9"
7   Making regular payments under Wage Earner Plan or similar arrangement
8   Repossession. (Indicate if it is a voluntary return of merchandise by the customer.)
9   Bad debt; place for collection; skip

Except for TRW Credit Data, which has a more detailed system for recording usual manner of payment,[16] the codes shown above are standard throughout the credit-reporting industry. Moreover, credit grantors have been working together to make the ratings they report to credit bureaus comparable,[17] although the significance of these ratings for credit decisions still varies with different credit grantors. This is but one example of industry efforts to standardize credit-related information.

The second item regularly disclosed to credit bureaus—amount owing—is significant because it enables credit grantors to avoid consumers who are already or may become overextended. Amount owing has always been exchanged freely among credit grantors, but only on direct inquiry either from credit grantor-to-credit grantor, or from credit bureau-to-credit grantor on behalf of another credit grantor. Only in the last few years have credit grantors routinely reported it to credit bureaus.

One result of this routine reporting is to make the credit evaluation process more efficient. Another is to concentrate information that historically was scattered among credit grantors until needed for a specific purpose. Still another result is to facilitate or improve processes such as "prescreening" mailing lists[18] and continuous monitoring of accounts for signs of overextension.

In addition to the regular reports, most credit grantors also notify credit bureaus of other events bearing on the credit relationship. For example, when an account limit is changed, when an account becomes delinquent or a delinquency is paid, when an inactive account is purged from the credit grantor's files, or when a customer dies, credit bureaus will normally be notified.

Not all credit grantors with open-end accounts routinely disclose all of

---

[16] Submission of TRW Credit Data, "Credit Datagram History Issue," Credit Reporting Hearings, August 4, 1976.

[17] Written statement of Associated Credit Bureaus, Inc., Credit Reporting Hearings, August 4, 1976, pp. 10-11.

[18] According to the Federal Trade Commission, "Prescreening is the process by which a list of potential customers is submitted to a credit bureau which then audits the list by deletion of those names that have an adverse credit record. Normally, such lists would be used for mail order solicitation or credit card solicitation." 16 C.F.R. 600.5 Effective February 23, 1973, 38 Federal Register 4947. The use of credit-bureau files to evaluate individuals on a mailing list is further discussed in Chapter 4.

the above customer information to credit bureaus. For example, American Express provides no customer information to credit bureaus, except in response to a specific request. In testimony before the Commission, American Express representatives said that when a credit bureau asks for a reference, the company supplies its card holder's name and address, membership date, highest amount of credit extended during the last six months, and an indication as to whether the account has been maintained satisfactorily, unsatisfactorily, or is the subject of some pending action.[19] American Express does not respond directly to the requests of other credit grantors for information about its card holders. Atlantic Richfield Company testified that its policy is similar, although it will disclose information to another credit grantor if the card holder insists.[20]

Reports to credit bureaus on closed-end accounts are less frequent than those on open-end accounts. The monthly account balance for a closed-end account is predetermined by the credit agreement. Once a credit bureau records the terms of a new closed-end account, the credit grantor need only report on changes in the account's status, such as delinquencies, repossessions, charge offs,[21] and final completion of the contract.[22]

Depository institutions (e.g., commercial banks, savings and loan associations, and credit unions) testified that they distinguish between their credit and their depository relationships when disclosing information to credit bureaus and other credit grantors. For example, Continental Illinois National Bank and Trust Company of Chicago testified that it will freely disclose information about credit customers to the "legitimate credit-grantor community," but will not even verify the existence of a savings account, let alone disclose the account balance to credit bureaus or other lenders.[23]

Bay View Federal Savings and Loan Association of California gave the Commission some insight into the disclosure practices of a large savings and loan institution. When it gets a telephone request for information about a savings account, it verifies the caller's identity by returning the call after checking the telephone directory. It will give a credit grantor the names of all owners of the account, the date the account was opened, the "low-hi" balances, and, for any account closed within the year, the closing date. When the request covers more than one account, each account is described separately.

Bay View Federal testified that it will not respond to a written request for information about a savings account unless the request is accompanied by the depositor's signed authorization. Even then, the bank will only verify items specified in the request, such as balance as of a particular date, the

---

[19] Written statement of American Express Company, Credit-Card Issuers Hearings, February 11, 1976, p. 7.

[20] Written statement of Atlantic Richfield Company, Credit-Card Issuers Hearings, February 11, 1976, p. 7.

[21] A credit grantor will "charge off" a delinquent account when its efforts to collect the outstanding balance prove unsuccessful, or when it learns that an individual has been adjudicated bankrupt.

[22] Written statement of Continental Illinois National Bank and Trust Company of Chicago, Depository and Lending Institutions Hearings, April 21, 1976, p. 5.

[23] *Ibid.*, p. 6.

date the account was opened, and the names of other parties on the account. Most written requests come from welfare agencies, outside auditors, and other banks. Bay View Federal keeps copies of them all, and a record of the disclosures made in response to them.[24]

At Western Electric Employees Federal Credit Union (WEEFCU), no information about a member's depository account is provided in response to an inquiry from a third party without first notifying the member. When an inquiry about an account comes in, WEEFCU discloses ". . . only that the person is on payroll deduction and that the account is current."[25] (The member is immediately notified of any inquiry and any disclosure.) No adverse information is disclosed unless the inquirer obtains the member's explicit authorization. A Western Electric representative explained: "Ordinarily, we disclose . . . information to third parties only upon written request of the credit union member."[26]

The bylaws of the National Credit Union Administration stipulate that:

> The officers, members of committees, and employees of [a] credit union shall hold in confidence all transactions of [the] credit union with its members and all information respecting their personal affairs, except to the extent deemed necessary by the [credit union] board in connection with the making of loans and the collection thereof.[27]

These bylaws help to shape the disclosure policy of Federal credit unions, and the bylaws of State-chartered credit unions contain similar provisions.[28]

The Lender's Exchange

Consumer finance companies are a source of closed-end credit for many Americans. In addition to the disclosures they routinely make to credit bureaus and other creditors, finance companies maintain an industry index called the Lender's Exchange. According to FinanceAmerica Corporation:

> The Lender's Exchange is a nonprofit, cooperative organization which serves as a clearinghouse for information among members, and membership is limited to licensed lenders engaged in the business of making loans . . . .
> The Exchange functions to assist lenders in identifying

---

[24] Written statement of Bay View Federal Savings and Loan Association, Depository and Lending Institutions Hearings, April 22, 1976, pp. 5-6.

[25] Written statement of Credit Union National Association, Depository and Lending Institutions Hearings, April 21, 1976, p. 8.

[26] Ibid., p. 9.

[27] Article XIX, Section 2 of the standard form of Federal credit union bylaws, as set forth in National Credit Union Administration (NCUA) Regulation Section 701.14(e). See also NCUA Regulation Sections 720.3, "Information Made Available to the Public" and 720.4, "Unpublished, Confidential, and Privileged Information."

[28] Written statement of Credit Union National Association, Depository and Lending Institutions Hearings, April 21, 1976, p. 11.

individuals who already have existing obligations . . . unlike a credit bureau, the Lender's Exchange does not keep records of indebtedness [i.e., the outstanding balance owed] to members or nonmembers and has no information on an individual's paying habits.[29]

An inquiring lender must provide the exchange with the applicant's name, address, date of birth, Social Security number, present place of employment, and occupation. These categories of information are maintained by the Exchange, and it therefore has some similarity to a credit bureau's files. As a practical matter, however, it simply serves as a pointer for lenders who want to know which other lenders have outstanding loans or applications from an individual. The function of this index, in other words, is to alert lenders to possible overextension and to facilitate direct communication among them about it.[30] An individual's name is removed from the Lender's Exchange when a member company reports that it was listed in error, or that the loan application has been declined, or that the obligation has been paid in full.[31]

DISCLOSURES TO COLLECTION AGENCIES

A grantor of open-end credit can take various steps to curtail credit abuse. When a credit-card account becomes delinquent, the card issuer notifies both the card holder and one or more credit bureaus and identifies the account in its authorization system's "negative file." It may also notify an independent authorization service. If the delinquency continues, the card issuer may try to retrieve the card or collect the unpaid balance, or both, or it may turn the account over to a collection agency.

There are firms that specialize in retrieving the credit cards of card holders whose privileges are revoked. Bank of America characterizes card-retrieval firms as investigative agencies, and gives them the following information: card holder's name, last-known address, account number, and, in some instances, last-known employer's address.[32] Bank of America puts no restrictions on the use of card-holder information by investigative agencies either during the retrieval efforts or afterwards.

Some of these investigative agencies may also prepare background reports for insurance underwriters, so that disclosures made to them for a collection purpose could jeopardize the card holder's insurance application. Such second- and third-order impacts underscore the importance of giving card-retrieval firms information only on individuals who actually have failed to meet a credit obligation.

When Bank of America assigns an account to a collection agency, it

---

[29] Written statement of FinanceAmerica Corporation, Depository and Lending Institutions Hearings, April 21, 1976, pp. 18-19.

[30] The Lenders Exchange is designed to facilitate direct inquiries among its subscribers. In contrast, as credit bureaus receive more information about individuals, their subscribers' need to communicate among themselves seems likely to disappear.

[31] Written statement of FinanceAmerica Corporation, Depository and Lending Institutions Hearings, April 21, 1976, p. 20.

[32] Written statement of Bank of America, Credit-Card Issuers Hearings, February 11, 1976, p. 15.

provides the following information: the card holder's name, account number, and payment history, plus any other possibly useful information on the card holder's original application, e.g., name and address of closest relative. Again, there are no restrictions on how a collection agency may use this information either during or after collection. As a consequence, information may be disclosed to potential users who have no role at all in the credit relationship.

Other credit grantors testified before the Commission that they, too, employ investigative agencies, both for locating card holders and for obtaining payment from them. Because such agencies are subject to the Fair Credit Reporting Act (FCRA),[33] the credit grantor must notify the card holder that an investigation of him may be conducted. To meet the FCRA requirement, some credit grantors include in their letters to customers with delinquent accounts paragraphs like these:

> This is to advise you . . . that an investigation may be made whereby information may be obtained through personal interviews with neighbors, friends, or others with whom you are acquainted. Such an investigation may be found necessary by us to aid in our efforts to collect the outstanding balance on your account.
>
> You have the right to make a written request within a reasonable period of time for a complete and accurate disclosure of additional information concerning the nature and scope of this investigation.
>
> Why make it difficult? Pay now or call us for suitable terms.[34]

The implied but nonetheless obvious threat in these statements is that unless the delinquent pays, interviewers will inevitably reveal information damaging to his reputation and job security.[35] The threat of disclosing a person's financial difficulties to his friends, neighbors, or employer before a debt is on public record raises fundamental questions about the confidentiality of the debtor-creditor relationship. The fact that collection efforts are sometimes initiated on the basis of inaccurate information, or directed at the wrong person, makes its doubtful legitimacy all the more questionable.

DISCLOSURES TO GOVERNMENT AGENCIES

A credit grantor's records about an individual can tell a great deal about his expenditures, possessions, lodging and eating habits, and travel.

---

[33] 15 U.S.C. 1687 *et seq.* See Chapter 8 for a discussion of investigative-reporting agencies and the Commission's recommendations concerning them.

[34] Written statement of Federal Trade Commission Staff, Credit-Card Issuers Hearings, February 12, 1976, p. 29, footnote 33.

[35] The National Commission on Consumer Finance concluded: "Threat to job security and application of social pressure are not proper methods to induce payment of debt. Until such time as a debt has been reduced to judgment, it should be a private matter between the debtor and creditor. Any communication regarding a debt to the debtor's employer or neighbors or others without the debtor's consent is an invasion of the debtor's privacy and is not a legitimate collection practice." The National Commission on Consumer Finance, *Consumer Credit in the United States,* 1972, p. 39.

They may also tell something about the individual's associates, as some credit cards are used for billing long-distance telephone calls. This kind of information has obvious value for government agencies with investigative, regulatory, or law enforcement missions.

A government agency can gain access to a credit grantor's records about an individual by various methods: court order and judicial subpoena (a writ carrying the force of legal compulsion); administrative subpoena[36] (a writ backed by the threat of binding judicial enforcement, but holding no actual legal penalty for noncompliance); pursuant to compulsory reporting statutes or regulations;[37] and through informal requests made by letter or telephone or in person.

In deciding which of these procedures to use in any particular instance, an agency must weigh their relative efficiencies. The compulsory procedures are more certain, but the informal procedures are less costly. The time and talent used in getting a single judicial subpoena could probably produce dozens of informal inquiries. Moreover, unlike a compulsory procedure, even the broadest informal request for information need not be justified to a court. Agencies understandably tend to rely on informal procedures more than on compulsory ones, especially if they have a sympathetic working relationship with the credit grantor.[38]

No statute regulates the voluntary disclosure of a credit grantor's records to government agencies and, as far as the Commission could determine in public hearings and research, many credit grantors have no consistent policy concerning such disclosures. In a Commission survey of local and national credit-card issuers other than banks, approximately half of the 26 that responded had no explicit policy. Moreover, the policies described to the Commission varied widely.

For example, one card issuer said that it honors all government inquiries except those made by telephone, while another averred that it discloses no record information except as required by "compulsory process."[39] Some credit grantors alert a customer when they receive a formal government inquiry, a subpoena, for example, but because many government inquiries do not appear to be made that way, the practical effect of such a policy is necessarily limited. Moreover, no statute, regulation, or judicial ruling now obligates any credit grantor, except a bank in California, to advise an individual that information from his account records has been given to a government agency; a credit grantor does so entirely at its own discretion.

Except for the Internal Revenue Service, no government agency at any

---

[36] Sometimes referred to as an "administrative summons."

[37] See Chapter 9.

[38] For example, the Federal Bureau of Investigation investigates crimes committed against a federally insured bank and also routinely checks criminal histories of prospective bank employees.

[39] Compulsory process includes an administrative summons, judicial subpoena, and court order.

level notifies the individual that it wants or has obtained access to his credit records.[40] Indeed, agencies usually take the position that notifying an individual may prompt him to alter his pattern of activity or to destroy evidence, and thus specifically asks the credit grantor not to tell him.

Moreover, the evidence before the Commission suggests that, as a general rule, government agencies can expect credit grantors to assist them voluntarily in their search for records. The 26 firms that responded to the Commission's survey collectively have more than 80 million credit cards in circulation. The survey asked each respondent how many times during the last two years it had complied with various types of requests for information about individual card holders from: (1) the Internal Revenue Service (IRS); (2) the Federal Bureau of Investigation (FBI); (3) the Securities and Exchange Commission (SEC); (4) the Department of Justice (divisions other than the FBI); (5) the Central Intelligence Agency (CIA); (6) other Federal agencies; (7) State law enforcement agencies; (8) other State agencies; (9) local law enforcement agencies; (10) other local agencies; and (11) congressional committees. Six of the firms that responded—Diners Club, Exxon, Gulf (for one of its two credit-card record systems), Mobile, Chevron, and Dayton-Hudson—were able to provide statistics for 1974 and 1975.

Of a total of 1,474 such disclosures the six firms made during the two-year period, 66 percent were made to Federal agencies, 25 percent to local government entities, and the remaining 9 percent to State agencies. Of the disclosures to Federal agencies, 438 or 45 percent were to the FBI, and of those, 99.5 percent were in response to informal FBI requests; that is, requests made on letterhead stationery, during personal visits by agents, or by telephone. These data strongly suggest that the FBI's usual mode of direct access to card-holder records is *not* through one of the forms of compulsory process mentioned above.

Approximately 16 percent (239) of the total number of disclosures the six card issuers made in 1974 and 1975 were to the IRS. In contrast to the FBI, however, the IRS relied heavily on formal procedures, and in particular the administrative subpoena, which was the vehicle for 65 percent of its successful requests to the six firms.

The Department of Justice (divisions other than the FBI) ranked third among the agencies named as recipients by the six firms. It used judicial subpoenas to obtain 68 percent of the 104 disclosures made to it.

The SEC and the CIA each received only two of the reported disclosures. Diners Club acceded to two administrative subpoenas from the SEC, while Gulf twice disclosed card-holder records to the CIA after receiving a personal visit or telephone call. Thirteen percent of the reported disclosures were to other Federal agencies, the Federal Energy Administration and the Postal Service accounting for many of them. Sixty-nine percent of the disclosures in this category were made in response to a personal visit or a telephone call.

At the State and local level, more than 98 percent (189) of the

---

[40] See Chapter 9 for a discussion of recent changes in the Internal Revenue Code concerning the use of the administrative summons to collect information.

disclosures made were to local law enforcement agencies in response to informal requests. Based on these data, it would appear that local law enforcement agencies, like the FBI, make most of their requests informally.

In sum, 1,070 of the 1,474 requests complied with by the six firms that kept records of their disclosures to government agencies did not entail any form of legal compulsion or even the prospect of compulsion. Rather, they were made informally in letters, personal visits, or by telephone.

The Commission recognizes that these data were provided by a small number of firms and thus, at best, only illustrate practices and suggest patterns of behavior. As the Commission's inquiry also established, however, accurate estimates of the number of credit-grantor disclosures to government agencies are impossible to make because many credit grantors keep no records of such disclosures.

Consumer-credit records, particularly those necessary for a credit-card account, are, as noted above, an ever richer source of detailed information about individuals. For government agencies to tap this source is a relatively recent development and one which cannot be dismissed lightly. The Commission addresses this issue more fully in Chapter 9.

CREDIT BUREAUS: THE GATEKEEPERS

A credit bureau[41] is essentially a clearinghouse for information supplied by credit grantors and collection agencies, and culled by the bureau itself from public records. Although there have been credit bureaus since the late 19th century, the advent of open-end credit coupled with new applications of computers and telecommunications has increased their importance both to the credit grantor and to the consumer.

A credit bureau satisfies one of the credit grantor's basic needs: a centralized source of information about an applicant's ability and willingness to pay. In recent years, automation has enabled some credit bureaus to monitor an individual's performance in a variety of credit relationships, thereby fulfilling another of the credit grantor's needs: to be on the alert for changes in an individual's financial situation which might affect his ability to meet obligations already incurred.

There are approximately 2,000 credit bureaus in operation today. Although most are small local monopolies serving communities of 20,000 or fewer households,[42] computerization has allowed a few to operate virtually nationwide. The five largest—TRW Credit Data, TransUnion, Credit

---

[41] Prior to the Fair Credit Reporting Act of 1970, credit grantors were served by "credit bureaus" and insurance companies were served by "inspection bureaus." The FCRA introduced the common nomenclature of "consumer-reporting agencies." However, the law recognizes the substantive difference between the credit and insurance areas, and it is important to bear this distinction in mind. Fundamentally, they differ from inspection bureaus with respect to type of subscribers (credit grantors rather than insurers), the type of information reported, their methods of collection, and some of their sources. For a discussion of inspection bureaus, commonly referred to in this report as "investigative-reporting agencies," see Chapter 8.

[42] Written statement of Associated Credit Bureaus, Inc., Credit Reporting Hearings, August 4, 1976, p. 1.

Bureau, Inc., Chilton Corporation, and Credit Bureau of Greater Houston—together maintain more than 150 million individual credit records. Moreover, because the large nationwide (and regional) bureaus often compete within the same geographic area, a current record on a great many Americans is maintained by more than one bureau.

Except for TRW Credit Data's limitations on the types of public-record information it reports,[43] there is consensus within the industry as to the categories of information on an individual a bureau should maintain and report. These include: *identifying information,* usually the individual's full name, Social Security number, address, telephone number, and spouse's name; *financial status and employment information,* including income, spouse's income, place, position, and tenure of employment, other sources of income, duration, and income in former employment; *credit history,* including types of credit previously obtained, names of previous credit grantors, extent of previous credit, and complete payment history; *existing lines of credit,* including payment habits and all outstanding obligations; *public-record information,* including pertinent newspaper clippings, arrest and conviction records, bankruptcies, tax liens, and law suits; and finally *a listing of bureau subscribers that have previously asked for a credit report on the individual.*[44]

Although credit grantors are a credit bureau's principal subscribers, and regulation of the industry is mainly predicated on credit grantors' need to exchange information, other important bureau clients include other credit bureaus, collection agencies, inspection bureaus, insurance companies, employers, landlords, and law enforcement agencies.[45] In other words, a credit bureau report will be available to subscribers with whom the individual has no credit relationship, although it cannot be assumed that the individual himself knows that.

Credit reports are the principal revenue producer for most credit bureaus, but the modern bureau also provides a number of other services. Most have at least a debt collection division.[46] Some automated bureaus "pre-screen" mailing lists to be used in targeted marketing campaigns. Some of the larger automated bureaus offer an account-monitoring service which automatically warns a subscriber if activity in an individual's file indicates that his credit worthiness ought to be reexamined. An unusual payment

---

[43] TRW Credit Data limits its reporting of public-record information to legal items that bear upon the financial standing of an individual, such as bankruptcies, tax liens and judgments. TRW Credit Data does not maintain information concerning arrests, indictments, or convictions. Written statement of TRW Information Services, Credit Reporting Hearings, August 4, 1976, p. 5.

[44] Submission of Associated Credit Bureaus, Inc., "Sample Copy of Form 100 Showing Typical Credit Report," Credit Reporting Hearings, August 4, 1976.

[45] These subscribers were legitimated by the Fair Credit Reporting Act in part because no distinction was drawn between credit bureaus and inspection bureaus other than the type of report prepared. Nonetheless, the Fair Credit Reporting Act was intended to limit, if only in broad terms, the availability of credit and inspection reports.

[46] Of the 1,800 credit bureaus belonging to Associated Credit Bureaus, Inc., 1,100 have debt collection divisions. Written statement of Associated Credit Bureaus, Inc., Credit Reporting Hearings, August 4, 1976, p. 20.

pattern, charging the limit on several credit cards, and divorce are the kinds of activity that trigger a warning.[47] Finally, some credit bureaus have developed check authorization[48] and medical billing services.[49]

Several factors account for these changes in the credit-reporting industry. Central to the explosive growth of the automated bureaus has been the growth of consumer credit itself, most notably in automobile financing and in the variety of open-end credit plans developed by retailers, by credit-card companies, and, most recently, by commercial banks.[50]

Changes in credit-granting methods bring new forms of credit reporting. The spread of open-end credit redefines the credit risk, which must now be measured by the total amount of credit available to an individual rather than by the amount of debt he has already incurred. As a result, credit grantors are beginning to rely on credit bureaus not only for information to use in making the inital decision to grant or deny credit, but also as monitors of the successful applicant's performance across a variety of credit relationships.[51]

Once credit grantors began to computerize their records, credit bureaus had to follow suit, and a bureau with the capacity to receive and report credit information in computerized form[52] also acquired the capacity to serve multiple markets. This change introduced competition to an industry previously composed of local monopolies.[53] Many local bureaus with manual record keeping and limited geographic coverage have been forced out of business or into cooperative arrangements with other bureaus.[54]

Much of this change has occurred since passage of the Fair Credit Reporting Act which has had its own, independent impact on the industry. Most importantly, the Act encourages specialization. The cost of complying with the Act's requirements regarding investigative reports has forced most

---

[47] Other items which may trigger a warning by the credit bureau include: death notice, bankruptcy filing, divorce filing, non-responsibility notice, new address on a "watch subject," new employment on a "watch subject," and major and minor "derogatory" reports from credit grantors. See written statement of Chilton Corporation, Credit Reporting Hearings, August 4, 1976.

[48] *Ibid.*, p. 27.

[49] Credit Bureau Inc. of Georgia, a subsidiary of Equifax, Inc., provides a service called "Professional Administrative Processing System." Two basic services are involved: (1) posting accounts, payments, and charges for physicians; and (2) preparation of insurance claim forms for the doctor's signature. The first service requires a physician to provide information indicating the purpose of the office visit, e.g., x-ray, consultation, or immunization. Based on codes, a bill is prepared and sent to the patient. Written statement of Credit Bureau Inc. of Georgia, Credit Reporting Hearings, August 5, 1976, p. 20.

[50] At the end of 1976, 7,889 financial institutions participated in BankAmericard/Visa and 8,594 participated in Master Charge. More than 74 million card holders belonged to the two systems and accounted for a gross dollar volume in excess of $24 billion during 1976. More than 855 million sales slips were processed to achieve this volume by the two bank-card associations. See American Bankers Association, "ABA Bank Card Letters," March 1977.

[51] In addition to the alert or warning services discussed above, credit grantors also use credit bureaus to review periodically, e.g., once every 12 months, an individual's credit standing.

[52] There are approximately 200 automated credit bureaus in the United States.

[53] Written statement of Associated Credit Bureaus, Inc., Credit Reporting Hearings, August 4, 1976, p. 1.

[54] *Ibid.*, p. 3.

of the bureaus that previously performed both credit-reporting and investigative functions to choose one area or the other. As a consequence, the proportion of investigative reports that credit bureaus prepare for employers, for example, has markedly decreased.[55] Finally, the growing percentage of people who abuse credit or try to defraud the credit system influences the kind of services credit bureaus provide.

INFORMATION FLOWS IN THE CREDIT-REPORTING INDUSTRY

The credit bureau is a natural outgrowth of a cooperative credit system. Each credit grantor helps minimize the risk to other credit grantors by contributing its information about applicants to a central repository. In addition, a credit bureau may collect and report information from public-record sources, debt-collection agencies, and interviews with individuals who come to the bureau to learn about the contents of its files on them.

Information flows into, within, and out of credit bureaus in the form of reports. The same information may be used to prepare a standard credit profile, contribute to a credit guide,[56] trigger a warning to a group of subscribers, or locate a debtor.

While the telephone greatly influenced the collection and dissemination of credit information, most of it still flowed on paper until the late 1960's. Today, many credit information channels are automated, especially those to, from, and within major national and regional credit-granting institutions. Bureaus large and small are pooling resources in various ways. For example, Associated Credit Bureaus, Inc., the credit bureau trade association, helps small bureaus improve their competitive position by putting the automated files of large credit-granting institutions onto microfiche for distribution to bureaus whose records are not automated.[57] In areas where they do not compete, two major automated bureaus have agreed to switch a subscriber's inquiry automatically from one to the other when the one receiving it has no file on the individual.[58]

Various factors limit both the amount of activity in which a credit bureau participates, and the variety of services it offers. These include its level of automation, the geographic area it serves, the number of contributing credit grantors, the number of individuals on whom it maintains files, and economic conditions in its market area. The Commission has taken these differences into account in developing its recommendations, though

---

[55] Letter from Associated Credit Bureaus, Inc. to Privacy Protection Study Commission, March 3, 1977.

[56] Credit guides are coded lists of individuals prepared for credit grantors by credit bureaus. Credit guides approved by the Federal Trade Commission must be limited to good credit risks; have the key to coding systems under tight control at the credit grantor's place of business; be used after an application is initiated by an individual; and result in a disclosure pursuant to 15 U.S.C. 1681m(a) if a credit guide is the basis for an adverse decision. See submission of Chilton Corporation, Credit Reporting Hearings, August 4, 1976.

[57] Ibid., p. 22. Associated Credit Bureaus, Inc. also provides a centralized service for collection divisions and recently developed a computerized medical billing service for manual credit bureaus.

[58] Submission of Chilton Corporation, Credit Reporting Hearings, August 4, 1976.

the problems the recommendations address are commonly found throughout the credit-reporting industry.

THE OPERATIONS OF A CREDIT BUREAU

The reach of the credit-reporting industry is illustrated by its trade
association's classification of contributors to credit bureau files. It includes:
automobile dealers; banks; clothing, department, and variety stores;
finance agencies; grocery and home furnishings dealers; insurers; jewelry
and camera stores; contractors; lumber, building materials, and hardware
suppliers; medical-care providers; national credit-card companies and
airlines; oil companies (credit-card divisions); personal services other than
medical; mail-order houses; real estate agents; hotel keepers; sporting goods
and farm and garden supply dealers; utilities; fuel distributors; government
agencies (e.g., the Federal Housing Administration and the Veterans
Administration); wholesalers; advertisers; and collection agencies.[59]

CREATING AND MAINTAINING CREDIT BUREAU FILES

When a person applies for credit for the first time, it is unlikely that
any credit bureau has a file on him. The credit bureau, however, promptly
uses the information given the credit grantor on the individual's application
to establish one, or if one already exists, to update it.

For a credit bureau to create its files and keep them current, it must
maintain continuing contact with its sources of information. It needs the
information credit grantors provide about each of their active accounts,
both in routine reports and in the specialized reports described earlier. Its
contacts also include other credit grantors; other credit bureaus; employers,
landlords, and references listed on the individual's credit application; and
often public records and collection agencies.

Legal records, particularly ones pertaining to suits and judgments,
bankruptcies, arrests and convictions, divorces, and property transactions,
are the most significant public-record sources for a credit bureau's files.
Interested parties, such as a credit grantor engaged in a suit, may supply
public-record information, and some credit bureaus use public-record
reporting services.[60] Newspapers are also sources of public-record information for credit bureaus.[61]

The Fair Credit Reporting Act gives an individual the right to find out
the nature and substance of what a credit bureau's file on him contains.[62]
Some bureaus interview those who inquire about the contents of their

---

[59] Submission of Associated Credit Bureau, Inc., "Common Language of the Consumer
Credit Industry," Credit Reporting Hearings, August 4, 1976.

[60] Such services may range from large-scale companies that systematically review public-
record sources to a courthouse clerk doing a records search as a part-time job.

[61] Newspaper articles may be clipped and retained but with automation affecting the manner
of storing information newspapers are relied on more for items such as notices of non-
responsibility and death.

[62] The inadequacies of this right are discussed in the next section of this chapter.

records as a way of developing new information and as a check on information already on file.

Reports from collection agencies pertaining to debts that have been placed for collection are another means of updating a credit file. Because most collection agencies are owned by credit bureaus, and because the fact of having an account placed for collection has great significance for an individual's credit record, this updating procedure is the way credit bureaus often learn about accounts placed for collection by doctors and other collection agency clients who do not routinely disclose information to credit bureaus.[63]

If a credit grantor asks a credit bureau for information neither the bureau nor its usual sources can provide, the bureau may turn to other credit grantors in order to obtain it. Bureaus also check with other credit grantors when a subscriber wants the most current possible picture of an individual's credit situation, and call employers to verify salary and other employment-related information.[64]

QUALITY CONTROLS

No description can do justice to the dynamic interchange of information that credit reporting represents. Nor can it convey the magnitude of operational problems the bureaus have had to face in recent years. Correctly identifying an individual is chief among the problems that the automated bureaus have had to address. With information from hundreds of sources on literally millions of individuals being compiled and collated in one place, identification methods, some of which partially rely on the Social Security number, must be improved over methods that are adequate in smaller scale operations.[65] Proper matching of information in existing files with information coming from outside sources is especially important, and special efforts have been made to assure it.[66]

Matching reports with inquiries has also been a problem for the large automated bureaus. In the early days of automation, one automated bureau tried to solve it by reporting information on more than one individual when more than one of its files could meet the inquiry's specifications.[67] Recently, some automated credit bureaus have developed sophisticated systems for making sure that inquiries and files are correctly matched. The Commission was not able to determine whether all large credit bureaus have been equally successful in coping with this common problem. One thing that does seem

---

[63] Submission of Chilton Corporation, Credit Reporting Hearings, August 4, 1976.

[64] *Ibid.*

[65] Written statement of TRW Information Services, Credit Reporting Hearings, August 4, 1976, p. 8.

[66] *Ibid.;* see also written statement of Chilton Corporation, Credit Reporting Hearings, August 4, 1976, pp. 6-10.

[67] This practice obviously created problems for the applicant whose credit record might not be used by the credit grantor. More importantly, the declined individual would be sent to the credit bureau with no assurance that the same credit file reviewed by him was also used by the credit grantor.

clear is that credit bureaus find the Social Security number a helpful tool for verifying identity.

The Fair Credit Reporting Act requires credit bureaus to have "reasonable procedures" to assure the accuracy of the information they report to their subscribers.[68] The updating procedures described in the preceding section, together with special precautions to assure the accuracy of public-record information,[69] are considered by credit bureaus to constitute "reasonable procedures." The timeliness of information in bureau reports is defined by the Act's statutory standards for obsolete information.[70]

Due to FCRA requirements, space limitations, and rapid decay in the value of certain credit information, credit bureaus must also regularly purge their files. Except for bankruptcies, all "adverse" information more than seven years old is usually purged. While the FCRA only limits the *reporting* of such information, prudent business practice dictates purging it to avoid the cost of storing and segregating it, and to prevent inadvertent reporting of it for which the credit bureau would be liable. One advantage of computerizing credit records is that information can be purged automatically, efficiently, and continuously according to programmed criteria.[71]

The FCRA has promoted completeness of records by giving an individual the right to file an explanatory notice of dispute with a credit bureau when he questions the accuracy of information in its files. Nonetheless, not all credit bureaus include the individual's statement in a credit report. Some simply indicate that a statement of dispute has been filed and that the credit grantor may inquire further if it so desires.[72] The relevance of information in credit reports is determined by the subscribing

---

[68] No specific standards exist for "reasonable procedures." The Federal Trade Commission staff has noted two general types of problems associated with this requirement. The first deals with the collection of information, for example, recording suits and not recording their disposition. The second, and in their view more complex, deals with the storage and retrieval systems used for information once collected. Written statement of Federal Trade Commission staff, Credit-Card Issuers Hearings, February 12, 1976, p. 19, footnote 21.

[69] Information from public-record sources usually requires a status check to assure its accuracy.

[70] Section 605 of the Fair Credit Reporting Act (15 U.S.C. 1681c) defines "obsolete" information as follows: (1) bankruptcies which, from the date of the judicial decision of the most recent bankruptcy, antedate the report by more than14 years; (2) suits and judgments, which from date of entry, antedate the report by more than 7 years; (3) paid tax liens which, from date of payment, antedate the report by more than 7 years; (4) accounts placed for collection or charged off which antedate the report by more than 7 years; (5) records of arrest, indictment, or conviction of crime which from date of disposition, release, or parole, antedate the report by more than 7 years; and (6) any other adverse item of information which antedates the report by more than 7 years. The above restrictions, however, do not apply when a consumer report is to be used in connection with: (1) a credit transaction which involves, or may reasonably be expected to involve, a principal amount of $50,000 or more; (2) the underwriting of life insurance involving, or which may reasonably be expected to involve, a face amount of $50,000 or more; or (3) the employment of an individual at an annual salary which equals or which may reasonably be expected to equal $20,000 or more.

[71] Written statement of Chilton Corporation, Credit Reporting Hearings, August 4, 1976, p. 15.

[72] This is one example of how computerized operations are less flexible than a manual operation and thus of how they may be making some consumer protections ineffective.

organizations. Thus, primarily for economic reasons, credit bureaus try to report only information that is both necessary and relevant to the decisions in which their reports are used.

Despite these quality controls, mistakes can and do happen. Consequently, the following standard disclaimer usually appears on a credit report:

> This information is furnished in response to an inquiry for the purpose of evaluating credit risk. It has been obtained from sources deemed reliable, the accuracy of which this organization does not guarantee. The inquirer has agreed to indemnify the reporting bureau for any damage arising from misuse of this information and this report is furnished in reliance upon that indemnity. It must be held in strict confidence, it must not be revealed to the subject reported on, except by a reporting agency in accordance with the Fair Credit Reporting Act.[73]

USES AND DISCLOSURES OF THE CREDIT-REPORTING FILE

A credit grantor may ask a credit bureau for a full credit report, for a report of only the information currently held by the bureau, or for a report covering only some specific aspect such as a single credit reference, employment and credit experiences, credit experiences only, or nothing more than previous residential address. In addition, insurance companies and their inspection bureaus may want credit reports for a variety of purposes. They may use a report to confirm the information on an insurance application, or for clues as to an individual's place of employment or previous address. An insurer may also want the substantial information about an individual's current financial situation a credit report provides in order to avoid "overinsuring" him.[74] For inspection bureaus, credit reports are an important source of public-record information which inspection bureaus need but do not regularly compile.[75]

Employers are a third major category of credit report users. In addition to reporting employment history information, an employer may ask a credit bureau to find out such information as the individual's reason for leaving a previous employer and whether the previous employer would rehire him. Employers often ask credit bureaus for information pertaining to an individual's education, including grades and class rank.[76]

Collection agencies are still another major category of credit report users.[77] The FCRA permits them to use a credit report in reviewing or collecting an amount owed on an account. *[15 U.S.C. 1681b(3)(A)]* A credit

---

[73] Submission of Associated Credit Bureaus, Inc., "Sample Copy of Form 100 Showing Typical Credit Report," Credit Reporting Hearings, August 4, 1976.

[74] For a discussion of the information needs of insurance underwriters, see Chapter 5.

[75] Written statement of Equifax Services, Credit Reporting Hearings, August 3, 1976, p. 14.

[76] Submission of Associated Credit Bureaus, Inc., "ACB Report for Employment Purposes," Credit Reporting Hearings, August 4, 1976.

[77] Written statement of Associated Credit Bureaus, Credit Reporting Hearings, August 4, 1976, p. 20.

report can give a collection agency a great deal of helpful information, such as the debtor's address, place and type of employment, income level, and total outstanding debt. Because notifying employers is a common practice in the collection business, knowing where an individual currently works is especially helpful.

Government agencies are a special subset of credit-bureau subscribers. The FCRA permits government access to credit bureau files for any purpose, including law enforcement, where there is a court order or the information requested is identifying information limited to an individual's name, current and former addresses, and current and former places of employment. Government agencies, however, can still purchase reports like anyone else if they want them for credit or employment-related purposes, or to determine eligibility for certain licenses and benefits. Such access is specifically provided for in the "permissible purposes" section of the FCRA. Federal agencies falling within this last category include the Federal Housing Administration, the Veterans Administration, the Federal Bureau of Investigation, the Civil Service Commission, and the Defense Investigative Service.

METHODS OF REPORTING

Traditionally, credit reports were mailed to subscribers. Today, the mail is used mainly by an institution sending an individual's application to a credit bureau for verification, or when an intermediary such as a report broker collects and sends reports to a large national credit grantor.[78]

The telephone is widely used for reporting credit information. Most credit bureaus have trained telephone operators to receive calls from subscribers. When the caller has been adequately identified (for billing as well as for confidentiality reasons), the credit bureau operator reads the contents of the individual's file to the inquiring subscriber. Subscribers have special forms for recording these oral transmissions. What is important to note about this method, however, is that it deprives the credit bureau of control over the way information is actually recorded at the subscriber's end. The bureau has no way of knowing if the subscriber makes a mistake in transcribing or fails to record some of the reported information.

A third transmission method is by a computer. The subscriber makes its inquiry with a typewriter-like device in its office, which transmits the inquiry to the bureau and also displays or prints out the bureau's response. Identification and authorization codes are programmed into the computer system to bar automatically unauthorized disclosures. The previously mentioned computer switch that two of the major automated bureaus recently installed is an elaboration of this method. Another variation is the service now being marketed by TRW Credit Data which uses the subscriber's point scoring formula to process individual applications. Information is retrieved from TRW Credit Data files only when the

---

[78] For a discussion of the role and operation of the nation's largest report broker, see written statement of Credit Bureau Reports, Inc., Credit Reporting Hearings, August 4, 1976.

applicant's score warrants it. This has the effect, in some instances, of suppressing the disclosure of credit-bureau information to the subscriber.[79]

COPING WITH FRAUD

Individuals have discovered ways to use a credit bureau to defraud credit grantors. Recently, the systems of TRW Credit Data and Credit Bureau, Inc. were each used to fabricate favorable credit records.[80] Credit bureaus take various precautions against such acts. For example, they screen prospective subscribers on the basis of their need for credit bureau reports.[81] Some large automated credit bureaus have set up separate departments for updating credit files, and some give polygraph tests to employees suspected of improperly altering credit reports.[82] Most automated credit bureaus also employ a wide range of physical, administrative, and technical precautions to prevent fraud.[83]

TRENDS IN CREDIT REPORTING

The testimony of industry witnesses before the Commission identified some significant trends. One that both an industry trade association and large national credit grantors have been promoting is movement toward a standardized format for routine disclosures to credit bureaus.[84] As nationwide credit grantors consolidate their data-processing programs into regional or national data-processing centers, national and regional credit-reporting firms have been established to service them. Because credit grantors deal with more than one credit bureau, however, they favor standardized reports to minimize inconvenience and error. The trade association also favors standardized formats to facilitate the distribution of information from regional and national credit grantors to small local credit bureaus.[85]

The development of large automated credit bureaus has started a trend toward centralization of information about individuals. Some manual bureaus have had to close, while others have service agreements with automated bureaus in order to get the advantages of computer technology without losing their autonomy.[86]

The accelerating pace at which information circulates within the credit-reporting world today suggests another trend. First mail set the pace,

---

[79] Submission of TRW Information Services, "The Time to Automate Your Credit Application Processing is NOW," Credit Reporting Hearings, August 4, 1976.

[80] In both cases, the fraud was perpetrated with the aid of credit-bureau employees.

[81] 15 U.S.C. 1681e requires, in part, credit bureaus to have procedures that require that " . . . prospective users of the information identify themselves, certify the purposes for which the information is sought, and certify the information will be used for no other purpose."

[82] Submission of Chilton Corporation, Credit Reporting Hearings, August 4, 1976.

[83] Submission of Associated Credit Bureaus, Inc., "Credit Reporting Industry Security Standards," Credit Reporting Hearings, August 4, 1976.

[84] Written statement of Associated Credit Bureaus, Inc., Credit Reporting Hearings, August 4, 1976, p. 10.

[85] *Ibid.*, p. 19.

[86] *Ibid.*, p. 3.

then the telephone, but the advent of computers with their processing capability means that credit grantors can tap credit bureau files without either the help or the knowledge of bureau employees. A logical next step is the elimination of practically all human intervention, both in answering inquiries and in evaluating credit applications. The TRW Credit Data experiment mentioned earlier is a significant step in this direction.[87]

The information that is now regularly reported to credit bureaus also shows how information flow is changing. For example, the amount owing on a particular account could always be obtained from credit grantors, but at the cost of some effort and time. Now that credit bureaus routinely store current amount-owing information, the time and effort needed to retrieve it is close to zero.[88]

The marketing and monitoring services now offered by automated credit bureaus demonstrate how improving a record-keeping system can multiply the uses made of it. As society becomes more dependent on open-end credit, credit-reporting agencies can also be expected to refine their ability to monitor individuals' use of credit for both control and marketing purposes.

The credit bureaus that offer billing services for doctors, and check-authorization services for banks and merchants, illustrate a trend toward diversification in the credit-reporting field. One possible reason for this kind of diversification is that it permits automated credit bureaus to make use of their computer facilities in ways that are not subject to Fair Credit Reporting Act requirements.

There is also an increased realization that concern for the individual subject of a credit bureau report benefits the industry. In contrast to the usual practice before passage of the FCRA,[89] some credit bureaus today voluntarily give an individual a copy of their credit reports on him. This and a few other harbingers suggest a progressive approach to consumer relations. Unfortunately, however, this trend is far from universal, as the next section of this chapter shows.

THE INDIVIDUAL IN THE CREDIT RELATIONSHIP

Preceding sections have examined personal-data record keeping in credit granting and credit reporting. This section describes problems individuals encounter as a consequence of the way credit records are made, kept, and used, and of weaknesses in the protections currently available to them.

---

[87] Submission of TRW Information Services, "The Time to Automate Your Credit Application Processing is NOW," Credit Reporting Hearings, August 4, 1976.

[88] Written statement of Associated Credit Bureaus, Inc., Credit Reporting Hearings, August 4, 1976, p. 45.

[89] See *The Credit Industry*, Hearings before the Subcommittee on Antitrust and Monopoly of the Committee on the Judiciary, U.S. Senate, 90th Congress, 2d Session, 1968; also, *Fair Credit Reporting*, Hearings before the Subcommittee on Consumer Affairs of the Committee on Banking and Currency, U.S. House of Representatives, 91st Congress, 2d Session, 1970.

CONTROL OVER THE COLLECTION OF INFORMATION

Credit grantors extend credit selectively. They need personal information about applicants in order to evaluate their risk. Individuals who apply for credit in effect consent to an intrusion on their privacy by the credit grantor. Whether the degree of intrusiveness is commensurate with the risk the credit grantor is being asked to assume is a question that has never been systematically addressed. Nonetheless, various laws enacted for other purposes, as well as the cost of compiling and keeping credit records, have served to limit the scope of the credit grantor's inquiry in recent years.

The Fair Credit Reporting Act has limited the scope of inquiry since 1971 by prohibiting credit bureaus from reporting certain categories of adverse information if the information is more than seven years old. Bankruptcies, however, may be reported for 14 years.[90] Other categories of adverse information currently reported by most credit bureaus are regulated in some States. For example, in California, New Mexico, and Kentucky, arrests and indictments that do not ultimately result in convictions may not be reported.[91] In New Mexico, a conviction may not be reported following a grant of full pardon.[92] Virginia and Florida bar the reporting of an outstanding debt as unpaid or delinquent if it is being disputed by the individual. It should be noted, however, that these restrictions only relate to the *reporting* of information by credit bureaus. A credit grantor who obtains such information from some other source, is free to use it as the basis for credit decisions.

The Equal Credit Opportunity Act, as amended, and its implementing regulations *[12 C.F.R. 202]* have also curbed the collection of certain types of information. The Act proscribes the use of race, sex, marital status, and some other kinds of information in making decisions about the granting of credit. It does so on the grounds that the use of such information in arriving at credit decisions is unfair rather than on the grounds that collecting it is an unwarranted intrusion on personal privacy. The changes resulting from enactment of the law and its amendment underscore the fact that individual efforts to limit the scope of the credit grantor's inquiry are not always enough.

From the Commission's point of view, there are a number of arguments for further government regulation of the collection of personal information by credit grantors. First, an applicant for credit is not well informed about the scope of the inquiry to which he will be subjected. Although most credit application forms state that the credit grantor will verify the information provided in the application, they do not identify which institutions and people will be asked for verification or what additional information will be sought.

Second, and perhaps more important, the more an individual needs credit, the harder it is to withhold any information the creditor may ask for, no matter how irrelevant. With the growing need for credit, the applicant

---

[90] See note 70.
[91] Calif. Civ. Code §1785.13; N.M. Stat. Ann. §50-18-6(5); Ky. Rev. Stat. §331.350.
[92] N.M. Stat. Ann. §50-18-6(5).

usually worries only about getting it. Later, when he can turn his attention to the import of certain questions, the application process has already been completed.

CONTROL OVER THE CONTENT OF RECORDS

Although their scope and particular requirements differ, the Fair Credit Reporting Act and the Privacy Act of 1974 share a common aim: that the policies and practices of record-keeping institutions minimize unfairness to individuals in the collection, maintenance, use, and disclosure of records about them. Fairness in record keeping is also an implicit objective of the Fair Credit Billing Act and, to a lesser degree, of the Equal Credit Opportunity Act, especially as it relates to the credit-history records maintained by credit bureaus. *[12 C.F.R. 202.6]*

Existing legal protections establish some minimum ground rules for interaction between individuals and the various institutional record keepers involved, but provide only partial, and sometimes self-defeating, solutions to the problems they were intended to address. Odd as it may seem that laws should be needed to guarantee an individual access to a record about himself, a way to have inaccurate information corrected, or a right to be told the reasons why credit was refused, the legislative history is replete with examples showing that governmental intervention is, indeed, necessary.[93] For all the effort needed to produce current protections, record-keeping problems continue to plague individuals in their consumer-credit relationships. One reason is that many of the legal requirements imposed on credit grantors and credit bureaus do not apply until the individual makes certain specific requests. To protect only those who are fully aware of their rights in the credit relationship leaves a great many individuals at a disadvantage. A brief review of existing law and business practice shows why.

What can an individual learn from a credit grantor regarding the basis for an adverse decision? When an individual is the subject of an adverse credit decision, *[15 U.S.C. 1691(d)(3)]* the credit grantor is required to notify him of his *right* to learn the reason(s) why, and, if information reported by a credit bureau was the basis for the decision, it must give the individual the bureau's name and address. *[15 U.S.C. 1681m(a)]* The credit grantor need not volunteer its reasons, however; the individual must specifically ask for them, despite the burden of additional correspondence this imposes on both parties.

When an individual asks specifically for reasons, credit grantors typically respond with a form letter or preprinted checklist, models of which have been prepared by the Federal Reserve Board. As to information the credit grantor obtained from sources other than credit bureaus, the individual is entitled to learn only its nature and, again, only if he specifically asks. *[15 U.S.C. 1681m(b)]*

Even more significant is what an individual may *not* learn from a

---

[93] *Ibid.*; also *Consumer Information,* Hearings before the Subcommittee on Consumer Affairs of the Committee on Banking, Currency, and Housing, U.S. House of Representatives, 94th Congress, 1st Session, 1975.

credit grantor. A credit grantor is not obligated to disclose to the individual the contents of any credit report that served as the basis for the adverse decision. In fact, a credit bureau's contract with each of its subscribers usually prohibits the subscriber from disclosing such information directly to the individual.[94] If the individual wants to try to figure out which items in a credit report were responsible for the adverse decision, he must inquire at the credit bureau. Nor is the credit grantor required to reveal the identity of any sources other than credit bureaus that contributed to an adverse decision. If the adverse decision was based on information from some other type of source, the credit grantor must disclose the nature (but not the substance) of the information to the individual if the individual asks within 60 days, and must tell the individual at the time the decision is made that he has a right to ask, but the source(s) need not be revealed.[95] Thus, in no case is the individual entitled to learn from the credit grantor the actual items of information supporting the specific reason(s) the credit grantor gives for its adverse decision.

What can an individual learn from a credit bureau regarding the basis for an adverse decision? The credit bureau must tell the individual the nature and substance of its report on him, the sources of the information in it, and the identities of all recent recipients of reports. *[15 U.S.C. 1681g(a)]* As noted earlier, some credit bureaus allow the individual to see his credit file and, in some cases, to make a copy of it. Some will mail a copy to the individual.[96] Such practices are, however, entirely voluntary and far from universal. The credit bureau, in other words, can legally choose not to apprise the individual of the specific words and phrases in the report, and not to let him see the report or copy it for further analysis. Not even the credit bureaus that provide service nationwide are required to mail a copy of a report to the individual. The Fair Credit Reporting Act does stipulate, however, that a credit bureau may not charge for any mandated disclosures to the individual if the individual has recently been notified that he was denied credit on the basis of one of its reports. *[15 U.S.C. 1681j]*

From the individual's standpoint, current law and practice are deficient in a number of respects. First, it forces him to spend a great deal of time and, in some instances, money, chasing after information that is already in the hands of the credit grantor. Second, even if the individual is able to see and copy the entire credit bureau file on him, the file may not include the information that influenced the credit grantor's decision. This can happen if the bureau reports orally to the credit grantor and the credit grantor makes a mistake in taking it down, or if the credit bureau revises its own file after forwarding its report to the credit grantor. Finally, the role of the credit report and the individual's rights *vis-a-vis* the credit bureau are not

---

[94] The standard industry report, prepared by Associated Credit Bureaus, Inc., contains the following: "It [the information] must be held in strict confidence, and must not be revealed to the subject reported on, except by reporting agency in accordance with the Fair Credit Reporting Act."
[95] Except in the case of a "consumer investigative report" if the information is adverse.
[96] Written statement of TRW Information Services, Credit Reporting Hearings, August 4, 1976, p. 15.

normally known by the individual at the time he must decide to contact the credit bureau.

How can an individual get a record corrected or amended? Arrangements between credit grantors and credit bureaus for routine monthly disclosure of information about active accounts have contributed greatly to the efficiency and utility of credit-reporting services. There are, however, some disadvantages for individuals. Credit bureaus note a credit grantor's rating of an individual's manner of payment and report it to their other subscribers. Until quite recently, credit bureaus might report an account delinquent when in fact the individual had not paid his account with one creditor because of a billing dispute. A legitimate dispute with one creditor could thus cause difficulty for him with others. The recently enacted Fair Credit Billing Act forbids reporting a disputed account as delinquent during the 90-day period in which the individual may legally withhold a disputed payment. *[15 U.S.C. 1666]* Credit grantors now report such accounts as being *in dispute* rather than delinquent, and other credit grantors (but only credit grantors, not all users of credit reports) are forbidden to use the dispute as grounds for refusing an individual's credit application. *[15 U.S.C. 1691(a)(3)]*

The Fair Credit Billing Act also prescribes procedures for resolving billing disputes. Although these procedures have helped individuals, they too are inadequate in several respects. When a credit grantor notifies a credit bureau or any other organization that an account is in dispute, it seldom sends either the individual's letter notifying it that a dispute exists or any other statement of the individual's version of the facts of the dispute. Furthermore, neither the credit bureau nor any credit report user is obligated to seek an explanation from the individual, and there is no requirement that the individual be notified that his dispute with the credit grantor has entered various credit-reporting systems. If the dispute continues beyond 90 days, credit grantors are then permitted to report the individual's account as being *both disputed and delinquent* and thereafter, but only thereafter, the credit grantor must notify the individual when it apprises anyone of the account's status, and give the name and address of recipients. *[15 U.S.C. 1666]*

Once either a dispute or a delinquency has been reported to a credit bureau, the Fair Credit Reporting Act provides a way for the individual to get a statement of his version of the facts in every subsequent report that mentions it. *[15 U.S.C. 1681i(c)]* The individual must specifically ask that this be done, however, and cite the Fair Credit Reporting Act, rather than the Fair Credit Billing Act, as his authority for asking. This assumes, of course, that he is familiar with both statutes and can distinguish between them, and also that he knows the credit bureaus to contact during the dispute settlement period, which, as suggested above, he has no way of knowing. Further, as indicated earlier, not all credit bureaus include the individual's statement in a credit report. Some simply indicate that a statement of dispute has been filed and that the recipient may inquire further if he so desires.

With no way of making sure he has a complete list of those who received information about a billing dispute, an individual cannot be sure of any limit on the damage to his credit, even after a dispute is resolved. He may settle, compromise, win, or even get vindication in court, but the credit grantor is still under no obligation to so notify the recipients of its dispute and delinquency reports. A credit bureau will try to keep its record of disputed accounts up to date, especially if a dispute escalates into a law suit, but in doing so it cannot always count on assistance from the credit grantor that originally reported the dispute.

In sum, procedures for settling billing disputes have four major deficiencies. First, institutions other than credit grantors that receive a dispute notice during the 90-day grace period are not prohibited from using it as the basis for an adverse decision, nor are they required to seek the individual's version of the facts of the dispute. Second, credit grantors do not have to inform individuals that a dispute indicator gets into the credit-reporting system during the 90-day dispute-settlement period. Third, an individual who wants to exercise his Fair Credit Reporting Act rights to have his own version of the facts of a dispute filed with a credit bureau must take all the initiative himself and cannot learn the name and address of credit bureaus that receive the dispute information during the 90-day settlement period. Fourth, credit grantors are not obligated to report resolutions of disputes in the individual's favor.

The FCRA, as noted above, prohibits credit bureaus from reporting adverse information that is more than seven years old, except in the case of bankruptcies. The Act does not, however, define "adverse" nor has any specific definition of the term been established by regulation. Since the credit-reporting industry is legally liable for reporting obsolete adverse information, it has, perforce, adopted its own definition. In general industry usage, the term "adverse" applies to information about bankruptcies, suits and judgments, tax liens, arrests and convictions, and to the information that a credit account is more than 90 days overdue.

A serious deficiency of the FCRA is its failure to assure the correction of adverse information erroneously disclosed by a credit grantor to a credit bureau. The situation is even worse with respect to credit cards, where the negative consequences of reporting erroneous adverse information to an independent authorization service can be even more certain than when such information is reported to credit bureaus. Representatives of independent authorization services told the Commission that they and their clients comply with the Fair Credit Reporting Act as far as possible.[97] What this means in practice is that if an individual's credit card is declined at an airport, for example, he will be given the name of the authorization service and left to deal with it directly as best he can. If the authorization service was indeed acting on the basis of erroneous information, the individual will have to suffer until he can get the error corrected.

This example highlights an important point. *As information in systems is used more and more to take preemptive action against individuals, institutional record-keeping policies and practices must become preventive*

---

[97] Written statement of TRW Validata, Depository and Lending Institutions Hearings, April 21, 1976, p. 6.

rather than curative. Emerging information system capabilities and uses are making irrelevant the FCRA approach of rectifying errors made on the basis of inaccurate information *after* the "adverse decision" has been made.

CONTROL OVER THE DISCLOSURE OF INFORMATION IN RECORDS

The credit relationship demands cooperation, both among institutions and between institutions and individuals. Credit grantors regularly share information about their individual customers because it is to their mutual advantage to do so, and because, in many instances, it is to the advantage of the individual. Given this inherent need for information exchange, can an individual legitimately expect the records generated about him in the context of the credit relationship to be treated as confidential?

Industry spokesmen consistently maintain that the individual who applies for credit implicitly consents to the exchange of information about him among credit grantors. Because credit application forms almost invariably request the names of a few credit grantors with whom the applicant already has a relationship, it is argued that the individual must know third-party sources will be contacted to verify and supplement the information he himself provides. The industry relies mainly on this implied consent to justify the free flow of information within it.

Although the Commission accepts the view that an individual should not expect absolute control over disclosures of the information about himself that credit grantors need if they are to establish or service a credit relationship, it believes that the individual should have an explicit, enforceable expectation of confidentiality. Achievement of this balanced objective is, however, undermined by the following practices.

First, while credit grantors themselves do not routinely disclose information about their customers to inquirers whose interests do not involve credit granting, their arrangements with credit bureaus allow for a substantial amount of disclosure for purposes unrelated to the granting of credit. Even assuming that an individual understands that information about his credit relationship will be shared among credit grantors, can it be assumed that he also knows it may be disclosed to employers, insurers, and government agencies? The Commission thinks not. Nor did any of the credit-bureau and credit-grantor witnesses who appeared before the Commission offer any evidence that individuals recognize a nexus between the reporting of credit information to a credit bureau for credit-related purposes and its subsequent uses for other purposes.

Second, the widespread acceptance of credit cards has created vast amounts of recorded information that is extremely useful to marketers. The data bases of both credit grantors and credit bureaus, particularly those who have automated their records, have emerged as an important institutional asset. Commercial banks and consumer-finance companies use their records on individuals to screen prospective customers for other commercial enterprises.[98] Credit bureaus refine marketers' mailing lists by weeding out individuals with unsatisfactory credit records. A consequence of these practices is that information derived from confidential relationships may be disclosed without the individual's knowledge, let alone authorization. The Commission's views on these practices and other marketing activities dependent on the compilation and use of mailing lists are discussed in Chapter 4.

Third, credit grantors disclose information to collection agencies without restrictions on subsequent use or disclosure by these agencies. As noted in the earlier discussion of credit grantor record-keeping practices, the implied threat that one's financial difficulties will be disclosed to neighbors and one's employer by a collection agency conflicts with the credit grantor's obligation to keep an individual's affairs confidential. Often the individual's expectation of confidentiality is outweighed by the desire of the credit grantor or its agent to protect itself against economic losses.

Fourth, although the Fair Credit Reporting Act regulates the disclosure of credit-bureau records to government agencies, disclosures by credit grantors are not now controlled. The individual simply has no legally recognized interest to be balanced against a governmental need for information about him held by a credit grantor, even when there are procedures for informing him of a pending disclosure that might be inimical to him. The Commission finds that the growing attractiveness of credit-card records to government investigators makes it more urgent than ever to strengthen the legal basis for an individual's expectation of confidentiality in his credit relationships. The broad issue of controlling governmental access to records held by various private-sector institutions is addressed in Chapter 9.

RECOMMENDATIONS

Information about an applicant has always been the basis for a consumer-credit decision, and there must always be records to document transactions. The emergence of point scoring and the newer forms of open-end credit, however, greatly increase dependence on records, profoundly affecting credit-related record-keeping practices. Today, many credit grantors accumulate a vast amount of detailed information about their individual account holders. Coupled with their growing reliance on modern record-keeping technologies, this accumulation of detail raises concerns about the content and quality of records, and about the degree of control an individual should have over their use and disclosure.

Records about individuals are also shared ever more widely as necessary credentials for an individual seeking credit, as essential tools for institutions' monitoring an individual's total indebtedness, and for other purposes such as marketing. As a result, ever larger amounts of recorded information are facilitating increasingly fine-grained decisions about an

---

[98] Written statement of FinanceAmerica Corporation, Depository and Lending Institutions Hearings, April 21, 1976, p. 25.

individual. This is evident not only in decisions to accept or reject a credit applicant, but also in the development of authorization systems that can preempt any credit-card transaction, large or small.

With respect to the legal protections the individual has recently acquired, the findings of the Commission clearly indicate that they are neither strong enough nor specific enough to solve the problems they were designed to address. In some cases, moreover, changes in record-keeping practices have already made them obsolete.

It is evident to the Commission that the credit consumer's prerogatives in the record keeping of credit grantors are being progressively attenuated. The individual's relationship with a credit grantor may be contractual, but the record-keeping practices that facilitate it now involve so many separate institutions that, confronted with this maze, the individual who is not versed in the law and the complexities of the credit system cannot protect himself against honest mistakes, let alone against deliberate abuses by credit institutions.

The recommendations that follow reflect more than a year's consideration of the privacy protection issues these aspects of the consumer-credit relationship raise. The recommendations are presented as they relate to the Commission's three broad policy objectives: (1) to minimize intrusiveness; (2) to maximize fairness; and (3) to create legitimate, enforceable expectations of confidentiality. The Commission believes they constitute a balanced approach to solving the specific problems identified in the preceding section on the place of the individual in the modern-day credit relationship, while at the same time satisfying the credit grantor's need to base its decisions about the individual on an accurate evaluation of his credit worthiness.

Intrusiveness

GOVERNMENTAL MECHANISMS

As noted in the section on the individual's place in the credit relationship, the Equal Credit Opportunity Act as amended, and its implementing regulations, are one form of public-policy response to the use of certain types of information as the basis for credit decisions. The ECOA, however, which proscribes the *use* rather than the *collection* of certain items of information, reflects a congressional concern with fairness rather than intrusiveness. Fairness may demand that items of information be collected even though they may not be used so as to be able to demonstrate that they are, in fact, no longer being used. For example, a credit grantor is hard put to prove that sex and race are not being systematically used to discriminate in its credit decisions unless it can show that it has, in fact, extended credit to women and minorities.

Protections against unwarranted intrusiveness make different and sometimes contrary demands on institutional record keepers. There the first thing that must be prohibited is collection, inasmuch as merely asking the question is intrusive. Use of certain information may also have to be prohibited to protect against unwarranted intrusion, but only to make sure that the item is totally excised from the decision-making process.

In the Commission's view, questions of this nature are best resolved on a case-by-case basis because of the sensitivity of government interference in private-sector information flows. The Commission also believes that all such determinations must be limited to future acts by the information collector, so as to avoid retroactive punishment for inquiries which at the time they were made were consistent with prevailing societal norms. So far, few items of information have been proscribed on grounds of unwarranted intrusiveness. Most such proscriptions have been aimed at eliminating unfair discrimination on the basis of characteristics that are readily observable, such as sex and race. Nonetheless, the Commission believes that society may in the future have to cope with objections to the collection of certain items of information about an individual on the grounds that they are "nobody's business but his own."

Accordingly, out of its desire to prevent unreasonable invasions of personal privacy, the Commission recommends:

Recommendation (1):

That governmental mechanisms should exist for individuals to question the propriety of information collected or used by credit grantors, and to bring such objections to the appropriate bodies which establish public policy. Legislation specifically prohibiting the use, or collection and use, of a specific item of information may result; or an existing agency or regulatory body may be given authority or use its currently delegated authority to make such a determination with respect to the reasonableness of future use, or collection and use, of a specific item of information.

The Commission believes that the mechanism proposed in *Recommendation (1)* will bring the issue of intrusive information collection practices to the surface and allow it to be dealt with responsibly. Random complaints should not be enough to justify government action. In each case, it will have to be shown that (1) there is a widespread problem; (2) the item in question is irrelevant to or unnecessary in the decision-making situation in which it is used; or (3) regardless of relevance, the item is objectionable enough to justify either legislation or action by a governmental institution that has been given specific authority to deal with such matters.

Because consumer credit is already regulated at the Federal level, the Commission believes that *Recommendation (1)* should be implemented primarily at the Federal level. The Congress should vest authority in the Federal Reserve Board, the Federal Home Loan Bank Board, and the other regulatory agencies responsible for enforcing the Fair Credit Reporting Act, to collect complaints from individuals about institutions subject to the regulations of those agencies, and to report to the Congress as to the need for additional legislation, if any, to control or regulate the collection, or collection and use, of particular items of information.

REASONABLE CARE IN THE USE OF SUPPORT ORGANIZATIONS

The Fair Credit Reporting Act requires a credit bureau to have procedures which assure that prospective subscribers have a legitimate need, as defined by the FCRA, for information about individuals. Indeed, a bureau's subscribers must certify that information they obtain from it will be used only for one of the permissible purposes specified in the Act. The FCRA, however, levies no requirement on any credit-bureau subscriber with respect to its selection of a reliable bureau. If a credit bureau flagrantly violates the FCRA, or is careless in its screening of new subscribers, the existing subscribers are under no obligation to sever their relationships with it. This is also the case with respect to a credit grantor's use of independent authorization services and collection agencies.

As in other areas into which it has inquired, the Commission firmly believes that implementation of its recommendations, together with existing laws, will be enhanced considerably if credit grantors have a strong incentive to assure that the activities of their support organizations are proper. Hence, the Commission recommends:

Recommendation (2):

That the Federal Fair Credit Reporting Act be amended to provide that each credit grantor must exercise reasonable care in the selection and use of credit bureaus, independent authorization services, collection agencies, and other support organizations, so as to assure that the collection, maintenance, use, and disclosure practices of such organizations comply with the Commission's recommendations.

If it could be shown that a credit grantor contracted for or used the services of a support organization with knowledge, actual or constructive, that the organization was engaging in illegal practices, an individual or the Federal Trade Commission (FTC) could initiate action against both the credit grantor and the support organization and hold them jointly liable for the support organization's actions.

Fairness

FAIRNESS IN COLLECTION

NOTICE REGARDING COLLECTION FROM THIRD PARTIES

The Commission believes the type of governmental mechanism called for in *Recommendation (1)* will be necessary mainly when the forces of the marketplace are not strong enough to mitigate concern about the propriety of certain inquiries. If market forces are to protect the individual credit customer, however, he must know what types of information a particular credit grantor may use as a basis for credit decisions. Otherwise, he has no way of judging whether to take his business elsewhere. The application form itself serves to apprise individuals of some of the information that will be gathered, but as previously noted, application forms provide only incomplete clues to the type or extent of inquiries that may be made of sources other than the individual himself.

Thus, to minimize the need for public-policy determinations concerning the propriety of credit-grantor inquiries about an individual, and to let the credit applicant know what divulgence he must make in order to obtain a favorable decision, the Commission recommends:

Recommendation (3):

That Federal law be enacted or amended to provide that when an individual applies for credit, a credit grantor must notify the individual of:

(a)   the types of information expected to be collected about him from third parties that are not collected on the application; and

(b)   the types of institutional sources that are expected to be asked to provide information about him.

This recommendation would require an individual to be apprised not only of the scope of the credit grantor's inquiry but also of the disclosures the credit grantor will ask others to make about him. The Commission recognizes that the credit grantor may inquire of some institutions with which the individual has a confidential relationship, including other credit grantors. When such institutions are *not* credit grantors, the Commission would expect the credit grantor to use an authorization procedure like the one called for in *Insurance Recommendation (8)* and *Employment Recommendation (16)*. When the inquiry is to another credit grantor, however, the interdependence of credit-granting institutions, and the likelihood that an individual will be aware of that interdependence as a consequence of the questions typically asked on a credit application, make the Commission believe that a stringent authorization procedure is not necessary.

With respect to the implementation of this recommendation, the Federal statute establishing the notification requirement should give regulatory authority to the Federal Reserve Board to supplement similar regulatory authority the Board now has under the Truth-in-Lending, Equal Credit Opportunity, and Fair Credit Billing Acts. The resulting Federal Reserve Board regulations could then be enforced by the agencies having authority over particular credit-granting institutions, as well as by the individual, as is currently provided in the Truth-in-Lending Act. Truth-in-Lending allows an individual to obtain damages for violation of standards promulgated by the Federal Reserve Board, either on his own behalf, or on behalf of a class.

NOTICE AS THE COLLECTION LIMITATION

The anticipated benefits of *Recommendation (3)* for the individual would be seriously negated if a credit grantor deviated from its notification to an applicant. Further, credit grantors depend on credit bureaus and other support organizations, whose collection practices could go considerably beyond what is stated in such a notice. Thus, to guard against these possibilities, the Commission recommends:

Recommendation (4):

That Federal law be enacted or amended to provide that a credit grantor must limit:

(a) **its own information collection practices in connection with an application for credit to those specified in the notice called for in *Recommendation (3)*; and**

(b) **its request to any organization it asks to collect information on its behalf to information and sources specified in the notice called for in *Recommendation (3).***

Recommendation (4) should be implemented in conjunction with *Recommendations (2)* and *(3)*. The purpose of this recommendation is to make clear that both the credit granter and any organization it utilizes to collect information on its behalf are equally subject to the limitations implicit in the notice required by *Recommendation (3)*.

FAIRNESS IN USE

ACCESS TO CREDIT GRANTOR RECORDS

If an individual suspects that inaccurate, incomplete, or obsolete information was the cause of an adverse credit decision concerning himself, the first thing he will want to do, indeed the first thing he must do, is find out what information the credit grantor used in making the decision. At the present time, however, a credit grantor is not obligated to reveal to such an individual anything other than the reasons for the decision and the nature of the information that was the basis for it, and then only if the information came from someone other than a credit bureau. In no case is the individual entitled to learn from the credit grantor the actual items of information that supported the decision. Moreover, if the information came from a credit bureau the individual may never be able to confront the specific items, since the credit bureau may have updated its file and thus no longer have them. To solve this problem, and to establish the basic statutory framework for *Recommendation (6)*, below, the Commission, therefore, recommends:

Recommendation (5):

That Federal law be enacted or amended to provide that an individual shall have a right to see and copy, upon request, all recorded information concerning him that a credit grantor has used to make an adverse credit decision about him.

This recommendation would not provide an individual with a see-and-copy right applicable to all aspects of a credit relationship at any time, but rather is focused on the adverse decision situation when the individual most clearly needs such a right. In contrast to other areas in which the Commission recommends a much broader right of access, it concluded that the decision to deny a credit application, to offer credit on other than standard terms, or to modify an existing credit agreement, are the points where existing law and business practice do not give an individual access to information about himself which is available to the credit grantor. Also, they are the points at which the individual has no regular, convenient means of correcting errors. Once the credit relationship is established, and particularly when it is open-ended, the individual has his own copies of the information that accumulates in the credit grantor's records about him. It should be noted, moreover, that *Recommendation (5)* is not intended to add any new record retention requirements.

ADVERSE CREDIT DECISIONS

The Commission also believes that the credit grantor should be obligated to explain its adverse decision to an affected individual. Current procedures described in the earlier discussion of what an individual can learn from a credit grantor regarding the basis for an adverse decision are patently inadequate. Accordingly, the Commission recommends:

Recommendation (6):

That Federal law be enacted or amended to provide that a credit grantor must:

(a) **disclose in writing to an individual who is the subject of an adverse credit decision:**
    (i)   **the specific reason(s) for the adverse decision;**
    (ii) **the specific item(s) of information, in plain language, that support the reason(s) given pursuant to (a)(i);**
    (iii) **the name(s) and address(es) of the institutional source(s) of the item(s) given pursuant to (a)(ii); and**
    (iv) **the individual's right to see and copy, upon request, all recorded information pertaining to him used to make the adverse decision; and**
(b) **inform the individual of his rights provided by the Fair Credit Reporting Act, when the decision is based in whole or in part on information obtained from a credit bureau.**

Recommendation (6) departs from current legal requirements in that it would obligate the credit grantor to disclose, *automatically, all* of the reasons, supporting items of information, sources, and additional rights the individual needs if the Commission's fairness objective and, for that matter, the objective of existing law is to be fulfilled. Additionally, the recommendation coordinates the notification requirements of the Fair Credit Reporting Act with those of the Equal Credit Opportunity Act so that differences in timing will not confuse the individual or unnecessarily complicate inquiries to the declining credit grantor, other credit grantors, and credit bureaus.

The automatic disclosure of items of information that support the specific reasons given is important because without such disclosure it may be impossible for the individual to determine whether the decision was based on inaccurate, obsolete, or incomplete information. The names and addresses of institutional sources should be disclosed so that an individual can correct at the source erroneous information that has affected him adversely and may continue to do so.

The Commission recognizes that most contracts between credit bureaus and their subscribers forbid the subscriber to disclose information obtained from the bureau directly to an individual. The Commission also recognizes the credit bureau's concern that it be allowed to correct inaccurate information for which it is responsible. Nonetheless, the primary goal of this recommendation is to make it possible for an individual to discover the basis for an adverse decision. To simply shunt the individual to the credit bureau where he can request disclosure of the information in its files may leave him uninformed as to the real basis for an adverse decision and will certainly complicate his efforts to discover it. It is the Commission's understanding that a credit grantor that uses point scoring would necessarily have to disclose all items of information it used in scoring the individual.

The Commission considered requiring automatic disclosure of all information, not just the items that support the reasons given, but found such wholesale disclosure unnecessary to achieve the Commission's primary objective. However, an individual who is not satisfied with the reasons and supporting items of information for an adverse decision should have a right to see and copy, *upon request,* all information about himself that is available to the decision maker. Thus, the Commission considers use of the right established by *Recommendation (5)* as underlying this recommendation but unnecessary in most situations.

Finally, the Commission is concerned about deficiencies in the way individuals who have been declined credit are apprised of their rights pursuant to the Fair Credit Reporting Act. An individual told that a credit bureau provided information that contributed to an adverse credit decision must decide whether to contact the bureau, but current law does not require that he be told what the FCRA permits him to require of the credit bureau. The Commission views this failure to apprise the individual of his FCRA rights, and of the bureau's responsibilities to him before he decides whether to follow up, as a self-defeating feature of the Act. If the intent of the Act is to bring individuals and credit bureaus together, and if this can occur only at the initiative of the individual, then the notice the Act requires a credit grantor to give an individual about whom an adverse decision has been made should be more explicit about what the individual can expect if he takes the initiative.

The Commission believes an individual should be given the ability to force a credit grantor to perform the duties owed to him by making a credit grantor that fails to comply liable to the individual. An individual should be able to sue a credit grantor in Federal court or another court of competent jurisdiction if the credit grantor failed to perform one of the duties set forth in *Recommendation (5)* or *(6).* This would include suit for failure to state specific reason(s) for an adverse decision when the individual has cause to believe that the real reason is other than the one stated by the credit grantor. The court should have the power to order the credit grantor to comply and to award attorney's fees and court costs to any plaintiff who substantially prevails. If it could be shown that the credit grantor willfully or intentionally denied the individual any of the rights *Recommendations (5)* and *(6)* would give him, the court should have the power to award up to $1,000 to the individual.

Systematic denials of access by credit grantors could be subject to enforcement by the Federal Trade Commission and the other agencies that currently have enforcement authority under the Fair Credit Reporting and Equal Credit Opportunity Acts. The remedy would be an order directing a credit grantor to disclose records upon request. Once the FTC or other agency issued such an order, the credit grantor would then be subject to the usual enforcement mechanisms available to the agency to secure compliance with its orders.

The burden should be on the individual to describe reasonably the documents sought and the credit grantor should be able to defend itself on the basis that it could not reasonably locate or identify the records sought by the plaintiff. For example, an individual could sue for any document developed as the result of an application for credit if the individual could reasonably identify the date and the nature of the application. If, however, an individual requested any information that relates to him in a file, and could not identify with some specificity the circumstances pursuant to which such a file was developed, the credit grantor would not be under an affirmative obligation to search through every record to locate a possible passing reference to the individual. Like *Recommendation (5), Recommendation (6)* is not intended to add any new record retention requirements.

ACCESS TO CREDIT BUREAU AND INDEPENDENT AUTHORIZATION
SERVICE RECORDS

If an individual so requests, the Fair Credit Reporting Act requires a credit bureau to disclose to him the "nature and substance" of all information it maintains about him. This requirement was intended to allow an individual to find out the contents of the credit file on him as a first step, and only a first step, in the process of protecting himself against the adverse consequences of inaccurate, incomplete, or obsolete information compiled and reported about him by credit bureaus. The efficacy of the FCRA hinges largely on the ease with which an individual can take this first step. Unless an individual can confront the contents of a credit file on him in a manner that is not unduly burdensome, the benefit of other protections guaranteed by the Act with respect to correcting or disputing a file's contents may never be realized.

Both critics and supporters of disclosure, including the credit-bureau trade association, recognize that disclosing only "nature and substance" of an individual's credit record can easily create anxiety and uncertainty for him. Some members of the credit-reporting industry have exceeded the minimum requirements of the FCRA by giving a copy of their credit reports to individuals who make a personal visit to them. In the Commission's view, this practice places an unwarranted burden on the individual. At a minimum, it causes the individual to take time out to visit the credit bureau and, in a mobile society served increasingly by national credit bureaus, could well require both expense and time. That, of course, is even more likely to be the case when an independent authorization service is involved, since such services are even less likely to have conveniently located offices. Thus, the Commission recommends:

Recommendation (7):

That the Federal Fair Credit Reporting Act be amended to provide that, upon request by an individual, a credit bureau or independent authorization service must:

(a) **inform the individual, after verifying his identity, whether it has any recorded information pertaining to him; and**

(b) **permit the individual to see and copy any such recorded information, in plain language, either in person or by mail; or**

(c) **apprise the individual of the nature and substance of any such recorded information by telephone; and**

(d) **permit the individual to use one or the other of the methods of access provided in (b) and (c), or both if he prefers.**

The credit bureau or independent authorization service may charge a reasonable copying fee for any copies provided to the individual.

Recommendation (7) would not alter procedures currently used by credit bureaus to identify individuals prior to disclosing information to them. The Commission assumes that both automated credit bureaus and independent authorization services will use computer software to prepare copies of credit reports.

The recommended amendment to the FCRA should allow an individual to sue a credit bureau or independent authorization service that fails to comply with the requirements of *Recommendation (7)* for specific performance and collect attorney's fees and court costs if he substantially prevails. This could be in addition to his action for recovery of damages under the existing terms of the FCRA.

FAIRNESS IN DISCLOSURE

INACCURACIES REPORTED TO CREDIT BUREAUS AND AUTHORIZATION SERVICES

Although existing laws regulate the flow of information from credit-granting institutions to credit bureaus, there are no requirements which focus specifically on inaccurate information a credit grantor may disclose to a credit bureau or independent authorization service.

The Fair Credit Reporting Act provides one approach to coping with negative consequences of inaccurate information, but it unfortunately fails to take account of the fact that in many instances credit grantors disclose information to more than one credit bureau or authorization service. Therefore, while the individual can correct inaccurate information, or file a statement of dispute concerning information at one credit bureau or service, he is not well enough informed nor is he likely to have the ability to avoid the unnecessary negative consequences of having inaccurate information disclosed to several of them.

The development of account monitoring services by automated credit bureaus is another reason to be concerned about the propagation of corrections *before* inaccurate information adversely affects an individual. These services expand the range of negative consequences to the individual beyond simply the denial of an application for credit; such information can jeopardize existing credit relationships. Therefore, the Commission recommends:

Recommendation (8):

That the Federal Fair Credit Reporting Act be amended to provide that if a credit grantor learns it has reported any inaccurate information about an individual to a credit bureau or independent authorization service, it must notify the credit bureau or authorization service within a reasonable period of time so that the credit bureau or authorization service can correct its files.

Although the Commission realizes that the phrase "within a reasonable period of time" is open to interpretation, the alternative would appear to be a regulatory agency with authority to establish specific time limits, along the lines of the regulations implementing the Fair Credit Billing Act. While this may be necessary eventually, the Commission hopes it will not; that the Fair Credit Billing Act experience will be an incentive to credit grantors to initiate corrections within periods of time that are reasonable.

PREVENTION OF INACCURACIES IN AUTHORIZATION SERVICE RECORDS

An individual whose credit-card account is incorrectly reported to an independent authorization service can experience serious difficulties which the Fair Credit Reporting Act does little to ameliorate. The FCRA contemplates an adverse credit decision of a different sort (e.g., rejection of an application) involving a different type of service organization (e.g., a credit bureau), so its protections are primarily curative. An independent authorization service, on the other hand, acts preemptively, and often speedily, with the result that preventive rather than curative protections are needed. Thus, to allow the FCRA to take *explicit* account of this new application of computer technology to consumer-credit decision making, the Commission recommends:

Recommendation (9):

That the Federal Fair Credit Reporting Act be amended to provide:

(a)   **that a credit-card issuer must have reasonable procedures to assure that the information it discloses to an independent authorization service is accurate at the time of disclosure; and**

(b)   **that an independent authorization service shall be subject to all requirements of the Act, except the requirement to disclose corrected information to prior recipients upon completion of a reinvestigation of disputed information.**

Given the fact that once an error in an independent authorization service record is discovered, the damage has already been done, and indeed usually cannot be remedied, a requirement that previous recipients be notified of any corrections would, in most instances, be gratuitous. If a credit-card issuer or independent authorization service fails to meet the requirements called for in *Recommendation (9),* it should be liable for actual damages in the event an individual is harmed by its failure.

DISCLOSURES TO COLLECTION AGENCIES

The notation in an individual's credit record that his account has been placed for collection, like a similar disclosure to an authorization service, is unambiguously adverse to an individual's credit reputation. Unlike information flows from a credit grantor to a credit bureau, however, information flows to collection agencies are currently unregulated. Moreover, as indicated in one of the first sections of the chapter, it is the practice of some collection agencies to send an individual threatening letters and to contact him at his place of employment. These tactics are both annoying and embarrassing, and completely unwarranted in the case of an individual who has been reported in error. Unless, however, the credit grantor tells the collection agency to desist, the individual may not be able to escape the collection agency's badgering. Thus, the Commission recommends:

Recommendation (10):

That the Federal Fair Credit Reporting Act be amended to provide that a credit grantor must have reasonable procedures for notifying a collection agency within a reasonable period of time if an individual has been referred to the agency as a delinquent debtor on the basis of inaccurate information; also, if a debt previously referred to a collection agency has been satisfied, or a satisfactory partial payment has been made, the credit grantor must so notify the collection agency within a reasonable period of time and provide the individual with proof of its notification.

The Commission has not addressed the larger question of what constitutes proper treatment of individuals in the conduct of legitimate collection efforts. The complexity of this issue merits a fuller examination than the Commission's resources permitted.

The Commission considered a recommendation that would restrain credit grantors or collection agencies from revealing the existence of a delinquent debt to other than the individual before the debt has been entered on a public record. It rejected this proposal, however, because of the lawsuits, sometimes even more damaging to an individual's reputation, which such a requirement would encourage.

If harm results from a credit grantor's failure to comply with the requirements called for in *Recommendation (10)*, the credit grantor should be liable for actual damages.

DISCLOSURE OF PREVIOUS CREDIT BUREAU INQUIRIES

Credit bureaus compile detailed information about an individual's various credit relationships, including the identity of his credit grantors, his total outstanding debt, and his payment habits. In addition, the Fair Credit Reporting Act requires a credit bureau to keep a list of all recipients of its credit reports so that an individual who wants to know can find out who has inquired about him during the preceding six months. Today, a credit report often contains the identity of all of those recipients as well as the identity of all recipients with whom the individual has, in fact, established a credit relationship. While a seemingly innocuous practice, some credit grantors in fact compare inquiries with relationships established, and where a relationship has not been established conclude that the individual's application must have been rejected. Although this conclusion is not totally reliable, it is certainly one possible interpretation, and can be the cause of an adverse credit decision.

The Commission views the practice of including previous inquiries in reports to credit grantors as unfair because of the broad range of eligibility requirements among credit-granting institutions. The Commission finds no reason to stigmatize an individual, either directly or by implication, by disclosing the identity of prior recipients of a credit report, except as a protection against fraud. Thus, the Commission recommends:

Recommendation (11):

That the Federal Fair Credit Reporting Act be amended to provide that a credit bureau must not disclose to its subscribers information about previous inquiries concerning an individual except the number and date of inquiries received.

Recommendation (11) would not affect the FCRA requirement that a credit bureau *retain* the identity of credit-report recipients and the date of disclosure. This information would still be collected and available to the individual but not to others.

Expectation of Confidentiality

CONFIDENTIALITY OF CREDIT-GRANTOR RECORDS

As noted earlier in this chapter, information is shared widely within the credit community and is disclosed to institutions that are not credit grantors either directly by credit grantors or indirectly through credit bureaus. Although the need for such disclosure is understandable, an individual's expectation of confidentiality with respect to a consumer-credit relationship can be distorted by the failure of most credit grantors to apprise him of their disclosure policies. More importantly, an individual has no legally recognized interest in the records maintained about him by a credit grantor and, consequently, cannot prevent a disclosure that may be inimical to him. Therefore, the Commission recommends:

Recommendation (12):

That Federal law be enacted or amended to provide:

(a) that a credit grantor must notify an individual with whom it has or proposes to have a credit relationship of the uses and disclosures which are expected to be made of the types of information it collects or maintains about him; and that with respect to routine disclosures to third parties which are necessary for servicing the credit relationship, the notification must include the specific types of information to be disclosed and the types of recipients;

(b) that information concerning an individual which a credit grantor collects to establish or service a credit relationship, as stated in the notification to the individual called for in (a), must be treated as confidential by the credit grantor; and thus any disclosures to third parties other than those necessary to service the credit relationship must be specifically directed or authorized by the individual, or in the case of marketing information, specifically described in the notification;

(c) that an individual must be considered to have a continuing interest in the use and disclosure of information a credit grantor maintains about him, and must be allowed to participate in any use or disclosure that would not be consistent with the original notification, except when a credit grantor discloses information about an individual in order to prevent or protect against the possible occurrence of fraud; and

(d) that any material changes or modifications in the use or disclosure policies of a credit grantor must be preceded by a notification that describes the change to an individual with whom the credit grantor has an established relationship.

Recommendation (12) is intended to make explicit the individual's expectation of confidentiality. It recognizes the need for routine disclosures and allows for such disclosures without authorization if the individual is aware that they may occur. An example of a routine disclosure would be the credit grantor's monthly disclosure to credit bureaus. One advantage of this approach is that, with a few exceptions, it leaves the basic decisions on disclosure policy to credit grantors and their customers. For such a policy to be worked out in the marketplace, however, individuals must be informed of institutional practices.

The notification requirement in *Recommendation (12)* establishes the basic ground rules for disclosure of information about an individual. To the extent that credit grantors inform their clients of information flows within the credit community, such flows would not be impeded. An authorization is recommended only for those disclosures which are an exception to the individual's expectation of confidentiality as established by the notification given at the beginning of the credit relationship.

The individual needs a continuing, legally assertable, interest in the uses and disclosures of information about him so that he can defend himself against demands for information levied on the credit grantor by persons who are not in any way parties to the credit relationship. The rationale for this assertion is fully explained in Chapter 1.

The Commission does not endorse an absolute right of control by the individual, as noted in numerous instances throughout this report. In this context, the Commission is sensitive to the credit grantor's need to disclose information about an individual to prevent or protect against the occurrence of fraud. In such instances, the credit grantor should not be bound by its duty of confidentiality and the corresponding requirement to obtain the individual's authorization.

In addition to enacting the recommendation, the statute should give the Federal Reserve Board regulatory authority similar to the regulatory authority it now has under the Truth-in-Lending, Equal Credit Opportunity, and Fair Credit Billing Acts. The resulting Federal Reserve regulations could then be enforced both by the agencies having authority over particular credit-granting institutions, and by the individual, as is currently provided under the Truth-in-Lending Act, which as indicated earlier, allows an individual to seek damages for a violation of standards promulgated by the Board, either on his own behalf or on behalf of a class.

CONFIDENTIALITY OF CREDIT-BUREAU RECORDS

Credit bureaus facilitate the exchange of credit information. Industry spokesmen have consistently argued that the individual implicitly consents to and benefits from this exchange. The Commission accepts both the basic need for a free flow of information among credit grantors and the implied consent of individuals to it, but the Commission rejects the view that individuals also consent to the free flow of credit information outside the credit system. In short, the Commission sees no justification for unfettered access to credit information by employers, insurance companies, licensing authorities, or other institutions. Thus, the Commission recommends:

Recommendation (13):

That the Federal Fair Credit Reporting Act be amended to provide that information concerning an individual maintained by a credit bureau may be used only for credit-related purposes, unless otherwise directed or authorized by the individual.

Implementation of this recommendation would require that the "permissible purposes" clause of the Fair Credit Reporting Act be changed so that purposes other than credit evaluation, account reviews, pre-screening, and debt collection would require an explicit authorization. This requirement comports with the Commission recommendations pertaining to records maintained by support organizations that service insurers and employers.

*   *   *   *   *   *   *

A NOTE ON THE COMMERCIAL-CREDIT RELATIONSHIP

Commercial establishments seek credit from banks, other commercial enterprises, and government agencies like the Small Business Administration. In fact, businesses commonly sought and received extensions of credit long before most individuals sought such credit extensions. Commercial-credit grantors, like consumer-credit grantors, collect information from and about applicants in order to evaluate their credit worthiness. When a business applies for credit, personal information about the individuals involved in the business may be collected and evaluated in making the decision to grant or deny credit to the business. Although decisions made by commercial-credit grantors primarily affect business entities, rather than individuals, they inevitably affect the livelihood of the individuals who own or operate the entities. The impact of commercial-credit decisions on individuals is particularly acute when the business seeking credit is a partnership, sole proprietorship, or closely held corporation.

While the Commission heard testimony on the record-keeping practices of commercial-reporting services, it had neither the time nor the resources to study in any detail the practices of commercial-credit *grantors*. Thus, the Commission's examination of commercial credit granting focused on the role of commercial-reporting services in the collection and evaluation of information bearing on credit worthiness. Like consumer-reporting agencies, commercial-reporting services collect information about applicants for credit from a variety of sources and report this information to their subscribers, the credit grantors. Unlike consumer-reporting agencies, however, commercial-reporting services are not subject to the Fair Credit Reporting Act; and thus individuals and firms about whom they collect information cannot avail themselves of the Act's existing protections against unfairness in record keeping.

Although the Commission has generally interpreted its mandate to include an examination of the impact of record keeping on individuals and to exclude inquiry into the effect of record keeping on legal entities, such as corporations, the boundary between record keeping that affects individuals and that which affects legal entities is not always entirely clear. This is particularly true in the case of commercial-credit granting. For example, a great deal of personal information about a sole proprietor who seeks credit will be collected in order to evaluate his business' general condition and, in particular, its ability to pay a debt. A decision about whether to grant or deny credit to a sole proprietor inevitably has great import for the individual who owns the firm. Thus, the Commission considered it important to examine the record-keeping practices of commercial-reporting services to determine what their impact on individuals is and to assess whether legal protections against unfairness to individuals in the commercial-credit relationship are necessary.

COLLECTION OF INFORMATION BY COMMERCIAL-REPORTING SERVICES

There are two main types of commercial-reporting services. The first type—which can be characterized as investigative—involves the collection of information about an applicant firm from its past and current creditors, as well as from a variety of other sources during the course of an investigation carried out by representatives of the commercial-reporting organization. Dun and Bradstreet and Equifax Services are the primary providers of this first type of service.

The second type of commercial-reporting service involves only the collection of information about an applicant firm from other credit grantors with which the firm has, or once had, a credit relationship. This second type of service is provided by TRW Business Credit Services for the National Association of Credit Management, as well as by other smaller firms.

An examination of the information collection practices of Dun and Bradstreet provides a good illustration of investigative commercial-reporting services. Dun & Bradstreet (D&B) collects information about commercial enterprises from a variety of sources and uses it to evaluate the current condition and future prospects of an enterprise. The most important source of information for D&B is the owners or managers of the business under investigation. Interviews with them naturally suggest other sources of information about the business, including banks, landlords, public records, the firm's major suppliers, and other creditors. Companies under investigation usually cooperate with D&B by naming other sources of information and authorizing the collection of information from them. Dun & Bradstreet executives state that more than 95 percent of businesses under investigation cooperate in this manner.[99] On the other hand, if a company does not cooperate in an investigation, that fact may be reported to its prospective credit grantors. A reported failure to cooperate, or D&B's inability to produce a report because of a lack of cooperation, can arouse suspicions about a company's credit worthiness, and have a chilling effect on its ability to obtain credit. Thus, a company might prefer to cooperate in the preparation of a negative report rather than be reported as uncooperative or as a firm on which no report exists.

Dun & Bradstreet investigators are instructed to inquire into eight areas in collecting information for their reports:[100]

1. Who owns the business?
2. What is the business-related background of the owners?
3. Where did the business get its capital, and how much?
4. What exactly do they do in their business?
5. What does their business owe and own?
6. How are they operating?
7. What do the figures mean?
8. How does the company pay?

An examination of these eight areas gives some insight into the nature and scope of a D&B commercial report.

---

[99] Testimony of Dun and Bradstreet, *Credit Reporting and Payment Automation Services*, Hearings before the Privacy Protection Study Commission, August 5, 1976, p. 591 (hereinafter cited as "Credit Reporting Hearings").

[100] Dun and Bradstreet, *Eight Keys to Basic Business Reporting*, Revised August 1976.

WHO OWNS THE BUSINESS?

The Dun & Bradstreet employee manual states:

unless people granting credit know with whom they are dealing, they have no way of knowing who is responsible for the payment of bills . . . the very first essential in investigating a business is to find out precisely who owns it. In addition, we check the ownership whenever an investigation is made, or whenever an inquiry is received which indicates a possible change in the ownership of the business.[101]

In answering the question "Who owns the business?," D&B investigators use the interview with a company's owners or executives as the first source of information. They then seek further documentation of ownership from sources such as incorporation papers and records of licenses. In the absence of satisfactory documentation of ownership from these sources, investigators are urged to have each owner or partner sign a financial statement of the company with his signature and title. Dun & Bradstreet will not issue a financial rating (known as a Capital and Credit Rating), an important factor in its report, until the firm has provided satisfactory assurances of ownership. This provides an incentive for company executives to disclose and document ownership fully.

WHAT IS THE BUSINESS-RELATED BACKGROUND OF THE OWNER?

A D&B investigation of the business-related background of the owner of a business must account for the individual's activities during each year from the time he was 21 until the present. Investigators are cautioned to be suspicious of any gaps in the description of a businessman's background. If the individual under investigation was once employed by others, the name of the employer, dates of employment, and description of the job record are obtained from the individual, if possible, and verified with previous employers.

The Dun & Bradstreet investigator may occasionally have to seek information about business-related background from sources other than the individual. The D&B manual states, "suppose the person . . . doesn't want to talk about his or her business experience? What then? Well, in the smaller town you can find people who know the business person, or just as important, may not know him or her. In the larger cities, go to the nearby bank, landlord, or someone who must have done business with the person. They'll know something about prior business background."[102]

In addition to information regarding the individual's business background, D&B investigators seek information regarding his education, marital status, and, most significantly, any involvement in criminal activity or bankruptcies. According to D&B, investigators do not collect informa-

---

[101] *Ibid.*, p. 7.
[102] *Ibid.*, p. 11.

tion regarding " . . . an individual's personal health, lifestyle, or . . . his personal financial dealings."[103]

While D&B constantly updates the information in its reports and discards obsolete information, information about criminal convictions of the owner or managers of a company under investigation are maintained and reported to credit grantors indefinitely by Dun & Bradstreet. Only if the conviction has been expunged or reversed, or the individual has been pardoned, will the mention of it be omitted from a report. Dun & Bradstreet reports pending criminal charges to subscribers as well until the charges are disposed of by a dismissal, acquittal, or a notation on the record that no further prosecution is intended. Arrests not followed by a complaint, affidavit, or indictment may be reported for six months and then dropped from the report.[104]

WHERE DID THE BUSINESS GET ITS CAPITAL, AND HOW MUCH?

Inquiries regarding where the business got its capital and how much capital it has become intensely personal because it involves inquiries about how much money an entrepreneur has and from where the money was obtained. Investigators for Dun & Bradstreet are, however, urged to think of such questions as business rather than personal inquiries.

> Now we are going to ask you whether you might hesitate to ask a person how much money is invested in the business and where he or she got it. Does it seem a "personal" question to you? It isn't. We are asking business questions for business reasons. We are asking the same questions the prospective supplier would ask if *he* or *she* calls on the new business person.[105]

WHAT EXACTLY DO THEY DO IN THEIR BUSINESS?

The D&B manual notes "this information is about the easiest to obtain."[106] In many cases, a great deal of the information necessary to answer this question can be obtained by an investigator's visit to the business premises. As the manual also notes, most people are proud of their business and are delighted to describe it to a willing listener. This portion of a D&B report does not usually contain personal information about the owners or executives of a company.

WHAT DOES THEIR BUSINESS OWE AND OWN?

It is difficult for an investigator to compile this information without obtaining a balance sheet and other financial statements from the company. Thus, the active cooperation of the firm under investigation is normally required to answer this question. Dun & Bradstreet instructions to its

---

[103] Testimony of Dun and Bradstreet, Credit Reporting Hearings, August 5, 1976, p. 587.
[104] Dun and Bradstreet, *op. cit.*, p. 12.
[105] Dun and Bradstreet, *op. cit.*, p. 15.
[106] *Ibid*, p. 17.

employees seem to indicate, however, that companies resist turning over copies of their financial statements to outsiders, such as D&B investigators. Thus, Dun & Bradstreet's instructions to employees focus on tactics that might be used to convince a firm that is under investigation to produce its financial statements for examination by D&B. The instructions include lists of reasons why the company's cooperation with D&B is wise, sample letters from retailers outlining some of the advantages that accrue to businesses as a result of disclosing information to D&B, and other assertions from firms that cooperation with credit investigators leads to increased sales and profits. Investigators are furnished with blank authorization forms that company executives can sign to authorize bankers and accountants to disclose company financial records to investigators. In the event that a business refuses to disclose information to D&B, investigators are urged to make their own on-site estimate of visible assets.

How are They Operating?

If the owners or managers of a business have disclosed its balance sheets and other financial data to the D&B investigator, he can use it to answer the question "How are they operating?." The investigator attempts to determine business trends by analyzing net worth and sales figures, and evaluates management efficiency by scrutinizing indicators, such as rate of merchandise turnover and return on invested capital. Investigators are apparently able to obtain sales and profit figures more easily than indebtedness and asset figures. For this reason, Dun & Bradstreet investigators are urged to ask for sales and profit figures and then use them as a basis for other computations.

What do the Figures Mean?

In answering inquiry 7, "What do the figures mean?", investigators must develop an assessment of the company's standing in the business world and its prospects. This is far from an exact science and is difficult even for professionally-trained accountants and financial analysts. Dun & Bradstreet bases its projections almost entirely on a company's past performance.

How Does the Company Pay?

The willingness and ability of a company to meet its credit obligations is the single most important information that the buyers of commercial credit reports are seeking. Therefore, commercial reporting services such as Dun & Bradstreet will go to great lengths to contact each creditor, large and small, to gather information regarding a company's creditworthiness. In determining how well a company meets its obligations, Dun & Bradstreet investigators use information from the company under investigation to learn who its creditors are. The creditors themselves are the primary source of information in answering this inquiry.

A change in payment habits is often the first indication of a change in a company's financial situation. A company encountering financial difficulties will often create what are essentially unauthorized, interest-free, short-term loans by systematically deferring payment on its accounts payable. Such activity may reflect the attitudes of the company's executives toward its expected future performance.

In sum, a Dun & Bradstreet commercial report is a detailed report about a business which includes information about its owners or managers as well as an analysis of the company's financial condition and performance.

Equifax, Inc., the information services conglomerate discussed earlier and in Chapter 8, offers investigative commercial reporting services similar in most respects to those offered by Dun & Bradstreet. The information collected by Equifax does not appear to be substantially different from that contained in Dun & Bradstreet's reports. One significant difference between Dun & Bradstreet and Equifax, however, is that

> Equifax has designed its Business Credit Report to give [its subscribers] specific information on *medium and small size* business-es.[107] (emphasis added)

Dun & Bradstreet's work involves the collection of information about large firms as well as small- to medium-size companies. Thus, concerns about the impact of the record-keeping practices of commercial-reporting services on individuals are especially pertinent in the case of Equifax because they specialize in providing information about small firms—sometimes owned by a single individual—to credit grantors.

The second type of commercial reporting service examined by the Commission is TRW's National Credit Information Service (NACIS), operated on behalf of the National Association of Credit Management. NACIS differs from the services offered by Dun & Bradstreet and Equifax because it does not investigate firms but merely compiles information obtained from commercial credit grantors and reports this information to other credit grantors. In addition, NACIS collects and reports information about a firm's relationships with banks. In essence, NACIS operates an automated clearinghouse for commercial credit information. Unlike Dun & Bradstreet and Equifax, NACIS provides no evaluative information about firms to credit grantors, such as an assessment of a business' creditworthiness, nor does NACIS provide credit grantors with information about the business-related background of a company's owners or managers.

PROTECTIONS FOR INDIVIDUALS AND FIRMS

Commercial-reporting services are not subject to the Fair Credit Reporting Act. Thus, subjects of commercial reports are not entitled by law to learn the nature and substance of the information in the report or to file a statement disputing information in the report. Nor are commercial reporting services subject to restrictions on the reporting of obsolete information, or constraints on the use or disclosure of the reports it prepares, but commercial credit grantors are generally subject to the Equal Credit Opportunity Act, as amended. Regulations implementing the Act *[12 C.F.R.*

---

[107] Equifax, Inc., *Equifax Business Credit Report*, March 1977, p. 1.

202.3(e)(2)] require commercial credit grantors to tell an applicant firm the specific reasons it has been declined credit *if* the firm makes a written request for the reasons within 30 days after it has been notified of the adverse decision. Thus, commercial reporting services are generally not subject to any laws governing fairness in record keeping, and the record-keeping practices of commercial credit grantors are prescribed at the Federal level only by the Equal Credit Opportunity Act. In its testimony before the Commission, however, representatives of Dun & Bradstreet said that its policies regarding its commmercial reports conform in some respects to the provisions of the Fair Credit Reporting Act. For example, Dun & Bradstreet representatives testified:

> Any time a company wishes to see what we are saying about it, we will give the firm a copy of our report. On occasion, where a report contains information which would reveal the names of individual firms which have provided information on how a company pays its bills, we do not disclose that particular information without the consent of the supplier.[108]

They also testified that if:

> . . . we have received adverse information, and the businessman challenges our conclusions or data, we will gladly reinvestigate the disputed facts and report back to him . . . . If substantive changes are made, we send the revised report to all appropriate subscribers.[109]

Moreover, Dun & Bradstreet representatives told the Commission that:

> . . . we regularly interview the businesses we report on and afford them opportunities to confirm, augment and correct the information we have about them.[110]

Dun & Bradstreet's practice, as noted above, is to interview the owners or managers of a business that is under investigation. As a consequence,

> Businesses are fully aware that we are writing the report and part of [the] reporter's job in the initial interview is to get across the reason why we are doing it.[111]

Finally, Dun & Bradstreet's agreement with its subscribers specifies that the use of its commercial reports must be limited to busi̇ness decisions relating to a firm or its stockholders, directors, officers, partners, proprietors or employees in their capacity as such and that:

> It is expressly prohibited to use such information as a factor in establishing an individual's eligibility for (1) credit or insurance to

---

[108] Testimony of Dun and Bradstreet, Credit Reporting Hearings, August 5, 1976, p. 588.
[109] *Ibid.*, pp. 588, 590.
[110] *Ibid.*, p. 594.
[111] *Ibid.*, p. 612.

be used primarily for personal, family, or household purposes, or (2) employment.[112]

In response to questioning by the Commission regarding whether subscribers ever violate this agreement and use information about an individual contained in commercial reports for the purpose of making decisions about him, rather than about the firm he owns or with which he is associated, a Dun & Bradstreet representative stated:

I cannot say categorically, but if there are any, it [sic] is very few.[113]

The Commission did not explore whether TRW and Equifax follow the kinds of procedures described above, and thus it cannot draw general conclusions about the adequacy of the record-keeping policies of these two commerical reporting services. The Commission notes, however, that Dun & Bradstreet is by far the largest of the commercial-reporting services, and thus its policies have great significance within the industry.

A court case involving abuses arising from the use of information about the owner of a commercial enterprise, as well as information about the enterprise itself, to make business-related decisions lends support for the recommendations the Commission makes below. The case in point involved Michael Goldgar.[114] In 1961, Goldgar was an owner of a conglomerate of companies including clothing stores and supermarkets, as well as other enterprises. According to Goldgar, a bankruptcy petition was filed against one of his companies in 1962 while he was out of the country. Goldgar returned to the United States and discovered that the bankruptcy petition was invalid. Dun and Bradstreet had, however, reported to credit grantors that Goldgar's company was bankrupt, as well as other derogatory information about Goldgar himself. This report, according to Goldgar, damaged the reputation of his companies and resulted eventually in actual bankruptcy. Goldgar then took Dun and Bradstreet to court. In reviewing the verdict against Dun and Bradstreet, the Supreme Court of New York State noted that as a consequence of D&B reporting "a false rumor was bruited about that Goldgar was leaving the country and could not meet his bills." The court noted, in sum, that:

The record presents the picture of a feud carried on by defendant, the well known credit rating organization, against one Goldgar who had incurred defendant's ill-will. Concededly, defendant was "out to get" Goldgar and the corporate conglomerate he was attempting to erect. Unfortunately, for Goldgar and his two chief companies, Dejay and Star, dissemination of derogatory information about *him* and his enterprises brought them crashing down into bankruptcy. Had this come about as a result of straightforward and honest credit reporting, that would have been the end of the matter. Unfortunately for defendant, the record discloses that its coup was

---

[112] Dun and Bradstreet, "Terms of Agreement."
[113] Testimony of Dun and Bradstreet, Credit Reporting Hearings, August 5, 1976, p. 510.
[114] *National Apparel Adjustment Council et al. v. Dun & Bradstreet, Inc.*, No. 6836 (N.Y. Sup. Ct. App. Div., lst Dept., April 1973).

accomplished by intrigue, deliberate assault on a business, planted rumor, and reckless disregard of consequences, going far beyond what the trial justice characterized as no more than a high degree of incompetence.

The Goldgar case illustrates that personal information about the owners or executives of a company can form part of the basis for an adverse commercial credit decision. The Goldgar case also demonstrates the need for procedures to assure that information collected and reported by commercial-reporting services is accurate. Finally, this case confirms the Commission's belief that an individual who is the subject of a commercial credit report should be able to see the report and request its correction. Without such a right, the firm's owners and managers may not be able to determine what information is being used to make adverse credit decisions affecting the business and to assure that inaccurate information in the files of a commercial-reporting service is corrected or amended.

CONCLUSIONS AND RECOMMENDATIONS

The Commission believes that the impact of the record-keeping practices of commercial credit grantors and commercial-reporting services have significance for individuals, as well as for the business entities with which they are associated. If credit is denied to a partnership, sole proprietorship, or closely held corporation, the consequences for the sole proprietor, partner, or owner may be grave. Moreover, the basis on which a commercial credit decision is made may involve personal information about individuals who own or manage a business, and personal information in a commercial report that is circulated widely may affect an individual's own reputation or career.

Intrusiveness

Commercial credit grantors, like consumer credit grantors, collect and use personal information about individuals in making credit decisions. Although the consumer credit grantor's interest is primarily in information about individuals, and the commercial credit grantor's inquiries focus on businesses that are seeking credit, information about individuals may enter into decisions about the extension of commercial credit. When a sole proprietorship or partnership applies for credit, a great deal of the information necessary to make a credit decision concerns, and is collected from, the individual or individuals who own the business.

Thus, the concerns about intrusive inquiries by credit grantors that were described in the section of this chapter dealing with consumer credit may arise as well in the commercial credit relationship. Therefore, the Commission believes that governmental mechanisms should exist to consider the extent to which an individual should be required to submit to inquiries about him as a consequence of an application made by a firm that he owns or with which he is associated. The Commission recommends:

Recommendation (14):

That governmental mechanisms should exist for individuals to question the propriety of information about individuals collected or used by commercial credit grantors, and to bring such objections to the appropriate bodies that establish public policy. Legislation specifically prohibiting the use, or collection and use, of a specific item of information may result; or an existing agency or regulatory body may be given authority or use its currently delegated authority to make such a determination with respect to the reasonableness of future use, or collection and use, of a specific item of information.

Fairness

Although the Commission believes that the procedures established voluntarily by Dun & Bradstreet to permit the owners or managers of a firm to see commercial reports, to dispute their accuracy, and to request their correction are entirely laudable, it finds that such procedures are not entirely sufficient to protect individuals from unfairness in the use of commercial reports. Voluntary procedures that permit a firm's owners or managers to inspect and request correction of a commercial report can be modified or done away with altogether whenever a commercial-reporting service finds them too costly or burdensome, and some commercial-reporting services may never voluntarily establish such procedures in the first place. Therefore, the Commission believes that Federal legislation to establish see-and-copy rights is necessary. Moreover, the Commission believes that a commercial credit grantor should be required by law to tell the managers or owners of a firm that is the subject of an adverse commercial credit decision based in whole or in part on information about individuals contained in a commercial report *which* commercial-reporting service provided the report to the credit grantor, and of the individual's rights to see, copy, and request correction of the report. Without such a notification by the commercial credit grantor, the firm's owners or managers may be unable to determine the source of the commercial report, and may not know of the rights that would be afforded the individual or firm if the Commission's recommendations were adopted.

Therefore, the Commission recommends:

Recommendation (15):

That the Congress amend the Fair Credit Reporting Act to provide that, upon request, a commercial credit grantor must disclose in writing to an individual who is associated with a firm that is the subject of an adverse credit decision, based in whole or in part on information provided by a commercial-reporting service, where such information pertains in whole or in part to that individual;

(a) the name and address of the commercial-reporting service that provided the information; and

(b)   the individual's rights provided by law with respect to a commercial-reporting service.

Recommendation (16):

That the Congress amend the Fair Credit Reporting Act to provide that, upon request by an individual, a commercial-reporting service must:

(a)   inform the individual, after verifying his identity, whether it has any recorded information pertaining to him connected with a report about a firm;
(b)   permit the individual to see and copy any such recorded information, except the identity of sources, in plain language, either in person or by mail;
(c)   apprise the individual of the nature and substance of any such recorded information by telephone; and
(d)   permit the individual to use whichever of the methods of access provided in (b) and (c) he prefers. The commercial-reporting service may charge a reasonable copying fee for any copies provided to the individual.

Recommendation (17):

That the Congress amend the Fair Credit Reporting Act to provide that an individual has a right to correct or amend information pertaining to him that is maintained by a commercial-reporting service or is provided an opportunity to file a concise statement of disagreement with the commercial reporting service.

Three details of these recommendations deserve special mention. First, the word "individual" as used in this recommendation and in succeeding recommendations in this section means the owner, manager, or other employee of a firm that is the subject of a commercial report, and who is mentioned in the report concerning the firm.

Second, the Commission's recommendations would not require that subjects of commercial reports be told the sources of information in the report. Commercial-reporting service and credit-grantor representatives argue that permitting the subjects of commercial reports to learn the identity of sources of the information in them would either "dry up" sources of information, or reduce the candor of sources' disclosures. For example, a letter from Robert Morris Associates (an association of commercial credit grantors) to the Commission stated that revealing the identity of the sources of information in a commercial-credit report

... would pose a serious threat to the meaningful exchange of credit information, reducing it to the reporting of favorable, or no information, which would lead to poor loan decisions and the perpetration of fraudulent business activities. The effect on the economy would be massive if the flow of credit information is curtailed.[115]

In other areas the Commission has studied in detail, it has rejected similar arguments. Because the Commission was not able to explore this area in enough detail to prove or disprove these arguments, however, it believes that commercial-reporting services should not at this time be required to reveal to individuals or firms the identity of the sources of information in a commercial report. The Commission does believe, however, that the subject merits further study, and so recommends below.

Third, the burden should be on an individual seeking access to information maintained by commercial-reporting services to reasonably describe the records sought by identifying the firm(s) with which he has been associated and about which they may have reports.

The Commission also believes that commercial-reporting services should be required by law to have reasonable procedures to assure the accuracy of the information in their reports.

Therefore, the Commission recommends:

Recommendation (18):

That the Congress amend the Fair Credit Reporting Act to provide that commercial-reporting services must have reasonable procedures to assure the accuracy of information pertaining to individuals included in reports produced by them.

As noted above, *Recommendations (14), (15), (16),* and *(17)* call for amendment of the Fair Credit Reporting Act. This approach parallels the one recommended by the Commission in the section of this chapter dealing with consumer credit. The Commission believes that an individual should be able to sue a commercial-reporting service for failure to comply with one of these recommendations. The court should have the power to order the commercial-reporting service to comply and to award attorney's fees and court costs to any plaintiff who substantially prevails. If it could be shown that the commercial-reporting service willfully or intentionally denied the individual any of the rights *Recommendations (14), (15),* and *(16)* provide him, or failed to institute and follow the procedures called for in *Recommendation (17),* the court should have the power to award up to $1,000 to the individual.

In addition, the Commission believes that the Federal Trade Commission should be able to enforce the recommended measures when systematic or repeated failures to comply by a commercial-reporting service occur. The remedy would be a FTC order directing the commercial-reporting service to comply, and the FTC could use the statutory powers it currently has to force compliance.

---

[115] Letter from Jerome L. Roderick, Director, Credit Division, Robert Morris Associates to the Privacy Commission, April 15, 1977.

THE NEED FOR FURTHER STUDY

The Commission believes that further study is required to evaluate certain issues regarding the record-keeping practices of commercial credit grantors that either were not addressed at all, or were not addressed fully, by the Commission. Accordingly, the Commission recommends:

Recommendation (19):

That further examination of the need for additional requirements appropriate for commercial credit granting and credit reporting record-keeping practices be undertaken.

With respect to commercial credit granting, the following specific areas should be examined:

(a) information collection practices;

(b) the need to protect the identity of sources other than commercial-reporting services; and

(c) the adequacy of credit grantors' explanation of adverse credit decisions, pursuant to the Equal Credit Opportunity Act.

With respect to commercial-reporting services, the following specific areas should be examined:

(a) the time limits for reporting certain types of information, e.g., arrests and convictions;

(b) the need to protect identity of sources; and

(c) the use of commercial-reporting services for insurance underwriting and other decisions.

The Commission's recommendations regarding commercial reporting and commercial-credit granting are not as extensive as those it has made in the consumer credit area. The Commission did not explore the commercial-credit relationship in great detail, and businesses are more likely than most individuals to be able to exert pressure to obtain redress when they have been harmed by the record-keeping practices of commercial-credit grantors or reporting services.

Nonetheless, the Commission believes that owners or managers of businesses should be given basic legal rights *vis-a-vis* their records: the right to learn which commercial-reporting services produced a report that formed the basis of an adverse credit decision; and the right to see, copy, and request correction of commercial reports. Without such basic rights, an attempt by a firm's owners or managers to learn the source of an erroneous report and to obtain correction of it may be long and arduous. Thus, the Commission's recommendations provide simple mechanisms by which affected individuals and their firms can make their concerns known and seek redress when they are harmed by unfair record-keeping practices.

Chapter 3

The Depository Relationship

As Justice William O. Douglas once observed, "The banking transactions of an individual give a fairly accurate account of his religion, ideology, opinion, and interest . . . ."[1] Moreover, the emergence of a checking account as an economic and social diary for many individuals is one reason why commercial banks are acutely aware of the need to keep their clients' financial affairs confidential. Yet, as noted in Chapter 1, the Supreme Court, in *U.S. v. Miller*,[2] recently rejected the notion that such expectations of confidentiality are either warranted or legally enforceable.

The Supreme Court decision comes at a time when electronic funds transfer services, and other developments in personal-data record keeping, promise far-reaching consequences for the type of individually identifiable documentation entrusted to depository institutions. For these among many reasons, the Commission felt compelled to examine the record-keeping practices of depository institutions and to reexamine the assumptions underlying depository practices.

DEPOSITORY INSTITUTIONS

Depository institutions—that is, commercial banks, savings and loan associations, mutual savings banks, and credit unions—are financial intermediaries[3] acting as go betweens for suppliers and borrowers of money and for payers and payees. In simplest terms, when an individual deposits his money with such an institution, the institution becomes his agent and the records resulting from the relationship exist primarily to document transactions. For example, when an individual writes a check, the bank pays on the basis of that order. The check is the individual's instruction to the bank and provides an accounting to protect both the individual and the depository institution.

Americans have long thought that the details of an individual's financial affairs are nobody's business but his own unless he chooses to reveal them. The record-keeping policies and practices of depository institutions visibly reflect this view. Depository institutions testified that

---

[1] *California Bankers Association v. Shultz*, 416 U.S. 21, 94 S. Ct. 1494, 39 L. Ed. 2d 812 (1974).

[2] *United States v. Miller*, 425 U.S. 435 (1976).

[3] Written statement of First National City Bank (Citibank), *Credit-Card Issuers and Reservations Systems*, Hearings before the Privacy Protection Study Commission, February 11, 1976, p. 13. (Hereinafter cited as "Credit-Card Issuers Hearings.")

they are cautious in responding to inquiries concerning even the mere existence of an account.[4] The number of institutions that have self-imposed policies for notifying individuals when government agencies are seeking account information further indicates their concern. Nonetheless, information about depositors is available for purposes other than accounting. New banking services, such as overdraft protection for checking accounts[5], and concern about fraud contribute to data availability. The demands of governmental agencies responsible for regulatory oversight, law enforcement, welfare administration, and other public-sector programs also affect the level of disclosure by depository institutions.

The proliferation of personal banking service records parallels the phenomenal growth of open-end consumer credit[6] over the past several decades. As a consequence, commercial banks keep a much broader range of transactions for a significantly larger population than they did only a few years ago. The combined increase in personal checking accounts and penetration of the open-end credit market described in Chapter 2 has made commercial banks major repositories of information about the activities and relationships of millions of people.

Commercial banks have begun to market services that guarantee the availability of funds to the recipient of a check. Such authorization, or "check-guarantee," services protect the depositor against having his personal checks refused by retailers, and protect the retailer against loss from forged checks and from checks returned because there are not sufficient funds in an otherwise legitimate account. These services create a new type of economic risk for depository institutions, making them more selective—and more inquisitive—about applicants for checking accounts. For the individual, the process of applying for these new types of depository services, in some instances, resembles the process of applying for open-end consumer credit,[7] and applications for ordinary checking accounts are now being declined at times on the basis of information provided by independent check-guarantee services and credit bureaus.

In response to the increasing frequency of fraudulent and overdraft checks written during the past decade, other types of institutions have also developed services for guaranteeing checks. They are functionally similar to the independent credit-card authorization services discussed in the preceding chapter and basically maintain information on individuals who have fraudulently used checks or have outstanding unpaid checks. Such institutions also may keep a log of check-writing activity for a brief period to be

---

[4] Written statement of Continental Illinois National Bank and Trust Company of Chicago, *Depository and Lending Institutions*, Hearings before the Privacy Protection Study Commission, April 21, 1976, p. 5 (hereinafter cited as "Depository and Lending Institutions Hearings"); also, written statement of Bayview Federal Savings and Loan Association, Depository and Lending Institutions Hearings, April 22, 1976, pp. 5-6; and, written statement of Credit Union National Association, Depository and Lending Institutions Hearings, April 21, 1976, p. 8.

[5] "Overdraft protection" is a pre-established line of credit to assure that a checking account does not get overdrawn.

[6] For a discussion of this growth, see Chapter 2.

[7] See Chapter 2.

able to report to subscribers the total number and amount of checks written by an individual on whom an inquiry is made.

An independent check-guarantee service may verify that an individual does not have any outstanding checks for which payment was refused by the individual's bank; or the service may guarantee, or insure, that the check will be honored. If the individual's bank refuses payment, the service will meet the obligation and then collect the funds directly from the individual.

It should be noted that a check-guarantee service can combine in one organizational framework functions normally associated with depository institutions, insurers, credit bureaus, collection agencies, and credit-card authorization systems.[8] The development of these multifaceted services illustrates how traditional relationships between individuals and institutions can blur in the coming decades. Although it may be premature to address such matters, the Commission believes that the President and the Congress should be attentive to the long-term effects they may have on individuals. At the very least, future framers of protective legislation will be faced with a new set of definitional problems.

THE BANK SECRECY ACT OF 1970

The Currency and Foreign Transactions Reporting Act of 1970, the so-called "Bank Secrecy Act,"[9] requires depository institutions to retain certain records on individuals and to report certain types of financial transactions to the Federal Government. The law was enacted largely in response to a concern over the use of secret foreign bank accounts to evade American laws. At the same time, however, Congress also recognized that the required records could be helpful to many law enforcement, regulatory, and tax administration authorities. Government agencies came to view the Bank Secrecy Act as a kind of insurance policy, guaranteeing that copies of checks and certain other documentation would be available if needed.

Bankers and civil libertarians have challenged the Act on the grounds that it raises fundamental questions about the confidential relationship between depository institutions and their customers and the relationship between government and citizens in a free society.[10] While the Commission addresses these concerns in Chapter 9, the Act is discussed here only as it affects the record-keeping practices of depository institutions.

---

[8] See written statement of Telecredit, Inc., *Credit Reporting and Payment Authorization Services*, Hearings before the Privacy Protection Study Commission, August 5, 1976. (Hereinafter cited as "Credit Reporting Hearings.")

[9] 31 U.S.C. 1051-1122

[10] *Amend the Bank Secrecy Act*, Hearings before the Subcommittee on Financial Institutions of the Committee on Banking, Housing, and Urban Affairs, U.S. Senate, 92d Congress, 2d Session, 1972; *The Effect of the Bank Secrecy Act on State Laws*, Hearings before the Subcommittee on Financial Institutions of the Committee on Banking, Housing, and Urban Affairs, U.S. Senate, 93d Congress, 2d Session, 1974; *Bank Failures, Regulatory Reform, and Financial Privacy*, Hearings before the Subcommittee on Financial Institutions of the Committee on Banking, Currency, and Housing, U.S. House of Representatives, 94th Congress, 1st Session, 1975.

The regulations issued by the Treasury Department[11] pursuant to the Bank Secrecy Act can be divided into four categories: (1) those pertaining to the record-keeping practices of banks and other financial institutions; (2) those requiring reports of currency transactions, foreign financial accounts, and the international transportation of monetary instruments; (3) those requiring financial institutions to verify the identity of their customers; and (4) those requiring persons having foreign financial accounts to report them to the government and to maintain records on them.

The first category requires banks, savings and loan associations, securities brokers, dealers in foreign currency, agents of foreign banks, and certain other financial institutions to retain the original or a copy of a record of each extension of credit in excess of $5,000 (except for credit secured by real estate), and the original or a copy of a record of each instruction given or received concerning the transmission out of the United States of more than $10,000 in credit, funds, currency, or other monetary instruments, checks, or securities. *[31 C.F.R. 103.33]*

A bank or other similar institution, such as a savings and loan association, credit union, or agent of a foreign bank must also retain a copy of the following: (1) documents granting signature authority over each deposit or share account; (2) account statements; (3) checks and other charges in excess of $100 that are posted to accounts (only checks drawn on certain high-volume accounts are exempt); (4) each check or other item in excess of $10,000 transmitted outside the United States; (5) each check or draft in excess of $10,000 drawn on or issued by a foreign bank which is paid by the domestic bank; (6) each check in excess of $10,000 received directly from a foreign financial institution; (7) records of each receipt of currency, other monetary instrument, securities, checks, or credit received from a foreign financial institution; and (8) records necessary to reconstruct a checking account and to furnish an audit trail for each transaction over $100. *[31 C.F.R. 103.34(b)]*

The Securities and Exchange Commission regulated the record keeping of securities brokers long before the Treasury Department issued its regulations implementing the Bank Secrecy Act. The Treasury regulations, however, added the requirement that the brokers obtain a signature card or similar document establishing trading authority over an account, and that they make a reasonable effort to obtain a Social Security number for each account. *[31 C.F.R. 103.35]*

One of the reporting requirements that affects the record-keeping practices of private financial institutions is only a modification of the longstanding requirement, in effect for more than 25 years, that financial institutions report to the Internal Revenue Service (IRS) any unusual domestic currency transaction involving more than $2,500. The new regulation raises the threshold amount from $2,500 to $10,000, and adds a penalty for willful failure to report. *[31 C.F.R. 103.32, .25(a), .47, .49]*

A new reporting requirement mandates reports on the international transportation of currency and certain monetary instruments in excess of

---

[11] 31 C.F.R. 103.

$5,000. A traveller carrying that amount with him must file a report with the U.S. Customs Service when he enters or leaves the United States. If the amount is transported in some other manner, a report must be filed with Customs before the monetary instrument enters or leaves the country. Conversely, a United States resident who receives $5,000 or more from overseas must file a report within 30 days after the money arrives. *[31 C.F.R. 103.23, .24(b)]*

Another reporting requirement of interest actually went into effect before Treasury issued its regulations. On the 1970 Federal income tax return, the IRS included a question concerning the ownership or control of foreign financial accounts and required any person who had such an account to file a separate schedule describing it. Under Treasury's regulation, such persons are also required to retain certain specified records of the account.

The precept "know your customer" is widely accepted in financial circles. The Treasury regulations reinforce it by requiring financial institutions to verify and record the identity of any person for whom they handle a reportable transaction, and by specifying minimum identification procedures. The identity of someone who is not a depositor may be verified by examining a driver's license, passport, or other document normally accepted as positive identification, but financial institutions must also make a reasonable effort to obtain a Social Security number or other taxpayer identification number for each entity identified with a deposit account.

Checks and other charges in excess of $100 must be microfilmed and retained for five years. The $100 minimum was supposed to exempt the vast majority of checks written by individuals, but selecting out checks in excess of $99 has proved so expensive that most banks microfilm all checks.[12]

THE SERVICE ROLE OF FEDERAL FINANCIAL REGULATORS

The fact that some financial regulatory agencies provide information-processing services for those they regulate distinguishes the depository area from other spheres of government regulation. The Federal Communications Commission, for example, does not provide the common-carrier facilities through which broadcasting networks distribute their programs, nor do State Insurance Commissioners operate computers for processing insurance companies' claims. In banking, however, Federal Reserve District Banks and Federal Home Loan Banks both provide important, though fundamentally different, record-keeping services for commercial banks and savings and loan associations.[13]

Since 1913, the Federal Reserve District Banks have cleared checks among the nation's commercial banks. Although they do not clear all checks, their services play a significant role in the movement of money from

---

[12] Written statement of American Bankers Association, Depository and Lending Institutions Hearings, April 22, 1976.

[13] Written statement of Board of Governors of the Federal Reserve System Staff, Depository and Lending Institutions Hearings, April 22, 1976; written statement of Federal Home Loan Bank Board Staff, Depository and Lending Institutions Hearings, April 22, 1976.

one part of the country to another. For years, this payments mechanism has depended on the physical movement of paper, with millions of individually documented transactions flowing through it every day. Concern over confidentiality was seldom expressed, since the paper glut alone was expected to protect an individual depositor's anonymity. However, changes in the form of such transfers to include electronically recorded entries, as discussed later in this chapter, have begun to undermine confidence in the continued preservation of confidential transactions as they pass through the Federal Reserve System.

Because savings and loan associations lack the payment powers of commercial banks, their record keeping does not usually cover transfers of funds among institutions, and thus is significantly less complicated than that of the commercial banks. Certain Federal Home Loan Banks, however, operate data-processing facilities as a service to savings and loan associations that are too small to support a data-processing facility of their own or are inconveniently far from a commercial data-processing service bureau.

The Commission has paid particular attention to the service role of these Federal financial regulators because of its concern with a continued public presence in the development and operation of electronic funds transfer services. The basis for this concern and the Commission's recommendation with respect to it is set forth in a later section of this chapter. First, however, the specific problems posed by the record-keeping practices of depository institutions today must be considered along with the Commission's recommendations with respect to them.

RECOMMENDATIONS

In contrast to the consumer-credit relationship, the depository relationship is not regulated with respect to determining eligibility for services and to use of third parties for information to make decisions about such eligibility. However, the introduction of new depository services involving economic risk for depository institutions, coupled with the *Miller* decision's effect on the confidential status of depository records, have persuaded the Commission that this lack of clear rights and responsibilities is undesirable for both depository institutions and their customers; the recommendations that follow reflect this conclusion.

The Commission's recommendations are presented in terms of its three recommended public-policy objectives: (1) to minimize intrusiveness; (2) to maximize fairness; and (3) to create a legitimate, enforceable, expectation of confidentiality.

GOVERNMENTAL MECHANISMS

Because of the greater risk banks assume when they offer check-guarantee services and append lines of credit to depository accounts, individuals can no longer count on getting a bank's depository services even if they apply with cash in hand. Although the evaluation of an individual who applies for a depository service does not appear to be as complex or as extensive as it is when he applies for consumer credit, there are parallels.

The Equal Credit Opportunity Act, as amended,[14] curbs the collection of some information about individuals by consumer-credit grantors, but depository institutions are under no such constraint. However, the Commission found no evidence that depository institutions collect items of information which could be considered excessively intrusive, and for this reason finds it unnecessary to recommend that governmental mechanisms should exist for individuals to question the propriety of information collected or used by depository institutions, or to bring such objections to the attention of bodies responsible for public policy. The need for such mechanisms may arise in the future, and the Commission suggests continued attention to developments bearing on the intrusiveness issue.

REASONABLE CARE IN THE USE OF SUPPORT ORGANIZATIONS

Because of the similarity between applying for some new types of depository services and for open-end consumer credit, and because, as noted earlier, an independent check-guarantee service can combine functions normally associated with insurers, credit bureaus, collection agencies, credit-card authorization systems, as well as depository institutions, the Commission believes that implementation of its recommendations regarding depository institutions will be enhanced considerably if depository institutions have a strong incentive to assure that the activities of their support organizations are proper. Hence, the Commission recommends:

Recommendation (1):

That the Federal Fair Credit Reporting Act be amended to provide that a depository institution must exercise reasonable care in the selection and use of credit bureaus, independent check-guarantee services, and other support organizations, so as to assure that the collection, maintenance, use, and disclosure practices of such organizations comply with the Commission's recommendations.

If it could be shown that a depository institution contracted for or used the services of a support organization with knowledge, actual or constructive, that the organization had been engaging in illegal practices, an individual, the Federal Trade Commission, or other appropriate enforcement agency could initiate action against both the depository institution and the support organization and hold them jointly liable for the support organization's actions.

---

[14] 15 U.S.C. 1691 *et seq.*

Fairness

FAIRNESS IN COLLECTION

NOTICE REGARDING COLLECTION FROM THIRD PARTIES

Although the Commission believes that there is currently no need for governmental mechanisms to question the propriety of information collected or used by depository institutions, the individual's participation in striking a balance between the amount of information he must divulge about himself and the service he expects in return does need to be strengthened. Thus, the Commission recommends:

Recommendation (2):

That Federal law be enacted or amended to provide that when an individual applies for a depository service, a depository institution must notify the individual of:

(a)   the types of information expected to be collected about him from third parties and that are not collected on the application; and

(b)   the types of institutional sources that are expected to be asked to provide information about him.

The recommended measure, like the parallel measure recommended for consumer credit, ensures that the individual will be told the scope of an inquiry before agreeing to it. The usual institutional sources to be queried are the individual's employer and the depository institutions with which he has or once had a relationship. The emergence of independent check-guarantee services and the new reliance on credit bureaus introduce additional institutional sources, and this recommendation also applies to them.

The Commission believes that this recommendation can best be implemented by giving additional authority to the Federal Reserve Board to supplement similar regulatory authority it now has under the Truth-in-Lending, Equal Credit Opportunity, and Fair Credit Billing Acts. The resulting Federal Reserve Board regulations could then be enforced both by the enforcement agencies with authority over particular depository institutions, and by the individual as currently provided in the Truth-in-Lending Act which allows an individual to seek damages for violation of standards promulgated by the Board either on his own behalf, or on behalf of a class.

NOTICE AS THE COLLECTION LIMITATION

The Commission is concerned that a depository institution's practices and those of its support organizations conform with the individual's expectations pursuant to *Recommendation (2)*. Therefore, the Commission recommends:

Recommendation (3):

That Federal law be enacted or amended to provide that a depository institution must limit:

(a)   its own information collection practices in connection with an application for a depository service to those specified in the notice called for in *Recommendation (2)*; and

(b)   its request to any organization it asks to collect information on its behalf to information and sources specified in the notice called for in *Recommendation (2)*.

Recommendation (3) should be implemented in conjunction with *Recommendations (1)* and *(2)*. Its purpose is to make clear that both the depository institution and any organization the depository institution utilizes to collect information on its behalf are equally subject to to the limitations implicit in the notice called for in *Recommendation (2)*.

FAIRNESS IN USE

ACCESS TO DEPOSITORY RECORDS

An individual needs a right of access to records about himself compiled for the purpose of making depository decisions just as he needs it for other decisions about him. The need grows more urgent as depository institutions depend on information from third parties, such as independent check-guarantee services. Without such access, the individual has no control over the accuracy and completeness of the information that is used, and has no way of discovering errors or other inaccuracies in the information another institution has provided. Thus, the Commission recommends:

Recommendation (4):

That Federal law be enacted or amended to provide that an individual shall have a right to see and copy, upon request, all recorded information concerning him that a depository institution has used to make an adverse depository decision about him.

The recommendation recognizes the individual's right of access only to the records about himself which enter into an adverse decision. In the adverse decision situation, the individual is affected by information that does not stem from transactions directly related to the depository account. The Commission recognizes that an individual presently receives copies of records with respect to his depository account on a periodic basis, usually in the form of monthly statements and cancelled checks or receipts for deposits and withdrawals. The implementation of this recommendation is discussed under *Recommendation (5)* below.

ADVERSE DEPOSITORY DECISIONS

The Commission has concluded that a depository institution should be obligated to explain its adverse decisions to the affected individuals. Unlike credit grantors, depository institutions have no procedures for fulfilling this obligation, and neither the Fair Credit Reporting Act nor the Equal Credit Opportunity Act applies to decisions denying an individual a depository service. Therefore, the Commission recommends:

Recommendation (5):

That Federal law be enacted or amended to provide that a depository institution must:

(a) **disclose in writing to an individual who is the subject of an adverse depository decision:**
   (i) **the specific reason(s) for the adverse decision;**
   (ii) **the specific item(s) of information, in plain language, that supports the reason(s) given pursuant to (a)(i);**
   (iii) **the name(s) and address(es) of the institutional source(s) of the item(s) given pursuant to (a)(ii); and**
   (iv) **the individual's right to see and copy, upon request, all recorded information pertaining to him used to make the adverse decision; and**
(b) **inform the individual of his rights provided by the Fair Credit Reporting Act, when the decision is based in whole or in part on information obtained from a credit bureau or independent check-guarantee service.**

The value of *Recommendation (5)* will be more apparent as depository institutions become more selective in opening depository accounts. Inequities stemming from the fact that no law now allows an individual easily to learn the reasons for an adverse decision, the information items behind those reasons, or the identity and whereabouts of institutional sources are discussed extensively in the preceding chapter. The inclusion of independent check-guarantee services in subparagraph (b) assumes the adoption of *Recommendation (6)*, below.

Recommendations (4) and *(5)* could be implemented either through amendment of the Fair Credit Reporting Act or the banking laws. An individual should be able to sue in Federal court or another court of competent jurisdiction if the depository institution fails to perform. This right should include the right to sue for failure to state specific reason(s) for a specific decision where the individual has cause to believe that the reason is other than the one(s) stated by the depository institution. The court should have the power to order the depository institution to comply and to award attorney's fees and court costs to any plaintiff who substantially prevails. If it could be shown that the credit grantor willfully or intentionally denied the individual any of the rights *Recommendations (4)* and *(5)* would give him, the court should have the power to award up to $1,000 to the individual.

Systematic denials of access by depository institutions could be subject to enforcement by the Federal Trade Commission and other agencies[15] that currently have enforcement authority under the Fair Credit Reporting and Equal Credit Opportunity Acts. The remedy would be an order directing a depository institution to disclose records upon request. Once the FTC or other agency issued such an order, the depository institution would then be subject to the usual statutes available to enforce such orders.

The burden should be on the individual to reasonably describe the documents sought and the depository institution should be able to defend itself on the basis that it could not reasonably locate or identify them. For example, an individual could sue for disclosure to him of any document developed as a result of an application for a depository service if the individual could reasonably identify the date and nature of the application. If, however, an individual requested any information that relates to him in a file, and could not identify, with some specificity, the circumstances pursuant to which such a file was developed, the depository institution would not be under any affirmative obligation to search every record to locate a possible passing reference to the individual.

REGULATION OF INDEPENDENT CHECK-GUARANTEE SERVICES

Independent check-guarantee services are arguably excluded from the Fair Credit Reporting Act because they do not influence credit or other decisions, such as employment and insurance. The Commission finds, however, that independent check-guarantee services affect individuals in the same way as do credit bureaus and inspection bureaus. The Federal Trade Commission staff has advised independent check-guarantee services that they *are* subject to the provisions of the FCRA, but this interpretation lacks the force of law. The Commission believes that the law should explicitly cover independent check-guarantee services, exempting them only from those FCRA requirements that are not appropriate. Therefore, the Commission recommends:

Recommendation (6):

That the Federal Fair Credit Reporting Act be amended to provide that an independent check-guarantee service shall be subject to all requirements of the Act, except the requirement to disclose corrected information to prior recipients upon completion of a reinvestigation of disputed information.

The rationale for the exception in this recommendation is the same as the rationale for the exception in *Recommendation (9)(b)* in the previous chapter on credit grantors and independent authorization services—namely, that once an error in an independent check-guarantee service record is

---

15 Under the pertinent provisions of the FCRA *[15 U.S.C. 1681s(b)]* and the ECOA *[15 U.S.C. 1691c(a) & (c)]*, twelve agencies have some administrative enforcement responsibility, ranging from traditional financial regulators such as the Federal Reserve Board to agencies such as the Civil Aeronautics Board and the Department of Agriculture.

discovered, the damage has already been done and usually cannot be remedied. Hence a requirement that previous recipients be notified of any corrections would, in most, cases, be gratuitous. If an independent check-guarantee service fails to meet the requirements called for in *Recommendation (6)*, it should be liable for actual damages in the event an individual is harmed by its failure.

INACCURATE REPORTS TO INDEPENDENT CHECK GUARANTEE SERVICES

The subscribers of an independent check-guarantee service are its principal sources of information. The subscriber list of Telecredit, Inc., the nation's largest check-guarantee service, includes automobile dealers, airlines, hotels, gasoline stations, commercial banks, department stores, car-rental agencies, and other retailers across the country. Other fruitful sources of information, less frequent but not less significant, are law enforcement agencies that track down stolen and forged checks.[16] Thus, an independent check-guarantee service's sources of information can be as diverse as those of credit bureaus.

The consequences of having one's name and identification adversely reported to an independent check-guarantee service are clear and certain; a subscriber to the service will not honor your check. The Commission is concerned about errors that may occur and the unfairly preemptive actions that they can cause. Accordingly, the Commission recommends:

Recommendation (7):

That the Federal Fair Credit Reporting Act be amended to provide that if a contributor learns it has incorrectly reported an individual to an independent check-guarantee service, it must notify the check-guarantee service within a reasonable period of time so that the service can correct its files.

As with *Recommendation (6)*, a contributor that incorrectly reports an individual to an independent check-guarantee service and fails to correct the error after it is discovered should be liable for actual damages in the event that an individual is harmed by its failure to do so.

Expectation of Confidentiality

CONFIDENTIALITY OF DEPOSITORY RECORDS

As with other confidential relationships, an individual's expectation of confidentiality in his depository relationship can be at best impressionistic unless a depository institution apprises him of its disclosure policies. Further, it must again be emphasized that an individual currently has no legally recognized interest in the records maintained about him by a depository institution and therefore cannot prevent a disclosure of them that may be inimical to him. Thus, the Commission recommends:

---

[16] Written statement of Telecredit, Inc., Credit Reporting Hearings, August 5, 1976.

Recommendation (8):

That Federal law be enacted to provide:

(a)   that a depository institution must notify an individual with whom it has or proposes to have a depository relationship of the uses and disclosures which are expected to be made of the types of information it collects or maintains about him; and that with respect to routine disclosures to third parties which are necessary for servicing the depository relationship, the notification must include the specific types of information to be disclosed and the types of recipients;

(b)   that information concerning an individual which a depository institution collects to establish or service a depository relationship, as stated in the notification to the individual called for in (a), must be treated as confidential by the depository institution; and thus any disclosures to third parties other than those necessary to service the depository relationship must be specifically directed or authorized by the individual, or in the case of marketing information, specifically described in the notification;

(c)   that an individual must be considered to have a continuing interest in the use and disclosure of information a depository institution maintains about him, and must be allowed to participate in any use or disclosure that would not be consistent with the original notification, except when a depository institution discloses information about an individual in order to prevent or protect against the possible occurrence of fraud; and

(d)   that any material changes or modifications in the use or disclosure policies of a depository institution must be preceded by a notification that describes the change to an individual with whom the depository institution has an established relationship.

In addition to enacting the recommendation, the statute should give the Federal Reserve Board regulatory authority similar to the regulatory authority it now has under the Truth-in-Lending, Equal Credit Opportunity, and Fair Credit Billing Acts. The resulting Federal Reserve regulations could then be enforced both by the enforcement agencies having authority over particular depository institutions, and by the individual, as currently provided in the Truth-in-Lending Act, which allows an individual to seek damages for violation of standards promulgated by the Board, either on his own behalf or on behalf of a class.

ELECTRONIC FUNDS TRANSFER SERVICES

The phrase Electronic Funds Transfer (EFT) includes several related techniques for processing and documenting deposits, withdrawals, and transfers of money with the aid of computers and telecommunications. Point-of-sale services and Automated Clearing House (ACH) Services are currently prominent examples. Variations in EFT services depend largely on the size and type of depository institution, the regularity of the payments to be processed, the purpose and complexity of the financial transaction, regulatory and other legal restraints, and the willingness of consumers to indulge business and governmental institutions in their search for new financial services.

Point-of-sale services are probably the form of EFT most visible to the individual. They offer the individual a convenient way to use the funds he has on deposit without having to visit the depository institution or draw a check or draft on his account. Some point-of-sale services simply allow the withdrawal of funds, as for example, when an individual receives cash at a supermarket and purchases his groceries with the cash. More sophisticated services allow the individual, at the location and time of purchase, to move funds electronically from his account to the merchant's account in exchange for goods or services that he would otherwise pay for with cash, check, or credit.

The information-processing technology necessary for providing point-of-sale services is similar in many respects to that used extensively by credit-card issuers. The ubiquitous plastic card has been borrowed from the credit-card world and enhanced with a *personal identification number,* a unique number known only to the account holder and his financial institution and intended to safeguard against unauthorized transfers of funds. Point-of-sale services depend on telecommunications and computer systems in the same manner as credit-card issuers use them for authorizing transactions, transmitting information among various institutions, and keeping track of credits and debits.[17] If a point-of-sale service involves many combinations of merchants and financial institutions, switches route each transaction to the appropriate financial institution, a technology also employed successfully by the two national bank-card associations.[18] In light of many existing credit-card systems, it seems that the novelty of most point-of-sale services for the individual will be a new way to make withdrawals of deposited funds. Point-of-sale services may eventually involve all types of depository institutions, i.e., commercial banks, savings and loan associations, mutual savings banks, and credit unions. However, to understand how these services work, one need only look at their impact on commercial banks and savings and loan associations.

Commercial banks have long offered their customers convenient access to deposits by means of checking accounts.[19] Checking accounts,

---

[17] Written statement of Dee W. Hock, President, National BankAmericard, Inc., and John H. Reynolds, President, Interbank Card Association, Credit-Card Issuers Hearings, February 11, 1976.

[18] As the following passage emphasizes, the techniques that make electronic exchange possible have been utilized quite successfully for bank-card operations: "EFT is emerging and coming fast . . . . Much has been learned in processing credit cards that will be useful in electronic funds transfer systems. Pre-authorized credits, sales authorization and interchange will be necessary." Western States Bankcard Association, *Annual Report 1975,* p. 1.

[19] Uniform Commercial Code § 3-108. See *Independent Bankers' Association of America, et al. v. Smith,* Doc. No. 75-0089 (D.C. Cir., March 23, 1976).

however, have two main drawbacks. For the banks, there is the cost of processing a glut of paper;[20] and for the individual, there is the reluctance of merchants to accept personal checks, a reluctance which has been rising with the number of fraudulent and overdraft checks.[21] Point-of-sale services promise to reduce both drawbacks. For some commercial banks, check-authorization services are a first step toward developing the computer and telecommunications capability necessary for a mature point-of-sale service.[22] Consumer acceptance will, however, determine how far such services can go in eliminating personal checks.[23]

Savings and loan associations and other thrift institutions ordinarily lack the payment powers necessary to offer their customers the convenience of checking accounts.[24] Point-of-sale services give them a way of overcoming this obstacle. One observer of EFT developments summarized this transformation of savings and loan accounts as follows:

> Electronic technology confuses payment powers limitations as well as doing away with the necessity of creating a negotiable instrument for purposes of conveying payment orders from account holder to financial institution. As a result, the technologies present two intriguing options to users. The account holder can turn any account into a "payment account" by dealing in cash if machines are strategically and conveniently located, or the account holder could, by electronically ordering the institution to do the paying for him by appropriate debits and credits to accounts, eliminate the use of cash or paper . . . .[25]

Automated Clearing House services also transfer funds electronically. Their principal purpose as presently constituted is to effect debits and credits of a recurring nature between institutions; for example, payrolls, insurance premiums, social security benefits, and payments for utilities and mortgages. The main differences between point-of-sale services and ACH services, now and for the foreseeable future, are in the type of transactions processed, details of processing, and institutional control over the systems.

---

[20] In 1970, an estimated 21.5 billion checks were written on demand deposit accounts in commercial banks in the United States. Approximately one billion additional checks were written by the Federal government. It has been estimated that the total cost to society of the check payment system is $10 billion annually. See Arthur D. Little, *The Consequences of Electronic Funds Transfer: A Technology Assessment of Movement Toward a Less Cash/Less Check Society,* Chapter 4, June 1975.

[21] Written statement of Telecredit, Inc., Credit Reporting Hearings, August 5, 1976, p. 1.

[22] Written statement of First National City Bank (Citibank), Credit-Card Issuers Hearings, February 11, 1976, p. 2; also, written statement of Continental Illinois Bank and Trust Company of Chicago, Depository and Lending Institutions Hearings, April 21, 1976, pp. 2-5.

[23] For some thoughtful comments concerning EFT from the consumer's perspective, see Peter H. Shuck, "Electronic Funds Transfer: A Technology in Search of a Market," *Maryland Law Review,* Volume 35, Number 1, 1975.

[24] The major exception to this general rule is the negotiable order of withdrawal (NOW) account. The orders of withdrawal are negotiable instruments but draw on interest-bearing accounts rather than demand deposits. Some States, such as New York, have granted checking-account powers to State-chartered thrift institutions.

[25] Stephen M. Ege, "Electronic Funds Transfer: A Survey of Problems and Prospects in 1975," *Maryland Law Review,* Volume 35, Number 1, 1975.

Typical ACH transactions are recurring pre-authorized transfers between institutions, as when social security recipients have their benefits deposited directly into their bank accounts each month. Such services arguably offer the most efficient, cost-effective, and convenient method of processing the innumerable government and commercial transactions that must be repeated regularly on fixed schedules. Telecommunications have not been essential to ACH operations in their early stages of development because each debit and credit does not need an authorization, as in point-of-sale services, nor does it need to be posted instantaneously to an account. However, ACHs across the country are being linked together by telecommunications to facilitate interregional exchange.[26]

Institutional control over ACH services differs from institutional control over point-of-sale services in that Federal Reserve district banks operate the computer and communications facilities used by all but two of them. To a large extent, Federal Reserve district banks also determine pricing of ACH services and liability for errors. *Most significant from the personal privacy viewpoint, the Federal Reserve System, which acts as a fiscal agent of financial institutions and the Treasury Department in some respects, is not constrained by either its government or its commercial clients, much less by any individual bank client, from disclosing information about a bank customer's account to other government agencies.*[27]

IMPACT OF ELECTRONIC FUNDS TRANSFER ON FINANCIAL RECORDS

Commercial banks and savings and loan associations presently stand at the threshold of a vast development in point-of-sale services. Significant effects of such development on institutional record keeping are clearly predictable based on experiences with credit cards. Expansion undoubtedly means that: (1) information about individuals recorded by financial institutions will include more details than otherwise required; (2) the records will become more centralized and the details will be more easily retrieved than they are now; and (3) financial records will expand to include items of information not ordinarily considered payment data.

It is important to note that the increased scope of the records generated by EFT may well include more than simply information necessary to transfer funds. Indeed, there are pressures which could eventually transform EFT systems into generalized information transfer systems. In the commercial environment, for example, accounting and administrative data will probably flow with various recurring payments; e.g., related benefit and tax withholding information could accompany wage

---

26 "NACHA/Federal Reserve Set Plans for Nationwide ACH 'Pilot' Exchange, Action Expected to Stir Concern as Implications Unfold," *Payment Systems Action Report*, Volume 1, Number 6, July 26, 1976.

27 Submission of Board of Governors of the Federal Reserve System Staff, Depository and Lending Institutions Hearings, April 22, 1976, p. 4. Part 261.6(b) of the Board's Rules regarding availability of information provides for the release of reports or examination of banks "to other agencies of the United States for use where necessary in the performance of their official duties." In Part 261.7 of its Rules, the Board has established procedures for responding to duly issued subpoenas.

payments. Consumer transactions are likely to relay information concerning the purpose of the transaction along with essential payment data to payee and payer alike. While such developments are not inevitable, the pressures to move in this direction are high. The economic incentives to combine payment and administrative information are great from both payer and payee point of view. It would eliminate the need for a great deal of paper documentation or the need for a duplicate information transfer system. Given the emergence of an increasingly competitive market for financial services and the potential cost savings for public and private institutions alike, there would seem to be little reason for providers of EFT services to refuse to accept the additional information flow.

For savings and loan associations, point-of-sale services also expand both the number and content of the records they keep and make the recorded information more readily available. The number grows because customers who no longer have to visit their savings and loan association in order to make a withdrawal or deposit will use their accounts more often, and each use generates a record. The content will grow because a point-of-sale transaction at, say, a supermarket requires that the record of that transaction be expanded to include at least the identity of the supermarket, and probably the time, date, and location of the transaction; the record may also expand further to include a description of items purchased. Finally, point-of-sale services will increase reliance on sophisticated information technologies, in many cases altering the form in which information is recorded and stored, and easing retrieval of it by those who control access to it. The great preponderance of savings and loan associations already have terminal-oriented computer systems, and point-of-sale services will simply further this trend. For savings and loan associations not currently automated, however, point-of-sale services will generate electronic records where none currently exist.[28]

With commercial banks, point-of-sale development is not likely to expand appreciably either the number of records they keep or the content of their records, since records of checking services contain much of the necessary point-of-sale information. Clearer descriptions of transactions may be needed for verification by the consumer, but the data base maintained for a checking account is probably adequate for point-of-sale purposes.

Commercial banks have already invested heavily in information technology for processing the volume of paper generated by checking accounts; the main difference made by adding point-of-sale services will be to increase substantially the uses commercial banks can make of them. New point-of-sale services will further decrease the banks' reliance on paper, as their permanent records come to include a higher fraction of electronic records of point-of-sale transactions and a lower one of microfilmed checks. Since it is far quicker and easier to search and retrieve information from electronic records than from voluminous paper documentation and microfilm, the utility of an information base that is already recognized as useful

---

[28] Written submission of the U.S. League of Savings Associations to the Privacy Protection Study Commission, June 2, 1976.

for many purposes apart from banking, from marketing to law enforcement, will be considerably enhanced.[29]

Expanding point-of-sale services will also have other less specialized effects. Even the most primitive point-of-sale services depend on accurate identification to assure that only authorized individuals have access to an account. Given the paramount importance of controlling access, providers of point-of-sale services will predictably demand more personal characteristics (e.g., fingerprints or characteristics of one's signature) to verify the identity of an account holder, giving financial record keepers additional information.

When banks and other financial institutions began issuing credit cards, the number of locations where their payment records originate and where copies of them must be kept multiplied.[30] Since most of the new makers and keepers of these records are not financial institutions, more and more of the records historically controlled by such institutions are now also retained and available for use by others. *This drift is significant insofar as one recognizes the existence of a confidential relationship between an individual and his bank and the obligation that flows to the record keeper as a result of the relationship. One public policy consequence is that identical records may be retained by different record keepers with whom an individual has different types of relationships and thus different expectations of confidentiality.*[31]

Very significant for personal privacy is that point-of-sale transactions must be monitored, and monitoring transactions could become an effective way of tracking an individual's movements.[32] Large-scale credit-card systems already monitor frequency of card use and point-of-sale services extend the range of potential surveillance.

Finally, there will be a significant impact if ACH services become a

---

[29] The Bank Secrecy Act was passed explicitly recognizing that financial records would be used for nonfinancial purposes. In particular, the findings statement for Section 21(a)(1) reads: "The Congress finds that adequate records maintained by insured banks have a high degree of usefulness in criminal, tax, and regulatory investigation proceedings. The Congress further finds that photocopies made by banks of checks, as well as records kept by banks of the identity of persons maintaining or authorized to act with respect to accounts therein, have been of particular value in this respect."

[30] Unlike checks, which are governed by Articles 3 and 4 of the Uniform Commercial Code, credit-card transactions are governed by the Federal and State laws discussed in Chapter 2, and by contracts among card issuers and merchants. To get payment for purchases made with credit cards and to protect themselves against errors, merchants retain copies of credit-card transaction records.

[31] The importance of recognizing an expectation of confidentiality as the touchstone for protecting the individual's interest in his records is discussed extensively in Chapter 1. Two recent California Supreme Court decisions, *Burrows v. Superior Court*, 13 Cal.3d 238 (1974) and *Valley Bank of Nevada v. Superior Court*, 15 Cal.3d 652 (1975) have upheld and clarified the theory that a bank customer has and should have a reasonable expectation of confidentiality and privacy in his bank records and, conversely, that a bank has a duty to take reasonable steps to preserve such confidentiality.

[32] See James B. Rule, *Value Choices in Electronic Funds Transfer Policy*, prepared for the Office of Telecommunications Policy, Executive Office of the President, October 1975; also footnote 8.

major vehicle for processing transactions that originate in point-of-sale services.[33] As point-of-sale services penetrate different regional markets, the need for interregional exchange of data will arise just as did the need for interregional clearance of checks. Thus, the scope of ACH services could expand considerably, not only functionally, but also geographically to include a much greater share of individual transactions. Since such transactions are the raw material for piecing together personal profiles of individuals, ACH expansion into point-of-sale services would intensify the threat to personal privacy.

It should not be assumed, however, that extension of ACH services to include point-of-sale transactions is necessary for them to pose a threat to privacy. Even in the limited use for recurring payments, such as social security benefits or wages, an ACH service poses all three privacy problems inherent in a fully developed EFT environment: (1) its records include more personal details than traditional systems of payment transfer; (2) the information in its records is more centralized; and (3) it transfers more information than would ordinarily be considered payment data.

The first step in linking ACH services across regions has been initiated by the Federal Reserve district banks. Because the Board of Governors of the Federal Reserve System has not yet decided how far it will expand its provision of EFT services,[34] point-of-sale services under Federal Reserve System auspices must be considered a possibility. Indeed, this possibility is a central concern of the Commission.

RECOMMENDATIONS

The use of electronically recorded transactions for marketing is a well established practice of a variety of organizations, including retailers and financial institutions. Current market practice is to draw upon the vast pool of credit-card transactions and credit-bureau files, and more generalized sources of demographic information, such as census tracts. Point-of-sale services will dramatically expand the base of electronically recorded transactions that marketers can tap. It will not, however, create a new demand for such information; that demand already exists.

The disclosure of financial records to government agencies is another well established practice of the institutions that will provide or use EFT services. For savings and loan associations, point-of-sale services will create a new source of information for government agencies. For commercial banks, point-of-sale services reduce a major incentive to resist inquiries by government authorities because of the cost of searching microfilmed check records. Simply by changing the means of information storage and retrieval, point-of-sale services exacerbate the government-access problem which has existed long before the introduction of EFT.

---

[33] Comments of the Office of Telecommunications Policy before the Board of Governors of the Federal Reserve System, in the matter of Proposed Amendment of Regulation J, March, 1976.

[34] Letter from Arthur F. Burns, Chairman of the Board of Governors of the Federal Reserve System to the Privacy Protection Study Commission, November 1, 1976.

The practice of using point-of-sale services to locate an individual is not yet widespread, but already at least one nationwide independent check-guarantee service is deriving revenue from it.[35] If, for example, the wanted individual offers to pay by check at a store that subscribes to this authorization service, he is asked for his current address, which is promptly reported to the client who wants to locate him.

Marketing, law enforcement, and locator services are only a few of the many collateral uses for EFT records. The Commission's general recommendations with respect to depository relationships are designed to give an individual both access to and some control over the disclosure of information that an EFT environment would accumulate about him. However, the Commission also urges the adoption of the three recommendations immediately below as part of the overall regulation of electronic funds transfer services now being considered by legislatures and regulatory bodies at both the Federal and State level.

CENTRALIZED FINANCIAL INFORMATION FLOWS

The Commission recognizes that electronic funds transfer services inevitably create and retain some records which cannot be controlled by the institutions from which the individual can reasonably expect confidentiality. Institutional arrangements already formed for automated clearinghouses and shared point-of-sale systems introduce new sources of electronically recorded information that centralize, if only briefly, information otherwise segregated among diverse depository institutions. The Commission is concerned about the far-reaching consequences of these centralized financial information flows because of the scope of the records that is expected to develop and the manner in which information about individuals or groups of individuals may be accumulated on a selective basis.

Beyond the fundamental problem of the accumulation and centralization of detailed information, there are two additional threats that such an EFT environment raises. First, there is the well perceived one of electronic eavesdropping, though not necessarily at the relatively unsophisticated and illegitimate level of wiretapping. It is technically possible through electronic means to monitor the flow of information through an EFT network, and to capture items of interest on a selective basis. While this would require a sophisticated technical approach, it is nonetheless possible and could lead to a rapid-response capability for locating an individual, or to a capability for building a comprehensive record on an individual's movements, buying habits, and so forth. Equally important, it could be accomplished without surreptitious entry into the system by anyone given access to the computer facilities that sort and direct the flow of information.

The second privacy threat also arises from the fact that EFT services will require an extensive data communications network. While the detailed implementation of such a network may vary from one EFT application to another, each one must accumulate certain items of information about the traffic that flows through it. For accounting and billing purposes, as well as

---

[35] Written statement of Telecredit, Inc., Credit Reporting Hearings, August 5, 1976.

for controlling and operating a network, some portion of the information flowing through it must be retained within it. To illustrate, the telephone company automatically captures for all long distance connections the calling and called numbers, the duration of the call, and the time and date. Technically, the telephone network could also capture the voice conversation, but does not need to do so and in fact is prohibited by law from capturing it. In an EFT environment, however, this might not be so; for technical convenience a particular network design might capture everything that flowed through it.

Whether an EFT network captures all the information flowing through it or only certain items or even portions of items, there is a risk that the resulting pools of information will become attractive sources of personally identifiable information for use in ways inimical to personal privacy. Because the response time of present EFT systems is hours or days, the temptation to use them to surveil an individual's movements is minimal. A transaction-oriented EFT system, however, will be much more dynamic, and will have to respond in seconds if it is to fulfill its function. Thus, the temptation to surveil may increase markedly.

For these reasons, the Commission believes that protection must be afforded individually identifiable information flowing through an EFT data communications network. Accordingly, the Commission recommends:

Recommendation (9):

That individually identifiable account information generated in the provision of EFT services be retained only in the account records of the financial institutions and other parties to a transaction, except that it may be retained by the EFT service provider to the extent, and for the *limited period of time*, that such information is essential to fulfill the operational requirements of the service provider.

An EFT data network not only deals with the original details of a transaction, but also may add or derive additional items of information. For example, the time-of-day or a running transaction number may be added; patterns of credit-card usage or frequency of particular activity can be derived. The Commission intends that both primary transactional information and derivative information created by the operation of the data network be subject to the restrictions of *Recommendation (9)*. In essence, the Commission has concluded that information generated by an EFT system, like information which is the product of check or credit-card transactions today, should be available only from the parties to the transaction and, subject to the restrictions of appropriate expectations of confidentiality, from the financial institutions which maintain accounts for those parties. Further, the Commission seeks, through the measure suggested above, to limit the potential for misuse or improper disclosure of information by the service provider by eliminating the presence of identifiable information in the system (at the "switch," "clearinghouse," or other exchange point, for example) to the extent practicable.

ACCURACY OF ELECTRONIC TRANSACTIONS

How to assure the accuracy of recorded information and reduce untoward effects of inaccurately recorded transactions was discussed in Chapter 2. Individuals are legally protected by the Fair Credit Billing Act against some of the untoward consequences of credit-card errors. Although a point-of-sale service for making withdrawals is operationally similar to a credit-card system, the individual has no comparable legal protection when disputing the accuracy of an electronic transaction. Therefore, the Commission further recommends:

Recommendation (10):

That procedures be established so that an individual can promptly correct inaccuracies in transactions or account records generated by an EFT service.

GOVERNMENT OPERATION OF EFT SERVICES

EFT services will produce qualitative changes in the information base available to various institutions and, in turn, will affect the demands placed on those institutions for financial records. EFT therefore adds to the urgency of the need to strengthen protections for personal privacy in the manner advocated throughout this report. The Commission's concern with EFT as a threat to personal privacy goes beyond its effect on depository record keeping as dealt with in the preceding section of this chapter. The Commission sees governmental provision of EFT services as a dangerous direction.

The surveillance potential of an EFT system becomes much more formidable, in the Commission's estimation, if government operates the facilities than when the service is controlled by private parties. When any government entity processes financial records which document the private affairs of individuals, the likelihood and opportunities for other government agencies to obtain and possibly misuse those records increases. *Current problems with government access to bank records are minor compared with the potential threat to privacy posed by government operation of EFT facilities.* As such services become more sophisticated and documentation and surveillance capability increases, government operation of EFT systems will become, in the Commission's view, an unparalleled threat to personal privacy. The current paper-based clearing system, though largely operated by the Federal Reserve, is not a useful source of information for government agencies because the checks being cleared cannot easily be retrieved on a selective basis. The situation changes when the Federal Reserve uses telecommunications technology for processing private transactions. Commission staff learned in an interview with Federal Reserve officials that the Department of Justice, for example, has requested that the Federal Reserve supply it with information from records of transactions between private parties where the Federal Reserve employed telecommunications to effect the funds transfer. The IRS has a much more limited information resource than the Federal Reserve would if it operated an EFT system; yet it has been abused for harassment and political advantage. While in our system of taxation there is a compelling need for government to manage the information flow on which the system depends, there seems to be no analogous rationale compelling government to provide EFT services for private parties.

A secondary problem focuses on the activities of the Federal Reserve Board of Governors and district banks. As mentioned above, the Federal Reserve has played a dominant role in the development of EFT, most notably by providing ACH services. For the Federal Reserve to continue, indeed increase, its control over facilities for EFT is unwise, in the Commission's view, particularly in view of the possible meshing of ACH services with point-of-sale services. Unless the Federal Reserve limits its EFT operations and begins divestment now, the inertia of economic circumstance may destroy the policy choice, leaving the Federal Reserve as the basic provider of services used by financial institutions to transfer funds and support point-of-sale services. Therefore, the Commission recommends:

Recommendation (11):

That no governmental entity be allowed to own, operate, or otherwise manage any part of an electronic payments mechanism that involves transactions among private parties.

The Commission's position does not suggest that there be no government regulation of EFT services. Without addressing such matters as the existing Federal regulatory structure for depository institutions, competition in the provision of EFT services, or the impact of an integrated national EFT system on capital markets, the Commission believes that regulation of the financial community should not be tied to government operation of an electronic payments system. If a monopolistic and thus closely regulated EFT system does emerge, the agencies which will have to provide oversight should not also operate its facilities.

Actual provision of services to a particular industry has often created unavoidable conflicts for the government agencies that act as that industry's watchmen or regulators. Too deep an involvement in day-to-day operation results either in a growing lack of responsiveness to consumer and public-policy concerns, or in a domination by the regulator which discourages efficiency and innovation, and fosters static patterns of response.[36] An example of the former problem can be found in the Interstate Commerce Commission's response to the congr●sional policy mandated by the Railroad Reform Act. The consequences of domination are reflected in the problems which recently spurred reform of the Atomic Energy Commission and the restructuring of U.S. nuclear research, development, and regulation.

In addition, given the communications aspect of EFT delivery systems, and the potential for them to evolve into more general information transfer services, the responsibility to regulate its development ought to be

---

[36] See Roger Noll, *Reforming Regulation*, (Washington, D.C.: Brookings Institution, 1972).

shared with the FCC or with a similar regulator who has communications as a principal mandate. From a privacy perspective, the traditional safeguards for individual messages transferred by way of electronic communications are the first step toward the protections needed in an EFT environment.

Finally, even if government operation of facilities for EFT services were determined to be desirable, the Federal Reserve Board and its related financial regulators are hardly the appropriate agencies to do it. Financial regulators such as the Federal Reserve are not as accountable to outside authorities as other governmental organizations; self-discipline is the only real restraint on their activities. An exception to the canons of governmental accountability to such external authorities as the Congress and the President may be justified insofar as Federal Reserve activities pertain to monetary policy and bank supervision, but hardly to activities which impinge on personal privacy.

Chapter 4

Mailing Lists

Each week the U.S. Postal Service delivers 2.3 pieces of unsolicited direct mail to the average American household.[1] To think of the flow and the impact of direct mail in terms of the average household, however, is misleading, since direct-mail users employ every stratagem money can buy to avoid sending their messages to an average house. The difference between profit and loss, between election and defeat, is skill in winnowing from a list of thousands or millions the names and addresses of the people most likely to buy a product, vote for a candidate, or contribute to a fund. Even a direct-mail campaign that starts with the advantage of a revolutionary product, a non-revolutionary candidate, or an appealing charitable cause must plan to break even on less than two percent positive response. It cannot realistically expect more, and is the object of wide imitation and envy if the response rate reaches five percent.

Even with a two percent average rate of return, however, direct-mail advertising is the major marketing tool of many enterprises. About $4.6 billion are spent annually for the materials and postage, and the total volume of business generated through direct mail approaches $60 billion.[2] More than 2.5 billion catalogs touting every conceivable type of goods are mailed each year, and an estimated $10 billion a year of the sum Americans contribute to organized philanthropies is raised by direct mail.[3] A good index of the importance of direct mail to the national economy is its standing among the competing advertising media: direct mail comes third, its users spending on it about half the total amount spent on newspaper advertising and about three-quarters of the total spent on televised promotions. After that come magazines and radio, each drawing about half as many dollars as direct mail.[4]

Section 5(c)(2)(B)(i) of the Privacy Act of 1974 directs the Commission to report to the President and the Congress on whether an organization engaged in interstate commerce should be required to remove from its

---

[1] Testimony of U.S. Postal Service, *Mailing Lists*, Hearings before the Privacy Protection Study Commission, (hereinafter cited as Mailing Lists Hearings), December 11, 1975, pp. 246-251.

[2] Testimony of Direct Mail Marketing Association (DMMA), Mailing Lists Hearings, (I) November 12, 1975, p. 6.

[3] *Ibid.*, p. 7.

[4] *Ibid.*, p. 6.

mailing list the name of an individual who does not want to have his name on it.[5] This chapter answers the question, summarizes the findings of the Commission's study of the mailing-list industry, and presents the Commission's recommendations.

WHAT IS A MAILING LIST?

Strictly speaking, a mailing list is nothing more than a list of names and addresses used to prepare labels or envelopes for mailing. The names can come from almost anywhere: from public records like the telephone directory, newspapers, or State Motor Vehicle Registries; from private organization records like the customer files of a retailer or the donor files of a charity; from lists of people who respond to magazine and radio advertisements; from convention rosters and trade association directories; or from salesmen or friends.[6] The key fact to understand about mailing lists, however, is that they are almost never free-standing; they are names and addresses of individuals who have some type of association, usually an active one, with a public or private organization. *To be on a mailing list, an individual's name must first find its way onto another list or into a record system that has been developed for some purpose other than mailing.* Indeed, once a mailing list, in the strict sense of the term, is disassociated from the master list or file it was culled from, its value rapidly declines because there is no longer any easy way to add new names to it or to correct or otherwise adjust the information in it.

WHO MAINTAINS A MAILING LIST?

Although there are list brokers who specialize in arranging rentals and exchanges of lists,[7] the Commission's analysis leads to the conclusion that *the maintainer of a mailing list is the organization that keeps the records from which the mailing list is extracted*; that is, the organization that uses information in its own files to assemble, add to, or correct a mailing list. This definition includes credit grantors and credit bureaus that allow their files to be used to select names for someone else's mailing,[8] and any organization that permits others to include their solicitations in its own customer mailings—for example, a credit grantor that allows a home appliance retailer to put an advertising flier in the envelope with the credit grantor's

---

[5] Privacy Act of 1974, Pub. L. No. 93-579, §5(c)(2)(B)(i) (codified as a note to 5 U.S.C. 552a).

[6] Testimony of the Reuben H. Donnelley Company, Mailing Lists Hearings, (II) November 12, 1975, pp. 5-6, 17-19; Testimony of R. L. Polk and Company, Mailing Lists Hearings, (I) November 12, 1975, pp. 113-114, 119, 121; Testimony of the Privacy Journal, Mailing List Hearings, December 10, 1975, p. 10.

[7] Testimony of National Business Lists, Inc., Mailing Lists Hearings, (II) November 12, 1975, pp. 53, 54.

[8] For a more detailed description of "pre-screening," see below.

monthly bill. The definition excludes list brokers, computer service bureaus,[9] and other middlemen in direct-mailing operations.

The testimony of witnesses before the Commission suggested three categories of organizations that fit this definition of a list maintainer: public record compilers; private record compilers; and government agencies.

PUBLIC RECORD COMPILERS

An individual's name and address turn up in various places that make them public, for example, in city directories, membership lists, and newspapers and publications like *Who's Who*. For some list compilers, however, no public record is a more useful starting point than the telephone book. One major public record compiler collects every year the names and addresses of everyone in the country who has a published telephone number. In some cases, these telephone book lists are themselves used to develop mailing lists, but typically they are merged or crosschecked with information that other public record compilers have developed by purchasing or renting copies of the records in State and local government files.

The records of State and local government agencies give details on such things as the year, make, and model of the registered automobiles at a given address, or whether anyone at that address has a hunting or fishing license, owns property elsewhere in the area, or has registered to vote. From such details, a mailing-list user can draw quite useful inferences. How many and what kinds of cars an individual owns, for example, is one indication of the individual's income, rough perhaps, but useful to a list compiler.

Julian Haydon, Vice President and General Manager of R. L. Polk and Company, Inc., described how that major public record compiler develops its basic file:

> We compile from official State records in 40 States[10] a car owner list of 43,500,000 names; a truck owner's list of 11,400,000; a motorcycle owner's list of 2,600,000; and a monthly list of new car buyers averaging about 480,000. The information contained in the motor vehicle list is: *owner's name and address; year, model, make, series, body style and number of cylinders of vehicle; vehicle identification number* (used in safety recall programs); and *license plate number* (which is currently not used).
>
> From this information, the following selection factors are developed: sex, inferred from the first name, *type of dwelling*, i.e., single or multiple, . . . inferred (from) the number of surnames found at a given address; *price class of car owned, based on year, model, make and series; current market value of the cars owned (CMV)*, based on

---

[9] In a typical form of list rental or exchange, the list owner sends its list on tape to a service bureau which uses it to address envelopes for the user and then returns the tape to the list owner without the user even physically possessing it.

[10] Testimony of R. L. Polk and Company, Mailing Lists Hearings, (I) November 12, 1975, pp. 121-22. At the time of the testimony there were 40, at this publication there are 36 states that permit motor vehicle records to be used in the manner described.

year, model, make and series (there are 10 CMV classifications). CMV "0"means that the car is rated to have an average value of less than $150. CMV "1" is $150 to $349, and so on, up to CMV "9," with an estimated value of $3,450 or more); *multiple car ownership,* based on two or more cars registered at the same name and address
. . . .

From our city directories,[11] we develop the following information: *name of household head* (from this we infer sex); *spouse's name* (from this and occupation, we infer marital status); *address; telephone number; single or multiple dwelling; owner or renter; occupation of household head; number of children under 18; number of persons in the household; the year at which we first found the household at this address; and the year in which the dwelling first appeared in our canvass.*[12] [Emphasis supplied.]

The Reuben H. Donnelley Corporation, another major public record compiler, also described to the Commission how it assembles its mailing-list information on some 60 million American households:

We start with the compilation of a national list of approximately 52 million residence telephone subscribers. We buy all published telephone directories as input to this compilation. We compile *name and address; telephone number; . . . sex or title,* if available; . . . and, because of the technique of compilation, are able to include . . . *length of residence* for each name.

Separately we obtain from R. L. Polk and Co. . . . their national list of motor vehicle registrants. This currently includes approximately 45,000,000 automobile owners' names at residence address. As part of this record, we get *name; address; sex or title, . . . number of autos owned;* and, for the two most recent autos owned, *make, year, series, body style, price-class, and number of cylinders.* We then computer merge the telephone and auto lists in CDS (City Delivery Service) areas to produce the so-called Donnelley Quality Index, or DQI— an unduplicated list of approximately 60,000,000 households . . . .[13] [Emphasis added.]

This 60 million-household list is then further refined through the use of census tract data. Although the Census Bureau never makes information public that would identify a specific individual or household, and although its statistical tables are never so fine-grained as to allow individual households to be identified, a public record compiler can get from Census Bureautables enough data to characterize a geographic area as small as 275 housing units in terms of the median income, educational level, occupation-

---

[11] *Ibid.*, p. 122. From city directories, Polk compiles information on 27 million households.
[12] *Ibid.*, p. 123.
[13] Testimony of Reuben H. Donnelly Company, Mailing Lists Hearings, (II) November 12, 1975, pp. 17-22.

al characteristics, median number of washing machines owned, and median number of children.[14] Thus, Donnelley can break down its master file by matching up every name with its proper census tract, and then break it down further by tract characteristics such as median income, median number of large appliances per household, and the like.[15]

The amount of detailed information amassed by public record compilers like R. L. Polk and the Reuben H. Donnelley Corporation, and the variety of demographic descriptors they have developed for paring their lists, enable their clients to keep the cost of a mail campaign within profitable bounds. Mailing-list users do not want the entire Donnelley list of 60 million names and addresses. Each user wants only the names of people who fit its image of someone likely to respond to its particular message or appeal.[16] Moreover, as one witness told the Commission:

> . . . [T]hat type of list [the Donnelley and Polk list] is low man on the totem pole when it gets down to selling a product to a special market. For example, if I were the advertising manager of Black & Decker and had a new handy-dandy hand tool to sell, and I had a choice of the most sophisticated breakdown Donnelley could give me and the names of the most recent buyers of *The Popular Mechanics Home Handyman Encyclopedia*, I know where I'd start. I'd take the buyers.[17]

PRIVATE RECORD COMPILERS

The reason the advertising manager would take the buyers is simple: cost. No mailer can afford to waste postage on people who are not even going to look at what it sends them, and it would prefer not to waste postage on people who are probably not going to do whatever it is it wants them to do. According to spokesmen for the mail-marketing industry, the best predictor the mailer can go by is whether an individual has previously bought, joined, or donated by mail.[18] The section below on selectivity gets back to this point.

---

[14] *Ibid.*, pp. 19-22.

[15] Donnelley described this process as follows: "After acquiring the tables made available by the Census Bureau of Census tracts and other geographic areas, including incidentally the block group and/or enumeration district mentioned earlier, which is a subdivision of the tract averaging about 275 housing units, the smallest entity with which we work, we process these tables according to our own requirements and now maintain a set of census tapes, as well as something we call our Geographic Statistical File. This latter file is a disc-stored set of approximately 42 census and list-descriptive statistics for each tract or smaller geographic entity. If, for example, we want to select all tracts with a median income of $12,000 or more, and reporting a median of 3.5 persons per household or more, this file will produce a list of these tracts on tape. This tape can then be matched against our DQI list file, which has appropriate header indicators to identify all addresses by tract, to output all addresses on mailing labels that fall within the desired tracts." *Ibid.*

[16] *Ibid.*, p. 12.

[17] Testimony of Association of American Publishers, Mailing Lists Hearings, (II) November 12, 1975, pp. 84-5.

[18] *Ibid.*, pp. 86-87; Testimony of Reuben H. Donnelley Corporation, Mailing Lists Hearings, (II) November 12, 1975, p. 5.

A few mailing-list compilers keep tabs on an individual's responses to direct-mail campaigns themselves, but the usual sources of information on who responds are the files of retailers (particularly those that sell by mail), and associations and charities. Not all such organizations rent or exchange the names and addresses of their customers, members, or donors. Major retailers that make sophisticated marketing uses of their own customer files do not allow them to be used by any other mailer,[19] and there are organizations that rent lists from others but do not make their own files available to other mailers.[20] Prominent among the many that do rent, lend, or exchange the use of their lists are magazine publishers, mail-order and catalog sales companies, public-interest groups, political campaign organizations, and charities. Moreover, the fact that so many do underscores an important point. *One of the easiest ways for an individual to get his name on a lot of mailing lists is to respond to a direct-mail solicitation.* There are other ways, such as being named in a public record, or mailing back the subscription form inserted in a magazine purchased at a newstand, but responding to a solicitation received through the mail is the surest. That is something the people who complain about getting mountains of "junk mail" often do not understand. Chances are that the individual who is most inundated with unsolicited mail responds to some of it; if he did not, his name would not be in the customer, member, and donor files from which so many mailing lists derive.

GOVERNMENT AGENCY COMPILERS

When a firm like R. L. Polk acquires records from, say, a State motor vehicle registry, it is doing no more than any citizen could do. State public record statutes make many such records available for the cost of copying. Or a public record statute may require an agency to allow anyone who asks to do so to copy names and addresses from whatever lists it keeps for its own mailings. In some States and localities, it is also possible to purchase or copy ready-to-use mailing lists. Some State and local government agencies compile lists of names and addresses for the express purpose of selling them to direct-mail users. A government agency may offer for sale a list of all current holders of fishing licenses, for example, or of licensed barbers or plumbers.

The rules that affect the mailing-list practices of government agencies at all levels are among the murkier areas of public law. At the Federal level, for example, there are records and lists which must clearly be made available to any member of the public who asks for them, but the availability of many others to the public is uncertain. Under the Federal Freedom of Information Act, an agency may deny a request for the information it maintains about an identifiable individual if it can sustain its

---

[19] Testimony of Sears, Roebuck and Company, *Credit-Card Issuers*, Hearings before the Privacy Protection Study Commission, February 12, 1976, p. 307.

[20] Testimony of Project HOPE, Mailing Lists Hearings, December 10, 1975, pp. 226-29.

opinion that to do otherwise would constitute a clearly unwarranted invasion of the individual's personal privacy.[21] This provision of the law has spawned a number of court cases involving lists of names and addresses, or records that could easily be transformed into lists of names and addresses.

In one case the courts allowed a list of the names of those who participated in an election supervised by the National Labor Relations Board to be disclosed to a law professor who was doing research on such elections. *[Getman v. N.L.R.B., 450 F.2d 670 (D.C.Cir. 1971)]* The Court of Appeals for the District of Columbia determined that the nature and importance of the research warranted this disclosure. A later decision involving the release of government information for the purposes of direct-mail solicitation went the other way. The Third Circuit Court of Appeals held that the government's release of the registration cards of persons making wine for personal consumption was not a disclosure required by the Freedom of Information Act. *[Wine Hobby U.S.A., Inc. v. IRS, 502 F.2d 133 (3dCir. 1974)]* The purpose—commercial mail advertising—did not justify invading the personal privacy of individual registrants by releasing their names and addresses.

Subsection (n) of the Privacy Act of 1974[22] forbids a Federal agency to market mailing lists for profit but the Freedom of Information Act and other Federal statutes say that numerous Federal agency lists can be copied on request. For example, citizens-band (CB) radio licenses are, by Federal law, a matter of public record. Moreover, because CB licensees like to be able to find one another, the Federal Communications Commission makes a computer-accessible directory of their names, addresses, and frequencies available, for the cost of copying, and updates it biweekly. Anyone can get a copy of the directory from the National Technical Information Services (NTIS), a purveyor of government documents, and the NTIS will break the list down by geographic area. The purpose of all this is to enable the public to find out easily who the CB license holders are, but obviously the directory is also extremely useful to marketers of CB equipment.[23]

The Privacy Act has had some effect on the availability of Federal agency records and lists that are or could be used by mailers. For example, the Drug Enforcement Agency now releases its lists of registered handlers of controlled substances only to requesters who guarantee in writing that they will not use them for any purpose other than to verify registration numbers, and refuses any request that smacks of intent to use the list for solicitation or commercial purposes.[24] The Department of the Interior has stopped public disclosure of most of its mailing lists; for example, it no longer discloses the names and addresses of retiring employees to retirement organizations.[25] The Veterans Administration releases its mailing lists only to nonprofit

---

[21] 5 U.S.C. 552(b)(6).

[22] 5 U.S.C. 552a(n).

[23] Privacy Commission staff conversation with John Small, Federal Communications Commission, October, 1976.

[24] Drug Enforcement Administration, Privacy Act of 1974 Annual Report to the Congress, Part III (f), p. 12, June 21, 1976.

[25] Annual Report of the Department of the Interior on the Privacy Act of 1974, Part III (f), *Sale or Rental of Mailing Lists*, p. 7, April 29, 1976.

organizations with functions directly related to the conduct of Veterans Administration programs or the utilization of benefits.[26] Other agencies, however, maintain lists of individuals with whom they have repeated contact. These may be project directors, business executives, college presidents, and the like, and there are lists of persons who ask to be included in their general mailings. These lists may be available at cost to anyone who asks for them, and the names of those who ask to be put on the general mailing list may sometimes be passed on to other government agencies for their use.[27]

At the State level, 14 States[28] now restrict the use of motor vehicle registration information for commercial mailing purposes in one way or another. The restrictions are usually implemented either through Department of Motor Vehicle regulations or through contracts with list compilers. Under a restricted contract, a compiler like R. L. Polk can collect information from the registry of motor vehicle owners for statistical purposes but cannot use or rent it for commercial mailing. The one exception is that the information may be used for mailing safety and engine emission recall notifications to vehicle owners. Most of the other States consider the records of the motor vehicle registry public records just like all other public records (e.g., licenses and mortgages), and thus they may be used by public record compilers to create mailing lists.

How Does a Name Pass From List to List?

The close connection between a mailing list and the source list or file from which it is drawn helps to explain an important feature of mailing-list development—the matter of list rental and exchange. As noted earlier, few mailing lists are ever completely severed from their source. Even public record compilers and government agencies regularly update their lists by checking them against the record systems they were taken from originally. Otherwise, the lists would soon be obsolete.

Many people seem to think that mailers get their names by copying them from the lists of other mailers. In fact, just the opposite is the case. List owners, by and large, do not permit their lists to be copied or even physically transferred to anyone else. What they do is make a rental or exchange agreement for the *use* of a list. The agreement usually expressly forbids copying it, and the other party seldom obtains physical possession of it. One of the two most common procedures is for the list owner to get the mailing envelopes and material from the renter and do the addressing and mailing itself. The other is for the list owner to give the list to a mailing house (often a computer service bureau) which then addresses and mails the promotional material given it by the renter, and returns the list to the owner. In neither

---

[26] Veterans Administration, Privacy Act of 1974, Annual Report for Calendar Year 1975, Part III (f), *Sale or Rental of Mailing Lists*, p. 4, April 30, 1976.

[27] National Science Foundation, Annual Report to Congress under the Privacy Act of 1974, Part III (f), *Sale or Rental of Mailing Lists*, April 22, 1976; see also United States Nuclear Regulatory Commission, Privacy Act Implementation Report, Part III (f), p. 8, April 30, 1976.

[28] Massachusetts, Washington, New Jersey, Hawaii, Nevada, Wyoming, Ohio, Connecticut, Pennsylvania, South Dakota, Missouri, Virginia, Alaska, and Arkansas.

case, however, is information about any individual on the list directly transferred from the files of the list owner to the files of the list user.[29] Consider the following example. John Smith is a customer of D. J. Higgenbottom, Inc., a mail-order marketer of gardening supplies; Smith's name is on Higgenbottom's mailing list for offers. One fall, Higgenbottom, Inc. rents the use of its own mailing list to Do-It-Yourself Industries, which has a new line of easy-to-assemble greenhouses. A mailing house does the addressing and mailing and Smith receives a direct-mail solicitation from Do-It-Yourself. A month later, Do-It-Yourself updates its own mailing list, adding to it the names and addresses of all its new customers, including Smith. Then, in November, the Wooly & Muffler Company, a purveyor of outdoor clothing, rents use of the Do-It-Yourself mailing list. Smith receives an ad from them, and purchases, say, a pair of fur-lined rubber boots, thereby getting his name added to Wooly & Muffler's customer file and eventually to its mailing list. When Tropical Tours, Inc., rents use of the Muffler list in December, Smith may break the chain by throwing its advertisement in the wastebasket, muttering wonderment as to how so many vendors get his name and address. In fact, the only one of them who knew Smith existed at first was Higgenbottom, Inc. Do-It-Yourself would never have known him if Smith had not filled in a Do-It-Yourself order blank, and so on down the chain to Tropical Tours, which still has no clue to Smith because he did not respond to its mailing.

That the individual is mainly responsible for the progress of his name from mailing list to mailing list is hard for most people to grasp, and mailing-list users do not go out of their way to enlighten them. By the time Smith tossed Tropical Tours' vacation package in the wastebasket, he was probably getting advertisements from all the other firms that had rented use of the Higgenbottom, Inc., Do-It-Yourself, or Wooly & Muffler lists, making him more concerned than ever about how his name seems to be bandied about.

WHO USES MAILING LISTS?

Traditionally, the small merchant with only a few items to sell has been the biggest user of rented lists. Even today, 200,000 of the 300,000 holders of third-class bulk-mail permits are companies doing less than half a million dollars worth of business annually.[30] Size, however, is no longer the characteristic that most clearly distinguishes the direct-mail user from other types of advertisers. As one witness before the Commission testified:

Our commercial clients and their purposes in renting our lists

---

[29] See, for example, the description of Project HOPE's direct-mail operations, Testimony of Project HOPE, Mailing Lists Hearings, December 10, 1975, pp. 226-27.

[30] Fewer than 30 of the nation's top 100 advertisers appear on the U.S. Postal Service list of its 6,000 top users of third-class mail. At a cost of 6.1 cents for each additional piece, direct-mail solicitation comes well within the budgets of many smaller businesses. Charitable and non-profit organizations operate under a Federal subsidy, paying only 1.8 cents to mail a message third-class. Testimony of Reuben H. Donnelley Company, Mailing Lists Hearings, (I) November 12, 1975, p. 7; Testimony of U.S. Postal Service, Mailing Lists Hearings, December 11, 1975, p. 268.

include magazine publishers to secure new subscribers; automobile companies to distribute new car catalogs and promotional pieces and to secure new credit accounts, make discount offers and secure new members in travel clubs; . . . insurance companies to sell insurance directly or to develop leads; retail stores to announce new stores, advertise sales, and secure credit accounts; charitable organizations to raise funds; research firms to determine consumer likes and dislikes about such things as automobile design, dealers and service; and package goods firms to distribute free samples or . . . discount coupons.[31]

Political and charitable organizations and public interest groups are also substantial users of direct mail. The Postal Service claims that in 1974, approximately $20 billion, or 80 percent of all contributions to nonprofit charitable and public interest organizations were raised through activities in which direct mail played a role.[32]

Government agencies are yet another user of mailing lists—their own and lists they rent from outside sources. One major government use of mailing lists is for sending out questionnaires to facilitate studies of various kinds.[33]

Most small-business users of mailing lists use them for advertising rather than for selling, to invite a prospective customer to come into the store to buy something rather than to make a purchase by mail. A great deal of the mail addressed merely to "Occupant" is of this sort, and when a customer shows up the mailer has no way of knowing whether he came because of the mailed advertisement or just happened to be passing by. As subsequent sections of this chapter argue, the fact that so many mailing-list users are of the one-way variety is one of several justifications for holding the record keeper in whose files the name originates, rather than the users of lists derived from those files, responsible for removing a name from a list.

---

[31] Testimony of R. L. Polk and Company, Mailing Lists Hearings, (I) November 12, 1974, p. 123.

[32] Testimony of U.S. Postal Service, Mailing Lists Hearings, December 11, 1975, p. 249.

[33] Testimony of R. L. Polk and Company, Mailing Lists Hearings, (I) November 12, 1975, pp. 115-16. The Commission also heard testimony on FBI, IRS, and State police uses for purposes other than mailing. Among the examples offered were: when a make or model of car has to be identified in large numbers, the FBI asks R. L. Polk to "furnish the names and addresses of everyone who owns a 1965 Chevrolet Impala in a certain county, Ibid, pp. 127, 141; a similar type of inquiry by the California Highway Patrol, Ibid., p. 116; and unconsummated IRS negotiations with a major business list compiler for the purpose of identifying non-filers of tax returns, Ibid., p. 116; Testimony of National Business Lists, Inc., Mailing Lists Hearings, (II) November 12, 1975, pp. 63-64, 70; Testimony of the U.S. Internal Revenue Service, Mailing Lists Hearings, December 11, 1975, pp. 310 ff. Properly speaking, however, these are not uses of mailing lists but rather of the underlying record systems from which mailing lists are developed. One public-record compiler testified that government agencies use its lists because "We have organized the information, standardized it, and have it readily available on magnetic tape. We control the computer and can cooperate quickly. In some States, the Department of Motor Vehicles has to get in line to use the computer or doesn't have the right programs." Testimony of R. L. Polk and Company, Mailing Lists Hearings, (I) November 12, 1975, pp. 146-47; Testimony of the Virginia Division of Motor Vehicles, Mailing Lists Hearings, December 10, 1075, pp. 163, 166. The issue of government access to private-sector record systems is dealt with in Chapter 9.

SELECTIVITY: THE KEY FACTOR

One reason that firms and organizations rent and exchange the use of their mailing lists is that they want to expand the number of people who buy through the mail. Joan Manley, a group vice president of Time, Inc. and head of its mail-order book division, told the Commission that it is good business for Time, Inc. to make its lists available for use by other direct mailers. Said Manley:

Our main reason for making them available is to enlarge the universe of active mail-order buyers. Our experience shows that the more one has purchased by mail, in the past, the more likely he is to appreciate the real value and the convenience of doing business by mail.[34]

The main reason most mailers want to rent and exchange use of their lists, however, is that, given a choice, a direct-mail user would almost always prefer to send his messages to a selection of people who appear likely to respond to them, and for a large number of mailers that means to people who have a history of responding to direct-mail solicitations. Publishers Clearing House President, Louis Kislik, put it this way:

Publishers Clearing House predominantly sells magazine subscriptions by mail and we do it by sending mailing pieces to our own past customers and to people on other lists that we rent through the normal list rental procedure. The mailings are very large-scale . . . . During the course of the year I estimate that we reach something over 40 million households . . . . The outside lists that we get are predominantly lists of people who have taken a mail-order action. We find that they are very much more productive for us and that is of course the name of the game. That produces the most orders.[35]

Richard Krieger, on behalf of the Association of American Publishers, summed it up even more bluntly:

. . . the best direct-mail campaign is the one that mails the least. This is a business necessity. In addition to rising costs generally, direct mailers are faced with quantum jump increases in postage. A piece of mail to an individual who doesn't want to buy is wasted, and to direct mailers the elimination of this kind of waste is absolutely essential.[36]

The Reuben H. Donnelly testimony also emphasized the cost factor.

Assume that a publisher sponsors the mailing of a subscription offer. Typically, his current cost for the mailing list, printing,

[34] Testimony of Time, Inc., Mailing Lists Hearings, December 11, 1975, p. 350.
[35] Testimony of Publishers Clearing House, Mailing Lists Hearings, (I) November 12, 1975, pp. 99-100.
[36] Testimony of Association of American Publishers, Mailing Lists Hearings, (II) November 12, 1975, p. 87.

mailing services, and postage might approximate 12 cents per piece mailed. Assume an expected response of two percent as the result of mailing to all 60 million households on our list. This would result in a mailing cost of $6 per subscription received. This might or might not be acceptable in terms of the publisher's economics. Assume, however, that some technique exists for selecting a more than averagely responsive subset of the mailing list, which, as the result of testing can be expected to return a three percent rather than a two percent rate. The immediate result is a decrease from $6 to $4 per subscription received.[37]

There are many ways of selecting "a more than averagely responsive subset of the mailing list." One of the simplest methods is the demographic one used by the public record compilers. To illustrate from testimony before the Commission:

If one were promoting lawn care or gardening items, an immediate choice would be to mail to single-family housing units rather than apartments. While there is no guarantee that each single-family residence is an active gardener, and that apartment dwellers do not garden, experience and reason insist that the probability of success is materially increased by this selectivity.[38]

Another method, equally simple, is to combine the names of people who have responded to several independent direct-mail solicitations into a single list and then pick out those that have responded most frequently. Typically, this kind of culling results in what is known among direct-mail users as a "hit list." Sometimes a list broker creates such a list as a way of promoting his particular line of business. What the broker does is get a group of list owners to agree to let him match their separate customer, member, or donor mailing lists to produce a single unduplicated list of "multiple buyers" which the broker then offers to other direct-mail users for a rental fee. For example, a list broker may get several companies in the mail-order nursery business to let him merge their customer lists into a single unduplicated list of people who have purchased nursery products two, three, or four times during the preceding year. Subject to conditions set by the list owners, and with the understanding that each owner will receive a pro-rata share of any proceeds from the rental of the new list, the broker then offers it to other direct-mail users. Owners and renters both benefit from this type of arrangement because, in addition to the rental fees that accrue to the list owners, each owner involved gets the use of an unduplicated list of people who have already demonstrated their responsiveness to direct-mail solicitations. Outside users of the hit list also benefit, since the customer responses to a mailing come back not to the broker or list owner, but to the user who then adds their names to its own list of customers.

The methods get more complicated when a list owner or user starts combining demographic characteristics, such as median number of single-family households in a census tract or ZIP code area, with the "recency of response" criterion. The circulation manager for a popular monthly magazine testified of one such operation in which a small group of magazine publishers sends the names and addresses of their new subscribers to a public record compiler whose lists they use in their mass advertising campaigns. In return, the public record compiler sends each of them an evaluation of their subscribers broken down by demographic characteristics and recency of responses to mailings by the other members of the group. These reports do not identify individual subscribers, nor do they identify the other magazines a publisher's subscribers are also receiving. They do, however, give each publisher an idea of the demographic characteristics of its subscribers who also subscribe to other mass circulation magazines, so that the next time the publisher rents the use of one of the public record compiler's mass lists the publisher can rent names and addresses of only people with two important characteristics: (1) a propensity to subscribe to the publisher's own magazine, and (2) a propensity to respond to any mail advertisements for a mass circulation weekly or monthly of the sort marketed by that particular group of publishers.[39]

A further refinement is introduced by what might be called a "multiple-response compiler." The multiple-response compiler is like the public record compiler in that it maintains a record system whose principal purpose is developing mailing lists for use by others. The specialty of the multiple-response compiler, however, is lists of people its own files show have responded to a variety of different types of direct-mail solicitations. The Richard A. Viguerie Co. of Falls Church, Virginia is a multiple-response compiler. The firm handles both political fund-raising solicitations and subscription campaigns that aim at people with conservative political views. Viguerie's firm, which maintains a master file of seven million names, sent out 65 million pieces of mail in 1975.[40]

The Viguerie Company often handles all aspects of a mailer's solicitation: design, testing, mailing, and the actual receipt of replies.[41] This last—receipt of the replies—allows the firm to keep track of the responses of the individuals whose names and addresses are in its master file. Viguerie described the operation as follows:

> If it is a name that has responded to a mailing, we have the month and the year that they responded. And, of course, their name and address and ZIP code. We have the amount of their contribution, and many times, we have the source of where the name came from. In other words, if we rented a magazine list of businessmen, we have a notation that this is a person who is a businessman. So that he is

[39] Testimony of McCall Publishing Company, (II) November 12, 1975, pp. 109-120.
[40] Testimony of Richard A. Viguerie Company, Inc., Mailing Lists Hearings, December 10, 1975, p. 129.
[41] Ibid., pp. 117-120.

going to be interested in subscribing to business publications perhaps or some such as that.[42]

The notation that "this is a person who is a businessman" results from coding the item to be returned by the recipient (such as a postcard or an order form) in a way that identifies the source of the list from which the individual's name originally came. Thus, if the Viguerie Company rents the use of a list from subscribers to a sporting magazine for use in marketing sporting equipment on behalf of one of its clients, it will put a code on the return order form which identifies the individual as a subscriber to the magazine. If the individual does not respond to the advertisement for sporting goods, his name will not get into the Viguerie files, but if he does, the Viguerie firm, through which his order will pass on its way to the sporting goods vendor, will note in its files the fact that he bought sporting goods *and* the fact that he subscribes to the magazine.

Because of the type of clients it has, the Viguerie files may also contain information on an individual's political opinions. The firm conducts surveys on behalf of political candidates, sometimes in conjunction with fund raising campaigns, and notes in its files how an individual responds. Said Viguerie in his testimony before the Commission:

> . . . It is just very general, very basic information. You know, it is a half-dozen items: name and address of the person, along with Mr. or Mrs. or sex; the fact they contributed to client A. . . . If they say I can't send money today but I agree with your position, they are put into the file with that notation, also; and if they say "Go jump in the lake," we have got that in there, too. That is basically the information we have along with the amount—if they did send a contribution—we record the amount of contribution and the time they sent it.[43]

This type of mailing-list compiler contrasts with the one described earlier that the small group of publishers uses because, as Viguerie testified, it is "mostly a record-keeping effort . . . to pinpoint special interests or philosophical inclinations."[44] Both, however, raise the same problem—namely, that the individuals who respond to advertisements or solicitations do not know that their actions are being noted in the files of a firm that specializes in developing mailing lists for use by others.

Selectivity is not only the key element in almost any direct mailing. Along with rising postal rates, it is also the principal force for change in the way mailing lists are developed. Chapter 2 refers to the fact that commercial banks, consumer-finance companies, and credit bureaus sometimes let their records on individuals be used to refine marketers' mailing lists by selecting from a large undifferentiated list the names of those with a propensity to buy certain kinds of items, or deleting the names of those who have unsatisfactory credit records and thus are undesirable prospects for a direct-mail

---

[42] *Ibid.*, pp. 117-118.
[43] *Ibid.*, pp. 137-140.
[44] *Ibid.*, p. 137.

marketer. This type of selection, called "prescreening" when a credit bureau's files are used, has two consequences that are of interest here: first, an action of a consumer that has nothing to do with direct-mail operations may get him onto or off of a mailing list; second, confidential information about an individual in the files of a credit grantor, commercial bank, or credit bureau may be disclosed to a list user.

The Federal Trade Commission defines "prescreening" as:

> the process by which a list of potential customers is submitted to a credit bureau which then audits the list by deletion of those names that have an adverse credit record.[45]

Kenneth Larkin, Senior Vice President of the Bank of America, explained how one such operation works:

> In accordance with the Federal Trade Commission's interpretation of the permissible uses of prescreening mechanisms, Bank of America . . . uses credit-reporting agencies for the purpose of expanding its card holder base. The Bank provides the credit-reporting agency with its credit criteria (i.e, annual income, number of open credit accounts, lack of experience with past due accounts, no BankAmericard account, . . .) and the credit-reporting agency matches the Bank's criteria against a name list containing desirable income characteristics . . . by various Federal census tracts for the State of California. By agreement, the credit-reporting agency submits to the Bank a list of those individuals who meet the Bank's criteria. The Bank, by letter, invites these persons to become BankAmericard holders by signing and returning the lower portion of the letter.[46]

Larkin emphasized that Bank of America "does not open an account or send a credit card unless and until it receives a signed response from the invitee," and if a person receiving an invitation does not respond within 90 days, the Bank "makes no further use of the information." He added that if the invitee indicates that he does not wish to receive a credit card, the Bank so informs the credit bureau to assure that the individual will not again be invited to become a BankAmericard holder.[47]

The example brings out two important points: one, to screen names on a public record list for a bank the credit bureau uses information about the individual's relationships with other credit grantors rather than information about their previous responsiveness to direct-mail campaigns; and two, the credit bureau actually sends the Bank the names and addresses on the screened list. In other words, there is a transfer of names and addresses from one organization to another of the names and addresses of individuals who have no role in the transfer and no knowledge of it. In the Bank of America case, the consequences for the individuals involved are no different than if

---

[45] 16 C.F.R. 600.5 Effective February 23, 1973, 38 *Federal Register* 4947.

[46] Testimony of Bank of America, Credit Cards and Reservations Systems Hearings, February 11, 1976, p. 30.

[47] *Ibid.*

the bank orders a credit report on them, but it is not hard to think of situations in which the consequences would be different.

Consider a simple example. Suppose a bank agreed to include a power-boat dealer's advertising brochure along with its monthly statements to individuals who have more than $10,000 on deposit. If any one recipient of the brochure subsequently turns up at the dealership and displays the brochure, the dealer will immediately surmise something about the individual which could directly affect their bargaining, and, most important-ly, which the individual no doubt thinks is a confidential item of information known only to himself and his bank.

This example is not as far-fetched as it may seem. If a retailer stuffs its monthly bills with advertising provided by an insurance company, the insurance company can safely assume that most of the individuals who respond to the stuffer have the general characteristics (such as average income, average number of dependents, average indebtedness) of the retailer's clientele. Moreover, if the retailer is willing, there is nothing to prevent the insurance company (or any other marketer, for that matter) from arranging to have the retailer stuff a highly selective subset of billings, perhaps the subset of those with incomes over $20,000 who have purchased fancy accessories for their automobiles or whose purchases indicate that they like to travel. Any number of such parameters can be used to help target a mailing on a market likely to be receptive to it, but the individual whose name is bobbing around in all these transactions has no say in them at all. No doubt many of the individuals who receive the advertising messages that are sent using screening techniques are pleased to know about the products and services being offered and happy to be able to take advantage of them. Few realize, however, that in the process personal information about them may be disclosed to an organization before they make any move to establish a relationship with it.

To some extent, prescreening and the selection methods like it are nothing more than an embellishment on the way direct-mail marketing has always operated. It has always been possible for a list user to acquire details about respondents to its mailings. If a list user wants to know something additional about anyone who responds to one of its mailings, all it has to do is confine its mailing to the names on a list rented or borrowed from one particular source.

In the Higgenbottom, Inc. example, there were a number of opportuni-ties for information about Smith's purchases to be transferred from firm to firm, and thus from mailing list to mailing list, without his knowledge. For instance, if Do-It-Yourself Industries had offered its list in segments, and the Wooly & Muffler Company had rented use of only the portion containing the names of recent purchasers of cold-weather gardening equipment, then when Smith responded to Wooly & Muffler's advertising campaign, Wooly & Muffler, could have made the notation that Smith was a winter gardener. It would be a guess, but more likely than not an accurate one, and if correct, would have added an item of information about Smith to the Wooly & Muffler file without Smith's knowledge. As a practical matter, however, Wooly & Muffler would not have bothered to do so. Industry spokesmen emphasized to the Commission that it would be uneconomic for a direct-mail marketer to take so much trouble unless the firm derived a substantial percentage of its income from the rental of its lists, or perhaps knew a number of mail-order houses that wanted to rent the use of a list of people who had recently purchased both cold-weather gardening equipment and a pair of fur-lined rubber boots.

The capacity to screen a list using the files of a credit grantor threatens to change this incentive structure, however, by making it possible for a mailer to rent the use of record systems that already contain a great deal of detail about an individual's purchasing behavior. Moreover, as Chapter 3 points out, electronic funds transfer technology promises to so increase the number of systems containing highly detailed records that the day may come when most mailing lists will be screened through them rather than by using the old-fashioned "recency of response" techniques. Such a development need not be viewed with alarm if the screening procedures block the disclosure of confidential information from one organization to another without the individual's consent. At present, however, there is no demand for attention to the problem screening procedures pose, since few individuals have any idea how mailing lists are developed, with or without screening, and even fewer know how to go about keeping their names and addresses from getting on lists they do not want to be on.

How to Keep a Name Off a Mailing List

If an individual does not want to receive unsolicited direct mail he can keep his name off most lists by becoming a modern-day hermit—by paying cash for all his purchases, not owning a car, giving to charities anonymously, always buying magazines at newstands, never responding to a door-to-door survey, never signing a petition or a guest book, never registering to vote, and never attending a meeting, conference, or newsworthy social event. Even so he may still get a certain amount of unsolicited mail addressed to "Occupant," but not much because "Occupant" mailings are not selective enough for most mailers.

There are to be sure less anti-social ways for an individual to choke off his direct-mail traffic, provided he knows of them. The Commission learned of four others: an individual can send a personal letter of objection to every organization he suspects is renting or otherwise making his name available to direct mailers; he can exercise the "negative check-off option" that some organizations offer him; he can lodge his request not to receive mail with the Mail Preference Service, a centralized delisting program operated by the Direct Mail/Marketing Association; and he can use the delisting service the Post Office maintains for individuals who do not want to receive obscene advertising. What he must *not* do, if he wants his correspondence to have any effect, is write to the organization that sends him unsolicited mail without having first established a relationship with him, because, as explained earlier, the user of a list normally does not have his name until he responds to its advertisement or solicitation. Moreover, he must *not* ask that his name be *removed* from the mailing list, but rather that in the records used to develop the mailing list a notation be put next to his name indicating that he does not want it to be used for direct-mail marketing or solicitation. That will assure that his name will be omitted from any list another organization is permitted to use.

DIRECT CORRESPONDENCE

If an individual believes a retailer, a magazine, or any other organization with which he has established a relationship, is making his name and address available for use by others in their direct-mail campaigns, he can write to the organization, asking that it put a notation in its records on him indicating that he does not want his name so used. Every organization that testified at the Commission's mailing list hearings, including the public record compilers, said that it would respond to such a request. The catch is that people do not know this opportunity is available to them, nor do they know which of the many organizations they have relationships with is renting, lending, or exchanging the use of their names.

THE NEGATIVE CHECK-OFF OPTION

The American Express Company and *Computerworld*, a weekly newspaper, both testified that they routinely inform their customers of their practice of making their customers' names and addresses available for mailing use by other organizations and give every customer an opportunity to object to having his name so used. The negative check-off is far more useful to individuals than the other three methods because the organizations offering it identify themselves to their customers as list renters and tell the individual exactly what to do if he objects to them renting his name to someone else. In the American Express case, moreover, the individual can also elect not to receive any advertising from American Express. It is easy for organizations that communicate with their customers at regular intervals in the normal course of their operations to offer the negative check off. American Express and *Computerworld* both renew their relationships with their customers annually and offer the check-off opportunity at that time. Not surprisingly, the negative check-off also seems to be more popular with customers, members, or donors who are already likely to be sensitive to the privacy issue. The percentage of *Computerworld* customers who exercise their negative check-off option, for example, is ten times greater than that of American Express customers.[48] Said the witness from American Express:

> The program was started just about one year ago by notices that accompanied new and renewal American Express cards. The notice advised the recipients that they were subject to mailings by non-affiliated firms and that they had the option of having their names removed from these listings, as well as the listings we use for our own services and merchandise mailings.

---

[48] Testimony of American Express Company, Mailing Lists Hearings, (I) November 12, 1975, p. 68; Testimony of ComputerWorld, Mailing Lists Hearings, December 11, 1975, p. 406.

I would like to emphasize that in the past it had always been our policy to remove from our lists the names and addresses of any person who wrote to us requesting us to do so. Now for the first time we were advising them formally of this practice, and even giving them a vehicle to send back to us if they chose. The results of these mailings were both interesting and enlightening. Since November of 1974, we have sent out approximately 5.6 million notices and have received approximately 58 thousand written responses, just over one percent.

Of these responses about 40 percent or 23 thousand wished to continue receiving our own merchandise offerings but did not wish to receive offerings from non-affiliated companies. You may also be interested in the reasons given by a sample of those one percent who responded negatively. About 60 percent of them who asked for the removal of their names did so because they did not wish their names and addresses transferred to another.

Another 20 percent wanted removal because they felt it would help the postal system by stopping excess mail, thus resulting in reduced postage rates. An additional ten percent asked for removal because they did not wish to be tempted to purchase merchandise or in some instances to have their spouses tempted. An additional ten percent were miscellaneous reasons, difficult to categorize.[49]

The offer of a negative check-off option may not reach all of an organization's customers, members, or donors. Many people have a well developed propensity not to read "junk mail," and so miss even the stuffer in an envelope that offers them a way of receiving less of it.[50] Publishers, mindful of the rule of thumb that a smart advertiser does not change the subject in the middle of a message, worried that the negative check-off message might distract the prospective customer from their advertising messages, although they had no persuasive evidence that the maxim applied in this case.[51] This is of concern to publishers and other organizations whose mailings to customers, unlike those of American Express, always contain some kind of advertising or solicitation message. If the negative check-off message should prove detrimental to advertising and solicitation messages, these organizations would be reluctant to offer it, as they would then face a choice of weakening their promotion or making a special mailing at substantial extra cost. Public-interest groups argued for keeping the check-off procedure flexible. For them, the thank-you letters they send for donations received and their newsletters and annual reports appear to be the best vehicles to use in offering their members and donors the negative check-off option.

Public record compilers pointed out that because they have little direct

---

[49] Testimony of American Express Company, Mailing Lists Hearings, (I) November 12, 1975, p. 68.
[50] *Ibid.*, pp. 69-73.
[51] *Ibid.*

contact with the public, their clients, the list users, would have to take the extra trouble of sending them the names of new list-user customers who indicate they do not want their names used for direct mailing. Even so, the customer request might not be fulfilled, since the public record compilers renew their basic files once a year and have no way of knowing that John Smith who lived at a certain address in Chicago last year is the same John Smith who lives this year in San Francisco. In other words, a notation next to Smith's name at the Chicago address does not get carried forward to the same Smith at a San Francisco address unless Smith tells the public record compiler he has moved. Smith, of course, cannot do that, because he does not know which public record compiler has his name and probably does not even know such organizations exist. Multiple-response compilers, which also have no direct communication with the individuals whose names are in their records, are in the same position.

The negative check-off in some form is nonetheless the most convenient method for the individual to use, and is not without benefit to the organization that offers it. American Express said that it offers the check-off "primarily for enhanced customer good will and improved customer relations," but added:

> We believe that our program improves understanding and delays misconceptions regarding use of mailing lists, as well as providing easy recourse for that small percentage of consumers who wish to have their names removed from our lists. There are peripheral benefits, too; among others, reducing the costs of our own mailings and improving returns on direct-mail advertising. We have no regrets about our decision to institute this program and will be continuing it into the future . . . .[52]

THE MAIL PREFERENCE SERVICE

The cost of mailings may make most mailers sympathetic to any program that takes off the lists the names of people who do not want to be on them, but it is not always the most compelling consideration. If, for example, a list source has 24 million names for rent, picking out a tenth of one percent of them—24 thousand—can cost more than any resulting response rate would be worth. Nor is it easy to persuade proponents of the direct-mail medium that there really are people who cannot be coaxed into buying something by mail. Mailers want to keep the hardcore objectors off their lists,[53] but they do not want to lose anyone who might be turned into a prospect if they can only get the right message to him.[54] This pervasive bias in favor of keeping the messages flowing is reflected in the workings of the industry's centralized delisting operation—the Mail Preference Service (MPS).

The MPS works this way. Say Jones, who wants less unsolicited mail,

---

[52] *Ibid.*, p. 69.
[53] *Ibid.*, p. 76.
[54] Testimony of Direct Mail/Marketing Association, Mailing Lists Hearings, (I) November 12, 1975, pp. 56-57.

learns of the MPS and writes to the Direct Mail/Marketing Association (DMMA) in New York to request a "Name Removal Form." By return mail he receives the form along with a pamphlet describing the MPS which paints the ramifications of his request for name-removal in tones that might cause anyone to have second thoughts. He is told, for example, that his action will probably cause him to "get fewer new product samples, coupons or special offers" and "receive fewer mailings offering chances to enter sweepstakes and other contests." Jones holds firm in his resolve to renounce such golden opportunities, and sends the completed form back to the DMMA. In case he had changed his mind, however, the DMMA also provided him with a form on which he could ask to have his name *added* to other mailing lists. Whichever step he takes, his name and address are put on computer tape and circulated on a regular basis to the 1,200 or so association members who participate in the MPS.

The MPS has been publicized during the last two years in national circulation magazines like *Time* and *Better Homes and Gardens.* Its advertisements are not the sort a direct-mail marketer trying to get customers would use, but a reader who perseveres will find out how the MPS works and the pros and cons of accepting its offer. One of the biggest disadvantages, and one that is shared by all four of the existing methods of curtailing the amount of direct mail an individual receives, is that the choice for the individual is strictly binary: he either does nothing, in which case he may be inundated with mail, or he takes advantage of one of the four methods open to him and gets little or no mail. MPS efforts to make the individual aware of that choice, so that his decision can be an informed one,[55] are apparently successful. At the time of the Commission's hearings, the DMMA had received requests from 135,137 individuals for the name-removal form. Of those, only about 56 thousand had filled out the form and sent it back; another 37,643 had asked for the add-on form, and 25 thousand of those had filled it out and sent it back.[56]

In addition, the procedure for getting on the MPS lists is cumbersome. The individual must first write for a form, and when it comes, fill out and return it. The direct-mail marketers who testified before the Commission were quick to protest the prospect of any regulation that would require them to add extra steps to their original solicitations to customers, but the MPS adds steps that require the individual to persevere.

A simple, one-step procedure, perhaps using a form included as part of the MPS advertisements in mass circulation magazines, would no doubt generate a much bigger response. Moreover, the MPS form requires an individual to write his name and address only once and in a standardized format which may or may not be the way it appears on one mailing list or another. Hence, the probability that the MPS tape will serve to catch his name and address every time they appear on a list developed or used by a DMMA member is a product of many factors including how uniformly the individual signs his name, how often he changes his address, how accurately they are transcribed onto lists, and how sophisticated a matching program

[55] *Ibid.*, pp. 36-42; 54-57.
[56] *Ibid.*, p. 38.

the DMMA member has. Thus the best procedure would be one whereby an individual could send the MPS the address labels from his unsolicited mail so that his name and address could be put on the MPS master tape in all the variety that turns up in his mailbox. This was suggested to the Commission by a public record compiler for whom the MPS is the only practical conduit for receiving messages from individuals who do not want it to rent their names and address.[57]

THE U.S. POSTAL SERVICE (USPS)

Two Federal statutes, one directed at pandering advertisements *[39 U.S.C. 3008]*, and the other at sexually oriented advertising *[39 U.S.C. 3010]*, provide ways for an individual to stop the flow of unsolicited mail from particular types of sources. The pandering advertisements statute allows an individual to get a court order forbidding a mailer to send him erotic material. Since the definition of "erotic" is left to the individual, an individual could perhaps use the statute to stop the flow of any kind of unsolicited mail from any source. However, anyone who tries to block the flow of material that nobody would consider erotic by this means must risk ridicule, since the proceeding to obtain the court order is a public one. USPS witnesses testified that as of the date of the Commission's hearings, it had received 475 thousand applications for court orders and logged approximately 6,000 violations.[58]

The second statute, the so-called obscenity law, takes a different approach. It directs the USPS to maintain a list of individuals who do not want to receive a statutorily defined class of sexually oriented material, and forbids a mailer to send that class of material to anyone who has been on the USPS list more than 30 days. The statute also requires the mailer to put a notice on the outside of the mailed item indicating that it is classified as sexually oriented advertising. The enforcement provisions of this statute are currently being challenged on constitutional grounds.

As explained in Chapter 1, it appears that there are no constitutional barriers to having the USPS carry out the wishes of an individual who does not want to receive a particular type of mail so long as the individual alone makes the decision about what he will or will not receive. USPS witnesses, however, recommended against enlarging the USPS role in this regard. They pointed out that to do so would require a government agency to maintain still another file on individuals, and a file dealing with matters as sensitive as what an individual does not want to read at that.[59] The file, moreover, would have to be copied and distributed periodically to the 300 thousand-odd holders of third class bulk mail permits, and in order to assure accurate name matches, the USPS would probably have to require all direct mailers to use a standardized mailing label. Altogether, the administrative cost to

---

[57] Testimony of Reuben H. Donnelley and Company, Mailing Lists Hearings, (II) November 12, 1975, p. 43.
[58] Testimony of the U.S. Postal Service, Mailing Lists Hearings, December 11, 1975, p. 279.
[59] *Ibid.*, pp. 262-64.

the Postal Service would be close to intolerable, and the cost to mailers prohibitive.

RECOMMENDATIONS

The Commission was specifically directed to report to the President and the Congress on:

whether a person engaged in interstate commerce who maintains a mailing list should be required to remove an individual's name and address from such list upon request of that individual. *[Section 5(c)(2)(B)(i) of P.L. 93-579]*

After much deliberation the Commission concluded that the answer to this question should be "no." That is, the Commission recommends:

Recommendation (1):

That a person engaged in interstate commerce who maintains a mailing list should *not* be required by law to remove an individual's name and address from such a list upon request of that individual, except as already provided by law.

The Commission's principal reason for reaching this conclusion is that the balance that must be struck between the interests of individuals and the interests of mailers is an especially delicate one. As a public record compiler put it in a letter to the Commission:

The founders of this nation promoted a unified front against England through Committees of Correspondence. Since the beginning mail has been a vital element in promoting business and ideas.[60]

Numerous witnesses testified to the importance of direct mail to non-profit organizations, to the champions of unpopular causes, and to many of the organizations that create diversity in American society.[61] It was also pointed out the new Federal election law *[2 U.S.C. 441a]* makes candidates virtually dependent on the small contributions which direct mail campaigns are the only practical way to raise.[62]

Dr. William B. Walsh, Director of Project Hope, testified that Project Hope's direct-mail program:

. . . is the most efficient method of reaching large numbers of individuals who may wish to support its work. Unlike commercial product manufacturers who can support vast advertising budgets

---

[60] Written statement of R. L. Polk and Company, Mailing Lists Hearings, (I) November 12, 1975, p. 22.

[61] Testimony of Craver and Company, Mailing Lists Hearings, December 10, 1975, pp. 210-211, 218; Testimony of Richard A. Viguerie Company, Inc., Mailing Lists Hearings, December 10, 1975, p. 107; Testimony of Common Cause, Mailing Lists Hearings, December 10, 1975, pp. 44-45.

[62] Testimony of Common Cause, Mailing Lists Hearings, December 10, 1975, pp. 46-47.

through the sales price of their product or service, Project Hope, as a non-profit institution, cannot afford major space advertising or radio and television campaigns. Project Hope uses direct mail to inform its present donors of program activity and progress and to locate new donors through the use of commercially available rented lists. The direct-mail program continues to be the largest single source of contributions to the Foundation. Through the use of rented lists, the prospect portion of the direct-mail program has enabled Hope to build a donor file of several hundred thousand individuals.[63]

Industry representatives also emphasized the economic importance of direct mail, pointing out that 70 percent of all magazine subscriptions are sold by direct mail and, as noted earlier, that the total volume of business generated through direct mail approaches $60 billion annually. While these figures are open to debate, there can be no doubt that direct-mail marketing has substantial economic significance.

Another reason for this recommendation is also largely economic. The Commission is persuaded that current technology cannot make a universal, legally enforceable name-flagging requirement economically feasible. The name-matching problem is a serious one, and any remedy proposed today would only create additional, and probably more serious, problems. It could, for example, necessitate a Federal regulation mandating a standard format of addressing all mail, not just direct mail. It could require the USPS to set up a data bank on individuals who do not want their names and addresses used for direct mailings. And if the costs of mailing continue to rise at anything like the present rate, organizations that now depend on direct mail for getting their messages will undoubtedly shift to telephone solicitation, a much greater nuisance to individuals than unsolicited mail.

Similarly, a statute requiring all organizations to offer a negative check-off option if they rent, lend, or exchange the names of their customers, members, or donors would have to reach further than appears at first blush. It would no doubt have to define the content of the offer precisely, require the offerer to make some acknowledgement that the individual's request has been received, and set a time limit for the organization's compliance. Such requirements demand uniformity where diversity is now the rule, and would greatly increase the cost burden of some organizations—public interest groups, for example—that can ill afford to bear it.

Focusing on the basic issue brings all these arguments into perspective. Strictly speaking, removing a name from a mailing list is *not* what one wants to accomplish. Rather, the basic mailing list issue is *whether an organization that maintains records on individuals and makes a practice of allowing other organizations to rent or borrow their names and addresses for use in direct-mail marketing or solicitation should have an obligation to notify the individuals that it does so and give each of them the opportunity to indicate that he does not want his name so used.* In general, the Commission believes that an individual should have a way to prevent information about him ostensibly collected for

---

[63] Testimony of Project HOPE, Mailing Lists Hearings, December 10, 1975, pp. 226-27.

one purpose from being used for another purpose to which he objects. The Commission did not go so far as to assert that an individual should have a unilateral right to control the uses to which recorded information about him is put. The individual's interest in controlling the use of recorded information about himself must be balanced against organizational and societal needs. In its examination of mailing-list operations, the Commission found that among the record-keeping organizations that maintain records about individuals with whom they have some direct relationship, it is a common practice to allow the individuals' names and addresses to be used by others without even telling the individuals that this is their practice. The Commission can find no overwhelming societal justification for such a state of affairs which, in effect, allows an organization complete discretion to decide whether and to whom it will rent or exchange its mailing lists.

Except for one,[64] none of the witnesses in the Commission's mailing list hearings were willing to acknowledge that privacy issues are involved in direct-mail marketing practices at all. Some were willing to admit that unsolicited mail could be a nuisance, an annoyance, or even an abomination—but not a trespass on personal privacy. If an individual does not wish to read his unsolicited mail, they argued, he has an easy option—throw it in the trashcan.[65] Even the USPS took this view. Robert Jordan, Director of its Office of Product Management, told the Commission:

> We can find no evidence that the present use of mailing lists in the direct-marketing process constitutes a significant or peculiar invasion of privacy. The economic pressures of the marketplace provide mailers with a strong incentive to direct their advertisements away from those individuals who might find them annoying. By its very nature, direct mail must be aimed at individuals who have some desire to receive it. Moreover, the recipient of unwanted mail matter has the option of throwing it away. Indeed, an individual probably finds it easier to avoid reading his mail than to escape from any other form of advertising.[66]

Many witnesses also argued that "good business practice" demands that organizations be responsive to their customers' wishes. No one wants a dissatisfied customer and no one wants to mail to an individual who is not going to be responsive.

The Commission would agree that *receipt* of mail is not the issue, but it also believes that the individual subject of a record has a stake in how that record is used as deserving of recognition as the record keeper's, and that therefore there should be close correspondence between his expectation of the uses that will be made of information about him and the uses that are actually made of it. In addition, there is, as explained earlier, the strong push for greater selectivity in the use of records about individuals to develop mailing lists. That drive, coupled with new technological capabilities, could

---

[64] Testimony of Privacy Journal, Mailing Lists Hearings, December 10, 1975, p. 8.

[65] Testimony of Time, Inc., Mailing Lists Hearings, December 11, 1975, pp. 343; Testimony of American Express Company, Mailing Lists Hearings (I), November 12, 1975, p. 65.

[66] Testimony of U.S. Postal Service, Mailing Lists Hearings, December 11, 1975, pp. 253-54.

change the character of the way direct-mail operations are conducted, a change even some of the witnesses agreed would be troubling.[67]

In the chapters of this report which include recommendations for creating a legitimate, enforceable expectation of confidentiality for the individual[68] the Commission addresses the problems posed by the use of records containing confidential information to screen mailing lists. This is a basic recommendation which the Commission makes, with certain modifications, in every area for which it urges creation of a lawful expectation of confidentiality. The Commission, however, does not believe that the organizations which owe individuals a duty of confidentiality are the only ones that should adhere to the principle that information collected for one purpose may not be used for other purposes unless the individual is first notified and given a chance to protest. All organizations that keep records about individuals should adhere to it.

The organization representatives who testified before the Commission argued almost unanimously that established procedures are adequate for handling all problems related to the receipt of unsolicited direct mail. Even the USPS took this position, pointing out that postal regulations already protect against socially objectionable and fraudulent offers.[69] The Commission, however, disagrees. It finds existing procedures either too limited in their scope, too cumbersome, or too poorly understood to be effective. The individual is by and large ignorant of the side effects of ordering, joining, or contributing through the mails; and few of the organizations that seek his purchases or his support do much to enlighten him. As many of them testified, they stand ready to comply with the individual's wishes—if he can find them—but do not see it as any part of their obligation to tell him where to look for them.

On the other hand, the Commission is sensitive to the fear that regulation of current practice may destroy direct-mail operations, and to the argument that the potential it sees for serious, systematic abuse of mailing list practices is still largely no worse than a potential. There are many different ways an individual could be notified of list-rental and exchange practices. However, it is unlikely that any one method can be applied across the board without making it impossible for some direct-mail operations to function. Since the industry avowedly stands ready to experiment with various notice alternatives and, to respect the wishes of any customers, members, or donors who do not want to be on lists, the problem is to find effective, economically feasible ways for organizations to let the public know what their list rental and exchange policies are, and to notify individuals of any deviations; and for individuals who object to notify organizations of their objection. These are problems of method, not of principle, and only require organizations to assume responsibility for solving them.

---

[67] Testimony of Publishers Clearing House, Mailing Lists Hearings, November 12, 1975, pp. 91, 103; Testimony of ComputerWorld, Mailing Lists Hearings, December 11, 1975, pp. 430-31.
[68] Chapter 2 on the consumer-credit relationship; Chapter 3 on the depository relationship; and Chapters 5 and 7 on, respectively, the insurance and medical-care relationships.
[69] Testimony of U.S. Postal Service, Mailing Lists Hearings, December 11, 1975, p. 253.

The Commission believes that the record keeper with which the individual has a relationship should accept responsibility for notifying him and seeing that his objections, if any, are respected. However, because it is acutely aware of the difficulty and the undesirability of forcing record keepers to assume that responsibility, and because so many appear to be willing to assume it voluntarily, the Commission believes that voluntary implementation is likely to be a successful as well as adequate solution to the problem. Thus, the Commission recommends:

Recommendation (2):

That a private-sector organization which rents, sells, exchanges, or otherwise makes the addresses, or names and addresses, of its customers, members, or donors available to any other person for use in direct-mail marketing or solicitation, should adopt a procedure whereby each customer, member, or donor is informed of the organization's practice in that respect, including a description of the selection criteria that might be used in selling, renting or exchanging lists, such as ZIP codes, interest, buying patterns, and level of activity, and, in addition, is given an opportunity to indicate to the organization that he does not wish to have his address, or name and address, made available for such purposes. Further, when a private-sector organization is informed by one of its customers, members, or donors that he does not want his address, or name and address, made available to another person for use in direct-mail marketing or solicitation, the organization should promptly take whatever steps are necessary to assure that the name and address is not so used, including notifying a multiple-response compiler or a credit bureau to whom the name and address has been disclosed with the prospect that it may be used to screen or otherwise prepare lists of names and addresses for use in direct-mail marketing or solicitation.

The Commission considered the binary nature of all the current delisting methods and concluded that if the individual is to have a fair basis for deciding whether he wants to ask that his name not be used, organizations will have to include in the recommended notices the selection criteria they allow to be used in developing mailing lists from their records. An individual may have no objection, for example, to having his name rented as a donor to a particular charity, in principle, but might still object to being put on a list of donors who contribute more than $500 a year.

Since some of the record systems used to develop or screen mailing lists today are maintained by organizations that have no direct contact with the individuals whose names and addresses are in their files, the Commission also recommends that a record keeper notify any multiple-response compiler or credit bureau to which it discloses its list information of the objections it receives from individuals. The Bank of America testimony on prescreening illustrates how easy it is to notify a credit bureau, and those who employ a multiple-response compiler to do their mailings should be able to handle the notification task equally simply.

The fit between this recommendation and the confidentiality recommendations in other chapters should be noted. Those recommendations generally call for some kind of advance notice of the kinds of disclosures the record keeper expects to make without asking for the individual's authorization. *Recommendation (2)*, above, is intended to supplement such requirements; not to supplant them. Thus, a credit grantor, insurer, or depository institution that owes a duty of confidentiality to the individuals on whom it maintains records would be legally required to include in its initial notice the disclosures it normally makes for marketing purposes, but its compliance with *Recommendation (2)*, above, would otherwise be voluntary.

A word also needs to be said about the meaning of "organization" as the term is used in *Recommendation (2)*. The recommendation does *not* contemplate the free exchange of names and addresses between a private-sector organization's subsidiaries and affiliates. As emphasized in Chapter 1, the Commission believes that regardless of the level at which an organization is defined as a unit for the purpose of complying with the Commission's several sets of recommendations, an individual must be assured that information about him collected and maintained in connection with one record-keeping relationship will not be made available for use in connection with another. If two affiliated companies define themselves as a unit but perform two different functions—one extending credit and the other selling insurance, for example—information about customers must not flow between them without adherence to the notice, authorization, and other requirements called for in the Commission's recommendations. Likewise, a corporate affiliate in, say, the retailing business should not rent or lend the names and addresses of its customers to another affiliate to market insurance unless the retailer informs its customers that it intends to do so and gives them an opportunity to indicate that they do not want their names used for that purpose.

GOVERNMENT AGENCY RECORDS

The records on individuals maintained by State and local government agencies are the principle source of the information public record compilers use to develop mailing lists. Unlike a multiple-response compiler, the public record compiler is not well situated to receive and take account of an individual's objection notices forwarded to it by its client organizations. The public record compiler renews its record system annually, and has no way of knowing whether John Smith in San Francisco this year is the same John Smith who last year in Chicago asked one of the compiler's clients to see that the compiler noted his objection to unsolicited mail. Furthermore, unless a public record compiler does its clients' mailings for them, it will not have control over the form individuals' responses take and thus may not be able to match the name and address on an objection notice with any name and address in its files. The name-matching problem can be particularly acute for a public record compiler.

The Commission considered several different ways of informing a public record compiler that an individual does not want his name on lists.

Mailing Lists

153

One is to have the public record compiler send a notice to each individual named in its records, but this would be inordinately costly. Another is to have each State and local government agency offer a negative check-off option to individuals whose names appear in its public records. This would run afoul of the objectives of public-record statutes, since it would require an agency to distinguish between an individual acting as a public record compiler's representative and the same individual asking for information in his capacity as a private citizen. An agency can make such a distinction when it enters into a contract with a public record compiler, but it otherwise can be difficult both to make and to justify. Moreover, to have the negative check-off apply to all public requests for access to a record, so as to avoid having to distinguish between different types of requestors, would even further undermine the purpose of public-record statutes.

Fortunately there is an alternative which takes account of the compiler's and its clients' desire for selectivity. The Commission concluded that if it is possible to rely on the mailing list user's much stressed desire not to send messages to individuals who do not want to receive them, it should be enough to note next to an individual's name on a public record that he does not want his name used for marketing or solicitation. The public record compiler would still be able to copy the record, just as any other member of the public can, but it would be on notice that the individual had objected to having his name on a list, and presumably, for economic reasons, would not include that name on lists it develops for its clients.

Accordingly, the Commission recommends:

Recommendation (3):

That each State review the direct-mail marketing and solicitation uses that are made of State agency records about individuals and for those that are used for such purposes, direct the State agency maintaining them to devise a procedure whereby an individual can inform the agency that he does not want a record pertaining to himself to be used for such purposes and have that fact noted in the record in a manner that will assure that the individual's preference will be communicated to any user of the record for direct-mail marketing or solicitation. Special attention should be paid to Department of Motor Vehicle records and the practices of agencies who prepare mailing lists for the express purpose of selling, renting or exchanging them with others.

* * * * * * *

The Commission believes that the recommendations in this chapter will significantly contribute to dispelling public ignorance of, and concern about, how individuals' names get onto and off of mailing lists. The individual who wants to receive no mail at all will not be satisfied. Even if every organization in the country complied, he would still get some mail addressed to "Occupant." The Commission, however, does not believe that the mere receipt of mail is the problem. Finding out "how they got my name" is the problem and the Commission believes it has found the way to let the individual know.

Chapter 5

The Insurance Relationship

The activities of the nation's 4,700 insurance companies touch the lives of all Americans in a variety of ways. Two out of three Americans have life insurance protection;[1] 90 percent of the civilian population under age 65 is covered by individual or group health insurance policies;[2] and 15 million are covered by the pension plans that life insurers offer.[3] It is estimated that almost 90 percent of the registered automobiles in the country are insured,[4] and few homes are without insurance coverage. In 1975, the premiums Americans paid for life, health, and pension coverage amounted to $58.6 billion[5] and property and liability insurance premiums amounted to another $50 billion.[6] The companies, for their part, paid out an estimated $75 billion in claims and policyholder benefits.[7]

The central function of insurance is to spread the economic burden of unforeseen financial losses by using the premiums paid by many insureds to pay for the losses sustained by a few. Some forms of insurance protection are mandated by law or business practice. For example, a number of States require car owners to carry auto insurance. Mortgage lenders require borrowers to carry fire insurance. Contractors are required to provide surety bonds to protect their clients against failures to perform and some fields of employment require fidelity bonds. Other forms of insurance, such as life, health, malpractice, and product and other liability coverages, are virtually mandatory in the minds of many people. Indeed, the cost and availability of insurance influence the character of society as well as the economy. It affects personal lives, life-styles, and even living standards.

Because the chief functions of an insurer—underwriting and rating risks and paying claims—are decision-making processes that involve evaluations of people and their property, the insurance industry is among

---

[1] American Council of Life Insurance, *Life Insurance Fact Book*, (New York: American Council of Life Insurance, 1976), p. 9.

[2] Health Insurance Institute, *The Source Book of Health Insurance Data 1974 - 1975*, (New York: Health Insurance Institute, 1975), p. 19.

[3] American Council of Life Insurance, *op. cit.*, p. 38.

[4] Automobile Insurance Plan Services Organization, *AIPSO Insurance Facts for 1977*, (New York: Automobile Insurance Plan Services Organization, 1977), p. 4.

[5] American Council of Life Insurance, *op. cit.*, p. 55.

[6] Insurance Information Institute, *Insurance Facts*, (New York: Insurance Information Institute, 1976), p. 12.

[7] American Council of Life Insurance, *op. cit.*, pp. 9 and 52; information obtained orally from A.M. Best and Co.

society's largest gatherers and users of information about individuals. This chapter reports the results of the Commission's inquiry into the personal-data record-keeping practices of insurance companies and the support organizations that provide them with various services, including record keeping.

The chapter begins with a short description of the industry, its sources of information about individuals, and the role that support organizations play in gathering and disseminating such information. This is followed by an examination of the way records about an individual affect his place in the insurance relationship today, and of the problems industry record-keeping practices pose from a privacy protection viewpoint. Finally, after summarizing current legal restraints on the record-keeping practices of insurance institutions and support organizations, the Commission, in the last section, presents and explains its specific recommendations for change. As in other chapters of this report the Commission's recommendations are arranged in terms of its three recommended public-policy objectives: (1) to minimize intrusiveness; (2) to maximize fairness; and (3) to create a legitimate, enforceable expectation of confidentiality.

INSURANCE INSTITUTIONS AND SUPPORT ORGANIZATIONS

There are essentially two types of insurance companies: stock companies owned by shareholders and mutual companies owned by policyholders. (Blue Cross and Blue Shield are nonprofit associations which policyholders join.) Although the largest life insurance companies are of the mutual type, the total amount of life insurance protection in force is about equally divided between stock and mutual companies. In the property and liability insurance business, the largest company is also a mutual company, but stock companies account for over 70 percent of premium volume.

Multiple-line insurance institutions are those with affiliate companies writing both life and health and property and liability coverages. The largest property and liability insurers are affiliates of multiple-line institutions, as are the largest life insurers since the expansion of some mutual companies into property and liability lines.

Companies sell insurance in four ways: by direct mail; through an exclusive agent; through an independent agent; or through a broker. While the exclusive agent represents only one company, the independent agent may have agreements with several companies, and the broker is a legal representative of his clients rather than the companies with which he places business. Agents are paid commissions or fees by companies rather than by clients. For simplicity of discussion, however, all will here be referred to as *agents*.

From a privacy protection viewpoint, insurers differ more significantly in terms of product line than they do in terms of ownership and company structure. The application form for the simpler types of life and health insurance sold by direct mail typically asks for little information. Name, address, age, sex, occupation, a statement certifying that the applicant has not had certain illnesses within a stated period of time and is currently in good health, and the beneficiary's name usually suffice. This is possible because policies sold by direct mail are relatively small ones, the population buying them is comparatively large, and they tend to be for limited coverages. Thus, the spread of risk of illness and death on which the premium rates are predicated is maintained.

In contrast, insurance sold through agents typically requires more information from and about the applicant and other insureds. Such coverages tend to be broader, more varied, and often need to be tailored to the particular needs of the applicant. Of all insurance sold through agents, the type requiring the least personal information is group insurance, which is underwritten on an aggregate rather than an individual basis, i.e., over time the premium rate is determined by the illness and death experience of the entire group.

Because the experience of large groups is statistically more reliable, the experience of many small groups may often be combined in determining premium rates. Doing so, however, demands more care in offering group insurance to smaller firms than in offering it to larger ones, lest the people in low-risk groups inadvertently subsidize those in high-risk ones. Care is also exercised in soliciting large accounts, but only as to the aggregate mix of occupations or other gross characteristics of the members of the group. Thus, while group insurance by its nature is markedly less dependent on information about the individual than on any other types of insurance, the amount of detail that can be dispensed with will depend on the size of the group involved.

As to individual life, health, and property and liability insurance that is sold through agents, the amount of information collected about individual applicants and insureds can be extensive. Moreover, the way it is collected, used, and disclosed is somewhat different in life and health underwriting than in property and liability underwriting. These differences, and the privacy protection problems they create, are principal themes of this chapter.

LIFE AND HEALTH INSURERS

Life and health insurers and their agents have different reasons for collecting and using information about individuals than property and liability insurers. In the first place, people often have to be persuaded to buy life insurance, whereas there is a ready market for property and liability coverage. Moreover, because life insurance is often sold as part of a package of financial planning services offered by agents, a life insurance prospect may be asked to divulge much information about himself even before the application is completed. For example, when insurance is used in estate building or estate conservation, the agent collects detailed information about the prospect's net worth, income, career prospects, and personal goals. When business life insurance[8] is being considered, extensive information about the financial condition of the firm or its principals is required. As a result, some life insurance agents have more comprehensive knowledge about a client's financial affairs than perhaps anyone else.

Most importantly, life insurance is a contract which binds a company to pay claims or benefits unless the policyholder fails to pay premiums when due, or unless the company can prove fraud or material misrepresentation during a limited "contestable period," generally two years after which a claim must be paid even if the application turns out to have been fraudulent. Thus, before entering into such a contract, the insurer wants an accurate health history, often supplemented by a medical examination to determine current health status, financial status information to protect against overinsurance, and enough information about personal habits to judge whether they might shorten the applicant's life. If the applicant has a significant health impairment, he is subjected to an extensive underwriting investigation to determine whether insurance can be issued to him, and if so, at what rate.

With most individual health insurance, there is less pressure to gather information about the applicant than in life insurance. Unless an individual health policy is the type that is not cancelable, the company can protect itself by increasing the price or declining to renew coverage at expiration. (Some health policies are guaranteed renewable but with the understanding that the company may increase the price at the time of renewal.) Nonetheless, detailed medical-record information is gathered in order to decide whether to accept the risk in the first instance, and how much to charge. Medical-record information is also an obvious consideration in writing disability insurance. Because these coverages are more susceptible than life insurance to abuse by insureds, companies want information concerning an applicant's character and his propensity for a disabling accident or illness. Occupation is also an important consideration—the loss of a finger is more disabling for a surgeon than a businessman—and the amount of disability income protection provided needs to be related to earned income.

The applicant and agent are the primary sources of information in underwriting life and health insurance. Because each has a financial interest in seeing the sale completed, however, investigative-reporting agencies (inspection bureaus) and other outside sources are often used to check the accuracy and completeness of the information applicants and agents provide. The types of inquiries these investigations typically involve and the manner in which inspection bureaus conduct them are described in Chapter 8. Here it is enough to point out that they can involve contacts with neighbors, employers, associates, bankers, and creditors; reviews of medical

---

[8] Business life insurance is life insurance purchased for the benefit of the business itself, e.g.: (1) to indemnify the business for the loss of a key employee; (2) as a source of funds to buy back or purchase ownership of a firm upon the death of a partner or key employee; or (3) as a source of funds in order to discharge financial responsibility pursuant to a contractual agreement.

records obtained from doctors or hospitals; and checks of public records for evidence of financial or legal difficulties.

Life and health insurers and investigative-reporting agencies acting on their behalf often contact third-party sources that have a confidential relationship with the applicant or insured, such as doctors, accountants, or lawyers, and thus an authorization is required before the information can be released. Typically, an applicant is required to sign such an authorization as a condition of having his application considered; is informed, as required by the Fair Credit Reporting Act (FCRA),[9] that an investigative report may be obtained; and is notified that information may be reported to the Medical Information Bureau (see below).

Normally, life insurance and medical expense claims are paid when a death certificate or medical bills are submitted. Claims for disability-income benefits are verified with the claimant's physician and employer and may be investigated more thoroughly if the claim appears questionable. The insurer's need for medical-record information in processing claims and the issues it raises for public policy on the confidentiality of the medical-care relationship are discussed in Chapter 7.

The Medical Information Bureau (MIB)

Like credit grantors, life and health insurers have organizations whose record-keeping services allow them to learn something about an applicant's previous contacts with other companies in the industry. The Medical Information Bureau (MIB) is an unincorporated, nonprofit trade association set up to facilitate the exchange of medical-record information among life insurers. Nearly 700 U.S. and Canadian life insurers subscribe to it and use it as an important source of information in underwriting life and health policies and in processing life and health claims.[10]

Each member company agrees to send the MIB a code anytime it develops information on an individual concerning certain medical and other conditions of some underwriting significance, except that companies are no longer supposed to report information developed in processing a claim. These codes are maintained by the MIB for seven years. Typically, a member company, on receiving an application, asks the MIB to check its files for information on the individual. If a code is found, it is sent to the inquiring company, which may then seek further details from the company that originally reported it, provided, however, that the inquiring company has first conducted its own investigation (e.g., a medical examination) to verify the reported condition. These "requests for details," which must be channeled through the MIB, are limited to 15 percent of the number of reports each company has submitted within the past year.[11] In 1975, there

---

[9] Fair Credit Reporting Act, 15 U.S.C. 1681 *et seq.*

[10] Written statement of the Medical Information Bureau (hereinafter cited as "MIB"), *Insurance Records*, Hearings before the Privacy Protection Study Commission, May 19, 1976, p. 11 (hereinafter cited as "Insurance Records Hearings").

[11] *Ibid.*, pp. 5-6.

were 75,000 of them out of a possible 300,000.[12]

The MIB does not investigate on its own, nor does it attempt to verify any information reported to it.[13] MIB Rule 9 specifies that member companies must report information regardless of the manner or form in which they acquire it.[14] Because many life insurers are also health insurers, information discovered in the course of health as well as life underwriting may thus be reported to the Bureau.

About 95 percent of the coded information contained in the MIB files is considered to be "medical." Only five percent is classified as nonmedical information, such as "reckless driving," "aviation," or "hazardous sport."[15] Currently, the MIB maintains information on 11 million individuals. Approximately three percent of all life applicants are uninsurable while six percent are "ratable."[16] In 1975, member companies submitted 2.45 million reports to the MIB,[17] and 17.5 million requests for information, while the MIB sent out 3.6 million responses.[18]

The Medical Information Bureau has been a controversial organization ever since its existence came to public attention in the mid-1960's. One of the most controversial aspects has been its use of the so-called *nonmedical* codes. In testimony before the Commission, the Bureau's Executive Director and General Counsel identified five: (1) reckless driving confirmed by the proposed insured or by official State or provincial (Canadian) motor vehicle bureau reports; (2) aviation with the proposed insured only as the source; (3) hazardous sport with the proposed insured only as the source; (4) nonmedical information where the source is *not* a consumer report (i.e., an inspection bureau report); and (5) nonmedical information received from a consumer report and not confirmed by the proposed insured.[19] He told the Commission that the fifth nonmedical code (nonmedical information received from a consumer report) could only refer to reckless driving, aviation, and hazardous sport and would not give life-style information.[20] In a letter sent to the Commission later, however, he states that "further review of MIB coding instructions shows that these nonspecific codes may also be

---

[12] *Ibid.*

[13] According to the report of a 1975 interview with then MIB Executive Director, Joseph C. Wilberding, the information companies were reporting to the Bureau came from the following sources: 33 percent from physicians, hospitals, or medical organizations; 15 percent from inspection bureau reports; and 53 percent from insurance forms filled out by the applicant himself or by the insurance agent, or from medical exams required by the companies. Mark Reutter, "Private Medical Records Aren't So Secret," *Baltimore Sun*, Juiy 13, 1975, "Trend" Section, pp. 1-4.

[14] MIB, "General Rules," *Handbook and Directory*, 1971, Rule 9. Since the Privacy Protection Study Commission hearings, the MIB has changed its rules. Rule 9 has been replaced by Rule D.2, which states that: "Underwriting information involving any impairments listed in the MIB Code Book and received by members from original medical or other sources, from official medical records, or from the applicant during the course of an application for personal life or health insurance must be reported to MIB regardless of the underwriting decision."

[15] Written statement of the MIB, Insurance Records Hearings, May 19, 1976, p. 10.

[16] *Ibid.*, p. 3.

[17] *Ibid.*, p. 4.

[18] *Ibid.*, p. 5.

[19] Testimony of the MIB, Insurance Records Hearings, May 19, 1976, pp. 236 - 38.

[20] *Ibid.*, p. 240.

used to report other types of nonmedical information, such as 'age,' 'environment,' 'foreign residence or travel,' 'occupation,' and 'finances.'"[21] Another object of controversy has been a code for reporting information about an individual's health, which, because of source, does not conform to the definition of medical-record information in the Fair Credit Reporting Act, i.e., information obtained from licensed physicians or medical practitioners, hospitals, clinics, or other medical or medically related facilities. *[15 U.S.C. 1681a(i)]* Such information could be reported in one of two ways. First, it could be reported by noting the specific code for the condition involved together with an additional symbol indicating that the information does not come within the FCRA definition.[22] Or second, as indicated in Executive Director Day's letter, it could be reported by using a code for "medical information received from a consumer report, not confirmed by the proposed insured or medical facility . . . ."[23]

On October 28, 1976, some months after the discussion of these matters in the Commission's hearings, the MIB informed the Commission that it was proposing the following changes to its code list. First, it was deleting three codes: (1) nonmedical information where the source is *not* a consumer report; (2) nonmedical information received from a consumer report not confirmed by the proposed insured; and (3) medical information received from a consumer report not confirmed by the proposed insured or a medical facility. The MIB assured the Commission that in the future "medical impairments may be reported only if information or records are received from the applicant or from licensed physicians, hospitals, clinics, or other medical or medically related facilities." It further stated that the three eliminated codes "will no longer be transmitted to member companies and will be purged or subjected to a 'no report order.'"[24]

Second, the remaining nonmedical codes (reckless driving, aviation, and hazardous sport confirmed by the proposed insured) may now only be reported to the MIB if such activity has occurred within the three years preceding the application at hand.[25] This was in response to the complaint that very old information could get into MIB files; that the practice of purging information *reported* more than seven years ago does not mean that all events or conditions coded in MIB records *occurred* within the previous seven years. For example, a reckless driving conviction that occurred 20 years ago could be noted in MIB records if a company reported it within the previous seven years.

Finally, the MIB also proposed to change the code which reports medical information obtained from a Federal agency to read "medical information obtained from a Federal medical source."[26]

A further source of controversy has been that codes dropped in the

---

[21] Letter from Neil M. Day, Executive Director and General Counsel, MIB, to the Privacy Protection Study Commission , September 30, 1976.

[22] Testimony of the MIB, Insurance Records Hearings, May 19, 1976, p. 279; Letter from Neil M. Day, MIB, to the Privacy Commission, September 30, 1976, p. 4.

[23] Letter from Neil M. Day, MIB, to the Privacy Commission, September 30, 1976, p. 4.

[24] Letter from Neil M. Day, MIB, to the Privacy Commission, October 28, 1976, p. 4.

[25] *Ibid.*

[26] *Ibid.*

past, as far as reporting requirements were concerned, are nonetheless still in the MIB file and thus can still be reported to MIB members. In reaction to this criticism, the MIB informed the Commission that the following discontinued codes will be purged or subjected to a "no report order": "'information obtained through a disability or health claim,' 'nonconformity,' 'age,' 'environment,' 'foreign residence or travel,' 'occupation,' 'insurance hazard,' and 'finances,'" and, of course, the three nonmedical codes mentioned above.[27]

Finally, the entire MIB system is predicated on the rule that the receiving company may not base an adverse underwriting decision on the information received from the MIB, but must make its own independent investigation.[28] Rule 14 reads:

> The information received through the Bureau shall not be used in whole or in part for the purpose of serving as a factor in establishing an applicant's eligibility for insurance.
>
> The application of this rule means that: (a) an application for insurance shall never be denied nor shall any charge therefore be increased wholly or partly because of information received through the Bureau and (b) all information received through the Bureau shall only be used as an alert signal.[29]

MIB's Executive Director told the Commission that ". . . Rule 14 is strictly adhered to by members who are regularly visited under the Company Visit Program."[30] When questioned, however, he agreed that the requirement to conduct an independent investigation may mean simply going to an investigative agency and getting old information that was once before the basis for an MIB report.[31] (Presumably this problem will be alleviated by the proposed elimination of inspection bureaus as authorized sources of certain types of information.) As to the Company Visit Program, moreover, it became apparent that Rule 14 may not be as strictly observed as the MIB would like to believe.

From time to time MIB staff members visit member companies to make certain that underwriters understand the Bureau's rules and to check on compliance with them.[32] A typical visit includes a check and review of the member's security arrangements and an "audit" of 20 randomly selected files.[33] Two major kinds of violations are looked for: (1) requests for details on MIB codes that have been submitted without first conducting the

---

[27] *Ibid.*, p. 5.
[28] Written Statement of the MIB, Insurance Records Hearings, May 19, 1976, p. 5.
[29] MIB, "General Rules," *Handbook and Directory*, 1971, Rule 14. This is now Rule D.4, which reads: "Underwriting information received from MIB shall be used to alert members of the need for further investigation of the applicants insurability. In the interest of sound underwriting and to avoid unfair competitive practices in the underwriting of risks, MIB record information shall not be used as the basis for establishing an applicant's eligibility for insurance." MIB, "General Rules," 1977, Rule D.4.
[30] Written statement of the MIB, Insurance Records Hearings, May 19, 1976, p. 13.
[31] Testimony of the MIB, Insurance Records Hearings, May 19, 1976, p. 250.
[32] Written statement of the MIB, Insurance Records Hearings, May 19, 1976, p.7.
[33] *Ibid.*, p. 16.

required independent investigation; and (2) adverse underwriting decisions that have been made solely on the basis of an MIB code (i.e., violations of Rule 14).[34] In a letter following his hearing testimony, the Executive Director told the Commission that in 1975, "161 member companies were visited and 3,200 underwriting files were examined . . .," but that "in fact only fifteen violations [of Rule 14]" were discovered.[35] Since the MIB sends out 3.5 million positive responses to company queries each year this means, if the sampling procedures permit such extrapolation, that overall there were approximately 15,000 violations of Rule 14 in 1975.

The efficacy of the investigation procedure was also questioned by the Commission. Each year the Company Visit Program looks at about 3,000 files (three companies per week, 150 companies per year, 20 files per company).[36] Because companies may have several regional offices, however, and because at the rate of 150 companies per year it would take five years to cover all the members, a considerable amount of slippage could go undetected.

Thus, in response to the Commission's expression of concern, the MIB has proposed the following changes. Each MIB member will now be required to adopt formal procedures to protect the confidentiality of MIB information. In addition, starting in 1977, each member must conduct at least annually "a self-audit program to determine whether it has complied with MIB's constitution and rules and whether its internal procedures have protected the . . . confidentiality of MIB information." In addition, the MIB investigation program, "will be expanded during the course of 1977 to include review of the results of members' self-audits." Such a review will include an on-premise inspection of internal procedures instituted by companies to implement certain aspects of MIB policy.[37]

Whether this voluntary program will be effective remains to be seen. The Commission, however, took the proposed changes into account in making its recommendations regarding insurance institutions and support organizations and believes that it has also found several ways of reinforcing the MIB initiative.

The Impairment Bureau

The Impairment Bureau, a service of the National Insurance Association, is another support organization that exists solely to facilitate communication among life and health insurers. The Impairment Bureau, however, differs from the Medical Information Bureau in several important respects.

In the first place, the Impairment Bureau's membership is much smaller and while all of its member companies may forward information to it, only five do so on a regular basis. Second, information about an individual is only sent to the Impairment Bureau when his application has been declined. Third, each member regularly receives a report on every

[34] Testimony of the MIB, Insurance Records Hearings, May 19, 1976, p. 235.
[35] Letter from Neil M. Day, MIB, to the Privacy Commission, September 30, 1976, pp. 2, 5.
[36] Testimony of the MIB, Insurance Records Hearings, May 19, 1976, pp. 245-47.
[37] Letter from Neil M. Day, MIB, to the Privacy Commission, October 28, 1976, pp. 1-3.

declination reported to the Bureau without having to ask for information on any particular individual. The Bureau compiles the information it receives on sheets which contain approximately 60 entries per page. Each entry contains the name of the applicant, his date and place of birth, the date of the rejection, a coded entry representing the cause of the declination, a coded entry representing the name of the reporting company, and the city and State where the applicant resides. This information, on approximately 2,000 declined applicants a year, is sent every other month to all member companies.

Like MIB records, Impairment Bureau records contain some information on conditions other than medical ones. Unlike the MIB, however, the Impairment Bureau does not have any specific rules to govern the use of the information it disseminates to member companies or the functioning of the Impairment Bureau itself. Each company may use the declination information as it sees fit and could, for instance, decline an applicant on the basis of the previous declination alone. On the other hand, the Impairment Bureau does not retain copies of the information submitted to it and has not done so since 1964. It merely compiles and distributes information to its members on the basis of the reports it gets from them. Once it has performed this function, the incoming reports are destroyed.[38]

PROPERTY AND LIABILITY INSURERS

In contrast to most life insurers, a property and liability insurance company has a ready market among people concerned about the replacement cost of tangible assets or about protecting themselves against liability claims brought by others. A property and liability company, moreover, can increase the price charged a policyholder or effectively cancel the risk by declining to renew coverage at the expiration of each contract period. Yet, as in the case of life and health insurance, detailed information is needed to decide whether to accept the risk in the first instance and how much to charge.

With property insurance, the items to be insured need to be identified accurately and valued, and the degree of care taken to protect them against fire, theft, or loss established. Since these coverages are also susceptible to abuse and fraud, the company wants to know enough about an applicant to make a reasonably confident estimate of his probable loss characteristics. Because liability insurance protects a policyholder against legal damages he may incur through negligence, underwriters consider it important to know, in the case of homeowners coverage, whether his home is well maintained and reasonably free of hazards, or to know, in the case of automobile insurance, whether he and others regularly using the car are responsible drivers. Although the applicant and agent are again primary sources of such

---

[38] This description of the Impairment Bureau is based on a letter from Charles A. Davis, Executive Director, National Insurance Association, to the Privacy Commission, May 17, 1976; and a Privacy Commission staff interview with Clarise Hall, National Insurance Association, August 27, 1976.

information, a company often checks the information they provide through an inspection bureau report or other sources considered more impartial.

The types of information needed to underwrite automobile insurance include name, address, date of birth, marital status, sex, occupation, driver's license number, use of vehicle, any physical impairments, how long licensed (if less than three years), and information regarding any accident or moving traffic violations in the past three years. State motor vehicle department records are often checked to verify the driving record of the applicant and members of his family. Some companies also require a physician's statement for elderly or physically impaired drivers. Finally, automobile underwriters sometimes order an investigative report on an applicant to find out whether his character, mode of living, and reputation in the community, may, in the judgment of the underwriter, influence the frequency of claims or the applicant's "defendability" in court. In other words, these reports are used by an auto insurer to determine whether the premium at which a policy may be issued is the correct one, but also, if highly derogatory information is uncovered, whether the policy should be issued, or if it has already been issued, whether it should be renewed.

For underwriting other forms of personal property and liability insurance, such as homeowners' policies, personal property floaters, fire policies, and boat policies, information requirements vary widely. To prepare and issue homeowners and fire policies, for example, the information required would include type of construction, age of dwelling, and distance to the nearest fire hydrant and fire department. For certain properties, an appraisal of their value may be required.

Information is, of course, also sought in the settlement of property and liability claims. Usually, this involves no other contact beyond the insured, the police or fire authorities, and the repair concerns involved in placing the property back in its original condition. Where the policy covers bodily injuries, however, contact may be made with the attending physician, the hospital, or other providers of medical services regarding the nature and extent of the injuries and the reasonableness of fees charged for services. In those few situations involving suspected fraud, the investigative activity may involve more extensive interviewing which can include witnesses, discussions with local law enforcement officials, and securing other background information that may be necessary to prepare for an effective defense if the claim is denied.

The investigation of claims or losses to determine the policyholder's liability to others (i.e., "third-party claims") will generally result in greater information gathering. A very detailed and complete investigation will frequently be made to determine the insured's responsibility for injury or damage and the degree or extent of such injury or damage. The role of inspection bureaus and private investigative agencies in the settlement of property and liability claims is briefly described in Chapter 8.

THE LOSS INDEXES

In the processing of claims, the indexes of the American Insurance

Association (AIA) may be checked to determine whether the claimant has had a series of prior losses or is submitting claims for the same loss to other companies. These indexes cover fire, burglary and theft, and fine arts losses, as well as third-party personal or bodily injury claims arising under automobile, homeowners, malpractice, and worker's compensation policies.[39] Many property and liability companies in the industry subscribe to the loss indexes. When a claim is filed, the insurer reports basic information on the claim to the proper index and, in return, receives from the index a copy of any previously filed reports on the claimant. In addition, the insurer, on the basis of such a report, can go to the company that filed it for further information.

The Fire Marshal Reporting Service

The Fire Marshal Reporting Service (FMRS) reports to fire marshals in 27 States on fire claims its members have paid. In addition, the FMRS maintains an index on reported fire losses in every State which any member can use to determine the prior loss record of a claimant as a check, for example, on arson. Membership in the Service is available to all interested insurance companies in the United States. At present 189 belong.[40]

Unlike reports made to the other indexes, reports made to the Fire Marshal Reporting Service are made after the claim has been paid. Reports are mandatory in those 27 States where the Fire Marshal must be notified of all losses above a minimum amount ranging from $10 to $250. Otherwise, the Service accepts reports of losses in amounts of $250 or more. Currently, there are 1,067,000 loss reports on file, all of them generated within the previous six years.[41]

Like Index System records (see below), Fire Marshal Reporting Service records are obtainable solely for the purpose of processing claims. "For a subscriber's authorized reporting office to initiate a search, the office must be handling and report a claim under the lines of coverage serviced . . . ."[42] The requirement that records be used only for claims purposes is enforced by requiring an index card from the inquiring subscriber before making any search or giving out any information.

The Burglary and Theft Loss Index

The Burglary and Theft Loss Index is maintained separately from the Fire Marshal Reporting Service, but membership in the FMRS entitles a company to receive reports from both systems. By using the Burglary and Theft Index, a member may detect simultaneous claims on the same item or a claim on a loss for which the claimant has previously been reimbursed. Part of the Burglary and Theft Loss Index is the Fine Arts Loss Index whose

---

[39] Testimony of the American Insurance Association (hereinafter cited as "AIA"), Insurance Records Hearings, May 21, 1976, pp. 755, 764 - 66.
[40] Ibid., pp. 764 - 65.
[41] Ibid., p. 765.
[42] Ibid.

function is to expose fraudulent claims involving art objects and to help locate missing ones that have been the subject of prior claims.[43]

The National Automobile Theft Bureau

The National Automobile Theft Bureau is a service organization sponsored, operated, and supported by approximately 500 insurance companies writing automobile, fire and theft insurance. The primary objectives of the Bureau are to assist in the recovery of stolen automobiles, to investigate automobile fire and theft losses which may be fraudulent, and to promote programs designed to prevent or reduce such losses. The Bureau operates as a national clearinghouse for stolen car information. Member companies report automobile thefts to the Bureau and the Bureau notifies member companies of recoveries, which are made primarily from police tow-away pounds.

According to its operations manual, the Bureau maintains the following record systems:

- *National Stolen Vehicle File.* This contains all Bureau members' reports on stolen vehicles and is used to detect fraudulent theft claims when several companies provide theft coverage on the same vehicle. Subfiles include information on impounded vehicles and stolen parts.
- *National Salvage File.* Records in this system indicate the disposition of all late model vehicles sold for salvage by member companies. Each entry of a salvage record creates an automatic inquiry against the master file by vehicle identification number, State license number, named insured, and salvage purchaser. Inquiries to the system may detect dual insurance coverage, multiple losses by a named insured, fraudulent claims based on the use of salvage documents or counterfeit documents on nonexistent vehicles.
- *Manufacturers' Production Records.* These are used in verifying that a vehicle was actually produced, and may also be used to find the dealer to whom a particular vehicle was originally sold. Each of the major U.S. manufacturers provides them to the Theft Bureau on microfilm.

The Index System

The Index System accumulates and makes available to its subscribers records concerning third-party personal and bodily injury claims. The Index System is maintained solely for use in claims processing. Ten branch offices serve all 50 States, the District of Columbia, the Commonwealth of Puerto Rico, and the Virgin Islands.[44] Subscribers report claims to the office servicing the territory where the incident occurred. Receipt of a properly

---

[43] *Ibid.*, p. 766.
[44] *Ibid.*, p. 756.

completed index card from a subscriber triggers a search of the Index. If the search turns up prior submissions on the claimant, the subscriber will be sent a photocopy of all of them.

The Index System is decentralized. Searches are normally limited to the records of the receiving branch office. Where the submitted index card shows that the claimant lives or once lived in the geographic area of another office, however, the inquiry is automatically referred to that other office for further checking and disclosure directly to the inquiring company of any record found.[45] The Index System "Instructions for Subscribers" says that "each subscriber is expected to cooperate by furnishing information contained in its claims files to other subscribers . . .,"[46] and also permit the insurer who has been asked for information to ask, in turn, for information from the inquirer. This allows two insurers who are in the act of settling claims by the same individual to communicate with each other.

There are two limits to these exchanges of claims information directly between insurers. First, "the exchange of information on [auto-related] medical payment, death and disability claims is at the discretion of the subscriber."[47] Second, "the Inquiry Form is to be used only in cases where *substantial claims* are involved to relieve subscribers of unnecessary work in procuring and examining closed files."[48] (Italics in the original.)

Reports to the Index System must be limited to claims of the following types: automobile liability (including uninsured motorists); automobile accident reparation (or personal injury protection); liability other than automobile, including liability claims under homeowners, commercial, multiple peril, yacht, pleasure craft, and aircraft policies; claims based on false arrest, assault and battery; malpractice claims; and worker's compensation claims. Worker's compensation claims are supposed to be reported only when they involve: (1) disability due to amputation, back injury, disfigurement, dislocation, eye injury, fracture, head injury, hernia, loss of hearing; (2) injuries with possible lost time payments of $500; (3) occupational diseases with possible medical and lost time payments of $1,000; (4) lost time claims by longshoremen and construction workers; or (5) a suspicion of fraud. A report *must* be made on any claim falling in these areas, except that reports on auto-related medical, death and disability claims are discretionary.[49]

Subscription to the Index System is open to "all insurance companies writing bodily injury liability coverages without regard to membership in the American Insurance Association."[50] To belong to the System, one must either be a liability insurer where liability claims are made against an

---

[45] American Insurance Association, "The Index System: Instructions for Subscribers," May, 1974, p. 2; Testimony of AIA, Insurance Records Hearings, May 21, 1976, p. 757.
[46] AIA, "Instructions for Subscribers," p. 3.
[47] *Ibid.*, p. 3.
[48] *Ibid.*
[49] *Ibid.*, p. 1.
[50] Testimony of AIA, Insurance Records Hearings, May 21, 1976, p. 755.

insured, or a self-insurer (such as an employer) which may have liability claims made directly against it.[51] About 26 percent of the Index System subscribers are self-insurers, but they represent a very small percentage of those that report.[52] In total, the Index System currently has 1,183 subscribing insurers and self-insurers and maintains records on approximately 28 million bodily injury claims reported during the System's six-year report retention period.[53]

A witness from the Index System offered some anecdotal evidence of its efficacy in uncovering fraud. One story tells of an elderly woman who constantly sustained minor injury to her mouth because of glass in a sandwich.

> In appearance, she resembled the classical image of . . . [a] grandmother—unassuming, nondemanding, doing a public service by calling attention to a deficiency in an insured's kitchen with no intent of making a fuss. From the viewpoint of the insurance carrier, liability was there; the demand was modest. The settlement was simple and uncomplicated. In fact . . . the insurance company almost had to force payment upon the claimant to accept any compensation for her inconvenience and minor injury.
>
> The sad truth was that "grandma" was a professional claimant. In her purse, she carried glass fragments which she would place in her mouth to cause a laceration. She would, then, call the waiter, display the physical evidence of the glass bit and the bloody napkin. Her manner would be mild and full of concern for other diners who might not be so fortunate in sustaining only a minor injury. She was literally in the claim business.
>
> Fortunately, in her travels, she did establish a pattern of reports involving subscribers [to the Index System] which led to an investigation of her activities and . . . agreement to divert her activities to more constructive lines.[54]

INFORMATION FLOWS FROM INSURANCE INSTITUTIONS

Both life and health and property and liability insurers routinely disclose information about an applicant or insured to the agent, to the extent necessary to service the policy; to reinsurers (when a company underwriting a large policy wants to reduce its exposure to loss); to an insured's physician; to inspection bureaus to facilitate the preparation of an investigative report; and to other types of investigators asked to prepare such reports. Because insurance is often required to buy a house, operate a car, pursue a career, or conduct a business, they may also disclose information about an individual to loan institutions and employers.

Further, life and health insurers, as indicated in the preceding sections, also disclose information to the Medical Information Bureau or the

---

[51] *Ibid.*, p. 769.
[52] *Ibid.*, p. 773.
[53] *Ibid.*, p. 756.
[54] *Ibid.*, pp. 760 - 61.

Impairment Bureau, and may provide details to another member insurer when requested to do so. Property and liability insurers, for their part, routinely notify the loss indexes of certain claims, and, in some cases, may notify the Insurance Crime Prevention Institute (see below).

Some potential insureds are judged to be so likely to produce adverse claim experience that they cannot obtain insurance in the normal manner. The driver with a poor record poses two problems. The first is meeting his own acute need for financial protection and perhaps his ability to qualify legally as a registered vehicle owner. The second is protecting society from the harm which an unsafe driver is likely to inflict on others. State "assigned-risk" insurance plans were formed to provide coverage to a driver whom companies consider an unacceptable risk and thus can require information about him to be disclosed to the administrators of the plan as well as to the insurance company to which his application is assigned.

Both life and health and property and liability insurers may release information about individuals to State insurance department officials in response to inquiries or complaints, and in the course of periodic examinations of company underwriting practices and procedures by such officials. Independent auditors employed by an insurance company make similar checks for the same purpose. In addition, because insurance companies are repositories of detailed information about individuals, their records are often requested by Federal as well as State government agencies and law enforcement authorities.

Finally, to make it possible for residents and property owners in high risk locations to purchase insurance against losses due to crime, civil disorders, and floods, partnerships have been formed between insurers and government agencies which make it necessary for insurers to disclose information about individuals to the agencies participating in such programs.

INFORMATION FLOWS FROM SUPPORT ORGANIZATIONS

The extensive flow of information about individuals into and out of organizations that conduct underwriting and claims investigations for insurers is described in Chapter 8. Medical Information Bureau rules, however, require a court order before information about an individual may be disclosed to anyone other than a member insurance company and while the property and liability loss indexes will be satisfied with a subpoena, rather than a court order,[55] they normally disclose information in their records only to a subscribing insurer submitting a properly prepared index card in connection with a current claim. The exceptions to this policy are the disclosures the Index System makes to the Marine Index Bureau and the disclosures any of the indexes may make to the Insurance Crime Prevention Institute (ICPI).

As indicated earlier, subscribers to the Index System are told to report

---

[55] A witness told the Commission that the loss indexes receive about 100 subpoenas a year from government agencies and that while for many they have no information to disclose, when they do have information they comply. *Ibid.*, p. 776.

lost-time claims filed by longshoremen. One reason for this is to make such information available to the Marine Index Bureau, whose subscribers are vessel owners. The owner of a vessel is responsible for its seaworthiness, which includes the quality of the crew.[56] In addition, an index may disclose information about an individual to the Insurance Crime Prevention Institute. As one witness from the indexes told the Commission: "We are an indicator. If the reports from the index system discern a pattern that might be of interest to the carrier or the ICPI . . . it is referred to them."[57] According to the testimony, however, an index would not send unsolicited reports to the ICPI unless it receives "four within a relatively short period of time of the same nature," or unless, in a two-claim situation, "the accident occurred on the same date with different insurers or at a different place with the same injury." Alternatively, the ICPI may come to an index and ask for a search, in which case it is treated in the same manner as any subscriber.[58]

The Insurance Crime Prevention Institute

The Insurance Crime Prevention Institute is a nonprofit corporation which operates as a trade association to uncover insurance fraud for property and liability insurers. The ICPI has its headquarters in Westport, Connecticut, maintains regional offices in New York City, Chicago, and Los Angeles, and has investigators stationed in major cities throughout the country.[59] Membership is open to property and liability insurance companies licensed in any of the 50 States.[60] Currently its membership is made up of 312 companies that underwrite 70 percent of the casualty and property insurance business.[61]

ICPI's purpose is to prevent and detect fraudulent insurance claims. Its focus is solely on criminal fraud, and the Institute's bylaws specifically prohibit it from assisting companies in claims settlement or civil actions incident to settlements.[62] Typically, an Institute investigation begins when a member sends information on a claim which the company suspects may involve criminal fraud. Other investigations are initiated by the ICPI based on information it receives from various sources, such as law enforcement agencies, "inside tipsters,"[63] or the loss indexes. In either case, however, the ICPI has complete control over its investigative activities, and may decline or initiate investigations as it sees fit.

If an ICPI investigation produces reasonable evidence of fraud, the

---

[56] *Ibid.*, p. 769.

[57] *Ibid.*, p. 768.

[58] *Ibid.*, p. 772.

[59] Statement of the Insurance Crime Prevention Institute (hereinafter cited as "ICPI"), Insurance Records Hearings, May 21, 1976, p. 1.

[60] ICPI, "By-Laws," Art. III, § 1.

[61] Written statement of ICPI, Insurance Records Hearings, May 21, 1976, p. 1; Testimony of ICPI, Insurance Records Hearings, May 21, 1976, p. 776.

[62] Written statement of ICPI, Insurance Records Hearings, May 21, 1976, p. 1; ICPI, "ICPI 1975," p. 2; ICPI, "By-Laws," Art. I.

[63] Written statement of ICPI, Insurance Records Hearings, May 21, 1976, p. 1.

matter will be "reported to a public law enforcement agency for whatever action it deems to be appropriate."[64] The ICPI investigator may go to insurance companies or an index for information. Going to an index will, of course, lead the investigator back to the insurers that have had claims filed by the individual under investigation. The investigation may consist of interviewing the claimant, verifying medical statements, verifying lost-wage statements, or searching police or court records.[65]

The Director of the ICPI testified that the Institute

> exercises extreme care in referring its investigative findings to law enforcement agencies . . . . Each case is checked for completeness of investigation and sufficiency of evidence before the investigator is authorized to present his report to a law enforcement agency. Aside from considerations of fairness to the subject of the investigation, civil tort law provides adequate incentive for caution.[66]

Where there is evidence of professional misconduct, such as where a physician inflates a bodily injury insurance claim, the ICPI can also make its file available to licensing authorities.[67]

ICPI characterized its relationship with the law enforcement community in its testimony as that of a "citizen coming forward with evidence of a crime."[68] The Institute will sign criminal complaints to initiate prosecution in instances where an insurance company has been the victim of a fraud and, when it does so, will voluntarily give a copy of its file to law enforcement officials. As the ICPI Director testified:

> It is a generally recognized exception to the principle of confidentiality that an insurance company, finding itself to be the victim of a fraudulent claim, may voluntarily release the pertinent records of that transaction to the police to obtain criminal justice . . . . The Institute, in effect, does no more than to perform this task for the insurance company.[69]

Occasionally, law enforcement officials will come to the ICPI for information:

> If there is a large arson in the Bronx on Sunday night, on Monday morning we are going to get a call to ask if we have a file on the owner . . . . If it is a legal and valid investigation, we will assist them in getting the information.[70]

The ICPI employs approximately 70 full-time investigators, most with

---

64 *Ibid.*
65 Testimony of ICPI, Insurance Records Hearings, May 21, 1976, pp. 776 - 77; ICPI, "ICPI - 1975."
66 Written statement of ICPI, Insurance Records Hearings, May 21, 1976, p. 2.
67 ICPI, "A Prosecutor's Introduction to ICPI," p. 4.
68 Written statement of ICPI, Insurance Records Hearings, May 21, 1976, p. 2.
69 *Ibid.*, citing *Burrows v. Superior Court*, 13 Cal. 3d. 238, 245 (1975) as by analogy providing an exception from the rule of confidentiality.
70 Testimony of ICPI, Insurance Records Hearings, May 21, 1976, pp. 784 - 85.

law enforcement backgrounds, and is licensed as a private detective agency in those jurisdictions which require licensing.[71] It investigates about 6,000 cases each year. In 1976, this resulted in the indictment of about 600 people. According to the testimony, it concentrates on two main areas of criminal fraud. The first is the ambulance-chasing attorney or the doctor who exaggerates claims, and the second is organized crime.[72]

THE INDIVIDUAL IN THE INSURANCE RELATIONSHIP

As is evident from the preceding sections, the insurance industry is highly dependent upon recorded information about individuals. This dependence creates a number of privacy protection problems, some of which are inherent in the insurance system, but can be controlled, and some of which present real or potential abuses that need to be eliminated.

THE INTRUSIVENESS OF CERTAIN COLLECTION PRACTICES

Insurance underwriting involves two separate decisions: (1) whether the insurer wants to insure the applicant at all (selection); and if so, (2) at what price and terms (classification). The need to make these two judgments dictates the kind and quality of information an insurance institution collects and maintains about an individual applicant or policyholder.

In making these two types of decisions insurers look to physical hazards—medical hazards in life and health underwriting and in property and liability underwriting, the condition of the property, its use, and its surroundings. Underwriters also look to what is termed moral hazard. Evaluation of moral hazard is made by examining attributes of the applicant which suggest a greater than average likelihood of a loss occurring or the potential for unusual severity of loss—either an absence of a desire on the part of the individual to safeguard himself or his property from loss or a positive willingness to create a loss or to deliberately inflate a claim.

Thus, it is not surprising that the evaluation of moral hazards, particularly in property and liability underwriting, is the area where the greatest number of objections to insurers' information collection practices have been raised. An inquiry may cover drinking habits, drug use, personal and business associates, reputation in the community, credit worthiness, occupational stability, deportment, housekeeping practices, criminal history, and activities that deviate from conventional standards of morality, such as living arrangements and sexual habits and preferences. Because the relevance of many of these particulars can be hard to demonstrate, and because the judgment as to their relevance is often left to the underwriter handling a particular case, their propriety has become subject to question.

From the standpoint of many applicants and insureds, the dichotomy between the individual's privacy interest and the insurer's interest in evaluating risk is probably not as great as it seems at first glance. The low-

---

[71] Ibid., p. 778; Written statement of ICPI, Insurance Records Hearings, May 21, 1976, p. 1; ICPI, "ICPI-1975," p. 9.

[72] Testimony of ICPI, Insurance Records Hearings, May 21, 1976, pp. 786-87.

risk applicant benefits from an underwriting evaluation that results in unusual risks being eliminated or written at a higher premium because that keeps the cost of his insurance down. The Commission was continually reminded that it is in the interest of the applicant to have complete and accurate information on which this judgment can be based so that he can be insured at the proper rate; that the insurer must be able to evaluate the risk it is being asked to assume if premium charges are to bear a reasonable relationship to expected losses and expenses for all insureds within a similar classification.

Economic forces may, however, work against a given individual. Because insurers compete against each other for the better risks, they do not have much incentive to look behind some of the criteria they use to sort the good risks from the bad. If their experience suggests, for example, that slovenly housekeepers make poor automobile insurance risks, they tend to be wary of all slovenly housekeepers. The problem, in other words, is not that the category of information lacks predictive value in all instances, but rather that it is applied too broadly.

Another source of concern in the area of intrusive collection practices stems from the use of so-called pretext interviews and other false or misleading information-gathering techniques. This concern was brought into sharp focus by recent publicity concerning Factual Service Bureau, Inc. (now Inner-Facts, Inc.), an investigative-support organization whose services were used by insurers in a number of cities throughout the country. Factual Service Bureau employees regularly misrepresented their identity and purpose in order to obtain medical-record information from hospitals and other medical-care providers without authorization. The insurers that used Factual Service Bureau should have known that it employed such intrusive techniques and generally engaged in questionable methods of information collection. Factual Service Bureau openly advertised its ability to procure confidential information about an individual without his authorization.[73] Thus, even the insurers who had no actual knowledge of the techniques being used by Factual Service Bureau on their behalf may be said to have condoned its activities by their silence or failure to investigate more fully the practices and techniques used.

The Factual Service Bureau case also illustrates a broader problem which results from the apparent lack of restraint exercised by insurers over the support organizations they use to collect information about individual applicants, insureds, and claimants. In the claims area particularly, where a great deal of money may be at stake or where the suspicion of fraud may be high, many insurance companies have tended to look the other way while hiring support organizations that use questionable information collection practices and techniques.

---

[73] A Factual Service Bureau advertising flyer asks, "Have you been denied medical authorization by a claimant? Does the claimant's attorney withhold medical information from you, or submit only 'partial' medical records? If either of the above is true, let Factual Service develop the true medical picture. We have specialized in background medical investigations for over two decades."

UNFAIR COLLECTION, USE, AND DISCLOSURE PRACTICES

Because of their acknowledged dependence upon information about individuals, insurance institutions are reluctant to deprive themselves of inexpensive access to it. There are few restrictions within the industry on the sharing of personally identifiable information or on obtaining it from sources outside the industry. This is true of insurance institutions and support organizations alike, and can lead to some highly questionable collection, use, and disclosure practices.

As indicated earlier, the Medical Information Bureau, until recently, retained claims information even though it no longer allowed it to be reported, and inserted a "failure to find impairment previously reported" code rather than deleting the impairment reference. To maximize the utility of information already collected, insurance institutions also piggyback on the information collection and use practices of other insurance institutions and support organizations. This dependence adds to the widespread exchange of information throughout the industry, not only by organizations like the Medical Information Bureau and the Impairment Bureau but by investigative-reporting agencies (inspection bureaus) and other insurance-support organizations that save and reuse the information they collect. Thus, once a mistake enters the system, its adverse effects are likely to proliferate, resulting in repeated unfairness to the individual.

The competition among insurance institutions has generally militated against adequate sensitivity to the fairness issue in record keeping. To be sure, this situation has been changing as particular companies have promulgated privacy protection principles to be followed in the conduct of their business. Except for the support organizations subject to the Fair Credit Reporting Act, however, record-keeping practices still remain by and large discretionary within the industry.

Insurance institutions and their support organizations have been concerned about certain types of disclosures to third parties and about data security problems. The admitted purpose of these safeguards, however, is to protect the business privilege as a limited defense to common law actions of defamation. Thus, they do little to constrain exchanges of information about individuals within the industry or to control the quality of the information used.

The lack of attention to fairness issues in record keeping about individuals has resulted in the structuring of information flows and uses so that *neither the insurance institution nor the individual applicant, insured, or claimant is responsible for the quality of the information used.* The individual is at a disadvantage because record-keeping practices within the industry are opaque from his point of view. He currently enters into an insurance transaction without being aware of the relationship's implications for his personal privacy because he does not understand how extensive or intrusive information gathering may be. Nor does he know the consequences of the notices on his application—for example, that the Medical Information Bureau notice means information about him may be reported to the Bureau not only from the application itself, but also as a consequence of the underwriting investigation the insurer may conduct. Because he lacks adequate knowledge of the practices followed, the individual cannot make the forces of the marketplace work for him. He is not given an opportunity to weigh the relative benefits which might be obtained through the insurance transaction against the personal cost of revealing and having others reveal information about him.

Nor does the individual always know why the insurer is collecting information about him, or when it is being collected for purposes unrelated to establishing his eligibility for an insurance benefit or service. Insurers frequently collect marketing and actuarial information through the application. When a claim is filed, they may collect information for the purpose of reviewing the propriety of a treating doctor's fees or procedures as well as the eligibility of the particular claimant or the particulars of the specific claim. They may collect additional information to determine the advisability of continuing to market a particular kind of insurance. Yet, they do not normally advise the individual that this is being done.

The individual is also placed at a disadvantage when he is asked to sign a form authorizing the release of recorded information about himself, because he is not specifically apprised of what he is consenting to. The commonly used blanket authorization form, in essence, authorizes the release of all information about the individual in the hands of anyone. Moreover, the type of authorization form currently used by insurance institutions typically has no stated purpose or expiration date, and may not be limited either as to the scope of the investigation or as to the sources of information. This again reflects the natural reluctance of insurance institutions to deprive themselves of easy access to any potentially useful information, or to decide in advance what information is needed for what purpose.

As far as fair use is concerned, the relationship between the individual and an insurer is often unnecessarily and undesirably attenuated. Information he provides about himself is only partly the basis for the decision made about him, and the decision is made by someone he does not know and with whom he normally has no direct interaction. In addition, records maintained by a variety of institutions within and without the industry may be brought to bear on the decision about him, while he believes he is only dealing with one such institution. That one institution, moreover, assumes no obligation to give him access to the information compiled about him or to afford him the opportunity to correct or amend information he believes to be inaccurate.

Under the existing system, the individual cannot adequately protect himself against the use of poor quality information in making underwriting decisions about him. Frequently, the individual is not told the reason for an adverse insurance decision. The insurance laws and regulations of many States require insurers to disclose to the individual (in some cases, only on request) the general reasons for *cancelling* or *refusing to renew* a personal automobile insurance policy. Few States, however, require insurance institutions to give individuals the reasons for a *declination* or a *rating*.[74] If the reason and supporting information for an adverse underwriting or rating decision do not arise out of a report prepared by a support organization subject to the disclosure provisions of the Fair Credit Reporting Act, the individual may be unable to find out why the decision was made, or whether inaccurate or incomplete information was at fault.

Life and health insurance institutions generally advise an applicant of the information that led to an adverse underwriting or rating decision only if they consider the information harmless (e.g., hazardous occupation, obvious health impairment). Typically, however, the specific items of information and their source are not revealed unless they came from a support organization subject to the Fair Credit Reporting Act, or from the applicant himself. When an individual requests a specific explanation for an adverse decision and the basis was medical-record information, most life insurers will divulge the information, but only to the applicant's personal physician. However, they virtually never tell the individual the specific reasons and supporting information for an adverse decision when the information concerns his character, morals, or life-style.

In property and liability insurance, an adverse decision may or may not lead to the insurer divulging the reasons and supporting information to the applicant. As in the life and health area, whether the *insurer* considers the information to be harmless will be a factor. With the exception of the State automobile insurance laws and regulations mentioned above, however, the consumer has no legal right to be told the reasons or information supporting an adverse insurance decision.

When an individual contacts the Medical Information Bureau, he or his physician, in the case of medical-record information, only learns the summary data that has been reported about him.[75] He does not learn how the reporting insurance company translated the underlying information into a code, and while he is told where the underlying information is, he, unlike another insurer, cannot get it automatically from the reporting company.

If the adverse decision was based on information in a report prepared by an inspection bureau, the Fair Credit Reporting Act only requires the insurer to tell the individual the organization's name and address. *[15 U.S.C. 1681m]* The individual has the right to learn the "nature and substance" of the information about him in the inspection bureau's files, but this is no assurance that he will be able to identify the reason for the adverse decision or the particular items of information on which it was based. To go to the inspection bureau is time-consuming for the individual and may effectively prevent him from getting on firm enough ground to ask for reconsideration of the decision if it turns out that there was erroneous information in the

---

[74] William J. Giacofci and John A. Andryszak, "Summary of State Insurance Laws and Regulations Serving to Protect the Individual's Right to Privacy," Maryland Casualty Company, July 1976.

[75] Testimony of the MIB, Insurance Records Hearings, May 19, 1976, pp. 265-67. The Federal Trade Commission believes that the MIB is subject to the Fair Credit Reporting Act and thus must give access. While the MIB denies this, it nonetheless grants access and thus the issue has not been brought to a head.

report. *To have a real voice in the quality of information on which decisions are based, the individual needs to know the reasons for the adverse action and the specific items of information that support the reasons.*

The Commission is also concerned that the mere fact of a previous adverse underwriting decision may unfairly stigmatize an individual who applies later for comparable insurance. Without knowing the reasons for it, some insurers use the mere fact of a previous declination or other adverse decision by another insurer as the basis for rejecting an applicant.[76] Yet a previous declination may have nothing to do with the individual's qualifications where, for instance, the insurer that declined him did so only because it had decided to restrict its underwriting in a certain area. Thus, when an insurer acts on the fact of a previous adverse decision alone, it may reject an individual whom it would otherwise have accepted if accurate and complete information were developed. Stigma may also result when an individual has previously purchased insurance from a "substandard" insurer or through an "assigned-risk" plan, even though the reasons for such previous action may not involve the individual or his eligibility directly.[77]

The Commission has not found that this problem exists in life and health insurance underwriting to the degree that it clearly does in personal property and liability insurance. Property and liability insurance applications often ask the individual whether he has previously been declined or rated, but rarely ask the reason for the rejection, presumably because, under the current system, the applicant will seldom know. A high percentage of the reasons may, in fact, relate to adverse characteristics possessed by the individual applicant or insured, as opposed to a general market condition unrelated to the individual's characteristics. Present practice, however, fails to distinguish between the two types of rejections.

Accepting from lay sources information that only a professional is competent to report is another questionable practice that stems from an insurer's reluctance to deprive itself of any information that may turn out to be useful. Medical-record information is crucial to life and health insurance underwriting and to claims processing. Collection of such technical information from anyone other than the individual himself, a medical source, or a close family member invites inaccuracies. Nevertheless, some insurers not only seek information concerning an individual's health from agents, or from the individual's neighbors, friends, and associates, but also use it as the basis for declining his application. Such information may also be communicated to other insurers. Until recently, the Medical Information

76 Written statement of Federal Insurance Administration, Department of Housing and Urban Development, Insurance Records Hearings, May 20, 1976, pp. 6 - 11; Department of Transportation Study, "Motor Vehicle Crash Losses and Their Compensation in the United States;" Testimony of Benjamin Lipson, Insurance Records Hearings, May 20, 1976, pp. 407-09.

77 Written statement of Federal Insurance Administration, Department of Housing and Urban Development, Insurance Records Hearings, May 20, 1976, p. 9; Department of Transportation Study, "Motor Vehicle Crash Losses: Their Compensation in the United States." p. 68.

Bureau accepted medical information obtained from lay sources, and the Impairment Bureau and the property and casualty loss indexes still do.[78]

Although support organizations such as the Medical Information Bureau have rules with respect to the type and quality of information reported to them, the rules are difficult to implement and enforce. The MIB, for example, has no way of knowing, except through periodic audits of member companies, whether medical or other information reported to it has come orginally from an authorized source. Thus, it cannot effectively control the quality of information in its files. Nor does the Bureau keep a complete accounting of all the disclosures,[79] the result being that it cannot always propagate corrections when inaccuracies are discovered. The property and liability loss indexes also have no way of knowing whether a subscriber has falsely filed an index card without having a real claim, or whether, once received by an insurance institution, the index information is used for other purposes, such as underwriting, or making a personnel decision.[80]

Perhaps the best example of the inability of support organizations to regulate the use of the information they provide is the Medical Information Bureau's rule which prohibits the use of a Bureau report, intended only as an alert, as the basis for declining an applicant.[81] Compliance with this rule has not been carefully audited in the past, and testimony before the Commission by the MIB indicates that as a result of the MIB's own audits there is evidence that some life insurers do render adverse decisions based solely on Medical Information Bureau codes.[82] Furthermore, the reinvestigation requirement the MIB imposes on its members can be satisfied by going to an inspection bureau and getting information on file there—the same information which another insurer may have used to decline the applicant.

To some extent these problems are endemic to data exchanges, like the MIB, that are controlled by their users. Being wholly dependent, they cannot be expected to enforce their rules against those who sustain them. The end result, however, is that poor quality information can, in a variety of ways, cause an individual to be denied an insurance benefit or privilege for which he would otherwise be eligible. The insurer may lose too, by forfeiting a customer or by having its relationship with an existing policyholder deteriorate. Obsolete, inaccurate, or incomplete information serves no one.

THE ABSENCE OF A STRICT DUTY OF CONFIDENTIALITY

There is an understandable public concern about the confidentiality of records about individuals that insurance institutions and their support

---

[78] Testimony of the MIB, Insurance Records Hearings, May 19, 1976, p. 263.
[79] *Ibid.*, pp. 235-36; 244-58.
[80] Testimony of the AIA, Insurance Records Hearings, May 21, 1976, p. 771.
[81] MIB, "General Rules," *Handbook and Directory*, Rule 14. Rule 14 is now Rule D.4.
[82] Testimony of the MIB, Insurance Records Hearings, May 19, 1976, pp. 234-36; 244-58. The Commission has no testimony from the Impairment Bureau on this issue, but problems no doubt exist with its subscribers as well. This would seem especially true since the Impairment Bureau lacks even those safeguards and rules under which the Medical Information Bureau operates.

organizations maintain. As previously noted, the collection of information about an individual without his full knowledge of the scope of the inquiry and its consequences may weaken the relationship between the insurer and the individual. The individual may be deterred from applying or may mistrust the insurer when he does apply. The Commission heard testimony that some people do not buy insurance for fear that the resulting information flow will come back to haunt them, either in a subsequent insurance decision or through disclosure to their employer.[83] Others do not use their benefits—for instance, psychiatric coverage—for fear claims information will not be held in strictest confidence.[84] In addition, the individual may be more likely to lie about information which he feels may go beyond the insurer. Confidentiality has become such a concern that some who maintain records about individuals, such as doctors and psychologists, are increasingly reluctant or unwilling to disclose the information in them, even when authorized to do so by the individual.[85] Other sources, such as neighbors and associates, may also refuse to provide information or may provide inaccurate information.

Although insurance institutions and support organizations now assume some responsibility for the confidentiality of the information they collect and maintain on individuals, earlier parts of this chapter show the extent to which personally identifiable information is disclosed by numerous insurance industry organizations. Within the industry, information sharing occurs on a routine basis. Moreover, information may be disclosed to those outside the industry without the individual's knowledge.[86] The Commission believes that the key to solving this important problem is to create an enforceable expectation of confidentiality which clearly delineates the circumstances under which an insurance institution or support organization may disclose information about an individual without his authorization.

CURRENT LEGAL RESTRAINTS ON RECORD-KEEPING PRACTICES

STATE INSURANCE REGULATION

The primary regulatory mechanisms for overseeing the activities of insurance institutions are at the State level. State regulation has developed around two basic aims: (1) maintaining the solvency of individual insurance companies; and, (2) assuring fair business practices and pricing. Although interest in the record-keeping practices of insurance institutions has increased in the last few years, few States have focused significant attention on the privacy protection problems the Commission has identified. No

---

[83] Written statement of Benjamin Lipson, Insurance Records Hearings, May 20, 1976, p. 7.

[84] *Ibid.*, p. 8; Testimony of Jerome S. Beigler, American Psychiatric Association, Insurance Records Hearings, May 20, 1976, pp. 358-360.

[85] Testimony of Jerome S. Beigler, American Psychiatric Association, Insurance Records Hearings, May 20, 1976, pp. 370-73.

[86] Testimony of the Index System, Insurance Records Hearings, May 21, 1976, p. 769; Testimony of Jerome S. Beigler, Insurance Records Hearings, pp. 361, 372; Written statement of the Blue Cross Organizations, Insurance Records Hearings, May 20, 1976, p. 5.

State, to the Commission's knowledge, has enacted privacy protection legislation which would affect insurance record-keeping practices. Moreover, regulation of insurance record-keeping practices at the State level is limited because State Insurance Departments do not have regulatory authority over most insurance-support organizations.

There are, however, existing regulatory mechanisms at the State level which could be used to implement some of the Commission's insurance recommendations. These include the unfair trade practices provisions of State insurance laws, and the authority State Insurance Commissioners have been given over the contents of those application forms which are considered part of the policy.

Most States have passed a version of the Model Unfair Trade Practices Act.[87] These laws are applicable to all types of insurance and are designed to protect the insurance consumer by prohibiting insurance institutions from engaging in a wide range of practices specifically defined by the Act to be unfair. The Act includes prohibitions against false advertising, defamation of competitors, boycotts, fraudulent financial statements, rebates, and unfair discrimination. Many States have added to this statute an Unfair Claims Practices Act which protects claimants by forbidding unreasonable claim settlement practices, including misrepresentation, delays in claim payments, and claim settlement offers which are so low as to compel claimants to institute litigation to collect their claims.

The Model Act provides the State Insurance Commissioner with several mechanisms to enforce the prohibition against defined unfair trade practices. The Commissioner has the authority to promulgate regulations identifying the methods of competition or practices which come under the specific prohibitions enumerated in the Act. In addition, the Commissioner may hold a hearing and issue a cease and desist order whenever he believes an insurer is engaging in one of the unfair practices. Monetary penalties or suspension or revocation of a company's license may also be imposed for a violation of the defined unfair trade practices where the insurer knew or should have known that it was in violation of the Act.

In addition to the Commissioner's powers to enforce defined unfair trade practices, the Model Act also provides that he may hold hearings on any act or practice which he believes is unfair, even though the practice is not specifically defined in the Act. If, after a hearing, an undefined act or practice is found to be unfair, the Commissioner may issue a cease and desist order. The Model Act, however, does not empower the Commissioner to add by regulation new acts to the defined unfair trade practices, or to impose monetary penalties for engaging in undefined unfair trade practices.

Some States already make use of the Unfair Trade Practices Act prohibition against unfair discrimination to regulate record-keeping practices. The regulations, however, are limited in scope and, in almost all instances, are concerned with the use of information in the underwriting process rather than its actual collection. For instance, the Privacy Commission heard testimony on the regulation of the relevance of information used

---

[87] Note: e.g., Cal. Ins. Code §§ 790.01, et seq. ; Mass. Gen. Laws Ann., ch. 93a; Vt. Stat. Ann. tit. 63, § 2451; Ill. Rev. Stat., ch. 121 1/2, § 261.

in the underwriting process from a representative of the California Insurance Department. California has used its regulatory authority under its unfair trade practices laws to prohibit unfairly discriminatory practices on account of sex, marital status, unconventional life-styles, and sexual orientations differing from the norm. The California Department normally does not attempt to prohibit collection; rather, it acts on an *ad hoc* basis to prohibit the *use* of certain criteria in underwriting decisions upon the receipt of complaints from insurance consumers.[88]

Because the Model Unfair Trade Practices Act is applicable to all lines of insurance and contains strong enforcement provisions, it can serve as an appropriate regulatory mechanism for several of the Commission's recommendations. It will, however, be necessary to amend the Act to define certain unfair record-keeping practices as unfair trade practices. These unfair practices would then be subject to the full range of regulatory and enforcement authority granted Insurance Commissioners under the Model Act, including the power to hold hearings and issue cease and desist orders, and to impose monetary penalties.

Many State Insurance Commissioners have an additional power which could assist in the implementation of certain of the Commission's recommendations. In many States, Commissioners have the authority to approve policy forms. In the case of life and health policies, application forms are considered a part of the policy, so they would be subject to the Commissioner's approval. Thus, Insurance Commissioners in a number of States would be in a position to monitor and enforce the Commission's notification, authorization, and previous adverse decision recommendations insofar as life and health insurance are concerned.

FEDERAL REGULATION

The Federal government has only one law which affects the record-keeping practices of the insurance industry—the Fair Credit Reporting Act. The FCRA governs the use of inspection bureau reports prepared by support organizations in connection with underwriting decisions by insurers, and thus its effect on insurance institutions is limited to their role as users of such reports. There are also a few State fair credit reporting statutes similar to the Federal one. The Commission believes that amending the Fair Credit Reporting Act is a good mechanism to implement many of its recommendations that are beyond the scope of the present Act, including some of its insurance recommendations. The scope of the Act could be broadened, and its title and enforcement framework could be altered to reflect the new scope presented by some of the Commission's recommendations. In addition, the oversight functions presently given to the Federal Trade Commission could be expanded, thus avoiding the necessity of creating a new Federal agency to oversee implementation of those Commission recommendations which are proposed for adoption by amendment of the FCRA.

---

[88] Testimony of the California Department of Insurance, Insurance Records Hearings, May 20, 1976, pp. 496-98.

THE COMMON LAW

The final constraint upon record-keeping practices in the insurance industry is provided by the common law actions of defamation and privacy. Defamation provides liability for damage to reputation caused by the publication of untrue information about an individual. The tort of invasion of privacy provides liability under certain circumstances for, among other things, public airing of private information about an individual. Insurance institutions and support organizations may be able to raise a qualified privilege in defense of such actions.

In recognition of the need for a free flow of information in commercial transactions, most States have recognized a qualified business privilege which provides a defense for otherwise defamatory statements when made to the proper parties, in a proper manner, and for a valid business purpose, except if the statement is false and made with malicious intent to injure the individual to whom it refers. Similarly, there is a qualified privilege for invasion of privacy actions. These limits on common law actions enable insurance institutions and support organizations to exchange information for legitimate purposes relatively free of legal restraints. As noted earlier, however, the privilege is available only when information is disclosed to someone deemed to have an interest in it. It is for this reason that insurance institutions and their support organizations are careful to guard against the disclosure of information to anyone outside of the industry.

RECOMMENDATIONS

The Commission's approach to the problems described in this chapter has been to focus on strengthening and balancing the relationship between the individual insurance applicant, policyholder, or claimant and the insurance institution with whom he deals. As indicated at the outset, the Commission's recommendations have three objectives:

(1) to create a proper balance between what an individual is expected to divulge about himself to a record-keeping organization and what he seeks in return (to minimize intrusiveness);

(2) to open up record-keeping operations in ways that will minimize the extent to which recorded information about an individual is itself a source of unfairness in any decision about him made on the basis of such information (to maximize fairness); and

(3) to create and define obligations with respect to the uses and disclosures that will be made of recorded personal information (to create a legitimate, enforceable expectation of confidentiality.)

In the insurance area, as in others it has studied, the Commission also believes that giving an individual certain rights without placing corresponding obligations on the institution with whom he has the primary record-keeping relationship is not likely to bring about adequate remedial action. Thus, the Commission believes that insurance institutions and insurance-support organizations must assume greater responsibility for their personal-data record-keeping practices. In some cases, this can be accomplished by bringing the forces of the marketplace to bear on record-keeping policy and practice, through voluntary adoption of standards set forth in this report, or through court action by individuals to enforce their rights. In others, government agencies should also be called upon to play monitoring and corrective roles. The Commission believes that both parties will benefit from this approach. The individual's position with respect to the records the insurance relationship generates about him will be strengthened, while insurers and insurance-support organizations will be assured of obtaining the kind of information that promotes fair and efficient operations. Greater confidence in insurance institutions and their role in society should result from opening up the process in this way.

One of the major reasons legislation is needed is that the individual is currently at a disadvantage in the insurance relationship. Some of the Commission's recommendations have attempted to protect the applicant, policyholder, or claimant by placing certain restraints on the insurer—limiting certain collection techniques, creating standards for the authorization forms used, and requiring reasonable procedures in the collection, use, and disclosure of information about an individual. The Commission's aim, however, is not so much to constrain insurance institutions and support organizations as it is to enhance the position of the individual so that he can protect his own privacy interests. To this end, the Commission has concluded that the insurer should inform the individual of the scope of its underwriting inquiry by a clear notice and an adequate authorization form; that the subject of an investigative report should be interviewed if he so desires; and that a mechanism should be created whereby the individual can question the propriety of a specific type of inquiry made in connection with an insurance decision about him. These recommendations are designed to give the individual a central role in the record-keeping practices (including information collection) of the insurance industry.

The ability of the individual to protect himself depends upon the knowledge he has of the records that are made about him. Thus, an individual should have access to a record about himself and a mechanism should exist whereby disputes concerning the accuracy of such a record can be settled. Access and correction rights are also needed to enable the individual to protect himself from investigations which exceed the scope of the notice he is given at the time he seeks to establish a relationship with an insurer, and to assure that the records maintained about him are accurate, timely, and complete. In addition, the individual should be informed of the reasons for an adverse decision about him and the specific information which supports those reasons, so that he can protect himself from unfair treatment resulting from the use of inaccurate, obsolete, or incomplete information.

This approach is not simply intended to be a procedural one. Rather, it is intended that the dynamics of the relationship between the insurer and the individual, rather than action by a legislature or regulator, will create certain standards governing the collection, maintenance, use, and disclosure of information by insurance institutions and support organizations. The Commission believes that notice, access, dispute, and an enforceable expectation of confidentiality are the tools an individual must have if he is to play an effective role in preventing the record-keeping practices of insurance institutions and support organizations from trespassing on his privacy interests. Armed with them, he can exert constructive pressure upon an insurer or agent. Even where the abuse concerns an insurance-support organization, pressure will be most effective on the insurer or agent, because the individual has a direct relationship with them, and because the prospect of adverse publicity that could affect the insurer's position in the market-place provides the insurer with more incentive to be responsive than the support organization.

Overall, the Commission believes that the strategy it proposes for implementing these recommendations is a reasonable and practical one in that it:

- uses existing regulatory and legislative mechanisms to the maximum extent possible;
- keeps the cost of administration and compliance at acceptable levels;
- provides inducements to comply willingly so that disputes over compliance can be kept to a minimum; and
- provides reasonable protection against liability for unintentional failure to comply, coupled with appropriate penalties for willful failure to comply.

As previously noted, because insurance is regulated primarily by State Insurance Departments, the Commission believes that the responsibility for implementing some of its recommendations should be properly lodged at the State level. In addition, the personal-data record-keeping practices of insurance institutions are also regulated to some extent by the Federal Fair Credit Reporting Act which the Commission believes is the proper vehicle for implementing recommendations that aim to strengthen the insurance relationship by eliminating artificial distinctions between the record-keeping practices of insurance institutions and the record-keeping practices of their support organizations. Finally, for reasons that are fully elaborated in Chapter 9 on government access to records about individuals maintained by organizations in the private sector, the Commission has concluded that the enforceable expectation of confidentiality it recommends must be implemented by Federal statute.

It should be noted, moreover, that the recommendations to be implemented by Federal statute, including those that would be implemented by amending the Fair Credit Reporting Act, give the individual actionable rights against insurance institutions and support organizations. The Commission has explicitly rejected the establishment of a Federal regulatory structure that could be quite costly both to the taxpayer and to the insurance industry. Instead, by making those who do not comply civilly liable for their failure to do so, and by making it comparatively easy for such actions to be brought, the Commission believes that a strong incentive for systemic reform will be created without subjecting those who favor reform to unnecessarily costly government regulation. The burden will fall on those who by their actions willfully and repeatedly disregard their responsibilities rather than on those who make a good faith effort to comply fully. In short, the implementation of the Commission's recommendations is designed to place an increasing financial burden on those companies who encourage costly disputes by resisting openness, or who fail to adopt reasonable procedures to control the collection, use, or disclosure of records about individuals.

Finally, insurance institutions should not be unduly exposed to liability which arises only because of the openness of the process. The objective of the Commission's recommendations is to cleanse the system of decisions based on inaccurate or incomplete information; not to create windfall recoveries for bad information or practices of the past.

Definitions for some of the terms used in the recommendations and discussion which follow may be found in the glossary at the end of this chapter.

Intrusiveness

The Commission's first three recommendations address the scope and character of the inquiry to which an insurer may require an individual to submit as a condition of establishing or maintaining an insurance relationship. Because insurance is concerned with the protection of individuals or personal property, the process of granting insurance coverage necessarily involves intrusions on personal privacy. The question is simply (or perhaps not so simply) how much of an intrusion and by what methods.

GOVERNMENTAL MECHANISMS

For some years now, controversies over the propriety of asking certain kinds of questions of an individual have generally centered on the relevance of the information sought to the decision to be made. For example, the Privacy Act of 1974 requires each Federal agency to limit its collection, maintenance, use and dissemination of information about individuals to that which "is relevant and necessary" to a purpose the agency is required to perform by statute or Executive Order.[89] The California Insurance Department, relying on its authority to prevent unfairly discriminatory practices, investigates the relevance of certain items of information used by insurers doing business in the State and may prohibit the use of any item whose relevance to underwriting decisions or pricing cannot be demonstrated to the Department's satisfaction.

A related, and in many respects more difficult, question concerns inquiries which, while demonstrably relevant, are objectionable on other grounds. Legislatures may prohibit, and have prohibited, the use of certain

---

[89] 5 U.S.C. 552a(e)(1).

items of information on fairness grounds. Race, for example, has been excluded as an eligibility or rating criterion for life underwriting even though its relevance to life expectancy can be demonstrated.[90] On the other hand, the Privacy Act of 1974 strives, not very successfully, to ban the collection and use of information pertaining to an individual's exercise of his First Amendment rights on the grounds that such inquiries by government agencies constitute an unwarranted invasion of personal privacy, i.e., that they fail the test not of relevance or fairness, but of propriety.[91]

Thus far, there have been few instances in which items of personal information have been proscribed on grounds of impropriety, i.e., unwarranted intrusiveness. In the insurance area, California has come close in proscribing the collection and use of information concerning "moral life-style."[92] The California approach is almost unique among State insurance regulatory authorities and all the California Department's other investigations, except for "moral life-style," have turned on other issues, such as fairness. In some cases regulation has not been necessary because the impropriety of certain types of inquiries is universally recognized. An example would be collection of information about an individual from his priest, minister, or rabbi.

It should be noted, moreover, that fairness and propriety issues usually cannot be dealt with in the same way. As briefly discussed in Chapter 2, when fairness is the overriding concern, such as in the Equal Credit Opportunity Act as amended, [15 U.S.C. 1691 et seq.], continued collection of certain information may be necessary to demonstrate that it is no longer being used to make decisions about individuals. For example, one cannot show that sex and race are not being systematically used to make credit decisions unless one can show that credit has been extended to women and minorities in proportion to their relative numbers in the credit grantor's market. And the most practical way to do that may well be to have the credit grantor record the sex and race of all applicants. This, however, is much different from situations where impropriety is the reason for proscribing information. There, the first act must be to prohibit collection, since the problem lies primarily in the asking of the question. Use may also be prohibited in such a situation but only to make sure that the information is totally excluded from the decision-making process.

The Commission believes that, in the future, society may have to cope with objections to the collection of certain information about an individual on the grounds that it is "nobody's business but his own." In some cases, these propriety issues may be resolved by prohibiting an inquiry on the grounds that it is irrelevant, but in others, where relevance can be

[90] See, for example, *Vital Statistics of the United States, 1972, Vol. II—Morality, Part A*. Table 5-3, Expectation of Life at Single Years of Age by Color and Sex, United States, 1972 (pp. 5-8), published by U.S. Department of Health, Education and Welfare, Public Health Service, Health Resources Administration, National Center for Health Statistics, Rockville, Maryland: 1976.

[91] 5 U.S.C. 552a(e)(7).

[92] Testimony of the California Department of Insurance, Insurance Records Hearings, May 20, 1976, p. 497; Letter from Angele Khachadour, California Department of Insurance, to the Privacy Commission, July 30, 1976. California Department of Insurance, Ruling No. 204.

demonstrated, proscription may be necessary on propriety grounds alone. In the Commission's view, questions of this nature are best resolved on a case-by-case basis. One must be concerned about undue government interference in such controversies. The Commission believes, moreover, that all such determinations must be prospective, so as to avoid retroactive punishment for behavior which at the time was wholly consistent with prevailing societal expectations and norms. However, the Commission also believes that institutional mechanisms are needed so that such questions can be raised and resolved.

Insurers have historically enjoyed considerable latitude in determining what information is and is not necessary to a given decision about an individual. Underwriting is far from an exact science. Moreover, industry spokesmen argue that the cost of collecting information is a powerful enough incentive to collect only relevant information. Yet others claim that insurance institutions collect a great deal of information whose relevance is questionable. Indeed, the industry has been criticized for *not* taking advantage of its actuarial and computer expertise to refine its relevance criteria.

To a large extent, the relevance-propriety issue in insurance stems from some insurers' belief that they should insure only those of "high moral character," and should shun those whose mode of living differs from what society considers normal. In a society as diverse as ours, however, determining what "society considers normal" is no easy task, and relying on the independent judgment of underwriters to make this determination has led to considerable difficulties.

The Commission is mindful of the complexities that lie beneath the surface of the relevance-propriety issue in the insurance area. It is aware that a few States have taken an interest in certain insurance-related inquiries. Most, however, have not. The Commission, moreover, is not fully persuaded that the problem can be handled exclusively through market mechanisms. Although *Recommendation (5)* (see below) seeks to set corrective market forces in motion, the necessity of insurance in today's society may make it difficult for individuals to make their objections felt. Furthermore, should there be sentiment in favor of banning a particular category of inquiry, irrespective of its relevance, some way will have to be found for society to estimate and consider the cost involved in such an action and the way in which the cost will be distributed. Thus, in light of all these considerations, and out of its desire to eliminate unreasonable invasions of personal privacy, the Commission recommends:

Recommendation (1):

That governmental mechanisms should exist for individuals to question the propriety of information collected or used by insurance institutions, and to bring such objections to the appropriate bodies which establish public policy. Legislation specifically prohibiting the use, or collection and use, of a specific item of information may result; or an existing agency or regulatory body may be given authority, or

use its currently delegated authority, to make such a determination with respect to the reasonableness of future use, or collection and use, of a specific item of information.

To implement this proposal, the Commission recommends that each State Insurance Commissioner collect individuals' complaints and questions concerning the propriety of particular types of inquiries, prepare periodic summary reports on the number of questions and complaints by category, and make them available to legislative bodies. If already authorized by the legislature, the Commissioner may take action. In California, for example, the legislature empowered the Commissioner to promulgate rules and regulations under the unfair trade practices article of the State insurance laws and the Commissioner then used that authority to declare discrimination based on sex, marital status, or sexual orientation a prohibited practice.[93] *[§790.03 and 790.10 of the California Insurance Code].* The rules the Commissioner adopts may prohibit the use of certain information in one line of insurance but not in another. Furthermore, within a given line of insurance, the Commissioner might allow certain information to be used as the basis for rating or determining risk, but not unless it has an impact on one or the other. For example, inquiry into the fact of cohabitation might be relevant in determining *use of a vehicle,* a valid rating criterion, but the mere fact of cohabitation, unrelated to vehicle use, could not be the basis of an underwriting or rating decision.

Currently, most Insurance Commissioners could address the use of irrelevant information under their general authority to hold hearings and issue cease and desist orders in connection with undefined unfair trade practices. The Commission believes, however, that the rule-making technique is fairer and more effective than looking one at a time at possible violations of a general prohibition against unfair trade practices. Not only will more insurers than the one offender have a say in the wisdom of the Commissioner's proposed prohibition, but the Commissioner's decision will only be subject to the narrow judicial review generally applied to rule-making decisions. The Federal Insurance Administrator could also collect the reports compiled by the State Insurance Commissioners and periodically report on them to the Congress.

An alternate and not mutually exclusive suggestion is that the Federal Insurance Administrator, or another appropriate Federal entity, collect complaints concerning the propriety of insurance inquiries directly from individual consumers and from time to time report and make recommendations on them to the Congress. It is not recommended, however, that the Federal Insurance Administrator have the rule-making authority urged for State Insurance Commissioners, since regulation of information practices within the insurance industry is currently a State function.

PRETEXT INTERVIEWS

As indicated earlier, Factual Service Bureau obtained some of its

---
[93] *Ibid.*

information through pretext interviews or other false or misleading representations.[94] A pretext interview is one in which the inquirer (1) pretends to be someone he is not; (2) pretends to represent someone he does not; or (3) misrepresents the true purpose of the interview. Mere silence on any or all of these points would not normally constitute a pretext interview. Indeed, an investigator could refuse to identify himself, his client, or the purpose of the inquiry, letting the person of whom the inquiry is being made infer whatever he wishes from such behavior. Nonetheless, an investigator dressed in a white lab coat making inquiries of a clerk in a hospital medical records room would be conducting a pretext interview if he allowed the clerk to assume he was a properly credentialed medical professional.

As pointed out in several chapters of this report, the Commission believes that some investigative practices are unreasonably intrusive, or at least have a high potential for depriving an individual of even a modicum of control over the disclosure of information about himself. An investigator conducting a pretext interview clearly raises that prospect. Thus, out of its desire to prevent unreasonable invasions of privacy resulting from the *techniques* used to collect information about individuals, the Commission recommends:

Recommendation (2):

That the Federal Fair Credit Reporting Act be amended to provide that no insurance institution or insurance-support organization may attempt to obtain information about an individual through pretext interviews or other false or misleading representations that seek to conceal the actual purpose(s) of the inquiry or investigation, or the identity or representative capacity of the inquirer or investigator.

This recommendation would apply to all insurance inquiries—whether for underwriting or first- or third-party claims. The prohibition would be enforceable by the Federal Trade Commission (FTC) against organizations that collect information by means of pretext interviews. An organization would be able to defend itself against an FTC action on the basis that it had taken reasonable steps and instituted reasonable procedures to prevent such activity. The use of pretext interviews should be made a civil offense, punishable by fines and cease and desist orders.

REASONABLE CARE IN THE USE OF SUPPORT ORGANIZATIONS

The reported practices of Factual Service Bureau also raise a legitimate concern about the care with which insurance institutions select and use the services of support organizations. An institution should not be totally unaccountable for the activities of others who perform services for it. The Commission believes that an insurance institution should have an affirmative obligation to check into the *modus operandi* of any support

---

[94] Testimony of Dale Tooley, District Attorney, Denver, Colo., *Medical Records*, Hearings before the Privacy Protection Study Commission, June 11, 1976, pp. 456 - 511.

organizations it uses or proposes to use; and that if an insurance institution does not use reasonable care in selecting or using such organizations, it should not be wholly absolved of responsibility for their actions. Moreover, a like obligation should obtain where one support organization uses the services of another.

Currently, the responsibility of an insurance institution for the acts of a support organization depends upon the degree of control the insurance institution exercises over the support organization. Most insurance-support organizations are independent contractors who traditionally reserve the authority to determine and assure compliance with the terms of their contract. Thus, under the laws of agency, an insurer may be absolved of any liability for the illegal acts of a support organization if those acts are not required by the terms of the contract.[95] In the Commission's opinion, the Factual Service Bureau case illustrates why this is not desirable. Accordingly, to deal with the responsibility of the institution that uses others to gather information about individuals for its own use, the Commission recommends:

Recommendation (3):

That the Federal Fair Credit Reporting Act be amended to provide that each insurance institution and insurance-support organization must exercise reasonable care in the selection and use of insurance-support organizations, so as to assure that the collection, maintenance, use, and disclosure practices of such organizations comply with the Commission's recommendations.

If it could be shown that an insurance institution had hired or used a support organization with knowledge, either actual or constructive, that the organization was engaging in improper collection practices, such as pretext interviews, an individual or the Federal Trade Commission could initiate action against both the insurance institution and the support organization and hold them jointly liable for the support organization's actions.

Fairness

THE REASONABLE PROCEDURES OBJECTIVE

As a general objective guiding the personal-data record-keeping practices of insurance institutions and their support organizations, the Commission recommends:

---

[95] See, e.g., *Milton v. Missouri Pacific Ry. Co.*, 193 Mo. 46, 91 S.W. 949 (1906); *Inscoe v. Globe Jewelry Co.*, 200 N.C. 580, 157 S.E. 794 (1932). However, recent decisions in a few jurisdictions indicate that under certain circumstances, one who contracts with a private investigator may not thereby insulate himself from liability for unlawful acts committed by the investigator by merely arguing that they were outside the scope of the contract. *Ellenberg v. Pinkerton's, Inc.*, 124 Ga. App. 648, 188 S.E. 2d 911 (1972); *Noble v. Sears, Roebuck and Co.*, 33 Cal. App. 3d 654, 109 Cal. Rptr. 269, 73 A.L.R.3d 1164 (1973).

Recommendation (4):

That each insurance institution and insurance-support organization, in order to maximize fairness in its decision-making processes, have reasonable procedures to assure the accuracy, completeness, and timeliness of information it collects, maintains, or discloses about an individual.

Subsection 3(e)(5) of the Privacy Act of 1974 requires each Federal agency to

collect, maintain, use and disclose[96] all records which are used by the agency in making any determination about any individual with such accuracy, relevance, timeliness, and completeness as is reasonably necessary to assure fairness to the individual in the determination.

This provision is a requirement on management wholly independent of the rights the Act gives an individual. For a Federal agency whose administrative procedures are subject to congressional oversight, it is an appropriate requirement.[97] The same, however, cannot be said of its applicability to the private sector.

As pointed out in Chapter 1, the Commission believes that the mix of rights and obligations its private-sector recommendations would establish are in themselves incentive enough to foster the kind of management attention to personal data record-keeping policy and practice that subsection 3(e)(5) of the Privacy Act requires. Thus, the Commission does not recommend that *Recommendation (4)* be incorporated in statute or regulation. Rather it envisages *Recommendation (4)* being implemented automatically as a consequence of the adoption of the other recommendations in this section, particularly *Recommendations (10), (11), (12), (13),* and *(16),* on access, correction, adverse decisions, disclosure of information from proper medical sources, and *Recommendations (5), (6),* and *(17),* on notice and disclosure.

The adoption of these recommendations will promote the maintenance of reasonable procedures by insurance institutions to assure the accuracy, completeness, and timeliness of information and provide a means whereby information collected, maintained, or disclosed may be corrected or updated by the individual.

FAIRNESS IN COLLECTION

NOTICE REGARDING COLLECTION FROM THIRD PARTIES

As indicated in the discussion of *Recommendation (1)*, the Commission believes that the type of governmental mechanism called for should be used mainly in instances where the forces of the marketplace are not strong

---

[96] The Act's definition of "maintain" includes all four record-keeping functions: collection, maintenance, use, and dissemination.

[97] For more detailed discussion of this requirement, and the problems agencies have had implementing it, see Chapter 13.

enough to induce the elimination of objectionable items from the insurer's scope of inquiry—for example, items that are demonstrably relevant but nonetheless objectionable on the grounds of propriety. To make market forces work to the advantage of the insurance purchaser, however, he must know the type of information that may be developed and considered in the decision-making process for an insurance transaction. Otherwise, he has no way of judging whether to take his business elsewhere. The application form itself serves to apprise the individual of some of the information that will be gathered about him, but as previously pointed out, the application normally gives at best only faint clues as to the type of inquiry that may be made of sources other than the individual himself.

Thus, to minimize the need for public-policy determinations as to the propriety of an insurer's inquiries about an individual, as well as inform the individual of the disclosures that must be made in order to obtain a favorable decision on his insurance application, the Commission recommends:

Recommendation (5):

That an insurance institution, prior to collecting information about an applicant or principal insured from another person in connection with an insurance transaction, notify him as to:

(a)   the types of information expected to be collected about him from third parties and that are not collected on the application, and, as to information regarding character, general reputation, and mode of living, each area of inquiry;

(b)   the techniques that may be used to collect such types of information;

(c)   the types of sources that are expected to be asked to provide each type of information about him;

(d)   the types of parties to whom and circumstances under which information about the individual may be disclosed without his authorization, and the types of information that may be disclosed;

(e)   the procedures established by statute by which the individual may gain access to any resulting record about himself;

(f)   the procedures whereby the individual may correct, amend, delete, or dispute any resulting record about himself;

(g)   the fact that information in any report prepared by a consumer-reporting agency (as defined by the Fair Credit Reporting Act) may be retained by that organization and subsequently disclosed by it to others.

Recommendation (5) would not apply to information collected for first- or third-party claims or for marketing purposes where the information is collected prior to the initial application. In all other cases, however, it would provide the individual with information about the scope of inquiry to which he is agreeing; the manner in which the inquiry will be conducted (e.g., through interviews of neighbors and associates) and the disclosures other institutions may possibly make in response to an inquiry from the insurer or an insurance-support organization. Most importantly, it would apprise the individual of the types of uses that may later be made of information without his authorization—for example, of medical-record information acquired by the insurer, or of "adverse information" acquired and retained by an investigative-reporting agency—while at the same time anticipating his need or desire to see and copy, or correct, information developed in the course of the inquiry. Thus, the recommendation would provide the individual with a detailed map of the information flows attendant upon the relationship he proposes to establish with the insurer.

It should be noted, moreover, that the subsection (a) requirement to notify as to "each area of inquiry" when information regarding character, general reputation, and mode of living is to be collected from a third party anticipates a level of specificity finer than currently considered acceptable under the Fair Credit Reporting Act. Furthermore, while the recommendation does not apply to information collected in connection with first- or third-party claims or for marketing purposes prior to the time the individual submits his application, the subsection (d) requirement to notify the individual of those parties to whom the information may be disclosed without his authorization would include notice of the fact that information on first-party property and liability claimants is sometimes disclosed to the loss indexes and the Insurance Crime Prevention Institute.

While unanimously agreeing that the type of notice called for in *Recommendation (5)* is necessary to solve the problems it addresses, the Commission was concerned about its practicality. One insurer, however, drafted an example which showed that the requirements of *Recommendation (5)* could be met by a notice that is neither unreasonably lengthy nor unreasonably complex.

As to implementation, while the Fair Credit Reporting Act governs notice requirements to some extent, Insurance Commissioners can also independently monitor industry compliance through their hearing authority under unfair trade practices laws as well as their authority to approve certain application forms. Finally, *Recommendation (5)* may be self-enforcing because *Recommendations (11)* and *(12)*, if adopted, will give the individual a right to have information beyond the scope of the notice given him deleted from any resulting underwriting or support-organization record about him.

NOTICE AS THE COLLECTION LIMITATION

The notice given pursuant to *Recommendation (5)* will be useless if the insurer's inquiry goes beyond what the notice anticipates. Furthermore, as indicated in the discussion of *Recommendation (3)* on reasonable care in the selection of support organizations, one of the problems with the insurance relationship is the degree to which it is attenuated by the insurer's frequent reliance on independent contractors in gathering information about individuals.

Thus, to assure that there will be consistency between the scope, techniques, and sources described in the *Recommendation (5)* notice and the actual inquiry that takes place, the Commission recommends:

Recommendation (6):

That an insurance institution limit:

(a)   its own information collection and disclosure practices to those specified in the notice called for in *Recommendation (5)*; and

(b)   its request to any organization it asks to collect information on its behalf to information, techniques, and sources specified in the notice called for in *Recommendation (5)*.

Like the notice recommendation itself, this recommendation does not apply to information collected in connection with first- or third-party claims or for marketing purposes where the information is collected prior to the initial application. Compliance with *Recommendation (6)* could be verified through the correction procedures called for in *Recommendations (11)* and *(12)* as well as Insurance Department examinations. If an individual finds that the insurer has information beyond that specified in the notice, the individual should be able to have it deleted from his record.

INFORMATION FOR MARKETING AND RESEARCH

Subsection 3(e)(3) of the Privacy Act of 1974 requires agencies to advise individuals whether the divulgence of particular items of information is mandatory or voluntary and the consequences of refusing to divulge them. The mandatory and voluntary concepts, however, have little meaning in the private sector, inasmuch as an individual's divulgences are all "voluntary" and an insurance institution can make "mandatory" anything it wishes. As a practical matter, an individual may have little choice but to comply with whatever requests for information are made of him. An example of the trepidation this can cause will be found in the discussion of the Blue Cross-Blue Shield psychiatric claims form in Chapter 7, on the medical-care relationship. Since this is so, insurance institutions should at least indicate on their application forms any requested information which is unnecessary for insurance coverage determination purposes but which is sought for marketing, research, or other purposes. Otherwise individuals will have no way of knowing whether such inquiries are necessary, and thus whether they should bring pressure on the insurer to make the inquiries truly voluntary. Accordingly, the Commission recommends:

Recommendation (7):

That any insurance institution or insurance-support organization clearly specify to an individual those items of inquiry desired for marketing, research, or other purposes not directly related to establishing the individual's eligibility for an insurance benefit or

service being sought and which may be used for such purposes in individually identifiable form.

This recommendation, which would not apply to third-party claim transactions, should be voluntarily complied with by insurers and support organizations. While the determination of what is required to establish eligibility is left to the individual company and will undoubtedly vary to some degree, fairness to the individual requires that he be apprised of those items of information desired, but not required by the company to determine acceptability or price.

AUTHORIZATION STATEMENTS

The authorization forms used by the insurance industry determine what information insurance institutions and their support organizations can obtain from those with whom an individual has a confidential relationship. Many authorization forms now in use are so broad as to constitute an invitation to abuse. Many do not indicate that they will be used by investigative-reporting agency representatives to develop inspection reports or acquire medical-record information to be transmitted to the insurer. Many do not indicate that they will be used to get credit reports, or information from banks and other organizations.

Although today, banks, employers, and some other types of record-keeping organizations may be willing to disclose certain information about an individual without his authorization, the Commission's recommendations with respect to those types of organizations would make obtaining the individual's prior authorization necessary. When that happens, as well as in those situations where record keepers have confidential relationships with individuals today, such as in the medical-care relationship, the record keeper on whom the duty of confidentiality rests will be the final arbiter of what constitutes a valid authorization. As a practical matter, however, such a record keeper may be hard-pressed to refuse to honor a broadly worded authorization if the result is grave inconvenience to the individual or refusal to reimburse the record keeper for services already rendered to the individual. Thus, to set the standards whereby those who have a duty of confidentiality to an individual may properly be asked to disclose information about him to others, the Commission recommends:

Recommendation (8):

That no insurance institution or insurance-support organization ask, require, or otherwise induce an individual, or someone authorized to act on his behalf, to sign any statement authorizing any individual or institution to disclose information about him, or about any other individual, unless the statement is:

(a) in plain language;
(b) dated;
(c) specific as to the individuals and institutions he is authorizing to

disclose information about him who are known at the time the authorization is signed, and general as to others whose specific identity is not known at the time the authorization is signed;

(d)   specific as to the nature of the information he is authorizing to be disclosed;

(e)   specific as to the individuals or institutions to whom he is authorizing information to be disclosed;

(f)   specific as to the purpose(s) for which the information may be used by any of the parties named in (e), both at the time of the disclosure and at any time in the future;

(g)   specific as to its expiration date which should be for a reasonable period of time not to exceed one year, and in the case of life insurance or noncancelable or guaranteed renewable health insurance, two years after the date of the policy.

The requirements of *Recommendation (8)* are not as severe as they may seem. Life and health insurance institutions regularly obtain authorizations as a part of their applications. Because of the individual's need for insurance, he exercises little bargaining power over the terms of the authorization. If a claim is involved, the authorization is obtained as a condition to considering the claim. It does the claimant little good to refuse to sign the authorization, for then he must go through the burden of suing the insurer, and even then much of the information will be available during discovery. Because insurers can basically dictate the terms of the authorization, the Commission concluded that the terms of the authorization needed to be specified so that the individual would know what he was agreeing to have disclosed, and so that those who held information of a confidential nature would know that they had received a valid authorization from the individual to release information to others.

Subsection (f) is especially important because it provides the individual with a description of the uses that may subsequently be made of information obtained about him pursuant to authorization. One particular example is that an individual would have to be told that information obtained from a medical-care provider in connection with underwriting may later be used for claim purposes.

Subsection (c) requires the authorization to be as specific as possible. It must specifically name those individuals and organizations authorized to release information about him who are known at the time the authorization is obtained. But if, for instance, an insurer subsequently learns of an attending physician whom the individual has not revealed, then the more general language of the authorization can be used with regard to that physician. Returning to the individual every time an insurer learned of a new source would be expensive and, in some cases, distressing to the individual, since it could delay processing of his application. Moreover, the subsequently identified source, a physician, for example, would still only be asked to disclose information of the sort described pursuant to subsection (d) and for the purpose specified pursuant to subsection (f). In addition, the individual would ultimately be able to identify every record-keeper contact by exercising the access rights Commission *Recommendations (10)* and *(13)*, below, would give him.

Subsection (g) limits the validity of the authorization to a reasonable period of time not to exceed one year. The only exceptions to this are for life insurance and noncancelable or guaranteed renewable health insurance where an authorization signed in connection with an application would be valid for two years from the date of the policy. Those types of policies, it will be remembered, are contestable for two years after they are issued and during that period an insurer needs to be able to protect itself from fraud or misrepresentation at the time of application.

Recommendation (8) would be implemented through the refusal of a holder of confidential information to release it unless presented with a valid authorization. It has also been suggested to the Commission that the National Association of Insurance Commissioners or the Commission on Uniform State laws might well develop standard authorization forms to achieve and facilitate the desired uniformity. Further, it should be noted that the necessary generality permitted by parts of *Recommendation (8)* need not apply to an insurance institution that obtains an authorization from an applicant, insured, or claimant permitting it to release confidential information to others. In that case, the authorization form can and should be specific as to what information, to whom, and for what purpose.

INVESTIGATIVE INTERVIEWS

As a general policy, the Commission believes that record-keeping institutions should strive as much as possible to collect information about an individual from the individual himself, rather than rely primarily on third-party sources. Furthermore, where an investigative report is being prepared, such a practice should not just be encouraged; it should be required if the individual so wishes.

Although inaccuracies in investigative reports prepared by inspection bureaus were a major stimulus to enactment of the Fair Credit Reporting Act, it has not been possible to determine whether the Act has substantially reduced the error rate. The major purposes of an investigative report are to: (1) verify information supplied by the applicant or his agent; and (2) develop information about the applicant's character, general reputation, and mode of living—lines of inquiry which must perforce involve a certain amount of subjective evaluation. Moreover, as Chapter 8 points out, it has been alleged that some reports get prepared without the investigator ever contacting anyone at all. Whatever the merits of that controversy, requiring an interview with the subject of a report as an affirmative requirement will help to resolve it and, if industry spokesmen are correct about the usefulness of interviews with report subjects, such interviews will improve the quality of the information inspection bureaus transmit to their insurer clients.

Thus, the Commission recommends:

Recommendation (9):

That the Federal Fair Credit Reporting Act be amended to provide that any insurance institution that may obtain an investigative report on an applicant or insured inform him that he may, upon request, be interviewed in connection with the preparation of the investigative report. The insurance institution and investigative agency must institute reasonable procedures to assure that such interviews are performed if requested. When an individual requests an interview and cannot reasonably be contacted, the obligation of the institution preparing the investigative report can be discharged by mailing a copy of the report, when prepared, to the individual.

This recommendation would not apply to any investigative report about an individual made in reasonable anticipation of civil or criminal action, or for use in defense or settlement of an insurance claim. Nor would it require an interview in every instance, since the individual would have to request it and presumably would make himself available for the interview. Not all individuals will seek such an opportunity. When an individual requests an interview and cannot be contacted using reasonable procedures, the requirement for an interview can be discharged by mailing a copy of the report to him.

The Commission considered having the interview occur just prior to sending the report off to the insurer, on the theory that the individual would then be in a position to review the information which had been gathered and, if necessary, to correct, amend, or dispute it. However, the Commission concluded that the difficulties involved in making a personal contact at a specific time could work to the disadvantage of the individual anxious to get his insurance application processed. Furthermore, the report is often not prepared until the investigator returns to his office. An alternative, also considered and rejected, would have required that a copy of the report be sent to the individual at the same time it is sent to the insurer. This was rejected because of the cost involved (a copy of every report prepared would have to be sent, regardless of whether the report resulted in an adverse decision) and because the adoption of *Recommendations (10)* and *(13)*, below, would make the report available to the individual on a see and copy basis from either the insurer or the investigative-reporting agency.

In incorporating this requirement into the Fair Credit Reporting Act, it should be made clear that the interview requirement applies to underwriting investigations undertaken by insurers themselves as well as by inspection bureaus.

FAIRNESS IN USE

ACCESS TO RECORDS

Access to records, as a general concept of fair record-keeping practice, should be extended to insurance records. Allowing an individual to see and copy a record kept about him can be advantageous to the insurance institution as well as to the individual. As suggested earlier, the records an insurance institution maintains about individuals are numerous and can serve a variety of functions. Except for medical records (information from which insurers also maintain), an insurance institution's records may contain information on more dimensions of an individual's life than almost any other type of record the Commission has examined. Moreover, several of the Commission's other recommendations depend on the individual being able to have access to insurance records about himself at times other than when an adverse underwriting decision has been made about him. For example, the notice requirement proposed in *Recommendation (5)*, and the limitation on collection practices in *Recommendation (6)*, depend on the individual being able to find out what information has been collected about him. And, as in other areas, the authorization statement an individual is asked to sign allowing an insurer to disclose information about him will be a meaningless piece of paper if he cannot learn what he has authorized to be disclosed.

Currently, an individual does not have a legal right to see or even learn the nature and substance of information maintained about him by an insurer, or by any insurance-support organization not subject to the Fair Credit Reporting Act. Moreover, the FCRA only requires an investigative-reporting agency to disclose to an individual the "nature and substance" of information in a report it has prepared about him. *[15 U.S.C. 1681g(a)(1)]* The Medical Information Bureau voluntarily gives an individual access to the summary data it maintains on him, if he so requests, but the individual has no legal right of access to anything held by an insurer, and thus, may not be able to figure out why the MIB record says what it does, or get the insurer that caused the MIB record to be created to correct errors in it.

To overcome these deficiencies, the Commission recommends:

Recommendation (10):

That the Federal Fair Credit Reporting Act be amended to provide:

(a)   **That, upon request by an individual, an insurance institution or insurance-support organization must:**
  (i)   **inform the individual, after verifying his identity, whether it has any recorded information pertaining to him; and**
  (ii)   **permit the individual to see and copy any such recorded information, either in person or by mail; or**
  (iii) **apprise the individual of the nature and substance of any such recorded information by telephone; and**
  (iv)   **permit the individual to use one or the other of the methods of access provided in (a)(ii) and (iii), or both if he prefers.**

The insurance institution or insurance-support organization may charge a reasonable copying fee for any copies provided to the individual. Any such recorded information should be made available to the individual, but need not contain the name or other identifying

particulars of any source (other than an institutional source) of information in the record who has provided such information on the condition that his identity not be revealed, and need not reveal a confidential numerical code.

(b)   That notwithstanding part (a), with respect to medical-record information maintained by an insurance institution or an insurance-support organization, an individual has a right of access to that information, either directly or through a licensed medical professional designated by the individual, whichever the insurance institution or support organization prefers.

As far as insurance institutions are concerned, it is the Commission's intention that this right of access be to any reasonably described information about the individual. In the case of an applicant, for example, commonly used identifiers such as name and address, coverage requested, and possibly date of application, ought to be enough to identify the record requested. The fact that information on one individual is contained in a record on another would not preclude the first from being able to see and copy it so long as he can provide the requisite identifier. Also, an individual should be able to see and copy information about other people in a record pertaining to himself if it is pertinent to his relationship with the insurer. For example, a husband who has an automobile policy that insures both him and his wife should be able to review his entire file, including any information in it about his wife. Conversely, as an insured, the wife should be able to see anything in the file on either herself or her husband.

The proposed right of access would extend to all records about an individual that are reasonably retrievable. Thus, it would include all information in a credit or investigative report, except that the identity of a non-institutional source (for instance, a neighbor or associate) need not be revealed where such a source provided information on the condition that his identity not be revealed. The individual, however, would have full access to all information such a source provided.

This, it will be noted, is a major departure from current practice wherein an insurer is customarily constrained from disclosing the contents of an investigative report to the individual by provisions in its contract with the inspection bureau. In the future, if the Commission's recommendations are adopted, such contractual constraints will not be possible. Moreover, neither the insurer nor the inspection bureau will be able to withhold the identity of any *institutional* sources.

The proposed right of access would also extend to medical-record information held by an insurer or insurance-support organization, although either organization would have the option of disclosing information to the individual through a licensed medical professional designated by the individual. The medical professional would be obligated to allow the individual to see and copy it upon request by the individual.

Finally, to make his access right convenient to exercise, the recommendation would allow an individual or a licensed medical professional designated by him pursuant to subsection (b), to see and copy records in person or by mail, or to have their nature and substance disclosed by telephone. This, too, is a departure from current practice inasmuch as the recommendation applies to support organizations as well as insurers, and the Fair Credit Reporting Act does not currently require an inspection bureau to provide the individual with a copy of an investigative report.

It should be noted that this recommendation would not apply to any record about an individual compiled in reasonable anticipation of a civil or criminal action, or for use in settling a claim while the claim remains unsettled. After the claim is settled the recommendation would not apply to any record compiled in relation to a third-party claimant (i.e., a claimant who is not a principal insured or policy owner) except as to any portion of such a record which is disseminated or used for a purpose unrelated to processing the claim. The exception for records compiled in reasonable anticipation of civil or criminal litigation would apply regardless of whether the insurance institution or support organization envisions being a plaintiff or defendant (in a civil action) or a complainant in a criminal proceeding. For example, an insurance institution or support organization may be compiling information to prove arson on the part of a first-party claimant. The insurer may have already paid the claim but is considering prosecution. When such an action is no longer reasonably contemplated, the first-party claimant's access right would be established.

When information is compiled in connection with the settlement of a first-party claim, and negotiations are in progress or contemplated, allowing access prior to settlement would unbalance the existing legal rights of both parties. However, once the first-party claim has been settled, the Commission believes that there is no sound justification for continuing to deny access.

The Commission does see the need to distinguish between first- and third-party claimants. *Recommendation (10)* creates a very limited right of access for a third-party claimant. Whereas the first-party claimant has a contractual relationship with the insurer, the third-party claimant, by definition, occupies an adversary role and has not entered into a relationship with the insurer. Only where information compiled in the course of a third-party settlement is used for a purpose other than settling the claim should the claimant be allowed access to such information. The principle involved is that non-claim decisions should not be made about an individual on the basis of records whose contents he cannot know. However, where the individual claimant is in an adversary negotiation with the record keeper, and existing law creates certain rights of access in the course of litigation, an exception to the general right of access recommended by the Commission can be justified. Information can be given to loss indexes and others solely for claim purposes without violating this exception to access by the individual.

Since *Recommendation (10)* would be implemented by amending the Fair Credit Reporting Act, an individual would be able to compel production of a record by an insurance institution or support organization through litigation brought in Federal court or another appropriate court. The right would be similar to the one given a citizen by the Federal Freedom of Information Act. The plaintiff would have to prove that he requested and was denied reasonably described records about himself in the possession of the insurance institution or support organization, and the burden would be on the institution or support organization to present any reason why the statute would not be applicable. Courts would have the power to order the insurance institution or support organization to disclose the particular record or records sought and to award reasonable attorney's fees and other litigation costs to any plaintiff who substantially prevailed.

Systematic denials of access by an insurance institution or support organization could be subject to Federal Trade Commission enforcement, in which the remedy would be an order directing the institution or support organization to produce records upon request by individuals. Once the Federal Trade Commission issued such an order, the insurance institution or support organization would then be subject to the usual enforcement mechanisms available to the FTC to secure compliance with its orders.

An alternative to this approach, in the case of insurance institutions, is to encourage the States to enact amendments to the unfair trade practices sections of their insurance laws to give State Insurance Commissioners the authority to enforce the requirements of this recommendation, and of the correction and adverse decision rights that *Recommendations (11)* and *(13)* would create. If a State failed to enact such legislation, the Federal Trade Commission would then be able to exercise its enforcement proceedings, using its normal enforcement mechanism with respect to systematic failures in that particular State.

An individual would have no right to money damages based solely upon a denial of his access right under *Recommendation (10)*. The burden would be on the individual to reasonably describe the document sought and the insurance institution or support organization could defend on the basis that it cannot reasonably locate or identify the records sought by the plaintiff. For example, the individual could sue for any document developed as the result of an application for insurance if the individual could identify the date and nature of the application. If, however, an individual requested any information that relates to him in a file, but could not, with some specificity, identify the circumstances pursuant to which such a file would have been developed, the insurance institution would not be under an affirmative obligation to search manually through each and every document to locate a possible passing reference to the individual.

The Fair Credit Reporting Act currently creates the following limitation of liability protection:

> Except as provided in Sections 1681n and 1681o of this title, no consumer may bring any action or proceeding in the nature of defamation, invasion of privacy, or negligence with respect to the reporting of information against any consumer reporting agency, any user of information, or any person who furnishes information to a consumer reporting agency, based on information disclosed pursuant to 1681h or 1681m of this title, except as to false information furnished with malice or willful intent to injure such customer. *[15 U.S.C. 1681h(e)]*

The Commission believes that this type of protection should be extended to insurance institutions and support organizations in connection with recorded information furnished pursuant to either *Recommendation (10)* or *Recommendation (13)* concerning adverse underwriting decisions. In addition, because insurers, unlike their support organizations, make decisions about individuals, the Commission believes that they should not be liable to suit for retroactive coverage where an adverse underwriting decision is made on the basis of information which proves to be incorrect. Thus, an insurance institution or support organization should have no liability, including liability for defamation, invasion of privacy or negligence, with respect to information which had been disclosed to an individual, regardless of whether or not that information was created or furnished by the insurance institution or insurance-support organization, unless false information was furnished to third parties with malice or willful intent to injure the individual.

CORRECTION OF RECORDS

Giving an individual the right to see and copy a record created for the purpose of making a decision about him is of little value if it is not accompanied by a right to get erroneous information in the record corrected. Both the Privacy Act and the Fair Credit Reporting Act establish procedures whereby an individual can correct, amend, or dispute inaccurate, obsolete, or incomplete information in a record about himself. The insurance business stands to gain, moreover, from improving the quality of information about individuals available to it. When an individual is denied insurance on the basis of an inaccurate record about himself, the insurer also suffers through the loss of premium income. Finally, given the observed need to strengthen and balance the respective roles of insurer and individual within the context of the insurance relationship, and given the fact that there is information interchange among insurers (particularly as facilitated by inspection bureaus, the Medical Information Bureau, and the loss indexes), it is unrealistic to expect the individual to chase an error through every insurance-related record-keeping organization to which it may have been transmitted. The insurer, the primary record keeper, must assume its fair share of responsibility for that task.

Accordingly, to make the individual's right of access to an insurance record worthwhile, and to improve the quality of recorded information available to underwriters and others who make decisions about applicants and insureds, the Commission recommends:

Recommendation (11):

That the Federal Fair Credit Reporting Act be amended to provide that each insurance institution and insurance-support organization permit an individual to request correction, amendment, or deletion of a record pertaining to him; and

(a)   within a reasonable period of time:

(i)   correct or amend (including supplement) any portion
      thereof which the individual reasonably believes is not
      accurate, timely, or complete; and
(ii) delete any portion thereof which is not within the scope of
      information the individual was originally told would be
      collected about him; and
(b) furnish the correction, amendment, or fact of deletion to any
    person or organization specifically designated by the individual
    who may have, within two years prior thereto, received any such
    information; and, automatically, to any insurance-support
    organization whose primary source of information on individu-
    als is insurance institutions when the support organization has
    systematically received any such information from the insur-
    ance institution within the preceding seven years, unless the
    support organization no longer maintains the information, in
    which case, furnishing the correction, amendment, or fact of
    deletion is not required; and automatically to any insurance-
    support organization that furnished the information corrected,
    amended, or deleted; or
(c) inform the individual of its refusal to correct or amend the
    record in accordance with his request and of the reason(s) for
    the refusal; and
    (i)   permit an individual who disagrees with the refusal to
          correct or amend the record to have placed on or with the
          record a concise statement setting forth the reasons for his
          disagreement; and
    (ii) in any subsequent disclosure outside the insurance
          institution or support organization containing information
          about which the individual has filed a statement of
          dispute, clearly note any portion of the record which is
          disputed, and provide a copy of the statement along with
          the information being disclosed; and
    (iii) furnish the statement of dispute to any person or
          organization specifically designated by the individual who
          may have, within two years prior thereto, received any
          such information; and, automatically, to an insurance-
          support organization whose primary source of information
          on individuals is insurance institutions when the support
          organization has received any such information from the
          insurance institution within the preceding seven years,
          unless the support organization no longer maintains the
          information, in which case, furnishing the statement is not
          required; and, automatically, to any insurance-support
          organization that furnished the disputed information;
(d) limit its reinvestigation of disputed information to those record
    items in dispute.

Recommendation (12):

That notwithstanding *Recommendation (11)(a)(i)*, if an individual who is the subject of medical-record information maintained by an insurance institution or insurance-support organization requests correction or amendment of such information, the insurance institution or insurance-support organization be required to:

(a)   disclose to the individual, or to a medical professional designated by him, the identity of the medical-care provider who was the source of the medical-record information; and

(b)   make the correction or amendment requested within a reasonable period of time, if the medical-care provider who was the source of the information agrees that it is inaccurate or incomplete; and

(c)   establish a procedure whereby an individual who is the subject of medical-record information maintained by an insurance institution or insurance-support organization, and who believes that the information is incorrect or incomplete, would be provided an opportunity to present supplemental information of a limited nature for inclusion in the medical-record information maintained by the insurance institution or support organization, provided that the source of the supplemental information is also included.

Although *Recommendations (11)* and *(12)* appear complex, they contain only two key requirements:

• that an individual have a way of correcting, amending, deleting, or disputing information in a record about himself, regardless of whether the record is held by an insurance institution or by a support organization; and

• that the insurance institution or support organization to whom the request for correction, amendment, or deletion is made, shall have an obligation to propagate the correction, amendment, deletion, or statement of dispute in any subsequent disclosure it makes of the information to possible recipients within the previous two years whom the individual designates; and to any insurance-support organization which within the previous seven years has been a regular recipient of the type of information, or which was the source of the information.

Regular recipients would include support organizations such as the Medical Information Bureau, the Impairment Bureau, or the loss indexes. Sources would mainly be investigative-reporting agencies (inspection bureaus).

The obvious objective of the second set of requirements is to allow for a thorough cleansing of industry record systems when inaccurate information is discovered and, in the case of amended or corrected information, to provide measures of the completeness and validity of information used in making decisions about an individual, thereby reducing the number of adverse decisions made on the basis of inaccurate or incomplete information. Furthermore, *Recommendations (11)* and *(12)* also provide two important vehicles for enforcing compliance with *Recommendations (5)* and *(6)* on pre-notice and limits on collection practices.

The requirement to delete information that falls outside the boundaries set by the notice called for in *Recommendation (5)*, not only from the insurer's records but also from the records of any support organization that has collected it, or to which it has been disclosed, not only gives the individual a means of holding the insurer to its declarations regarding the scope of the inquiry to be made about him, but also enhances the insurer's control over the record-keeping practices of its contractors. In addition, by closely wedding the scope of a support organization's inquiry on behalf of each of its clients to each client's specified needs, the net effect of this requirement should be to allow an insurer that spends money on refining its relevance criteria and information collection techniques to avoid subsidizing other insurers that have not done so. At the present time, the relationship between insurer and investigative-reporting agency, for example, is loose enough to allow the reporting agency to use an inquiry on behalf of one insurer to gather information that can be marketed to others. Today, apparently, this is not a serious problem, because there are broad similarities among the kinds of reports insurers order. If *Recommendation (5)* succeeds in making privacy protection policy an element in insurers' competition for customers, however, fairness demands that the more socially responsible insurers not have to subsidize the practices of their less conscientious competitors.

In addition, subsection (d) limits the reinvestigation of disputed information to the items in dispute. The purpose of this provision is to prevent the dispute mechanism from becoming an occasion for a wholly new intrusion merely because of the questioned accuracy of one item.

As to *Recommendation (12)*, the rationale and explanation for it will be found in the discussion of *Recommendation (8)* in Chapter 7 on the medical-care relationship.

Like *Recommendation (10)*, neither *Recommendation (11)* nor *Recommendation (12)* would apply to any record about an individual compiled in reasonable anticipation of a civil or criminal action, or for use in settling a claim while the claim remains unsettled. After the claim is settled, moreover, these recommendations would not apply to any record compiled in relation to a claimant who is not an insured or policy owner, except as to any portion of such a record which is disseminated or used for a purpose unrelated to processing the claim. Nor are these recommendations intended to replace entirely the current Fair Credit Reporting Act reinvestigation and dispute requirements. Although *Recommendation (11)* would extend the current six-month limitation on an inspection bureau's obligation to propagate corrections, amendments, and disputes, it is not intended that this recommendation supplant existing Fair Credit Reporting Act requirements to reinvestigate and record the current status of information (unless the complaint is frivolous) or to delete information which can no longer be verified.

The Fair Credit Reporting Act should be amended to allow an individual to sue to force compliance with *Recommendations (11)* and *(12)* and be entitled to reasonable attorney's fees and other litigation costs if he substantially prevails. This would be the sole remedy in the event an insurance institution or support organization fails to comply with the requirements of *Recommendations (11)* and *(12)*, except that an intentional or willful refusal to comply could result in up to $1,000 in damages. The alternatives for Federal Trade Commission or State regulatory enforcement when there are repeated violations have been discussed above in conjunction with *Recommendation (10)* on access and apply equally here.

ADVERSE UNDERWRITING DECISIONS

An underwriting decision cannot be fair if it is made on the basis of inaccurate information. Both the individual and the insurance institution have a common objective in this regard. Currently, however, an insurer that makes an adverse underwriting decision about an individual is not required, in most cases, to give any clues as to the information that supported it. If the information came from an investigative-reporting agency or a credit bureau, the insurer must identify the agency or bureau and furnish its address but nothing more. Furthermore, as explained earlier, being able to find out from a support organization the "nature and substance" of information it reported to the insurer is no guarantee that the individual will be able to relate what he learns to the decision that was made on the basis of it. The "nature and substance" of an investigative report may sound harmless to a rejected applicant. How is he to know that something in it, if explained in greater detail, might have caused the adverse decision to come out the other way? Or if something in the report is inaccurate, how is he to know whether it was that particular item that caused the adverse decision and thus the one that needs to be followed up?

Because the investigative-reporting agency's sources (including institutional sources) need not be disclosed to the individual, he also has no way of knowing to which sources he should go to get an inaccuracy corrected in a manner which will persuade the insurance institution that information the support organization reported was erroneous. Nor is the insurer under any obligation to disclose its own independent sources, such as the Medical Information Bureau, or the Impairment Bureau, or a source identified *through* the Medical Information Bureau. Finally, if the individual is venturesome enough to try to get inaccurate information corrected, he is expected to make the decision to do so without necessarily knowing what his rights are under the Fair Credit Reporting Act.

Thus, in order to bring insurance practices in line with current or recommended practice in other areas the Commission has examined, the Commission recommends:

Recommendation (13):

That the Federal Fair Credit Reporting Act be amended to provide that an insurance institution must:

(a)   disclose in writing to an individual who is the subject of an adverse underwriting decision:
     (i)   the specific reason(s) for the adverse decision;
     (ii) the specific item(s) of information that support(s) the reason(s) given pursuant to (a)(i), except that medical-record information may be disclosed either directly or through a licensed medical professional designated by the individual, whichever the insurance institution prefers;
     (iii) the name(s) and address(es) of the institutional source(s) of the item(s) given pursuant to (a)(ii); and
     (iv) the individual's right to see and copy, upon request, all recorded information concerning the individual used to make the adverse decision, to the extent recorded information exists;

(b)   permit the individual to see and copy, upon request, all recorded information pertaining to him used to make the adverse decision, to the extent recorded information exists, except that (i) such information need not contain the name or other identifying particulars of any source (other than an institutional source) who has provided such information on the condition that his or her identity not be revealed, and (ii) an individual may be permitted to see and copy medical-record information either directly or through a licensed medical professional designated by the individual, whichever the insurance institution prefers. The insurance institution should be allowed to charge a reasonable copying fee for any copies provided to the individual;

(c)   inform the individual of:
     (i)   the procedures whereby he can correct, amend, delete, or file a statement of dispute with respect to any information disclosed pursuant to (a) and (b); and
     (ii) the individual's rights provided by the Fair Credit Reporting Act, when the decision is based in whole or in part on information obtained from a consumer-reporting agency (as defined by the Fair Credit Reporting Act);

(d)   establish reasonable procedures to assure the implementation of the above.

Recommendation (13) is similar to the recommendation regarding adverse credit decisions in Chapter 2. It is, however, even more of a departure from current practice in that insurers generally have not had to disclose the specific reasons for their adverse underwriting decisions. On the other hand, *Recommendation (13)* differs from its counterpart in the credit area in that, like *Recommendation (10)*, above, it takes account of the fact that not all sources of information used to make an insurance decision about an individual are institutional ones and further, that some adverse insurance decisions may be made on the basis of medical-record information. It is linked to *Recommendations (11)* and *(12)* through *subsection (c)*, which requires that the insurer apprise the individual of its own correction, amendment, deletion, and dispute procedures, and to *Recommendation (4)* in requiring that the insurer establish reasonable implementation procedures.

It should be noted that *Recommendation (13)* applies only to adverse underwriting decisions, which the Commission has defined as follows:

- With respect to life and health insurance, a denial of requested insurance coverage (except claims) in whole or in part or an offer to insure at other than standard rates; and with respect to all other kinds of insurance, a denial of requested insurance coverage (except claims) in whole or in part, or a rating which is based on information which differs from that which the individual furnished; or
- a refusal to renew insurance coverage in whole or in part; or
- a cancellation of any insurance coverage in whole or in part.

Since *Recommendation (13)* would be implemented by amending the Fair Credit Reporting Act, an individual would be able to obtain a court order from a Federal court or other court of competent jurisdiction to force an insurance institution to perform any one of the duties called for if he could prove that the insurance institution had failed to do so. This would include incomplete disclosure of the specific reasons and underlying information. The court would have the power to order the insurance institution to comply and to award attorney's fees to any plaintiff who substantially prevailed. Such an action would be the individual's sole remedy, except that the court should also have the power to award up to $1,000 to the plaintiff if it is shown that the institution intentionally or willfully denied the individual any of the rights *Recommendation (13)* would give him.

As noted in the discussion of *Recommendation (10)*, the Commission believes that a limitation of liability similar to that now provided by the Fair Credit Reporting Act should be extended to insurance institutions as well as insurance-support organizations. The implementation of *Recommendation (10)* would create no liability on the part of an insurance institution or support organization, including liability for negligence, defamation or invasion of privacy, unless the institution or support organization acted with malice or willful intent to harm the individual.

Like *Recommendations (10), (11),* and *(12), Recommendation (13)* depends primarily for its enforcement upon the individual's assertion of his rights. As noted above, however, the Commission proposes two alternate means of government enforcement where an insurance institution repeatedly or systematically denies the rights granted by *Recommendations (10), (11), (12),* and *(13)*. One alternative is that the Federal Trade Commission would have the authority to bring enforcement proceedings, using its normal enforcement mechanisms. The other would be for the States to be encouraged to enact amendments to the unfair trade practices sections of their insurance laws which would give State Insurance Commissioners the authority to enforce the requirements of these four recommendations. Should a State enact such legislation, the Federal Trade Commission would then be precluded from exercising its enforcement proceedings with respect to systematic failures in that particular State.

DECISIONS BASED ON PREVIOUS ADVERSE DECISIONS

In the following chapter, on record keeping in the employer-employee relationship, there are several examples of the harm that can result when actions taken against an individual by one record-keeping organization become the basis for decision making by another. The problem, however, is a general one and stems from the tendency of record-keeping organizations to make unwarranted assumptions about the validity and currency of information generated by other record-keeping organizations. Questions are seldom asked about how recorded information came to be and the caveats knowledge of those processes should evoke.

As explained earlier, insurers often ask an applicant whether any other insurer has ever declined him, refused to renew a policy, or insured him at other than standard rates. While life insurers seem to use this information as a guide to finding out more about an applicant, automobile insurers often decline applicants solely on the basis of an affirmative response to the question. In the Commission's opinion, this is grossly unfair. The bare fact of an adverse underwriting decision is an incomplete item of information; the reason for the decision is the important item and it is missing. Indeed, using the mere fact of a previous adverse decision as the basis for rejecting an insurance applicant is one of the clearest examples the Commission found of information itself being the cause of unfairness in a decision made on the basis of it. Thus, the Commission recommends:

Recommendation (14):

That no insurance institution or insurance-support organization:

(a)   **make inquiry as to:**
       (i)   **any previous adverse underwriting decision on an individual, or**
      (ii)   **whether an individual has obtained insurance through the substandard (residual) insurance market,**

    unless the inquiry requests the reasons for such treatment; *or*

(b)   **make any adverse underwriting decision based, in whole or in part, on the mere fact of:**
       (i)   **a previous adverse underwriting decision, or**
      (ii)   **an individual having obtained insurance through the substandard (residual) market.**

An insurance institution may, however, base an adverse

underwriting decision on further information obtained from the source, including other insurance institutions.

It will be remembered that in the explanation of *Recommendation (1)*, it was noted that when the fairness, as opposed to the propriety, of an item of information is at issue, one might both prohibit its use and require its collection. In *Recommendation (14)*, however, the Commission proposes that an insurer both cease to inquire and cease to use, the reason being that compliance will be principally monitored through the individual's exercise of his rights pursuant to *Recommendation (13)* on adverse underwriting decisions. State Insurance Commissioners should use their unfair trade practices authority, and their authority to review certain application forms to assure that adverse insurance decisions are no longer based on the mere fact of a previous adverse decision. They should also require that insurers collect information about prior declinations only when the reasons for the declination are also collected. The Commission hopes, however, that once the previous adverse decision problem is well enough and widely enough understood, voluntary measures, facilitated by exercise of the statutory rights proposed in *Recommendation (13)*, will assure universal compliance.

UNDERWRITING DECISIONS BASED ON INFORMATION FROM INDUSTRY DATA EXCHANGES

The Commission found that in life and health underwriting, there is less than perfect adherence to the industry's own rules regarding the use of information obtained from the Medical Information Bureau. According to MIB rules, no adverse underwriting decision is ever supposed to be made solely on the basis of an MIB "flag," but the record clearly indicates that efforts to achieve this have been weak and superficial.[98]

The problem here, of course, is the same one *Recommendation (9)* addresses, except for the fact that in this case the items of information in question are being obtained from an industry data exchange rather than from the individual himself, thereby multiplying by two the points at which errors could be made. Either the insurer that reports an item to the exchange, or the exchange in reporting it to still another company, could report it incorrectly. Because the item is only a flag, moreover, it is by its very nature without context; that is, it is an incomplete item of information. Accordingly, the Commission recommends:

Recommendation (15):

That no insurance institution base an adverse underwriting decision, in whole or in part, on information about an individual it obtains from an insurance-support organization whose primary source of information is insurance institutions or insurance-support organizations; however, the insurance institution may base an adverse underwriting

---

[98] Testimony of MIB, Insurance Records Hearings, May 19, 1976, pp. 244-54; 274-77.

decision on further information obtained from the original source, including another insurance institution.

This recommendation would apply to the Medical Information Bureau and the Impairment Bureau, but not to the loss indexes, since they do not supply information for use in underwriting decisions. In addition, the recommendation refers only to information about a particular individual and, therefore, would not govern the use of information obtained, for example, from a rating organization.

As with *Recommendation (14)*, voluntary compliance with this recommendation will be facilitated by exercise of the statutory rights proposed in *Recommendation (13)*, and also by any action taken by State Insurance Commissioners pursuant to their unfair trade practices authority referred to in the discussion of *Recommendation (14)*.

FAIRNESS IN DISCLOSURE

DISCLOSURES TO INDUSTRY DATA EXCHANGES

Life insurance companies have had a longstanding practice of reporting to the Medical Information Bureau or the Impairment Bureau information about an individual's health, which they have obtained from sources other than a licensed medical-care provider, or the individual to whom the information pertains. The same has been true of property and liability reporting on claimants to the loss indexes. In the case of the MIB and the Impairment Bureau, agents' reports and reports compiled by inspection bureaus, in part on the basis of interviews with neighbors and associates, have been a major source of such information. In the Medical Information Bureau this material was coded as "medical information" that because of source does not meet the requirements of the Fair Credit Reporting Act, and "medical information received from a consumer report, not confirmed by the proposed insured or a medical facility."[99]

As discussed earlier, this is an area in which the MIB Executive Committee took action following the Commission's hearings on the record-keeping practices of insurance institutions and insurance-support organizations. The MIB's action, however, does not affect the existing flow of "health status information" into the Impairment Bureau and the loss indexes. Moreover, as indicated in its discussion of *Recommendation (11)*, the Commission believes that the responsibility for the content of records maintained by industry data exchanges is properly placed on the reporting insurance institutions, since it is they who control the record-keeping policies of the data exchanges.

The chief problem with health status information is its unreliability. It is bad enough to be labeled as a pariah by those society considers qualified to do so, but it violates all canons of fairness to allow such labels to be attached by anyone, regardless of his qualifications. Accordingly, the Commission recommends:

---

[99] Submission of MIB, "Offical Code List of Impairments - 1962," *Insurance Records Hearings*, May 19, 1976, p. 1.

Recommendation (16):

That Federal law be enacted to provide that no insurance institution or insurance-support organization may disclose to another insurance institution or insurance-support organization information pertaining to an individual's medical history, diagnosis, condition, treatment, or evaluation, even with the explicit authorization of the individual, unless the information was obtained directly from a medical-care provider, the individual himself, his parent, spouse, or guardian.

This recommendation should be implemented in connection with *Recommendation (17)* concerning the confidential relationship between an individual and an insurance institution or support organization. It would become part of the duty of confidentiality owed to an individual by an insurer or support organization. Although support organizations like the loss indexes have little practical control over the source of medical information sent to them, it is expected that insurance institutions, in order to protect their own interests in not disclosing medical information in violation of subsection (b)(iv) of *Recommendation (17)*, will establish procedures to assure that only medical information obtained from a qualified source is communicated to a support organization or to another insurance institution.

Expectation of Confidentiality

The Commission's third policy objective is to establish and define the nature of the confidential relationship between an individual and the record-keeping institutions with which he can be said to have a relationship. A confidential relationship is one in which there is both an explicit limitation on the extent to which information generated by the relationship can be disclosed to others, and a prior mutual understanding by the parties involved as to what that limitation shall be.

Certain relationships (e.g., doctor-patient, attorney-client) have traditionally carried with them legally enforceable expectations of confidentiality, at least in particular types of circumstances.[100] These protections, moreover, have sprung from the breadth of inquiry and observation on which the success of the relationship depends. If one type of relationship requires more divulgence and probing than another, the latter, so the argument goes, should not be permitted to feed off the former at will. To allow that to happen is not only fundamentally unfair; it is also a violation of the ethics of the first relationship.

One sees this problem vividly today in the record-keeping dimensions of the doctor-patient relationship. It is present, however, in every area of personal-data record keeping where an individual must submit to the collection and recording of intimate details about himself in order to obtain some benefit or service. Furthermore, as the Commission argues in Chapter 9, if society is to solve the problems inherent in the compulsory disclosure of

---

[100] For a discussion of the doctor-patient testimonial privilege to most medical record-keeping situations, see Chapter 7.

information about an individual from one record-keeping relationship to another, it must limit the circumstances in which voluntary disclosures are permitted at the discretion of the record keeper. Otherwise, there is no point in restricting the circumstances under which a government agency, for example, may compel a record keeper to produce information it holds in its records on an individual. To make such restrictions sensible, as well as to assure the individual a role in determining when and to what extent they will be suspended, one must first impose a duty of confidentiality on the holder of the records.

With these considerations in mind, the Commission has concluded that each insurance institution and insurance-support organization should owe a duty of confidentiality to the individual on whom it maintains records. The amount, diversity, and character of the information gathered to establish and facilitate the insurance relationship is such as to warrant establishing such a duty of confidentiality. The insurance relationship, moreover, is extraordinarily important to society. Like the credit, depository, and medical-care relationships considered in other chapters of this report, it is one that is increasingly difficult for an individual to avoid. Yet the relationship cannot be maintained successfully if it is perceived as being inherently unfair or as disregarding the legitimate interests of the individuals who enter into it.

Currently, insurance institutions and their support organizations voluntarily assume some ethical responsibility for the confidentiality of the information they maintain on individuals. However, they do not uniformly respect the individual's legitimate desire to limit the disclosures they make about him, nor are they able to defend the integrity of their record-keeping relationships with individuals against certain demands made on them by extraneous parties. Thus, to create and define obligations with respect to the uses and disclosures that may be made of records about individuals, legitimate patterns of information-sharing within the industry and threshold conditions for the disclosure of such records to outsiders must be established.

Accordingly, the Commission recommends:

Recommendation (17):

That Federal law be enacted to provide that each insurance institution and insurance-support organization be considered to owe a duty of confidentiality to any individual about whom it collects or receives information in connection with an insurance transaction, and that therefore, no insurance institution or support organization should disclose, or be required to disclose, in individually identifiable form, any information about any such individual without the individual's explicit authorization, unless the disclosure would be:

(a)   to a physician for the purpose of informing the individual of a medical problem of which the individual may not be aware;

(b)   from an insurance institution to a reinsurer or co-insurer, or to an agent or contractor of the insurance institution, including a

sales person, independent claims adjuster, or insurance investigator, or to an insurance-support organization whose sole source of information is insurance institutions, or to any other party-in-interest to the insurance transaction, provided:

(i)   that only such information is disclosed as is necessary for such reinsurer, co-insurer, agent, contractor, insurance-support organization, or other party-in-interest to perform its function with regard to the individual or the insurance transaction;

(ii)   that such reinsurer, co-insurer, agent, contractor, insurance-support organization or other party-in-interest is prohibited from redisclosing the information without the authorization of the individual except, in the case of insurance institutions and insurance-support organizations, as otherwise provided in this recommendation; and

(iii)   that the individual, if other than a third-party claimant, is notified at least initially concurrent with the application that such disclosure may be made and can find out if in fact it has been made; and

(iv)   that in no instance shall information pertaining to an individual's medical history, diagnosis, condition, treatment, or evaluation be disclosed, even with the explicit authorization of the individual, unless the information was obtained directly from a medical-care provider, the individual himself, or his parent, spouse, or guardian;

(c)   from an insurance-support organization whose sole source of information is insurance institutions or self-insurers to an insurance institution or self-insurer, provided:

(i)   that the sole function of the insurance-support organization is the detection or prevention of insurance fraud in connection with claim settlements;

(ii)   that, if disclosed to a self-insurer, the self-insurer assumes the same duty of confidentiality with regard to that information which is required of insurance institutions and insurance-support organizations; and

(iii)   that any insurance institution or self-insurer that receives information from any such insurance-support organization is prohibited from using such information for other than claim purposes;

(d)   to the insurance regulator of a State or its agent or contractor, for an insurance regulatory purpose statutorily authorized by the State;

(e)   to a law enforcement authority:

(i)   to protect the legal interest of the insurer, reinsurer, co-insurer, agent, contractor, or other party-in-interest to prevent and to prosecute the perpetration of fraud upon them; or

(ii)   when the insurance institution or insurance-support

> organization has a reasonable belief of illegal activities on
> the part of the individual;
>
> (f) pursuant to a Federal, State, or local compulsory reporting
> statute or regulation;
>
> (g) in response to a lawfully issued administrative summons or
> judicial order, including a search warrant or subpoena.

In contrast to the corresponding recommendations with respect to credit grantors and depository institutions, wherein interpretative responsibilities would be assigned to existing regulatory authorities, the Commission recommends that the responsibility for enforcing the confidentiality duties of insurance institutions and support organizations be left exclusively to the aggrieved individual. The information flows in and out of the insurance industry, while extensive in some areas, appear less dynamic and thus less prone to change than those in the credit area, for example. As a result, there is less need for flexibility in establishing their legitimacy; that is, there is no need for an interpretative rule-making function.

The provisions of the recommended statute, however, should be explicitly drawn to allow an individual to sue an insurance institution or support organization and to obtain actual damages for negligent disclosures that violate the duty of confidentiality, even if there is no showing of an intentional or willful violation. Where an intentional or willful violation of the duty of confidentiality is established, the individual should, in addition to actual damages and court costs, including reasonable attorney's fees, be entitled to general damages of a minimum of $1,000 and a maximum of $10,000. A defense available to the defendant charged with *negligent* disclosure would be that it had established reasonable procedures and exercised reasonable care to implement and enforce those procedures in attempting to protect the interests of the individual. Where it could not meet such a test, the insurance institution or support organization would then be subject to actual damages and court costs, including legal fees, for any violations.

The statute should also make clear that *subsection (b)(iii)* would not apply to any record about an individual compiled in reasonable anticipation of a civil or criminal action, or for use in settling a claim while the claim remains unsettled. After the claim is settled, moreover, *subsection (b)(iii)* would not apply to any record compiled in relation to a claimant who is not an insured or policyowner (i.e., a third-party claimant), except as to any portion of such record that is disseminated or used for a purpose unrelated to processing the claim.

The first premise of the proposed statutory duty is that no record should be disclosed by an insurance institution or support organization without the authorization of the individual to whom it pertains. The Commission would expect, moreover, that the authorization statement used would be specific as to the information proposed to be furnished, to whom, and for what purpose. Nonetheless, as in other areas, the Commission has recognized the need to allow certain types of disclosures to occur without the individual's authorization. These exceptions can be divided into three categories:

- disclosures to protect the individual;
- disclosures the insurance institution or support organization must make in order to perform duties inherent in the insurance relationship or to protect itself from failure by the individual to meet the terms of the relationship; and
- disclosures to governmental authorities.

Subsection (a) of the recommendation falls into the first category. It permits disclosure without authorization to a physician for the purpose of informing the individual of a medical problem about which he may be unaware, and which an insurance institution or support organization may be reluctant to disclose to him directly. Making an exception for such situations seems justified by the benefit to the individual and by the minimal risk to personal privacy it involves, since the physician also stands in a confidential relationship to the individual.

The second category of exceptions concerns disclosures consistent with the insurer's rights and duties in its relationship with the insurance consumer. The duty of confidentiality, primarily for the benefit of the latter, should not unfairly burden the insurer's ability to fulfill its part of the bargain or to protect its own interests. By the mere fact of applying for insurance, maintaining a policy, or presenting a claim, the individual authorizes the insurer to perform certain functions. Thus, under *subsection (b)* of the Commission's recommendation, no authorization is required for disclosures to reinsurers, co-insurers, agents, contractors, insurance-support organizations, or any other party-in-interest, when disclosure is necessary for that person to perform a function concerned with the insurer's relationship with the insured. The insured should nonetheless be notified (see *Recommendation (5))* that such disclosures may be made and should be able to find out whether or not they have, in fact, been made (see *Recommendation (10)).*

In many cases, individually identifiable information is provided by an insurer to one or more other insurers who act as reinsurers of the first. The individual whose insurance policy is reinsured has no legal relationship with the reinsurer. The only party who has a contractual relationship with the insured is the insurer from whom the individual purchased the policy. Reinsurance is common within the insurance industry, and sometimes involves the transfer of individually identifiable information. Currently, however, the individual has no knowledge of this type of disclosure.

It would serve no purpose to require an applicant to expressly authorize the dissemination of information about him to a reinsurer. The individual who refused to authorize the disclosure would simply be denied the insurance. The reinsurer, moreover, would have the same duty of confidentiality as the original insurer and be subject to the same requirements for holding information in confidence.

The reinsurance situation is similar to other party-in-interest situations in which the Commission believes individual authorization should not be required for information disclosure. For example, the amount of one insurer's claim payment may be related to another's payment. In this case, where a pro-rata liability or other coordination of benefits clause exists, each insurer must be considered a co-insurer and should, therefore, be allowed to share necessary information, subject to the same restrictions as to notice and confidentiality outlined above. Other exceptions based on the party-in-interest concept would include cases involving subrogation,[101] as well as cases involving insurers who were potentially being defrauded by the same person.

All parties-in-interest referred to in *subsection (b)* would either already be bound by or would assume the same duty of confidentiality as the provider of the information—that is, they would not be permitted to redisclose the information without the individual's authorization, unless, in the case of any party-in-interest that is an insurance institution or insurance-support organization, the disclosure would be otherwise authorized under this recommendation. Only information necessary for the recipient to perform its function should be disclosed. Thus, for example, an independent claims adjuster should only be given the information needed to properly settle a claim. As already noted, *subsection (b)(iii)*, which requires notice and a way for an individual to find out whether a particular disclosure had been made, would not apply to cases expected to involve litigation or to claims situations. *Subsection (b)(iv)* incorporates *Recommendation (16)* as the Commission urged that it should, above.

One special concern of insurance institutions and insurance-support organizations is to detect and deter fraud. Privacy requirements should not be used to restrict an insurer's capacity to protect its interests, especially where fraud may be involved. Thus, no authorization is required under *subsection (b)* for the disclosure of information to the Insurance Crime Prevention Institute or other support organizations that operate as surrogates of the insurer in seeking to prevent fraud. Authorization is also not needed for disclosure to one of the loss indexes or other insurers when the purpose is to deter and detect insurance fraud. Conversely, *subsection (c)* could allow the loss indexes to continue to disseminate information to their subscribers without individual authorization. To require otherwise would be tantamount to destroying the loss indexes, since those intent on fraud would naturally refuse to agree to the disclosure.

Currently, "self-insurers" may subscribe to the loss indexes. These subscribers are neither insurance institutions nor insurance-support organizations within the Commission's or insurance regulatory officials' definitions. They are companies and governments that have chosen to retain some or all of their exposure to loss rather than to transfer it to an insurer. Since they are not insurance institutions or insurance-support organizations, they are not subject to the Commission's recommendations on such organizations. Nevertheless, the information from the loss indexes may continue to flow to self-insurers and should, therefore, be subject to a duty of confidentiality as provided in *subsection (c)(ii)*.

The third category of exceptions concerns disclosures to government. The Commission is aware that, for public policy reasons, information must be disclosed by insurance industry parties to law enforcement officials under

---

[101] Subrogation is the substitution of one party in place of another with reference to a lawful claim or right.

certain circumstances. Such disclosures would be permitted, provided they comply with the Commission's recommendations regarding government access to private-sector records, explained in Chapter 9.

One voluntary disclosure that is permitted without an authorization is to law enforcement officials when an insurance institution or insurance-support organization reasonably concludes, from information generated in its relationship with him, that an individual has violated the law or is suspected of fraud in connection with the insurance coverage. Certainly in this instance, the insurer should not be required to get the authorization of the individual.

Furthermore, insurance institutions are required to release information to State insurance departments which regulate the insurance industry. Insurance institutions and insurance-support organizations must also respond to Federal, State, and local compulsory reporting statutes and regulations. They have no choice but to disclose information when required by government under these circumstances. A requirement of authorization by the individual would be meaningless. The Commission recognizes, however, that insurance institutions, like other record keepers, should have some obligation to inform an individual that information will be routinely reported to government. Finally, insurance institutions and support organizations must respond to a lawfully issued administrative summons or judicial order, such as a subpoena or search warrant. While they have no choice but to comply with such legal process, and while the primary obligation to assure protection of an individual's rights should rest with government, as explored in Chapter 9, the insurance record keeper has certain responsibilities—primarily to assure the facial validity of the particular form of compulsory process served on it, and to limit its compliance to the specific terms of the order. If, for example, a subpoena requires disclosure of information on a certain date, an insurance institution or support organization should not disclose until that date. Restricted response of this type will permit the individual whose records were sought to exercise those rights the Commission recommends be granted in the context of government access.

*   *   *   *   *   *   *

Insurance protection is vital to most Americans. Much personal information is provided or developed through the process of providing needed insurance protection, properly pricing it, and in servicing insurance contracts, including the investigation and settlement of claims. The Commission believes that the recommendations in this chapter respect this need for information and strengthen the relationship between insured and insurer while promoting its three public-policy objectives.

GLOSSARY OF TERMS

Individual:

any natural person who is a past, present, or proposed named or principal insured (including any principal insured under a family or group policy or similar arrangement of coverage for a person in a group), policyowner, or past or present claimant.

Insurance Institution:

an insurance company (including so-called service plans like Blue Cross and Blue Shield and any other similar service plan), regardless of type of insurance written or organizational form, including insurance company regional, branch, sales, or service offices (or divisions or insurance affiliates), or insurance company solicitors; or agents and brokers.

Insurance-Support Organizations:

an organization which regularly engages in whole or in part in the practice of assembling or evaluating information on individuals for the purpose of providing such information or evaluation to insurance institutions for insurance purposes.

Insurance Transaction:

whenever a decision (be it adverse or otherwise) is rendered regarding an individual's eligibility for an insurance benefit or service.

Adverse Underwriting Decision:

(1)   with respect to life and health insurance, a denial of requested insurance coverage (except claims) in whole or in part, or an offer to insure at other than standard rates; and with respect to all other kinds of insurance, a denial of requested coverage (except claims) in whole or in part, or a rating which is based on information which differs from that which the individual furnished;

(2)   a refusal to renew insurance coverage in whole or in part; or

(3)   a cancellation of any insurance coverage in whole or in part.

Institutional Source:

an institutional source is any person who provides information as part of his employment or any other connection with an insurance institution.

Medical-Record Information:

information relating to an individual's medical history, diagnosis, condition, treatment, or evaluation obtained from a medical-care provider, from the individual himself, or from his spouse, parent, or guardian for the purpose of making a non-medical decision (e.g., an underwriting decision) about the individual.

Medical-Care Provider:

a medical professional or medical-care institution.

Medical Professional:

any person licensed or certified to provide medical services to individuals, including but not limited to, a physician, dentist, nurse, optometrist, physical or occupational therapist, psychiatric social worker, clinical dietitian, or clinical psychologist.

Medical-Care Institution:

any facility or institution that is licensed to provide medical-care services to individuals, including, but not limited to, hospitals, skilled nursing facilities, home-health agencies, clinics, rehabilitation agencies, and public-health agencies or health-maintenance organizations (HMO's).

Chapter 6

The Employment Relationship

A comprehensive study of the effects of record keeping on personal privacy must include records generated in the context of the relationship between employer and employee. The employment relationship affects most people over the greater part of their adult lives, and is basic to the economic and social well-being of our society. Loss of work is for most people a considerable hardship. Its consequences for an individual and for his family can be disastrous.

When an individual applies for work today, it is not unusual for the employer to ask him to divulge a considerable amount of information about himself, and to allow the employer to verify and supplement it. In addition, the individual may be examined by the company physician, given a battery of psychological tests, interviewed extensively, and subjected to a background investigation. After hiring, the records the employer keeps about him will again expand to accommodate attendance and payroll data, records concerning various types of benefits, performance evaluations, and much other information. All of this creates a broad base of recorded information about the employee which various entities unrelated to the employee-employer relationship will view as a valuable resource.

It is the creation, maintenance, use, and disclosure of these employee records which concern the Commission. At what point do inquiries about applicants and employees become unduly intrusive? What does fairness demand with respect to the uses and disclosures of records that support an employment decision? What expectation of confidentiality can an individual legitimately have with respect to the records his employer makes and keeps about him?

The Commission's examination of these questions has concentrated on the record-keeping practices of large private corporations. The Commission considered examining public-sector practices as well, but was dissuaded by time, budget, and the substantial amount of work already completed or in progress on personnel record keeping in the public sector. Several recent studies by Congressional committees and government agencies have examined public-sector employment practices, information collection techniques, and personal-data record systems.[1] The Commission's study of how the Privacy Act of 1974 affects record keeping in the Federal

---

[1] *The Use of Polygraphs and Similar Devices by Federal Agencies*, Report of the Government Operations Committee, U.S. House of Representatives, 94th Congress, 2d Session, 1976, p. 61;

government has illuminated the strengths and weaknesses of those privacy protection rules and procedures in the context of the Federal employment relationship. And the Project on Personnel Practices, Computers, and Citizens' Rights being carried out for the National Bureau of Standards by Professor Alan F. Westin, with partial Commission funding, has analyzed personnel record-keeping policy and practice in several agencies of Federal, State, and local government.

Within the private sector, the Commission also had to choose between looking at the record-keeping practices of a cross section of employers or confining its inquiry to the practices of sizeable organizations. The Commission concluded that concentrating on the employment-related record-keeping practices of larger organizations had some strong advantages. Although they constitute less than one percent of the many millions of businesses in the country, firms with over 1,000 employees account for more than 40 percent of total business employment.[2] Records also tend to matter more in large organizations. Because management can deal on the basis of personal knowledge or acquaintance with only a limited number of employees, records play an important role in employment decision making. Larger firms also tend to provide a wider range of benefits and frequently administer their benefit programs themselves. Thus, their records about applicants and employees contain more information than those of smaller employers. Of great importance to the Commission, moreover, was the fact that large private corporations lead in applying new information processing technologies to personal-data record keeping and thus have had to deal with privacy protection concerns earlier and more aggressively than most other organizations.

For these reasons, the analysis and recommendations that follow have focused on records generated in relationships between individuals and large, private-sector employers. The Commission does, however, believe that the limited amount of work it was able to do on the personnel record-keeping practices of small organizations warrants more general application of the principles underlying its recommendations.

THE EMPLOYEE-EMPLOYER RELATIONSHIP

The record-keeping policies and practices of private-sector employers are best understood by viewing them in the context of the employee-employer relationship. The legal framework of that relationship is contractual. That is, in theory, the employer and employee make a contract on mutually agreed terms, with termination equally available to both parties. The law of employment is based on the principles of employment at will and

---

Rights to Privacy of Federal Employees, Hearings before the Subcommittee on Retirement and Employee Benefits of the Committee on Post Office and Civil Service, U.S. House of Representatives, 93d Congress, 1st and 2d Session, 1974, p. 378; and *Government Dossiers: Survey of Information Contained in Government Files*, Report of the Subcommittee on Administrative Practice and Procedure of the Committee on the Judiciary, U.S. Senate, 90th Congress, 1st Session, 1967, p. 605.

[2] U.S. Department of Commerce, *1967 Enterprise Statistics*, (Part I, General Report on Industrial Organization), 1967.

mutuality of obligation. Accordingly, the contract can be summarily terminated by either party.

In the public sector, these principles have been modified by civil service rules, which stipulate that government employees can be discharged only for just cause established through due process. In the private sector, they have been modified by collective bargaining. Union-management contracts have established just cause criteria for discipline and dismissal which, along with the institutionalization of arbitration, provide due process protections for some employees. Over three-quarters of all private-sector employees, however, do not have such protections.[3]

A private employer today may demand that applicants and employees supply detailed information about any aspect of their lives, submit to tests and examinations, and authorize the employer to acquire whatever records it wants about them from other organizations. Further, courts in some instances have upheld an employer's right to fire employees for exercising basic civil rights and privileges, e.g., for refusing to give perjured testimony, or for serving on a jury.[4]. Thus, absent collective bargaining, there is no general framework in the private sector which could accommodate disputes about recorded information.[5] Federal employees had such a framework before the Privacy Act of 1974 was conceived, but employees in the private sector do not.

RECORDS THE RELATIONSHIP GENERATES

In a small organization the various items of information maintained about an employee are frequently mingled in one file, and the custodian of the file may perform a number of loosely related record-keeping functions. In a large organization, on the other hand, the need to deal in a consistent way with large numbers of employees, and to match applicant abilities with job requirements, calls for specialized functions and records. Over the years, personnel departments have expanded to handle not only recruitment, selection, and job placement but also, in many cases, industrial relations, benefit programs, occupational medicine and safety, and compliance with various Federal and State government requirements. All of these functions have record-keeping consequences for the individual applicant or employee.

Employee records are of necessity individually identifiable. Electronic data processing has streamlined personnel record keeping, but even large corporations still keep some of their employment records, particularly those involving subjective evaluations and those on applicants for jobs, in manual systems. Some of these records relate directly to employment, such as payroll records, grade and skill classifications, leave records, performance

---

[3] According to the Bureau of Labor Statistics, in 1974 employees who were members of unions or employee associations represented 29.1 percent of employees in non-agricultural establishments, and 24.5 percent of the total labor force. U.S. Department of Labor, Bureau of Labor Statistics, *Directory of National Unions and Employee Associations*, 1976.

[4] Kenneth Walters, "Employee Freedom of Speech," *Industrial Relations*, Vol. 15, No. 1 (February, 1976), pp. 26-43.

[5] Clyde W. Summers, "Individual Protection Against Unjust Dismissal, Time for a Statute," *Virginia Law Review*, Vol. 62, No. 3 (April, 1976), pp. 481-532.

evaluations, and promotion tables. Others, such as pension records, life and health insurance records, medical records, counseling records, and home-loan records, are tangentially related. The need to keep well organized, readily accessible records is all the more imperative because of skill specialization in the workplace, increasingly complicated bookkeeping requirements, and Federal and State government record-keeping and reporting requirements, especially those which require that the basis of an employment decision be carefully documented.

Some corporations establish specific guidelines for personnel record keeping and inspect all record-keeping units periodically. In others, however, subordinate managers control the records their units maintain and use, so that while central management may set general policy, it cannot vouch for compliance with it.

THE USE OF RECORDS IN EMPLOYMENT DECISION MAKING

To the Commission's knowledge, no systematic analysis of how employee records affect employment decisions has ever been made. After an extensive survey of the literature, one writer characterized employment decision making as a "black box" problem: an individual can find out what information was available, and can know the outcome, but he may not know what decision processes produced the outcome.[6] Nevertheless, a few general observations can be made.

In the first place, there are certain key decision-making points in the employment cycle: selection, placement, transfer, promotion, demotion, training, discipline, and separation. Second, there are great differences in how employee records are used in different industries. Different categories of employees, such as unionized and nonunionized workers, are affected differently by the records an employer keeps about them. For example, industries which recruit unskilled workers and train them to perform technologically advanced functions are likely to rely heavily on testing. Management and scientific and technical employees in any company are more likely than unskilled workers to be hired or promoted on the basis of colleagues' evaluations. Where there is a union contract, its terms frequently set criteria for making economically significant decisions about employees and, in such cases, reliance on records, both to make and to justify decisions, is common.

Unlike decisions based on insurance, credit, or medical records, however, the crucial employment decisions do not flow as a matter of course from recorded information, and thus it is virtually impossible to say for sure that an adverse decision was based on a record. In some cases, the records of several people are compared in arriving at decisions about applicants or employees, so that an employee's record standing alone cannot show why certain decisions were made about him. Moreover, there are occasions when the possibility of having to make a particular decision generates the keeping

---

[6] Michael Baker, "The Use of Organization Records in Decisions About Job Applicants and Employees," Unpublished memorandum to the National Bureau of Standards' Project on Personnel Practices, Computers, and Citizens Rights, July 11, 1976.

of a record, as when an employee's aberrant behavior is documented in order to *justify* an adverse decision about him.[7]

FORCES FOR CHANGE

External forces can impinge heavily on employment-related record keeping. Government action, technological change, evolving managerial viewpoints and techniques, perspectives and goals of business firms and labor unions, market forces, and change in the composition and character of the work force can all have an effect. Yet because policy must be future-oriented, it is important to try to identify significant trends.

GOVERNMENTAL ACTION

The blurring of boundaries between public and private institutions that has shaped the nation's economic life over the last three decades is not likely to be reversed. More frequent and extended interaction with government inspectors, auditors, and contract monitors makes it likely that records will be required to support a larger range of decisions, including personnel decisions. This is likely to make managers more careful about what goes into records.

The main focus of legislative and regulatory intervention affecting the employment relationship appears to be in the area of general welfare of employees rather than labor-management relations *per se*. The Equal Employment Opportunity Act *[42 U.S.C. 2000 et seq. (1972)]* and the Occupational Safety and Health Act (OSHA) *[29 U.S.C. 651 et seq. (1970)]* suggest the path this trend may take. The perception that an individual's rights and liberties need more protection in his relationships with private-sector institutions is becoming widespread. Fair information practice legislation, such as the Fair Credit Reporting Act *[15 U.S.C. 1681 et seq. (1971)]* and the California law that permits employees to have access to their personal records *[California Labor Code Sec. 1198.5]* reflects this disposition.

In addition, some protective labor legislation, such as the Employee Retirement Income Security Act (ERISA), *[P.L. 93-406, 88 Stat. 829 (1974)]* underscores the increasing importance of the employer's role as provider of social and economic benefits. Yet neither the actual requirements imposed by such legislation, nor the regulations issued by government agencies to implement it, account for its overall impact on the collection, use, and disclosure of information about employees. For example, the Equal Employment Opportunity Commission has not required employers to create or maintain any specific records on individuals,[8] and yet its actions in pursuit of its statutorily defined objectives have forced employers to create records in order to demonstrate compliance. If an affirmative action

---

[7] See, for example, Testimony of the Manufacturers Hanover Trust Company, *Employment and Personnel Records*, Hearings before the Privacy Protection Study Commission, December 16, 1976, pp. 693-695. (hereinafter cited as "Employment Records Hearings").

[8] See, for example, Testimony of the Equal Employment Opportunity Commission, Employment Records Hearings, December 17, 1976, p. 972.

program is required, as under the Rehabilitation Act *[29 U.S.C. 701 et seq. (1973)]* or the Age Discrimination in Employment Act *[29 U.S.C. 621 et seq. (1967)]*, or is voluntarily undertaken out of a sense of corporate responsibility, records are essential. State laws have also had an impact upon the collection of information about employees and, most particularly, about applicants.

The long-term impact of some of this legislation is still not clear, however. Currently, the Occupational Safety and Health Act (OSHA) appears to be one of the laws most likely to raise significant fair information practice concerns. It provides in part that where standards have been promulgated with reference to specific health hazards:

> where appropriate, any such standard shall prescribe the type and frequency of medical examinations or other tests which shall be made available, by the employer at his cost, to employees exposed to such hazards in order to most effectively determine whether the health of such employees is adversely affected by such exposure. *[15 U.S.C. 636(b)(7)]*

Results of these examinations or tests must be furnished to the employee's physician at the employee's request. They can also be made available to a prospective employer pursuant to authorization by the employee. This raises the prospect that an employee's medical records might follow him from job to job.[9] Some workers have already declined to take the physicals employers are required to make available, and it has been suggested that one reason for their refusal is their fear of the consequences of having a known disability documented in their records. While a full discussion of this potentially serious problem is beyond the scope of this chapter, it seems clear that using information about previous exposure to health hazards in making determinations about an individual's suitability for employment or promotion is not consistent with the protective intent of the OSHA statute.

The Commission foresees that government involvement in selected aspects of the private-sector employment relationship will increase. The impact on employment record-keeping practices will be mixed, but the overall effect will probably be continuous reinforcement of the incentive to make, keep, and use records about employees. Barring a fundamental reconceptualization of governmental policy affecting the private-sector employment relationship, the likelihood is that incremental changes will perpetuate existing trends. Thus, for the future as in the present, the important task is to eliminate and guard against dangers inherent in existing policy and practice.

GROWTH OF FRINGE BENEFITS

Further increase in the benefits and services provided by employers is likely to contribute to further government involvement in the employment

---

[9] Letter from the Ford Motor Company to the Privacy Protection Study Commission, January 14, 1977.

relationship. Fringe benefits have become a significant part of employee compensation in American industry. Beyond paid vacations and recreational programs, they now include pension plans, family health and medical benefits, and extended or supplementary unemployment insurance. For example, as of three years ago, the employers of some 65 percent of all private-sector, nonfarm workers offered pension plans.[10] This expansion increases the dependence of employees upon their jobs, and quite possibly their reluctance to change jobs, while, at the same time, adding to the amount and variety of information an employer maintains about employees.

Medical services and health and accident insurance are increasingly provided to employees and their families.[11] As elsewhere, limitations on the kind of information gathered in these contexts are few because almost any personal information may be related to an individual's health, and because the expected confidentiality of the patient-physician relationship serves to legitimate probing inquiries. In the employment context, however, the provision of medical services and the processing of medical insurance claims raise acute privacy protection problems.

In practice, corporate and professional ethics tend to discourage abuse. Yet, so long as there are no absolute barriers to an employer's use of its employee medical and insurance claims records, and as long as employers are in some cases *required* to use such records, a privacy problem of potentially major proportions exists. For example, Department of Defense Industrial Security regulations require employers to report any information that would reflect on the reliability of employees who work on classified projects.[12] Information on employees and their dependents in medical treatment or insurance claims files is not excluded from this requirement.

MANAGEMENT AND PERSONNEL MANAGEMENT

In large organizations with highly specialized divisions of labor and well-established standards and procedures governing performance in the workplace, personnel management strives for rational ways of making selection, assignment, and promotion decisions. Fair and equal treatment has been a major objective of personnel offices throughout the country.

It has been widely suggested, however, that this tendency is counter-productive for organizations in rapidly changing environments with highly skilled and educated workers, and with tasks that require constant development of new systems and products. The role of personnel management in such "post-bureaucratic" organizations is changing. Setting up temporary project-type organizations—firms within a firm—is a way of operating whose popularity is growing. Staffing is crucial in this type of organization, and standard personnel department placement techniques are

---

[10] Donald R. Beld, "Prevalence of Private Retirement Plans," *Monthly Labor Review*, Vol. 98, No. 10 (October 1975), pp. 17-20.

[11] Seymour Lusterman, *Industry Roles in Health Care*, (New York: The Conference Board, 1973).

[12] Department of Defense *Industrial Security Manual for Safeguarding Classified Information*, (DOD 5220.22-M), par. 6b(1).

often irrevelant in such situations. Thus, authority for personnel decisions may be increasingly transferred to the project manager whose principal concern is fitting the individual with the necessary skills into the work team.

There is a strong trend in management away from formal, rule-bound relationships and toward the encouragement of openness and the development of commitment. The implications of this trend for the protection of personal privacy are, however, unclear. While a focus on commitment, teamwork, and adaptability tends to create a consultant market for behavioral scientists, this does not mean that the pressures on management to justify its past and present decisions on the basis of detailed records will cease to grow. On the one hand, the so-called "behavioral approaches" to management tend to stress "the importance of collecting accurate, timely data about aspects of the organization not normally closely monitored—evidence as to employee job satisfaction, the accumulation of specialized knowledge and skills, signs of interdepartmental conflict, and the like."[13] Yet, on the other hand, their net effect may be to focus decisions concerning employees more sharply than at present on work-related matters.

TECHNOLOGICAL DEVELOPMENTS

Recent years have brought a tremendous increase in the capabilities of computer-based personnel systems. Use of these systems varies widely. The private organizations reporting to the Commission differed considerably in the extent to which they have automated their personnel files. To date, technological innovations in information storage, transfer, and display have not generally increased the amount of information about individual employees that is collected, maintained, or disclosed. Indeed, the Commission's inquiry indicates that adaptation to automated systems usually means that the information to be maintained in the data base is carefully screened for cost effectiveness. Furthermore, the emphasis on accuracy and timeliness of information associated with automated systems, and the practice of providing a print-out of the record for verification by the employee, have been positive factors from a privacy protection viewpoint.

While cost will always be a consideration, computer technology promises to remove many limitations on record-system development in the near future. Improved computer capabilities, micrographics, and new duplication and transmission techniques promise to make the capture, transmission, and retrieval of information more and more economical in comparison with manual processes, and more readily available in highly selective formats to geographically separated users. Although these technical capabilities will not in themselves present privacy protection problems, trends and developments associated with them may pose problems that do not exist today. The types of records maintained in easily retrievable form will expand, and it seems likely that behavioral science data concerning

<hr>

[13] George Strauss, R. E. Miles, and C. C. Snow, "Implications for Industrial Relations," *Organizational Behavior: Research and Issues*, (Madison, Wisc: Industrial Relations Research Association, 1974), p. 198.

employee attitudes and values will have an enhanced role in personnel decision making.

Instantaneous availability of information on employees at many locations may centralize some decisions now made locally; it certainly will raise the significance of need-to-know criteria in any policy governing disclosure of records within a firm. Centralization of files also increases the capability of organizations to respond to external requests for information about their employees. While the Commission's hearing record documents the reluctance of firms to disclose information about employees or former employees, easy retrieval may intensify pressures to make information available for purposes other than those for which they were originally collected.

In sum, the Commission subscribes to the view that information abuse does not flow automatically from advanced information technologies, and that better protections for personal privacy have often resulted from computerization.[14] Yet, it also has reason to believe that ready access to large amounts of recorded information tends to create incentives to use that information for purposes that are inconsistent with the purposes for which it was originally collected. Thus, capabilities of information-processing technologies to be available in the 1980's make it imperative that responsible policies and practices governing the use of information generated in the employee-employer relationship be developed promptly.

GENERAL RECOMMENDATIONS

As elsewhere, the Commission has formulated its recommendations on records generated by the employment relationship in the light of three broad public-policy objectives: (1) to minimize intrusiveness; (2) to maximize fairness; and (3) to create a legitimate, enforceable expectation of confidentiality. In contrast to other areas, however, the Commission envisages adoption of most of its employment-related recommendations by voluntary action. The exceptions are all instances in which statutory or regulatory action appears to be both necessary and feasible. For example, the Commission recommends a statutory prohibition against the use of some exceptionally intrusive techniques for collecting information about applicants and employees, such as truth verification devices and pretext interviews. It also recommends amendment of the Fair Credit Reporting Act to regulate further the conduct of background investigations on applicants and employees, and proposes legislative or administrative action to constrain some practices of Federal agencies which impinge on the private-sector employment relationship. In other recommendations, however, the implementation strategy the Commission recommends is by and large a voluntary one.

Private-sector employers maintain many different kinds of information about their employees in individually identifiable form. The use of that information in decision making about employees is, however, difficult for an

---

[14] Alan F. Westin and Michael A. Baker, *Databanks in a Free Society*, (New York: Quadrangle/The New York Times Book Company, 1972).

outsider to describe, particularly since employment decisions frequently are not solely based on recorded information. Both the scope of records and the elusiveness of their use distinguish employment record keeping from most other areas the Commission has studied.

Further, as stressed earlier, the absence of a general framework of rights and obligations that could accomodate disputes about recorded information places severe limitations on the extent to which rules governing the creation, use, and disclosure of employee records can be enforced. The Commission believes that flexibility in decisions about which job an employee is best suited to perform is essential to good management and should be constrained by public policy only to the extent that employers show themselves unable or unwilling to respond to concerns about the protection of employee privacy. Nonetheless, the enforcement problem is the primary reason why the Commission does not believe that many of the privacy protection issues the private-sector employee-employer relationship raises can be resolved by legislated record-keeping requirements.

One can conceive of approaches to enforcing rules the Commission recommends for voluntary adoption by means which do not involve the creation of new labor laws, but all of the ones the Commission considered, it found wanting. One might give an employee a right to sue for failure to produce records on request, for example, but such a right would hardly be effective where records are difficult to identify with any reasonable degree of specificity; where it is difficult to link adverse decisions to records; and where it is often difficult to determine even that a particular decision was adverse. Given this situation and the possibility of reprisals, it seems reasonable to expect that most employees would be unwilling to sue an employer for access to records, or for correction of erroneous records. Furthermore, without specific protections, record-keeping personnel might find themselves in an awkward bind, if, for example, persons with more status in the organization pressured them to divulge information they were required by law to keep confidential. If they complied, they would violate the law; if they refused, they might lose their jobs.

In many other areas the Commission has studied, there are either Federal or State bodies responsible for monitoring the operations and performance of particular industries, such as insurance and banking. In the employment area, however, enforcement through government monitoring of employment record keeping, or even through a system whereby an employee could complain to a government agency about his employer's failure to comply with privacy protection requirements, would require creation of a new government program. Given the great number of records that would be eligible for oversight under the Commission's recommendations, and the fact that the collection and use of records varies considerably among employers, it would be a massive task for any government agency to oversee effectively the internal record-keeping practices of private employers. Such intervention by government, moreover, could markedly change the character of the employee-employer relationship in directions the Commission has not considered itself competent to evaluate.

The Commission does, of course, recognize that a voluntary approach may not be effective. Indeed, a minority of the members of the Commission are convinced that it will not be. They do not agree that to give an individual a statutory right to see, copy, and correct a record an employer maintains about him must be, of necessity, to give him a right without a remedy. The entity the Commission recommends in Chapter 1 might give further consideration to this matter.

It should be noted that there are no legal barriers or conflicts with other laws that would prevent companies from voluntarily complying with the Commission's recommendations. In addition, the experience of companies that have complied voluntarily will no doubt guide future determinations as to the need for, and practicality of, legislative action. Thus, the Commission as a whole hopes that the analysis and recommendations in this chapter will move the society toward a better understanding of the issues involved, the remedies that might be possible, and the balances that need to be struck.

REVIEW OF RECORD-KEEPING PRACTICES

Although private-sector employers are increasingly aware of the need to control the collection, maintenance, use, and disclosure of information about employees, employer practices vary widely, as do their methods of conforming practice to policy. The Commission's hearing record illustrates this variety.

Some large corporations have developed comprehensive fair information practice policies that they have systematically communicated to their employees.[15] Others have developed practices to deal with some privacy protection concerns, but not others.[16] Most employers, however, have not undertaken any sort of systematic review of their employment record-keeping policies and practices with privacy protection in mind. If such studies are done, it is usually because of Equal Employment Opportunity Act requirements or because the firm wants to automate some of its employment-related record keeping.[17] Only rarely has the employee's perspective motivated reform of record-keeping practices, and in only a very few instances has an employer invited active participation by employees in revising its policies and practices.[18]

Several employers testified that they had created privacy protection

---

[15] See, for example, Submission of the Cummins Engine Company, "Employee Profile," Employment Records Hearings, December 9, 1976, p. 7; Submission of the Equitable Life Assurance Society of the U.S., "Privacy Principles, General Operating Policy No. 29," March 19, 1976; and Submission of International Business Machines, "Four Principles of Privacy," Employment Records Hearings, December 10, 1976.

[16] See, for example, Submission of the Proctor and Gamble Company, "Release of Information About Present or Former Employees," Employment Records Hearings, December 9, 10, 16, 17, 1976; and Submission of the Manufacturers Hanover Corporation, "The Standards We Live By," Employment Records Hearings, December 16, 1976.

[17] See, for example, Testimony of the Inland Steel Company, Employment Records Hearings, December 10, 1976, p. 369; and Testimony of the Cummins Engine Company, Employment Records Hearings, December 9, 1976, p. 2.

[18] See, for example, Testimony of the Cummins Engine Company, Employment Records Hearings, December 9, 1976, p. 13.

review committees to study and report on employment-related record-keeping practices. In some instances, these bodies have been given permanent advisory responsibilities.[19] Such high-level committees, however, are rare. Some corporations have issued statements of policy or principle which inform employees and the public of their concern about the employment records they maintain. Others, without making any formal statements, have instituted record-keeping procedures that take account of privacy protection concerns.[20] One major corporation testified that it had had a policy of allowing employees to have access to their records for years, but in reviewing its practices, discovered that its employees were unaware of the policy.[21] Nothing in the Commission's record suggests that such a finding is unusual.

Among organizations that have adopted policies or practices to regulate the handling of records about employees, few have any way of checking to see if they are being carried out uniformly.[22] Moreover, action taken at the corporate level is not always communicated to field offices, and few employers testified that they penalize record-keeping personnel for failure to comply with administrative instructions about the handling of employee records.[23]

The first step for employers who want to develop and execute privacy protection safeguards along the lines recommended by the Commission is to examine their current record-keeping policies and practices. The Commission also believes that employees should be represented on any group that undertakes such an examination.

Any review of current policy and practice should look carefully at the number and type of records held on applicants, employees, and former employees, and the items of information in each record. It should examine the uses made of employee records, their flow both within and outside of the employing organization, and how long they are maintained. Compliance with established policies and procedures should also be reviewed, particularly when a corporation has offices and plants in different States or in foreign

---

[19] See, for example, Testimony of the Equitable Life Assurance Society, Employment Records Hearings, December 9, 1976, p. 107; Testimony of the General Electric Company, Employment Records Hearings, December 9, 1976, pp. 226, 227; Testimony of the Cummins Engine Company, Employment Records Hearings, December 9, 1976, p. 10; and Submission of the International Business Machines Corporation, "The Managing of Employee Personal Information and Employee Privacy," Employment Records Hearings, December 10, 1976, pp. 8-9.

[20] See, for example, Testimony of the Inland Steel Company, Employment Records Hearings, December 10, 1976, pp. 332, 373.

[21] Testimony of the Ford Motor Company, Employment Records Hearings, December 16, 1976, p. 517.

[22] Alan Westin, "Trends in Computerization of Personnel Data," Part II, 1955-1976, Unpublished Report for the National Bureau of Standards' Project on Personnel Practices, Computers and Citizens Rights, p. 4; Testimony of the General Electric Company, Employment Records Hearings, December 9, 1976, pp. 267-268; Testimony of the Equitable Life Assurance Society, Employment Records Hearings, December 9, 1976, p. 133; and Testimony of Rockwell International, Employment Records Hearings, December 17, 1976, pp. 922-924.

[23] See, for example, Submission of General Electric, "Safeguarding Confidential Data," Unpublished memorandum to Major Appliance Group, June 21, 1976; and Testimony of the Inland Steel Company, Employment Records Hearings, December 10, 1976, p. 366.

countries. Finally, the review should determine whether, or in what situations, an employer systematically informs individuals of the uses and disclosures that are made of employment records about them. The Commission, in sum, recommends:

Recommendation (1):

That an employer periodically and systematically examine its employment and personnel record-keeping practices, including a review of:

(a)   **the number and types of records it maintains on individual employees, former employees, and applicants;**
(b)   **the items of information contained in each type of employment record it maintains;**
(c)   **the uses made of the items of information in each type of record;**
(d)   **the uses made of such records within the employing organization;**
(e)   **the disclosures made of such records to parties outside the employing organization; and**
(f)   **the extent to which individual employees, former employees, and applicants are both aware and systematically informed of the uses and disclosures that are made of information in the records kept about them.**

Once having initiated such a program, an employer should be in a position to improve, articulate, and communicate to its employees both its privacy protection policies and its internal arrangements for assuring that these policies are consistently observed.

ADHERENCE TO FAIR INFORMATION PRACTICE POLICY

Although consenting to the divulgence of information about oneself can have little meaning for an individual who needs a job, an employer's adherence to a fair information practice policy can alleviate an applicant or employee's sense of uncontrolled exposure to intrusion on his personal privacy. The preliminary health questionnaire used by the IBM Corporation, for example, includes a detailed explanation of its purpose.[24] The Cummins Engine Company's employee profile form, a copy of which is routinely sent to all employees, lists all possible users within the corporation, tells which information on the form goes to which users, and invites employees to address questions to the record system manager or the personnel office.[25] Other employers follow similar procedures.[26]

If, however, a category of employment records is not shared with

---

[24] Submission of International Business Machines, "Preliminary Health Questionnaire," Employment Records Hearings, December 10, 1976.

[25] Submission of Cummins Engine Company, "Employee Profile," Employment Records Hearings, December 9, 1976.

[26] See, for example, Submission of J. C. Penney, "Drug Screen Report," Employment

applicants and employees as a matter of policy, prevailing practice appears to be for employers not even to inform employees that such a category of records exists. Some employers indicated to the Commission that employees, in their opinion, have no legitimate interest in knowing of the existence of certain records, such as evaluations of employee "potential" used for management planning or records associated with security investigations.[27] This position is hard to defend, since it argues for record-keeping systems whose very existence may be concealed, a posture with respect to minimum standards of fairness in personal-data record keeping that even the investigative agencies of the Federal government have not vigorously put forward. Nonetheless, there are many who will still try to defend it.

In the Commission's view, an employer's fair information practice policy must recognize eight basic obligations:

(1) *to limit the employer's collection of information about applicants and employees to matters that are relevant to the particular decisions to be made and to avoid items of information that tend to stigmatize an individual unfairly.* This can be a difficult judgment to make as there is little agreement on the characteristics that suit an individual to a particular job. The J.C. Penney Company has recently made an interesting attempt to limit its information collection to relevant items, and as a result, the firm's new employment application no longer asks about such things as leisure activities, military history, convictions (except for specific offenses), physical or mental condition, or alien status.[28]

(2) *to inform all applicants, employees, and former employees with whom it maintains a continuing relationship (such as retirees) of all uses that may be made of the records the employer keeps on them.* This makes it possible for individuals to understand the record-keeping aspects of their employment relationships and thus, as indicated earlier, to alleviate any sense they may have of uncontrolled intrusion on their personal privacy.

(3) *to notify employees of each type of record that may be maintained on them, including records that are not available to them for review and correction,* so that employees need not fear that hidden sources of information are contributing to decisions about them;

(4) *to institute and publicize procedures for assuring that individually identifiable employment records are (a) created, used, and disclosed according to consistently followed procedures; (b) kept as accurate, timely, and complete as is necessary to assure that*

Records Hearings, December 10, 1976; and Submission of General Electric Company, "Medical History," Employment Records Hearings, December 9, 1976.

[27] See, for example, Testimony of the Ford Motor Company, Employment Records Hearings, December 16, 1976, pp. 559, 560. In addition, every corporate witness testified that some of its employment records were unavailable to employees.

[28] Submission of J. C. Penney, "Application Form," Employment Records Hearings, December 10, 1976.

they are not the cause of unfairness in decisions made on the basis of them; and (c) disclosed within and outside of the employing organization only according to stated policy;

(5) *to institute and publicize a broadly applicable policy of letting employees see, copy, correct, or amend, and if necessary, dispute individually identifiable information about themselves in the employer's records;*

(6) *to monitor the internal flow of individually identifiable employee record information,* so that information is available only as actually needed according to clearly defined criteria;

(7) *to regulate external disclosures of individually identifiable employee-record information in accordance with an established policy of which employees are made aware,* including specific routine disclosures such as disclosures of payroll tax information to the Internal Revenue Service and disclosures made without the employee's authorization in response to specific inquiries or requests to verify information about him; and

(8) *to assess its employee record-keeping policies and practices, at regular intervals, with a view to possibilities for improving them.*

In sum, as an overall framework for addressing fair information practice concerns in the employment relationship, the Commission recommends:

Recommendation (2):

That an employer articulate, communicate, and implement fair information practice policies for employment records which should include:

(a) limiting the collection of information on individual employees, former employees, and applicants to that which is relevant to specific decisions;

(b) informing employees, applicants, and former employees who maintain a continuing relationship with the employer of the uses to be made of such information;

(c) informing employees as to the types of records that are being maintained on them;

(d) adopting reasonable procedures to assure the accuracy, timeliness, and completeness of information collected, maintained, used, or disclosed about individual employees, former employees, and applicants;

(e) permitting individual employees, former employees, and applicants to see, copy, correct, or amend the records maintained about them;

(f) limiting the internal use of records maintained on individual employees, former employees, and applicants;

(g) limiting external disclosures of information in records kept on individual employees, former employees, and applicants, including disclosures made without the employee's authorization in response to specific inquiries or requests to verify information about him; and

(h) providing for regular review of compliance with articulated fair information practice policies.

SPECIFIC RECOMMENDATIONS

With a few important exceptions, the Commission's specific recommendations on record keeping in the employee-employer relationship also embody a voluntary scheme for resolving questions of fairness in the collection, use, and dissemination of employee records. The reasons for not recommending statutory implementation of many of these recommendations should by now be clear. The Commission does, however, believe that employees, like other categories of individuals, should have certain prerogatives with respect to the records that are kept about them, and the recommendations below, if adopted, would serve to define those prerogatives as a matter of practice.

Intrusiveness

Some of the information an employer uses in making hiring and placement decisions is acquired from sources other than the individual applicant or employee. In addition to former employers and references named by the individual, such third-party sources may include physicians, creditors, teachers, neighbors, and law enforcement authorities.

One way to keep an employer's inquiries within reasonable bounds is to limit the outside sources it may contact without the individual's knowledge or authorization, as well as what the employer may seek from the individual himself. To do so, however, is to grapple with long and widely held societal views regarding the propriety of inquiries into an individual applicant or employee's background, medical history, credit worthiness, and reputation. As the Commission has agreed elsewhere in this report, the intrusions on personal privacy that seem to be taken for granted in many of the record-keeping relationships the Commission has studied usually begin with the criteria we, as a society, accept as proper ones for making decisions about people. Thus, while the Commission was struck by the extensiveness of the inquiries some employers make into matters such as medical history, it concluded that so long as society considers the line of inquiry legitimate, judgments about how extensive it should be must be largely aesthetic.

The same was not true, however, with regard to some of the *techniques* that are used to collect information about applicants and employees. There the Commission found a few it considers so intolerably intrusive as to justify banning them, irrespective of the relevance of the information they generate.

TRUTH VERIFICATION DEVICES

The polygraph examination, often called the lie-detector test, is one technique the Commission believes should be proscribed on intrusiveness grounds. The polygraph is used by employers to assess the honesty of job applicants and to gather evidence about employees suspected of illegal activity on the job. An estimated 300,000 individuals submitted to this procedure in 1974.[29]

The main objections to the use of the polygraph in the employment context are: (1) that it deprives individuals of any control over divulging information about themselves; and (2) that it is unreliable. Although the latter is the focal point of much of the continuing debate about polygraph testing, the former is the paramount concern from a privacy protection viewpoint. During the 93rd Congress, the Senate Subcommittee on Constitutional Rights concluded that polygraph testing in the context of *Federal* employment raises intrusiveness issues of Constitutional proportions.[30] Similarly, the Committee on Government Operations of the House of Representatives emphasized the "inherent chilling effect upon individuals subjected to such examinations," and recommended that they no longer be used by Federal agencies for any purpose.[31]

Advocates of banning the polygraph in employment describe it as humiliating and inherently coercive and suspect that some employers who use it do so more to frighten employees than to collect information from them.[32] Use of the polygraph has often been the subject of collective-bargaining negotiations and has even inspired employees to strike. The Retail Clerks Association, with more than 700,000 members, urges its locals to include anti-polygraph provisions in all contracts.[33]

Other truth-verification devices now on the market, such as the Psychological Stress Evaluator (PSE), pose an even greater challenge to the notion that an individual should not be arbitrarily deprived of control over the divulgence of information about himself. Like the polygraph, the PSE electronically evaluates responses by measuring stress. Unlike the polygraph, the PSE uses voice inflections to measure stress and thus may be used without the individual knowing it is being used.[34] The use of such devices in the employment context, and the practices associated with their use, are, in the Commission's view, unreasonable invasions of personal privacy that should be summarily proscribed. The Commission, in effect, agrees with the conclusions of the two Congressional committees that have examined this issue as it arises in the Federal government and, therefore, recommends:

Recommendation (3):

That Federal law be enacted or amended to forbid an employer from

---

[29] *Privacy, Polygraph, and Employment*, Report of the Subcommittee on Constitutional Rights of the Committee on the Judiciary, U.S. Senate, 93d Congress, 2d Session, November 1974, p. 3.
[30] *Ibid.*, pp. 9-14.
[31] *Op. cit.*, House Committee on Government Operations, p. 46.
[32] *Ibid.*, p. 38.
[33] Testimony of the Retail Clerks International Association, Employment Records Hearings, December 17, 1976, p. 1009.
[34] Joseph F. Kubis, "Comparison of Voice Analysis and Polygraph as Lie Detection Procedures," (Report for U.S. Army Land Warfare Laboratory, August 1973) p. 6.

using the polygraph or other truth-verification equipment to gather information from an applicant or employee.

The Commission further recommends that the Congress implement this recommendation by a statute which bans the manufacture and sale of these truth-verification devices and prohibits their use by employers engaged in interstate commerce. A clear, strong, Federal statute would preempt existing State laws with less stringent requirements and make it impossible for employers to subvert the spirit of the law by sending applicants and employees across State lines for polygraph examinations.

PRETEXT INTERVIEWS

The Commission also finds unreasonably intrusive the practices of investigators who misrepresent who they are, on whose behalf they are making an inquiry, or the purpose of the inquiry. (These so-called "pretext interviews" are discussed in some detail in Chapter 8.)

Because background checks in connection with the selection of an applicant or the promotion or reassignment of an employee are not criminal investigations, they do not justify undercover techniques. Nor, according to testimony before the Commission, are pretext interviews necessary to conduct adequate investigations in the employment context. Witnesses from private investigative firms repeatedly said that extensive information about an applicant can be developed without resorting to such ruses.[35] Accordingly, in keeping with the posture it took on pretext interviews in connection with insurance underwriting and claims investigations, the Commission recommends:

Recommendation (4):

That the Federal Fair Credit Reporting Act be amended to provide that no employer or investigative firm conducting an investigation for an employer for the purpose of collecting information to assist the employer in making a decision to hire, promote, or reassign an individual may attempt to obtain information about the individual through pretext interviews or other false or misleading representations that seek to conceal the actual purpose(s) of the inquiry or investigation, or the identity or representative capacity of the employer or investigator.

Amending the Fair Credit Reporting Act in this way would be a reasonable extension of the Act's goal of assuring that subjects of investigations are treated fairly.

---

[35] See, for example, Testimony of Pinkerton's Incorporated, *Private Investigative Firms*, Hearings before the Privacy Protection Study Commission, January 26, 1977, p. 156 (hereinafter cited as "Private Investigative Hearings"); and Testimony of Wackenhut Corporation, Private Investigative Hearings, January 26, 1977, pp. 53-54.

REASONABLE CARE IN THE USE OF SUPPORT ORGANIZATIONS

An employer should not be totally unaccountable for the activities of others who perform services for it. The Commission believes that an employer should have an affirmative obligation to check into the *modus operandi* of any investigative firm it uses or proposes to use, and that if an employer does not use reasonable care in selecting or using such an organization, it should not be wholly absolved of responsibility for the organization's actions. Currently, the responsibility of an employer for the acts of an investigative firm whose services it engages depends upon the degree of control the employer exercises over the firm. Most investigative reporting agencies are independent contractors who traditionally reserve the authority to determine and assure compliance with the terms of their contract. Thus, under the laws of agency, an employer may be absolved of any liability for the illegal acts of an investigative firm if those acts are not required by the terms of the contract.[36] Accordingly, to establish the responsibility of an employer which uses others to gather information about applicants or employees for its own use, the Commission recommends:

Recommendation (5)

That the Federal Fair Credit Reporting Act be amended to provide that each employer and agent of an employer must exercise reasonable care in the selection and use of investigative organizations, so as to assure that the collection, maintenance, use, and disclosure practices of such organizations comply with the Commission's recommendations.

If *Recommendation (5)* were adopted, and it could be shown that an employer had hired or used an investigative firm with knowledge, either actual or constructive, that the organization was engaging in improper collection practices, such as pretext interviews, an individual or the Federal Trade Commission could initiate action against both the employer and the investigative firm and hold them jointly liable for the investigative firm's actions.

Fairness

Unfair practices can enter into employment record keeping in four main ways: (1) in the kinds of information collected for use in making decisions about individuals; (2) in the procedures used to gather such information; (3) in the procedures used to keep records about individuals accurate, timely, and complete; and (4) in the sharing of information across

---

[36] See, e.g., *Milton v. Missouri Pacific Ry. Co.*, 193 Mo. 46, 91 S.W. 949 (1906); *Inscoe v. Globe Jewelry Co.*, 200 N.C. 580, 157 S.E. 794 (1931). However, recent decisions in a few jurisdictions indicate that under certain circumstances, one who employs a private investigator may not thereby insulate himself from liability for torts committed by the investigator by merely arguing that they were committed outside the scope of the employment. *Ellenberg v. Pinkerton's, Inc.*, 125 Ga. App. 648, 188 S.E.2d 911 (1972); *Noble v. Sears, Roebuck and Co.*, 33 Cal. App. 3d 654, 109 Cal. Rptr. 269, 73 A.L.R. 3d 1164 (1973).

the variety of record-generating relationships that may be subsumed by the employment relationship.

FAIRNESS IN COLLECTION

When employers ask applicants and employees for more personal information than they need, unfairness may result. The process of selecting among applicants generally involves step-by-step disqualification of applicants on the basis of negative information. Where jobs require routine skills, or where many apply for a few vacancies, items of information that have little to do with job qualifications can become the basis for sifting among otherwise undifferentiated applicants. An arrest or conviction record remote in time or pertinence to the job being sought, or a less-than-honorable military discharge, are items of information that can be used in that way.

The cost of collecting information tends to limit what employers collect, but cost is not an effective deterrent when the item is easily obtained. Moreover, in employment, as well as in other areas in which records influence decisions about individuals, too much deference is often paid to records generated by other institutions. Unwarranted assumptions can be made about the validity and currency of information that other organizations record and disseminate. Questions are seldom asked about how the record came to be. As a result, records created by other institutions for their own decision-making purposes can unfairly stigmatize an individual. In the extreme case, they can set in motion a series of events which permanently exclude an individual from the economic mainstream, condemning him to marginal employment for a lifetime. Again, arrest, conviction, and military discharge records are principal culprits in this regard.

USE OF ARREST INFORMATION

Arrest information raises perplexing questions of fairness. Although the Commission's hearing testimony indicates that many employers no longer use arrest information in their employment decisions, a great many still do.[37] The use of arrest information in making employment decisions is questionable for several reasons. An arrest record by itself indicates only that a law enforcement officer believed he had probable cause to arrest the individual for some offense; not that the person committed the offense. For instance, an individual may have been arrested for breaking and entering a building, while further investigation revealed that he had the owner's permission to be in the building. Constitutional standards specify that convictions, not arrests, establish guilt. Thus, denial of employment because

---

[37] Written statement of American Civil Liberties Union, Employment Records Hearings, December 9, 1976, p. 5; and testimony of Sorrell Wildhorn, Rand Corporation, Private Investigative Hearings, January 26, 1977, p. 237. See also the testimony of Charles S. Allen, Jr., President, Armored Car Division, Contract Carrier Conference, American Trucking Association, and Donald J. Jarvis, Vice President - Secretary and General Counsel, Burns International Security Service. *Criminal History Records*, Hearings before the Law Enforcement Assistance Administration, U.S. Department of Justice, December 11, 1975 (transcript on file at LEAA).

of an unproved charge, a charge that has been dismissed, or one for which there has been an adjudication of innocence, is fundamentally unfair.

There is a balance to be struck between society's presumption of innocence until proven guilty and its concern for security. When it has been forced to strike that balance in the past, laws have been enacted declaring that arrests for certain offenses *must* be considered in choosing among applicants for certain kinds of employment.[38] While such action is clearly the obverse of a ban on the use of arrest information in employment decision making, it can be treated as a limit on the collection and use of such information. Accordingly, the Commission recommends:

Recommendation (6):

That except as specifically required by Federal or State statute or regulation, or by municipal ordinance or regulation, an employer should not seek or use a record of arrest pertaining to an individual applicant or employee.

In addition, to give this recommendation force, the Commission further recommends:

Recommendation (7):

That existing Federal and State statutes and regulations, and municipal ordinances and regulations, which require an employer to seek or use an arrest record pertaining to an individual applicant or employee be amended so as *not* to require that an arrest record be sought or used if it is more than one year old and has not resulted in a disposition; and that all subsequently enacted statutes, regulations, and ordinances incorporate this same limitation.

Where an *indictment* is outstanding, *Recommendations (6)* and *(7)* would allow an employer to use it, even if a year had passed without disposition of the charge. Without the limitation *Recommendation (7)* would impose, however, the use of an arrest record is doubly unfair in that the information is untimely as well as incomplete. Because of rules requiring that cases be dropped if there is not a speedy trial and because the prosecution frequently drops cases where it does not have sufficient evidence to bring them to trial, the record of such cases may remain without disposition, and therefore be incomplete.

OCCUPATIONAL LICENSING

Many jurisdictions have occupational licensing laws that require an

---

[38] See, for example, California Labor Code Sec. 432.7(e)(1) and (2).

applicant to be of good moral character, the definition of good moral character being left to administrative boards or the courts to determine.[39] Commonly, these bodies define an arrest record as pertinent to assessing moral character. The Commission obviously believes that an arrest record *per se* is an uncertain indicator of character; that if arrest records are to be sought, the language of the statute or regulation should specifically state both the type of occupation for which such information is necessary and the type of offense that is relevant to the required assessment of moral fitness. To do otherwise, in the Commission's view, is to invite unfair discrimination. Accordingly, the Commission recommends:

Recommendation (8):

That legislative bodies review their licensing requirements and amend any statutes, regulations, or ordinances to assure that unless arrest records for designated offenses are specifically required by statute, regulation, or ordinance, they will not be collected by administrative bodies which decide on an individual's qualifications for occupational licensing.

THE LAW ENFORCEMENT ASSISTANCE ADMINISTRATION ROLE

The Commission believes that it will be difficult to stop the inappropriate use of arrest information in employment decision making unless the dissemination of such information by law enforcement agencies and criminal justice information systems is restricted. Although no national policy or Federal legislation deals comprehensively with the collection, storage, and dissemination of criminal justice information by law enforcement authorities, some State laws do, and a start in the direction of formulating a national policy has been made. The Omnibus Crime Control and Safe Streets Act of 1968, as amended in 1973, contains some loose protections against unfair uses of records in State criminal justice information systems. It specifies that if arrest information is maintained, disposition information should also be maintained where feasible; that there should be reasonable procedures for assuring the accuracy of the information maintained and disseminated; that the subject of the information should be allowed to review it and challenge its accuracy; and that the information should only be used for lawful purposes. *[42 U.S.C. 3771(b)]* Even with this statute, however, and the Law Enforcement Assistance Administration regulations implementing it *[28 C.F.R. 20.21]*, criminal histories are still too readily available to employers. Criminal justice information systems at State and local levels frequently do not have the capacity to disseminate only conviction information or records of arrest for specific offenses. Few are able to update arrest and disposition information promptly. The systems as they have developed often are incapable of making fine-grained distinctions between an arrest with pending disposition and one which has been recently

---

[39] See, for example, *Purdon's Pennsylvania Statutes Annotated: Professions and Occupations, Title 63*, and Code of Laws of South Carolina 56-1305 ("Licensing of Pharmacists"), 1952.

dismissed. Thus, while it is feasible to correct information in a system after a year or so, the status of an arrest may be inaccurately recorded during the intervening period.

The Commission has not found a solution to this problem, but believes that the Law Enforcement Assistance Administration can and should do so. Accordingly, the Commission recommends:

Recommendation (9):

That the Law Enforcement Assistance Administration study or, by its grant or contract authority, designate others to study, alternative approaches to establishing within State and local criminal justice information systems the capacity to limit disclosures of arrest information to employers to that which they are lawfully required to obtain, and to improve the system's capacity to maintain accurate and timely information regarding the status of arrests and dispositions.

RETENTION OF ARREST INFORMATION

Because of the stigma attached to having an arrest record, and because arrest information is primarily used in hiring, the Commission believes that no employer should keep an arrest record on an individual after he is hired, unless there is an outstanding indictment or conviction. Accordingly, the Commission recommends:

Recommendation (10):

That when an arrest record is lawfully sought or used by an employer to make a specific decision about an applicant or employee, the employer should not maintain the record for a period longer than specifically required by law, if any, or unless there is an outstanding indictment.

CONVICTION RECORDS

The problems conviction records present in employment decision making are different from those presented by arrest information. A conviction is a societal judgment on the actions of an individual. Unlike arrest information, a conviction record is not incomplete.

Federal and State laws sometimes require employers to check the conviction records of applicants for jobs in particular industries. Banks, for example, are required by the Federal Deposit Insurance Corporation to have the FBI check every job applicant for conviction of crimes involving dishonesty or breach of trust. *[17 C.F.R. 240.17 f. -2]* Similarly, the Department of Transportation requires the trucking industry to find out whether a would-be driver has been convicted of reckless driving. *[49 C.F.R. 391.27]* The Bureau of Narcotics and Dangerous Drugs requires drug manufacturers to check the conviction records of all job applicants. *[21 C.F.R. 1301.90, 1301.93]*

Nevertheless, uneasiness among employers about the relevance of conviction records to employment decisions is growing. Some employers have stopped collecting them;[40] others have reworded their application forms to inquire only about convictions relevant to the position for which an individual is applying. For example, the J.C. Penney Company now asks an applicant to list only convictions for crimes involving a breach of trust.[41] Other employers specify felonies only or exclude traffic offenses, and some ask applicants to list only felonies committed during the past five years.[42]

Thus, to encourage employers to take steps voluntarily to protect individuals against unfair uses of conviction records in employment decision making, the Commission recommends:

Recommendation (11):

That unless otherwise required by law, an employer should seek or use a conviction record pertaining to an individual applicant or employee only when the record is directly relevant to a specific employment decision affecting the individual.

RETENTION OF CONVICTION RECORDS

Once conviction information has been collected and used in making a particular decision, retaining it raises still another fairness issue. The Commission has recommended that arrest-record information be destroyed after use, but the need for conviction information may recur, as when an employee is being considered for bonding or a position of trust. For the employer to have to seek the same information again and again would inconvenience both employee and employer.

Two witnesses before the Commission, IBM and General Electric, testified that they request conviction information on a perforated section of the application form. The personnel department tears off this segment and either seals it or maintains it separately from the individual's personnel file before circulating the form to potential supervisors.[43] Thus, conviction information is not available in making decisions except when it is specifically required. The Commission believes this practice is a sound one, and thus, recommends:

Recommendation (12):

That where conviction information is collected, it should be maintained separately from other individually identifiable employment

---

40 Cummins Engine Company, interview with staff, November 4, 1976.

41 Submission of J. C. Penney Company, "Application Form," Employment Records Hearings, December 10, 1976.

42 See, for example, Submission of International Business Machines, "Application Form," Employment Records Hearings, December 10, 1976.

43 See, for example, Submission of International Business Machines, "Application Form," Employment Records Hearings, December 10, 1976; and Submission of General Electric Company, "Application Form," Employment Records Hearings, December 9, 1976.

records so that it will not be available to persons who have no need for it.

MILITARY-RECORD INFORMATION

SPN Codes. The use some employers make of military discharge records, and of the administrative codes found on the Department of Defense (DOD) form known as the "DD-214," raises still another set of fairness issues. Of particular concern is the use of the separation program number (SPN) codes that the DOD assigned to all dischargees beginning in 1953. These codes may indicate many things, including an individual's sexual proclivities, psychiatric disorders, discharge to accept public office, or status as sole surviving child. The DOD uses them in preparing administrative and statistical reports and in considering whether an individual should be permitted to re-enlist. The Veterans Administration uses them to determine eligibility for benefits. Employers, however, also use them, and in the employment context they can do a great deal of harm.

SPN codes are frequently assigned on the basis of subjective judgments which are difficult for the dischargee to challenge. Until recently, the codes had different meanings in each branch of service, and they have been changed several times, leaving them prone to misinterpretation by employers not possessing the proper key. (Although employers are not supposed to know what the SPN codes mean, many have found out as a result of leaks from the agencies authorized to have them.)[44]

In 1974, the DOD tried to stop unfair use of SPN codes by leaving them off its forms and offering anyone discharged prior to 1974 an opportunity to get a new form DD-214 without a SPN code. This solution has several defects. For one thing, not all pre-1974 dischargees know of the reissuance program. For another, a pre-1974 DD-214 without a SPN code may raise a canny employer's suspicion that the applicant had the SPN code removed because he has something to hide.

Inasmuch as this problem still seems to be a significant one, the Commission believes that the DOD should reassess its SPN code policy. The Department might consider issuing new DD-214 forms to all dischargees whose forms presently include SPN codes. Although such a blanket reissuance could be costly, without it employers will continue to draw negative inferences from the fact that an individual has exercised his option to have the SPN code removed. In any case, SPN code keys should stay strictly within the DOD and the Veterans Administration.

Issuing new DD-214s and tightening code key disclosure practices, however, will not resolve the problem if employers can continue to require that dischargees applying for jobs authorize the release of the narrative descriptions in their DOD records. The most effective control over this information would be a flat prohibition on its disclosure to employers, even when the request is authorized by the applicant. This would have to be done

---

[44] *Need for and Uses of Data Recorded on DD Form 214 Report of Separation from Active Duty*, Report of the Subcommittee on Drug Abuse in Military Services of the Committee on Armed Services, U.S. Senate, January 23, 1975.

in such a way as not to preclude individuals from requesting narrative descriptions from the DOD for their own purposes, since they are entitled to do so under the Privacy Act.[45]

Military Discharge Records. The military discharge system, as it works today, still influences employment opportunities. There are five types of discharges: honorable, general, other than honorable, bad conduct, and dishonorable. General and other than honorable discharges are products of an administrative process which usually includes the right to a hearing before a board and a subsequent right of administrative appeal. Bad conduct and dishonorable discharges, on the other hand, are only given after a full court-martial.

In practice, it appears that employers tend to disregard the distinction between the administrative discharge and discharges resulting from courts-martial.[46] Thus, any discharge except an honorable one can be the ticket to a lifetime of rejected job applications. Nor is that accidental. The DOD has intentionally linked discharge status to future employment as an incentive to good behavior while in the service.[47]

It can be argued that military service is just another kind of employment, and that discharge information is no different from information about any other past employment which applicants routinely release to prospective employers. Military service and civilian employment are not, however, comparable, since few civilian jobs involve supervision of almost every aspect of an employee's life.

On March 28, 1977, the Secretary of Defense announced a program for reviewing Viet Nam era discharges. It applies to two categories of individuals: (1) former servicemen who were discharged during the period August 4, 1964 to March 28, 1973, and who, if enlisted, received an undesirable or general discharge, or if an officer received a general or other than honorable discharge; and (2) servicemen in administrative desertion status whose period of desertion commenced between August 4, 1964 and March 28, 1973, and who meet certain other criteria. The discharge review portion of this program gives eligible veterans six months to apply for possible upgrading if positive service or extenuating personal circumstances appear to warrant it. The program aims at adjusting inequities that occurred during a particularly troubled period in our nation's history. It does not, however, address all the problems mentioned above. It does not extend to veterans with honorable discharges that carry possibly stigmatizing SPN codes. Nor does it apply to anyone separated from service with a general or undesirable discharge after March 28, 1973, although the normal channels for administrative review of such discharges are open to such individuals.

---

[45] Letter from Walter W. Stender, Assistant Archivist for Federal Records Centers, General Services Administration National Archives and Records Service, to the Privacy Protection Study Commission, March 3, 1977; see also, General Services Administration "Release and Access Guide for Military and Personnel Records at the National Personnel Records Center," December 30, 1976.

[46] See, for example, Testimony of the Ford Motor Company, Employment Records Hearings, December 16, 1976, p. 585.

[47] Letter from D. O. Cooke, Deputy Assistant Secretary of Defense, to the Privacy Protection Study Commission, January 18, 1977.

Thus, despite this welcome initiative, the Commission recommends:

Recommendation (13):

That Congress direct the Department of Defense to reassess the extent to which the current military discharge system and the administrative codes on military discharge records have needless discriminatory consequences for the individual in civilian employment and should, therefore, be modified. The reassessment should pay particular attention to the separation program number (SPN) codes administratively assigned to dischargees so as to determine how better to limit their use and dissemination, and should include a determination as to the feasibility of:

(a) **issuing new DD-214 forms to all dischargees whose forms currently include SPN numbers;**

(b) **restricting the use of SPN codes to the Department of Defense and the Veterans Administration, for designated purposes only; and**

(c) **prohibiting the disclosure of codes and the narrative descriptions supporting them to an employer, even where such disclosure is authorized by the dischargee.**

NOTICE REGARDING COLLECTION FROM THIRD PARTIES

The background check is the most common means of verifying or supplementing information an employer collects directly from an applicant or employee. Some employers have their own background investigators,[48] but many hire an outside firm. The practices of private investigative firms are discussed in detail in Chapter 8. The discussion here focuses on the employer's responsibility when it conducts such an investigation itself, or hires a firm to do so in its behalf.

A background check may do no more than verify information provided by an applicant. It may, however, seek out additional information on previous employment, criminal history, life style, and personal reputation. The scope of such a background check depends on what the employer asks for, how much it is willing to pay, and the character of the firm hired to conduct the investigation. The Fair Credit Reporting Act (FCRA) protects the subject of certain types of pre-employment investigations by providing ways for him to keep track of what is going on and contribute to the investigative process. The Act's protections, however, do not extend to many applicants and employees, and the FCRA pre-notification requirement and the right of access the Act affords an individual to investigative reports are both too limited.

The FCRA requires that an individual be given prior notice of an employment investigation, but only if the investigation relates to a job for

---

[48] See, for example, Testimony of the Ford Motor Company, Employment Records Hearings, December 16, 1976, p. 531; and Testimony of Rockwell International, Employment Records Hearings, December 17, 1976, pp. 953, 955, 957.

which he has formally applied and only if the employer retains outside help for the investigation. It does not require that an individual be told the name of the investigating firm, the types of information that will be gathered, the techniques and sources that will be used, or to whom information about him may be disclosed without his authorization. Furthermore, there is no requirement that the individual be notified if the information is or may be retained by the investigative agency and perhaps used by it in whole or in part during subsequent investigations it conducts for other employers or other users. Nor does the Act, as a practical matter, give an individual an opportunity to prevent the investigation, to suggest alternative sources, or to contradict the investigative agency's interpretation of what it discovers about him. The Act does require that an applicant be told when an adverse decision has been based on information in an investigative report and that he be given a chance to learn the nature and substance of the report, but these requirements only apply in situations where prior notice of the investigation is also required. *[15 U.S.C. 1681d, g]* That is, an individual need not be told anything if he has not applied for the job or promotion that has prompted the investigation, or if the investigation was conducted by the employer rather than by an outside firm. Thus, to strengthen the notice requirements of the FCRA as they protect individuals being investigated in connection with employment decisions, the Commission recommends:

Recommendation (14):

That the Federal Fair Credit Reporting Act be amended to provide that an employer, prior to collecting, or hiring others to collect, from sources outside of the employing organization the type of information generally collected in making a consumer report or consumer-investigative report (as defined by the Fair Credit Reporting Act) about an applicant, employee, or other individual in connection with an employment decision, notify the applicant, employee, or other individual as to:

(a) the types of information expected to be collected about him from third parties that are not collected on an application, and, as to information regarding character, general reputation, and mode of living, each area of inquiry;

(b) the techniques that may be used to collect such types of information;

(c) the types of sources that are expected to be asked to provide each type of information;

(d) the types of parties to whom and circumstances under which information about the individual may be disclosed without his authorization, and the types of information that may be disclosed;

(e) the procedures established by statute by which the individual may gain access to any resulting record about himself;

(f) the procedures whereby the individual may correct, amend, or dispute any resulting record about himself; and

(g)   the fact that information in any report prepared by a consumer-
reporting agency (as defined by the Fair Credit Reporting Act)
may be retained by that organization and subsequently disclosed by it to others.

If *Recommendation (14)* were adopted, the current FCRA enforcement
mechanisms would apply to employers who do their own investigations, as
well as to investigative agencies. Employers argue that not letting a
candidate for a job or promotion know he is being investigated protects him
from disappointment. In the Commission's view, that argument is overridden by considerations of fairness to the individual. The purpose of requiring
a notice of investigation is to alert an individual before information about
him is collected. The purpose of requiring specific items in the notice is to
apprise the individual of the extent of the intrusion. The purpose of the
notice regarding access, correction, and amendment procedures is to assure
that applicants and employees know that these rights exist and how to
exercise them.

NOTICE AS COLLECTION LIMITATION

The anticipated benefits of *Recommendation (14)* for the individual
would be negated if an employer deviated from its notification. Moreover,
many employers depend on investigative-reporting agencies whose collection practices could go considerably beyond what is stated in such a notice.
Thus, to guard against these possibilities, the Commission recommends:

Recommendation (15):

That the Fair Credit Reporting Act be amended to provide that an
employer limit:

(a)   its own information collection and disclosure practices to those
specified in the notice called for in *Recommendation (14)*; and
(b)   its request to any organization it asks to collect information on
its behalf to information, techniques, and sources specified in
the notice called for in *Recommendation (14)*.

Like the notice recommendation itself, the existing Fair Credit
Reporting Act enforcement mechanisms would be available to individuals
when the limitations on notice have been exceeded either by employers or
investigative firms. Consequently, an applicant or employee would be able
to pursue Fair Credit Reporting Act remedies when an employer or
investigative firm collected information from third parties or used techniques of collection other than as stated in the notice. Also, if an individual
finds that the consumer investigative report has information beyond that
specified in the notice, he should be able to have it deleted from his record.

AUTHORIZATION STATEMENTS

In many instances an employer must have an applicant or employee's permission before it can get personal information about him from other persons or institutions. In general, physicians and hospitals do not disclose individually identifiable information about a patient without the patient's specific written authorization. As a consequence of the Family Educational Rights and Privacy Act of 1974 (see Chapter 10), educational institutions no longer respond to an employer's inquiries about a current or former student without the individual's consent. Testimony before the Commission indicates that employers themselves are becoming reluctant to disclose information about their former employees to other employers.[49]

Nonetheless, many employers' job application forms still include a release which the applicant must sign, authorizing the employer to acquire information from organizations or individuals that have a confidential relationship with the applicant.[50] Or, as noted in Chapter 8, an investigative firm may require that the employer get releases from employees to facilitate its inquiries on the employer's behalf. As in the insurance area, these authorizations are usually broad; and few warn that the information collected could be retained and reported to subsequent clients of the investigative firm.

When any authorization or waiver of confidentiality is sought from an applicant or employee, fairness demands that it be limited both in scope and period of validity. It should bear the date of signature and expire no more than one year from that date. It should be worded so that the individual who is asked to sign it can understand it, and should specify the persons and institutions to whom it will be presented and the information that each will be asked for, together with the reasons for seeking the information.

Requiring this degree of specificity in authorizations should not unduly hamper legitimate investigations and will go far to improve the quality of the personal information held not only by investigative firms and employers, but by other keepers of individually identifiable information as well. Accordingly, the Commission recommends:

Recommendation (16):

That no employer or consumer-reporting agency (as defined by the Fair Credit Reporting Act) acting on behalf of an employer ask, require, or otherwise induce an applicant or employee to sign any statement authorizing any individual or institution to disclose information about him, or about any other individual, unless the statement is:

(a)   in plain language;

---

[49] See, for example, Testimony of International Business Machines, Employment Records Hearings, December 10, 1976, p. 315; Testimony of Manufacturers Hanover Trust Company, Employment Records Hearings, December 16, 1976, pp. 678-679; and Testimony of Civil Service Commission, Employment Records Hearings, December 10, 1976, p. 414. Exception to this general practice may occur when an employee is terminated for cause, in which case this fact may be released. Testimony of Ford Motor Company, Employment Records Hearings, December 16, 1976, pp. 517-518, 599.

[50] See, for example, Testimony of General Electric Company, Employment Records Hearings, December 9, 1976, p. 252.

(b) dated;

(c) specific as to the individuals and institutions he is authorizing to disclose information about him who are known at the time the authorization is signed, and general as to others whose specific identity is not known at the time the authorization is signed;

(d) specific as to the nature of the information he is authorizing to be disclosed;

(e) specific as to the individuals or institutions to whom he is authorizing information to be disclosed;

(f) specific as to the purpose(s) for which the information may be used by any of the parties named in (e) at the time of the disclosure; and

(g) specific as to its expiration date which should be for a reasonable period of time not to exceed one year.

It should be noted that the necessary generality permitted by parts of *Recommendation (16)* need not apply to an employer that obtains an authorization from an applicant, employee, or former employee permitting it to release confidential information to others. In that case, the authorization form can and should be specific as to what information may be disclosed, to whom, and for what purpose.

FAIRNESS IN USE

ACCESS TO RECORDS

Fairness demands that an applicant or employee be permitted to see and copy records an employer maintains about him. Allowing an employee to see and copy his records can be as advantageous to the employer as to the employee. As discussed earlier, employment records in the private sector are generally regarded as the property of management.[51] Except where limited by State statute, as in Maine[52] and California,[53] or where controlled by collective-bargaining agreements, all the rights of ownership in employment records vest in the employer. Although many firms permit, and some even encourage, employees to review at least some of the records kept about them, there is no generally accepted rule.[54] Where records are factual, e.g., benefit and payroll records, or where they are the sole basis for making a decision about an individual, such as in a seniority system, the advantages of employee access to assure accuracy are rarely disputed. However, many employers do not give their employees access to promotion tables, salary schedules, and test scores. Some employers believe that employee access to

---

[51] Letter from the Association of Washington Business to the Privacy Protection Study Commission, November 22, 1976; and Letter from The Standard Oil Company to the Privacy Protection Study Commission, October 18, 1976.

[52] Maine Rev. Stat. Ann. Tit. 5, Sec 638; Tit. 30, Sec. 64 and 2257.

[53] California Labor Code, Sec. 1198.5.

[54] See, for example, Testimony of General Electric Company, Employment Records Hearings, December 9, 1976, p. 235; Testimony of Cummins Engine Company, Employment Records Hearings, December 9, 1976, pp. 58-59; and Testimony of Inland Steel Company, Employment Records Hearings, December 10, 1976, pp. 370-373.

information may weaken their position when they are potentially in an adversary relationship with an employee, e.g., in a dispute regarding a claim for benefits. Most employers do not want employees to have access to information they believe requires professional interpretation, such as medical records and psychological tests. In addition, employers are reluctant to give employees access to information supplied by sources requesting an assurance of confidentiality. While testimony before the Commission suggests that this last problem is diminishing as reliance on references diminishes,[55] in the academic community, where candidates for tenure are traditionally evaluated by unidentified peers, concern about access to letters of references is great.[56]

Although union contracts rarely address the access issue, where formal grievances are filed, the records supporting management's decisions must, by law, be shared with the union and with the grievant. Also, certain information, such as seniority, salary, and leave, must be posted.[57] Unions have won access to particular records in specific circumstances by arbitration, and even where there is no union some employers have grievance and arbitration procedures. Without a union, however, employees who complain of violations of an internal policy on employee access to records have little protection from reprisals and no right of appeal if their complaints are ignored.

Furthermore, a right to see, copy, and request correction or amendment of an employment record is of little value, so long as an employer is free to designate which records will be accessible and to determine the merits of any dispute over accessibility or record content. Nonetheless, a well-considered access policy, consistently carried out, is strong evidence of an employer's commitment to fair practice protections for personal privacy. Such a policy gives an employee a way to know what is in records kept about him, to assure that they are factually accurate, and to make reasoned decisions about authorizing their disclosure outside the employing organization.

While recognizing that periodic evaluations of employee performance contain subjective information developed by the employer for its own use, the Commission believes that employees should have a right of access to those records also. Many employers do, in fact, share performance evaluations with their employees, as guidance on how to improve perfor-

---

[55] See, for example, Testimony of General Electric Company, Employment Records Hearings, December 9, 1976, pp. 279-280; and Testimony of Cummins Engine Company, Employment Records Hearings, December 9, 1976, p. 68.

[56] See, for example, Testimony of Harvard University, Employment Records Hearings, December 17, 1976, pp. 864-902; Letter from Jean Mayer, President, Tufts University, to Roger W. Heyns, President, American Council on Education, August 9, 1976; and Sheldon Elliot Steinbach, "Employee Privacy, 1975: Concerns of College and University Administrators," *Educational Record*, Vol. 57, No. 1, 1976.

[57] Labor Management Relations (Taft-Hartley) Act, 29 U.S.C. 141 *et seq.* (1947). For case citations, see Clyde W. Summers, *op. cit.*

mance is generally regarded as one of the more important functions of these evaluations.[58] The employee's interest in these records is obvious, since negative evaluations can deny an employee opportunities for promotion or placement. They may also disqualify him from entering the pool of employees from which such selections are made. Furthermore, records pertaining to employee performance are usually maintained in individually identifiable form and could be disclosed in that form to outside requestors.

When it comes to evaluations of an employee's *potential*, however, the testimony suggests that the resulting records frequently are not shared with employees.[59] The Commission finds it difficult to justify the difference in treatment. Performance evaluations and evaluations of potential are intimately related. Moreover, where an employee does not have access to both, supervisors can evaluate an employee one way to his face and another way behind his back, so to speak, making it impossible for him to assess his standing.

The Commission recognizes a valid difference between performance and potential evaluations when a separate set of records pertains to employees thought to have a *high potential* for advancement. Since such records are mainly a long-range planning tool of management, employees should not necessarily have a right to see and copy them, whether or not they are maintained in individually identifiable form. The mere existence of such records, however, should not be kept secret from employees.

Another type of evaluation record an employer might justifiably withhold from an employee is the security record concerning an ongoing or concluded investigation into suspected employee misconduct. Although employees have a right to know that their employer maintains security records, a general right to see, copy, and request correction of such records would seriously handicap security investigations. Nonetheless, as the Commission contends later in this chapter, access should be allowed to any information from a security record that is transferred to an individual's personnel file.

The Commission strongly believes that employees should be able to see and copy most employment records. If an individual cannot conveniently do this in person, he should be able to arrange to do so by mail or telephone, provided the employer takes reasonable care to assure itself of the identity of the requestor. Nonetheless, as the Commission has already emphasized, to legislate a right of access to records without a more general scheme of rights to protect the employee who exercises it could be futile. When the employee-employer relationship is defined by collective bargaining, access to records is an obvious topic for contract negotiation and the resulting provisions would then be binding on the parties. When, however, employee access rights are not defined by contract, or enforceable by a

---

[58] See, for example, Testimony of Cummins Engine Company, Employment Records Hearings, December 9, 1976, pp. 46-47; Testimony of Equitable Life Assurance Society of the U.S., Employment Records Hearings, December 9, 1976, pp. 131-132; and Testimony of J. C. Penney Company, Employment Records Hearings, December 10, 1976, p. 464-465.

[59] Testimony of Manufacturers Hanover Trust Company, Employment Records Hearings, December 16, 1976, p. 653.

government agency with rule-making powers, individual employees are in a poor position to resist their employer's refusal to honor their access and correction rights. As indicated earlier, there were differences within the Commission as to whether such a right need be a right without a remedy, and thus a right that should not be legislated. Recognizing that employers have discretion to determine which records they will make available to their employees, the Commission believes that employers should develop and promulgate access and correction policies voluntarily. Accordingly, the Commission recommends:

Recommendation (17):

That as a matter of policy an employer should

(a) designate clearly:

   (i) those records about an employee, former employee, or applicant for employment (including any individual who is being considered for employment but who has not formally applied) which the employer will allow such employee, former employee, or applicant to see and copy on request; and

   (ii) those records about an employee, former employee, or applicant which the employer will not make available to the employee, former employee, or applicant,

except that an employer should not designate as an unavailable record any recorded evaluation it makes of an individual's employment performance, any medical record or insurance record it keeps about an individual, or any record about an individual that it obtains from a consumer-reporting agency (as defined by the Fair Credit Reporting Act), or otherwise creates about an individual in the course of an investigation related to an employment decision not involving suspicion of wrongdoing;

(b) assure that its employees are informed as to which records are included in categories (a)(i) and (ii) above; and

(c) upon request by an individual applicant, employee, or former employee:

   (i) inform the individual, after verifying his identity, whether it has any recorded information pertaining to him that is designated as records he may see and copy; and

   (ii) permit the individual to see and copy any such record(s), either in person or by mail; or

   (iii) apprise the individual of the nature and substance of any such record(s) by telephone; and

   (iv) permit the individual to use one or the other of the methods of access provided in (c)(ii) and (iii), or both if he prefers,

except that the employer could refuse to permit the individual to see and copy any record it has designated as an unavailable record pursuant to (a)(ii), above.

ACCESS TO INVESTIGATIVE REPORTS

The Fair Credit Reporting Act requirement that an employer notify an individual when information in an investigative report was the basis for an adverse employment decision about him is inadequate. That an individual, so notified, can go to the investigative-reporting agency that made the report and demand to know what information is in it gives him some protection. *[15 U.S.C. 1681h]* The Commission believes, however, that in employment, as in insurance, the subject of an investigative report should have an affirmative right to see and copy it, and to correct, amend, or dispute its contents. When corrections, amendments, or dispute statements are entered into a report by an employer, it should so inform the investigative-reporting agency so that its records may also be altered. Finally, it is important for an individual to be notified in advance of his right to see, copy, correct, amend, or dispute a proposed report, and of the procedures for so doing.

The Commission's recommendations in Chapter 5 on the insurance relationship specify that the subject of an investigation has a right to see and copy, in two places, the report prepared by a support organization in connection with an underwriting investigation: at the office of the insurer that ordered it, and at the office of the firm that prepared it. Hence, the Commission does not recommend that the insurer or investigative agency routinely provide the individual with a copy of the report, either before or after using it to make a decision about him. To do so would be costly because of the volume of reports insurers order, many of which do not result in adverse decisions, and because *Insurance Recommendation (13)* on adverse underwriting decisions, would immediately expose a report that did result in such a decision.

In the employment context, however, several considerations urge a different approach. First, all the evidence available to the Commission indicates that there are far fewer investigative reports prepared on job applicants and employees than on insurance applicants.[60] Second, the Commission's recommendations on employment records provide no guarantee that an employee will be able to see and copy an investigative report on himself that remains in an employer's files after he is hired, even though the report could become the basis for an adverse action in the future. Third, while the Commission considered tying a see-and-copy right to the making of an adverse employment decision, it rejected the proposal because the relationship between items of information and employment decisions is not always clear enough to make such a right meaningful. Fourth, it seemed to

---

[60] See Chapter 8 of this report; See also, for example, Testimony of Equifax Services, Inc., *Credit Reporting and Payment Authorization Services,* Hearings before the Privacy Protection Study Commission, August 3, 1976, pp. 162-163; Testimony of Wackenhut Corporation, *Private Investigative Hearings,* January 26, 1977, p. 29; and Testimony of Inland Steel Company, Employment Records Hearings, December 10, 1976, p. 349.

the Commission that for a rejected applicant to exercise a see-and-copy right would be awkward at best.

Hence, to balance an employer's legitimate need to collect information on applicants and employees through background checks against the procedural protections needed to insure fairness to the individual in making such investigations and using the information so acquired, the Commission recommends:

Recommendation (18):

That the Fair Credit Reporting Act be amended to provide:

(a)   that an applicant or employee shall have a right to:
    (i)   see and copy information in an investigative report maintained either by a consumer-reporting agency (as defined by the Fair Credit Reporting Act) or by the employer that requested it; and
    (ii)   correct, amend (including supplement), or dispute in writing, any information in an investigative report maintained either by a consumer-reporting agency (as defined by the Fair Credit Reporting Act) or by the employer that requested it;
(b)   that an employer must automatically inform a consumer-reporting agency (as defined by the Fair Credit Reporting Act) of any correction or amendment of information made in an investigative report at the request of the individual, or any other dispute statement made in writing by the individual; and
(c)   that an employer must provide an applicant or employee on whom an investigative report is made with a copy of that report at the time it is made by or given to the employer.

ACCESS TO MEDICAL RECORDS

The medical records an employer maintains differ significantly in character and use from the other records created in the employee-employer relationship. Responsibility for giving physical examinations to determine possible work restrictions and for serving as primary medical-care providers is falling ever more heavily on employers, giving them increasingly extensive medical files on their employees. These records, and opinions based on them, may enter into employment decisions, as well as into other types of non-medical decisions about applicants and employees. Hence, the Commission believes that access to them should be provided in accordance with the Commission's recommendations on medical records and medical-record information in Chapter 7. That is, *when an employer's relationship to an applicant, employee, or former employee is that of a medical-care provider,*[61] the Commission recommends:

---

[61] The term "medical-care provider" includes both "medical-care professionals" and "medical-care institutions." A "medical-care professional" is defined as "any person licensed or

Recommendation (19):

That, upon request, an individual who is the subject of a medical record maintained by an employer, or another responsible person designated by the individual, be allowed to have access to that medical record, including an opportunity to see and copy it. The employer should be able to charge a reasonable fee (not to exceed the amount charged to third parties) for preparing and copying the record.

However, when the employer's relationship to an applicant, employee, or former employee is *not that of a medical-care provider*, the Commission recommends:

Recommendation (20):

That, upon request, an individual who is the subject of medical-record information maintained by an employer be allowed to have access to that information either directly or through a licensed medical professional designated by the individual.

In Chapter 7, where the rationale for these recommendations is presented in detail, "medical-record information" is defined as:

Information relating to an individual's medical history, diagnosis, condition, treatment, or evaluation obtained from a medical-care provider or from the individual himself or from his spouse, parent, or guardian, for the purpose of making a non-medical decision about the individual.

As to *Recommendation (19)*, the Commission would urge that if a State enacts a statute creating individual rights of access to medical records pursuant to *Recommendation (2)* in Chapter 7, it encompass within the statute medical records maintained by an employer whose relationship to applicants, employees, or former employees is that of a medical-care provider.

ACCESS TO INSURANCE RECORDS

In their role as providers or administrators of insurance plans, employers maintain insurance records on employees and former employees and their dependents. Since the considerations governing access to these records are largely the same as when the records are maintained by an insurance company, the Commission believes that employer policy on access to them by the individuals to whom they pertain should be consistent

---

certified to provide medical services to individuals, including, but not limited to, a physician, dentist, nurse, optometrist, physical or occupational therapist, psychiatric social worker, clinical dietitian or clinical psychologist." A "medical-care institution" is defined as "any facility or institution that is licensed to provide medical-care services to individuals, including, but not limited to, hospitals, skilled nursing facilities, home-health agencies, clinics, rehabilitation agencies, and public-health agencies or health-maintenance organizations (HMOs)."

with the recommendation on access in Chapter 5. Accordingly, the Commission recommends:

Recommendation (21):

That an employer that acts as a provider or administrator of an insurance plan, upon request by an applicant, employee, or former employee should:

(a) inform the individual, after verifying his identity, whether it has any recorded information about him that pertains to the employee's insurance relationship with him;
(b) permit the individual to see and copy any such recorded information, either in person or by mail; or
(c) apprise the individual of the nature and substance of any such recorded information by telephone; and
(d) permit the individual to use whichever of the methods of access provided in (b) and (c) he prefers.

The employer should be able to charge a reasonable copying fee for any copies provided to the individual. Any such recorded information should be made available to the individual, but need not contain the name or other identifying particulars of any source (other than an institutional source) of information in the record who has provided such information on the condition that his or her identity not be revealed, and need not reveal a confidential numerical code.

It should be noted that this recommendation as it would apply to insurance institutions (see Chapter 5) would not apply to any record about an individual compiled in reasonable anticipation of a civil or criminal action, or for use in settling a claim while the claim remains unsettled. After the claim is settled, the recommendation would not apply to any record compiled in relation to a a third-party claimant (i.e., a claimant who is not an insured, policy owner, or principal insured), except as to any portion of such a record which is disseminated or used for a purpose unrelated to processing the claim.

Inasmuch as this recommendation and *Recommendation (25)*below, are proposed for voluntary adoption by employers, it should be noted that there is a gap in the Commission's recommendations regarding records generated in the insurance relationship (Chapter 5) and that it may affect a substantial number of individuals, given the proportion of the workforce currently insured under employer-provided or employer-administered group plans. Thus, while the Commission hopes that employers will voluntarily adopt *Recommendation (21)* and *(25)*, it also hopes that because their adoption must be voluntary, employers will not seize on self-administered insurance plans as a way of avoiding the statutory access and correction requirements recommended for insurance records in Chapter 5.

As to medical-record information maintained by an employer as a consequence of its insurance relationship with an individual employee or former employee, the Commission's intention is that *Recommendation (20)* apply.

CORRECTION OF RECORDS

Any employee who has reason to question the accuracy, timeliness, or completeness of records his employer keeps about him should be able to correct or amend those records. Furthermore, the procedures for correcting or amending employment records should conform to those recommended in other chapters of this report. For example, when an individual requests correction or amendment of a record, the employer should notify persons or organizations to whom the erroneous, obsolete, or incomplete information has been disclosed within the previous two years, if the individual so requests. When the information came from a consumer-reporting agency (as defined by the Fair Credit Reporting Act), any corrections should routinely be passed on to that agency so that its records on an applicant or employee will also be accurate. When the employer rejects the requested correction or amendment, fairness demands that the employer incorporate the employee's statement of dispute into the record and pass it along to those to whom the employer subsequently discloses the disputed information, as well as to those who need to know the information is disputed in order to protect the individual from unfair decisions being made on the basis of it. Moreover, if an employer attempts to verify allegedly erroneous, obsolete, or incomplete information in a record, it should limit its investigation to the particular items in dispute.

The Commission does not intend that the correction or amendment procedures alter any existing retention periods for records or require employers to keep an accounting of every disclosure made to a third party. However, when an employer does keep an accounting of disclosures to third parties, for whatever purpose, it should let an employee use it in deciding to whom corrections, amendments, or dispute statements should be forwarded. Accordingly, the Commission recommends:

Recommendation (22):

That, except for a medical record or an insurance record, or any record designated by an employer as an unavailable record, an employer should voluntarily permit an individual employee, former employee, or applicant to request correction or amendment of a record pertaining to him; and

(a) **within a reasonable period of time correct or amend (including supplement) any portion thereof which the individual reasonably believes is not accurate, timely, or complete; and**

(b) **furnish the correction or amendment to any person or organization specifically designated by the individual who may have, within two years prior thereto, received any such information; and, automatically to any consumer-reporting agency (as**

defined by the Fair Credit Reporting Act) that furnished the
information corrected or amended; *or*

(c)   inform the individual of its refusal to correct or amend the
record in accordance with his request and of the reason(s) for
the refusal; and

   (i)   permit an individual who disagrees with the refusal to
correct or amend the record to have placed on or with the
record a concise statement setting forth the reasons for his
disagreement;

   (ii) in any subsequent disclosure outside the employing
organization containing information about which the
individual has filed a statement of dispute, clearly note
any portion of the record which is disputed, and provide a
copy of the statement along with the information being
disclosed; and

   (iii) furnish the statement to any person or organization
specifically designated by the individual who may have,
within two years prior thereto, received any such information; and, automatically, to any consumer-reporting
agency (as defined by the Fair Credit Reporting Act) that
furnished the disputed information; and

(d)   limit its reinvestigation of disputed information to those record
items in dispute.

The procedures for correcting and amending insurance and medical
records which the Commission recommends in Chapters 5 and 7 should be
voluntarily adopted by employers who maintain such records. Thus, with
respect to a medical record maintained by an employer whose relationship
to an employee is that of a medical-care provider, the Commission
recommends:

Recommendation (23):

That an employer establish a procedure whereby an individual who is
the subject of a medical record maintained by the employer can
request correction or amendment of the record. When the individual
requests correction or amendment, the employer should, within a
reasonable period of time, either:

(a)   make the correction or amendment requested, or

(b)   inform the individual of its refusal to do so, the reason for the
refusal, and of the procedure, if any, for further review of the
refusal.

In addition, if the employer decides that it will not correct or amend a
record in accordance with the individual's request, the employer
should permit the individual to file a concise statement of the reasons
for the disagreement, and in any subsequent disclosure of the disputed
information include a notation that the information is disputed and
the statement of disagreement. In any such disclosure, the employer

may also include a statement of the reasons for not making the requested correction or amendment.

Finally, when an employer corrects or amends a record pursuant to an individual's request, or accepts a notation of dispute and statement of disagreement, it should furnish the correction, amendment, or statement of disagreement to any person specifically designated by the individual to whom the employer has previously disclosed the inaccurate, incomplete, or disputed information.

As with *Recommendation (19)*, the Commission would urge that if a State enacts a statute creating individual rights regarding the correction of medical records pursuant to *Recommendation (2)* in Chapter 7, it encompass within the statute medical records maintained by an employer whose relationship to applicants, employees, or former employees is that of a medical-care provider.

In addition, when an employer maintains medical-record information about an individual applicant, employee, or former employee, the Commission recommends:

Recommendation (24):

That notwithstanding *Recommendation (22)*, when an individual who is the subject of medical-record information maintained by an employer requests correction or amendment of such information, the employer should:

(a)   disclose to the individual, or to a medical professional designated by him, the identity of the medical-care provider who was the source of the medical-record information;

(b)   make the correction or amendment requested within a reasonable period of time, if the medical-care provider who was the source of the information agrees that it is inaccurate or incomplete; and

(c)   establish a procedure whereby an individual who is the subject of medical-record information maintained by an employer, and who believes that the information is incorrect or incomplete, would be provided an opportunity to present supplemental information of a limited nature for inclusion in the medical-record information maintained by the employer, provided that the source of the supplemental information is also included.

Although *Recommendations (22), (23)* and *(24)* appear complex, they contain only two key requirements:

•   that an individual have a way of correcting, amending, or disputing information in a record about himself; and

•   that the employer to whom the request for correction or amendment is made shall have an obligation to propagate the resulting correction, amendment, or statement of dispute in any subsequent disclosure it makes of the information to certain prior or subsequent recipients.

Finally, with respect to the correction or amendment of insurance records maintained by an employer, the Commission recommends:

Recommendation (25):

That when an employer acts as a provider or administrator of an insurance plan, the employer should:

(a)   permit an individual to request correction or amendment of a record pertaining to him;

(b)   within a reasonable period of time, correct or amend (including supplement) any portion thereof which the individual reasonably believes is not accurate, timely, or complete;

(c)   furnish the correction or amendment to any person or organization specifically designated by the individual who may have, within two years prior thereto, received any such information; and, automatically, to any insurance-support organization whose primary source of information on individuals is insurance institutions when the support organization has systematically received any such information from the employer within the preceding seven years, unless the support organization no longer maintains the information, in which case, furnishing the correction or amendment would not be necessary; and, automatically, to any insurance-support organization that furnished the information corrected or amended; *or*

(d)   inform the individual of its refusal to correct or amend the record in accordance with his request and of the reason(s) for the refusal; and

   (i)   permit an individual who disagrees with the refusal to correct or amend the record to have placed on or with the record a concise statement setting forth the reasons for his disagreement;

   (ii)   in any subsequent disclosure outside the employing organization containing information about which the individual has filed a statement of dispute, clearly note any portion of the record which is disputed and provide a copy of the statement along with the information being disclosed; and

   (iii)   furnish the statement to any person or organization specifically designated by the individual who may have, within two years prior thereto, received any such information; and, automatically to an insurance-support organization whose primary source of information on individuals is insurance institutions when the support organization has received any such information from the employer within the preceding seven years, unless the support organization no longer maintains the information, in which case, furnishing the statement would not be necessary; and, automatically, to any insurance-support organization that furnished the disputed information; and

(e) limit its reinvestigation of disputed information to those record items in dispute.

FAIRNESS IN INTERNAL DISCLOSURES ACROSS RELATIONSHIPS

Just as fairness must be a concern of employers when gathering information from external sources, they have a duty to see that information generated within the several discrete relationships subsumed under the broad employee-employer relationship is not shared within the employing organization in ways that are unfair to the individual employee.

As a rule, employers large enough to have separate functional units for personnel, security, insurance, and medical-care operations have voluntarily taken steps to assure that the records each of these units generates are maintained separately and not used improperly. The biggest problems are in small organizations that cannot realistically segregate record-keeping functions. Another potential problem is the impact of technology which could make retrieval of information stored in a common data base by unauthorized persons easier than is currently the case.

PERSONNEL AND PAYROLL RECORDS

As personnel planning and management systems have become more elaborate, so have the personnel files and payroll records an employer keeps on its employees. This is not to say that all employees expect personnel and payroll records to be held in confidence within the employing organization. Some may not; but out of consideration for those who do, the Commission believes that an employer should limit the use of personnel and payroll record information to whatever is necessary to fulfill particular functions. Therefore, the Commission recommends:

Recommendation (26):

That an employer assure that the personnel and payroll records it maintains are available internally only to authorized users and on a need-to-know basis.

SECURITY RECORDS

Security records differ from personnel records in that they frequently must be created without the employee's knowledge. Sometimes the information in them is inconclusive; sometimes the problem that precipitated the security record is not quickly resolved. Nonetheless, an employer may have to keep security records in order to safeguard the workplace or corporate assets. As a rule, employers document any action resulting from security investigations in the individual's personnel file, but do not include the details leading up to the action.[62]

Security departments usually work with personnel departments in the course of investigating incidents involving employees.[63] When the security function is separate from the personnel department, however, security records are generally not available to management and are frequently, though not always, filed by incident rather than by name, at least until the case is resolved.[64] Since security records maintained apart from personnel records can have little impact on personnel decisions about an employee, and since employee access to security records could substantially hamper legitimate security investigations, allowing the employee to see and copy them while they are being maintained as security records seems hard to justify. If, however, information in the security record of an employee is to be used for other purposes, such as discipline, termination, promotion, or evaluation, fairness demands that the employee have direct access to it. Thus, the Commission, again taking the voluntary approach, recommends:

Recommendation (27):

That an employer:

(a)   **maintain security records apart from other records; and**
(b)   **inform an employee whenever information from a security record is transferred to his personnel record.**

MEDICAL RECORDS AND MEDICAL-RECORD INFORMATION

As indicated earlier, an employer may maintain both medical-record information and medical records: the former as a consequence of requiring it as a condition of employment, placement, or certification to return to work; the latter as a consequence of providing various forms of medical care, including routine physicals. However collected, there is a case for requiring employers to restrict the circulation of medical records and medical-record information outside the medical department. Corporate physicians are sincerely concerned about possible misuses of the records they maintain. No matter how hard they may strive to be independent of the employing organization their allegiance is ultimately to the employer.

Many large employers have procedures that guarantee the confidentiality of medical-record information in all but the most extreme circumstances; and many corporate medical departments only make recommenda-

---

[62] See, for example, Testimony of Inland Steel Company, Employment Records Hearings, December 10, 1976, p. 388; Testimony of Ford Motor Company, Employment Records Hearings, December 16, 1976, p. 576; and Testimony of International Business Machines, Employment Records Hearings, December 10, 1976, p. 309.

[63] See, for example, Testimony of Cummins Engine Company, Employment Records Hearings, December 9, 1976, p. 19; and Testimony of Ford Motor Company, Employment Records Hearings, December 16, 1976, p. 556.

[64] See, for example, Testimony of Inland Steel Company, Employment Records Hearings, December 10, 1976, p. 388; and Testimony of Ford Motor Company, Employment Records Hearings, December 16, 1976, p. 576.

tions for work restrictions, carefully refraining from passing on any diagnosis or treatment details in all but the most extreme circumstances.[65] Nevertheless, it is the duty of the corporate physician to tell his employer when he finds in an individual a condition that could negatively affect the interests of the employer or other employees.[66] Furthermore, employers rely on corporate physicians for evaluation of an applicant or employee's health in making hiring and placement decisions. A further complication arises if, as often happens, the corporate physician also provides regular medical care for employees outside of the employment context, perhaps functioning as the family doctor.

An employee availing himself of medical services offered by his employer does so at some risk to the traditional confidential relationship between physician and patient, unless great care is taken to insulate that relationship from the usual work-related responsibilities of the medical department. Thus, when a medical department provides voluntary physicals or routine medical care for employees, the resulting records should be maintained separately from the records generated by work-related contacts and should never be used to make work-related decisions. This is a difficult policy to enforce and can work only where management understands and respects the need to separate the compulsory and voluntary functions of the medical department. Thus, the Commission recommends:

Recommendation (28):

That an employer that maintains an employment-related medical record about an individual assure that no diagnostic or treatment information in any such record is made available for use in any employment decision; and

Recommendation (29):

That an employer that provides a voluntary health-care program for its employees assure that any medical record generated by the program is maintained apart from any employment-related medical record and not used by any physician in advising on any employment-related decision or in making any employment-related decision without the express authorization of the individual to whom the record pertains.

---

[65] See, for example, Testimony of Dr. Bruce Karrh, Assistant Medical Director, du Pont de Nemours and Company, Employment Records Hearings, December 17, 1976, pp. 782-783; and Testimony of Dr. Norbert Roberts, Medical Director, Exxon Corporation, Employment Records Hearings, December 17, 1976, p. 785. This is also the policy of the Ford Motor Company and the Atlantic Richfield Company. See "Employee Records & Personal Privacy: Corporate Policies & Procedures," McCaffery, Seligman & von Simpson, Inc., November, 1976, pp. 105, 139.

[66] See, for example, Testimony of Ford Motor Company, Employment Records Hearings, December 16, 1976, p. 587; and Testimony of Dr. Bruce Karrh, Assistant Medical Director, du Pont de Nemours and Company, Employment Records Hearings, December 17, 1976, pp. 781-783.

INSURANCE RECORDS

Insurance claims records often contain information about medical diagnosis and treatment. This information is given to the employer to meet a need of the employee; that is, to protect the employee against loss of pay due to illness or to arrange for medical bills to be paid. Where an employer either self-insures or self-administers a health-insurance plan, it necessarily maintains a significant amount of information about employees and their families. Some of this information can be useful in making personnel decisions, especially if it gives details of the diagnosis or treatment of a mental condition, a terminal illness, or an illness which drains the emotions of an employee. Testimony before the Commission indicates that many employers guard claims information carefully, apparently understanding how unfair it is to make an employee choose between filing a legitimate insurance claim and jeopardizing future employment.[67] Some physicians say, however, that this kind of information is available for use in personnel decision making,[68] and there is evidence of its unauthorized use in making decisions unrelated to claims payment.[69]

In its consideration of insurance institutions and the records they maintain, the Commission saw how important a confidentiality policy is to insureds. It believes that such a policy is no less important when the insurance plan is administered by an employer. Although it may be difficult to segregate insurance claims records completely, fairness demands that the claims process be walled off from other internal functions of the employing organization.

Employment-related insurance, such as disability or sick pay, usually involves the corporate physician in claims processing, as it is his function to evaluate the medical evidence on which the claim is based. Thus, corporate physicians must have access to information about these claims. They do not, however, have to use information thus obtained in making decisions that are unrelated to the claim. If asked for an opinion of a candidate for transfer to a job at a new location, for example, the physician can determine a person's physical capacity by examination without delving into claims records for clues to potential medical problems. Nor should these records influence other employment decisions, such as determinations of tenure, promotion, or termination. Accordingly, the Commission recommends:

Recommendation (30):

That an employer that provides life or health insurance as a service to its employees assure that individually identifiable insurance records are maintained separately from other records and not available for use in making employment decisions; and further

---

[67] See, for example, Testimony of Inland Steel Company, Employment Records Hearings, December 10, 1976, p. 334; and Testimony of General Electric Company, Employment Records Hearings, December 9, 1976, pp. 248-250.

[68] "Confidentiality and Third Parties," The American Psychiatric Association Task Force of June 1975, Appendix Vol. H, p. 53.

[69] *Ibid.,* p. 55.

Recommendation (31):

That an employer that provides work-related insurance for employees, such as worker's compensation, voluntary sick pay, or short- or long-term disability insurance, assure that individually identifiable records pertaining to such insurance are available internally only to authorized recipients and on a need-to-know basis.

Expectation of Confidentiality

Employers have regular access to more information about employees than do credit, depository, or insurance institutions; yet there are no legal controls on the disclosure of employment information. The confidentiality of these records is maintained today solely at the discretion of the employer and can be transgressed at any time with no obligation to the individual record subject.

Evidence before the Commission indicates that, although there is no legal requirement for them to do so, private-sector employers tend to protect information about employees against disclosure.[70] In part, this is because answering requests for such information can be a substantial administrative burden with no compensating advantage to the employer. In part, it is because employers fear common law actions brought for defamation or invasion of privacy. Such restraints, however, are uneven at best; and there are circumstances under which almost any employer routinely discloses the information in its employee records, as, for example, in response to inquiries from law enforcement authorities.[71]

The question of how much confidentiality can be expected of employers for information in their employment records is significant. Because of the amount and nature of the information held, the pressures under which it is usually collected, and the diverse circumstances in which it could be used, the creation of an expectation of confidentiality is at least as important in the employee-employer relationship as in any other relationship the Commission studied. Furthermore, while there is generally no valid business-related reason to disclose this information, modern technology, as discussed earlier, is making the process of disclosure much easier than it has been. Thus, the employee needs protection against the disclosure of information outside of the employing organization.

Although employees, as a rule, recognize that employment information will be used within the employing organization for a variety of purposes, and that they cannot be notified of and asked to approve each use, they should be able to assume that this rather free flow will be contained within the boundaries of the employing organization. The expectation that

---

[70] All employers who testified to the Commission have policies limiting the disclosure of information about employees, although there is some variation from employer to employer regarding what information is disclosed.

[71] See, for example, Testimony of the Equitable Life Assurance Society of the United States, Employment Records Hearings, December 9, 1976, p. 125; Testimony of Inland Steel Company, Employment Records Hearings, December 10, 1976, p. 390; and Testimony of Ford Motor Company, Employment Records Hearings, December 16, 1976, pp. 540-541.

the confidentiality of information about them will be respected as to outside requestors depends on certain assurances on the part of employers.

The Commission believes that an employer has an obligation to inform its employees as specifically as possible of the kinds of information about them that may be disclosed both during and after the employment relationship. This means that at the beginning of the relationship, the employer should tell the applicant or employee what information about him may be disclosed. This communication is essential to protect the individual's right to determine what information he will divulge in case disclosure in some particular quarter could embarrass or otherwise harm him.

NOTICE REGARDING EXTERNAL DISCLOSURES

An employer should notify each applicant and employee of its policies regarding the disclosure of *directory information*, that is, basic factual information freely given to all third parties. The applicant or employee should also be informed of disclosures that may be made pursuant to statute or collective-bargaining agreements, and of the procedures by which he will be notified of or asked to authorize any other disclosures. Because information may have to be released under subpoena or other legal process, employees should be assured prior notice of subpoenas where possible in sufficient time to challenge their scope and legitimacy. Chapter 9 on government access to records about individuals examines this problem and recommends placing the notice burden on the party issuing the subpoena.

In sum, the Commission recommends:

Recommendation (32):

That an employer clearly inform all its applicants upon request, and all employees automatically, of the types of disclosures it may make of information in the records it maintains on them, including disclosures of directory information, and of its procedures for involving the individual in particular disclosures.

THE EMPLOYER'S DUTY OF CONFIDENTIALITY

As the first premise of a responsible confidentiality policy, disclosures to any outside entity without the employee's authorization should be prohibited. Exceptions can then be made for directory information, subpoenas, specific statutory requirements, and disclosures made pursuant to collective-bargaining agreements.

Directory Information. Although employers do not, as a rule, object to giving employees some control over the disclosure of information in records the employer keeps on them, they fear that requiring consent in every instance will be unmanageably burdensome. To alleviate this fear, and in recognition of the fact that most external disclosures of information from employment records are made in the interest of the employee rather than of the employer, the Commission believes that disclosure by an employer of a limited category of factual data without employee authorization can be justified. This category, which the Commission has designated as "directory information," should include only information an employer considers reasonably necessary to satisfy the vast majority of third-party requests. That is, it might include the fact that an individual is or has been employed by the employer, the dates of employment, the individual's present job title or position, and perhaps wage or salary information. This is not to suggest, however, that every employer should freely disclose all of these items. The Commission commends employers whose disclosure policies are even more limiting.

Disclosures for Law Enforcement Purposes. Law enforcement authorities frequently ask employers for information about employees. In addition to the items designated as directory information, they often seek an individual's dates of attendance at work, home address, and, in some cases, personnel and payroll records. Reasonable as it may seem to some to give properly identified law enforcement authorities access to information in employee files, there can be no employee expectation of confidentiality without limits on such access. The Commission's hearing record suggests that most law enforcement requests for information can be met by disclosing directory information, the employee's home address, and specific dates of attendance at work.[72] When law enforcement authorities need more extensive information than that, they can obtain it by means of a subpoena or other legal process; requiring them to do so would reinforce realistic expectations of confidentiality for employment records without unduly burdening either law enforcement authorities or employers. It would also allow an employer to give a consistent response to all law enforcement requests.

Conversely, the Commission believes that an employer should remain free to disclose information about an individual applicant, employee, or former employee to law enforcement authorities if it has reason to believe that actions of the individual threaten the employer's property or the safety or security of other employees, or if it suspects an employee of engaging in illegal activities, whether or not those activities relate to his employment. Such disclosures, in the Commission's view, should not be considered violations of an employee's reasonable expectation of confidentiality.

Other Disclosures. In addition to the types of disclosures dicussed above, an employer must fulfill the obligations set by its collective-bargaining contracts. When an employer retains an outside agent or contractor to collect information about an employee or group of employees, the employer must be in a position to disclose enough information for the agent or contractor to perform its legitimate functions. The agent or contractor, however, should be prohibited from redisclosing such information, and the employee should be able to find out that it has been disclosed. In addition, when a physician in an employer's medical department, or one retained by the employer, discovers that an employee has a serious medical problem of which he may not be aware, the physician should be free to disclose that fact to the employee's personal physician.

---

[72] See, for example, Testimony of Ford Motor Company, Employment Records Hearings, December 16, 1976, pp. 539, 592.

In contrast to its duty of confidentiality recommendations with respect to credit, insurance, and medical-care record keeping, the Commission is not prepared to urge that the employer's duty of confidentiality be established by statute or regulation. The absence of legal barriers to voluntary implementation by an employer, coupled with the fact that the employee-employer relationship is not one in which the record keeper is performing a service for the individual, justifies, in the Commission's view, a voluntary approach. This is not to say that there should be no legislative or regulatory action at all. Chapter 9, on access to records by government agencies, calls for legislating constraints on access to records about individuals when the record keeper is not bound by a statutory duty of confidentiality. In addition, when an employer does perform services for employees or former employees, such as providing life and health-insurance coverage or medical care for employees or former employees who want it, the Commission's recommendations with respect to those types of record-keeping relationships could also be made applicable to employers. Earlier in this chapter, the Commission has suggested how the access and correction rights that would prevail in a normal insurance or medical-care relationship might be applied to an employer by extension. Likewise, the duty of confidentiality recommended for insurers and medical-care providers could be made applicable to employers to the extent that the relationship with an applicant, employee, or former employee mirrors those types of relationships. In the main, however, the Commission believes that the employer's duty of confidentiality, at least with respect to those records that are peculiarly the product of the employment relationship, can be implemented by voluntary compliance reinforced by mutual agreements, such as through collective-bargaining contracts. Accordingly, the Commission recommends:

Recommendation (33):

That each employer be considered to owe a duty of confidentiality to any individual employee, former employee, or applicant about whom it collects information; and that, therefore, no employer or consumer-reporting agency (as defined by the Fair Credit Reporting Act) which collects information about an applicant or employee on behalf of an employer should disclose, or be required to disclose, in individually identifiable form, any information about any individual applicant, employee, or former employee, without the explicit authorization of such individual, unless the disclosure would be:

(a)   **in response to a request to provide or verify information designated by the employer as directory information, which should not include more than:**
   (i)   **the fact of past or present employment;**
   (ii)   **dates of employment;**
   (iii) **title or position;**
   (iv)   **wage or salary; and**
   (v)   **location of job site;**
(b)   **an individual's dates of attendance at work and home address in**

response to a request by a properly identified law enforcement authority;

(c) a voluntary disclosure to protect the legal interests of the employer when the employer believes the actions of the applicant, employee, or former employee violate the conditions of employment or otherwise threaten physical injury to the property of the employer or to the person of the employer or any of his employees;

(d) to a law enforcement authority when the employer reasonably believes that an applicant, employee, or former employee has been engaged in illegal activities;

(e) pursuant to a Federal, State, or local compulsory reporting statute or regulation;

(f) to a collective-bargaining unit pursuant to a collective-bargaining contract;

(g) to an agent or contractor of the employer, provided:

  (i) that only such information is disclosed as is necessary for such agent or contractor to perform its function for the employer;

  (ii) that the agent or contractor is prohibited from redisclosing the information; and

  (iii) that the individual is notified that such disclosure may be made and can find out if in fact it has been made;

(h) to a physician for the purpose of informing the individual of a medical problem of which he may not be aware; and

(i) in response to a lawfully issued administrative summons or judicial order, including a search warrant or subpoena.

DISCLOSURES OF OSHA RECORDS TO PROSPECTIVE EMPLOYERS

A confidentiality problem mentioned earlier in this chapter derives from the Occupational Safety and Health Act (OSHA), which mandates that an employer provide medical surveillance of employees known to have been exposed to certain hazardous environments or substances. This, of course, requires the employer to keep records of medical examinations and other tests made to find out if a worker's health has been adversely affected. The Commission's hearings showed that some employers have already established procedures for exchanging medical surveillance records of workers known to have had such exposures.[73] A worker's former employer may disclose such a record to a prospective employer solely in the interest of continued protection of the worker's health, but the possibility remains that the prospective employer may discriminate against the worker because of its fear that previous hazardous exposure may lead in time to partial or complete disability.

The central problem with these disclosures from one employer to another is that the use of medical surveillance records as a measure of

---

[73] Letter from C. Hoyt Anderson, Director Personnel Relations and Research Office, Ford Motor Company, to the Privacy Protection Study Commission, January 14, 1977.

employability is not a use for which the information is collected and thus is inherently unfair. Accordingly, the Commission recommends:

Recommendation (34):

That Congress direct the Department of Labor to review the extent to which medical records made to protect individuals exposed to hazardous environments or substances in the workplace are or may come to be used to discriminate against them in employment. This review should include an examination of the feasibility of:

(a) **restricting the availability of records generated by medical examinations and tests conducted in accordance with OSHA requirements for use in making employment decisions; and**
(b) **establishing mechanisms to protect employees whose health has been affected by exposure to hazardous environments or substances from the economic consequences of employers' decisions concerning their employability.**

*   *   *   *   *   *   *

The Commission's recommendations assign employers an important task: to adopt policies and practices regarding the collection, use, and disclosure of information on applicants, employees, and former employees without being forced to do so by government. Unless each employer has a conscientious program on which applicants and employees can rely to safeguard the records the employer keeps about them, the voluntary approach recommended in this chapter will prove unsuccessful. Thus, a future commission or legislative bodies may have to consider compulsory measures, with all the disadvantages for the employee-employer relationship that would entail.

When asked how he thought industry would respond to guidelines for voluntary compliance in developing policies and procedures on employment record keeping, a witness representing the Ford Motor Company said:

Certainly it has the merit of allowing various corporations to develop guidelines that are appropriate to their situations . . . there is a wide diversity of situations and there are numerous ways by which the principles of privacy could be implemented . . . I would simply want to take a hold on determining whether at some later date legislation is necessary. The suggestion is that we start with the voluntary and determine to what extent the compulsory may be necessary based on experience.[74]

The Commission shares that view.

Finally, the Commission also believes that its recommendations with respect to the employment relationship, or at least the concepts on which

---

[74] Employment Records Hearings, December 16, 1976, p. 528.

they are based, apply equally to Federal, State, and local governments and their employees.[75]

---

[75] A more complete discussion of the topics of this chapter will be forthcoming in a separately published appendix volume.

Chapter 7

Record Keeping in the Medical-Care Relationship

Americans made an estimated one billion, 56 million visits to physicians during 1975, an average of 5.1 visits for each person in the country. Approximately 720 million of these visits occurred in physicians' private offices, while another 136 million took place in the clinics and emergency rooms of hospitals. Inpatient admissions accounted for a large percentage of the remainder.[1] In addition, in 1974, more than a million individuals, approximately five percent of the U.S. population aged 65 and over, resided in nursing homes.[2] Each of these contacts with a medical-care provider generated a new medical record,[3] or added information to an already existing record. Considering that the recommended minimum retention period for a medical record today is 10 to 25 years,[4] these numbers seem staggering. Yet, even more staggering is the realization of how many people besides the medical-care providers[5] who create a medical record have access to it at the same time that the patient himself is by and large denied access to it.

Indeed, the way in which medical records are created and used has undergone radical change in the last 50 years,[6] a change that is both a result and a cause of significant alterations in the character of the medical-care

---

[1] 1975 data conveyed to staff of the Privacy Protection Study Commission by staff at the National Center for Health Statistics.

[2] National Center for Health Statistics, *Health: United States 1975*, (Rockville, Maryland: Department of Health, Education, and Welfare, 1975), p. 3.

[3] Section 5(c)(2)(A) of the Privacy Act of 1974 authorized the Commission to include "medical records" in its examination of governmental and private-sector record-keeping policies and practices.

[4] Testimony of the American Hospital Association, *Medical Records*, Hearings before the Privacy Protection Study Commission, June 10, 1976, p. 83 (hereinafter cited as "Medical Records Hearings").

[5] The term *medical-care provider* has been used throughout the chapter to refer to both *medical professionals* and *medical-care institutions*. For the Commission's purposes the term *medical professional* refers to any person licensed or certified to provide medical services to individuals, including, but not limited to, a physician, dentist, nurse, optometrist, physical or occupational therapist, psychiatric social worker, clinical dietitian or clinical psychologist. The term *medical-care institution* means any facility or institution that is licensed to provide medical-care services to individuals, including, but not limited to, hospitals, skilled nursing facilities, home-health agencies, clinics, rehabilitation agencies, and public-health agencies or health-maintenance organizations (HMOs).

[6] In a survey conducted in 1918, the American College of Surgeons discovered that only 89

relationship itself. This chapter explores the nature of the transformation and its implications for the protection of personal privacy.

The first section briefly identifies the keepers and users of medical records and medical-record information.[7] The second section shows why medical record-keeping practices are making the medical-care relationship progressively more fragile, underscoring the need for better statutory and regulatory protections. The third section contains general and specific recommendations that seek a proper balance among the various interests that come to focus in the medical-care relationship today.

KEEPERS AND USERS OF MEDICAL RECORDS

In the early part of this century, physicians, most of them practicing alone, delivered 85 percent of all medical services in the country. Today less than five percent of the providers of medical-care services are physicians.[8] It has been estimated that in most hospitals today only a third of a patient's hospital medical record is created by the attending physician.[9] In addition, there have been major changes in the way medical care is paid for, and these changes, together with corollary efforts to monitor and improve the quality of medical care, have had and continue to have profound effects both on the flow of medical-record information and on the way medical records are maintained.

Private health-insurance coverage has risen steadily over the last 25 years. In 1950, third-party payment covered about a third of personal health expenses; in 1975, two-thirds, including almost 90 percent of hospital expenses and 61 percent of physicians' services was covered.[10] So many of

---

out of 5,323 hospitals registered in the U.S. by the American Medical Association kept ". . .accurate and complete case records. . .written for all patients and filed in an accessible manner." Edna K. Huffman, *Medical Record Management*, (Berwyn, Ill: Physicians Record Co., 1972), p. 21.

[7] For the purposes of this study, the Commission has defined a *medical record* as a record, file, document, or other written material relating to an individual's medical history, diagnosis, condition, treatment or evaluation which is created or maintained by a medical-care provider. Conversely, the term *medical-record information* is used here to refer to information obtained from a medical record or from the individual patient, his spouse, parent, or guardian, for the purpose of making a non-medical decision about him. The circumstances in which medical-record information is gathered, maintained, and used to make non-medical decisions are summarized in this chapter, but details will be found in the chapters on insurance, employment, public assistance and social services, and research and statistics. The Commission's detailed recommendations regarding medical-record information held by such third-party users will also be found in those chapters. As in all other aspects of the Commission's inquiry, the attention here is to medical records and medical-record information collected, maintained, used, and disseminated in individually identifiable form.

[8] Alfred M. Freedman, "Protection of Sensitive Medical Data," *Patient Centered Health Systems*, Michael A. Jenkin, ed., (Minneapolis, Minnesota: Society for Computer Medicine, 1975), p. 3.

[9] Testimony of the American Hospital Association, Medical Records Hearings, June 10, 1976, p. 84.

[10] National Center for Health Statistics, *op. cit.*, p. 3.

these payments are now made under group policies that employers either administer or finance, or both,[11] that employers have begun to rival insurance companies as major keepers and users of medical-record information. Tax revenues also cover an increasing share of the nation's health-care bill. In 1974 Medicare and Medicaid together accounted for three-fifths of the total government expenditure for medical services, with 71 percent and 37 percent of their funds, respectively, going for services provided by hospitals.[12]

The magnitude of these public and private expenditures has focused attention on controlling the cost and monitoring the quality of medical services with the medical record becoming the primary instrument for cost control and quality assessment. Today, third-party payers not only want to know whether services billed to them are wholly or partially covered, but also whether they were consistent with the medical problem stated on the claim form, or indeed have been performed at all. To answer those questions in any particular instance the third-party payer may need copies of the entire record when only a particular episode of treatment is at issue. In 1972, the Congress in P.L. 92-603 authorized the formation of Professional Standards Review Organizations (PSROs) to monitor the appropriateness, quality, and outcome of the services provided to beneficiaries of the Medicare, Medicaid, and Maternal and Child Health Programs. The professional review mandated by the PSRO legislation depends upon information in the medical record being precisely documented, and in standardized form so that it can readily be retrieved. Since the program is not yet fully operational, its effectiveness cannot yet be evaluated, but if the PSRO program succeeds in controlling medical-care costs, private-sector third-party payers will undoubtedly develop similar programs or use the PSRO. The Congress, too, is watching PSRO performance with an eye to its implications for proposed legislation to create a universal health insurance program, covering all aspects of medical care.

It must be understood, of course, that these impositions on the presumed confidentiality of the physician-patient relationship are not without precedent. Mandatory filing of birth and death certificates is a form of intrusion into the physician-patient relationship that has long been accepted as socially justified by the need for population statistics and epidemiological research. Today vital statistics records provide a vast data resource for many research and statistical activities. When communicable diseases were a major cause of death, legislation was enacted requiring that medical-care providers report information about individual cases to public-health authorities. Many States now also require medical-care providers to report cases of cancer and other diseases in which an environmental or occupational factor is suspected, and some require reports on drug addiction, gunshot wounds, child abuse, and other violence-related injuries. The justification for each of these intrusions into the medical-care

---

[11] *Ibid.*, p. 60. By 1970 employers were paying all of the group-health premiums for 39 percent of the families covered by such plans, and at least partially paying the premiums for 53 percent more.

[12] *Ibid.*, p. 2.

relationship is that society's need for information outweighs the individual's claim to personal privacy in that particular case.

Through expenditures in support of medical research, both government and the private sector indirectly contribute to third-party intrusions into the medical-care relationship. As Chapter 15 points out, government funding supports most of the organized research and statistical activities in this country and medical research accounts for a high proportion of the research expenditures of government and many of the large private foundations. Federal rules governing the funding of medical research require the informed consent of the individuals who participate in it as research subjects, but do not require their consent when medical records are reviewed and abstracted for retrospective epidemiological research studies.

Epidemiological research was originally concerned with the cause and prevention of infectious diseases,[13] but during the last two decades the focus of the discipline has expanded to include the chronic, noninfectious diseases, such as emphysema and cancer, which have emerged as primary causes of illness and death in this country. Because these conditions typically cluster in time and place at a rather low level of intensity; because their progression may be slow; and because their causes are frequently insidious, studying them often requires medical surveillance of a substantial population at widely disparate points in time. For example, an epidemiologist who wants to know whether a particular chemical employed in certain industrial processes was causally associated with bladder cancer might well be required to survey a large number of employees who have been exposed to the chemical at five-year intervals for at least 20 years. Such a task, however, would be impractical, if not impossible, without recourse to the medical records of the population being studied.

There are few statistics indicating the number of requests for medical-record information that are not directly related to the delivery of medical care, but testimony before the Commission suggests that the number is high. For example, the director of the medical record department at a 600-bed university teaching hospital testified that he receives an estimated 2700 requests for medical-record information each month, some 34 percent of them from third-party payers, 37 percent from other physicians, eight percent in the form of subpoenas and 21 percent from other hospitals, attorneys, and miscellaneous sources.[14] The attorney for a large and well known medical clinic testified that the clinic receives an estimated 300,000 requests for medical-record information a year, some 88 percent of them patient-initiated requests relating to claims for reimbursement by health insurers.[15] Representatives of a California photocopying firm told the Commission that in 1975, their firm photostated 365,000 medical records for the State disability insurance program. This same firm, which acquires medical-record information pursuant to patient authorization for use

---

[13] Epidemiology is the medical science responsible for investigating the impact of both man's genetic endowment and his environment on his physical health.

[14] Testimony of Andrew Bailey, Director, Medical Record Department, Stanford University Hospital, Medical Records Hearings, June 10, 1976, p. 98.

[15] Written statement of Mayo Clinic, Medical Records Hearings, August 25, 1976.

primarily by lawyers and insurers, has amassed a microfilm library of approximately 780,000 records.[16]

The results of a 1970 survey of requests directed to the offices of California psychiatrists are equally revealing. Of the 346 respondents, 89 percent reported that they had been asked for medical-record information by insurance companies, 56 percent by schools, and 49 percent by employers.[17]

These figures give some idea of how heavily a variety of institutions in our society have come to depend upon the information in medical records in order to perform their basic functions. They also suggest that medical-record information is now the key to many societal gatekeeping functions.[18] This is clearly revealed when the individual with venereal disease is denied a marriage license; when the person with heart disease is denied life insurance; when the epileptic is denied employment; or when a convicted felon is sent to a mental hospital instead of to prison. There are, however, many less dramatic and thus less visible examples. Chapter 6, on record keeping in the employer-employee relationship, describes some of the ways in which medical-record information figures in assignment and promotion decisions. The chapter on public assistance and social services takes special note of how medical-record information influences eligibility determinations. An incident recounted later in this chapter illustrates that much harm can come to an individual when medical-record information being used for research is casually disclosed to another. Indeed, as Westin has observed:

> . . . the outward flow of medical data . . . has enormous impact on people's lives. It affects decisions on whether they are hired or fired; whether they can secure business licenses and life insurance; whether they are permitted to drive cars; whether they are placed under police surveillance or labelled a security risk; or even whether they can get nominated for and elected to political office.[19]

The Commission agrees that the secondary use of medical records "raises the sharpest clash between society's interest in protecting medical confidentiality and its interest in a wide variety of other important functions . . . "[20] Yet this clash is not easy to resolve or even mitigate. From a privacy protection point of view, however, the confidentiality of the medical-care relationship has been seriously eroded and clearly needs to be restored. Simply blocking third-party access to medical-record information is not the answer. New balances must be struck, recognizing not only that existing law and public policy on the subject are inadequate but also that many of the

---

[16] Written statement of Micro-Reproduction Services, Inc., Medical Records Hearings, August 26, 1976.

[17] Written statement of Maurice Grossman, M.D., Clinical Professor of Psychiatry, Stanford University, Medical Records Hearings, June 11, 1976, p. 4.

[18] "Gatekeeping function," as the term is used in this report, connotes the use of recorded information to determine whether individuals should be allowed to enter into different types of social, economic, and political relationships, and if so, under what circumstances.

[19] Alan F. Westin, Computers, Health Records, and Citizen's Rights, (Washington, D.C.: United States Department of Commerce, 1976). p. 60.

[20] Ibid., p. 60.

gatekeeping and credentialling functions that depend on information derived from medical records are essential.

THE FRAGILITY OF THE MEDICAL-CARE RELATIONSHIP

The physician-patient relationship is an inherently intrusive one in that the patient who wants and needs medical care must grant the doctor virtually unconstrained discretion to delve into the details of his life and his person. As a practical matter, because so much information may be necessary for proper diagnosis and treatment, no area of inquiry is excluded. In addition to describing the details of his symptoms, the patient may be asked to reveal what he eats, how much he drinks or smokes, whether he uses drugs, how often he has sexual relations and with whom, whether he is depressed or anxious, where and how long he has worked, and perhaps what he does for recreation. Moreover, he is expected to submit to as much direct observation and recording of what is observed as his condition suggests and as the confines of the medical-care setting permit. As the Executive Director of the American Medical Record Association observed to the Commission, "a complete medical record [today] may contain more intimate details about an individual than could be found in any single document."[21]

Like all records, the medical record is in part a memory aid. It serves to remind the physician of conditions discovered, drugs prescribed, tests and treatments administered, and the charges levied. Earlier in this century, when most medical professionals were family physicians in solo practice, the typical medical record was simply a small ledger card with entries showing the dates of the patient's visits, the medications prescribed, and the charges. The physician was usually able to file the intimate details of a patient's medical or emotional condition in the "safe crevices of his mind."[22] In contrast, a modern hospital medical record may easily run to a hundred pages. The records of a family physician may still hold information on ailments and modes of treatment, but also now note the patient's personal habits, social relationships, and the physician's evaluation of the patient's attitudes and preferences, often in extensive detail.

A great many factors contributed to this marked transformation in medical record-keeping practices. The information needs of third-party users have already been mentioned. Other factors include the progress of medical knowledge and the professional specialization it has fostered; the propensity of the American public to move around, making the medical record the principal instrument for assuring continuity of medical care; and the increasing use of medical records in judicial proceedings, especially in

---

[21] Medical Records Hearings, June 10, 1976, p. 137.
[22] Natalie Davis Spingarn, *Confidentiality*, (Washington, D.C.: American Psychiatric Association, 1975), p. 1. See also, Carmault B. Jackson, "Guardian of Medical Data," *Prism*, Vol. 2 (June 1974), pp. 40-41.

malpractice suits, where the content of a medical record is often the physician's only real defense.[23] Today's physician, in short, must learn more and remember more about his patients than his predecessors. To aid memory and to meet the demands for precise documentation, he incorporates more and more of what he learns about patients in their medical records.

Many argue that the efficacy of the medical-care relationship is directly related to the patient's confidence that the information recorded in the course of the relationship will go no further. As one witness told the Commission,

> Patients would be reluctant to tell their physicians certain types of information which they need to know in order to render appropriate care, if patients did not feel that such information would remain confidential.[24]

This may well be true; certainly it has the ring of common sense. If it is true, however, one can only conclude that patients are poorly informed about the information flows that often stem from their relationships with medical professionals.

Physicians have recognized their duty to keep information about patients to themselves since time immemorial. The following clause of the Hippocratic Oath merely acknowledged a principle already rooted in the ethos of ancient Greece:

> Whatever, in connection with my professional practice, or not in connection with it, I see or hear, in the life of men, which ought not to be spoken abroad, I will not divulge, as reckoning that all such should be kept secret.[25]

Physicians still subscribe to that oath, but in practice modern society requires of them frequent and sometimes substantial departures from it. The ethical code of the American Medical Association, for example, acknowledges that physicians must abandon their duty of confidentiality when required by law to disclose information about a patient, and when in the physician's judgment, he must do so in order to protect the welfare of the patient or of the community.[26] Yet, even these major exceptions do not adequately convey the idea of the outward flow of information generated within the context of the medical-care relationship today. They take no note, for instance, of the breadth of many of the authorization statements patients are now routinely asked to sign or of the complex balances that must be struck in deciding when the welfare of the community should take

---

[23] It has been estimated that medical-record information is used as evidence in about three-quarters of all civil cases and in about one-quarter of all criminal trials. Harold L. Hirsch, "Medical Records—Medicolegal Implications," *Southern Medicine*, Vol. 63, No.4 (August 1975), p. 11.

[24] Testimony of the American Medical Association, Medical Records Hearings, June 10, 1976, p. 179.

[25] Cited in Robert M. Veatch, et. al, *The Teaching of Medical Ethics*, (New York: Hastings Center Publications, 1973), p. 146.

[26] *Ibid.*, pp. 145-46.

precedence over the welfare of a patient. As a set of ethical precepts, moreover, they do not reach beyond the intimate physician-patient relationship which in today's world constitutes only one segment of the medical-care relationship.

In making these observations, the Commission is aware that the physician's ethical duty to protect the records he keeps about his patients is also established in law. Nineteen States have regulations, statutes, or case law recognizing medical records as confidential and limiting access to them.[27] In 21 States, a physician's license may be revoked for willful betrayal of professional secrets.[28] These statutes, however, do not generally apply to medical-care providers other than physicians, and although the codes of ethics of most allied health professions reaffirm the principle of confidentiality, the codes can impose only a moral, not a legal, obligation. Moreover, although a few courts have recognized that a patient has a cause of action against the physician who discloses information about him without his permission, as Westin notes, there is no reported U.S. case in which a physician or hospital had to compensate a patient for an injury resulting from breach of confidentiality.[29]

More important, the typical statutory prohibition against the disclosure of medical-record information by medical professionals is focused on protecting the professional, not the patient. It prevents the professional from being compelled to testify or to produce records about a patient in court proceedings and before grand juries, and in the 43 States that have some form of testimonial privilege, the protections have gradually been extended from oral communications to records such as medical reports, X-rays, and laboratory tests. With this broadening of the privilege has also come an increasing number of exceptions to it, justified in large part by the belief that the privilege has all too frequently been invoked merely to conceal information that would be neither embarrassing to the patient, nor counter-therapeutic, nor destructive of the physician-patient relationship if it were disclosed.[30]

The most important thing to remember about the testimonial privilege

---

[27] Richard Henry, ed. "A Summary of Freedom of Information and Privacy Laws of the 50 States," *Access Reports* (December 1975), p. 1.

[28] Ann H. Britton, "Rights to Privacy in Medical Records," *The Journal of Legal Medicine*, Vol. 3, No. 7 (July-August 1975), p. 32.

[29] Westin, *op. cit.*, p. 29. Analysis of the relevant case law also indicates that gaining a judgment against a physician for an unauthorized disclosure of medical-record information is no mean feat. There are only 16 jurisdictions in the United States that have adjudicated cases pertaining to a physician's liability for the disclosure of confidential information. In these cases, a cause of action for unauthorized disclosure has been justified under a number of different theories: breach of statutory duty; invasion of privacy; libel; malpractice; breach of trust; and breach of contract. (John J. Fargo), "Medical Data Privacy: Automated Interference with Contractual Relations," 25 *Buffalo Law Review* 493 (August 1976). See also Judith Lenable Elder, "Physicians and Surgeons: Civil Liability for a Physician Who Discloses Medical Information Obtained Within the Doctor-Patient Relationship in a Nonlitigation Setting," 28 *Oklahoma Law Review* 658-673, No. 3 (Summer, 1975).

[30] In his treatise on evidence, Wigmore argued that the privilege is not justified. Ninety-nine percent of the cases in which it has been invoked, he noted, involve personal injury cases where the patient voluntarily placed the extent of his injury before the court; actions on life insurance policies where the deceased was alleged to have misrepresented his health to the insurer; or

is that it has virtually nothing to do with normal, everyday use and disclosure of records maintained by a medical-care provider. The discretion to disclose or not to disclose, in most circumstances, resides solely with the provider. The courts by and large uphold that autonomy [31]

It is true that physicians customarily obtain a patient's authorization before revealing information about him to someone who is not in a position to compel such disclosure legally, but evidence presented to the Commission suggests that this safeguard, too, is weak. As described in Chapters 5 and 8, an investigation by a team of television reporters in late 1975 prompted a Denver, Colorado, grand jury to look into the local activities of a Chicago firm that specialized in obtaining medical-record information on individuals *without* authorization. The firm, then called "Factual Service Bureau" and now known as "Inner-facts," provides a variety of investigative services, but its speciality appears to have been the surreptitious acquisition of medical-record information from hospitals and physicians. Insurance claims investigators and lawyers used this information for a variety of purposes: to estimate how much their companies should reserve to cover particular claims; to assure that a claimant has not exaggerated the gravity of an illness or injury or inflated his lost earning capacity; and to detect other fraud. While in many cases they could have obtained the same information through normal channels, some claims personnel apparently felt there were justifiable reasons for avoiding the normal methods of acquiring it. That a firm like Factual Service Bureau could be successful, at least until it came under scrutiny by the Denver grand jury, appears to have been due in no small measure to the laxity of hospital security measures.

In June, 1976, the Denver grand jury received permission of the Colorado court to issue a special report to the Privacy Protection Study Commission. It said in part:

> From the evidence, it is clear that the problem with respect to the privacy of medical records in this jurisdiction exists in many other cities and jurisdictions across the nation . . . [However,] the grand jury believes that there is no one, simple law which can be enacted or action taken to prevent future abuses and unlawful activities concerning medical records. Rather, what is needed is a combination of voluntary self-regulation by institutions, health care provi-

---

actions on wills where the deceased's mental capacity was in question. Thus, in none of these instances could one say that the absence of the privilege would have hindered the individuals involved from seeking medical care, while in all of them the medical-record information sought was necessary to reach a decision. Wigmore, *Evidence* § 2380a (McNaughton rev. 1961).

[31] For example, in *Clark v. Geraci, [208 N.Y.S. 2nd 564 (S. Ct. N.Y. 1960)]*, an employee, seeking an excuse for his absenteeism, asked his physician to provide a general medical excuse. In doing so, however, the physician also disclosed that the employee was an alcoholic, thereby causing the employee to be dismissed. According to the court, the employee's request for a general excuse constituted a waiver by estoppel, authorizing the disclosure for an undistorted account of the employee's condition, including his alcoholism. In another case, *Hague v. Williams, [181 A.2nd (N.J., 1961)]*, a court construed an application for life insurance as a waiver of confidentiality. In this case, an infant's pediatrician told an insurance company that the child suffered from a congenital heart defect, even though he had never made this condition known to the baby's parents.

ders, the insurance industry, and the legal profession. Appropriate state and federal laws . . . should be enacted or amended to better accomplish the goal of protecting medical records.[32]

The Factual Service Bureau case points up a serious weakness in the protections offered by the authorization procedures used by medical-care providers. Nonetheless, it is not the only weakness, or even the most important for the majority of individuals on whom medical-care providers maintain records. Other Commission witnesses described how the form a patient is now routinely asked to sign authorizing the medical-care provider to disclose medical-record information about him is often so broadly worded that the patient, in effect, signs away all control over what is disclosed and what may be done with it thereafter. A noted authority on the confidentiality of psychiatric records told the Commission that knowing or suspecting that their medical records will be reviewed by outsiders keeps many people from seeking treatment for their illnesses, especially when the illness is psychiatric in character.[33]

An incident that occurred midway in the Commission's work illustrates how intense this concern can be. In 1976, Blue Cross-Blue Shield, in cooperation with the National Institute of Mental Health, the Civil Service Commission, and the American Psychiatric Association, initiated a study to monitor claims and assess the appropriateness of psychiatric services provided to members of the Blue Cross-Blue Shield Federal Employee Benefit Program. The study required a form containing detailed psychiatric information to be submitted along with the standard claim for reimbursement under the program. The outcry was immediate. Claimants feared that the details of their illness and treatment would find their way into Federal personnel files. Phone calls and letters to local public-interest groups, to the press, to the Congress, and to the Privacy Commission caused Blue Cross-Blue Shield to reconsider the need for some of the most objectionable items of information. Bowing to pressure from Congress and the threat of a lawsuit, Blue Cross-Blue Shield has since developed a new reporting form. Meanwhile, however,, some unknown number of Federal employees failed to file such claims for fear of losing jobs or security clearances.

One must ask whether such a public outcry would have resulted from a request for detailed information about disorders other than psychiatric ones. Because of the social stigma attached to mental and nervous disorders in our society, even the fact of admission to a psychiatric hospital or disclosure of the name of the attending physician in a general hospital can have untoward consequences for an individual.

The former Chairman of the American Psychiatric Association Task Force on Confidentiality, told the Commission that his colleagues "are all

---

[32] Written statement of Dale Tooley, District Attorney, Denver, Colorado, Medical Records Hearings, June 11, 1976.

[33] Medical Records Hearings, June 11, 1976, p. 374. For examples of injuries suffered by patients as a result of breaches of confidentiality, see also, Maurice Grossman, *Confidentiality and Third Parties*, (Washington, D.C.: American Psychiatric Institute, 1975).

minimizing the amount of information that goes into the chart to protect the patient."[34] The Joint Commission on the Accreditation of Hospitals, in recognition of the extraordinary sensitivity of psychiatric records, has recommended special procedures for filing, storing, and providing authorized access to them.[35]

Psychiatric records are not the only concern, however; other medical records are also considered to be particularly sensitive. In recent years special Federal statutes have been enacted governing the disclosure of medical-record information pertaining to alcohol and drug abuse.[36] The National Center for Health Statistics attributes the unreliability of its data on the incidence of venereal disease to physicians' refusal to make the required reports, fearing, for their patients, the social stigma that attaches to these conditions.[37] Nor does this exhaust the list of examples. Still others can be found in the growing literature on medical record-keeping practices and problems.[38]

Moreover, it is not clear that the nature of a patient's condition is the only factor that arouses anxiety about disclosure and its possible consequences. Because of the deference paid to expert opinion in our society, a physician's offhand comment or speculation about a patient can be taken as an authoritative statement by those making non-medical decisions about the patient. A 1974 article in a journal published by the American Medical Association describes a case in which a physician's discharge report to an employer contained a statement that the patient might have difficulty with money.[39] Although hardly a medical judgment, the remark permanently limited the individual's opportunities to advance in his firm. The co-director of a women's health center in Los Angeles gave the Commission still another illustration:

> The woman was hospitalized for an acute infection. While in the hospital, she was sent from her own room to the X-ray department, some distance away in the hospital. She was given her medical records, sealed in a manila envelope, and told to walk over to the X-ray department. On her way to X-ray, curiosity got the best of her and she opened the envelope to have a look at her condition via the medical record. She was astonished to see more information written

[34] Testimony of Jerome S. Beigler, M.D., Chairman, American Psychiatric Association Committee on Confidentiality, *Insurance Records*, Hearings before the Privacy Protection Study Committee, May 20, 1976, p. 371.

[35] Joint Commission on the Accreditation of Hospitals, *Accreditation Manual for Hospitals*, 1976 ed. (Chicago, Ill: JCAH, 1976) p. 98.

[36] Comprehensive Alcohol Abuse and Alcoholism Prevention, Treatment, and Rehabilitation Act of 1970, as amended by P.L. 93-282, and the Drug Abuse Office and Treatment Act of 1972, as amended by P.L. 93-282.

[37] National Center for Health Statistics, *op. cit.*, p. 257.

[38] Westin's 1976 study, previously cited, is the most recent contribution to the medical record-keeping literature on practices and problems.

[39] Ralph Crawshaw, "Gossip Wears a Thousand Masks," *Prism*, Vol. 2, No. 6 (June 1974), pp. 45-47.

in her record about the appearance of the friends who came to visit her in the hospital than about her medical condition.[40]

Whether such information had been or would be disclosed outside the hospital was not clear. Yet, the fact that it was in the record, the fact that it could have been disclosed, and the fact that the patient would normally have no way of knowing it was there, suggest why the medical-care relationship can be an extremely fragile one today.

One tends to forget that a patient usually has no way of knowing what is in a medical record about him, no way of controlling the accuracy or pertinence of the information it contains, and by and large no alternative but to allow others to have access to it when they ask permission to do so. As indicated earlier, consent to the disclosure of medical-record information about oneself is rarely voluntary. Usually the choice is between signing an authorization statement and foregoing a job or some indispensable service or benefit.[41] Under such circumstances an authorization can serve as a means of controlling the disclosure of information about oneself but never as a means of giving voluntary consent, and it can only serve as a means of control if the patient knows what it is he is authorizing to be disclosed. He rarely does, however. Just as custom prescribes an ethical duty of confidentiality for the medical-care provider, so also custom prescribes that the patient shall know nothing that is in the medical record except to the extent that the maker of the record chooses to tell him.

There is, of course, little consensus among medical professionals as to whether a patient should be allowed to learn the contents of his medical record and less as to whether he should be able to see and copy it. Forceful arguments for and against were presented in testimony before the Commission. The fears expressed by private-sector physicians and medical-care institutions were not unlike those of their Federal counterparts before the Privacy Act went into effect—fears which, by and large, have not been supported by experience. For example, one of the most commonly cited arguments in opposition to patient access is that it will lead to tremendous numbers of requests for records and thus greatly increase administrative costs while taking clerical and professional time to search for, prepare, and review records. Yet this has not been the case. A representative of the Health Services Administration of the Public Health Service testified that out of a total estimated patient population of five million, requests for records by

---

[40] Testimony of Feminist Women's Health Center, Medical Records Hearings, June 11, 1976, p. 323.

[41] In testimony before the Privacy Protection Study Commission, Dr. Catherine Elkin Rosen described an experiment she conducted to determine if the manner in which a consent form is presented affects the rate of compliance. From the study she concluded that individuals sign such forms only because they believe it will increase the likelihood of receiving services. Nearly all the clients in four mental health centers agreed to sign the authorization unless they were informed that they had the alternative of refusing. Testimony of Catherine E. Rosen Ph.D., Director, Research and Evaluation, Northeast Georgia Community Mental Health Center, Medical Records Hearings, June 11, 1976, p. 433. The results of this study have also been reported by Dr. Rosen in an article, "Signing Away Medical Privacy," The Civil Liberties Review, Vol. 3, No. 4, (Oct-Nov. 1976), pp. 54-59.

patients from the Bureau of Medical Services and the Indian Health Service have so far numbered around 3,000.[42] The Deputy Assistant Secretary of Defense for Administration provided no data on the numbers of requests for access to records but noted that only 20 requests for correction of medical records were received in a ten-month period by Department of Defense medical facilities.[43] The Administrator of St. Elizabeths Hospital, a large federally run psychiatric facility in Washington, D.C., estimated the number of requests for patient access during the first three months after the Privacy Act took effect at about 63.[44]

Others argue strongly for allowing an individual to have access to a medical record through a licensed physician designated by him, and still others express concern that patient access would have a detrimental effect on the content of the medical record itself. Nonetheless, the Director of the Public Health Service's Bureau of Medical Services told the Commission that the Privacy Act had the positive effect of encouraging physicians to record only information useful for patient care.[45]

Indeed, in the final analysis, the most persuasive line of reasoning favoring access turned on the concept of authorization. So long as it is thought acceptable, or even necessary, for an individual's past or present medical condition to be taken into account in making non-medical decisions about him, he will be asked to allow others to have access to his medical records or at least some of the information in them. As a practical matter, however, his authorization allowing such access by a third party will be meaningless so long as he does not know, and cannot find out, what is in the records. Both theoretically and practically, authorization is a meaningless procedure unless the individual knows what he is authorizing to be disclosed.

Finally, although much of the preceding discussion is focused on paper records, it is important to recognize that significant changes are occurring, both in the way information is organized in medical records, and in the way medical records are stored and retrieved. The "problem-oriented medical record" is perhaps the most important and widely accepted of recent attempts to standardize medical-record format. It allows all medical professionals involved in an individual's care to enter data and record observations on the same forms in the same manner. The problem-oriented format is adaptable to all medical-care settings from the physician's private office to the long-term chronic disease facility. More important, its standardized format lends itself easily to computerization and it was, in fact, initially developed with that purpose in mind.

Computerization of *medical records* in contrast to *medical-record information* is not a common phenomenon today. As hospitals and other larger medical facilities acquire and use computers for business office

---

[42] Written statement of the Health Services Administration, Public Health Service, DHEW, Medical Records Hearings, July 20, 1976.

[43] Testimony of the Department of Defense, Medical Records Hearings, July 21, 1976.

[44] Submission of the Public Health Service, DHEW, Medical Records Hearings, June 10, 1976.

[45] Testimony of the Health Services Administration, Public Health Service, DHEW, Medical Records Hearings, July 20, 1976, p. 125.

functions, however, a move toward computerization of the medical record itself becomes almost inevitable. A survey of some 6,000 hospitals conducted by the American Hospital Association in 1975 indicated that approximately 1,500 had in-house computers,[46] and the number undoubtedly has increased in the last two years with the advent of mini-computers and the growing experimentation with hospital information systems. Moreover, as Westin has pointed out in a study conducted for the National Bureau of Standards,[47] the flow of medical-record information between hospitals and third-party payers is already heavily automated and likely to become more so.

While this study showed that computerization has not yet led to greater collection of information or wider sharing of confidential records than heretofore prevailed in medical practice, it concluded that the creation of large automated information systems poses new problems and opportunities from a privacy protection viewpoint. The problems are centered around the need to spell out the rules under which personnel within a medical-care institution shall have access to all or part of an automated medical record and the necessary levels of physical security for automated records containing especially sensitive information (such as psychiatric records). The opportunities arise from the fact that an automated record can be adapted to a need-to-know policy more easily than a manual record.

These two trends—changing conceptions of the medical record and increasing automation—are important forces behind the Commission's conviction that now is the proper time to establish privacy protection safeguards for medical records that will enhance the integrity, and thus the efficacy, of the medical-care relationship.

RECOMMENDATIONS

The Commission's inquiry into the creation, maintenance, use, and disclosure of medical records and medical-record information led it to six basic conclusions.

First, medical records now contain more information and are now available to more users than ever before.

Second, the control medical-care providers once exercised over information in medical records has been greatly diluted as a consequence of specialization within the medical profession, population mobility, third-party demands for medical-record information, and the increasing incidence of malpractice suits.

Third, the comparative insulation of medical records from collateral uses, normal even a decade ago, cannot be entirely restored. Indeed, it appears that the importance of medical-record information to those outside of the medical-care relationship, and their demands for access to it, will continue to grow. Moreover, owing to the rising demand for access by third parties, coupled with the expense of limiting disclosure to that which is specifically requested by the non-medical user, there appears to be no

---

[46] Marcia Opp, "The Confidentiality Dilemma," *Modern Health Care,* (May 1975), p. 52.
[47] Westin, *op. cit.*

natural limit to the potential uses of medical-record information for purposes quite different from those for which it was originally collected.

Fourth, as third parties press their demands for access to medical-record information, the concept of consent to its disclosure, freely given by the individual to whom the information pertains, has less and less meaning. When an individual must choose between signing an authorization form and foregoing employment or insurance or public assistance, one cannot realistically speak of his signing voluntarily. This is not to say that authorization procedures are useless; to the contrary, they are essential instruments of control over the content and subsequent use of what is disclosed. In many situations, however, they should no longer be construed as evidence of consent freely given.

Fifth, although the content of a medical record is becoming harder to control at the same time that the number and kind of decisions in which it figures is growing, it is still rare for an individual to be allowed to see, much less copy, a medical record pertaining to himself or to check the accuracy, timeliness, or completeness of the information it contains.

Sixth, there are steps that can and should be taken: (a) to improve the accuracy, timeliness, and completeness of the information in a medical record; (b) to enhance the individual patient's awareness of the content and uses of a medical record about himself; and (c) to control not only the amount and type of information that is disclosed to other types of users, but also the conditions under which such disclosures are made.

The recommendations presented below are the Commission's answer to a balanced delineation of these steps. As with the Commission's other recommendations, they have three objectives: (1) to minimize intrusiveness; (2) to maximize fairness; and (3) to create a legitimate, enforceable expectation of confidentiality. Unlike the Commission's other recommendations, however, the recommendations set forth below are expected to have their greatest influence *outside* the medical-care relationship. For example, the Commission's recommendations are not focused on the intrusiveness of the medical-care relationship *per se,* but rather on the intrusiveness that can result from others being able to take advantage of the unusual extent of divulgence and recording of observations that the medical-care relationship entails. Similarly, the Commission's recommendations for letting the patient see, copy, and correct or amend his records are not primarily aimed at the consequences of inaccuracies or other deficiences in the records when used by a medical-care provider working within the context of the medical-care relationship.

The Commission has been moved to recommend rights of access and correction for the patient in recognition of the harm that can befall him as a consequence of inaccurate, obsolete, or incomplete medical-record information being available for use in the context of relationships he has with other kinds of record-keeping institutions. While the Commission is aware of the argument that giving a patient the right to review, discuss, audit, and obtain a copy of his medical record can have therapeutic value,[48] it does not consider the decision-making uses of medical records within the confines of the medical-care relationship to be within its competence. In fact, only in the confidentiality area do the Commission's recommendations speak directly to the dynamics of the medical-care relationship, but again, only as those dynamics are affected by the lack of a legitimate, enforceable, expectation of confidentiality.

GENERAL RECOMMENDATIONS

The Commission considered several ways in which its medical-record recommendations might be implemented and enforced. The alternatives considered ranged from a wholly voluntary approach to Federal legislation which, like the 1974 Drug Abuse and Alcoholism statutes,[49] would make compliance with the recommendations a requirement attached to the direct or indirect receipt of Federal funds. Ultimately, however, the Commission settled on an intermediate strategy of giving medical-care *institutions* the responsibility for seeing that the requirements are met as a condition of qualifying for Medicare or Medicaid reimbursement. Private practitioners would not have to meet these requirements, since under current law they are not subject to the qualification standards that apply to medical-care institutions. Nonetheless, as it becomes necessary for private practitioners to qualify for Federal reimbursement, either through expansion of existing regulations, or through other developments looking toward a national health insurance scheme, they, too, would be covered by the recommended measures.

The Commission believes that this strategy allows time and opportunity for the orderly resolution of differences between the institutionalized medical-care relationship and the private practitioner relationship, differences that directly affect the content and handling of medical records. Moreover, to begin with the institutional relationship is to begin where the greatest problems appear to exist at the present time.

Accordingly, the Commission recommends:

Recommendation (1):

That the Congress, through amendment of the Social Security Act,

---

[48] This argument has been espoused by the staff of the Given Health Care Center in Vermont and is supported by a study reported by them in *Applying the Problem Oriented Record*. One hundred people were given their medical records and asked to review and audit the "subjective" data in their file. Reportedly, 78 percent of the patients indicated changes in their living, eating, and drinking patterns and 97 percent indicated less worry about their health after review of their record. Richard E. Bouchard, et al. "The Patient and His Problem-Oriented Record," *Applying the Problem-Oriented System*, H. Kenneth Walker, J. Willis Hurst, and Mary F. Woody, eds. (New York: MEDCOM, 1975).

[49] Comprehensive Alcohol Abuse and Alcoholism Prevention, Treatment, and Rehabilitation Act of 1970, as amended by P.L. 93-282, and the Drug Abuse Office and Treatment Act of 1972, as amended by P.L. 93-282.

authorize the Secretary of Health, Education, and Welfare to promulgate regulations requiring:

(a) that medical-care providers whose services are paid for directly or indirectly under Titles XVIII and XIX of the Social Security Act develop specific procedures for implementing Commission *Recommendations (5), (7), (9), (10), (11), (12), (13), and (14)*;

(b) that such providers be required to show evidence of compliance with these recommendations as a condition of participation in the Medicare and Medicaid programs; and

(c) that all records of surveys of compliance with the procedures developed pursuant to the Commission's recommendations be a matter of public record and open to public inspection, provided, however, that the names or other identifying particulars of patients are deleted prior to public release.

This recommendation builds on existing regulatory mechanisms and current certification and accreditation processes. Subparagraph (c), however, goes beyond current practice regarding surveys carried out by the Joint Commission on the Accreditation of Hospitals (JCAH). Whereas surveys of Federal facilities and of institutions other than JCAH-accredited hospitals are open to public inspection under the Federal Freedom of Information Act, the results of JCAH surveys of medical-care institutions, by law, are not. Thus, unless the law were changed to provide for public inspection of those portions of a survey having to do with Title XVIII and Title XIX privacy protection requirements, the public would have no knowledge of hospital compliance. As repeatedly emphasized throughout this report, openness as to information policies and practices and accountability for such policies and practices are two of the most important protections for personal privacy. Both these protections would be absent if JCAH survey reports were allowed to remain secret.

The need for subparagraph (c) points up the major disadvantage of relying exclusively on the existing Title XVIII and Title XIX regulatory mechanisms; no actionable rights for individuals will be created as a result. Enforcement will depend solely on the effectiveness of certification and accreditation procedures, and the ability of individuals, as individuals, to induce the Department of Health, Education, and Welfare to investigate specific cases and institute sanctions where an institution has failed to discharge its responsibilities. In Chapter 9 on the education relationship, the deficiences of this type of approach are described, from the sanctioning agency's point of view as well as from the individual's. Hence, as a corollary to the action it urges on the Congress, the Commission also recommends:

Recommendation (2):

That each State enact a statute creating individual rights of access to, and correction of, medical records, and an enforceable expectation of confidentiality for medical records consistent with Commission recommendations in these areas.

The Commission strongly urges that the National Commission on Uniform State Laws, or another body of comparable mission and expertise, develop model State statutes that will provide for the individual a right to sue for access to a medical record about himself, to correct or amend erroneous, misleading, or incomplete information in a medical record, and a right to hold a medical-care provider responsible if it can be shown that the provider has not exercised reasonable care in protecting the confidentiality of the medical records it maintains about him. In addition, the Commission would urge that such statutes create a limitation of liability to protect the medical-care provider against actions brought for defamation, invasion of privacy, or negligence when a medical record or medical-record information is released pursuant to the requirements of the statute or to the DHEW regulations proposed in *Recommendation (1),* above. False information furnished with malice or willful intent to injure an individual would, of course, not be covered by such limitation.

Recognizing that there will be some medical-care providers that will not be subject to Medicare and Medicaid regulations, or, at least for a time, to State statutory requirements, the Commission also recommends:

Recommendation (3):

That any medical-care provider not subject to either of the Commission's two general recommendations on implementation voluntarily establish procedures to comply with the specific recommendations set forth below.

Finally, in light of the evidence presented to the Commission concerning the surreptitious acquisition of medical-record information from medical-care providers, the Commission recommends:

Recommendation (4):

That Federal and State penal codes be amended to make it a criminal offense for any individual knowingly to request or obtain medical-record information from a medical-care provider under false pretenses or through deception.

Safeguarding the confidentiality of medical records is properly the responsibility of the medical-care provider maintaining them. Yet, as noted earlier, at least one firm has specialized in obtaining medical-record information through subterfuge and was reported to have been successful in more than 90 percent of its attempts.[50] Indeed, the breaches of medical-record security which have come to the public's attention in the last few years have been dramatic and unsettling. The break-in at the offices of Daniel Ellsberg's psychiatrist, the publicizing of Senator Eagleton's past medical history, and the recent exposure of the theft of information by Factual Service Bureau are but three examples of blatant disregard for the

---

[50] Testimony of Dale Tooley, District Attorney, Denver, Colorado, Medical Records Hearings, June 11, 1976, p. 474.

confidentiality of medical records. Under these circumstances, to place the full onus of responsibility for the protection of medical records on the medical-care provider seems to the Commission to be unrealistic. Its responsibility must be reinforced by sanctions against the deceptive acquisition or theft of medical-record information.

SPECIFIC RECOMMENDATIONS

Inasmuch as the Commission has no recommendations that bear directly on the intrusiveness of the medical-care relationship itself, its first set of specific recommendations concerns fairness. The measures recommended here prescribe procedures for allowing a patient to see, copy, and correct or amend a medical record pertaining to himself, and for placing limits on the circulation of medical-record information within the immediate medical-care setting. Measures are also recommended to reinforce the expectation of confidentiality in the medical-care relationship by placing limits and conditions on those, other than a medical-care provider, who may acquire and use the information contained in a medical record.

Fairness

PATIENT ACCESS TO MEDICAL RECORDS

As noted earlier, one of the issues on which medical-care providers are least in agreement is whether a patient should be allowed to see and copy a medical record about himself. Nine States currently grant a patient the right to inspect and, in some instances, obtain copies of his medical records. Colorado clearly has the most liberal statutes in that they apply not only to hospital records, but also to records kept by private physicians, psychologists, and psychiatrists. The Colorado statutes grant the patient the right to obtain a copy of his records for a reasonable fee, without resort to litigation, and without the authorization of physicians or hospital officials.[51] An Oklahoma statute permits the patient to inspect and copy his medical records in both the hospital setting and the physician's office.[52] The difference between the Oklahoma and Colorado laws lies in the status of psychiatric records. Colorado provides for patient access to psychiatric records following termination of treatment, while Oklahoma excludes psychiatric records altogether.

Other States recognize a much narrower right of access. Florida law gives the patient the right to obtain copies of all reports of his examination and treatment, but applies only to records maintained by physicians, with no mention of hospital records.[53] By contrast, the statutes of Connecticut,

[51] Colo. Rev. Stat. § 25-1-801.
[52] Okla. Stat. Ann. tit. 76, § 19.
[53] Fla. Stat. Ann. § 458.16.

Indiana, Louisiana, and Massachusetts cover only a hospital record, and make no mention of records maintained by physicians.[54] Mississippi and Tennessee require the patient to show good cause before he can have access to his hospital records.[55] Ten States (Illinois, Maine, Missouri, Montana, Nevada, New Jersey, New Mexico, North Dakota, Utah, and Wisconsin) have vaguely worded statutes or regulations[56] that allow a patient, relative, physician, or attorney access to the patient's medical records. Of these 10 states, Nevada and New Mexico apply only to mental-health records. In New York, the patient need be shown only enough of the hospital record to indicate which physicians have attended him,[57] and in Ohio the hospital determines how much of the medical record the patient may see.[58] In Arizona the administrator or attending physician must consent before a patient can inspect his hospital records.[59]

In several other States legislation is now pending that would create a right of access for a patient similar to the one provided by the Privacy Act of 1974, i.e., a right to *see and copy* a medical record about oneself except in special situations.

The subsection of the Privacy Act that specifically refers to medical records states:

> In order to carry out the provisions of this section, each agency that maintains a system of records shall promulgate rules . . . which shall . . . establish procedures for the disclosure to an individual, upon his request, of his record or information pertaining to him, including special procedures, if deemed necessary, for the disclosure to an individual of medical records, including psychological records pertaining to him. *[5 U.S.C. 552a(f)(3)]*

The Office of Management and Budget guidelines for implementing the Privacy Act quote the legislative history of this provision as follows:

> If in the judgment of the agency, the transmission of medical information directly to a requesting individual could have an adverse effect upon such individual, the rules which the agency promulgates should provide means whereby an individual who

---

[54] Conn. Gen. Stat. Ann. § 4.104 (1969); Ind. Code Ann. § 34-3-15.5-4; La. Rev. Stat. Ann. § 44.31 (1951); Mass. Gen. Laws Ann. ch. 111 § 70 (1971).

[55] Miss. Code Ann. § 7146-53 (Supp. 1971); Tenn. Code Ann. § 53-1322.

[56] Ill. Ann. Stat. ch. 51 § 71; Maine: Letter from Robert B. Calkins, Assistant Attorney General to the Secretary's Commission on Medical Malpractice, June 19, 1972; Missouri Division of Health, Hospital Licensing Law, ch. 197; Montana Board of Health Regulations, §31.106; Nev. Rev. Stat. §433.721; N.J. Stat. Ann. §30:4-24.3; N. M. Stat. Ann. §32-2-18; N.D.- Rules and Regulations for Hospitals and Related Institutions R. 23-16-8S.1-.3; Utah Code Ann. §64-7-50; and Wis. Stat. Ann. §269.57(4).

[57] N.Y. Official Compilation of Codes, Rules and Regulations, §§ 720.20(p)(1971).

[58] *Wallace v. University Hospital,* 171 Ohio St. 487, 172 N.E.2d 459 (1961).

[59] Arizona Hospital Association Consent Manual, 1969.

would be adversely affected by receipt of such data may be apprised of it in a manner which would not cause such adverse effects.[60]

While the Privacy Act recognizes an individual's undeniable right to see and copy a medical record about him maintained by a Federal medical-care facility, it clearly allows special procedures where direct access could be harmful to him. The guidelines are vague about when special procedures are justified and silent about what they may be. Thus, it should not be surprising that the special procedures developed by the different agencies are not the same.

The Department of Health, Education, and Welfare has the most liberal procedures, providing for indirect access to records through a responsible individual, not necessarily a medical professional, designated by the patient. The Department of Defense procedure requires that arrangements be made for release of the record to a physician of the patient's choice. The Veterans Administration takes a middle ground, requiring that medical records containing "sensitive information" be "referred to a physician or other professional person with the necessary professional qualifications to properly interpret and communicate the information desired." The one caveat provided is that the selectee must either meet VA professional standards or be licensed in the appropriate professional specialty.[61]

The Commission's hearings failed to produce evidence that one procedure was more effective than another in protecting patients from any adverse consequences that might result from obtaining their medical records. Not one witness was able to identify an instance where access to records has had an untoward effect on a patient's medical condition. While the Department of Defense special procedure is clearly the most restrictive, DOD representatives estimated that the Department had released a record to a physician, rather than to the individual directly, in less than one percent of the cases where access had been requested.

The Commission considered a number of proposals for a special procedure to be followed when direct access might harm the patient. Some of these would stop short of the DHEW procedure allowing release of the record to any responsible person the patient may designate, whether the designee is a medical professional or not. Others would leave the patient's see-and-copy right unrestricted with respect to any information in his medical records that had been or might be disclosed for use in making non-medical decisions about him, but would prescribe special procedures in specified instances (e.g., psychiatric or terminal illness) when there is no possibility of such disclosure to third parties. In the end, however, the Commission concluded that no solution would be acceptable in the long run so long as it risks leaving the ultimate discretion to release or not to release in the hands of the patient's physician. In situations where the keeper of a medical record believes that allowing the patient to see and copy it may be

---

[60] Office of Management and Budget, *Privacy Act Guidelines*, issued as a supplement to Circular A-108, 40 *Federal Register*, 132, p. 28957.

[61] U.S. Veterans Administration, *Manual MP-1*, Part II, Chapter 21, Section 6.d.

injurious to the patient, the Commission concluded that it would be reasonable for the record to be given to a responsible person designated by the patient, with that person being the ultimate judge of whether the patient should have full access to it. In no case, however, should the physician or other keeper of the record be able to refuse to disclose the record to the designated responsible person, even where it is known in advance that the designated person will give the patient full access to it.

Accordingly, having weighed the evidence before it, and having considered the arguments pro and con, the Commission recommends:

Recommendation (5):

That upon request, an individual who is the subject of a medical record maintained by a medical-care provider, or another responsible person designated by the individual, be allowed to have access to that medical record, including an opportunity to see and copy it. The medical-care provider should be able to charge a reasonable fee (not to exceed the amount charged to third parties) for preparing and copying the record.

Although this recommendation stops short of guaranteeing that the patient will be allowed to see and copy everything in every medical record about him, it leaves the designee the option of giving the patient this guarantee. The Commission believes that the measure will encourage medical-care providers themselves to release records to patients whenever they can possibly do so in good conscience. In some sense, the recommended procedure harkens back to the time when family members and friends played a much larger role in patient care than they normally do today. In any case, it gives most patients a way of finding out what is in their medical records, and of knowing what others can learn about them from those records.

This discussion would be incomplete without a word about access to medical records by patients who are minors. As noted in Chapter 11 on the public assistance and social services relationship, most of the comments submitted to the Commission urged that a minor patient be given access to medical records concerning treatment he has sought on his own behalf, if State law permits him to obtain such treatment without the knowledge or consent of his parents. State laws usually deal with this question in connection with venereal disease, drug or alcohol abuse, pregnancy, and family planning, including abortion. The Commission believes that in these instances only the minors (and not their parents or guardians) should be given access to such records or portions of records so as not to discourage them from seeking necessary treatment.

The fee provision also raises a minor problem. *Recommendation (5)* would allow the medical-care provider to charge the individual a preparation or copying fee consistent with the fees it charges others for such services. This could mean anything from $1 to several hundred dollars. Obviously, the Commission would not want the right to see and copy a medical record to become a prerogative of the well-to-do, and thus urges medical-care providers to develop fee schedules flexible enough to match the varying financial circumstances of patients.

PATIENT ACCESS TO MEDICAL-RECORD INFORMATION

Elsewhere in this report the Commission recommends measures to assure an individual's right of access to a record maintained about him by an insurer, self-insurer, or insurance-support organization and further, that he be able to obtain on request a copy of all the information that served as the basis for an adverse insurance decision about himself. In another chapter, the Commission recommends that an employer voluntarily establish procedures whereby an individual can gain access to records the employer maintains about him. In the chapter on Public Assistance and Social Services, the Commission recommends enactment of a Federal statute requiring that the States, in turn, enact statutes permitting individuals to have access to records maintained by a public assistance or social service agency.

In all three instances, some of the records to which the individual would be given access are, or contain, medical-record information. The Commission would prefer that such third-party holders of medical-record information not distinguish it from any other information the individual asks to see and copy. The Commission recognizes, however, that as a practical matter an individual may not always find a medical record or a copy of medical-record information informative unless a medical professional interprets its technical language for him, and third-party keepers of medical-record information may not be able to provide such assistance. Thus, with respect to medical-record information, the Commission recommends:

Recommendation (6):

That upon request, an individual who is the subject of medical-record information maintained by an organization which is not a medical-care provider be allowed to have access to that information either directly or through a licensed medical-care professional designated by him.

It must be noted that this recommendation does not fall within the primary implementation strategy contained in *Recommendations (1), (2),* and *(3)* above. In the case of insurance institutions and insurance-support organizations, it would become part of the recommended general and specific rights of access to records to be established by Federal statute. In the private-sector employment situation, it would be implemented voluntarily by the employer. In the public assistance and social services area, it would become a right provided by State statute which, if the Commission's recommendations were followed exactly would have to distinguish between the social-services provider who is a medical-care provider—properly subject to the requirements of *Recommendation (5)* —and the social-services provider who is not a medical-care provider but who uses medical-record information. As to the latter, the statute should guarantee *direct* access lest it retreat from the current practice of allowing an individual to see, before or during a hearing, information used to make an adverse eligibility determination about him. (See Chapter 11.)

CORRECTION OF A MEDICAL RECORD

A main premise of a privacy protection policy is that an individual should be able to review the records made by others of information he has divulged, or has permitted to be divulged, and to correct any errors or amend any inadequacies in them. This premise is no less important for medical records than for other types of records, although much of the information in a medical record is put there by medical professionals. The individual may provide information, but he rarely enters it directly into the record; the medical professional normally does that. Thus, even with the most conscientious record keeping, there are ample opportunities for errors of fact or interpretation to creep into a medical record.

Within the medical-care relationship itself, such errors can usually be corrected before they do any harm. Once information has been disclosed to someone outside the relationship, however, not only is correction or amendment more difficult but the consequences of errors become increasingly difficult to avoid or reverse. This becomes a particular danger when, as previously noted, offhand comments and speculations which are irrelevant to a patient's medical history, diagnosis, condition, treatment, or evaluation are set down in medical records that become available for use in making a non-medical decision about him. Furthermore, while it is true that some portion of the information in a medical record may be beyond the patient's comprehension, not all of it will be. Accordingly, in recognition of the fact that the circulation of erroneous, obsolete, incomplete, or irrelevant medical-record information outside the confines of the medical-care relationship can bring substantial harm or embarrassment to the individual concerned, the Commission recommends:

Recommendation (7):

That each medical-care provider have a procedure whereby an individual who is the subject of a medical record it maintains can request correction or amendment of the record. When the individual requests correction or amendment, the medical-care provider must, within a reasonable period of time, either:

(a)   **make the correction or amendment requested; or**
(b)   **inform the individual of its refusal to do so, the reason for the refusal, and of the procedure, if any, for further review of the refusal.**

In addition, if the medical-care provider refuses to correct or amend a record in accordance with the individual's request, the provider must permit the individual to file a concise statement of the reasons for the

disagreement, and in any subsequent disclosure of the disputed information include a notation that the information is disputed and furnish the statement of disagreement. In any such disclosure, the provider may also include a statement of the reasons for not making the requested correction or amendment.

Finally, when a medical-care provider corrects or amends a record pursuant to an individual's request, or accepts a notation of dispute and statement of disagreement, it should be required to furnish the correction, amendment, or statement of disagreement to any person specifically designated by the individual to whom the medical-care provider has previously disclosed the inaccurate, incomplete, or disputed information.

The requirement to furnish a correction, amendment, or dispute statement to such previous recipients as the individual may designate evolves from a concern that medical-record information disclosed to third parties be as accurate, complete, and timely as possible. To expect a medical-care provider to convey a correction, amendment, or dispute statement to all previous recipients of information from a record would impose an unreasonable burden on the provider; yet the Commission is concerned that some steps be taken to minimize the extent to which medical-record information may become a source of unfairness to an individual. Therefore, it has recommended that only those specifically designated by the individual be furnished with the details of the correction, amendment, or statement of disagreement. The Commission believes this approach represents a reasonable balance. Moreover, because *Recommendations (10)* and *(14)* below call for two types of accountings of disclosures (notations and retained authorization statements), the Commission would expect those accountings also to be available to the individual to help him to decide to whom corrections, amendments, or statements of disagreement should be sent.

CORRECTION OF MEDICAL-RECORD INFORMATION

As with its recommendations on patient access, the Commission also debated the correction, amendment, and dispute issues as they relate to keepers of medical-record information. The problem is largely one of information erroneously or incompletely reported by a medical-care provider, or erroneously copied or interpreted for or by the recipient. For example, an investigative-reporting firm under contract to an insurer may be authorized to acquire information from the physicians and hospitals named on an individual's insurance application. If the investigative firm representative makes a mistake in copying information from a medical record, neither his firm nor the insurer has any way of knowing it unless and until the error precipitates an adverse insurance decision and perhaps not even then. Even if the error is detected later, the information may have been disclosed in the meantime to other insurers (with the individual's authorization), or to the

Medical Information Bureau where it will be retained, and thus constitute a potential problem for the individual for many years.

The Commission recognizes that the number of mistakes of this sort can be minimized by having a medical-care professional review and interpret records for agents of third parties, or by using photocopying techniques. Not all medical records today can be organized to allow easy photocopying, however, and at the same time assure that the inquiring third party receives only as much information as the individual has authorized it to receive. Nor is it always possible to have a professional available when records are reviewed by third parties. Thus, in some unknown number of cases, either a medical professional will have to prepare special reports for the ultimate recipient—in this example, the insurer—or a certain amount of hand copying by persons who are not medically trained will unavoidably continue. Even when a medical record can be photocopied without revealing more information than is meant to be disclosed, there is the danger that the third party representative making the copy will overlook portions of the record which, if known, would alter the insurer's decision.

The simplest solution would, of course, be to allow the individual to correct or amend medical-record information where it rests, in the files of the recipient-user. Yet the simplest solution is not always the most practical one. The insurer (or employer, or whoever the third-party record holder happens to be) may elect not to give the individual direct access to medical-record information about himself. *Recommendation (6)*, it will be remembered, gives the third-party record holder the option[62] of disclosing medical-record information either to the individual to whom it pertains, or to a licensed medical professional whom the individual designates. Hence, there may be no way for the third-party holder to cope with a correction or amendment request without, in effect, giving up its option to deal with the individual through a designated professional.

Moreover, despite what has been said about the tendency of some medical-care providers to record irrelevant information, it must be remembered that the medical record is a document to which unusual attention is given because it is created by persons who have special expertise. If an insurer could have confidence in an individual's own description of his medical situation, there would be no need to acquire information in his medical records. The insurer, however, cannot assume that the individual is either qualified or motivated to give an accurate description. The fact that the insurer cannot rely on the individual in this matter is both the reason why the insurer seeks to acquire medical-record information and the reason why the individual's claim that the information obtained is erroneous or otherwise inadequate cannot be taken at face value.

It may also happen that the medical-care provider who originally provided the contested information can no longer be consulted; for example, a physician may have retired, died, or moved out of reach, or the provider may simply not be willing to acknowledge that an error was made. In such situations, the Commission believes that the third-party holder of

---

[62] Except in the case of the social-service provider that uses medical-record information to make an (adverse) eligibility determination.

the allegedly inaccurate information should afford the individual a way of entering his corrections into the record as long as it also indicated that the changes were made without the concurrence of its original source. Accordingly, the Commission recommends:

Recommendation (8):

That when an individual who is the subject of medical-record information maintained by an organization whose relationship to the individual is not that of a medical-care provider requests correction or amendment of such information, the organization should disclose to the individual, or to a medical-care professional designated by him, the identity of the medical-care provider who was the source of the information; and further,

That if the medical-care provider who was the source of the information agrees that it is inaccurate or incomplete, the organization maintaining it should promptly make the correction or amendment requested.

In addition, a procedure should be established whereby an individual who is the subject of medical-record information maintained by an organization whose relationship to him is not that of a medical-care provider, and who believes that the information is incorrect or incomplete, would be provided an opportunity to present supplemental information, of a limited nature, for inclusion in the organization's record, provided that the source of the supplemental information is also included in the record.

SAFEGUARDS AGAINST UNAUTHORIZED DISCLOSURE

In other chapters of this report, the Commission considers various potential sources of unfairness to the individual when information is being used for the purposes for which it was collected. The Commission does not believe it necessary to do so here because institutional providers of medical care have traditionally given priority to protecting the individual in their own uses of patient records.[63] The several organizations in the field of medical records management are far more competent than the Commission to make judgments and recommend rules as to the proper content of a medical record, its proper uses, and the types of users to whom it should or should not be disclosed within the framework of the medical-care relationship. Thus, in this chapter, the Commission confines its examination of information management *within* the medical-care relationship to one

---

[63] According to the Director of the Professional Services Division of the American Medical Record Association, the total membership of the Association at the beginning of 1977 was approximately 19,500 individuals. It was estimated by the Bureau of Health Manpower of the Department of Health, Education, and Welfare in 1974 that there were 53,000 individuals employed in the management and administration of medical records, 11,000 of whom were working in an administrative capacity. U.S. Department of Health, Education and Welfare, *The Supply of Health Manpower* (Washington, D.C.: DHEW, 1974), p. 144.

obvious area of concern: the medical-care provider's role in assuring that the patient's legitimate expectations of confidentiality are not breached as a consequence of negligence on the part of medical professionals themselves. The dramatic instance, previously cited, of the Factual Service Bureau's unauthorized access to hospital medical records clearly highlights hospital internal records management as a problem area, although laxity in hospital records-management procedures was only part of the problem in that instance.

Hospital records are routinely available to hospital employees on request. Most of these people are medical professionals who need such access in order to do their jobs, but not all of them are. Besides the physicians, psychologists, nurses, social workers, therapists, and other licensed or certified medical professionals and paraprofessionals, there are nearly always medical students and other people in training programs conducted either by the medical-care institution itself or affiliated with the institution. These people, too, have access to medical records for training or job-related purposes, as do non-professional employees and voluntary workers. In fact, one of the Factual Service Bureau sources was an employee in the administrator's office of a Denver hospital.

The more people there are who have access to a medical record, the more people there are who can be approached by a firm like Factual Service Bureau. Since the patient cannot control access to or use of records about him *within* a medical-care institution, it follows that the responsibility for protecting the record from such abuse must be assumed by the institution. Thus, the Commission recommends:

Recommendation (9):

That each medical-care provider be required to take affirmative measures to assure that the medical records it maintains are made available only to authorized recipients and on a "need-to-know" basis.

Requiring the patient's authorization each time an employee of the institution needs access to his medical record would be impractical. The team approach to treatment demands that the professional staff have ready access to patient records. Employees whose functions are purely administrative or custodial, however, need access to only some of the information in a patient's record, for example, name, address, and whatever other information may be essential for preparing and submitting bills and claims or statistical and management reports. These employees do not need, and should not have, free access to detailed clinical information about patients.

The Commission urges accrediting bodies, licensing agencies, and professional associations to take the lead in establishing guidelines for affirmative measures to protect hospital medical records from unauthorized access. Affirmative measures might include routine call-back to verify the validity of telephone requests for records, requiring staff members and employees who request information or records from the medical-record department to identify themselves, prompt dismissal of any employee who violates the confidentiality of medical-record information, and a program to instruct new employees in the hospital's confidentiality policies.

Expectation of Confidentiality

DISCLOSURE BY MEDICAL-CARE PROVIDERS

The American Hospital Association (AHA), like the American Medical Association (AMA), claims for its membership the right to decide when disclosure of a patient's medical record is necessary to protect the individual or the community. According to *Hospital Medical Records,* an AHA publication:

> The medical record . . . is the property of the hospital, therefore, the hospital, subject to applicable legal provisions, may restrict the removal of the record from the medical-record files or hospital premises, determine who may have access to it, and define the kind of information that may be taken from it.[64]

Although courts have found the disclosure of medical-record information by a physician to be actionable in a number of different cases, they have also consistently held that such disclosures are justifiable if they are made either in the best interest of the patient or to foster a supervening societal interest. An individual can clearly bring suit against a physician and probably against any other medical-care professional for disclosing information in a medical record about him without his authorization, but he is likely to lose. Indeed, in one case involving the unauthorized disclosure of derogatory psychiatric information, a court went so far as to affirm that ". . . the responsibility of the doctor to keep confidences may be outweighed by a higher duty to give out information even though defamatory. . . ."[65]

Spokesmen for the medical-care professions argue that their discretion in making disclosures of the information in medical records is not a significant source of abuse. While the Commission is inclined to agree, the individual cannot rely on his expectation of confidentiality in any record-keeping relationship unless the restraints on disclosures are known, as the Commission argues in Chapter 9. As long as record keepers have complete discretion in making disclosures, the individual can have no basis for an expectation of confidentiality. Even if all record keepers were equally aware of their confidentiality obligation and equally conscientious in discharging it, the individual could not tell just what to expect since their perceptions of what the obligation entails would not necessarily be the same. Record keepers need not be denied all discretion in the matter; if enforceable limits are set on their discretion, the individual can build an expectation of confidentiality that corresponds with those limits.

Enforceable limits on voluntary disclosures of confidential information have advantages for the record keeper as well as for the individual. In

---

[64] American Hospital Association, *Hospital Medical Records* (Chicago: AHA, 1972), p. 8.
[65] *Berry v. Moench,* 331 P.2d 814 (Utah 1958).

fact, without them, both are often hard put to refuse demands for disclosure, and virtually helpless when the demand is part of a compulsory process.

The Commission believes that the medical-care relationship in America today is becoming dangerously fragile as the basis for an expectation of confidentiality with respect to records generated in that relationship is undermined more and more. A legitimate, enforceable expectation of confidentiality that will hold up under the revolutionary changes now taking place in medical care and medical record-keeping needs to be created and the Commission therefore recommends:

Recommendation (10):

That each medical-care provider be considered to owe a duty of confidentiality to any individual who is the subject of a medical record it maintains, and that, therefore, no medical care provider should disclose, or be required to disclose, in individually identifiable form, any information about any such individual without the individual's explicit authorization, unless the disclosures would be:

(a)   **to another medical-care provider who is being consulted in connection with the treatment of the individual by the medical-care provider;**

(b)   **to a properly identified recipient pursuant to a showing of compelling circumstances affecting the health and safety of an individual provided that:**

    (i)   **an accounting of any such disclosure is kept; and**

    (ii)   **the individual who is the subject of the information disclosed can find out that the disclosure has been made and to whom it has been made;**

(c)   **for use in conducting a biomedical or epidemiological research project, provided that the medical-care provider maintaining the medical record:**

    (i)   **determines that such use or disclosure does not violate any limitations under which the record or information was collected;**

    (ii)   **ascertains that use or disclosure in individually identifiable form is necessary to accomplish the research or statistical purpose for which use or disclosure is to be made;**

    (iii) **determines that the importance of the research or statistical purpose for which any use or disclosure is to be made is such as to warrant the risk to the individual from additional exposure of the record or information contained therein;**

    (iv)   **requires that adequate safeguards to protect the record or information from unauthorized disclosure be established and maintained by the user or recipient, including a program for removal or destruction of identifiers; and**

    (v)   **consents in writing before any further use or redisclosure**

> of the record or information in individually identifiable form is permitted;
>
> (d)   for an audit or evaluation purpose specifically required by law, provided that an accounting of such disclosures is kept and the individual who is the subject of the information being disclosed can find out that the disclosure has been made and to whom;
>
> (e)   for an audit or evaluation purpose not specifically required by law, provided that:
>
>   (i)   any further use or redisclosure of the information in individually identifiable form is prohibited;
>
>   (ii)   adequate safeguards to protect the medical-record information from unauthorized disclosure are established by the user or recipient including a program for removal or destruction of identifiers;
>
>   (iii)   an accounting of such disclosures is kept and the individual who is the subject of the information being disclosed can find out that the disclosure has been made and to whom;
>
> (f)   pursuant to a statute that requires the medical-care provider to report specific diagnoses to a public-health authority, and the individual is notified of each such disclosure;
>
> (g)   pursuant to a statute that requires the medical-care provider to report specified items of information about the individual to a law enforcement authority, and the individual is notified of each such disclosure;
>
> (h)   limited to location and status information (such as room number, dates of hospitalization, and general condition) provided that:
>
>   (i)   the patient or his authorized representative does not object to the disclosure; and
>
>   (ii)   such disclosure is limited to items specified in the general notice to the individual called for in *Recommendation (12)*; or
>
> (i)   pursuant to a lawful judicial summons or subpoena consistent with the recommendations of the Commission on government access.

The recommended duty of confidentiality would be established in the first instance through regulations promulgated by the Department of Health, Education and Welfare. To make the duty fully effective, however, it should be adopted by statutory enactment in each of the 50 States. If this is not done the individual patient will be dependent on the medical-care provider to protect him against compulsory process and other demands for his medical records or he will have to rely on the Department of Health, Education and Welfare to act on his behalf when a provider violates its duty of confidentiality to him.

The Commission recognizes that a duty established by State statute will not in most cases be effective against any conflicting requirements of Federal agencies to disclose medical-record information in individually identifiable form as a condition of participation in a Federal program. Thus, the final test of society's desire to create a viable basis for legitimate expectations of confidentiality in records about individuals generated in the context of the medical-care relationship, as in other contexts examined in this report, will be its willingness to adopt the Commission's recommendations on government access set forth in Chapter 9.

Exceptions to the Duty of Confidentiality

As noted earlier, it is no longer possible to restore the comparative insulation medical records enjoyed even a decade ago. Exceptions allowing disclosure without the individual patient's authorization are necessary here, as elsewhere, in order to strike a balance between the individual's right to personal privacy and society's countervailing needs for information about his medical condition. The rationale for each of the exceptions in *Recommendation (10)* is explained below.

Disclosures to Other Medical-Care Providers

The first exception the Commission weighed concerns the disclosure of medical-record information between medical-care providers. Currently, it is by no means routine for a provider referring a patient to another provider to ask the patient's written authorization to disclose the pertinent medical-record information about him to the second provider. Inasmuch as the second provider is no doubt directly involved in the diagnosis and treatment of the patient, the patient's authorization properly may be assumed. The Commission agrees that this is a proper assumption. It does not, however, find the assumption proper when information in the medical record of a patient is disclosed to a medical-care provider who has not had, or is not being consulted in connection with, a therapeutic relationship with the patient. In such a case, respect for the patient's legitimate expectation of confidentiality demands that disclosure be made only with the patient's written authorization or pursuant to one of the other exceptions in *Recommendation (10)*.

Disclosures to Protect Health or Safety

Exception (b) of *Recommendation (10)* recognizes that a medical-care provider clearly cannot be bound by a requirement to obtain the patient's authorization before disclosing medical-record information about him if such disclosure is necessary to avert or alleviate a serious threat to an individual's health or safety. Nonetheless, this exception is only justified by a compelling threat to someone's health or safety; a provider's desire to protect individuals' social or economic welfare or peace of mind is not enough. For example, a physician would not ordinarily be permitted to justify telling a patient's employer that the patient has cancer, although he might justify notifying an airline employer that a patient, who is one of its pilots, is suicidal.

Disclosures to Facilitate Research

Most medical-care providers routinely give medical professionals engaged in clinical or epidemiological research access to their patient records along with permission to abstract individually identifiable information and exchange that information with other researchers. Patient authorization for such access by researchers is not usually sought. Although a researcher's obligation to obtain an individual's informed consent to participate in any study that may expose him to physical or psychological harm is widely recognized, the researcher's obligation to obtain the patient's permission to use information in records about him has always seemed less compelling. For one thing, the practical difficulties are considerable. Patients are difficult to locate, and if asked for an authorization might refuse, thereby skewing the results of the study in unknown ways. Insistence on patient authorization would make many important studies impossible. The recent search for the cause of the "Legionnaires' Disease," for example, would have been doomed at the start if the researchers had had to obtain authorizations before reviewing medical records. As it was, some victims were not traced until months after the event. The diethylstilbestrol (DES) follow-up studies described in testimony before the Commission[66] are another example of epidemiological research that could hardly have been undertaken had the researchers been required to obtain patients' authorization prior to reviewing their medical records.

The research uses of medical records are not, however, without risk. As one witness told the Commission:

> . . . a researcher was doing a follow-up study of people who had been enrolled in a methadone maintenance program . . . . The contractor had the name and address of one particular individual who had been enrolled in the program several years previously, and the contractor went to the individual's residence. It was a Saturday night and the person was having a party and the contractor said, "Hi, I am so-and-so from such-and-such an organization, and we are doing a follow-up study of patients who had been enrolled in the methadone maintenance program."[67]

Another such incident which came to the Commission's attention involved the recontact of patients who had received treatment at an abortion clinic. In both instances the recontacts were unwelcome, resented, and extremely embarrassing to the persons contacted.

Contacting individuals for follow-up information after reviewing their medical records poses a unique problem, illustrating the need for some minimum conditions on disclosure and use of individually identifiable records for research and statistical purposes. Exception (c) of *Recommendation (10)* makes the researcher who wants access to this kind of information

---

[66] Testimony of the American Public Health Association and Mayo Clinic, Medical Records Hearings, June 10 and 11, 1976, pp. 297 and 567.

[67] Testimony of National Institute of Mental Health, Medical Records Hearings, July 20, 1976, p. 83.

accountable to the medical-care provider keeping the records and, through the provider, to the individuals concerned. Under this recommendation the researcher who wants access to medical-record information in individually identifiable form must show that he needs it for a worthwhile purpose; that access is vital to the fulfillment of that purpose; and that he can and will protect whatever expectation of confidentiality the patients had when the information was originally recorded. *Recommendation (10)(c)* comports with the Commission's recommendations in Chapter 15 pertaining to the disclosure and use of records about individuals for statistical or research activities funded in whole or in part by the Federal government.

Disclosures to Auditors and Evaluators

Exceptions (d) and (e) recognize that surveyors and reviewers regularly ask for and get access to medical records for such purposes as certifying the accuracy and adequacy of an institution's financial or administrative records; assessing the effectiveness of their medical, administrative, or financial management; and assuring their faithfulness to medical, legal, financial, and administrative standards. These examinations of records are part of the audits, certifications, accreditations, and licensure reviews and evaluations conducted by organizations like the Joint Commission on the Accreditation of Hospitals, Professional Standards Review Organizations, State and local public-health departments, and other government agencies. While such activities clearly serve the interests of the public that receives and subsidizes medical care, the Commission sees no need for the reports of auditors and evaluators to identify any individual patient directly or indirectly, nor does the Commission see any reason why the individual should be deprived of the knowledge that auditors and evaluators have had access to his records, and thus of any recourse in the event he is harmed by the disclosures they may make of information about him. Exception (d) recognizes that when audits and evaluations are specifically required by law, the medical-care provider is in no position to impose conditions on how information obtained from the medical records it maintains will be treated. In such cases, moreover, any subsequent uses and disclosures would be subject to the Commission's government access recommendations in Chapter 9. Exception (e) deals with the situation where the medical-care provider can set conditions for disclosure and recommends what those conditions should be.

Disclosures Pursuant to Compulsory Reporting Statutes

The original purpose of the State statutes that require the reporting of specific diagnoses to public health authorities was to help control the spread of communicable diseases. Today, however, many States require that in addition to communicable diseases, cases of cancer and other environmentally and occupationally related diseases also be reported. Mandatory reporting of births and deaths is universal and, in addition, some States require that gunshot and stab wounds, cases of child abuse, and other violence-related injuries be reported to law enforcement authorities.

While a significant number of States that require the reporting of venereal disease restrict, to some degree, the permissible uses and disclosures of such reports, over half the States provide no statutory protection for them.[68] One State which has such a reporting statute leaves it up to local health departments to decide whether such reports shall be open to public inspection, and another gives citizens the right to examine public records, including required reports of communicable diseases.[69]

Amendment of State statutes governing the use and disclosure of medical-record information obtained pursuant to public-reporting statutes is clearly the best way to prevent the irreparable harm to an individual that can result from misuse of such a report. Strengthening confidentiality protection would still not preclude the possibility that subsequent contact by agents of authorities to whom the information is properly reported will startle or embarrass an individual unnecessarily, particularly if the individual is not aware that a report was made. Thus, exemptions (f) and (g) require medical-care providers to notify an individual whenever information about him is disclosed pursuant to a public-reporting statute.

Disclosures to the Public

Many medical-care institutions that would under no circumstances divulge the details of a patient's diagnosis or treatment are quite comfortable about allowing the fact of admission, or the occurrence of a birth or death, to be publicized. It is normal hospital practice to tell anyone who inquires whether a patient has been admitted to a hospital and to indicate how serious the patient's current condition is.

In its *Guide for Cooperation with Communications Media*, the American Hospital Association takes the position that:

The hospital has the . . . obligation of pointing out to the patient that his hospitalization is likely to become known and . . . public acknowledgement will usually be in his best interests . . . [to assure] that accurate information [about] his condition will come from an authorized source.[70]

The Commission, however, believes that an individual patient's desire not to have his admission and general condition known should be respected. Exception (h) provides for limited disclosure of location and status information while at the same time giving the individual who objects a way of making his wishes known and binding. Limiting what may be disclosed to items specified in the notice called for in *Recommendation (11)* not only gives an individual a means of deciding whether he wishes to object to any

---

[68] Dennis Helfman, *et al*, "Access to Medical Records," *Appendix: Report of the Secretary's Commission on Medical Malpractice* (Washington, D.C.: Department of Health, Education, and Welfare, 1973), p. 181.

[69] Mass. Gen. Laws Ann. ch. 111, §111 (1971); Neb. Rev. Stat § 84-712 (1966).

[70] Cited in Westin, *op. cit.*, p. 77.

disclosure at all; it also reassures the individual who, while inclined *not* to object, is concerned about what may be disclosed if he takes no preventive action.

Disclosures Pursuant to Compulsory Process

A hospital or physician must surrender medical records or medical-record information when required by proper judicial process unless the disclosure is prohibited by statute. A psychiatrist testifying before the Commission urged the Commission to recommend a measure to protect patient records from indiscriminate court orders and subpoenas. He argued that information released pursuant to a court order or subpoena becomes a matter of public record; that grounds for issuing a subpoena are not always legitimate; and that not only patients but physicians and hospital officials are often so intimidated by the threatening documents they do not know they have legal rights against them. He recommended that at the very least subpoenas should include notification to the individual that he has a right to contest it, and how to do so.[71]

The Commission agrees strongly that an individual whose medical records have been subpoened should have an opportunity to be heard in court. It also recognizes that to provide that opportunity, existing Federal and State laws will have to be amended. Exception (i) represents the first step toward that end. Other steps are proposed in the Commission recommendations on government access in Chapter 9.

THE PRINCIPLE OF LIMITED DISCLOSURE

Medical professionals look upon the medical record as a tool of communication among themselves. It seldom crosses their minds that a patient's record may fall into the hands of someone who is neither trained to interpret it nor bound by the professional's ethics. Moreover, when a medical professional discloses information in a patient's record outside the medical community, neither he nor the patient who may grant permission for its disclosure can fully anticipate the ways in which the information may figure in non-medical decisions made about the patient.

The Commission, as noted earlier, is neither mandated nor qualified to question a medical-care provider's prerogative of putting into a medical record any item of information whose inclusion is professionally defensible. If medical-care providers are to maintain that prerogative, however, and if others who do not have a medical-care relationship with the individual are to continue to benefit from the extraordinary degree of divulgence and observation the medical-care relationship can entail, it is essential that each disclosure of information from a patient's record, with or without patient authorization, be strictly limited to the particular information needed for the user's particular stated purposes. Medical-care providers breach the confidential nature of the medical-care relationship whenever they send a

---

[71] Written Statement of Maurice Grossman, M.D., Clinical Professor of Psychiatry, Stanford University, Medical Records Hearings, June 11, 1976, p. 10.

copy of a patient's entire medical record to an insurer or employer instead of completing the claims form provided, or abstracting the specific information requested. Photocopying technology, in general, and portable copying machines, in particular, make this practice widespread.

When the patient has authorized disclosures, the authorization statement proposed in *Recommendation (13)* below will encourage the medical-care provider to place limits on the amount of information disclosed. It has also been suggested that a way to control the flow of information into and out of hospitals and physicians' offices is to develop a basic uniform medical record that would make it possible to comply with utilization and quality-care review requirements without disclosing an unnecessary amount of detail. Such a standardized record, however, is a long way off. Therefore, given the individual's inability to be certain that the information disclosed is no more and no less than indicated on the authorization statement he signs, and given the fact that a certain number of disclosures will necessarily take place without his authorization, the Commission believes that implicit in the medical-care provider's duty of confidentiality is an affirmative responsibility to limit the disclosure of information in a medical record to only that information which is specified on the authorization form or required by law. Accordingly, the Commission further recommends:

Recommendation (11):

That any disclosure of medical-record information by a medical-care provider, with or without the authorization of the individual to whom it pertains, be limited only to information necessary to accomplish the purpose for which the disclosure is made.

NOTICE OF DISCLOSURES WITHOUT AUTHORIZATION

To relieve apprehension about the disclosures that may be made of information in a medical record without the patient's authorization, as well as to inform a patient of the procedures by which he can ascertain whether particular disclosures have been made, the Commission recommends:

Recommendation (12):

That each medical-care provider be required to notify an individual on whom it maintains a medical record of the disclosures that may be made of information in the record without the individual's express authorization.

This recommendation is comparable to the notice recommendations made in other areas the Commission has examined. Ideally, the patient should be notified during his first contact with the medical-care provider and renotified whenever a new category of disclosures without authorization is created. The Harvard Community Health Plan, a health maintenance organization, is one medical-care provider that already provides its members with such a rudimentary form of notice in its service agreement. In the confidentiality provision of the agreement, the member is informed that his medical records will be kept confidential

> . . . except for use incident to bona fide medical research, . . . education, . . . use reasonably necessary in connection with the administration of the agreement [and that] such information will not be disclosed without the consent of the member, unless . . . required by law.[72]

Although this notice is not as specific as the one the Commission recommends, it demonstrates that such a notice requirement could be met.

DISCLOSURES PURSUANT TO AUTHORIZATION

As indicated in many chapters of this report, each time an individual applies for a job, for life or health insurance, for credit, or for financial assistance or services from the government, he agrees to relinquish some measure of personal privacy in return for the benefit he seeks. This cannot be helped, but all too often he is asked to sign away far more of his privacy than the situation warrants. Some authorization statements are so broadly worded as to require the recipient to "furnish any and all information on request."

The American Psychiatric Association takes the position that any blanket consent for the release of information from a medical record is unacceptable, since all consent for the disclosure of medical-record information should be "informed consent."[73] Such a standard appears to the Commission to be impractical. To speak of informed consent is to presuppose that the individual being asked to give it not only knows precisely what is being disclosed, but has the option both of refusing to divulge information about himself and preventing others from doing so. It also assumes that he can predict accurately who shall subsequently have access to the information and precisely how it will be used. In other words, to have given one's informed consent to a particular disclosure of information about oneself is to have fully understood the costs and benefits that will or even might result from such disclosure. Yet the individual who authorizes someone to acquire medical-record information about him rarely has the option of refusing to do so. Technically, most authorization statements are voluntarily signed, but the option of refusing varies inversely with the individual's need for the treatment, job, insurance, or social service he is seeking.[74]

Recognizing these natural limits of informed consent, the Commission recommends an authorization procedure along the lines prescribed in the DHEW regulations on the "Confidentiality of Alcohol and Drug Abuse Patient Records" *[42 C.F.R. 2]* as a working model for all authorization

---

[72] Harvard Community Health Plan, "Group Service Agreement," Section XII E.
[73] American Psychiatric Association, *Confidentiality and Third Parties* (Washington, D.C.: APA, 1975), p. 13.
[74] Testimony of Dr. Catherine E. Rosen, Medical Records Hearings, June 11, 1976.

statements presented to and accepted by a medical-care provider. The Commission recommends:

Recommendation (13):

That whenever an individual's authorization is required before a medical-care provider may disclose information it collects or maintains about him, the medical-care provider should not accept as valid any authorization which is not:

(a) **in writing;**

(b) **signed by the individual on a date specified or by someone authorized in fact to act in his behalf;**

(c) **clear as to the fact that the medical-care provider is among those either specifically named or generally designated by the individual as being authorized to disclose information about him;**

(d) **specific as to the nature of the information the individual is authorizing to be disclosed;**

(e) **specific as to the institutions or other persons to whom the individual is authorizing information to be disclosed;**

(f) **specific as to the purpose(s) for which the information may be used by any of the parties named in (e) both at the time of the disclosure and at any time in the future;**

(g) **specific as to its expiration date, which should be for a reasonable period of time not to exceed one year, except where an authorization is presented in connection with a life or non-cancellable or guaranteed renewable health insurance policy, in which case the expiration date should not exceed two years from the date the authorization was signed.**

This type of authorization statement provides assurance that an individual will understand what he is allowing to be disclosed, and why, but does not require that the voluntariness of his action be verifiable, nor does it assume that he can recognize every possible consequence of signing it. The medical-care provider should be responsible for having reasonable procedures to assure that authorizations presented to it satisfy the conditions of the recommendation. The medical-care provider should be able to use the exercise of such procedures as a defense where it later is claimed that the authorization is invalid. Subsection *(b)* of *Recommendation (13)* raises a small problem when the disclosure of medical-record information is authorized by a minor patient. The Commission feels strongly that where State law permits minors to obtain treatment for specific conditions without the consent of a parent or guardian the presumed confidentiality of the resulting medical-care relationship must be protected. Therefore, it would urge that in these instances, the minor patient alone be permitted to authorize disclosure of such information.

The exceptions to the one-year rule in subsection *(g)* take account of the two-year "contestable period" (see Chapter 5) in life insurance and the mentioned types of health insurance. It should be noted, however, that the corresponding recommendation in Chapter 5, *Insurance Recommendation (18)*, calls for the signature date on the authorization statement to be the same as the date of the policy, thereby limiting the period of validity to two years.

To enable the individual to verify the fact that an authorized disclosure has been made, the Commission further recommends:

Recommendation (14):

That each time a medical-care provider discloses information about an individual pursuant to a valid authorization, it be required to retain a copy of the authorization and, for the purpose of *Recommendation (5)* on patient access, treat it as part of the record(s) from which the disclosure was made.

National Health Insurance

Public and political pressure for a Federal health insurance program continues even as this report is issued. The Commission is acutely aware that the process of setting a national health insurance program into motion will open up unparalleled opportunities to reevaluate medical record-keeping policies and practices and hopes its recommendations will assist the public, medical- record keepers, and the Congress to that end.

In exploring the possible effects of such a program on existing use and disclosure of medical records, the Commission's staff reviewed 18 national health insurance proposals presented to the 94th Congress. These varied from the Kennedy-Corman bill (H.R. 21), which proposed a mandatory, government-administered program covering the entire population; to the AMA-supported Fulton bill (H.R. 6222), which proposed a Medicare-like system of private-sector intermediaries to administer premiums and reimbursements; to a voluntary, catastrophic health-insurance plan available only to individuals whose medical expenses exceed a specified amount (H.R. 1373, the so-called "Roe bill").

Of the 18 bills only five contained specific provisions to protect the confidentiality of the records that would be created by the program and even these were vague. Most of the five merely specified that all information collected and maintained for program purposes must be considered confidential. While it is too soon to say which, if any, of these various forms of national health insurance will be enacted into law, or how soon, the Commission sees a clear need to devise specific safeguards to prevent unfairness and protect the confidentiality of the medical-care relationship, whatever form such a program may take.

If current private and publicly funded health-insurance programs are any indication, a universal health-insurance program will likely involve the creation and retention of records beyond the control of the provider with whom the individual has a medical-care relationship. Thus, the Commission urges that the recommendations in this chapter be adopted and that any legislation providing for national health insurance include safeguards covering the acquisition and dissemination of medical records and medical-record information.

Chapter 8

Investigative-Reporting Agencies

A common denominator of many record-keeping institutions examined in preceding chapters is their dependence on support organizations to gather and maintain information that has protective value. Credit and inspection bureaus, independent credit-card authorization and check-guarantee services, the Medical Information and Loss Index Bureaus of the insurance industry, all exist to protect their clients from the individual who falsifies or fails to reveal significant information that could alter the credit, insurance, or employment decision to be made about him.

Some of these support organizations are simply clearinghouses that save their clients from having to contact one another directly. Credit-card authorization services and the Medical Information Bureau are prime examples. As explained in Chapters 2 and 5, the information in their files comes from their clients; they do not have their own independent sources. Other support organizations, however, use investigative techniques to gather the information they report about individuals. Although they, too, maintain files, they develop their information initially through interviews and inquiries of neighbors, business associates, employers, and other record-keeping institutions.

The purpose of this chapter is threefold: (1) to describe the practices of the various investigative support organizations so that their relationship to the decision-making processes of their clients may be clearly appreciated; (2) to explain in one place how the Commission's recommendations in other chapters address problems that the activities of investigative support organizations create; and (3) to outline for further study some areas the Commission has not been able to address but considers worthy of examination.

The chapter begins with an overview of the activities of two types of investigative support organizations on which the Commission was able to develop substantial detail: the *inspection bureaus* whose reports are primarily used in insurance underwriting; and the *private-investigative agencies* that principally make background inquiries about individuals for employers. This is followed by a section on investigative services performed in connection with the settlement of insurance claims or for an employer who believes it has internal security problems. Finally, the concluding sections summarize the Commission's recommendations in other chapters which affect the activities of investigative-reporting agencies and suggest problem areas that, in the Commission's opinion, merit further examination.

THE INSPECTION BUREAU: AN OVERVIEW

In insurance underwriting the company and the individual consumer strive for different ends—the individual, to acquire protection at the lowest possible cost; the company, to minimize its risk and control claims and administrative overhead. Moreover, because most insurance is sold through an agent field force that derives its income from commissions, a company wants some kind of independent check on the applicants or insureds and the information about them that agents submit. Inspection bureaus exist in large measure to satisfy these company needs for information about the individual with whom it has or proposes to have an insurance relationship.

The inspection bureau industry, like the credit-reporting business, is a concentrated one. Equifax Services, the industry giant, prepares over 15 million inspection reports each year.[1]

Originally insurance companies did their own inspection work. As business grew, however, multiplying the number of necessary inspections, they began to rely more and more on the bureaus. Because an inspection bureau can serve more than one company client in a given geographic area, it saves all its company clients money. Furthermore, when an insurance company orders an inspection report, it is not just purchasing an investigative capability to develop and verify information; it is also purchasing access to an existing reservoir of information on individuals who have previously been investigated, and this too constitutes an important cost-saving factor.

The services inspection bureaus perform are labor-intensive. While credit bureaus may profitably exploit the speed and efficiency of modern information-processing technology, it is hard to see how the computer can replace the inspection bureau field worker who specializes in interviewing neighbors and associates. Inspection bureaus are aware of this and, consequently, place a premium on the productivity of individual investigators. Pay scales are comparatively low. Costs must be kept down lest the companies lose their incentive to use bureau services. The general level of education and training required can be modest.[2] Inspectors are often part-time students, off-duty policemen, housewives, and retired persons. Advertisements for investigators indicate that to qualify, an individual need only have a high school diploma and a car.[3] Obviously, pressures to produce,

---

[1] Testimony of Equifax, Inc., *Credit Reporting and Payment Authorization Services*, Hearings before the Privacy Protection Study Commission, August 3, 1976, p. 163 (hereinafter cited as "Credit Reporting Hearings").

[2] The experience level and turnover rate of inspection bureau personnel is a matter of some question. Equifax, Inc., testified that about 64 percent of its field representatives had some college training, with approximately 25 percent holding at least a bachelor's degree, and that the average field representative had almost 12 years of company experience. (Credit Reporting Hearings, August 3, 1976, p. 163). However, a former supervisor with 15 years experience at Equifax asserted in a letter to the Senate Banking Committee that Equifax commonly employed investigators on a part-time basis who lacked the "investigative training for the types of decisions which they must make," a problem which was further complicated by an "extremely high" turnover rate. (Letter from Daniel P. Reiter to the Senate Banking Committee, August 5, 1976.)

[3] *Miami Herald*, June 11, 1974, p. 18-e.

coupled with low salary scales, can easily affect the quality of an inspection bureau's product.

TYPES OF INFORMATION COLLECTED

An insurance company generally uses an inspection report to help it answer two related types of questions: (1) whether to grant or continue coverage; and (2) if coverage is to be granted or continued, what is the proper price to charge. That is, in the absence of information it considers derogatory, an insurance company will normally proceed with the coverage requested, concerning itself only with items of information that may affect the premium it will charge. Or, if it has already written a policy, derogatory information in a subsequently provided report may be used as the basis for cancelling or refusing to renew the policy or for altering the premium. Automobile insurance, for example, almost always becomes effective immediately upon filing an application with a company or its agent. However, information in an inspection report the insurer subsequently acquires may cause it to charge the consumer a higher premium than he originally anticipated or cause the insurer to terminate the policy altogether.[4]

Because Equifax Services accounts for a major proportion of the inspection bureau business,[5] a review of its investigative manuals[6] and its report forms can offer substantial insight into the kinds of information insurance underwriters consider "adverse." Because of Equifax's dominant position in the inspection industry, a survey of its major reporting services should also afford a good understanding of typical bureau practices.

In addition to extensive questions covering the identity of the individual, details as to his past employment, driving record, finances, insurance history (including special ratings or previous declinations), Equifax inspectors are asked in different reports to respond "yes" or "no," and if "yes," to provide greater detail on questions, such as the following:

- Use alcohol? (If "yes," answer: (1) What? (2) How often? (3) How many? (4) Where? (5) Over what period of time?)
- Use(d) marijuana?

---

[4] See Chapter 5 for a discussion of the insurance underwriting process.

[5] According to the Federal Trade Commission, in 1970 the Retail Credit Company (Equifax, Inc.) produced approximately 26,000,000 consumer reports for credit, personnel, and other purposes, resulting in revenues in excess of $136,000,000. (United States of America before the Federal Trade Commission, in the matter of Retail Credit Company, Docket No. 8920, initial decision February 10, 1976, p. 10). In his opening statement in 1974 Senate hearings on the credit-reporting industry, Senator William Proxmire (D.-Wisc.) stated that ". . . the Retail Credit Company accounts for over two-thirds of the investigative reporting industry, and other firms within the industry have closely followed the practices and procedures of Retail Credit." (*Credit Reporting Abuses*, Hearings before the Subcommittee on Consumer Credit of the Committee on Banking, Housing, and Urban Affairs, U.S. Senate, 93d Congress, 2d Session, 1974, p. 1).

[6] Equifax, Inc., "Property Lines Manual," May 1975; "Life and Income Protection Manual," November 1974; and "Employment Reports Manual," March 1976.

- Use(d) narcotics, sedatives, depressants, stimulants, or hallucinogens?
- How was worth acquired? (Inherited, accumulated, or speculation)
- If other than married, does applicant reside with another person?
- Anything adverse about reputation, life style, or home environment?
- Do any of the following apply? Unfair business practices? Heavy debts? Domestic trouble?
- Reputation of business questionable?
- Any evidence of job instability?
- Personal reputation or associates questionable?[7]

While a "yes" answer to any of these questions is explained on the back of the form, the yes-no portion serves to "flag" items that meet the receiving insurer's concept of "adverse" information. (Inspection bureaus commonly develop different report forms for the different types of insurance each underwrites.)

Arguably, some of the information the inspection bureau's clients consider "adverse," "actionable," "declinable," "pertinent," or "significant," does not indicate an above-average insurance risk. While there are broad areas of overlap between what a community may hold to be negative characteristics and what may constitute a demonstrable risk to an insurer (for example, an alcoholic who is held in low public regard because of his behavior is also avoided by an automobile insurer), there are socially unacceptable traits that may have no bearing at all on risk in a particular line of insurance. A bearded, blue-jeaned resident of a small town might encounter some difficulty if his neighbors were asked to evaluate his "reputation" or "trustworthiness." Yet, the personal characteristics that set him apart may be of no importance in underwriting auto, life, or homeowner's insurance. An inspection report, however, does not make these fine distinctions, nor can it take account of the prejudices or other idiosyncracies of the people who are asked to make such subjective judgments, including, in many cases, the investigator himself.

INFORMATION COLLECTION METHODS

As indicated earlier, the use of personal interviews to gather information about an individual is one of the distinguishing characteristics of an investigative support organization. Inspection bureau field representatives generally interview an applicant's neighbors and business associates or fellow employees, as well as other sources that may be suggested along the way. As to the last, an interview with the applicant himself can be one of the most important sources of leads.

Unless specifically prohibited from doing so by the insurance company, or unless the bureau's own past experience with the applicant

---

[7] *Ibid.*

indicates that he will not be cooperative, an inspection bureau may attempt to interview him and some insurance companies require the inspection bureau to do so. Indeed, in some instances an inspection bureau does no more than verify information in the application directly with the applicant.

According to Equifax internal documents, the applicant can provide the following types of information in a direct interview:

- Health: history, attending/personal physicians, height/weight/waist measurement, impairments, smoking.
- Finances: exact income and worth figures or very close estimates. Personal financial statements.
- Occupation: details on employment status, business history, foreign travel, part-time jobs.
- Duties: a precise description of work performed.
- Identity: thorough identification of the applicant.
- Military: past or present connections.
- Spare Time: sports, hobbies, flying, club affiliations.
- Driving: record of accidents and violations.
- Drinking: description of drinking habits.
- Drugs: present or past use.
- Criminal Record: arrests and convictions.
- Other Coverage: amounts and carriers. Previous ratings and declinations.
- Financial Problems: details of problems or tips to same.
- References: name of personal acquaintances, bankers, permission to see accountants and attorneys.[8]

Inspection bureaus prefer that all interviews be conducted in person. Interviewing by telephone is discouraged, unless the purpose of the interview is to verify information obtained in an earlier investigation. Apparently, however, it is not strongly discouraged since the testimony of several former field representatives before congressional committees indicates that telephone interviews are, in fact, widely used for the simple reason that they save time.[9]

In an April 1975 *New Yorker* article, "Anything Adverse?," the Equifax "Manager Manual" was quoted on the techniques used to elicit

[8] Equifax, Inc., "Life and Income Protection Manual," November 1974, p. D-20.
[9] *Credit Reporting Abuses*, Hearing before the Subcommittee on Consumer Credit of the Committee on Banking, Housing, and Urban Affairs, U.S. Senate, 93d Congress, 2d Session, 1974.

information in an interview. The field representative "must not be afraid to ask personal questions"[10] and "should be sufficiently suspicious by nature to derive satisfaction from tracking down leads and developing the facts."[11] To this end:

> the top-notch Field Representative should be highly sensitive to the more subtle clues in the remarks of his sources and other behavior, perceiving their implications and adapting his own approach and conversation accordingly . . . . A sense of humor [will prove to be] a powerful instrument in the development of a warm, friendly relationship with sources. In fact some of the most pertinent personal information is sandwiched in between homey remarks and other small talk.[12]

According to the Equifax "Field Representative Manual," the interviewer should:

> . . . proceed from the impersonal to the personal. People do not readily talk to strangers about the personal reputation and morals of their friends and acquaintances. However, after first talking about impersonal areas (identity, employment, and health), they have less hesitancy to cover more personal matters.[13]

In addition to learning this basic interview strategy, the interviewer is instructed to ask open-ended questions, such as "How is he regarded?" instead of, "Is he well regarded?"; or "How much does he drink?," not "Does he drink?"[14] Because inspection field representatives are in the business of collecting rather than distributing information, all are strongly advised not to transmit to any sources the information acquired from other ones. In many cases, moreover, the name of the client, i.e., the insurance company, is not to be given. Indeed, in some cases, the source being interviewed will not be aware, even in a general sense, of the purpose of the interview.

Record searches are the second method by which inspection bureau field representatives collect information. Many records held by city, county, State, and Federal agencies are open to public inspection. Depending upon the locality, these may include police arrest blotters, civil and criminal court records, motor vehicle accident reports, records of driving convictions, and possibly even welfare rolls or other records concerning contacts with social service agencies.[15] Adverse information obtained from public records is of particular value to an inspection bureau. In addition to being unfavorable and, therefore, valuable to the bureau's clients, such information, in contrast to information obtained from neighbors or associates, does not require

---

[10] Equifax, Inc., "Manager Manual," as cited by Thomas Whiteside, "Anything Adverse?," *New Yorker*, April 21, 1975, p. 54.
[11] *Ibid.*
[12] *Ibid.*
[13] Equifax, Inc., "Field Representative Manual," April 1973, p. 29.
[14] *Ibid.*
[15] Equifax, Inc., "Claim Reports Manual," November 1975, pp. C-15 - C-17.

reverification under the Fair Credit Reporting Act (FCRA) when carried forward from one report to another (except where the report is for employment purposes). *[15 U.S.C. 1681l]* Further, public-record information alone does not meet the FCRA definition of a "consumer investigative report." *[15 U.S.C. 1681k]* Thus, a report containing information about anything from character and morals to business reputation and domestic difficulties can be prepared solely on the basis of public records without the individual who is the subject of it receiving the prior notification the FCRA otherwise requires.

Mindful of this, some inspection bureaus are now encouraging their clients to depend more upon information that can be gleaned from public records than on the "subjective information" heretofore gathered from neighbors and associates. As the President of O'Hanlon Reports, Inc., described the current situation to the Commission:

> Our business [has changed] drastically in the past three years from a time when subjective reports constituted as much as 80 to 85 percent of our business . . . . Today, subjective reports are less than 40 percent . . . and we do everything we can do to accomplish the point of getting the underwriting people and the insurance companies to allow us to make the short-form classification, the short-form dwelling reports, and so on, that do not require subjective information . . . . That is the future of the inspection business . . . . Use these other reports and stop making everybody liable for all kinds of problems . . . .[16]

As indicated in Chapter 2, credit reports are an important source of public-record information for inspection bureaus. Most inspection bureaus (like most private investigative firms) are eligible to subscribe to credit bureaus and some of the larger inspection bureaus own one or more.[17] In addition, if the inspection bureau has a signed authorization in hand, it can often get banks and accountants to make or confirm a reasonably accurate estimate of an individual's income. For underwriting life or disability insurance on self-employed individuals, this is particularly helpful as estimates of their income or worth might otherwise be difficult to obtain.

Besides interviews and record searches, inspection bureaus also use their own files as a basic source of information. In fact, in some cases, their own files are the only source they use. To get an investigation started, the insurance company must provide basic identifying information on the individual, and may, in addition, ask the bureau to verify other items the individual himself has already provided on the application form.

Equifax's Chairman told the Commission that at any given time his company will be maintaining files in its local offices on up to 25 percent of a

---

16 Testimony of O'Hanlon Reports, Inc., Credit Reporting Hearings, August 3, 1976, pp. 142-43.

17 Equifax, Inc., and Hooper-Holmes Bureau, Inc., own and operate major credit bureaus. See, for example, Testimony of Equifax, Inc., Credit Reporting Hearings, August 3, 1976, p. 150.

community's inhabitants with the nationwide total of files maintained being in the order of 39 million.[18] Because investigator expenses are the largest single contributor to the cost of preparing an inspection report, a bureau's files are a valuable cost-saving resource. The Fair Credit Reporting Act allows a bureau to report without verifying any information it has gathered through personal interviews within the previous three months, as well as any information it has obtained from public records. Older material must be reverified before it can be included in a current report, but it can also be used as leads to possible new information. This situation, plus the pressures on an investigator to work as quickly as possible, explains why the same adverse information can be reported again and again, and why a report containing false information can create recurring problems for an individual over a period of years.

It also explains why inspection bureaus tend to retain derogatory information in their files. Equifax policy calls for the destruction every thirteen months of reports made to life, auto, and property insurers, unless " . . . serious significant information is involved," in which case company manuals direct that such reports be kept for ten years. Motor vehicle reports are normally kept for five years from the date they are acquired, unless they are seriously unfavorable, in which case they, too, will be kept for ten years.[19] Since the FCRA imposes no time limit on the retention, as opposed to the reporting, of such adverse information, there is nothing other than cost to keep it from being kept in a bureau's files forever.

PRODUCTION PRESSURES: INCENTIVES FOR INVENTION

In February 1974, Mark S. Brodie testified before the Senate Banking, Housing, and Urban Affairs Committee that when he had worked briefly as a part-time Equifax investigator the previous year, his average workload was 15 cases per four-hour day, or about 16 minutes a case. Brodie described a procedure known in his office as "zinging":

A zing means you do nothing. You do not contact the investigatee. One does not go out on the street . . . he utilizes whatever information was supplied by the insurance company, and hopefully, looks up the insured in the phone book to assure that he lives there; then you just fill in the form.[20]

Another investigator, Dick Riley, who worked fifteen years for Equifax, also testified to the same practice, known in his office as "the crystal-ball

---

[18] Credit Reporting Hearings, August 3, 1976, p. 171.

[19] Equifax, Inc., "Reference File Information—How to Destroy and Expert Files," (Form 1912), June 1975.

[20] *Credit Reporting Abuses*, Hearing before the Subcommittee on Consumer Credit of the Committee on Banking, Housing, and Urban Affairs, U.S. Senate, 93d Congress, 2d Session, 1974, p. 11.

system," which "consists of quoting old reports, looking at [the information on] an inquiry, and determining that the individual 'looks okay.'"[21] Of course, "zinging" and "the crystal-ball system" have their pitfalls. Brodie told of one report that cited a source at a certain address which turned out to be a parking lot, and related an incident where an investigator "zinged" a report on an individual who was no longer living. Such practices are flagrant violations of corporate policy, but they apparently do occur.

Perhaps the most controversial aspect of inspection bureau operations is their use of production schedules for measuring the performance of field representatives. Discussions of production schedules usually begin with the proposition that it is impossible to speak of an "average" number of reports that can be completed by a "typical" field representative. Nevertheless, inspection bureaus do establish performance standards for their field representatives and successfully communicate the rewards and sanctions for exceeding or failing to meet them.[22]

Equifax has periodically conducted studies to determine the level of effort necessary to complete various types of reports.[23] In testimony submitted to the Commission,[24] Equifax representatives stated that regular life and automobile reports, the firm's two basic reporting services, are used to develop comparative measures of the time and effort that can be expended on its other reports and still produce a profit. Exceptions to these measures are allowed if a field representative has a preponderance of more (or less) complicated reports to prepare. Nonetheless, the economics of the firm's reporting services are such as to place constant pressure on management, and thus presumably on each field representative, to complete reports as quickly as possible. For its high-volume, low-cost reporting services, time is money for a firm like Equifax. Hence, the more reports that are produced within a given period of time, the more likely that the firm will be able to turn a profit without having to raise its prices.

In addition to the pressure to keep the number of reports high, critics have also alleged that Equifax keeps track of the amount of adverse information each report contains and that these statistics are translated by Equifax management and field workers into "adverse information quotas." The evidence on this point is confusing, in large measure because discussions of it in public forums have invariably failed to distinguish clearly between pressures to push up the number of reports produced and pressures to keep the *quality* of reports at acceptable levels. At one time Equifax apparently did keep statistics on the gross percentages of "protective" and "declinable" information in reports emanating from each field office. A December 15, 1972 memorandum from the Vice President for Operations, Southern Pacific Region, congratulates regional field office managers for having finished "in the upper third grouping in both total protective and

---

[21] *Ibid.*, p. 6.
[22] See Supplementary Statement of Retail Credit Company (Equifax, Inc.), *Fair Credit Reporting Amendments of 1975*, Hearings before the Subcommittee on Consumer Affairs of the Committee on Banking, Housing, and Urban Affairs, U.S. Senate, 94th Congress, 1st Session, 1975, pp. 233-35.
[23] *Ibid.*
[24] Written statement of Equifax, Inc., Credit Reporting Hearings, August 3, 1976, pp. 17-18.

percent declinable" in the second round of an intra-company survey called the "Life and Health Quality Profile." In addition, the memorandum went on to extol the "vast improvement" in both life and health and auto reporting "since they [sic] have been keeping this record back to 1968."[25] In sworn testimony before the Privacy Commission, however, Equifax representatives stated that "we no longer accumulate statistics concerning 'pertinent' information,"[26] and in a subsequent letter to the Commission indicated that they had formally ceased to do so in January 1976,[27] approximately eight months before testifying in the Commission's hearings. It has never been established, moreover, that competition among field offices, which the 1972 memorandum suggests the "pertinent information" statistics induced, was ever formally translated into adverse information quotas for individual field representatives. Nor need it have been.

One might well argue that the whole controversy over adverse information quotas misses the point by failing to recognize that adverse information is the inspection bureau's most salable product. Insurance companies have little use for innocuous commentary about applicants and policyholders. They are paying to find out whether there is anything about an individual which would warrant declining him or altering the premium he would otherwise be charged. From their point of view, it makes no difference whether "adverse" information is included in 10 or 30 or even 100 percent of the reports received. What they want is as thorough and accurate an investigation as they can get within the boundaries set by the price they are willing to pay. The proportions are irrelevant; the type of information and its quality are what counts.

It is true, of course, that both insurers and the investigative support organizations which service them share a less than rosy view of human nature. When asked if his firm's credibility would not be jeopardized if the amount of adverse information in its reports went down substantially over a period of time, Equifax's Chairman responded that in all probability it would "because we know the social behavior of our population is not improving that much."[28]

> . . . we know that if . . . [an investigator] works intelligently and carefully and conscientiously, . . . he is going to develop a rather substantial amount of information that we term as pertinent information, pertinent to the risk. . . . We have a rather homespun Executive Vice President who said that if you send a man to a blackberry field every day with a bucket and every day he came

[25] Equifax, Inc., "L & H [Life and Health] Quality Profile," Memorandum from Russell H. Beckett, Regional Vice President to Managers, December 15, 1972. Cited in *Fair Credit Reporting Act—1973*, Hearings before the Subcommittee on Consumer Credit of the Committee on Banking, Housing, and Urban Affairs, U.S. Senate, 93d Congress, 1st Session, 1973, p. 877.
[26] Written Statement of Equifax, Inc., Credit Reporting Hearings, August 3, 1976, p. 19.
[27] Letter from Equifax, Inc., to the Privacy Protection Study Commission, February 23, 1977.
[28] Credit Reporting Hearings, August 3, 1976, p. 235.

back with no blackberries, then you would notice that something was wrong.[29]

Such a statement, while neither proving nor disproving the quota allegation, makes a powerful point: that the underlying assumption of any inspection bureau investigation is that a certain amount of adverse information may be developed. This does not mean that adverse information *will* be developed in every instance but rather that an inspector should find adverse information on at least some applicants, because adverse information is assumed to be there to be discovered. If an inspector consistently finds nothing, or very little, the inevitable conclusion is that he has not done his job, not that the individuals he was assigned to investigate all happen to be sterling characters.

Understanding the natural emphasis of the inspection bureau's product also helps to understand a point made in the introduction to this report: that from a purist point of view, factual inquiries can involve more of an intrusion on an individual's personal privacy than subjective ones. The following February 1972 communication was directed to all Equifax field representatives:

Believe me -

It Makes the Difference

This Doesn't Tell the Story -
"Insured drinks to excess on weekends."
"Drinks to excess on special occasions."
"Drinks to feeling good and drives afterward."
"Drinks a few beers daily."
"Is criticized for being a heavy drinker."
"Used to drink a lot but quit."

We Haven't Done the Job Unless
        We've Found Out and Reported -
What he drinks.
How often he drinks - daily, weekly, monthly, 2-3 a year?
How much he drinks -
    If daily - how many, and where, and when?
    If on weekends - every weekend, or most, or 1-2 a month?
    If to excess - feeling good or loud and boisterous or intoxicated?
        - how often - daily, weekly, monthly, 1-2 a month, 2-3 a year?
Where he drinks - home, tavern, lounge, club, parties, on the job?
When he drinks - evenings, lunch, on the way home from work?
How long - if he quit, specifically when and why?

---

[29] *Ibid.*, pp. 236-37.

Does he drive afterwards?[30]

At first glance, such an exhortation to further prying may seem patently offensive. When one compares the first set of inquiries (deemed inadequate) with the second (considered desirable), however, one realizes that the latter is far more factual in its orientation than the former. Whether an individual would fare better with an insurer if the factual details of his drinking behavior were manifest (the second set of questions), in lieu of purely subjective characterizations of it (the first set), will depend on the company he is dealing with and the type of insurance he is seeking. The important point to grasp, however, is that intrusions on personal privacy of the sort in which inspection bureaus engage usually begin with the criteria we, as a society, accept as proper ones for making decisions about people; and that so long as society countenances certain lines of inquiry by certain types of record-keeping institutions, questions as to how far a line of inquiry may properly go are largely aesthetic. Indeed, if one prefers that decisions be made on the basis of facts rather than subjective evaluations, one should logically prefer that the line of inquiry be quite detailed as a protection against drawing inaccurate inferences.

THE PRIVATE INVESTIGATIVE AGENCY: AN OVERVIEW

While an inspection report can be the sole basis for making an adverse insurance decision, the background investigations that private investigative agencies conduct for employers are just a part of the information that is taken into account in making a decision about an individual. In most hiring situations, the employer will interview the applicant directly, using the private investigator only to verify information to be used in making the decision. In some cases, however, the results of a background investigation can be the determining factor. For example, an employer may engage the services of a private investigative agency to find out if an applicant or employee has an unsavory background or reputation of which the employer is unaware; to see if there is criminal behavior in the applicant's background which may be relevant to the job applied for; or perhaps to check out an employment history that itself raises questions.

Another factor that distinguishes a preemployment investigation from the underwriting investigation conducted by an inspection bureau is that the criteria for accepting an applicant for employment are quite different from those governing insurance decisions. Whereas an insurance company makes a profit by accepting all comers who do not present unreasonable risk, there is a limit to the number of individuals an employer can hire. Hence, the employer must select the "best" candidate from the current pool of available applicants, which means, in turn, that the employer must rely on more information than just what an investigative agency gathers.

The information market that has evolved to meet the specific needs of employers also tends to be much more expensive than the market for

---

[30] Equifax, Inc., "It Makes a Difference," Memorandum from Quality Analysis Division to "Fellow Workers," February 1972.

inspection bureau services. Unless it is performed for a client already on retainer for other services, such as investigations of inventory losses or off-hour security guards, Pinkerton's, Inc., the nation's largest private investigative agency, will not accept a preemployment investigation which involves less than a day's billing. The average time billed by Per-Mar Security, a smaller firm, has been estimated at about a day and a half, and some investigations can run as long as three to four days.[31] From an employer's point of view, this can be advantageous. If an employer believes a particular individual is likely to do a good job, it does not want him disqualified by inaccurate or incomplete information, even if that means paying extra to assure a careful, thorough inquiry. Yet because the cost of gathering high-quality information can also outweigh its value in decision making, some employers have ceased to engage the services of investigative agencies, while others use them only for highly sensitive or key management positions.

In contrast to the inspection bureau workforce, the workforce of the private investigative agency is a skilled one. Instead of some use of part-time students, housewives, and retired persons, the private investigative agency tends to hire people who have previously worked for government law enforcement and investigative agencies. That is, it employs, on a full-time basis, a well trained individual who is acquainted with standard investigative practices and knows how to access public, as well as private, sources of information.[32] Moreover, because of the background of their employees, many private investigative firms do not require training programs for their new investigators, whereas most inspection bureaus provide basic instruction in interviewing and record-searching techniques.

Inspection bureaus also do a certain amount of preemployment work, although most of their reports, perhaps as many as 50 percent, are on applicants for employment in the insurance industry. Equifax Services, for example, does enough preemployment investigations to justify a separate division of the company. However, the reports it prepares are generally similar to its inspection reports, and the information in them is drawn from the same types of sources, including the same company files.[33] Equifax's instructions to investigators preparing preemployment reports parallel those to its field representatives preparing inspection reports, except for the extra stress they place on employment history and their observation that the applicant usually is not interviewed. Preemployment reports prepared by inspection bureaus also tend to be much cheaper than the ones prepared by private investigative firms, suggesting that they play a different role in the hiring decision or are ordered on a different level of applicant or employee. Thus, in the remainder of this section, the focus is on the more expensive private investigative report, save for a few instances in which comparisons with inspection bureau practices seem important enough to be noted.

---

[31] Testimony of the Wackenhut Corporation, *Private Investigative Firms*, Hearings before the Privacy Protection Study Commission, January 26, 1977, p. 213. (Hereinafter cited as "Private Investigative Hearings").

[32] Testimony of the Wackenhut Corporation, Private Investigative Hearings, January 26, 1977, p. 40.

[33] Credit Reporting Hearings, August 3, 1976, p. 247.

TYPES AND METHODS OF INFORMATION COLLECTION

Although preemployment reports emphasize past employment experience more than an insurance inspection report does, they lay stress on the same categories of "adverse" or "derogatory" information. Private investigative firms seek information on drinking habits, associates, drug use, personal habits, possible criminal behavior, personal reputation, and other items that might not show up in the records of a previous employer, or be volunteered by an applicant. Pinkerton's, Inc. testified that in a neighborhood check, they examine "primarily reputation and character." "We would even describe a house," said one witness, "whether it is well maintained, the grass is cut, depending upon the type of position."[34] Although they said they would not ask specific questions about sexual activities or preference, Pinkerton witnesses also said they would specifically inquire about current and past drug use and alcohol consumption.[35]

In its operations manual, one major private investigative firm directs its investigators to keep the following "basic and fundamental" points of inquiry in mind at all times:

(1) Character - general traits; reputation as to sobriety; honesty; trustworthiness; reliability; discretion; or lack of such qualities.

(2) Associations - types of persons, groups, or organizations, or movements with which person has been affiliated, with particular concern as to whether his associations have been undesirable in any way.

(3) Qualifications and ability - specific inquiry concerning qualifications and ability is essential.[36]

Beside compiling information through interviews, private investigative agencies also make inquiries of other record keepers. Included in one private investigative firm's list of "general sources of information" are the following: banks; collection agencies; small loan companies; savings and loan associations; land title companies; Federal narcotic agencies; postal authorities; the Internal Revenue Service; the Immigration and Naturalization Service; the Securities and Exchange Commission; the Department of Justice; the Department of Health, Education, and Welfare; State Comptrollers and tax offices; local school authorities; universities and other education facilities; and probation officers.[37] Although access to some of these records must be conditional upon obtaining the written authorization of the subject of the investigation, this is not explicitly provided for in the firm's manual. Moreover, it is widely alleged that because of the previous

---

[34] Testimony of Pinkerton's, Inc., Private Investigative Hearings, January 26, 1977, p. 157.

[35] Ibid.

[36] Until recently, investigators were also instructed to examine "loyalty," which was defined as, "actions or statements reflecting person's loyalty to employer; also, attitude and allegiance to the United States." The identity of this private investigative firm has been kept confidential at its request.

[37] The identity of this private investigative firm has been kept confidential at its request.

government employment of so many of their investigators, private investigative agencies are able to circumvent established authorization procedures.

The best example of this is the access which they are generally assumed to have to the centralized criminal history files maintained by State and local criminal justice agencies. The three private investigative firms which testified before the Commission all asserted that they have access to such files only where the law permits. However, Sorrell Wildhorn, a Rand Corporation analyst who has conducted the most far-reaching independent study of private investigative agencies to date, told the Commission that many private security executives freely admit to having access to ". . . the records of public law enforcement agencies . . . in jurisdictions in which policy or statutes prohibit such access."[38] It is said that to keep an employer from knowing about such practices, investigators commonly report the criminal history information as though it had been obtained from a police blotter or court records.[39]

Finally, the Wackenhut Corporation told the Commission that it used to maintain extensive files at its Coral Gables, Florida, headquarters on possibly "subversive" political activity, and other related information, and that these files were checked in the course of all background investigations, including preemployment investigations. The files, which Wackenhut no longer holds but to which its investigators still have access, were based on a collection of information, known as the "Barz Lag List," which Wackenhut purchased in February, 1966. Barz Lag, a retired naval officer, had monitored House of Representatives Internal Security Committee hearings and similar proceedings to sort out "derogatory-type" information on individuals for black-listing purposes.[40] Wackenhut purchased the Barz Lag material partly at the urging of some of its employer clients and partly out of its own desire to corner the private-sector market for such information. Subsequently, Wackenhut supplemented the Barz Lag files through an extensive newspaper clipping and general information-gathering program. Local offices, including the Washington, D.C., branch, were instructed to clip newspaper reports of political demonstrations or unrest—such as the civil rights and anti-Vietnam war protests of the late 1960's—as well as other events which might be of future interest. Patterned after the central files of the FBI, the information was indexed by individual and by subject, allowing a quick central-file check in the course of each background investigation the firm conducted. For a time, this file capacity was considered a major asset in marketing Wackenhut investigative services. However, when few employers expressed interest in it, Wackenhut donated it to the Church League of America, a political group which claims to hold "the largest and most comprehensive files on subversive activity, with the single exception of the FBI."[41] Today Wackenhut continues to use the Church League files when there seems to be a need to do so, but they are apparently not much in

38 Private Investigative Hearings, p. 237.
39 Ibid.
40 Testimony of the Wackenhut Corporation, Private Investigative Hearings, January 26, 1977, pp. 44, 63-89.
41 The Church League of America, What is the Church League of America? undated, p. 4.

demand. Pinkerton's and Per-Mar both testified that they have never maintained files of this nature, nor have their preemployment background reports ever contained information on political activities.[42]

Apparently employers, unlike insurers and credit grantors, are not much interested in sharing information about applicants and their backgrounds. This was demonstrated by a Wackenhut witness who testified that Wackenhut once considered establishing a central databank that employers could use to check out applicants and current employees:

> . . . we felt that there was a need on the part of business and industry to have a central index where they could secure information regarding the background of the individuals involved in various types of criminal as well as subversive activities; and we at one time contemplated setting up a procedure whereby, for example, we might accumulate information on individuals who are employed in the retail field, or people employed in the transportation industries, and provide a central index of information regarding those persons.[43]

The plan was abandoned, however, for lack of employer interest. The employers contacted were neither prepared to contribute information to the databank nor to pay for the service it would make possible. Apparently, the employer's desire for a high-quality, thorough, investigation, tailored to its specific needs, is a real one; and high-quality investigations cannot be reliant on a central databank. Moreover, there are more employers than insurers, and thus a much less concentrated demand for reports on applicants. Indeed, Wackenhut, the nation's third largest private security firm, testified that it currently maintains only about 70,000 files containing information on subjects of investigations done for clients.[44] Pinkerton's, Inc., the country's oldest and largest security firm, and Per-Mar Security, a much smaller firm, both testified that they do not centrally index reports done by local branch offices, nor do they retain investigative reports very long.[45] In fact, Pinkerton's testified that unless a preemployment report is needed for litigation or possible prosecution, it is destroyed as soon as the client pays the bill.[46]

On the other hand, private investigators doing preemployment work do have access to the information reservoirs maintained by the support organizations that service insurers and credit grantors. Employers, like insurers, view an individual's credit history as an important indicator of trustworthiness and responsibility; and credit bureaus, as a rule, have not

---

[42] Testimony of Pinkerton's, Inc., Private Investigative Hearings, January 26, 1977, p. 147; and testimony of Per-Mar Security, Inc., Private Investigative Hearings, January 26, 1977, p. 196.

[43] Testimony of the Wackenhut Corporation, Private Investigative Hearings, January 26, 1977, p. 43.

[44] *Ibid.,* p. 24.

[45] Testimony of Pinkerton's, Inc., Private Investigative Hearings, January 26, 1977, p. 144; and testimony of Per-Mar Security, Inc., Private Investigative Hearings, January 26, 1977, p. 191.

[46] Testimony of Pinkerton's, Inc., Private Investigative Hearings, January 26, 1977, p. 144.

been reluctant to share information in their records with insurers and employers who are willing to pay for it. Hence, private investigators and inspection bureau representatives both rely on credit-bureau records in writing their reports, and as leads to further sources of investigation.

Moreover, for some reason, private investigative agencies will not identify a credit bureau as the source of information in a preemployment report. One major firm's investigative manual says that:

Information obtained from Dun and Bradstreet and from various credit bureaus should be treated as coming from a confidential source and should not be reported in the language of the credit agency. This information should be reported in the language of the investigator, disguising its origin.[47]

One consequence of this, of course, is to make it impossible for either the employer or the applicant to trace an error back to its source.

There is also some evidence that private investigative agencies have access to inspection bureau files. A senior employee of one of the larger investigative agencies told the Commission staff that it is not uncommon for an investigator to establish a "source" relationship with an inspection bureau, but again always disguising the source.

INVESTIGATIVE SERVICES IN ADVERSARY SITUATIONS

In addition to conducting underwriting and preemployment investigations, inspection bureaus and private investigative agencies both provide special investigative services to assist insurers in the settlement of certain types of claims. Private investigative agencies may also offer extensive "loss prevention" services to employers. In both instances, experienced and highly trained investigators are assigned to the case; and in some cases mechanical surveillance devices may be used.

Transfer to the "special investigations" claims unit is considered a promotion for the inspection bureau field representative, and the reports they prepare are carefully checked before they are delivered. Claims settlement and loss prevention investigations are adversary situations which may lead directly to a court room, so the evidence standards of both client and investigator are high. Moreover, the potential savings to the insurance company or employer are great. Fraud is estimated to be involved in hundreds of millions of dollars worth of insurance claims each year. While even the most complete investigation rarely results in a prosecution for criminal fraud, a good investigation can frequently force a fraudulent claim to be dropped or produce a much-reduced settlement. Similarly, it is estimated that well over three-fourths of all business inventory shortages are the result of theft by employees. Theft from retail establishments alone amounted to an estimated $7.2 billion in 1976.[48] Thus, even a very expensive investigation can turn out to be cost-effective.

Where large amounts of money are at stake, investigators may use

---

[47] The identity of this private investigative firm has been kept confidential at its request.
[48] U.S. Department of Commerce, *Cost of Crimes Against Business*, O.B.R.A., 1976.

unusual techniques. In a personal injury case, standard investigative practice is to conduct an "activities check," which may involve covert surveillance of the individual, possibly photographic surveillance. Along these lines, investigators working for a company with theft or other problems may place an "intelligence agent" undercover in the company's work force to observe the activities of other employees. Whether or not this produces direct results, the sense that it may be going on can have a desirable inhibiting effect.

Pretext interviews in claims investigations are another routine practice. Wackenhut witnesses described how one such interview might be conducted:

> Well you might, for example, call up and ask the lady of the house, who apparently is the claimant in connection with the matter, what type of detergent or soap she might use in laundering her wash, and she would tell you. And you would indicate to her without even disclosing what company you are with and who you represent that you would like to come out on Monday morning or whenever she does her washing in order to take some pictures of her using that product. And, then you would appear on the scene and she would wash. And, you would have a person who has a serious back injury who is claiming a large amount of money from the insurance company, who proceeds to wash and hang up her wash on the washing line. That might be one example.[49]

Because of the importance of medical-record information in claims settlments, Equifax Services Claims Department maintains special card files on "medical sources." A source card generally indicates the most opportune times for obtaining information from the doctor, whether an authorization is commonly required, the doctor's attitude toward insurance companies, and so forth.[50] Of the 11,000 hospitals accredited in the United States and Canada, Equifax estimates that its agents are able to make a personal review of the records in all but 1,200, the 1,200 being known in the business as "problem hospitals."[51]

An extreme example of the use of pretexts to gain access to medical records without authorization was provided in testimony by the Denver, Colorado, District Attorney during the Commission's Medical Records Hearings in Los Angeles.[52] Factual Service Bureau, Inc., (FSB) a private investigative agency headquartered in Chicago but with offices scattered around the country, was said to have made the unauthorized acquisition of medical-record information for use in investigating and settling third-parties insurance claims its "bread and butter" business. According to the evidence presented to the Commission, this was apparently done by phoning a hospital records room, pretending to be a doctor, or by paying a strategically

---

[49] Private Investigative Hearings, January 26, 1977, p. 54.

[50] Equifax, Inc., "Claim Reports Manual," November 1975, p. B-3.

[51] Ibid., p. C-11.

[52] Testimony of Dale Tooley, Medical Records, Hearings before the Privacy Protection Study Commission, June 11, 1976.

placed hospital employee to spirit the records out. FSB also claimed to be able to acquire records from the "IRS and financial sources," creating the impression that it could penetrate both.

Although aspects of Factual Service Bureau's *modus operandi* are described in several parts of this report, two points are important here. First, while the Commission realizes that the type of practices in which Factual Service Bureau engaged are rarely, if ever, used in underwriting or preemployment background investigations, and further that they are not typical even in most claims investigations, the fact that there was any kind of market for such a service should be a matter of great concern. Second, it must be understood that the reports Factual Service Bureau prepared were not subject to any of the requirements of the FCRA by virtue of the fact that they were developed in connection with claims investigations which the Act does not reach.

COMPLIANCE WITH THE FAIR CREDIT REPORTING ACT

At the time it was enacted, the primary objective of the FCRA was to improve the accuracy, timeliness, and completeness of the information credit bureaus, inspection bureaus, and private investigative firms report to their clients. To this end the Act made it possible for the subject of an investigation to review and challenge information in the report that results from the investigation. Implementation of these provisions, however, has not been without its problems; and the Act today remains a much less effective protection for the individual consumer than he needs. The reasons why this is so in the credit area are explained in detail in Chapter 2, and the chapters on insurance and employment record keeping (Chapters 5 and 6) highlight similar problems in those areas.

Based upon the testimony it has taken and the analysis of the extent to which the FCRA comports with the Commission's three recommended policy objectives regarding intrusiveness, fairness, and expectation of confidentiality, the Commission has concluded that additional legislative action is clearly needed. While the practices of investigative-reporting agencies have certainly changed significantly over the past six years, and although it appears that the practices of some inspection bureaus and private investigative firms now meet not only the objectives of the Act but also the objectives of the Commission's recommendations, this is not universally so, nor has the process by which it has sometimes come about been a reassuring one.

This is sharply illustrated by the experiences of one Commission witness who sought to challenge the information in an inspection bureau report which prompted cancellation of his auto insurance.

The Millstone Case

In August 1971, journalist James C. Millstone moved from Washington, D.C. to St. Louis, Missouri, to assume the post of news editor for the *St. Louis Post Dispatch*. He asked his insurance agent to place automobile insurance for him. A policy with Firemen's Fund took effect on November 15. A few days later, Millstone received a form notice that a personal investigation would be made in connection with the new policy. On December 20, Firemen's Fund informed Millstone's agent that the policy would be canceled as a result of information turned up in an inspection report prepared by O'Hanlon Reports, Inc.

Because the agent was willing to vouch for him, and because of Millstone's standing in the community, Firemen's Fund was shortly thereafter persuaded to ignore the report and reinstate Millstone's policy. However, getting the report itself cleaned up was not so easy. On December 22, 1971, Millstone went to the St. Louis office of O'Hanlon Reports. The office manager told him that he was entitled to know what was in his own report, but that O'Hanlon was by law allowed 10 days to produce the information. When Millstone protested, the manager called O'Hanlon's New York Headquarters and let Millstone speak to one Kenneth Mitchell. Mitchell told Millstone that the file was in the mail from St. Louis to New York and would be made available as soon as possible. As it later came out in court, however, Millstone's file was actually in the St. Louis office when he visited it and was only mailed to New York after he left.

Six days later, when Millstone returned to the St. Louis office, the manager read from a single sheet the purported contents of Millstone's file. The disclosure sheet, prepared by David K. Slayback, Vice President of O'Hanlon, said in part:

> The file shows that you are very much disliked by your neighbors at that location [Millstone's Washington residence] and were considered to be a "hippy type." The file indicates that you participated in many demonstrations in Washington, D.C., and that you also housed out-of-town demonstrators during demonstrations. The file indicates that these demonstrators slept on floors, in the basement, and wherever else there was room on your property. The file shows that you were strongly suspected of being a drug user by neighbors, but they could not positively substantiate these suspicions. You are shown to have had shoulder-length hair and a beard on one occasion while living in Washington, D.C. The file indicates that there were rumors in the neighborhood from three previous residences in Washington, D.C. prior to living at the 48th Street, N.W. location.[53]

This disclosure was read to but not shown or given to Millstone for his own examination.

Shocked, Millstone disputed virtually all of the information disclosed to him and demanded an explanation of several of the allegations. The office manager told Millstone he had no further information and could not answer Millstone's questions. He said that his instructions from the New York office were to read the disclosure sheet and note any item disputed by Millstone. The actual report from which the disclosure was abstracted was

---

[53] *Millstone v. O'Hanlon Reports, Inc.*, 383 F. Supp. 269, 271 (1974).

neither produced nor quoted. The manager, however, called New York once again; and this time Millstone spoke to David Slayback. Slayback defended the method and propriety of the disclosure process and refused to expand on the statement that Millstone was strongly suspected of being a "drug user."

Slayback directed the manager of O'Hanlon's Silver Spring, Maryland, office, which had conducted the original investigation, to reinvestigate. The Silver Spring office took approximately three days to do so and report back to New York. A further abstract was prepared. The abstract based on the reinvestigation contained new charges and led to another series of meetings and telephone calls between O'Hanlon representatives and Millstone. In each conversation and meeting, Millstone asked to see his file but was refused.

Eventually, Millstone sued O'Hanlon. During the pre-trial discovery process, Millstone learned about critical comments concerning his wife contained in his file, but never previously disclosed to him, as well as additional derogatory allegations about himself.

One of the documents Millstone introduced as evidence at the trial was the handbook O'Hanlon issued to each branch office manager. The manual states in part:

> The important thing is to NEVER check the files in the presence of the consumer . . . prior to the time of your appointment with the consumer, you will have received the Statement of Disclosure from the Home Office. At the time of your appointment ANY and ALL information you may have relating to the consumer, such as copies of files, a copy of your statement, index cards, etc., are to be in your desk drawer out of SIGHT of the consumer. You are not to show anything or acknowledge that you have anything other than the Statement of Disclosure.
>
> Actual disclosure will be accomplished by reading the Statement of Disclosure to the consumer. The Statement is to be read word for word at your normal reading speed. It is not to be read slow enough for anyone to copy down word for word, nor is it to be read so fast that the consumer will not understand what you were saying. Part or all of the Statement of Disclosure may be reread if the consumer indicates he did not understand what you were telling him. The consumer and/or the person with him may not have a copy of the Statement, nor may they be allowed to read the Statement or touch it.[54]

It was disclosed that an O'Hanlon employee, Alexander Mayes, conducted the original investigation of Millstone. Mayes claimed to have spoken to four former neighbors of the Millstones on the block where they had lived in Washington, D.C. Of the four, one refused to speak to Mayes and two told him that they knew of trouble in the neighborhood but that they knew nothing firsthand and that they did not wish to be involved. All of the data in the Mayes report were purported to have come from one

---

[54] *Ibid.*, 272, 273.

neighbor, "McMillan," who was deceased at the time of the Millstone suit. Mayes averaged approximately 70 to 80 reports a week and spent from 10 to 30 minutes on each insurance investigation.

Millstone's character, reputation in the community, working and personal habits, and his family relationships were testified to by character witnesses of national reputation at the trial. These witnesses were entirely supportive of Mr. Millstone and contradicted the O'Hanlon report allegations totally.

The court found that Mayes had "knowingly included false information in the report," and further that O'Hanlon's,

> methods of reporting on consumers' credit backgrounds as shown at the trial were so slipshod and slovenly as to not even approach the realm of reasonable standards of care imposed by the statute [FCRA].[55]

Millstone was granted $2,500 in actual damages, $25,000 in punitive damages, and $14,000 in attorney's fees. The decision was appealed by O'Hanlon, but finally upheld in January 1976.[56]

While Mr. Millstone's experience by no means typifies the treatment of all or even a sizeable minority of the individuals investigated by inspection bureaus and private investigative agencies, it shows why the FCRA needs to be strengthened substantially. Only a small percentage of inaccurate information reports result in litigation, and many cases that go to court are settled before judgment. The Millstone case was filed in April 1972, within months after the Act took effect, and has established legal precedents of wide-reaching effect. Yet the case was not settled until the U.S. Court of Appeals rendered a decision four years later. Meanwhile, the inspection bureau vigorously fought each step of the way and apologized to Mr. Millstone only in August 1976 during its testimony before the Privacy Protection Study Commission.

Many consumers are still not aware that legal recourse is available to them and many who are will nonetheless try to cope with the damage done rather than bring suit. Litigation is expensive, uncertain, protracted, and possibly demeaning as one attempts to document one's own reputation. Further, as the *Millstone* case illustrates, some inspection bureaus, in complying with the access and dispute requirements of the FCRA first developed policies which discouraged all but the most persistent, and which had the effect of obscuring the actual content and sources of information in a report unless the aggrieved individual was willing to go to court. Only recently did they start allowing an individual to see and copy a corrected inspection report upon request, and some still do not allow the individual to do even that.

THE COMMISSION'S RECOMMENDATIONS

The activities of the investigative support organizations described in

---

[55] *Ibid.*, 275.
[56] 528 F.2d. 829 (8th Cir., 1976).

this chapter present a number of special privacy protection problems. In part because of the broadly worded authorization forms that applicants for insurance and employment are often asked to sign, the crucial role these organizations can play in the decision-making processes of insurers and employers is poorly understood by the public. As indicated in the chapters on the insurance and employment relationships, blanket, open-ended permissions for unnamed third parties to make almost any kind of inquiry about an individual tend to obscure the fact that an inspection bureau or private investigator, rather than the insurer or employer, may actually do the information gathering and perhaps retain the results for subsequent reporting to others. Moreover, the information gathered and reported may often disguise its source, thereby making it impossible to tell whether an individual's presumed confidential relationship with a record-keeping institution, such as a credit grantor, an insurer, a medical-care provider, or his employer, is, in fact, being honored.

Furthermore, in the insurance area, the economic incentive to assure that the information in an inspection report is accurate, timely, and complete has traditionally been weak. Although inaccurate or false information can lead a company to turn down an applicant who would otherwise qualify for average or even preferred rates, it takes a large number of policies lost as a result of inaccurate inspection reports to more than make up for a $50,000 claim settlement that might have been avoided if information developed by an inspection bureau report had been used as the basis for declining or refusing to renew. Clearly a service which will help a company avoid even a few substantial claims or which tends to raise premium income even a small amount is quite valuable. Indeed, it can make a great deal of difference to an insurer in terms of earnings and competitive position, thereby directing attention away from the fact that it can also be a cause of considerable unfairness to some unknown number of individuals whose reports contain inaccurate information.

Finally, to the extent that inspection bureaus rely on information in their own files in making reports, they can play a gatekeeping role that significantly affects an individual's ability to establish relationships with a large number and variety of record-keeping institutions. Where adverse information is kept on file for many years, an individual may never be able to avoid having certain lines of inquiry made about him, and thus never be able to escape the subjective judgments of others as to whether he still has the questionable characteristics that were once reported about him. While this may not have the same "chilling effect" on an individual as government inquiries about aspects of an individual's private life are reputed to have, it presents at least the danger of permanent, inescapable stigmatization.

In recognition of these problems, the Commission has made recommendations regarding the insurance and employment relationships which, if adopted, will markedly alter the role that investigative support organizations play in them. The recommendations would redistribute responsibility for the practices of inspection bureaus and private investigative agencies by requiring their users to exercise reasonable care in selecting and evaluating them, and, in addition, levy access and correction requirements on users which parallel those that would apply to report preparers. Equally important, the Commission's recommendations would enlarge the population of individuals entitled to the protections afforded by the FCRA, change the Act's access and correction requirements to make them better serve the interests of the individual, and regulate, to some degree, the investigative techniques that may be used by insurers, employers, and investigative support organizations that serve them.

REDISTRIBUTION OF RESPONSIBILITY

The Fair Credit Reporting Act establishes liability for the accuracy, timeliness, and completeness of investigative reports, but currently places it exclusively on the inspection bureaus and investigative agencies that prepare them. The user of a report bears no responsibility for the conduct of the investigative support organization that put the report together, nor is it under any obligation to inform the support organization when it discovers an error. Indeed, the likelihood that it will discover an error is low, since the FCRA only allows an individual to check and, if necessary, correct the copy of an investigative report that the support organization retains. The Act gives him no parallel right with respect to the same report in the hands of the insurer or employer user. The user's responsibility is limited to notifying the individual that a report may be requested, describing, upon request, the scope of the investigation, and, if an adverse decision results, notifying the individual of the name and address of the inspection bureau or private investigative agency that prepared the report.

The Commission's solution to this problem is to place the insurer and employer in a position of joint responsibility with the investigative support organization. While accountability for the contents of a report would remain with the organization that prepares it, the user would be liable if it repeatedly did business with any support organization that consistently engaged in objectionable practices. Moreover, by requiring the user, as well as the preparer of a report, to disclose its contents to the individual whom it concerns and to cope with certain types of deficiencies in it that the individual may allege, the user is given a strong incentive to deal only with support organizations that produce reports of high quality.

Some investigative support organizations currently have contracts with their users that make the user who discloses the contents of a report to its subject the liable party in any law suit that may result. The effect, of course, is to keep the user from disclosing anything to the individual, and the Commission's recommendation would therefore make such contracts null and void. Finally, the Commission's "expectation of confidentiality" recommendations and proposed authorization requirements are worded in such a way as to compel support organizations to live by the same ground rules on third-party access to reports as the insurers and employers who use them. In practical terms, this means that a report prepared on an individual for one purpose will no longer be useable for another purpose without his authorization, thereby giving him some control over the circulation of information about him which has been generated in service of markedly different record-keeping relationships he maintains or seeks to establish.

SCOPE OF THE FCRA

A second shortcoming of the FCRA is that its protections do not reach every individual who is the subject of an underwriting or preemployment investigation—notably any individual whom an insurer or employer investigates on its own or who is investigated in connection with a job for which he has not applied. The Commission has heard of no plausible rationale for preserving such a distinction and thus, through judicious wording of its various recommendations affecting the FCRA, has eliminated it.

ACCESS AND CORRECTION REQUIREMENTS

Perhaps the most blatant weakness in the FCRA is the impracticality of its provisions aimed at giving an individual a way of getting inaccurate, incomplete, or obsolete information in an investigative report corrected, amended, or deleted. As was evident in the *Millstone* case, requiring only that the "nature and substance" of a report be revealed to the individual effectively deprives him of his corresponding right to challenge its content. Thus, in its insurance and employment recommendations, the Commission proposes that the FCRA be amended to allow an individual to "see and copy" a report about himself, whether in the hands of the preparer or the user and regardless of whether they happen to be the same organization (as when an insurer or employer conducts its own investigation of an individual). In conjunction with this change in the Act, the Commission also recommends that the individual be able to receive a copy of a report in the mail, and, for reasons discussed in the chapter on the employment relationship, that an employer automatically send an applicant or employee a copy of any background report prepared on him. (Note that the Commission's recommendation on applicant interviews in the course of preparing underwriting reports could also be satisfied by mailing the applicant a copy of the report.)

Of equal importance is the corollary obligation the Commission's recommendations would place on an insurer or employer to propagate corrections, amendments, disputes, and deletions of information in a report back to the support organization from whence the information came. So, also, the Commission's recommendations that would prohibit the use of information concerning previous adverse insurance decisions, and the disclosure by insurance institutions and support organizations of information concerning an individual's health which has not been obtained from a medical-care provider or from the individual himself, or from his spouse, parent, or guardian, should serve to reduce the amount of damaging gossip in inspection bureau reports.

INVESTIGATIVE TECHNIQUES

Finally, the Commission has recommended Federal legislation that would (1) outlaw the use of pretext interviews in all insurance (including claims) and preemployment investigations; (2) prohibit an employer from using polygraph or other truth verification equipment to gather information from an applicant or employee; and (3) make it a criminal offense to seek to acquire medical-record information from a medical-care provider through false or misleading representations.

AN AGENDA FOR FURTHER STUDY

If accepted, the Commission's recommendations should go a long way towards improving the practices of inspection bureaus and private investigative agencies. There are, however, a number of problem areas that deserve further study.

In the employment area, particularly, further study is needed of the access which private investigators are alleged to have to computerized criminal histories maintained by public law enforcement agencies. If there is indeed a "buddy system" which facilitates unauthorized access to such records, it should be exposed and dealt with responsibly. Additional examination is also needed to assure that "blacklists" and reports concerning an individual's political beliefs and associations are not being used in making employment decisions. In this regard, the activities of organizations like the Church League of America need to be studied further.

The loss prevention services and background investigations for parties other than employers which many private investigative agencies offer their clients are still another category of activities that merits examination. The Commission has not been able to look at possible uses of private investigators to monitor union activity or the activities of individuals whose political views conflict with those of their employer or of any other investigative agency client. Finally, the effectiveness of requiring a private investigator to have a signed authorization in hand before he can acquire information in records maintained by an institution with whom an individual has a legally enforceable confidential relationship will be a crucial question for the future.

Adoption of the Commission's recommendations regarding investigative reporting agencies will involve some sweeping changes in current practice. The record of the last 10 years does not suggest that those changes will be easily wrought. Hence, in recognition of the impact that investigative-reporting activities can have on the lives of many individuals, the Commission believes that continued monitoring is not only advisable; it is essential.

Chapter 9

Government Access to
Personal Records and "Private Papers"

Discussion of the need to protect individuals from threats to personal privacy often conjures up ominous images of government agents conducting surreptitious investigations and compiling dossiers. Such images come forcefully to mind when one is concerned, as the Commission is, with preventing improper inquiry into and disclosure of records about individuals. While the tendency to equate threats to personal privacy with government action, and government action with clandestine police operations, is understandable, the evidence uncovered in the Commission's inquiry shows that such equations are not necessarily accurate.

The improper collection and use of information about an individual present as difficult problems when private institutions fail to observe the legitimate rights and expectations of the individual as when government fails; but, governmental intrusions on personal privacy have a longer and more dramatic history, both in law and in the public mind. Generous portions of the Bill of Rights were fashioned two centuries ago to assure that Americans would not again suffer the unwarranted intrusions by government which, in John Adams' mind, provided the spark that ignited revolution.[1] Protection from government intrusion, as exemplified in the Fourth and Fifth Amendments, has long been the primary public focus of privacy protection.[2] The desire to assure for the individual the quiet enjoyment of his home in part justifies such protection; but in equal part, individual rights securing privacy are also intended to safeguard the personal papers and other documentation that can illuminate the associations, interests, attitudes, and beliefs as well as actions of an individual.[3] Such information is valuable in a variety of forms of government coercion, ranging from criminal prosecution to less legitimate activities. Indeed, this second aspect of personal privacy is the focus of Fourth Amendment protection, the "search and seizure" standards which never fail to stir public

---

[1] Hiller Zobel and Kinvin Wroth (eds.), *Legal Papers of John Adams*, (Harvard University Press, Cambridge: 1965) Vol. 2, Case No. 44, pp. 106-144.

[2] John Eger, "Foreward" to Kent Greenawalt, *Legal Protections of Privacy*, Office of Telecommunications Policy (Washington, D.C.: 1976); Thomas I. Emerson, *The System of Freedom of Expression*, (New York: Vintage, 1970) pp. 544-48.

[3] See Note, "Formalism, Legal Realism, and Constitutionally Protected Privacy Under the Fourth and Fifth Amendments," 90 *Harv. L. Rev.* 945 (1977) (hereinafter cited as 'Formalism, Legal Realism . . . .").

interest and win extensive press coverage when debated in the Supreme Court.

These well publicized elements of Constitutional controversy and national history, perhaps inevitably, tend to focus on problems of law enforcement officers improperly gaining access to one's home or one's private records. Along with this emphasis on invasions of privacy by law enforcement comes a tendency to treat the issues as legal issues rather than policy ones, because, after all, the battleground for resolving those issues has traditionally been the courts. Earlier chapters of this report should dispel the impression that dangers to personal privacy are only products of government action, but the equation of government action with law enforcement activity needs to be tempered and the notion needs to be dispelled that resolving the basic privacy issues raised by government action demands a close attention to legal niceties.

The question of law enforcement, and the peculiar powers and opportunities to acquire information given government for that purpose, raise uniquely sensitive problems. Nonetheless, government's expanding role as regulator and distributor of largess gives it new ways to intrude, creating new privacy protection problems. By opening more avenues for collecting information and more decision-making forums in which it can employ that information, government has enormously broadened its opportunities to embarrass, harass, and injure the individual. These new avenues (and needs) for collecting information, particularly when coupled with applications of modern information technologies, multiply the dangers of official abuse against which the Constitution seeks to protect.[4] Recent history reminds us that these are real, not mythical, dangers.

The concern about governmental abuse which underlies traditional protections against government intrusion on personal privacy provides a focal point for exploring the particular balancing of interests which faced the Commission in reaching its recommendations on government access to private records as well as for emphasizing the need *not* to confine such deliberations within the narrow precincts of law. Though solutions must finally be fashioned into law, the choices made in arriving at such solutions are not mere legal choices; they are fundamental public-policy decisions— social and political value choices of the most basic kind.

The balance to be struck is an old one; it reflects the tension between individual liberty and social order. The sovereign needs information to maintain order; the individual needs to be able to protect his independence and autonomy should the sovereign overreach. The peculiarly American notions of legally limited government and the protections in the Bill of Rights provide broad theoretical standards for reaching a workable balance. But the world has a way of disrupting the particular balance struck in past generations; the theory may remain unaltered but circumstances change, requiring a reworking of the mechanisms which maintained the balance in the past.

---

[4] *Infra*, this Chapter, "Restricting Compulsory Reporting Requirements;" also, Chapter 13.

Current threats to personal privacy stem largely from changes in the way individuals go about their day-to-day business.[5] The Commission's inquiry did discover, however, that some threats are the result of government rewriting the rules of the game without letting the rest of the players know.[6] Both circumstances combine to erode the effectiveness of traditional protections for personal privacy and individual liberty.

Traditionally, the records an individual might keep on his daily activities, financial transactions, or net worth were beyond government reach unless the government could establish probable cause to believe a crime had been committed. If government were merely suspicious and wanted to investigate, such records were unavailable. The legal standards that protected them evolved in a world where such records were almost universally in the actual possession of the individual. Reflecting that reality, the law only barred government from seizing records in the possession of the individual.[7] As the record compiled by the Commission proves, that world no longer exists. Third parties, institutions or persons other than the individual, now keep a great many records documenting various activities of a particular individual. Indeed, these third parties keep records about the individual he would not ordinarily have kept in the past. Records for life and health insurance, for example, are repositories of highly intimate personal data, financial and familial as well as medical, which were virtually unknown until recent decades.

Financial records, particularly the information retained in demand deposit accounts, provide another instance where the changing patterns of life took the possession of information about himself out of the control of the individual. Of great importance, checking account records present a situation where alterations in record-keeping patterns have been exacerbated by government action. Until recently the account record maintained by one's bank frequently did not include a copy of each individual check, with the payee, date, and often place and reason for drawing the check clearly noted; rather, the record might simply have noted the dollar amounts of transactions and the date of processing by the bank.[8] The Bank Secrecy Act of 1970 and the Treasury regulations which give that law effect, however, now *require* depository institutions to keep copies of the checks an individual uses to draw on the funds in his account.[9] The checking account

---

[5] See, e.g., Chapter 2, "Consumer-Credit Relationship."

[6] *Infra*, this Chapter, "The Grand Jury Subpoena."

[7] *Boyd v. United States*, 116 U.S. 616 (1886); *Olmstead v. United States*, 277 U.S. 438, 474 (1928) (Brandeis, J., dissenting); *infra*, this Chapter, note 81.

[8] As Representative Patman explained during the debates preceding passage of the Bank Secrecy Act, a primary purpose of the Act was to "make uniform and *adequate* the present record-keeping practices, or *lack of record-keeping practices*, by domestic banks and other financial institutions," (emphasis added) 116 *Cong. Rec.* 16951 (1970); also, see remarks of Representative Stark, *Administrative Summons and Antidisclosure Provisions of the Tax Reform Act of 1976*, Hearings before the Subcommittee on Oversight of the Committee on Ways and Means, U.S. House of Representatives, 95th Congress, 1st Session, ser. 95-4, at 26 (February 24, 1977) (hereinafter cited as "U.S. House of Representatives, Hearings on Administrative Summons").

[9] 12 U.S.C. 1951 *et seq.*; 31 C.F.R. 103.

has become an intimate mirror of individual activity in a way it never was before the Bank Secrecy Act.

The existence of records about an individual that are not in his possession poses serious privacy protection problems, especially when government seeks access to those records. Record keepers can, often do, and sometimes must, disclose records about an individual to government without seeking the individual's approval, whether the disclosure is at the request of government or through the initiative of the record keeper; and, frequently no record of the disclosure is ever made. A government request made informally through a personal visit to the record keeper or by a telephone call, for example, may leave no trace in any record. The individual may never know that agents of the government have inspected his records. Except in a limited number of situations, neither the record keeper nor the government is obliged to notify him that his records were opened to government scrutiny. Even if the individual is given notice and documentation of the disclosure, he has no legal right to challenge the propriety of government access to his records, despite the possibility that the government agent might have been on a "fishing expedition."[10]

Historically, the courts have justified relatively unrestricted government access to records on individual activity kept by third parties by regarding such information as independent documentation of voluntary transactions between the individual and the record keeper.[11] Coupled with this concept of voluntariness, such records have not been viewed, and until recently rightly so, as the sorts of private records and personal papers that merit special protection because they illuminate an individual's associations, interest, attitudes, and beliefs, as well as actions. The privacy protections that help secure the independence and autonomy of the individual were not considered necessary. Courts and the public were comfortable with a legal standard that protected only records in the possession of the individual.

Today, the law remains unchanged even though new sorts of personal records, created to meet new circumstances, sometimes generated by government requirements, are vulnerable to seizure or inspection by government without the individual being able to intervene. A record keeper may volunteer information about an individual to government; or the Executive branch of government can compel production of such records with little trouble and often without supervision by the judiciary or anyone else.[12] Recently, the courts have begun to doubt the assumptions of voluntariness upon which they rest their refusal to extend basic constitutional protections to an individual when government seeks disclosure of records held by a third-party record keeper. Indeed, some judges have taken tentative notice of the realities of contemporary record keeping and the danger that allowing government to acquire such "third party" records

---

[10] See, e.g., *United States v. Miller*, 425 U.S. 435 (1976); *Kelley v. United States*, 536 F.2d 897 (9th Cir. 1976); compare, *Donaldson v. United States*, 400 U.S. 517 (1971); also, see *infra*, note 94.

[11] *Ibid.*

[12] *Infra*, this Chapter, "Regulating the Compelled Production of Records."

might disclose "intimate areas of personal affairs" protected by the Fourth and Fifth Amendments.[13]

Nonetheless, to wait on the courts to reweave the fabric of law and create protections for the individual is to adopt a policy of uncertain outcome. One cannot be sure the courts will become more flexible. One can be sure, however, that if the courts do extend protections, their efforts will be slow and piecemeal. Yet the society is faced with problems that demand decision and resolution. The world has altered and continues to change with increasing rapidity. As the Commission's study of Electronic Funds Transfer Systems suggests, existing problems with government access to records will be exacerbated by future developments; they will not go away.[14] Today, government has access to the most revealing personal records about an individual; yet the individual has no ability to thwart or even contest such access. Perhaps most important, they are situations in which the individual has no choice but to allow others to maintain records about him. Not to enter into the relationships that generate individually identifiable records would subject the vast majority of Americans to severe economic and social burdens, disrupting the ordinary course of their lives. Think, for instance, of the time and effort necessary to pay all bills in person, not to mention the risk involved in carrying enough cash to transact all personal business.

Further, and of increasing importance, there is little to impede government access to records about individuals held by third parties, particularly records the government requires third parties to keep. In its Depository and Lending Institution hearings, witnesses told the Commission that informal access to bank records, i.e., access without a subpoena or summons, was a favorite tool of government investigators. Indeed, the American Civil Liberties Union submitted testimony originally given before the House Judiciary Committee in July, 1975, which suggested that such informal or "voluntary" disclosure was "the means by which government normally procures access to confidential bank records."[15] The Internal Revenue Service testified that banks are usually cooperative in responding to a "friendly" summons.[16] Even when banks are somewhat less cooperative, however, little real impediment to government access occurs. Continental Illinois Bank, for example, seeks to notify the individual that his account records have been subpoenaed and does a "four corners" check of the validity of any summons received,[17] but, as explored below in more detail, neither action by the bank gives any real assistance to the individual. And,

---

[13] *California Bankers Assn. v. Schultz*, 416 U.S. 21, 78 (1975) (Powell, J., concurring).

[14] See Chapter 3, "The Depository Relationship," section on "Electronic Funds Transfer Services: An Overview."

[15] Written Statement of Hope Eastman, Associate Director, ACLU, *Depository and Lending Institutions*, Hearings before the Privacy Protection Study Commission, April 22, 1976, p. 5 (hereinafter cited as "Depository and Lending Institutions Hearings").

[16] Testimony of the Internal Revenue Service, Depository and Lending Institutions Hearings, April 22, 1976, pp. 777-830, and particularly pp. 804-07.

[17] Testimony of Continental Illinois Bank and Trust Company, Depository and Lending Institutions Hearings, April 21, 1976, p. 277.

the extent of concern exhibited by Continental Illinois for its customers is rare.

The Commission's hearings on the record-keeping practices of credit grantors and depository and lending institutions and its survey of credit-card issuers indicate that a large proportion of private-sector financial record keepers lack any policy on government access, not to mention a policy as fair as that of the Continental Illinois Bank.[18] In addition, what is labeled "policy" is frequently little more than a grant of discretion—to notify or not, to determine the validity of a subpoena or not—given to an office manager or perhaps someone lower in the heirarchy. Some record keepers even seem to have a policy of *not* notifying the individual or reviewing the validity of the subpoena. Such lack of policy, however, should not be viewed as unkindly as a first reaction might suggest. As American Express testified in February, 1976, it did not notify customers as a matter of course because it could not see what good it would do.[19] Though its position was not particularly well received by the public, American Express was right; notice to the customer does little good. Even if notified, the individual can do little to hinder government access, however illegitimate the purposes or improper the procedures.[20] The ground rules need to be changed if any good is to be done.

To effect that change successfully, a brief exploration of the arguments that have prevented the courts from extending constitutional protections for private papers to bank account and similar records will illuminate the range of policy decisions the Commission addressed and the basic choices that must be made.

THE LIMITS OF LEGAL PROTECTION: AN OVERVIEW

If records about individuals held by third-party record keepers are to be protected against government access, the law must change. In light of the inability of the courts to refashion the application of Constitutional theory, the change must come through legislative action.

VOLUNTARY DISCLOSURE AND COMPULSORY PROCESS

Government access to the account records of depository institutions provides an excellent example of the need for change and illustrates the importance of understanding current standards. In *United States v. Miller*,[21] the Supreme Court reaffirmed the traditional legal standard that customer account records in a bank are not the private papers of the customer. An

---

[18] See Chapter 2, "Consumer-Credit Relationship," section on 'Disclosures to Government Agencies", particularly the discussion of the credit-card issuers survey; also, generally, Depository and Lending Institutions Hearings, April 21-22, 1976.

[19] Testimony of American Express Company, *Credit-Card Issuers*, Hearings before the Privacy Protection Study Commission, February 11, 1976 (hereinafter cited as "Credit-Card Issuers Hearings").

[20] *Infra*, this Chapter, "Regulating the Compelled Production of Records"; "Formalism, Legal Realism . . . .," 90 *Harv. L. Rev.* 945, 964-85.

[21] 425 U.S. 435 (1976).

individual has neither ownership nor possession of such records, reasoned the Court; therefore, the records are simply the "business records of the bank." This line of argument and the precedents which have developed it extend back through the Eighteenth Century.[22] The crucial element in this traditional view is that the individual, lacking a "proprietary" interest in a bank's records of his account, has no legal right he can assert to challenge access to those records by government or anyone else.

In California, the legal status of bank account records has been altered. Interpreting a 1972 amendment to the State Constitution, the California Supreme Court ruled that "a depositor has a reasonable expectation [that] the information and documents he furnishes his bank in connection with his account will remain private."[23] Because of this legal expectation, the disclosure of bank records to government without "proper legal process" amounts to an illegal search and seizure under California law. Proper legal process, according to the developing judicial interpretation, means that the probable cause standard a search warrant must meet becomes the minimum standard government must establish when seeking to compel the production of bank records. Perhaps more important, government may not request and receive an individual's bank records from the bank without employing legal process, unless, of course, the individual consents.[24] Put simply, California law provides the individual with a "legitimate expectation of privacy," which gives him a protectible legal interest in his bank records and, given that interest, the legal tools to protect his records.

The contrast between the *Miller* decision and California law highlights two issues: (1) the question of "voluntary" disclosure of information by third-party record keepers, that is, the discretion to disclose to government without the compulsion of legal process; and (2) the necessity of a substantive standard an individual can assert to protect records about him.

However detailed and carefully structured limitations on compulsory disclosure to government may be, as long as government can request and receive information from records about an individual on an informal or voluntary basis, little real protection of personal privacy will be achieved. If a record keeper has the discretion to disclose voluntarily, it will be hard for record keepers, particularly in heavily regulated sectors such as banking, to resist pressures for "voluntary" compliance with government requests for information. Voluntary disclosure of information on individuals held by third parties must be limited if limitations on compelled disclosure are to mean anything.

Limiting voluntary disclosure involves two distinct, though related, steps. One is to require government agencies to use legal process to obtain records and to notify the individual that his records are being sought. This

---

[22] The lack of any assertable legal interest in bank notes themselves, not to mention records of banking transactions, except a limited protection against theft, is chronicled by Blackstone, *Commentaries*, Vol. 4, p. 234; also, *Ibid.*, Vol. 3, p. 382; S.F.C. Milsom, *Historical Foundations of the Common Law*, (London: Butterworth, 1969), p. 372.

[23] *Burrows v. Superior Court*, 13 Cal. 3d 238 (1974).

[24] *Ibid.*; also, *Valley Bank of Nevada v. Superior Court*, 15 Cal. 3d 652 (1975); *Carlson v. Superior Court*, 58 Cal. App. 3d 13 (1976).

procedural requirement would outlaw informal, clandestine, and undocu-
mented access by a government agency to an individual's record, assisting
effective oversight of government activity. The second step in curbing
voluntary disclosures is to levy a legally enforceable duty of nondisclosure
on record keepers who hold records in which an individual has or should
have a legitimate expectation of confidentiality. Where records are not the
sort the individual has a right to expect will be held in confidence, there is no
persuasive argument for making the record keeper liable, though an
argument remains for requiring legal process and notice by the government—the tendency to mount fishing expeditions and groundless investigations can only be tempered by effective oversight which requires documentation of investigative activities. But requirements of legal process and
notice alone cannot adequately recognize the individual privacy interest in a
record.

The second consideration, which emerges from contrasting California
law with the traditional status of bank records, is the need to provide the
individual with a legally recognized interest he can assert to protect records
about himself when government seeks to acquire them from a third party.
Granting the individual such an interest gives him (and the record keeper) a
basis for limiting voluntary disclosures of such records and forces government to meet certain criteria in order to obtain them. Without such a
protectible interest in his records, an individual given notice, standing, and
the right to challenge a government request for his records would have little
basis for any real challenge, other than to snipe at the facial validity of a
summons or subpoena and to question the government's adherence to the
proper procedural path. A grant of such procedural defense does not really
recognize the privacy interest of the individual; rather, it would create
complexity, delay, and expense for all parties while still leading almost
inevitably to disclosure to the government. While the requirement that
government use formal process and notify the individual when it seeks his
records may provide more effective oversight of government activity,
procedure alone gives the individual no tool to protect himself. So if one
accepts that an individual's bank records are to some extent his private
records, creation of a protectible interest, of a legitimate expectation of
confidentiality in those records, is essential.

One must not assume, however, that simply passing a statute that
provides an individual with a "legitimate expectation of confidentiality" is
enough. As the California experience illustrates, further definition of the
interest is necessary. Since the expectation in California is constitutionally
mandated, the courts there are employing traditional constitutional protections, such as those provided for private papers in the Fourth Amendment,
to define the parameters of the expectation. The Commission, on the other
hand, in areas where it believes such an expectation needs to be created, has
indicated what the definition of that expectation ought to be. For example,
in credit, insurance, and medical record keeping, where the vulnerability to
government access is similar, the Commission has recommended that an
individual be given a legitimate interest in protecting records about him

from unilateral disclosure by the record keeper and, in addition, that he be given a legitimate expectation of confidentiality in such records.

COMPULSORY REPORTING STATUTES

The problems of voluntary disclosure of records and access by government through summons or subpoena do not exhaust the varieties of currently legitimate government access to records about individuals that must be considered in fashioning protections for personal privacy. The number of statutes and regulations that require record keepers to collect, maintain, or report information about certain facets of their relationships with individuals mounts steadily and poses grave long-term dangers. In a few situations, the courts have found such compelled reporting and maintenance of records repugnant to Constitutional strictures on government action. Where a statute requires third-party record keepers, such as financial institutions, to supply information from an individual's records to government, or to maintain certain records for government inspection, however, the courts have not extended the Constitutional protections of the Fourth and Fifth Amendments to those records.[25] They are reluctant to do so largely because they still define the reach of individual interest in terms of ownership or possession of a record. This definition also makes courts uncomfortable with extending protection through the self-incrimination standard of the Fifth Amendment, though they have employed that rationale elsewhere to limit government reporting requirements laid directly on the individual.[26]

As long as there is no limit on government requirements that record keepers routinely report information about an individual, circumscribing voluntary disclosures and creating and defining a legitimate expectation of confidentiality would, in the long run, be a hollow protection for personal privacy. An effective protective umbrella must include limits on the manner and extent of government record keeping and reporting requirements.

SCOPE OF THE COMMISSION'S INQUIRY

The Commission's study of government access to records about individuals held by third parties was not limited to the activities of traditional investigative or law enforcement agencies. The Commission examined, in addition, the reporting requirements government has levied on keepers of records about individuals and also the requirements imposed on record keepers to maintain records open to government inspection. Finally, the Commission reviewed the power given a wide variety of agencies not ordinarily equated with law enforcement to compel the production of records for the purpose of assuring compliance with law or maximum efficiency in the delivery of services. This breadth of inquiry reflected the initial understanding of the Commission, confirmed by its findings, that

---

[25] *Infra*, this Chapter, "Restricting Compulsory Reporting Requirements."
[26] *Infra*, note 125.

information about individuals in the control of one agency tends to become a shared resource, available with little, if any, restriction, to other agencies.

Even with the deliberately wide focus of this study, however, much of the time and resources allocated to the project were spent tracing the practices of investigative agencies. In part, attention to investigative agencies grew out of the traditional concern for abuse in the government's exercise of police powers. The Commission recognized not only that the investigative agencies of government often seem to have an indiscriminate appetite for information about individuals, but also that they tend to be primary exploiters of information held by other agencies for other purposes.

In considering the question of government's exercise of its police powers, one must bear in mind that the ordinary information needs of most agencies of government can be met by seeking information directly from the individual and by inquiries to third parties which the individual authorizes. If a goverment agency satisfies its appetite for information by these means, its appetite can be controlled. Should the government agency act in an improper or unduly intrusive manner, the openness of the process would expose it to remedial action.

Such direct collection occurs where the intent of government is more or less benign; where the concern is supplying a benefit or monitoring compliance with law solely for the purpose of helping people to comply. When government seeks information for the purposes of enforcing compliance with law, however, the agents of government often collect information on their own initiative, through means other than submissions by individuals themselves. Ordinarily, such inquiries are carried out by traditional investigative agencies or by designated investigative or enforcement units of other administrative agencies. These agencies and units can seek the voluntary assistance of third parties who may hold information; or they can employ more powerful tools. The various forms of compulsory legal process, from administrative summons to judicial search warrant, enable agents of government to compel a record keeper to hand over information. On the Federal level, this power is theoretically circumscribed; such inquiries are proper only in response to a statutory command or in the course of investigating violations of statute. In State jurisdictions, investigations of violations of common law also justify the use of compulsory legal process to gather information.[27]

The right of government to mount independent inquiries and employ legal compulsion to secure necessary information is undoubted. The Constitution clearly recognizes the right of government to force the disclosure of information in the Fourth Amendment, but the right recognized is a limited one. The concept of "ordered liberty" which underlies our system of government circumscribes government's right to use its almost unlimited power to compel the production of information.[28] Perplexing and complex problems inherent in this limitation on government

---

[27] Note, "Common Law Crimes in the United State," 47 *Colum. L. Rev.* 1332 (1947).

[28] See *Entick v. Carrington*, 19 State Tr. 1407 (1765); also, *United States v. United States District Court*, 407 U.S. 297 (1972); *Chimel v. California*, 395 U.S. 752 (1969); *Aguilar v. Texas*, 378 U.S. 108 (1964).

information collection powers emerge most clearly in connection with the operation of investigative agencies.

The independent collection capabilities that government traditionally possesses gave rise to the constitutional and legal standards that are the foundations of our ideas about privacy. Such standards limit the process through which government investigators may exercise their collection powers and, to a more limited extent, prohibit government from collecting and using certain sorts of information. In large part, these restrictions on governmental activity grew out of the notion that the state monopoly on violence inherent in the police power has to be controlled—the individual citizen must not be without protection from the unique coercive powers of the state.[29]

Equally important, the voracious appetite of investigators for information causes them to collect and retain virtually any personal data uncovered unless the collection or retention is *clearly* illegitimate. This attention to avoiding what is improper, rather than accomplishing only what is necessary and proper, leads investigative agencies into abuses of citizens' rights.[30] More often than not, such rights are not clearly protected by the Constitution and have not been secured by statute. As explored earlier, for example, an individual's interest in his bank records is virtually unrecognized, nor does an individual have a right not to have records kept about him except where he is being investigated for violations of law or where he participates in the creation of the record.[31] The basic protections for citizens' rights were fashioned before the emergence of modern investigative agencies with their massive record-keeping systems. The actions of such agencies and their information management practices lend themselves to abuses not apparent when the present protections against government intrusion were developed. Nor was the ability of government to compel the reporting of personal information on a routine basis, and the subsequent capacity of investigators to employ such information for inquiries into an individual's activities, a question to which the nation addressed itself when first considering the protection of personal privacy and autonomy.

In this chapter and in the preceding chapters on record keeping in the private sector, the Commission outlines a policy framework for readjusting the mechanisms necessary to preserve the balance between individual liberty and social order in the light of present conditions. While the focus of

---

[29] See 1 *Annals of Congress* 424-450, 660-779; also, Thomas Jefferson, letter to James Madison, Julian Boyd (ed.), *The Papers of Thomas Jefferson* (Princeton: Princeton University Press,1958), Vol. 12, p. 440.

[30] See, e.g., the activities chronicled in *Intelligence Activities and the Rights of Americans: Book II*, Report of the Senate Select Committee on Intelligence Activities, S. Rep. No. 755, 94th Congress, 2d Session (1976), particularly at pp. 139, 142, 173-74, 178-79, 184, 197-98, 204, 220 (hereinafter cited as "U.S. Senate, Intelligence Activities"); also, the almost inevitable overzealousness of law enforcement investigators has been noted by the Supreme Court frequently, see, e.g., *Johnson v. United States*, 333 U.S. 10, 13-14 (1948); *Aquilar v. Texas*, 378 U.S. 108 (1964).

[31] The Privacy Act of 1974 attempts to set some limits, 5 U.S.C. 552a(e)(1), (e)(2), (e)(7), but, in light of certain exceptions to those limits, the requirements of the Act place few clear limitations on the practices of law enforcement agencies, see 5 U.S.C. 552a(e)(7), (j), (k); also, Chapter 13.

the Commission's attention in this area has been the Federal government, the broad public policy and specific recommendations presented in this chapter are, in the estimation of the Commission, equally applicable to State and local government.

ELEMENTS OF AN EXPECTATION OF CONFIDENTIALITY

PROHIBITING VOLUNTARY DISCLOSURE

In several areas of its inquiry, the Commission attempted to identify records about an individual kept by third parties in which it believes the individual should have a legitimate expectation of confidentiality—a right to expect that such records or the information in them would not ordinarily be disclosed without his consent. The Commission found that certain financial, insurance, and medical records fall in this category.[32] The Commission also believes that other areas of private activity, which could not be studied as carefully, create records outside the possession of the individual which deserve protection, one example being telephone toll records.

While toll records are not analogous, as checking account records are, to "private papers" within the meaning of the Fourth Amendment, they provide independent documentation of communications which, before the telephone, were considered uniquely private in character.[33] Indeed, our present legal system severely restricts access to the contents of such communications.[34] Since the mere fact of communication is often as revealing as the content, the Commission believes that toll records should be protected as well. The American Telephone and Telegraph Company has, in fact, already taken a step in that direction by refusing to disclose toll records in all but a few instances unless a subpoena commands it.[35] Moreover, telephone toll records are but one example of areas of record keeping that may be deserving of protection but into which the Commission did not have time to delve.

Whatever the record about an individual, however, if it is determined to be one in which a legitimate expectation of confidentiality should exist, then to secure that expectation the record keeper must be put under a duty not to disclose the information in the record without the consent of the individual unless required to do so by legal process or government reporting requirements. Simply saying that a record keeper may not disclose voluntarily, however, is not enough. Real protection demands that the individual have the means to prevent improper disclosures by a record keeper and secure redress against a record keeper who violates the basic

---

[32] See Chapters 2, 3, 5, and 7.

[33] See Alan F. Westin, *Privacy and Freedom*, (N.Y.: Atheneum, 1967) p. 330; *Commonwealth v. Lovett*, 4 Clark 5 (Pa., 1831).

[34] *Berger v. New York*, 388 U.S. 41 (1967); *Katz v. United States*, 389 U.S. 347 (1967); 18 U.S.C. 2510 *et seq.*

[35] Except in so-called "national security" situations; see Testimony of American Telephone and Telegraph Company, Credit-Card Issuers Hearings, February 12, 1976, pp. 46-50; letter from H.W. William Caming, Attorney, AT&T, to the Privacy Protection Study Commission, August 13, 1976, p. 2.

expectation of confidentiality. To an extent, the mode for obtaining such redress is set out in the Commission's recommendations regarding particular areas of record keeping. A critical further step is clear definition of the individual's legal interest in the record, of his expectation of confidentiality as it applies to the question of voluntary disclosure by the record keeper.

Under existing law, when documentary information is voluntarily supplied to law enforcement personnel in the course of investigation, such as wage records provided by an employer, the subject of such documentary evidence is presumed not to have a legal interest in the records. As the Supreme Court has noted, personnel files and the like are "records in which the . . . [individual] has no proprietary interest of any kind, which are owned by the third person, which are in his [third person's] hands, and which relate to the third person's transaction" with the individual.[36] For these reasons, the record keeper's right to volunteer the information in its records to the government is currently unrestricted.[37] Even documents obtained illegally by private parties, if acquired without government knowledge or complicity, may be turned over to and used by the government.[38]

As explored earlier in this chapter, and in several other sections of this report, not only is the record keeper free to disclose as a matter of theory, record keepers in sectors such as banking and credit make a practice of disclosing account information voluntarily to government agents. The Commission's survey of credit-card issuers and their disclosure practices confirmed testimony to this effect received during the Commission's hearings.[39] Representatives of Federal investigative agencies themselves corroborated the Commission findings that, with the exception of requests for telephone toll records and the records maintained by a limited number of banks, most of the requests they make for records are complied with informally. Frequently, government agencies maintain informal liaison with credit companies and banks to facilitate the flow of account information.[40]

These findings reinforce the conclusion that only when an individual can claim a legal interest equal to the California standard of a legitimate expectation of privacy is voluntary disclosure of his records by third-party record keepers securely limited. Recognition of such a legal interest places clear responsibility on the record keeper to assure against improper disclosure, to government or anyone else. If information is improperly disclosed, in other words, the record keeper is liable for damages or susceptible to injunctive relief. The fact that the record keeper is liable for improper disclosures of information held confidentially, however, does not mean that the government may use informal coercion to force "voluntary" disclosure, thus escaping liability. Indeed, if government were to coerce

---

[36] *Donaldson v. United States*, 400 U.S. 517 (1971).
[37] *Infra*, this Chapter, "Regulating the Compelled Production of Records."
[38] *Burdeau v. McDowell*, 256 U.S. 465 (1921).
[39] *Supra*, notes 15-19; Chapter 2, "The Consumer Credit-Relationship"; also, the ease with which government agents gain access to private records held by third parties was confirmed in interviews with officials of Federal investigative agencies conducted by Commission staff.
[40] Staff interviews with Special Agents of the Federal Bureau of Investigation, at Headquarters, Washington, D.C. on January 6, 1977.

disclosure, there would be little equity in holding the record keeper responsible. The Commission believes that as a corollary to prohibitions on voluntary disclosure by record keepers, stringent penalties should be established for inducing a record keeper or its employees to disclose information in which an individual has an expectation of confidentiality. Such an enforcement scheme should include the right to initiate an individual civil damage action against anyone who induces the breach of an expectation of confidentiality in records. The scheme should extend sanctions to all persons, not simply government agents.

A record keeper's duty not to disclose recorded information in which an individual has a legitimate expectation of confidentiality should not prohibit every disclosure. Obviously, there are circumstances in which the record keeper should have the discretion, or even the duty, to disclose. If the record subject injures the record keeper, for example, information may be disclosed by the record keeper to establish the fact of injury or to assist those investigating the injury. Protecting privacy does not mean completely insulating an individual; if he violates the terms of his relationship with a credit-card issuer, for example, he must be prepared to accept the costs of injury to that financial agent. In such circumstances, the record keeper should be free to disclose information about the individual necessary to assure full compensation for the injury and proper application of the law.

In addition, if a record keeper becomes aware from information generated in its relationship with an individual that he is engaged in illegal activity, then the record keeper should be under some obligation to disclose that information to proper authorities, as would any other citizen. For example, if a bank holds confidential documentary information which indicates that an individual is engaged in illegal transfers of funds to a foreign nation, the bank might be implicated as an accessory if one of its officers were aware of the transfer and the bank did not report it.[41] It is not the intent of the Commission to create a new testimonial privilege for bankers, insurers, or anyone else. Rather, the Commission seeks to fashion protection for *documentary* information about individuals which, were it not for Twentieth Century changes in social and economic organization, would have remained the private and protectible records of the individual. The observations of the record keeper and his employees concerning the actions of the individual which appear to be illegal are not, in the Commission's opinion, protectible information.

Finally, as outlined in the credit, depository, insurance, and medical records recommendations of the Commission, certain disclosures by the record keeper are necessary to maintain properly the relationship between record keeper and individual. Within the context of the prior notice provisions and redisclosure safeguards recommended in the chapters

---

[41] e.g., 18 U.S.C. 4; also, *Tournier v. National Provincial Union Bank* (1924), 1 K. 461, 473, 481 (C.A.).

dealing with those types of records, the Commission recognizes the legitimacy of such disclosures.[42]

A prohibition on voluntary disclosure provides the first element in the design of the expectation of confidentiality which the Commission recommends for certain records. To secure this first portion of the legal barrier that will protect records about an individual from improper incursion by government and others, the Commission recommends that as a general rule a private-sector record keeper maintaining records in which an individual has a legitimate expectation of confidentiality should not disclose information from such records without the consent of the individual, except under the specific circumstances discussed in the last few pages and articulated in the separate recommendations relating to each area of private-sector record keeping.

Concurrent with this limitation, the Commission, of course, recommends restrictions on how government may go about obtaining information about individuals from third-party record keepers. Those limitations on government access will be discussed below.

REGULATING THE COMPELLED PRODUCTION OF RECORDS

We thus conclude that under the statutes here applicable . . . that today that which we have previously considered to be administrative fishing expeditions are often permitted; and that administrative subpoenas may be enforced for investigative purposes unless they are plainly incompetent or irrelevant to any lawful purpose.[43]

The quotation above from a recent opinion of the United States Court of Appeals for the Tenth Circuit symbolizes the relative ease with which the Federal government today may compel the production of records about individuals. Whatever the scope or purpose of a subpoena, be it an administrative or judicial summons, compulsory process to obtain documentary information about an individual from a third party who maintains a record about, or on behalf of, that individual is virtually unchallengeable. Equally important from the perspective of safeguarding individual rights, certain portions of the process by which some judicial or administrative summons may be issued need reconsideration.

Though the Commission is most directly concerned with problems engendered by government access to records about individuals held by third parties, this examination of summons and subpoena power pays more than passing attention to the procedure by which any compulsory process is issued, whether to the individual or to an independent record holder. In large part, this scope of inquiry is appropriate because distinguishing between types of legal process on the basis of who receives the process would be spurious in procedural terms.

The processes of compulsion at the Federal level which the Commis-

---

[42] See Chapter 2, *Recommendation (12)*; Chapter 3, *Recommendation (8)*, Chapter 5, *Recommendation (17)*, Chapter 7, *Recommendation (10)*.

[43] *EEOC v. University of New Mexico*, 504 F.2d 1296, 1301 (10th Cir. 1974).

sion scrutinized fall into three broad categories: (1) administrative summons, (2) judicial subpoenas in the course of litigation, and (3) Grand Jury
subpoenas. These and the search warrant are the forms of legal process the
Federal government uses to compel the production of records or testimony.
The Commission is well aware of the bewildering variety of administrative
tools, from "inspection warrants" to "subpoenas," which fall under the
umbrella term, "summons." But as the discussion below explains, the
Commission found good reason to treat all such processes similarly.

Before examining the forms of administrative summons and judicial
subpoena, however, two questions must be disposed of: the definition of an
individual's legal interest in records which he has a right to consider
confidential; and, the rationale of the Commission in not including the use
of the search warrant in its considerations.

DEFINITION OF AN INDIVIDUAL'S LEGAL INTEREST

As the earlier portions of this chapter illustrate, an individual currently
has no legally recognized interest in certain records about him, though these
records may be ones in which the Commission has found that he ought to
have an expectation of confidentiality.[44] Without that legal interest, or
"legitimate expectation of privacy" as the courts have termed it, the
individual has no basis to challenge access to those records by government;
that is, no ability to protect his expectation of confidentiality. Whether
access to information about an individual is demanded by Grand Jury
subpoena to a bank,[45] by administrative summons to an accountant or
employer,[46] or by a subpoena during litigation directed to third parties, the
individual is without standing to contest and, even if he were given standing,
without substantive protections, constitutional or statutory, which he might
assert.

Attempts to provide the individual with protection through mere
procedural reform are, unfortunately, ineffective. The Tax Reform Act of
1976,[47] for example, provides a mechanism that was meant to help
individuals protect records in third-party hands from the administrative
summons of the IRS. The mechanism, however, does not accomplish that
purpose (though it does provide means for oversight of agency activity by
other institutions). The Tax Reform Act requires the IRS to give an
individual notice that a summons has been served on a third-party record
keeper and allows the individual both to stop the record keeper from
complying until a hearing is held and to intervene in any hearing or
enforcement proceeding. Such a notice, with standing and nothing more,
while it may deter baseless investigative activity, gives the individual little
with which to impede IRS access. In short, the recent amendments to the tax
code do not alter the inability of an individual to protect records about him
held by third parties, even in the limited context of IRS summonses. To be

---

[44] *Supra*, notes 10, 42.
[45] *United States v. Miller*, 425 U.S. 435 (1976).
[46] *Couch v. United States*, 409 U.S. 322 (1973); *Donaldson v. United States*, 400 U.S. 517 (1971).
[47] 26 U.S.C. 7609.

sure, the individual may go into court, but when he gets there he has nothing to say, because he has no legal interest to defend or to balance against the government's desire for the record.

The rationale for leaving the individual helpless in this situation was best articulated in the *Miller* decision; because he does not possess and control the records, the individual has no "proprietary" interest in them and, thus, no protectible legal interest of any sort, at least against the government.[48]

The emphasis the Supreme Court laid on the possessory relationship of the individual to the record in *Miller*, however, need not frustrate efforts to fashion a legally protectible interest for the individual. Previous Supreme Court decisions, in fact, had suggested that such an interest might be found. In *Donaldson v. United States*,[49] the Court rejected an employee's attempt to challenge an IRS summons for certain employment records because the summons was not directed to records "in the hands of anyone with whom the taxpayer had a confidential relationship of any kind"; the records sought were ones "in which the taxpayer has no proprietary interest of any kind, which are owned by the third person, which are in his [the third person's] hands, and which relate to the third person's business transactions with the taxpayer."[50] In short, the records sought were not held by someone from whom the individual might claim any duty to hold the record in confidence.[51] The Court did not, in *Donaldson*, restrict the possible reach of the individual's interest to possession alone. In a line of cases which the Court distinguishes from those involving records,[52] it recognized an interest in information not possessed or controlled by the individual.

Rejecting the notion that geographic suzerainty or a "proprietary" interest is necessary to protect communications from interception without a search warrant, the Supreme Court indicated in *Katz v. United States* that even without such traditional interests an individual had a legitimate expectation of privacy.[53] The Court noted that "the premise that property interests control the right of the government to search and seize has been discredited."[54] Thus, a legal and logical basis exists for recognizing an individual interest in records about him held by third parties, but the parameters of that interest have yet to be defined.

In the definition emerging as the California courts apply that State's constitutional protection for a "legitimate expectation of privacy" in bank records, the Commission sees the outline of the protectible legal interest that

---

[48] Against a private party, he may have some interest, in contract or through certain "common law" expectations; see *Milovich v. First Nat'l Bank*, 224 So.2d 759 (Fla. Ct. App. 1969); *Sparks v. Union Trust Co.*, 256 N.C. 478 (1962); *Peterson v. Idaho First National Bank*, 83 Idaho 578 (1961); also, *Brex v. Smith*, 104 N.J. Eq. 386 (1929).

[49] 400 U.S. 517 (1971).

[50] *Ibid.*, at 523.

[51] *Supra*, note 5.

[52] *Warden v. Hayden*, 387 U.S. 294, 304 (1967); *Berger v. New York*, 388 U.S. 41 (1967); *Katz v. United States*, 389 U.S. 347 (1967); for the distinction of "records" from "communications," see *Couch v. United States*, 409 U.S. 322 (1973); *United States v. Miller*, 425 U.S. 435 (1976); *Fischer v. United States*, 425 U.S. 391 (1976).

[53] 389 U.S. 347 (1967).

[54] Citing *Warden v. Hayden*, 387 U.S. 294 (1967).

will safeguard the individual while permitting the effective enforcement of law necessary for an ordered society. While the legal expectation enjoyed by an individual in California was first recognized in 1974 in *Burrows v. Superior Court*,[55] the substance of that expectation did not begin to emerge clearly until a year later in *Carlson v. Superior Court*.[56] Giving content to the expectation recognized by the California Supreme Court in *Burrows*, the California Court of Appeals (4th District) ruled that, "law enforcement officials may not gain access to an accused's private papers [in this case, bank records] by subpoena until there has been a judicial determination that there is probable cause to believe he has committed a criminal offense and that the papers and documents described in the subpoena would be material evidence in the case."[57] In other words, the Court of Appeals suggested that the State must establish both probable cause to believe a crime has been committed and the relevance of the records sought to that crime before the privacy interest of the individual in the records can be overborne.

The Commission endorses this approach, believing that records in which an individual has an expectation of confidentiality should not be accessible to government unless a compelling governmental interest, outweighing the individual's interest to be free from government intrusion, can be shown.

RECOMMENDATIONS

The first step in securing such an expectation was examined earlier in this chapter—the record keeper maintaining a confidential record must be placed under a duty not to disclose the record without the consent of the individual, except in certain limited circumstances. The specific limitations placed on record keepers in such areas as financial services,[58] medical care and insurance are set out elsewhere in this report.[59] Coupled with these obligations on third-party record keepers must be certain limitations on government action and certain rights which the individual can assert. Thus, as the second step in securing the expectation of confidentiality, the Commission recommends:

Recommendation (1):

That Congress provide an individual by statute with an expectation of confidentiality in a record identifiable to him maintained by a private-sector record keeper in its provision of financial services, medical-care, insurance, or telecommunications services, which statute should specifically require that the individual, in defense against compelled

---

[55] 13 Cal.3d 238 (1974).
[56] 129 Cal. Rptr. 650 (1976).
[57] *Ibid.*, at 655.
[58] The terms "financial service" and "financial institution" should be understood to mean those services and institutions covered by the recommendations of the Commission in Chapter 2, "Consumer-Credit Relationship," and Chapter 3, "The Depository Relationship."
[59] See Chapter 2, *Recommendation (12)*; Chapter 3, *Recommendation (8)*; Chapter 5, *Recommendation (17)*; Chapter 7, *Recommendation (10)*.

production of such a record pursuant to any administrative, judicial, or legislative summons, subpoena, or similar order be permitted—

(a)   to challenge the relevance and scope of the summons, subpoena, or order and to require from the government clear proof of the reasonable relationship of the record sought to the investigation, prosecution, or civil action in furtherance of which the summons, subpoena, or order was issued before a court may order disclosure of the record; and

(b)   to assert in protection of the record the protections for private papers and effects articulated in the Fourth Amendment, and the due process protections articulated in the Fifth Amendment, to the Constitution of the United States.

The Commission recognizes that the recommended measure does not reach fully the level of protection afforded an individual under California law. Section (b) of the recommendation creates a standard that may amount to somewhat less than probable cause; what the Commission recommends may not raise all requests for bank, credit, insurance, or health records to the level of a search warrant.[60] At the very least, however, it will force government to establish reasonable cause to believe that the record is relevant to prosecution of a violation of law before the legitimate expectation of the individual can be overridden.[61]

SEARCH WARRANTS

Turning from the definition of the legal substance of an individual's expectation of confidentiality, the question of search warrants can now be reviewed briefly. The protections against abuse of the search warrant by government officials are articulated in the Fourth Amendment to the Constitution.[62] For a magistrate to issue a warrant, the government must establish probable cause and describe with specificity the place to be searched and the materials to be seized. Although, in the search warrant situation, the individual has no opportunity to contest seizure of the records beforehand, he may be able to suppress the use of the information afterward, since government must meet the requirements of the Fourth

---

[60] See *Andresen v. Maryland,* 427 U.S. 463 (1976); *Beckwith v. United States,* 425 U.S. 321 (1976); *Fisher v. United States,* 425 U.S. 391 (1976); *United States v. Bisceglia,* 420 U.S. 141 (1975); given that an individual will have the right to challenge the summons before it can be enforced, a relativistic balancing test of government need and individual right will surely emerge, rather than a strict standard such as probable cause being placed on government.

[61] If the standards of *Bisceglia* and *EEOC v. University of New Mexico* are to be tightened at all, this is the minimum test government would have to meet.

[62] *The right of people to be secure in their persons, houses, papers, and effects, against unreasonable searches and seizures, shall not be violated, and no warrants shall issue, but upon probable cause, supported by Oath or affirmation, and particularly describing the place to be searched, and the persons and things to be seized. U.S. Const.,* amend. IV.

Amendment in order to employ the fruits of the warrant as well as to procure it.[63] Should the government act in violation of the constitutional strictures, clear channels for redress exist.[64] To the extent that requiring government to present a compelling need for a particular record helps secure an individual's expectation of confidentiality, the search warrant provides adequate protections.

Given probable cause, however, the government may employ a search warrant today to seize virtually any record about an individual, whether held by the individual or by a third party. No longer do there seem to be any personal documents inaccessible to government because they reveal "intimate areas of personal affairs."[65] The notion has vanished that some documents are as deserving of absolute protections as are the utterances protected absolutely through the combined strictures of the Fourth and Fifth Amendments.[66] Today, whatever a person may write down, to prepare his taxes or settle his mind, meant for only a few others or for no one else's eyes, government can have if government acts through the proper procedures. While this element of contemporary constitutional interpretation does not unduly disturb the Commission in regard to the records about individuals ordinarily kept by third parties in the course of a confidential relationship with an individual, such as bank records, the idea that papers in the hands of the individual have no sanctity is troubling. The Commission focused on more or less formalized record keeping in its study; it is unsure of how to go about defining the sort of papers that should be inviolate in the hands of the individual but urges the Congress, the courts, and legal scholars to continue working to resolve this issue and to mark out a clearer zone of impenetrable personal privacy.

Having proposed that the individual's interest in certain records be legally recognized, and having suggested that certain records which are personally held may need absolute protections, the Commission turned its attention to the procedures, legal and practical, by which government exercises its power to compel access to records.

PROHIBITION ON INFORMAL ACCESS

Returning for a moment to the question of informal access to personal records by government, the Commission's study showed that a wide variety of records about individuals are revealed to government without leaving a

---

[63] See *Mapp v. Ohio*, 367 U.S. 643 (1961); *Bivens v. Six Unknown Named Agents*, 403 U.S. 388 (1971); Oaks, "Studying the Exclusionary Rule in Search and Seizure," 37 *U. Chi. L. Rev.* 665 (1970); also *Katz v. United States*, 389 U.S. 347 (1967); *United States v. United States District Court*, 407 U.S. 297 (1972); see further (re: force and fraud), *Ker v. California*, 374 U.S. 23 (1963).

[64] *Mapp v. Ohio*, 367 U.S. 643 (1961); *Bivens v. Six Unknown Named Agents*, 403 U.S. 388 (1971).

[65] See *Andresen v. Maryland*, 427 U.S. 463 (1976); *Fischer v. United States*, 425 U.S. 391 (1976); *Boyd v. United States*, 116 U.S. 616 (1886); Note, "Formalism, Legal Realism . . .," 90 *Harv. L. Rev.* 945.

[66] See *Boyd v. United States*, 116 U.S. 616 (1886); and Note, "Formalism, Legal Realism. . ." 90 *Harv. L. Rev.* 945.

record that the disclosure was made and without the individual ever being aware of the disclosure.[67] While documentation of such disclosures will not directly help the individual protect his records, it will help in discovering improper or excessive acquisition of information by government. Access by Federal investigators to the records of private associations, retailers, employers, or local government agencies, for example, where government need not use compulsory process because there is no expectation of confidentiality, could be monitored. Such public documentation and consequent ability to monitor investigative collection activities may help to avert the dangers of clandestine compilation of unnecessary records such as those discovered in 1976 by the Senate Select Committee on Intelligence Activities.[68] To effect such documentation of government requests for personal records, the Commission, therefore, recommends:

Recommendation (2):

That any request for an individually identifiable record made to a private-sector record keeper or agency of another government jurisdiction by a government agency or its agents be made only through recognized legal process, such as an administrative summons or judicial subpoena, unless the request is made with the consent of the individual to whom the record pertains.

The Commission does not intend through this recommendation to cut off an investigator's ability to seek the testimony of parties with whom an individual under investigation may have had contact; nor does it want to eliminate the ability of the retailer, for example, to refresh his memory of contact with an individual from his own records. When government seeks a *copy* of a record, such as the charge record from a gas station or the hotel's copy of a guest's bill, it would have to use legal process. The Commission sees no reason why government should not leave a paper trail of its investigation just as the individual in our society leaves a trail of his activities. The value of personal records to agencies investigating the legitimacy of an individual's conduct suggests that similar documentation of government information collection activities will be equally valuable for investigating and assessing the legitimacy of governmental conduct. Finally, it should be recognized that requiring government to use legal process to obtain individually identifiable records does not mean that the individual can halt such access or create delays where he has no legitimate expectation of confidentiality in the record.

What are those forms of process which government must employ to obtain records, however; and, what limits does the Commission recommend placing on them? As outlined at the beginning of this section, government moves to obtain documentary evidence through three basic forms of process: administrative summons, judicial subpoena in the course of

---

[67] *Supra,* notes 15-19, 35, 40.
[68] U.S. Senate, *Intelligence Activities,* generally pp. 137-288.

litigation, and Grand Jury subpoena. There are common elements in the way the three are issued.

THE SUBPOENA AND SUMMONS

A subpoena or summons is simply a form which a government agent or attorney fills in to show who is commanded to appear, with what document or testimony, when, and where. For an administrative summons, the form is prepared by the agency for which the official filling it out works. For a judicial or Grand Jury subpoena, the form is obtained simply by asking the clerk of a district court for a blank. U.S. Attorney's offices, for example, often have boxes of blank Grand Jury subpoenas on hand. After it is filled in, the subpoena or summons is delivered to the person to whom it is directed, or the "addressee," who may comply with it, and, if he wishes, hand over the records requested immediately or as soon as he can get them together. The addressee, however, may decide not to comply with the request. If he refuses, the government must then take the matter before a magistrate if it wants to compel the addressee to disclose the specified information. At that point the addressee can challenge the propriety of the subpoena, either on the grounds of procedural deformity or on the basis of some protected legal interest he has in the information. The magistrate then determines the validity of the subpoena or summons and, if valid, orders the addressee to produce the information or be punished by fine or imprisonment. As this synopsis illustrates, the executive agency or investigator issues and delivers a summons or subpoena without prior judicial supervision or even knowledge; supervision comes into play only if the subpoena is challenged and there is a legally recognized basis for that challenge.[69]

If personal records are in the possession of the individual, as they usually were when the subpoena process developed,[70] a subpoena does not threaten the confidentiality of those records unduly. The individual could go into court and seek to stop unwarranted government seizure of his records. With so many personal records not within the individual's possession, and with the courts generally refusing to recognize the interest of the individual in records he does not possess, the subpoena and summons allow government to seize personal records without the possible intervention or even knowledge of the individual. Nor does the process allow the record keeper to assert a privacy interest for the individual or to raise questions which go much beyond whether the subpoena was filled out properly.[71] In effect, the subpoena has become a tool that government agents can use to seize the records of an individual without being required either to give him an opportunity to dispute this action before his privacy is invaded or to

---

[69] See, e.g., *United States v. Miller*, 425 U.S. 435 (1976); *Donaldson v. United States*, 400 U.S. 517 (1971); *United States v. Powell*, 379 U.S. 48 (1964).

[70] Theodore F.T. Plucknett, *A Concise History of the Common Law*, (5th Ed., Boston: 1956), pp. 683-684.

[71] *California Bankers Assn. v. Schultz*, 416 U.S. 21, 53 (1974); *United States v. First Nat'l Bank of Mobile*, 295 F.142, 143 (S.D.Ala. 1924), *aff'd, per curiam*, 267 U.S. 576 (1925).

establish a reasonable basis for the seizure (i.e., probable cause) before an impartial magistrate.[72] The protections of the Fourth Amendment against unreasonable search and seizure, meant to give individuals the assurance that the executive could not act in a high-handed and unchecked manner, seem to have been superseded. The procedures by which the various forms of subpoena and summons are issued tend to exacerbate this problem of unreviewed executive action. Government investigators today may decide what information they need and seize it without prior outside supervision.

THE ADMINISTRATIVE SUMMONS

The Commission reviewed more than 160 separate statutes which empower Federal authorities to compel the production of documents or records.[73] Though this sample represented a large proportion of the statutes granting some sort of summons power at the Federal level, it was by no means exhaustive.

The procedures by which administrative summons power is exercised ordinarily parallel those for issuing, serving, and adjudicating challenges to a judicial subpoena, whether the summons power is provided by statute to conduct investigations or to assist in adjudication of claims before an administrative tribunal. The term "administrative summons" as employed in this report, however, also encompasses broad record inspection powers under which an agency need employ no document to gain access to a record, at least so far as the statutory grant of power is concerned.[74]

Whatever the nature of the summons power in a particular case, however, the Commission found that it is uniformly given to administrative bodies who have enforcement or oversight responsibilities—in other words, to virtually every agency of government. The reach of such summons power is restricted to the compulsion of information which is arguably relevant to carrying out an agency's responsibilities.[75] The restriction, however, need not mean much. An IRS summons issued in a tax investigation, for example, may reach to any conceivable record about an individual. As U.S. Supreme Court Justice Stewart noted in reviewing IRS summons power in 1975,

virtually all persons or objects in this country may, of course, have Federal tax problems. Everyday the economy generates thousands of sales, loans, gifts, purchases, leases, deposits, mergers, wills, and

---

[72] See particularly the discussion of the use of the Grand Jury Subpoena *infra*.

[73] Most of the statutes reviewed were the product of a computer search conducted for the Privacy Protection Study Commission by the Congressional Research Service of the Library of Congress. A few of the statutes examined were obtained through manual research by Commission staff. Throughout this section of the text on Administrative Summons, the statutes cited in notes ordinarily will be examples of statutory structure and language rather than an exhaustive list of all Federal statutes which might illustrate the point at issue.

[74] 15 U.S.C. 49; 21 U.S.C. 880.

[75] The tenuous nature of the relevance which is necessary is illustrated in *United States v. Powell*, 379 U.S. 48 (1964); also, *FTC v. Texaco, Inc.*, 517 F.2d 137, 170 (D. C. Cir., 1975).

the like which suggest the possibility of tax problems for somebody. Our economy is tax relevant in almost every detail.[76]

The sources which may authorize the issuance of the summons run the gamut from the majority of the members of a governmental agency to any person designated by the highest official of the agency. Statutes grant the right to issue a summons to the following: agency, committee, subcommittee; chairman, president; vice-chairman, nondesignated committee member, designated committee member; designated department head, designated officer, designated representative, designated employee; examiner, claims agent, collections agent, appraiser, proper United States attorney, attorney representing the government, any agent of the FBI, any designated employee of any State, territory, or political subdivision; or, any designated person.[77]

Few of the statutes specify who must sign a summons in order for it to issue. The laws which do specify most often delegate the power to the chairman (or other head official) or individuals he may designate. Some statutes also go so far as to mention who may deliver the summons, but most of those simply permit delivery by any individual whom the issuer designates.[78] There is no statutory attempt to keep the power to issue a summons in the hands of those with supervisory responsibilities.

The range of records which may be compelled by an administrative summons is also broad. Many statutes simply grant the power of subpoena or of subpoena *duces tecum* without elaboration.[79] Others add such brief, general descriptions as "information," "records," or "documentary evidence." Others enumerate lengthy lists of compellable evidence, e.g., "books, papers, schedule of charges, contracts, agreements, or documents." The most common combination of words used in statutes is the phrase "books, papers and documents."[80]

A few statutes, but only a few, establish express limitations on summons power by excluding certain records from the reach of the summons. For example, the enabling legislation of the Food and Drug Administration gives broad powers to inspect records which are required to be kept by law and related documents, but specifically excludes financial data, sales data other than shipment data, or pricing data.[81] Ordinarily when statutes specify direct limitations on the summons power, they only reiterate common law or constitutional principles which would be applicable anyway, reaffirming preexisting limitations. In contrast, a few statutes establish additional procedural rights and set forth requirements of nondisclosure.[82]

The rare statute that prohibits disclosure does so to protect confiden-

---

[76] *United States v. Bisceglia*, 420 U.S. 141, 154 (1975) (Stewart, J., dissenting).
[77] 22 U.S.C. 1623; 12 U.S.C. 1464(d)(9); 7 U.S.C. 15, 115, and 136d; 15 U.S.C. 1173; 42 U.S.C. 405.
[78] 15 U.S.C. 4a.
[79] 12 U.S.C. 1464(d)(9).
[80] Over 20 percent of the statutes reviewed employed that phrase.
[81] 21 U.S.C. 880.
[82] 7 U.S.C. 87f; 18 U.S.C. 1968; 21 U.S.C. 374; 29 U.S.C. 161.

tial subject matter or trade secrets. In addition, the Freedom of Information Act articulates several reasons which justify a refusal to disclose specifically requested information. These statutes limit the conditions under which disclosure may be made. At least one permits disclosure to anyone if dissemination will aid the individual who gave the information.[83] Under most of the statutes granting summons power, however, the executive agency has virtually unlimited discretion to determine what information is sufficiently confidential or private to trigger nondisclosure requirements.[84]

In a majority of cases where statutory language limits the summons power, a broad "reasonableness" standard is employed. The statutes mandate that a summons be reasonable with respect to particularity, timeliness, and relevance (e.g., location, identity of custodian, good faith belief that the individual possesses the records). Fair housing legislation provides one example:

> The Secretary (of HUD) shall grant the petition (of the witness) if he finds that the subpoena requires appearance or attendance at an unreasonable time or place, that it requires production of evidence which does not relate to any matter under investigation, that it does not describe with sufficient particularity the evidence to be produced, that compliance would be onerous, or for other good reason.[85]

Some five percent of the statues reviewed contained this kind of limitation.

Rather than limiting administrative summons power, many statutes expand its reach even beyond the range permitted through judicial subpoena power. They increase government's ability to obtain information by restricting the scope of privileges, broadening inspection powers, increasing protection of informants, and offering preferential treatment for the agency seeking the information.[86] As discussed later in connection with government information reporting and record-keeping requirements, the statutory expansion of administrative ability to compel disclosure of information includes the power to enter and inspect records without even the formality of an official piece of paper.[87]

In effect, the scope and use of administrative summons power is left largely to administrative discretion. While most administrative summons do not appear to have been misused, only the goodwill and restraint of the innumerable officials empowered to issue and administer summons protect an individual from abuse. Unfortunately, some abuses of power have occurred.

The agents of the Internal Revenue Service, for example, have

---

[83] 45 U.S.C. 362.

[84] A few statutes do modify this ability by permitting the individual who is compelled to provide information to initiate an agency determination regarding what information may not be disclosed, though ordinarily only in the context of trade secret and similar information. See, e.g., 50 U.S.C. App. 6430.

[85] 42 U.S.C. 3611.

[86] 12 U.S.C. 1784; 15 U.S.C. 155.

[87] *Supra*, note 74.

exercised their power to issue summons in questionable and improper ways.[88] Former Commissioner Alexander attempted to prevent further abuses by restructuring the internal procedures for the issuance of a summons. At the same time, similar misuse of process by other agencies has not led to internal reform.[89] Even were administrative reform comprehensive, however, the individual cannot be sure of protection unless the Congress acts. Dependence on the restraint of executive officers alone is perilous.[90]

In addition to the dangers cited, the possibility of information flowing indiscriminately from the agency acquiring it to others leads to abuses of the administrative summons power. It is not only the information produced through reporting requirements which circulates widely within government; information obtained by agencies through their summons power for a specific purpose also flows to other agencies for unrelated use. As former Deputy Attorney General Tyler indicated to the Commission, information in the hands of the IRS, whether compelled through a reporting requirement or the summons power, is viewed as a general governmental resource.[91]

The courts have not acted to restrain the scope of administrative summons power, although some judges have expressed discomfort with the notion that "unreviewed executive discretion" may result in disclosure of records of "intimate areas of personal affairs" which could violate an individual's legitimate expectation of privacy.[92] However uncomfortable they may be, though, judges, especially the Supreme Court, have endorsed the expanding reach of administrative summons power.[93] Virtually no individually identifiable record in the control of a third-party record keeper is immune from an administrative summons; and, the individual is without a legally recognized interest which he may assert to protect a record about himself, even if it is a bank, credit, employment, insurance, or medical record. Furthermore, the present ability of government to compel disclosure of records administratively is so broad and ill-defined in scope that it permits what the Tenth Circuit characterized as "fishing expeditions" and what Justice Stewart has suggested is compulsory process based on "sheer speculation."[94]

In order to minimize the dangers created by the current unrestricted and ill-defined administrative summons power of Federal agencies, and to return to the individual some measure of control over records about him held by third parties, the Commission recommends:

---

[88] *Supra*, notes 15, 16, 18.

[89] Testimony of the Internal Revenue Service, Depository and Lending Institutions Hearings, April 22, 1976, pp. 785-86; *The New York Times*, April 20, 1975, IV, p. 4:5; June 11, 1975, p. 29:6; June 21, 1975, p. 1:5; also, S. Rep. No. 938, 94th Cong., 2d Sess., pp. 368-369 (1976).

[90] U.S. Senate, *Intelligence Activities*, pp. 14-15.

[91] Testimony of the Deputy Attorney General, United States Department of Justice, *Federal Tax Return Confidentiality*, Hearings before the Privacy Protection Study Commission, March 11, 1976, pp. 63-65.

[92] *California Bankers Assn. v. Schultz*, 416 U.S. 21, 78 (1975) (Powell, J., concurring).

[93] See, e.g., *United States v. Bisceglia*, 420 U.S. 141 (1975).

[94] *Ibid.*, at 158 (Stewart, J., dissenting); *EEOC v. University of New Mexico*, 504 F.2d 1296, 1301 (10th Cir. 1974).

Recommendation (3):

That Congress provide by statute that an administrative summons (or other form of compulsory legal process) issued by an administrative or executive authority of government to a private-sector record keeper in order to inspect or obtain an individually identifiable record shall be issued only

(a)   for the inspection of a record required to be maintained pursuant to a statute or regulation, or

(b)   for the investigation of violations of law where the evidence obtained by such administrative summons (or other form of compulsory process) will be used only for administrative action, civil enforcement, or criminal prosecution directly related to the statutory purposes for which such summons power was granted, except, where evidence of unrelated criminal activity is uncovered, the existence of such activity may be reported to a proper investigating authority who may then proceed to obtain such information from the record keeper pursuant to whatever legal processes are at its command; and

(c)   where a copy of the administrative summons is served by the administrative or executive authority of government upon an individual who (i) is, or is likely to become, the subject of investigation or enforcement proceedings, and (ii) is the subject of the record to be produced,

(d)   where the issuance of such a summons may only be made by officials of the issuing agency who are not field agents and who exercise supervisory authority and responsibility over the agents who will serve the summons, and

(e)   where an individual identified in the record and subject to notification under (c) above has standing to assert protections for those records in which he has an expectation of confidentiality as defined in *Recommendation (1)* above or any other defense provided by common law or statute;

except that,

(f)   an administrative summons may be issued without service upon the individual where the government shows to a court that service would:

(i)   pose a reasonable possibility that the record sought will be destroyed, or an attempt to destroy it will be made, by the record subject upon whom service of the summons is required; or

(ii)   pose a reasonable possibility that other evidence would be destroyed or become unavailable to government, jeopardizing the investigation; or

(iii) cause flight from prosecution by the individual upon whom service of the summons is required; or

(iv)   endanger the life or physical safety of any person;

provided that, before issuance of such a summons, the government must show the reasonable relationship of the record sought to the investigation in furtherance of which the summons is to be issued. Within a reasonable period of time after issuance of a summons without notice, the government must notify the subject of the record of the seizure. This provision ((f)) would not, however, apply to a record in which an individual has a legitimate expectation of confidentiality recognized by statute or common law.

The Commission believes that this recommendation would curtail the potential for invasion of personal privacy through unreviewed executive action. It would limit the unmonitored expansion of administrative summons power and return the decision to compel disclosure of documents to the supervisory level, where it belongs. In addition, the recommended measure would interfere little with the proper activities of law enforcement. While some inefficiency inevitably occurs when one seeks to safeguard personal privacy, the provisions of subparagraph (f) will minimize any additional burden on government. Finally, the Commission appreciates the arguments of law enforcement officials who suggest that motions to quash summons will result in delays, largely because of protracted appeals.[95] To avoid a potential bottleneck, the Commission suggests that a district court decision regarding enforcement of a summons should not be a final judgment from which an individual could take an interlocutory appeal, but should be appealable only as an evidentiary question after prosecution. Or, if no prosecution is brought, then an individual would be entitled to appeal the decision on the summons within 90 days after the close of the investigation, if he was notified while the investigation was continuing, or one year after being notified of the issuance of the summons, whichever comes first.

The Commission has tried to fashion protections for personal privacy without jeopardizing investigations in which the records of individuals are needed to establish the criminal conduct of a record keeper. If the individual is not the subject of investigation or is unlikely to be implicated publicly in any proceeding, government is not under a duty to serve such individuals when it subpoenas records. Cases of embezzlement or stock manipulation, for example, may require extensive analysis of individual account information to establish the illegal acts of the embezzler or manipulator.[96] Because such government access is not intended to produce action against the individual record subject, nor does it ordinarily disclose information in identifiable form, and because government does not usually retain account

---

[95] Testimony of Hon. Griffin Bell, Attorney General, United States Department of Justice, U.S. House of Representatives, *Hearings on Administrative Summons*, February 24, 1977, pp. 5-6; while the Commission understands the burden argument, it does not endorse the argument that an individual be given only one chance in any investigation to challenge government summons for his records, though the Commission is not opposed to the individual being required to challenge in the same proceeding a group of summons which were issued *at the same time.*

[96] The recently promulgated Federal Rules of Evidence reflect this need by providing for summaries of extensive business records, Fed. Rules Evid. Rule 1006.

information obtained for this purpose in its files, the Commission does not consider such access an unwarranted invasion of personal privacy.

THE JUDICIAL SUBPOENA IN THE COURSE OF LITIGATION

There is considerably more supervision of subpoenas and discovery orders issued in the course of a law suit than of those employed in furtherance of an administrative investigation. The common law strictures on relevance and scope have retained their currency.[97] As with any government request for records, however, the individual about whom records are maintained by a third party has limited ability to intervene in any attempt to force disclosure. His interest may be somewhat better represented in the context of litigation than it is in the context of an administrative summons or Grand Jury subpoena, since the record keeper is often a party to the litigation and thus more likely to protect the record vigorously. Nonetheless, it is still a long way from control over records about himself. In this circumstance, there can be little argument that giving the individual notice and standing when records about him are sought will cause undue delay or other burdens. For these reasons, the Commission recommends:

Recommendation (4):

That Congress provide by statute that a subpoena or other method of judicial summons, issued after indictment or information or after the filing of a complaint or other initital pleading, issued to a private-sector record keeper

(a) in order to obtain an individually identifiable record and
(b) where the record subject is, or is likely to become, a target of the investigation, a named party to the litigation, or otherwise publicly implicated in the proceedings, may be issued only where

    (i) service of the summons or subpoena is made upon both the individual identified in the record and the record keeper,

    (ii) the individual has standing to contest the summons or subpoena and to halt production of the record until his claims are litigated, and

    (iii) the individual is able to assert in protection of the record the defense provided by any legal expectation of confidentiality or other defense provided by common law or statute.

THE GRAND JURY SUBPOENA

Having dealt with the broad problems of summons and subpoena in

---

[97] See, e.g., *Hecht v. Pro-Football, Inc.*, 46 F.R.D. 605 (D.D.C. 1969); *Richards of Rockford, Inc. v. Pacific Gas & Electric*, 71 F.R.D. 388 (N.D.Calif. 1976).

the administrative and litigation contexts, the Commission turned to the
most powerful and perhaps most problem-ridden mechanism by which
government can compel the disclosure of records.

. . . The law vests the Grand Jury with substantial powers, because
the Grand Jury's investigative powers must be broad if its public
responsibility is to be adequately discharged. Indispensable to the
exercise of its power is the authority to compel the attendance and
the testimony of witnesses and to require the production of
evidence.[98]

The flavor of the passage above suggests the great deference, often
shading to veneration, paid to the Grand Jury. Included as a protection for
the individual in the Bill of Rights, it is an institution whose unique powers
the Supreme Court frequently reaffirms and protects. The first clause of the
Fifth Amendment guarantees the Grand Jury process because it is viewed as
"a basic guarantee of individual liberty," as "a barrier to reckless or
unfounded charges," and, in crisis times, as a critical protection against
abuse of the legitimate coercive power of the state.[99] In protecting the
Grand Jury, the courts have rejected attempts to limit its traditional power
of investigation on constitutional grounds.[100] Indeed, as Justice Powell
noted in 1974, "the Grand Jury . . . has traditionally been allowed to pursue
its investigative and accusatorial functions unimpeded by the evidentiary
and procedural restrictions applicable to a criminal trial."[101]

All of which is not to suggest that the power of the Grand Jury to
compel testimony and the production of evidence is without limits. The
requirement that each person give what evidence he possesses is conditioned
on that person's ability to assert a recognized privilege. But even constitutional privileges are not as absolute in the Grand Jury situation as they
might otherwise be.[102] To return to Justice Powell's analysis, for instance:
"Of course, a witness has no right of privacy before the Grand Jury."[103]

To balance these broad powers, the deliberations of the Grand Jury
are theoretically protected by a strict standard of secrecy. The requirements
of secrecy are designed to protect individuals into whose activities the
Grand Jury may inquire. While the Grand Jury can acquire a great deal of
personal and potentially embarrassing or damaging information, ordinarily
it cannot release that information to the world unless it is prepared to indict
an individual, to charge him with a particular violation of criminal law. If
the Grand Jury is unwilling to accuse a person of criminal conduct, then it
may not reveal the information it gathered.[104] Equally important, the Grand
Jury has no adjudicative function of its own; its capabilities end with

[98] *United States v. Mandujano*, 425 U.S. 564 (1976).
[99] *Ibid.; United States v. Calandra*, 414 U.S. 338 (1974); *Costello v. United States*, 350 U.S. 359
(1956).
[100] *United States v. Mandujano, supra*; *United States v. Calandra, supra*; *Blair v. United States*,
250 U.S. 273 (1919); see also, *Branzburg v. Hayes*, 408 U.S. 665 (1972).
[101] *United States v. Calandra, supra.*
[102] See, e.g., *Rogers v. United States*, 340 U.S. 367 (1951); *Branzburg v. Hayes*, 408 U.S. 665
(1972).
[103] *United States v. Mandujano, supra.*
[104] See *Wood v. Hughes*, 173 N.E.2d 21 (NY 1961); *In re Talerico*, 309 NYS2d 511 (1970).

indictment or presentment, with an accusation that a crime has been committed. The Grand Jury gathers information, but can use that information only to determine whether the force of the criminal law should be brought to bear against an individual, whether there is "probable cause to believe a violation of law has been committed"; the Grand Jury does not determine final guilt or innocence, whether a man should lose his liberty or otherwise be punished.[105]

While there has been a great deal of recent criticism of the Grand Jury and its use by prosecutors, both at the Federal and State levels, the Commission accepted the constitutional existence and recognized powers of the Grand Jury in pursuing its inquiry. The Commission's concern is to protect privacy, to balance the preservation of that interest against the legitimate demands of society, not to reform the institutional structure of our legal system. It can not ignore, however, the threats to individual privacy in what it views as improper use of Grand Jury powers by prosecutors and government agents. The improper uses of power which concern the Commission are not so much deliberate attempts to violate rights or circumvent the law as abuses that stem from the "ordinary" operations of the Grand Jury—operations which are, in fact, quite extraodinary, as the following brief survey of the historical and theoretical foundation of the Grand Jury's powers shows.[106]

In medieval England, the Sheriff of each county empanelled bodies of twenty-three men, called "le grande inquest," to inquire into and present to the King's Justices the names of those believed to have committed criminal offenses. By the Fourteenth Century the function of the inquest was clearly limited to accusation; a separate jury and judge tried the accused to establish guilt or innocence. To secure the broadèst range of inquiry for the Grand Jury and to assure that reputations would not be damaged simply because of inquiry or deliberation by the Jury, the jurors were pledged to secrecy. Indeed, that pledge of secrecy made no exceptions, even in favor of government.

The English migration to America brought with it the institution of the Grand Jury. In the first centuries of its existence in the new world it flourished. The Revolutionary generation especially revered the Grand Jury, using it to reject the initiation of prosecutions which the Royal government desired. As judges are fond of pointing out, the Grand Jury functioned as a bulwark of individual liberty. Its ability to protect subjects of investigation who were subsequently not accused was maintained; the duty of secrecy was jealously guarded. For these reasons, the Grand Jury was incorporated into the fundamental structure of the government of the United States in the Fifth Amendment to the Constitution. '

As the Grand Jury emerged into the industrial age, particularly the

---

[105] *Supra*, notes 98-100, particularly *U.S. v. Calandra*; *People v. Johnson*, 203 N.E.2d 399, 401 (Ill. 1965); *Fed. R. Crim. P.*, Rule 6(e).

[106] The discussion in this and the following paragraphs is largely drawn from Blackstone, *Commentaries*, Vol. 4, pp. 301ff.; Wm. Holdsworth, *History of English Law* (7th rev. ed. 1956), Vol. 1, pp. 321-323; Kennedy and Briggs, "Historical and Legal Aspects of the California Grand Jury System," 43 *Cal. L. Rev.* 251 (1955); Dession and Cohen, "The Inquisitorial Functions of Grand Juries," 41 *Yale L.J.* 687 (1932).

Twentieth Century, its institutional structure began to change. Investigations of official misconduct, violations of anti-trust laws, and white-collar crime created a need for collectors and analysts of information to assist the Grand Jury in determining who ought to be accused of crime. Those who provided such assistance were government investigative agents and government attorneys. While they assisted the Grand Jury, they were not jurors and thus not clearly covered by the duty of secrecy, except with respect to testimony actually given before the Grand Jury. In addition to this new class of persons privy to some, or all, of the information before the Grand Jury, the Jury began to request frequently not only testimony but records as well. Documentary evidence was often essential if the jurors were to judge reasonably whether or not to accuse someone of a crime.

Out of these circumstances came the current operational structure of the Grand Jury. Its broad power to compel testimony makes the Grand Jury an unusually powerful means of conducting investigations and gathering evidence, particularly at the Federal level. Except for the search warrant, with its stringent requirements of probable cause based upon oath or affirmation, the Grand Jury subpoena provides the only form of compulsory legal process that can be employed for general inquiries into violations of law. The administrative summons cannot. Even without the measure the Commission recommends for constraining administrative summons power, an administrative summons can be used only to compel production of evidence germane to the purpose of the particular statute which granted the summons power—though, as explored earlier, the reach of such a summons can be overly broad.

In the Federal setting the United States Attorney (or his Justice Department counterpart) ordinarily makes all decisions as to what witnesses will be heard by the Grand Jury. Prompted by government investigators, he also determines what documentary evidence will be subpoenaed. As representatives of Federal investigative agencies indicated to the Commission, agents often seek Grand Jury subpoenas for documents on their own initiative from a U.S. Attorney to assist in investigations not yet brought to a Grand Jury's attention.[107]

It is the attorney for the government who decides when a Grand Jury subpoena will be issued and who issues it. The evidence gathered by the subpoena is then organized by government attorneys and Federal agents before being presented to the Grand Jury. Indeed, documents obtained by Grand Jury subpoena ordinarily pass through the hands of investigative agents who prepare reports for the government attorneys describing the contents of the subpoenaed documents. In most cases, a copy of such a report also goes into the files of the investigative agency. FBI agents, for example, prepare an "Agent's Report 92" describing the contents of

---

[107] Much of the material in this and the following paragraph is based on discussions with attorneys from the Department of Justice and U.S. Attorney's Offices and with Federal Investigative Agents, particularly interviews with Special Agents of the Federal Bureau of Investigation at Headquarters, Washington, D.C. on January 6, 1977, and at San Francisco Field Office on January 24 and 26, 1977; see also, *United States v. Cox*, 342 F.2d 167 (5 Cir. 1965); *Marston's Inc. v. Strand*, 560 P.2d 778 (Ariz. 1977); *supra*, note 100.

documents obtained by Grand Jury subpoena in certain organized crime investigations. A copy usually, though not always, goes to the strike force attorney, as well as to the investigative files of the Bureau.[108]

When documents obtained pursuant to a Grand Jury subpoena are presented to the Grand Jury, they, and presumably the information in them, come under the seal of secrecy. When documents are not presented, as often happens, however, they become part of an investigative record which some argue is not under the requirements of secrecy and thus is open to less restricted use by the government. In any case, the reports which are made part of an investigative file are not considered information maintained under the Grand Jury seal.[109] Even information presented and sealed is generally available to government attorneys and any Federal agents assisting them, though they may not disclose the information except by court order or in the course of criminal prosecution based on an indictment issued by the Grand Jury.[110]

In essence, the Grand Jury subpoena *duces tecum* has become little more than an administrative tool, its connection with the traditional functions of the Grand Jury attenuated at best. One might characterize its current use as a device employed by investigators to circumvent the stringent requirements which must be met to obtain a search warrant. Documents are subpoenaed without the knowledge, not to mention approval, of the Grand Jury. Documents summoned in the Grand Jury's name may never be presented to it. Indeed, the evidence obtained may not even reach an attorney for the government; it may simply be examined and retained by investigative agents for unspecified future uses. The unique powers of inquiry and compulsion, theoretically justified by the secrecy and limited effect of Grand Jury deliberations, have become a generalized resource for Federal investigative activities. Its broad use is underscored by a recent Justice Department internal memorandum which cautioned United States Attorneys and Strike Forces "not to appear to abuse the Grand Jury subpoena power . . . so as to furnish an excuse for adverse legislative action."[111]

The *Miller* decision provides a further example of how far the use of the subpoena has been separated from the actual functioning of the Grand Jury. In that case, the government attorney issuing the subpoena ostensibly on "behalf" of the Grand Jury, did not even pay courtesy to form; he stated as the return date of the subpoena a day on which the Jury would not be

---

[108] Drawn from a variety of interviews with Federal attorneys and investigative agents, particularly an interview with Special Agents of the Organized Crime Section, FBI, at Headquarters, Washington, D.C. on January 6, 1977.

[109] See, e.g., *Granbery v. District Court*, 531 P.2d 390 (Colo. 1975), where the Colorado Supreme Court stated that the policy of secrecy for Grand Jury proceedings "is intended only to protect against disclosure of what is said and takes place in the Grand Jury room," documents *per se* do not fall under the Grand Jury seal; also, *Marston's Inc. v. Strand*, 560 P.2d 778 (Ariz. 1977).

[110] *Fed. R. Crim. P.*, Rule 6(e); *Dennis v. United States*, 384 U.S. 855 (1966); also, *California Penal Code* §938.1 regarding release of Grand Jury information after indictment.

[111] United States Department of Justice, Memorandum of September 8, 1976 from Assistant Attorney General Richard L. Thornburgh to all United States Attorneys and Strike Forces.

sitting. In addition, the subpoena was served and the specified records obtained and analyzed by Treasury agents, not the U.S. Attorney or his assistants. Finally, as the Supreme Court pointed out, "the record does not indicate whether any of the bank records were in fact presented to the Grand Jury."[112]

The erosion of the protections built into the Grand Jury process to insure against improper and indiscriminate use of the information which comes before it disturbs the Commission. The broad powers of the Grand Jury can be justified only by the traditional protections in which its process was cloaked. The Grand Jury should not be a tool for collecting information which may be used for whatever purpose the government chooses; it should be a vehicle for specific criminal investigations. In order to assure against future abuse of the powers of the Grand Jury, the Commission recommends:

Recommendation (5):

That Congress provide by statute that a record obtained pursuant to a Grand Jury subpoena:

(a)   shall be returned and actually presented to the Grand Jury under whose authority the subpoena was issued;

(b)   shall be employed only for the purposes of prosecuting a crime for which an indictment or presentment was issued by the Grand Jury sitting at the time the record was obtained;

(c)   shall be destroyed or returned to the record keeper if it was not used in the prosecution of a crime for which the Grand Jury issued an indictment or presentment or if it has not been made part of the official records of the Grand Jury maintained under the seal;

(d)   shall not be maintained, or its contents described in any record maintained, apart from the sealed records of the Grand Jury by any agency or officer, employee, or agent of such agency of government; and,

(e)   the information contained in such record shall be protected by stringent penalties for improper disclosure or maintenance, including penalties to be enforced by criminal prosecution (or the exercise of judicial contempt power).

In fashioning this recommendation, the Commission sought to avoid jeopardizing on-going investigations in which a Grand Jury about to expire has not issued an indictment. In such a case, the Grand Jury would be free to make a presentment to the judge, under seal or not, as it wished. The presentment would enable a second Grand Jury to continue the investigation. The Commission believes, however, that the recommended measure would effectively prevent government from using information obtained in a Grand Jury investigation for unrelated purposes. Indeed, to the extent the recommendation suggests the destruction and return of documents, the

---

[112] *United States v. Miller*, 425 U.S. 435 (1976); also, see the Court of Appeals opinion, 500 F.2d 751 (5th Cir. 1974).

Commission feels it will be particularly successful; information which is not available cannot be misused.

Having suggested the means for reestablishing and securing the traditional protections for an individual's privacy which should be part of the Grand Jury structure, the Commission does not believe it essential to extend the standards of notice and challenge it recommended for administrative summons and subpoenas in the course of litigation to every Grand Jury subpoena for records. In the administrative and litigation situations, to subpoena the record is tantamount to making it public. In the Grand Jury context, given the changes the Commission recommends, the fact of a subpoena does not necessarily mean the record will become public.

Even though the Grand Jury situation can be distinguished from the other forms of compulsory process, however, the Commission believes that the individual should be able to protect those records in which he has a legitimate expectation of confidentiality. The individual has rights even in the context of the Grand Jury; he may protect himself against self-incrimination, improper process, or the seizure of his private records. Since the records in which the Commission believes there is an expectation of confidentiality are ones which, were it not for the unprecedented changes in social and economic organization of this century, would be recognized as the private and protectible papers of the individual, the Commission feels that he ought to be able to protect those records from Grand Jury seizure just as he would from other government inquiries. For those reasons, the Commission recommends:

Recommendation (6):

That Congress provide by statute that a Grand Jury subpoena *duces tecum* (or other Grand Jury subpoena to acquire the contents of documentary evidence, whether by testimony or otherwise) issued

(a) to obtain an individually identifiable record,
(b) where a legally protectible expectation of confidentiality exists, such as the expectation recommended by the Commission for records of a credit grantor, depository institution, insurance institution, or health-care provider, and
(c) where the record subject is, or is likely to become, a target of the investigation, named in an indictment or presentment, or otherwise publicly implicated in the proceedings, may be issued only where
   (i)   service of the subpoena is made upon both the individual identified in the record and the record keeper,
   (ii) the individual has standing to contest the subpoena and to halt the production of the record until his claims are litigated, and
   (iii) the individual is able to assert in protection of the record the defenses provided by any legal expectation of confidentiality or other defense provided by common law or statute.

RESTRICTING COMPULSORY REPORTING REQUIREMENTS

Government requirements that record keepers, private and public, maintain additional records about individuals and report information from their records to government are increasing. More often than not, these requirements are designed to get information government legitimately needs—to provide health services, to assure against racial or sexual discrimination, to administer the tax laws, and the like.[113] Yet, this method of collecting information about individuals is fraught with greater potential for abuse, and threatens individual liberties and privacy more, than any other legitimate way government goes about gathering information.

The net of information reporting and record-keeping requirements is frequently spread wider than necessary; government finds itself with more information than it needs to carry out its responsibilities, and in a position to inspect or seize information which is not necessarily within its purview.[114] In addition, more record maintenance and reporting requirements inevitably mean greater government control of private-sector record keeping and, ultimately, more government control of information flow. Further, because much of the reporting and maintenance is mandated by the Federal government, but carried out by the States through federally funded activities, control of the information in government hands is centralized at the Federal level.

Progressive centralization makes access by government, particularly the Federal government, even less amenable to control. Traditionally, legal tools for protecting against government intrusion have checked neither the widening of the government's information net through reporting and record maintenance requirements nor the centralized control of record-keeping at the Federal level and the increasing ease of access by government to recorded information about individuals. The programmatic, piecemeal approach used to determine government information needs has not provided an effective forum in which to raise questions of whether government should seek as much information as it does or, indeed, whether there is some information it simply should not collect.

Perhaps the danger inherent in extensive information reporting and maintenance requirements levied by government is unheeded because its

---

[113] See, e.g., 2 U.S.C. 432 et seq. (regulation of election campaigns); 7 U.S.C. 136a (registration of pesticides); 12 U.S.C. 1749b (regulation of recipients of Federal insurance); 12 U.S.C. 1844 (regulation of bank-holding companies); 21 U.S.C. 355 (Food, Drug, and Cosmetic Act; licensing of drugs); 29 U.S.C. 431 et seq. (Labor-Management Act; regulation of unions and employers); 29 U.S.C. 626 (enforcement of age discrimination laws); 30 U.S.C. 821 (regulation of coal mine operators); 31 U.S.C. 1051 (Bank Secrecy); 42 U.S.C. 3769 (recipients of LEAA funds); 42 U.S.C. 299i (regulation of recipients of Public Health Service funds); 42 U.S.C. 300e-6 (regulation of recipients for health maintenance organizations); 42 U.S.C. 1786 (regulation of states and localities that accept Federal funds for nutrional assistance programs); 42 U.S.C. 1395mm (regulation of recipients of health maintenance organizations); 42 U.S.C. 2000e-8 (regulation of parties covered by Civil Rights Act); 47 U.S.C. 393 (regulation of recipients of funding for educational television and radio); Exec. Order No. 11246, 42 U.S.C. 2000e (regulation of parties who contract with the Federal government).

[114] See e.g., *Whalen v. Roe,*   U.S.   , 44 U.S.L.W. 4166 (1977); *EEOC v. University of New Mexico,* 504 F.2d 1296 (10th Cir. 1974).

specific elements have not been fitted together. The problem is not simply that government collects more information on individuals than it perhaps ought to; nor that the program-by-program method of granting power to collect information and then to judge the propriety of the collection is inadequate. Though these two elements must be understood to appreciate the dimensions of the danger, the problem is equally that the expanding reservoir of information government controls may be used for virtually any purpose once it gets into government custody. Information about individuals may be inadvertently or improvidently disclosed with consequent embarrassment or damage to the reputation of innocent persons. Perhaps worse, in a democratic society, is the ever present danger that someone in power may be tempted to use the information about individuals available to them for harassment or intimidation. In particular, government investigative agencies enjoy a unique ability to employ government's store of information about individuals with little restriction—most often for legitimate purposes but, as recent history reminds us, not always. The misuse of tax-return information by Federal investigators, for example, is well documented in all of the recent Administrations. The example, moreover, indicates that the pressure to engage in such activities comes as often as not from those charged with the oversight and management of investigative agencies.[115] Failure to appreciate that information frequently becomes a general governmental resource once it is in the hands of one agency, coupled with the failure to understand the dangers raised by the potential abuse of information in such an environment, is effectively illustrated by a recent decision of the United States Supreme Court.

The Flow of Information Into Government

On February 22, 1977, the Supreme Court upheld the constitutionality of a New York statute which required the reporting of every prescription for certain drugs and the inclusion of the reported information in a computerized central registry.[116] The specific purpose of the reporting and registry was to facilitate the investigation and enforcement of laws against the illegitimate use of narcotics. Patients, doctors, and two professional associations had challenged the portion of the statute which required that the identities of those receiving drugs be reported to the central registry. They argued that such reporting invaded the patient's privacy because the State had no need to maintain a record of the identities centrally. Indeed, during the first 20 months of operation under the statute with hundreds of thousands of identities registered, only once was the identification information relevant to an investigation of illegal activity. The challengers contended that the danger of improper disclosure and consequent damage to reputation, and the "chilling" effect of that danger on an individual's (or

---

[115] See, e.g., U.S. Senate, *Intelligence Activities*, pp. 115-116, 168, 181, 254-260, 280; a particular case in point was the ease with which FBI agents gained access to other government agencies' records on the Rev. Martin Luther King, Jr., U.S. Senate, *Intelligence Activities*, at p.220.

[116] *Whalen v. Roe, supra.*

doctor's) willingness to undertake drug therapy, was not balanced by sufficient public interest in the information to justify the central registry. The three judge panel which heard the case at the trial level agreed with the plaintiffs and found that "the diminution of a constitutionally guaranteed freedom is too great a price to pay for such a small government yield."[117]

Reviewing the lower court's ruling, the Supreme Court chose not to reevaluate the general issue of the constitutional propriety of requiring reporting of information about individuals for "legitimate" regulatory purposes.[118] Relying on past reasoning, the Court indicated that compelled reporting was to be distinguished from impermissible intrusions in violation of the Fourth and Fifth Amendments. The opinion noted that cases where intrusions were found illegitimate "involved affirmative, unannounced, narrowly focused intrusions into individual privacy during the course of criminal investigations" or circumstances where "there was an uncontroverted showing of past harm through disclosure."[119] The crux of the Court's opinion focused on the distinction it saw between the New York scheme and past schemes—the central *computerized* registry.[120] In assessing the threat to privacy created by the registry, the Court suggested that the considerations to be weighed were the dangers of "unwarranted disclosure of accumulated private data" and of inadequate "security provisions." In effect, the Court did not seem concerned with the intrusion created by collection but only with the potential for improper dissemination; even that concern seemed limited. Justice Stewart, in his concurrence, went so far as to suggest that the Constitution, to the extent it protects privacy, "does not recognize a general interest in freedom from disclosure of private information."[121]

Though litigants have long argued that reporting requirements imposed by government raise the same sorts of questions that would be raised by government searching your house or seizing your papers, their argument has carried little weight at the Federal level.[122] The Supreme Court consistently rejects it and restricts the reach of constitutional protections against government collection of information to certain limited aspects of reporting requirements.

Where the government requires an *individual* to report information about himself, the Court has found the Fifth Amendment protection against self-incrimination to provide some limitation on government power. In *Marchetti v. United States*,[123] the majority declared the wagering tax reporting system a violation of the Fifth Amendment privilege. As Justice Harlan reasoned for the Court, "The terms of the wagering tax system make quite plain that Congress intended information obtained as a consequence of registration and payment of the occupational tax to be provided to interested state prosecuting authorities." Since wagering was illegal in most

---

[117] *Roe v. Ingraham*, 403 F.Supp. 931 (3-judge Ct.)(S.D.N.Y. 1975).
[118] *Infra*, note 125.
[119] *Whalen v. Roe, supra.*
[120] *Ibid.*, at 4169-4170; also, see Justice Brennan's concurrence.
[121] *Ibid.*, at 4171.
[122] See, e.g., "Brief of Appellants Fortney H. Stark, Jr., et al.," *California Bankers Assn. v. Schultz*, 416 U.S. 21 (1974).
[123] 390 U.S. 39 (1968).

jurisdictions, continued the argument, such an intention amounted to a deliberate compulsion on a gambler to incriminate himself or be liable for failing to confess to illegitimate activity. Only a year later, however, virtually the same Court (with Justices Douglas and Black dissenting) refused to extend the rationale of *Marchetti* to the order form requirements of the marijuana and narcotic drug laws in *Minor v. United States*.[124] As Justice Douglas noted in his dissent, the issue was the same; the government had required an individual to report his own illegal activities or be liable for failing to incriminate himself. Indeed, the reporting forms which one needed to complete in the circumstances of *Minor* were never even prepared by the government—the statute was used solely as a prosecutorial "catch-22."

Though the standards of *Marchetti* and *Minor* may be difficult to reconcile, the broader protection given the individual under *Marchetti* is still quite limited. The *Marchetti* decision precludes compulsory reporting, and the use of information collected thereby, only when the mere fact of reporting amounts to incrimination. *In other words, reporting requirements are improper only to the extent that they leave an individual no choice but to incriminate himself.* In contexts where the reporting would not necessarily indicate illegal activity, reporting is proper even though compelled.

Where information about an individual must be reported by a *third party*, as in the case of the New York statute, the Supreme Court recognizes only the most nebulous constitutional protection. *The Court's only limitation on the scope of the reporting has been that the information be arguably relevant to the mission of the agency of government collecting it*.[125] This was the position the court took with respect to the New York drug reporting statute. Thus, even in the arena of medical or financial information (which most individuals consider peculiarly sensitive), the ability of government to compel reporting is restrained only by the requirement that information sought be "intimately related to . . . and obviously supportable as in aid of" an otherwise legitimate government activity.[126]

In the constitutional context, then, compelled reporting by government has been limited only to the extent that the reporting violates a narrow interpretation of Fifth Amendment protections against self-incrimination, or that the information sought is patently irrelevant to the proper activities of government.

The real danger to personal privacy from the vast store of personal information being accumulated by government is, in the eyes of the Supreme Court, the danger of improper dissemination. Preoccupation of the Court with questions of dissemination reflects its unwillingness to recognize the legal interest of an individual in records about himself held by third parties and its inaccurate understanding of how reported information may be used by government. The Court's approach, however, is understandable. By focusing on what government may do with information it has already collected, the courts have only to assess subsequent conduct on the basis of

---

[124] 396 U.S. 87 (1969).

[125] *United States v. Kahriger*, 345 U.S. 22 (1953); *Sonzinsky v. United States*, 300 U.S. 506 (1937).

[126] *United States v. Kahringer, supra.*

the actual harm caused by improper use or dissemination. Such an approach is judicially more comfortable than trying to assess possibilities and probabilities in advance, as they would have to do if they tried to judge the propriety of collecting the information in the first place and to balance the government's need for information against the individual's right to privacy.[127]

Unfortunately, individuals no longer possess all the records and information about themselves which they have a right to consider private. While the Supreme Court may be reluctant to recognize that bank account records, for example, are personal papers in which an individual has a legitimate expectation of privacy, society must give such recognition to those records if it is to preserve the delicate balance between the state and the individual. At least to the extent that an individual has a recognized and legitimate expectation of confidentiality, the Commission feels that third-party record keepers should not be required to report such information routinely. The same standard should prevail, in the Commission's view, even where the use of reported information is clearly limited and the dangers of abuse minimized.

The Flow of Information Within Government

To appreciate the relatively unrestricted flow of information within government and the dangers of that flow, the Supreme Court's consideration of the New York prescription reporting statute provides a useful starting point. In the course of its opinion, the Court assumed that the availability of reported information for purposes unrelated to the securing of "public health" would be restricted because the avenues for disclosure were restricted.[128] Restricted though the avenues for disclosure may appear to be on the surface of a reporting scheme, however, the availability of the information for specific investigative purposes generally opens up that record to law enforcement. The Court discusses "restrictions" on disclosure of drug users' identities by the State of New York; but, when an investigative agency legitimately obtains information for its investigation of a specific violation, such information goes into its files where the information is available when the same investigative unit inquires into other kinds of violations; and, the agents investigating possible violations of the New York drug laws were part of an agency which also investigates other violations of law. Further, the Court's reasoning does not take into account the routine cooperation and sharing of information by investigative units at all levels of government. Finally, the opinion fails to recognize that individuals have little, if any, power to protect themselves from improper use or disclosure *within* government.[129] In practice, then, government may require the

---

[127] See, e.g., *California Bankers Assn. v. Schultz*, 416 U.S. 21 (1974).

[128] *Whalen v. Roe, supra*, at 4168.

[129] Hearings before the Select Committee on Intelligence, U.S. House of Representatives, 94th Congress, 1st Session, pp. 977-79, 981, 1034-35, 1222-23 (1975); U.S. Senate, *Intelligence Activities*, pp. 254-262; also, see President's Commission on Law Enforcement and the

reporting of information for one purpose and use it for a second purpose—notably, criminal prosecution.

Equally important, the courts have found no constitutional limitation on the manner or extent of government disclosure of information about an individual, whether the disclosure is to the public, or to private entities, or within the confines of government. In the 1976 term, for instance, the Supreme Court ruled that there was no constitutional protection for an individual when a government official distributed copies of a leaflet which charged that the persons identified in it were "known" criminals, even though one of the individuals so identified had never been arrested or convicted of any crime.[130] Where the disclosure occurs between one agency of government and another, lower courts have held that there is no common law or constitutional restraint on such exchanges.[131]

While the implications of the free flow of information within government, particularly to or between investigative agencies, are described in Chapter 13, two aspects of that information flow must be considered here to determine how best to cope with the problems raised by government reporting and record-keeping requirements. The relatively unrestricted flow of information about individuals is endemic to both Federal and State government; the sharing of resources and the diffusion of authority and responsibility often require extensive exchange of information both within and between governments. The Commission recognizes the value of our existing architecture of government and understands that the very interdependence of agencies within the Executive Branch of the Federal government militates against unacceptable concentrations of power. The problem of intragovernmental information flow and public disclosure cannot be eliminated; but, the Commission believes that its dangers can be minimized.[132] Given the continuing danger of improper disclosure and use of information in government hands, the Commission believes it essential to limit requirements for the reporting of information about individuals maintained by third-party record keepers. Since the courts have made it clear that they do not feel it within their power to effect such limitation, any protection for personal privacy must be established by statute. Indeed, to the extent that protections against misuse of reported information or limitations on the scope of reporting currently exist, they are the product of legislation.[133]

That existing protections are the product of legislation is appropriate,

Administration of Justice, *The Challenge of Crime in a Free Society*, (Washington, D.C.: 1967), pp. 119-120, 266-267.

[130] *Paul v. Davis*, 424 U.S. 693 (1976).

[131] *Atchison, Topeka and Santa Fe Rwy. v. Lopez*, 531 P.2d 455, 467 (Kan. 1975); *Schulman v. N.Y.C. Health and Hospitals Corp.*, 355 N.Y.S.2d 782 (1975); see also Swan, "Privacy and Record Keeping: Remedies for the Misuse of Accurate Information," 45 *N.C.L. Rev.* 585 (April 1976).

[132] On minimization of these dangers, see also Chapter 14, "The Relationship Between Citizen and Government: The Citizen as Taxpayer."

[133] See, e.g., Tax Reform Act of 1976, 26 U.S.C. 6103; Census, 13 U.S.C. 9; Drug Abuse Prevention and Treatment Act, 21 U.S.C. 1102-1191; Child Abuse Prevention and Treatment Act, 42 U.S.C. 5101-5106.

since the problem of compulsory information reporting is the creature of legislation. In the past two decades, Congress has enacted hundreds of statutes which require, or permit, an administrative agency to require third parties to report information about individuals. As the Commission has found, it is futile to examine this problem as though each reporting requirement were an independent and unrelated scheme. Government is compelling record keepers to report information about individuals in unprecedented volume. In addition, the information reported covers a wider spectrum of individual activity than ever before, from health records to employment to financial activity. Most of that information becomes available for uses unrelated to the purpose for which it was reported. Even when government does not require reporting, it frequently mandates that records about individuals be kept and requires that they be open to inspection by government agents.

Record-keeping requirements for information about individuals are the statutory twin of compulsory reporting; ordinarily, when a record keeper reports information it must also retain that information. Further, statutes often require the retention of information which is not reported, but kept for possible inspection by government. Such record-keeping requirements raise many of the same questions as the reporting requirements. Government's access to the retained records is broad and virtually unassailable, particularly by the subject of the record. Even when legal process is ostensibly required for government to gain access to the records, such requirements provide little protection for an individual. Under the Bank Secrecy Act, for example, government agents may examine or seize account records without the account holder being able to object, even if the process by which the government proceeded was improper.[134] In other cases, Federal investigators have been permitted access to all the personnel and employment records of an organization, although they had no complaint justifying the examination nor any cause to believe that the records evidenced a violation of law.[135] Finally, access to records which are required to be kept by law may be predicated on statutory inspection provisions which exempt the investigator from obtaining legal process. Drug abuse control legislation, for example, states that government agents do not need a warrant to inspect books and records which the Attorney General (or his delegate) deems relevant or material to an investigation. This exemption from the need for legal process is provided even though the warrant in question is an administrative one which, under the statute, can be issued without probable cause. Such a warrant may be issued simply upon showing that there is "a valid public interest in the enforcement of this subchapter or regulations thereunder, sufficient to justify administrative inspections . . . ."[136]

The virtually unchallangeable power of government to gain access to records about individuals that a third party has been required to keep results, as do the reporting requirements, in information coming into government hands and becoming available for disclosure or reuse largely at

---

[134] *United States v. Miller*, 425 U.S. 435 (1976).
[135] *EEOC v. University of New Mexico*, 504 F.2d 1296 (10th Cir. 1974).
[136] 21 U.S.C. 880.

the discretion of government. Under most of the relevant statutes, a government agency has wide discretion to determine whether it will hold the information it acquires in confidence,[137] increasing still further the possibility of disclosure and future misuse.

Moreover, the Federal government does not limit the avenues through which it compels reporting of information or maintenance of records to direct requirements placed on third-party record keepers. Through a variety of programs, particularly those involving medical services and public assistance, the Federal government makes the States its collectors and record keepers by predicating Federal funding for State programs on fulfillment of such duties. Many of these funding schemes encourage, even obligate, State governments to collect more information about individuals than they otherwise would. The Medicaid program, for example, provides extra funding if the State agency administering the program agrees to adopt the Medicaid Management Information System (MMIS) information collection criteria.[138] Under them, medical-care providers must report detailed information on patients and their claims to the State authority. The extensive set of records then becomes available to Federal auditors or investigators, such as the newly created Fraud and Abuse Office in the Medicaid program, at their request. Predictably, given the financial incentives, most States have adopted the MMIS criteria.[139]

During the course of the Commission hearings on Medical Records, however, several witnesses testified that they do not consider the extensive collection of identifiable information mandated by programs such as MMIS necessary.[140] In particular, representatives of the Commission on Professional and Hospital Activities testified that there are viable alternatives to such massive reporting of information about individuals which would guard equally well against fraud and other abuses.[141] They advocated an auditing system by which the original records of the medical-care provider would be minimally abstracted and only that abstraction sent on to the Medicaid payer; the original record would continue to exist and be available for audit at any time; yet far less information would flow to government or any private insurer acting as a government intermediary.

Any reduction in the amount of information reported to government, such as the alternative to current practices suggested at the Commission's Medical Record Hearings, will correspondingly reduce the danger of abuse which inevitably accompanies the accumulation of information in government hands. The Commission suggests to the Congress, and to State

---

[137] e.g., 15 U.S.C. 1193; 7 U.S.C. 136f (trade secret); 15 U.S.C. 1944; 42 U.S.C. 1973g; 45 U.S.C. 362 (disclosable if it will aid individual); P.L. 94-106.

[138] 42 U.S.C. 1396(a)(3); 45 C.F.R. 250.90.

[139] Testimony of Medical Services Administration, Social and Rehabilitative Services, Department of Health, Education, and Welfare, *Medical Records*, Hearings before the Privacy Protection Study Commission, July 20, 1976, p. 218 (hereinafter cited as 'Medical Records Hearings").

[140] *Ibid.*, pp. 211-12, 222-23; Testimony of the Commission on Professional and Hospital Activities, Medical Records Hearings, July 21, 1976, pp. 462-65.

[141] Testimony of the Commission on Professional and Hospital Activities, Medical Records Hearings, July 21, 1976, pp. 462-65, 486-89.

legislatures, that they forego any future personal information reporting or record-keeping requirements unless a clear need for government to have the information exists, the need outweighs any privacy interest of the record subject, and there are no less intrusive alternatives for achieving the desired goal. In effect, the Commission believes that such an approach would result in statutes of greater utility and much less potential for harm than statutes like the drug reporting statute of New York State.

Not only are there extensive reporting and record-keeping requirements that make information about individuals available for government use, but few Americans are aware of the extent or nature of the identifiable information about themselves reported to government or kept at government's command. Some may know about one piece or another of the vast information requirements; but, those who begin to realize the breadth of information about them open to unimpeded government scrutiny are few. An individual has lost most of his control of what government can know about him. If the Bank Secrecy Act indicates the direction of future legislation, an individual may soon lose all control. The Commission hopes that legislators will recognize the impotence of the Constitution as currently interpreted to limit the reach of overbroad statutory commands to report personal information or to keep it on record. If they do, they will exercise extreme caution, particularly by limiting delegations of authority to executive officers to determine the scope of information reporting and the propriety of record inspection.

When reporting of individually identifiable information or the keeping of personal information are determined to be essential, the Commission recommends, in order to minimize dangers to personal privacy:

Recommendation (7):

(a)   **That where a private-sector record keeper is required to report information about an individual to an agency or authority of government, the scope of such reporting should be limited by Congress such that:**

   (i)   **each reporting requirement is expressly authorized in statute;**

   (ii) **each statutory provision clearly identifies the policies and purposes which justify the reporting it authorizes;**

   (iii) **each statutory provision details standards of relevance which must be met before the information must be reported;**

   (iv) **no information is reported in individually identifiable form unless such reporting is essential to accomplish the statutory policies and purposes which justify the reporting; and**

   (v)   **where individual identity is not reported by the record keeper, yet at some point such identification may be necessary to ensure compliance with law, identifiable records be maintained by the record keeper only for** inspection by authorized agents of the government upon presentation of a lawful summons or subpoena;

(b) that inspection by a government agency of records maintained pursuant to statute or regulation in individually identifiable form by a private-sector record keeper be permitted to occur

(i) only upon presentation and delivery of a copy of an administrative summons, provided that

(ii) the summons identifies the particular records and items of information to be made available for inspection by the agency;

(c) that a private-sector record keeper be required to notify an individual when he enters into a relationship with the record keeper that information concerning the relationship

(i) will be reported to agencies and authorities of government pursuant to statute or regulation, or

(ii) may be open to inspection by agencies and authorities of government;

(d) that individually identifiable information obtained by government through reporting or inspection required by statute or regulation should be unavailable for civil or criminal prosecution of violations of law not directly related to the statutorily identified purposes which justify the reporting or inspection;

(e) that an individually identifiable record required to be maintained by a private-sector record keeper pursuant to statute or regulation may be destroyed by the record keeper at any time after the statute of limitations expires for the specific violation justifying the reporting or maintenance of such record; and

(f) that an individually identifiable record collected by a government agency from information reported or maintained by a private-sector record keeper pursuant to statute or regulation be destroyed by the government agency at the time the statute of limitations expires for the specific violation justifying the reporting or maintenance of such record.

While directed explicitly at the personal information reporting and record-keeping requirements of the Federal government, this recommendation is equally applicable to the actions of State governments. At the State level, however, the Commission recognizes that Federal requirements generate a large part of the demand for personal information. In consequence of that recognition, the Commission intends that the recommendation apply equally to Federal requirements levied on State agencies which result in private record keepers reporting to State authorities as well as to requirements placed directly on private record keepers.

Equally important, except for sections (c) and (e), the recommended measures seek to limit the reach of government power and assure the legitimacy of government activity, placing the primary burden for securing the protection of personal privacy on the potential invader, government, rather than the record keeper. Section (a) recommends clear statutory authority for reporting or record-keeping requirements, eliminating potentially abusive executive discretion and providing in subsections (ii) and (iii) some standards through which the provisions of section (d) may be applied. Section (d) would permit government to take actions against fraud and other sorts of abuse within a program but would eliminate the use of records for unrelated purposes, *unless* Congress specifically provides in the authorizing legislation that the records ought to be available for other designated purposes. An example of such a provision can be found in the Tax Reform Act of 1976, which permits disclosure of tax-return information about a taxpayer provided to the IRS by a private-sector record keeper to Federal investigative agencies for use in non-tax investigations upon written request of the agency head. The Commission urges, however, that such deviation from the general rule be permitted rarely, if at all.

Finally, the requirements of sections (e) and (f) would eliminate records no longer needed for their original purpose but which in the future might cause the harassment or embarrassment of an individual. Records which do not exist cannot be abused.

STRIKING A REASONABLE BALANCE

In August, 1973, Commissioner Donald Alexander of the Internal Revenue Service abolished the so-called Special Service Staff (SSS) within that agency and impounded its records. The SSS, established in 1969, accumulated information about American citizens whom the executive branch considered politically unwelcome, initiated IRS investigations and audits of them, forwarded information about them to other Federal law enforcement and intelligence agencies, and received information about them from other agencies that sometimes had been collected through illegal or improper means.

Testifying before the Senate Select Committee on Intelligence Activities in October 1975, Commissioner Alexander told the Committee that he had kept the SSS files so that the Committee "could review . . . them, and see what sort of information was supplied to us on this [sic] more than 11,000 individuals and organizations," adding that "at the end of all these inquiries, I would like to take those files to the Ellipse and have the biggest bonfire since 1814." Seconding Mr. Alexander's sentiments, the Chairman of the Committee suggested that "it might be a more important bonfire than the Boston Tea Party when it comes to protecting individual rights of American citizens."[142]

Commissioner Alexander's bonfire, and the abolition of SSS, highlight a basic element of the practices of government agencies that led the Commission to recommend the measures explained in this chapter. Alexander's suggestion that the SSS files be burned implicitly expressed concern about the vulnerability of information in government hands to abuse, while also acknowledging that government can, and does, collect information about individuals it does not need for any legitimate purpose, and thus should not have.

The recommendations in this chapter provide a means of curbing

---

[142] U.S. Senate, *Intelligence Activities*, pp. 95-96.

indiscriminate government collection of information about individuals, whether through informal requests, compulsory legal process or compulsory reporting. Allowing the individual a voice in government access to records about him and requiring outside supervision of government collection activities should create accountability for those activities, helping to assure that the acquisition of information by government is proper.

The Commission recognizes that its recommendations do not reach all recorded information about individuals, nor do they allow an individual to participate in all decisions as to whether government should have access to records about him. The Commission has concentrated on providing protections for the most revealing records of individual activity, the kind of records that government traditionally has been required to justify its interest in before they may be opened to it. Even where a legitimate expectation of confidentiality is recommended, government may still use a search warrant to acquire a record without the individual's prior knowledge. The recommendations, however, would no longer allow the executive branch of government to acquire records about individuals without supervision; no longer, for example, would unreviewed executive discretion enable government agents to seize an individual's bank records.

While appreciating the efficiency arguments of law enforcement agencies, the Commission does not believe that convenience alone should control policy judgments when individual rights are at issue. The burden argument, moreover, is not totally convincing. The IRS already, as a matter of policy, employs some form of summons or subpoena to obtain access to records.[143] In addition, the United States Department of Justice acknowledges that an individual should at least be notified when his bank records are summoned,[144] though the Department does not believe that a citizen should be given a protectible legal interest with which to challenge a subpoena or summons. In large part, the Department's position assumes the goodwill and good intentions of investigative agencies and their executive branch overseers. Such an argument, always unacceptable in theory, seems less tenable in practice in the aftermath of the Vietnam era and Watergate.

The law enforcement and investigative community has already indicated that it feels that some of the recommendations go too far; civil libertarians will undoubtedly be concerned that the recommended restrictions are not strong enough. The Commission, however, has sought to strike a reasonable balance between protecting personal privacy and assuring that the goverment can do its job. Just as the Constitution does not prohibit all searches and seizures, the Commission does not suggest that government agents be absolutely prohibited from obtaining records about individuals. Government, however, will have to make its case before it can do so.

---

[143] *Supra*, note 16.

[144] Testimony of Hon. Griffin Bell, Attorney General, United States Department of Justice, U.S. House of Representatives, *Hearings on Administrative Summons*, February 24, 1977, pp. 5-6.

Chapter 10

Record Keeping in the Education Relationship

An individual's relationships with educational institutions help shape his personal development and may substantially affect the degree to which he can enter into and benefit from all other social and economic activities and relationships. The records about individuals that the education relationship generates affect almost everyone, for nearly every American has or will have spent some time in at least one educational institution.[1]

Within an educational institution, education records[2] form a background against which decisions about an individual student's status or progress are made, not only at the major turning points in his educational career, but also on a daily basis where they shape unobtrusive but significant decisions about him. Educational record-keeping practices, however, vary substantially by size of institution and sophistication of administrative practices. They also vary as students move along the continuum from pre-school toward post-graduate education, because the role of educational institutions varies along the same continuum.

Society grants educational institutions substantial authority over students and substantial freedom to gather, record, and use information about them without their consent or the consent of their parents. This is considered necessary if educational institutions are to provide basic instructional services and maintain an environment conducive to learning and personal development. Nonetheless, the authority to act in *loco parentis* carries with it the responsibilities of stewardship. Report cards, conferences, and parent-teacher associations are all devices by which educational institutions are held directly accountable to parents and students. In addition, through the election of school officials, as well as through licensing, accrediting, and the enactment of State education codes, educational institutions are held accountable to the society as a whole.

---

[1] "Educational institution" or "educational agency or institution" means any public or private agency or institution which is the recipient of funds under any Federal program for which the U.S. Commissioner of Education has administrative responsibility, as specified by law or by delegation of authority pursuant to law. The term refers to the agency or institution recipient as a whole, including all of its components (such as schools or departments in a university) and shall not be read to refer to one or more of those components separate from that agency or institution. 20 U.S.C. 1232g(a)(8).

[2] "Education records" are those records which: (1) are directly related to a student, and (2) are maintained by an educational agency or institution or by a party acting for the agency or institution. 20 U.S.C. 1232g(a)(4).

The accelerated pace of social change in recent decades has subjected the stewardship role of educational institutions to unprecedented stress. The population explosion of the past thirty years, the growing mobility of the American population, and the rapid increases in the breadth and specialization of knowledge have all had a direct impact on educational institutions. Parents, students, and society as a whole have developed new expectations as to the skills educational institutions should impart. Courses now cover subjects ranging from woodworking and driver education to regression analysis and zero-based budgeting. With this growth in size and scope of responsibility, have come bureaucratic forms of administration, larger budgets, mounting pressures to demonstrate effectiveness, and a heightened drive for autonomy and special prerogatives on the part of professional educators.

Over the last fifteen years, the Federal government has affected all levels of education through financial assistance programs aimed at helping educational institutions to meet their responsibilities, and also at using educational institutions to further other social purposes, such as equal opportunity. This has reinforced the educational system's own gravitation toward bureaucratic administration and professional specialization. It has also altered record-keeping requirements and practices, modified power balances within educational institutions, and made many educators wary of Federal regulation.

The combined impact of all these changes on record keeping about students has been the focus of Commission concern. Educational institutions make and keep more records about students today than ever before. More people participate in making and keeping education records, and more people outside the educational system want access to them for other than educational purposes. Moreover, the emphasis in educational record keeping has shifted from reporting progress to parents and supplementing personal contact in instructing and making decisions about students to serving not only as a management tool but also as a means of justifying an educational institution's actions and budget, and as a surrogate for personal contact with students. These changes have elevated the importance of education records in American society, and thus the importance of good school record-keeping practices.

The importance of educational record keeping today was formally recognized in 1974, when the Congress enacted the Family Educational Rights and Privacy Act (hereinafter FERPA). *[20 U.S.C. 1232g]* This legislation gives parents of minor students, and students who are over 18, the right to inspect, correct, amend, and control the disclosure of information in education records. It obliges educational institutions to inform parents and students of their rights, and to establish policies and procedures through which their rights can be exercised.

FERPA represents an alternative to the omnibus approach to regulating record keeping taken by the Privacy Act of 1974. The Privacy Act, applicable to all Federal agencies, levies a broad set of requirements on a diverse mix of records and record-keeping institutions. FERPA, in contrast, is targeted on education records, the individuals to whom they pertain, and the institutions that keep them.

FERPA, the Department of Health, Education, and Welfare (DHEW) regulations implementing it *[45 C.F.R. 99]*, and the activities of the Department in carrying out its responsibilities under the law, exemplify, albeit imperfectly, a novel regulatory strategy that might be termed "enforced self-regulation." The regulated institutions are responsible for developing and implementing policies and procedures that meet minimum requirements established by law. Those legal requirements state objectives for the development and implementation of local substantive and procedural requirements, but do not prescribe detailed substantive standards or impose fine-grained procedures. Such a strategy entails penalties for violations of locally established standards and procedures, but does not impose any particular interpretation of substantive standards. Rather, it relies on making an institution accountable to those whom it most directly affects without requiring either prior Federal approval of local policies and procedures or systematic Federal monitoring of each institution's performance.

To evaluate the merits of FERPA as a privacy protection statute, the Commission held public hearings in October and November 1976 to learn about the experiences of parents, students, professional educators, and educational institutions in complying with the law. At the time of the hearings, the Department of Health, Education, and Welfare's final FERPA regulations had been in effect less than nine months, although the statute had been in force for almost two years. Many institutions were still developing, or had only recently begun to implement, their FERPA policies and procedures.

In the Commission's view, however, the hearing testimony confirms the necessity and validity of most FERPA requirements and the potential effectiveness of "enforced self-regulation." The hearing record also indicates that some features of the statute and regulations make implementation difficult or dilute its effectiveness. Nonetheless, FERPA is apparently leading educational institutions to respect some basic record-keeping rights that were not uniformly accorded students or parents before the Act was passed.

Educators, parents, and students have generally accepted FERPA's principles despite some minor problems and misunderstandings, and the extreme sensitivity of educational institutions to Federal regulation. In spite of the substantial delay in issuing regulations and the resulting lack of awareness and even misunderstanding of the law, the testimony of educational institutions indicates that enforced self-regulation can take hold, and, if strengthened, can be an effective tool for striking the proper balance among individual, institutional, and societal interests.[3]

This chapter reports the results of the Commission's assessment of the Family Educational Rights and Privacy Act of 1974 and recommends some

---

[3] See, for example, written statement of Franklin and Marshall College, *Education Records*, Hearings before the Privacy Protection Study Commission, November 11, 1976, pp. 7-15; (hereinafter cited as "Education Records Hearings").

changes in the Act that will make it better able to achieve the Commission's public-policy goals of minimizing intrusiveness, maximizing fairness, and creating legitimate, enforceable expectations of confidentiality. The first section focuses on the role of record keeping about students. It summarizes the missions and functions of the various types of educational institutions and describes the records they keep and how they collect, use, and disclose information about individual students. This section also describes the testing and data-assembly service organizations whose highly specialized education records play a major role in post-secondary admissions and financial-aid decisions.

The second section describes the Family Educational Rights and Privacy Act, its accompanying DHEW regulations, and the experience to date in implementing the law. The third section assesses how well personal privacy is protected by FERPA, and presents the Commission's basic conclusions. The focus in the third section is on specific record-keeping problems that arise in the various types of educational institutions and the tools the individual currently has for coping with them. The final section recommends additional steps to clarify and strengthen FERPA as an instrument for achieving the basic objectives of the Commission as they relate to educational record keeping.

RECORD-KEEPING PRACTICES IN EDUCATION

Some 60 million students are currently enrolled in formal educational programs provided by educational institutions. As a student moves from one point to another in the education system, his path is blazed by records concerning his performance, his behavior, and his own, and often his family's, life circumstances. These records are created by an educational institution mainly to record the student's progress, to help make decisions about him, and to improve the effectiveness of the educational programs the institution provides.

Education records are generated in many different organizational settings from pre-school through post-graduate institutions. For most individuals, the educational experience is a progression through a number of organizations with differing missions, roles, functions, and authorities with respect to both the individual and society. It is important to recognize that the record-keeping practices of educational institutions reflect those differences.

The mission and role of an educational institution are key determinants of its record-keeping practices. The mission of a pre-school is to care for and nurture children and to lay a foundation for the academic tasks they will confront in elementary school. The elementary school's mission is nurturant and custodial, but also includes formal instruction in reading, mathematics, and other subjects. As the child moves through the elementary years, the school's custodial role is augmented by a greater concern for socialization. Gradually, the school's nurturant role is overshadowed by its role in developing fundamental academic skills until the junior high-school years, when the nurturant role disappears altogether. The custodial role remains as long as compulsory education laws force children to attend school, but the school's emphasis shifts towards maintaining the order necessary to carry out its academic mission.

The post-secondary educational mission is almost exclusively one of intellectual development and training; it includes only vestiges of custodial care and behavioral control. In most post-graduate and professional schools a concern with socialization reappears, but is much more narrowly focused on inculcating professional mores and ethics. Thus, while the instructional mission runs as a common thread throughout all schooling, there are, in fact as well as in law, two quite distinct educational systems in this country: elementary and secondary education on the one hand, and post-secondary education on the other.

ELEMENTARY AND SECONDARY EDUCATIONAL INSTITUTIONS

The ways in which record keeping about students in elementary and secondary education differs from record keeping about students in higher education can be understood by examining six features of the record-keeping relationship in the two systems: (1) the role of records in decision making; (2) institutional decision-making responsibilities and authorities; (3) variations in organizational settings; (4) the ways in which records are created and used; (5) record-keeping responsibilities and authorities; and (6) disclosure practices.

THE ROLE OF RECORDS IN DECISION MAKING

Elementary and secondary educational institutions share responsibility for the intellectual, social, and ethical development of a student with the student's parents and with others who deal with youth, such as child welfare and juvenile justice agencies. In pursuing this broad mission of child development, schools provide instructional services, regulate behavior, report to parents on academic performance and social conduct, diagnose student needs, and conduct special programs for students. The visible decisions they make concern matters such as class placement and promotion, eligibility for special educational programs (such as for handicapped or gifted children), eligibility for public assistance and social services programs (school breakfast and lunch programs, for example), and major disciplinary decisions, such as suspension or expulsion. Much less visible are the series of small decisions they make which subtly shape a student's educational career: decisions about the speed with which a child's development should be fostered in specific areas of academic course work or personal conduct, for example, or about the sanctions and rewards that should be used to discipline or encourage a child.

The main characteristic of decision making about students in elementary and secondary education is that it is contextual. Regardless of the philosophy of education a school espouses, elementary and secondary school professionals generally believe that decisions must be made on the basis of the "whole child"; that is, that intellectual and social development are intimately related. This encourages schools to assemble so much information about students that it becomes difficult to determine which information is or was the basis for a particular decision. Both in routine decision making, such as when class placement or promotion is at issue, and in decision making based on fairly specific criteria, such as when public assistance or social services eligibility must be decided or suspension or expulsion proceedings concluded, the practice is to look at such a multiplicity of factors that the relationship between specific items of information and the ultimate decision becomes increasingly unclear.

INSTITUTIONAL DECISION-MAKING RESPONSIBILITIES AND AUTHORITIES

Public schools are given broad authority to make decisions about students. Public elementary and secondary institutions must deal with all children. Admission is not selective, nor can public schools set performance standards that would eliminate certain students from the student body or narrow the variety of programs that will be offered. Thus, while they strive to cooperate with parents, the degree to which public schools share authority with parents has been largely left to schools to decide.

Most public educational institutions are special-purpose local governments created by State law, accountable to the people of the school district through locally elected and appointed school boards and school officials. State education laws place limits on the authority of schools, and prescribe due process procedures that order decision making and reinforce parental control. Nevertheless, a State code cannot regulate all placement and treatment decisions, and many such decisions are not visible enough to parents to induce their involvement. Parents of private and parochial school students have the option of withdrawing their children from the school if they dislike the manner in which the school exercises its authority, but beyond that, parents have little ability to control decisions made by elementary and secondary schools about their children, even in the private-school setting.

VARIATIONS IN ORGANIZATIONAL SETTING

Elementary and secondary education occurs in a diversity of organizational settings. Despite a strong trend toward consolidation, there are still more than 15,000 school districts in this country. Within and among districts there is also great variation in size, organizational complexity, types of special services offered, and intensity of involvement in economic and social issues, such as racial balance, drug use, juvenile crime, and cultural disadvantage. The Los Angeles Unified School District, for example, serves over 600,000 students. It has more employees providing administrative and special educational services than classroom teachers, different organizational structures for its instructional services than for its special ones, and its own police force to cope with juvenile crime problems. It also receives massive Federal funding.[4] In contrast, some small consolidated rural school districts serve fewer than 10,000 students, maintain a high teacher-to-suppport staff ratio, offer only a few special services, have few delinquency problems, and receive minimum Federal support.

Despite these differences in organizational setting, however, all schools today have some common characteristics that affect the way they collect, maintain, use, and disclose information about students.

- Schools are tending to rely more on records than on personal contact in arriving at decisions.
- As maintaining order and sharing decision making with parents become more difficult, school officials feel a greater need for autonomy and for confidentiality in communicating with other school officials.
- Policy-making functions have been increasingly centralized as a consequence of growth and consolidation of school districts, but administrative decisions and policy implementation remain decentralized and generally free of monitoring by a central authority.
- Children are assigned and treated according to special categories established on the basis of various characteristics and performance indicators.
- Educational personnel have become increasingly professionalized, and thus more attentive to the standards of their particular professional specialties than to those of the institution that employs them.
- Any school or school district is a microcosm of the community in which it exists and hence, to the degree that juvenile crime, racial conflict, drug and child abuse, and other social problems exist in communities, schools have to deal with them both alone and in cooperation with other community institutions.
- Because most school districts are overcommitted, driven by contradictory demands to deliver more services and cope with social problems while reducing costs or holding them constant, record-keeping problems cannot successfully compete with other demands for their time, attention, and resources.

CREATION AND USE OF RECORDS

The content of school records is to some extent required by State education laws and local school boards. Information such as the child's name and birthdate, immunizations, and a certain amount of descriptive information about family background at the time of enrollment are usually required. Thereafter, grades and credits are added to a student's record,

---

[4] Testimony of the Los Angeles Unified School District, Education Records Hearings, October 7, 1976, pp. 8-100.

along with health information, test scores, actions authorized by the school, parental authorizations or prohibitions, and family financial data. In addition, a student record now almost always includes information about the behavior and personality of the student, his social life; and the status, attitudes, and behavior of his family. For example, one school district's guidelines[5] allow the accumulation of information about

- family life—attitudes of parents toward the school, stability of the home, the social and economic status of the family;
- personal characteristics—aggressiveness, amount of attention demanded, reaction to sexual development; and
- social life—crushes, boy-girl relationships, kinds, numbers, and age of friends, and membership in churches, lodges, or fraternal organizations.

Much of the information about a student is kept at the school in a cumulative record, but some information—such as psychological test data, records of family visits by school social workers, eligibility for special programs—is maintained separately.

Methods of collecting information vary. Much of it is provided to the school directly by the student or his parents, while other information comes from test scores and teacher or administrative evaluations. So-called "anecdotal information" is created by the institution on its own initiative from observation of the student; from analysis, interpretation, and synopsis of information already on record; and from interpretations made by the person creating the record when information provided by the student or parent is insufficient.

Anecdotal information tends to be negative. Elementary and secondary institutions normally have resources available to them for the detection and treatment of special student problems. Thus, the task of detecting problems early and providing special treatment to remedy them creates a diagnostic bias toward negative information. This bias may grow when there are institutional or fiscal incentives to over-identify problems. It also can grow when the methods of diagnosing a problem leave room for interpretation, or when the person making the entry is not professionally qualified to report a diagnosis (e.g., the diagnosis of unruly children as hyperkinetic by people who are not medical professionals).

There are few limits on a school's internal use of education records in making administrative and instructional decisions about students. School authorities do not hesitate to seek and use whatever information about the student's background and personality might seem to bear on his academic performance. Even those special programs to which a child is assigned on the basis of some specific characteristic tend to use a broad base of information in making decisions about him once he is in the program. Individualized instruction, "mainstreaming" (i.e., incorporating education-ally handicapped children and programs designed especially for them into

---

[5] Los Angeles City School Districts, Division of Elementary Education, Guidance and Counseling Section, *Cumulative Record Handbook for Elementary Schools: A Guide for Teachers*, Tentative Edition, December 1968.

the normal classroom situation) and team teaching—all popular innovations in elementary and secondary education today—are likely to intensify rather than diminish this reliance on a large number of factors in evaluating a student.

Standards regarding the content and use of records often exist on paper but are rarely put into practice. The best information management practices are found in academic grading. Grades are systematically created by processes generally known to parents and students and are documented and regularly reported to them. For other types of records, however, there are few generally accepted standards of relevance or propriety. Administrative control of record keeping is minimal. While most institutions define what they consider to be basic information, individual educators generate a wealth of other records. For example, many individualized instruction programs require a diagnostic profile of each child to be used in making day-to-day instructional decisions about him. Without systematic quality control, however, the information in records of this type is bound to reflect the varying competencies of the professionals who create them.

Some elementary and secondary school districts have guidelines specifying the kinds of information members of the school staff may enter in a student's cumulative record. For example, a guideline might specify that entries include only firsthand observations, noting the time and place of the observation and the identity of the observer. To make such guidelines effective, however, the staff must be trained to follow them and student records must be systematically reviewed for compliance.

Given the multiple functions and broad responsibilities of elementary and secondary schools, the differences among them, and the emphasis on the whole child, there is understandable disagreement about what standards for record keeping should be. Even if standards for relevance, propriety, and reliability of information were firmly established, it would be difficult to monitor their application because record keeping in most school systems is so decentralized.

RECORD-KEEPING RESPONSIBILITY AND AUTHORITY

The authority of educational institutions to collect, use, and disclose information about students is even broader than their authority to make administrative and instructional decisions. State laws usually do not restrict the collection of information, nor do they surround the information that forms the basis of educational decisions with due process protections.

Local boards of education seldom involve themselves in developing record-keeping policies, leaving it to professional educators, whose primary concern is school management, to establish such policies. Educators, in turn, have given the matter little attention and have seldom consulted parents and students about what information is collected or how it is used. As records come to substitute for personal interaction, educators understandably come to view records as their own and view the involvement of parents and students in decisions about record keeping as a threat to their autonomy and an implied insult to their integrity.

PERSONAL PRIVACY IN AN INFORMATION SOCIETY

Disclosure Practices

Most elementary and secondary institutions have a tradition of treating records about students as "within the family," that is, as entrusted to the school for use by the school. The tradition is being challenged by both internal and external pressures. Increased specialization has divided responsibility within the school among teachers, psychologists, social workers, security personnel, and professional school administrators. Each type of school employee tends to have different relations to outside agencies and professionals. Thus, a school social worker, for example, relates as much to a colleague in a child welfare or corrections agency as he does to his school principal. Moreover, he often needs the assistance of professionals in those agencies who turn to him for assistance as well.

Some believe that schools exceed the limits of justifiable sharing of information about students or their families. For example, in school districts troubled by gang violence or drug abuse, school disciplinarians may informally share information about student behavior with local law enforcement agencies. In Maryland, for example, a county government began collecting information about students' families ostensibly to establish the students' eligibility to attend county schools, but the information was routinely shared with motor vehicle and taxing authorities for purposes having little or nothing to do with the educational mission of the school district.[6]

A school district may also transfer individually identifiable information from student records to other State agencies in order to establish the district's eligibility for categorical funds. In addition, school districts also share individually identifiable records with State and Federal agencies or their contractors for audit, program evaluation, research, and statistical purposes. Decisions to use student records for research purposes are usually made at the level of the individual school, whether or not policies regarding such use exist at the district level.

The Commission's findings indicate that practices with respect to research use of student records in elementary and secondary school districts vary widely.[7] In some districts the outside researcher is considered a nuisance. In others, it appears that close relationships exist between school personnel and university-based researchers who share a common interest in the use of student records for research purposes. In most cases, however, research has little or nothing to do with the immediate education of the child whose records are used, nor does it directly benefit the child or the school. While some schools seek parental consent before disclosing records for research purposes, or parental participation if the project entails the collection of new information, practices at the elementary and secondary level seem to present few barriers to the use of student records for research purposes.

---

[6] Elizabeth Becker, "Parents say 'School board is prying,'" *Washington Post*, May 6, 1976, Maryland Section, p. 6.

[7] Testimony of Stefan Javanovich of the Urban Policy Research Institute, Education Records Hearings, October 7, 1976, pp. 121-22.

Education records, like hospital records, public assistance and social services records, and other administrative records are becoming a valuable commodity for large-scale studies. Schools are finding it more difficult to resist research demands on their records or to control the conditions of use and redisclosure, especially if the research is sponsored by an agency that supplies them with funds.

PRINCIPAL RECORD-KEEPING PROBLEMS

While any generalizations about a world as large and diverse as elementary and secondary education must have numerous exceptions, the Commission's inquiry led it to the following general conclusions with respect to the records elementary and secondary educational institutions generate about students.

- School record-keeping practices are often anachronistic and institutional interests tend to overshadow the interests of students and parents in the collection, use, and dissemination of education records.
- Given the demand for curriculum reform, improvement of service delivery, and cost reduction, there is little incentive to devote the time, energy, or money to update or substantially modify record-keeping practices.
- The character of educational record-keeping systems (e.g., the range of information they include, its subjectivity, and the lack of criteria for relevance or propriety) create privacy problems for an individual whose ability to protect himself is weak.
- The authority of the institution, the uncertain relationship between decisions and information, and the institution's weak accountability to its students and their parents further diminish the individual's ability to cope.
- As educational records become more important, educational institutions tend to see control over them less as a stewardship on behalf of students than as a prerogative that cannot be shared with students and parents.
- The pressures for more collection and dissemination of information will continue, and there is little to counter them.

POST-SECONDARY EDUCATIONAL INSTITUTIONS

The primary mission of post-secondary institutions is academic and vocational, and focuses on the development of intellectual and technical skills. Because most students in institutions of higher education are adults, the institution shares responsibility for their development not with parents and other social institutions, but with the students themselves. Normally, institutions of higher education do not actively seek to identify students who are potentially eligible for assistance that supplements academic training. The institution may or may not assist a student in obtaining public assistance and social services, for example, but if it does, acceptance of those services by the student is voluntary; the institution does not have custodial responsibility.

The difference in institutional mission and responsibility is the key to understanding the differences between the record-keeping practices of elementary and secondary schools and those of post-secondary schools. In post-secondary education, the minimal institutional responsibility for socialization of the student and the lack of custodial responsibility creates a simpler and more differentiated set of relationships between the institution and the individual.

THE ROLE OF RECORDS IN DECISION MAKING

The limited and narrowly focused mission of post-secondary institutions results in a more limited and clearly defined set of functions and types of decisions. The primary functions are to provide instruction, to order a student's progression through a broad but highly standardized set of instructional programs, and to provide academic counseling. In addition, most post-secondary institutions provide a range of ancillary services such as medical care, financial assistance, and housing.

The majority of post-secondary institutions draw a clear line between instructional and ancillary services. The student's academic relationship with the institution is usually clearly segregated from his financial, medical, or housing relationships. The basic decisions that relate to admission, to evaluation of academic performance, and determination of eligibility for financial aid are characterized by highly rational, comparative decision making based upon well known criteria.

INSTITUTIONAL DECISION-MAKING RESPONSIBILITIES AND AUTHORITY

The relationship between a post-secondary institution and its students is voluntary and contractual in nature. Generally, the rights and responsibilities of both are spelled out in advance. Rules of conduct, and sanctions for violations, are made known to students. Academic requirements, in terms of required courses and performance levels, are clearly defined. Admission is usually selective except in some State systems, so most institutions can use performance standards to control enrollment. Individual institutions can also control the variety of programs they offer.

Post-secondary institutions have much broader authority than do elementary and secondary institutions. Public institutions are established and regulated by State law, but generally are delegated broad authority. Private institutions are subject to some government regulation, but it does not usually affect their authority over students. Nevertheless, post-secondary institutions have in recent years increasingly shared both responsibility and authority with students. The involvement of students in governance at the departmental, college, and even university level is common, especially insofar as program planning, standard setting, and developing due process mechanisms for decision making are concerned. Colleges and universities, particularly those that are public, have permitted, and in some cases encouraged, strong student organizations to negotiate with faculty and administrators on matters of mutual interest.

VARIATIONS IN ORGANIZATIONAL SETTING

There is a strong trend toward large and diversified public higher education systems with huge campuses. Some states like California have a university system in which each campus has a full array of undergraduate, graduate, and professional schools; a state college system in which each campus has a full complement of undergraduate institutions and some graduate and professional schools; and a number of community colleges. Nonetheless, there are still many private institutions, including sectarian or liberal arts colleges, with fewer than 1,000 students.

The size of student bodies in post-secondary schools can vary from a few hundred to 50,000. Some campuses are urban while others are located in communities with a smaller population than the campus. In the latter case, the community may be economically and socially dependent on the school. Some campuses have more than 100 departments offering specialized training and more than 15 quasi-autonomous schools or colleges. Some of the larger campuses have annual budgets of over $300 million and more than 10,000 employees. Most post-secondary schools have some kind of law enforcement unit or special arrangement with local law enforcement units. Some use Federal funds only for Basic Opportunity Grants for Handicapped Students; others receive up to 40 percent of their total budget from Federal agencies.

Again, however, there are certain characteristics common to all of these diverse organizational settings that affect the collection, maintenance, use, and dissemination of records about students.

- The larger the student body, the more likely it has been for an institution to rely on records rather than on personal contact in dealing with students, particularly at the graduate levels.
- In the last decade, post-secondary institutions have increasingly shared authority and responsibility with students.
- While growth has led to centralization of policy and administrative support functions, academic decision making about individual students remains highly decentralized.
- Ancillary services such as health care, psychological services, law enforcement, financial aid, and undergraduate admissions tend to be highly professional and completely separate from the academic decision processes, with independent record-keeping practices that are governed by the standards of the different professional groups involved.
- Universities and even small colleges, tend to be cities unto themselves; not microcosms of the communities in which they are located. Hence, relationships with community agencies are the exception rather than the rule.
- Colleges and universities, like elementary and secondary

schools, are caught between demands for more services and high fixed costs. Many engage in research and public service functions, both to support their graduate and professional programs and to meet public needs. These activities often strain their budgets and dominate their attention. Almost all are under tremendous pressure from State legislatures, students or alumni to curtail rising costs.

• Many post-secondary institutions are major employers, custodians of massive physical complexes, and major contractors for a variety of Federal agencies. As such, they must comply with Federal program requirements that tend to increase their costs, decrease management control at a time when they are pressed for management efficiency, and dominate much of their agenda. Federal requirements arising from anti-discrimination legislation, Federal procurement practices, occupational safety and environmental protection legislation, student-loan and other financial assistance programs have made post-secondary institutions wary of Federal regulation. Post-secondary institutions have also developed a tendency to concentrate on the letter rather than the spirit of Federal program requirements.

CREATION AND USE OF RECORDS

Post-secondary institutions maintain many different kinds of records about students. Some are centralized; others are created solely for the use of a department, committee, or individual faculty member. Some are conscientiously used for only one purpose; others are segregated in theory but are actually used widely for many purposes. Some are uniform in content, format, and method of collection; others differ widely in those respects. The problem for the individual in a post-secondary institution arises from the difficulty of finding out what records are being kept, by whom they are being kept, and for what purposes they are being used.

The records on students that are centralized are primarily academic records (e.g., courses, credits, grades, letters of recommendation), attendance records, and financial records. Such records seldom include much information about a student's family or social life, and only rarely include anything about a student's personality and behavior.

The centralized record about a student starts with admission. In most of the public undergraduate institutions, admissions is a fairly straightforward and simple process. The applicant supplies most of the information needed, including academic, financial, and health information, and often letters of recommendation to verify and supplement the academic record. Registrars' offices usually maintain the official academic record, which includes information regarding course work, credits earned, and grades. Health and financial records are maintained separately.

In private undergraduate institutions, and in both public and private graduate and professional schools, the admissions process generates a detailed record on the applicant, only part of which is supplied to the school by the applicant himself. Such records may include the results of faculty and staff interviews, letters of recommendation, indicators of expected performance generated from analysis of transcripts, ratings or rankings created by the admissions process, and documentation of the actions taken by admissions officers and committees with respect to the individual applicant. The admissions decisions of these institutions often allow for considerable exercise of professional judgment, unsupported by documentation. Admissions criteria often include vaguely defined attributes such as "character" and "morals."[8] Although some admission decisions are made on the basis of objective information, in many cases highly subjective data on applicants is collected and used. Institutional controls on the relevance, propriety, and reliability of the information collected do not appear to exist.

Letters of recommendation, whether written at the request of the applicant or the institution, play a role in some but not all admissions decisions. While there is great variation in attitudes toward the value of letters of recommendation, the professors preparing them, and the institutions receiving them have tended to treat them as confidential communications that should *not* be made available to the applicant.

Universities usually set minimum record-keeping requirements for colleges and academic departments, but academic record keeping outside the registrar's office is extremely decentralized. Colleges and universities have very few restrictions or even guidelines on content, format, or method of collecting information for records kept at the department or college level. There are, moreover, few incentives for an academic department to cede any professional or departmental control over record keeping to a centralized authority within the institution. This is especially true if control impinges on activities that faculty members perceive as professional prerogatives and which, therefore, crucially affect faculty-administration relationships. Nonetheless, problems such as grade inflation suggest that the professional standards of judgment in academic performance evaluation are inconsistent, relatively weak, and often of no great interest to those making such judgments. Faculty members are not specifically trained to evaluate student performance. While standards are difficult to set, and the evaluation process will always rely heavily on professional judgment, records of evaluators normally do not include the evidence underlying the judgments they contain.

As written records tend to be substituted for the unrecorded personal knowledge of faculty and administrators, "second-order" student records have been increasingly generated. An example of such second-order records are those created by teaching assistants to enable a faculty member to operate in a system which presumes he has personal knowledge of his students, even though his class may include 400 students. Another illustration is the records created by academic supervisory committees to develop and monitor a graduate student's curriculum. Such records may or may not be official, and they often differ within colleges or even within

---

[8] Testimony of the Medical School, University of California, Los Angeles, Education Records Hearings, October 8, 1976, pp. 556-58.

departments of the same institution. Information in these kinds of records is, however, almost always limited to academic performance and performance evaluation. They are not used for diagnosis or specialized treatment because students in post-secondary schools are expected to make decisions about courses without the benefit of someone else's analysis of special needs.

Ancillary services can be quite elaborate in post-secondary institutions. Many university counseling centers, for example, provide psychotherapy for students, and almost all maintain student health centers staffed by physicians. Many even have hospital facilities for student use. Financial aid services, too, may be quite extensive, and may generate extensive records about students and their parents. These financial records are not commingled with other centralized records, however, and information in them is rarely disclosed or used within the university for other than financial-aid purposes.

Post-secondary institutions usually keep disciplinary records on students, and many institutions have campus security units that maintain their own records. Student records are often shared between administrators responsible for discipline and campus security forces.[9] Such information does not affect academic decision making, although academic records are often used in evaluating students who have created a disciplinary problem. Nevertheless, there are few internal limits on the use of academic or disciplinary records. For example, the turbulent period of the late 1960's and early 1970's provided many examples of the ability of institutions to collect and use information about students in order to control them.[10] The boundaries between academic and disciplinary decision making are sometimes more nebulous than the institutions like to admit, and in times of political stress, professional ethics are a poor substitute for legal controls over the internal uses of records.

RECORD-KEEPING RESPONSIBILITY AND AUTHORITY

Post-secondary institutions have almost unlimited freedom to collect and use records about students. Few proscriptions regarding the collection or use of records appear in law or university policy. The public accountability structures in both public and private institutions, while powerful, are neither sufficiently focused on administrative questions nor responsive enough to students' interests to limit record-keeping autonomy. In practice, professional standards, and the recent trend toward student involvement in university governance, do provide some limits on institutional autonomy. As noted above, however, record keeping in higher education is predominantly a professional prerogative.

[9] Submission of National Student Association, Education Records Hearings, November 12, 1976.

[10] Testimony of National Student Association, Education Records Hearings, November 12, 1976, pp. 392-93.

DISCLOSURE PRACTICES

In post-secondary education, there is little occasion for information to flow beyond the bounds of the educational institution. Colleges and universities have a tradition of limiting the release of information about students to external organizations, in effect holding the information in "trust" for the students. Traditionally, they have released information regarding attendance, degrees received, courses taken, and honors received, but most will not transfer records of a student's academic performance or financial situation to other institutions unless a student requests that they do so.[11]

Much of the current demand for information in student records comes from commercial interests developing mailing lists, or from Federal agencies conducting research, evaluating programs, or auditing financial records. For example, controversy arose recently over the use of student information by the Veterans Administration (VA) in auditing VA student-aid programs administered by institutions of higher education. The VA auditors compare records of students who do not receive its funds with the records of students who do, and inspect student records without the consent of the students involved.[12] In at least one reported instance, records on students were physically removed from a school to another location where they were inaccessible to students.[13] Still, research using information in records on students in individually identifiable form in higher education is not extensive. In addition, while institutions may permit such use without the consent of the individual under certain circumstances, universities are usually quick to demand guarantees of confidentiality from the research-ers.[14]

The most sensitive disclosures made by post-secondary institutions are to law enforcement authorities. In the recent past, a number of universities have collaborated with law enforcement and intelligence agencies to generate and share information on the political activities of student radicals. Many post-secondary institutions depend on local law enforcement agencies for campus security and may share information with these agencies. This sharing occurs most often in institutions that have campus security units. These units, usually staffed by law enforcement professionals, are more likely to follow the professional law enforcement norm of widespread sharing of information with other law enforcement authorities than the norm of strict confidentiality generally followed by educational institutions. The information shared is often trivial—for example, the fine for a parking

---

[11] See, for example, Testimony of Goucher College, Education Records Hearings, November 11, 1976, pp. 276-77; Testimony of University of Maryland, Education Records Hearings, November 11, 1976, pp. 293-96; and Memoranda of staff interviews with admissions officials of the University of California, San Diego and the University of California, Los Angeles.

[12] See, for example, Testimony of Goucher College, Education Records Hearings, November 11, 1976, pp. 276-77; and Testimony of University of Maryland, Education Records Hearings, November 11, 1976, pp. 282-83.

[13] Memoranda of staff interviews with Mr. Frank Till, Director of Information Services of the National Student Association, July 1976.

[14] Testimony of Yale University, Education Records Hearings, November 11, 1976, pp. 68-69.

ticket given by a campus policeman may have to be paid to the local city government at the latter's offices, an arrangement which entails a record transfer of minimal import. In other situations, such as in cases involving drug traffic, major thefts, or threats of violence, the information shared may be much more extensive and consequential.

PRINCIPAL RECORD-KEEPING PROBLEMS

The Commission's inquiry led it to the following general conclusions with respect to the records post-secondary institutions generate about students.

- While the interests of educational institutions tend to over-shadow the interests of students in the collection, use, and dissemination of education records, the more balanced relationship between the post-secondary institution and the student tends to restrict the areas of potential harm to the student that can result from record-keeping practices.
- It is in those areas that have the greatest impact on a student's career, namely in academic performance evaluation and admission to graduate or professional school, that abuses are most likely to arise. It is in these decisions that judgment weighs most heavily, that the basis for decisions can be hard to identify, and that faculty prerogatives are strongest. Thus, a student may perceive that any effort to assert his interest in a record about himself may jeopardize his chances of a favorable evaluation.

TESTING AND DATA-ASSEMBLY SERVICE ORGANIZATIONS

As the number of persons seeking admission and financial aid began to tax the capabilities of post-secondary educational institutions, they formed coalition organizations such as the College Entrance Examination Board (CEEB) and the Law School Admissions Council to help collect and process the information used to make admissions and financial-aid decisions. Through these coalition organizations, post-secondary institutions have since fostered the growth of other organizations that test and assemble information on applicants. Best known among them are the Educational Testing Service (ETS) and the American College Testing Program (ACT).

Testing and data-assembly service organizations have become a gate through which a student's education records must pass if he is to gain admission to accredited institutions and to qualify for certain types of financial aid. The student must pay fees for taking tests and for having information assembled, stored, and forwarded to the educational institutions he designates. Because testing and data-assembly service organizations provide their services under contract to organizations like the College Entrance Examination Board and the Law School Admissions Council rather than to post-secondary institutions, policy regarding their record-keeping practices is set by the former rather than the latter, and the students they serve have no role whatsoever.

Testing and data-assembly service organizations are highly specialized and rely heavily on information supplied to them by the applicant. Their procedures for collecting, generating, and maintaining information are also highly automated. Their sophistication and technical proficiency make them sensitive to record-keeping issues and they have strong fiscal incentives for efficient and effective information management, and do not often make serious errors, but they sometimes have difficulty detecting the errors they do make.

Testing and data-assembly organizations usually inform an individual about the principal uses they make of the information they collect about him. Moreover, their policies generally limit the uses they make of their records to the purposes communicated to the individual. Testing and data-assembly organizations take special precautions to protect individually identifiable data when their records are used for research. They also have strong confidentiality standards. One such organization has repeatedly gone to court to resist attempts by the Internal Revenue Service to subpoena student financial data.[15] Nevertheless, a testing and data-assembly service organization is not in a position to assume total responsibility for record-keeping policies that would operate to safeguard the interests of the individual, since its policies reflect those of its clients, the coalition organizations representing post-secondary institutions. The Commission's hearing record indicates that the oversight post-secondary institutions exercise over the operations of testing and data-assembly service organizations tends to serve their own interests somewhat better than it does the interests of applicants.[16] Thus, although such organizations deal directly with individual applicants, and collect and process mountains of information about them, they are less accountable to the individuals on whom they keep records than any other type of record-keeping institution in higher education.

THE FAMILY EDUCATIONAL RIGHTS AND PRIVACY ACT

THE ORIGINS OF FERPA

The growing importance of records about students and of the record-keeping practices of educational institutions has not gone unnoticed. Litigation and the professional literature have drawn attention in recent years to the misuse of personal information in the placement of minority children in programs for the educationally handicapped.[17] Research has highlighted the impact of stigmatization on the educational achievements of children and has pointed to the impact on educational decisions of

---

[15] Testimony of Educational Testing Service, Education Records Hearings, November 12, 1976, pp. 301-19.

[16] Testimony of Ohio State University College of Law, Education Records Hearings, November 11, 1976, pp. 159-80.

[17] *Diana v. California Board of Education*, Docket No. C-70-37-RFP (N.D. Calif. 1970); *P. v. Riles*; 343 F. Supp. 1306 (N.D. Calif. 1972), *Aff'd* 502 F. 2d 963 (9th Cir. 1974).

erroneous or incomplete information about students. Court cases prior to the passage of FERPA in 1974 increasingly recognized that decisions made by schools can result in harm to students and that students and parents must therefore have a right of redress.[18]

Several studies carried out in the early 1970's documented record-keeping problems in both higher education and elementary and secondary schools. In 1970, the Russell Sage Foundation convened a conference on the Ethical and Legal Aspects of School Record Keeping to clarify principles for the management of elementary and secondary school records. Release of the conference report[19] was followed by a second conference on Student Records in Higher Education and a second report.[20] The recommendations in these reports helped to crystallize concern about the creation, use, and disclosure of school records.

The stimulus for the passage of FERPA was a 1974 study of the National Council of Citizens in Education (NCCE).[21] In this report the NCCE identified the following as the most prevalent abuses in elementary and secondary school record keeping:

- *carte blanche* access to school records by school personnel, law enforcement agencies, welfare and health department workers, and Selective Service Board representatives;
- lack or denial of the right of parents and students to inspect school records, to control what goes into them, and to challenge their contents;
- failure to obtain permission from parents before collecting information on students and their families (for example, before submitting students to psychiatric or personality tests);
- serious abuses in the preparation of student records that follow students throughout their educational careers; and
- failure to inform students and parents when, to whom, and why others are given access to records.

On May 14, 1974, Senator James L. Buckley succeeded in getting a floor amendment to the General Education Provision's Act of 1974 which aimed to correct these problems. The two main provisions of the amendment, which applied to any school that receives Federal funds through the U.S. Office of Education (Department of Health, Education, and Welfare), required procedures to assure students and parents access to those records and restricted disclosure of records to third parties. Although the amendment had not been the subject of Congressional hearings, it was adopted by

---

[18] *Goss v. Lopez*, 419 U.S. 565 (1975); *Wood v. Strickland*, 420 U.S. 308 (1975); *Wisconsin v. Yoder*, 406 U.S. 205 (1972).

[19] Russell Sage Foundation, *Guidelines for the Collection, Maintenance, and Dissemination of Pupil Records*, Report of a Conference on the Ethical and Legal Aspects of School Record Keeping, June 12-14, 1972.

[20] Russell Sage Foundation, *Student Records in Higher Education: Recommendations for the Formulation and Implementation of Record-Keeping Policies in Colleges and Universities*, June 12-14, 1975.

[21] National Committee for Citizens in Education, *Children, Parents, and School Records*, 1974, p. 309.

the conference committee on the General Education Provision's Act later that summer and signed into law on August 21, 1974.[22] At the time, few educators were aware of it.

During the weeks after its enactment, however, educational institutions and other interested parties around the country launched a massive letter-writing campaign to members of Congress. At this point, the Senate and House Education Subcommittees and the Department of Health, Education, and Welfare Legislative Office took the lead in working out a compromise measure, which Senator Buckley sponsored. Representatives of educational institutions and of parent and student groups contributed to the drafting of the revision, which became known as the Family Educational Rights and Privacy Act. It was passed by both Houses of Congress and signed into law in December 1974.[23]

The process by which FERPA was enacted had a significant impact on its subsequent implementation. Several factors are important in understanding this impact. First, professional educators were not involved in drafting the original legislation nor even aware of its existence. Although key groups were brought in during the redrafting, their role could only be responsive, not creative, and was, in the main, defensive. Because there had been no national debate or public hearings on the measure, and only a minimum of congressional debate, neither the affected parties (i.e., educational institutions, parents, and students) nor the Department of Health, Education, and Welfare, which had to develop regulations to implement the Act, received much guidance on the manner in which the Act should be interpreted.

Second, FERPA was primarily designed to address documented problems in elementary and secondary schools, but it was made applicable to higher education on the too simple assumption that the problems in both areas are similar and thus that the same principles would apply equally well in both places. Representatives of higher education who participated in drafting the compromise amendment considered the final version to be a vast improvement over the original measure. Nevertheless, they continued to be convinced that FERPA addressed a set of record-keeping problems that were different from those that arise in higher education and thus that the requirements of FERPA would create substantial burdens without benefiting students.

THE REQUIREMENTS OF FERPA

The principal requirements of FERPA are straightforward: they give a student or his parent the right to inspect and review, and request correction or amendment of, an education record maintained about him *[20 U.S.C. 1232g(a)(1) and (2)];* and give a student or his parents some measure of control over the disclosure of information from an education record about him *[20 U.S.C. 1232g(b)(1)].* FERPA obligates educational institutions to provide procedures for inspection and review of records within 45 days from

---

[22] P.L. 93-380.
[23] P.L. 93-568.

the time it receives a request for access to them. *[20 U.S.C. 1232g(a)(1)(A)]* It also exempts the following types of records from parent and student access:

- records maintained by law enforcement units of educational institutions, if such records are maintained separately from other education records and if no exchange of information between those records and other education records is permitted *[20 U.S.C. 1232g(a)(4)(B)(ii)];*
- medical or psychological treatment records maintained separately from other education records and used only for medical treatment purposes; provided, however, that such records may be seen by an appropriate professional of the student's choice *[20 U.S.C. 1232g(a)(4)(B)(iv)];*
- so-called "desk drawer notes;" that is, personal records of instructional, supervisory, or administrative personnel that are not shared with anyone else except a substitute *[20 U.S.C. 1232g(a)(4)(B)(i)];*
- confidential letters of recommendation that were in a student's record before the Act or to which the student has waived his right of access *[20 U.S.C. 1232g(a)(1)(B)(ii) and (iii)(I)];* and
- records about applicants who have never been students at the educational institution. *[20 U.S.C. 1232g(a)(6)]*

FERPA requires educational institutions to allow students or parents to have a hearing to challenge information in records they believe to be inaccurate, misleading, or otherwise in violation of their privacy rights. It also obligates an educational institution to correct or delete challenged information or, if it refuses to make the requested correction, to insert in the record the student or parent's written explanation regarding the disputed information. *[20 U.S.C. 1232g(a)(2)]*

In addition, FERPA requires written consent from a student or parent before a student's record or any personally identifiable information in it may be disclosed to a third party. Consent is not required, however, when the disclosure is to:

- officials of the educational institution acting in pursuit of a legitimate educational purpose *[20 U.S.C. 1232g(b)(1)(A)];*
- officials of schools or school systems in which the student seeks to enroll, provided the student is notified of the disclosure, given a copy of the record or information upon request, and has an opportunity to have a hearing to challenge the contents of the record or information *[20 U.S.C. 1232g(b)(1)(B)];*
- certain Federal and State agencies for auditing and evaluation purposes on the condition that no redisclosure of the record is made and it is destroyed when no longer needed *[20 U.S.C. 1232g(b)(1)(C), (E), and (4)(B)];*

- accrediting agencies for accrediting purposes *[20 U.S.C. 1232g(b)(1)(G)];*
- organizations conducting studies for educational purposes on behalf of educational institutions, on the condition that no redisclosure of the record is made and it is destroyed when no longer needed *[20 U.S.C. 1232g(b)(1)(F)];*
- in an emergency, when necessary to protect the health and safety of the student or other persons *[20 U.S.C. 1232g(b)(1)(I)];* and
- in response to a judicial order or lawfully issued subpoena, provided that parents and students are notified in advance of compliance with the order or subpoena. *[20 U.S.C. 1232g(b)(2)(B)].*

FERPA also permits an educational institution to disclose directory information (i.e., information about the identity or status of the student which has been publicly designated by the institution as directory information) without the consent of the student or his parent, provided the student or parent has had a reasonable opportunity to inform the institution that any or all of the information should not be released without the student's prior consent. *[20 U.S.C. 1232g(a)(5)]* An educational institution must keep an accounting of all disclosures requested or obtained, and allow a student or parent to review the accounting. *[20 U.S.C. 1232g(b)(4)(A)]*

FERPA instructs the Secretary of Health, Education, and Welfare to promulgate regulations to protect the rights of students and their families in surveys or data-collection activities conducted, assisted, or authorized by the DHEW or an educational institution. *[20 U.S.C. 1232g(c)]* Finally, it places a requirement on educational institutions to inform students and parents of their rights under the Act. *[20 U.S.C. 1232g(e)]*

FERPA applies to any institution receiving U.S. Office of Education funding and provides for the termination of such funding if an institution fails to comply with it and compliance cannot be secured voluntarily. *[20 U.S.C. 1232g(f)]* DHEW is required to set up an office and a review board to investigate, review, and adjudicate violations and complaints alleging violations. *[20 U.S.C. 1232g(g)]*

The Commission believes that FERPA represents a reasonably successful attempt to establish a clear set of minimum requirements for the protection of students' and parents' privacy rights. At the same time, its gives each educational institution considerable latitude in establishing its own procedures to fulfill these requirements. Ironically, FERPA's most specific provisions are the exceptions to its requirements, and most of them were added at the request of representatives of educational institutions and Federal agencies during the drafting of the compromise measure.

REGULATIONS IMPLEMENTING FERPA

In preparing the regulations, DHEW consulted extensively with representatives of educational institutions, and generally did not interpret the Act in such a way as to reduce the flexibility given educational institutions by the statute. The regulations require educational institutions and agencies to formulate a policy that specifies their procedures for effectuating the rights given students and parents by FERPA. Insofar as disclosure is concerned, the policy must specify rules and criteria for determining which educational purposes are legitimate and which school officials within the institution or agency can gain access to records. It must also specify what categories of information are to be considered directory information. The regulations include broad guidelines for hearing procedures, general conditions for disclosure in emergencies affecting the health and safety of an individual, and a definition of the term "student" that denies students in one component of an institution (an undergraduate college, for example) access to their admissions records in another component of the same institution (such as a law school or medical school).

The statute did not require DHEW to review and approve each institution's policies, or to pass judgment on the substance of policies when complaints are made, and the Department has not done so. Responsibility for judgments of that sort has been left to local institutions, and wisely so in the view of the Commission.

Experience in Implementing FERPA to Date

The implementation of FERPA has been plagued by confusion, misunderstanding, and delay. Because the Congress did not authorize additional funds for DHEW to implement the law, the Department has not been able to spend much money doing so. The Department's small Fair Information Practice Staff was designated as the office responsible for developing and promulgating the regulations required by the statute, answering questions and offering assistance in interpreting the statute and regulations, handling complaints about violations of FERPA requirements, and mediating solutions to conflicts over interpretations.

The FERPA regulations were not issued until June 1976, some 18 months after passage of the Act. Inadequate staffing and funding were not the only reasons for the delay. Extensive consultations with representatives of educational institutions took time, especially because many educators were still poorly informed about FERPA and resistant to Federal government regulation of any sort. As a consequence, many institutions did nothing to implement the Act pending the issuance of the regulations, while others attempted to develop policies based on interpretations derived from the Russell Sage and NCCE studies or those developed by their legal counsels.

The long delay generated confusion and misunderstanding that was not easily alleviated by issuing the regulations. While the DHEW staff was available to answer questions, not many educators turned to them for answers, and there was no systematic program to inform school officials or the public about the law. Rumors and misinterpretations have been widespread. For example, the Privacy Commission received an indignant complaint from an educator responsible for record-keeping policy in a large elementary and secondary school district who did not know that FERPA regulations, issued six months previously, had completely obviated the complaint.

Another serious implementation problem arose because FERPA was introduced into an environment that has come to expect the Federal regulatory role to be prescriptive. The underlying strategy of FERPA, which leaves to educational institutions most of the responsibility for defining the details of procedures to assure individual protection, has been viewed by educators as a weakness rather than a strength of the law. For example, the president of a local university recently complained to a reporter from the university's student newspaper that "the Buckley Amendment is one of the prime examples of poor legislation, poor administration and everything that goes into it. Just about every institution has a different interpretation of FERPA."[24]

What educators perceive to be ambiguity has led many of them to make unnecessarily labored and highly defensive interpretations of the law. Instead of taking the latitude afforded by the statute as a challenge to their professional skill, and as an opportunity for innovation in concert with parents, students, and colleagues, educators have turned to their legal counsels for safety. In many cases, legally sound advice has been unnecessarily burdensome and on occasion educationally unsound.

In the Commission's judgment, the major problem in implementing FERPA has been the lack of understanding among educators, parents, students, and the general public both about the requirements of the Act and the strategy of enforced self- regulation that underlies it. Where understanding of these factors exists, the Commission has found little objection on the part of educational institutions to either FERPA's principles or its requirements.[25] Contrary to their expectations, educators have found that offering students and parents access to their records does not unleash a tidal wave of demands for access and correction that immobilizes educational institutions. Implementing FERPA has not been burdensome for those institutions with sound record-keeping practices, or for those that have sought in good faith to develop policies consonant with the spirit of the law.[26]

A few of the complaints about unnecessary burdens are doubtless justified. Examples of possibly burdensome requirements include the requirement to keep a record available to students and parents of all requests for disclosure, whether granted or not *[20 U.S.C. 1232g(b)(4)(19)]*; the requirement to identify and list all record systems in a central place rather than simply requiring each component to have such a list available on request *[45 C.F.R. 99.5(2)(iv)]*; and the requirement to allow a student to restrict the disclosure of any or all categories of directory information. *[20*

---

[24] Jane McHugh, "GW Witholding Iranian Info," *The Hatchet*, February 17, 1977, p. 3.

[25] See, for example, Testimony of Franklin and Marshall College, Education Records Hearings, November 11, 1976, pp. 9-15; Testimony of San Diego Unified School District, Education Records Hearings, October 7, 1976, pp. 207-22 and pp. 250-59; and Testimony of University of California, Los Angeles, Education Records Hearings, October 8, 1976, pp. 487-89.

[26] Testimony of San Diego Unified School District, Education Records Hearings, October 7, 1976, pp. 252, 274-76.

U.S.C. 1232g(a)(5)(B)]; In addition, educators in some elementary and secondary schools have found restrictions on the sharing of information with social services agencies unnecessarily burdensome, and some schools at all levels have found it difficult to control access to student files by federally funded researchers.

Claims that FERPA imposes unreasonable costs appear to be largely rhetorical. Typical of the rhetoric is the statement of a university administrator that universities are "stockpiling lawyers like countries are stockpiling nuclear warheads in the cold war."[27] In reality, this administrator's own large State university has met the added burden of FERPA requirements by retaining the part-time services of an attorney who was also enrolled as a graduate student.

In response to the Commission's direct request for data on the cost of implementing FERPA, only one institution produced evidence of extra expenditures. Its estimate, after careful analysis, was that FERPA cost about one extra dollar per year per student and, in doing the analysis, it discovered several places in which the flexibility FERPA allows would enable it to cut even that cost without detriment to the individual student.[28] Had the cost of implementing FERPA been as great as the rhetoric would suggest, the Commission's request for data would surely have produced budgeting and planning documents reflecting the costs from institutions that had found them to be burdensome. While there are obviously some costs incurred in implementing the law—an extra page or two of printing, an extra form for those who wish directory information withheld, and the cost of discussions with faculty, staff, and administrators—it seems safe to infer that they are insignificant.

The cost of implementing FERPA depends of course on the quality of an institution's records and the efficiency of its record-keeping practices prior to the enactment of the statute. If the quality of an institution's records were so poor that it receives many requests to correct them, or is subjected to other legal action, then the cost of implementing FERPA might very well become substantial. The prospect of such costs provides a valuable incentive to develop better record-keeping policies and practices.

Even when policies are well conceived, difficulties can arise in implementing them. At the elementary and secondary school level, there are strong indications that in a large school district with a *uniform* policy, there is often little uniformity of *practice* among schools within the district. Parent and student groups have documented the allegation that student records are still being disclosed to law enforcement agencies without notice to, or authorization from, students or parents and that, in some cases, "desk

---

[27] Testimony of National Association of State Universities and Land Grant Colleges, Education Records Hearings, October 7, 1976, p. 252.
[28] Testimony of San Diego Unified School District, Education Records Hearings, October 7, 1976, p. 270.

drawer" notes have been used as official records, rather than solely as the personal records of a teacher.[29] Student groups testified to the Commission that universities or faculty members were subtly coercing students into waiving their right of access to letters of recommendation.[30] Further, the Commission could find little evidence that educational institutions are doing a very good job of informing students and parents of their rights under the Act.

The Commission found substantial evidence that neither parents nor educators consider the system for enforcing FERPA satisfactory, as it depends on complaints being filed with DHEW for mediation, and the only sanction for failure to comply with the law is withdrawal of all U.S. Office of Education funding. DHEW has not received many complaints, possibly because Washington seems too far away, or because the only available sanction is so harsh that it is rarely ever imposed and thus is not credible, or because the sanction would not in any case secure the desired result—prompt compliance. Educators resent, in principle, the idea of withdrawal of Federal funds and view its threat with disdain because it is not likely to be exercised.

THE INDIVIDUAL UNDER THE FAMILY EDUCATIONAL RIGHTS AND PRIVACY ACT

In spite of the limited and rather uneven implementation experience to date, the Commission was able to draw some reasonably reliable conclusions about the degree to which practices under FERPA meet the Commission's recommended public-policy objectives. The concerns expressed in its objectives are precisely those that led to the passage of FERPA: namely, minimizing intrusiveness; keeping recorded information from being a source of unfairness in decisions made on the basis of it; and establishing a legitimate, enforceable expectation of confidentiality. The complaints and abuses documented by parent and student groups, and the guidelines from the two Russell Sage studies cited above, also centered on these three objectives.

The statute, however, does not fully achieve the Commission's three objectives. There are significant gaps in its coverage of institutions and types of records, and the enforcement mechanisms it relies on are too weak to support its strategy of enforced self-regulation.

CONTROL OVER THE COLLECTION OF INFORMATION

FERPA seeks to minimize intrusiveness in several ways. It requires educational institutions that collect and maintain records about students to pay due regard to the "appropriateness" of information and the privacy rights of students. Currently, the only tool for enforcing it is the right of the

---

[29] Testimony of Stefan Javanovich, Urban Research Policy Institute, Education Records Hearings, October 7, 1976, pp. 121-24.

[30] Testimony of University of California Student Lobby, Education Records Hearings, October 8, 1976, pp. 563-70; and Testimony of National Student Association, Education Records Hearings, November 12, 1976, pp. 394-95.

student or his parent to inspect and challenge the contents of records. Although FERPA specifically requires the DHEW Secretary to issue regulations to protect the privacy of students and their families in connection with any surveys or data-gathering activities conducted, assisted, or authorized by an administrative head of an educational agency, the regulations have never been issued.

As the first section of this chapter indicates, intrusiveness in elementary and secondary schools is a serious problem, not only of surveys but also in the routine creation of records on students. An individual has little control over data collected directly from him, generated from observations of his behavior, or created by analysis of his student record. Yet FERPA does not address such collection and recording of information.

Reliance on access and correction as a remedy for intrusiveness has several deficiencies. Access and correction are at best remedial, not preventive, and do not address the problem of stigmatization. Parents are not and could not be notified of every entry made in the record of a student, so that substantial harm can be done before they can request correction of stigmatizing information. A student is stigmatized less by a particular item of information than by the composite impression the record as a whole conveys, which makes it difficult for parents to determine which items should be corrected or amended. An addendum to the record giving the student's or parent's side of the story seldom repairs damage to a student's reputation.

In addition, individual access to a record and the right to request that it be corrected cannot lead to preventive action in a highly decentralized system unless specific abuses are either concentrated in one location or are prevalent. If a serious abuse occurs only rarely, steps to prevent its recurrence may be taken only at the location where the abuse occurred, not throughout a system.

Intrusiveness is a problem of information collection. It is simply not realistic for students and parents to exercise control over what information is collected, but it is realistic for institutions to establish standards of propriety and relevance. Adequate standards not only minimize intrusiveness, but provide a context in which the individual can effectively exercise his right to challenge the content of a record, and thereby help the institution to maintain and improve its standards.

Intrusive surveys and other data collection activities are a major problem. Students are a captive population and as such are vulnerable not only to intrusive questioning but also to dangers that arise simply from too much questioning. As pointed out earlier, individuals in component units of decentralized systems often have the autonomy and incentive to authorize or engage in surveys and other data-collection activities. Part of the reason that DHEW has been slow to issue regulations applicable to these activities is that the Department has already promulgated regulations to protect the rights of all human research subjects *[45 C.F.R. 46 et seq.]* and is now in the process of revising them. Nevertheless, the regulations covering human research subjects apply only to DHEW funded activities, and leave to the data collector rather than the educational institution the responsibility of defining the interest of the individual in that research.

Although most of the data-collection activities in schools are sponsored by the Federal government, and the organizations carrying them out are covered by the research on human subjects regulations, some are not. Moreover, what the researcher, educator, and parent might consider appropriate may differ substantially. Parental complaints about intrusive surveys and other data-collection activities were one reason for the enactment of FERPA;[31] yet intrusive data-collection activities continue, notwithstanding DHEW's regulations regarding research on human subjects.

In post-secondary institutions, intrusiveness is not a major problem either in routine record keeping or in special data-collection activities. The organization and management of information by purpose and the comparatively clear standards for the content of records are important protections in themselves. The admissions process does, however, pose intrusiveness problems by virtue of the fact that FERPA places no obligation on an institution to establish standards of relevance and propriety with regard to the information collected and used in the admissions process, or to inform the applicant of the types of information that will be collected about him, and also by virtue of the fact that FERPA allows admissions records containing highly subjective information about him to be kept secret. *[20 U.S.C. 1232g(a)(6), (a)(B)(ii) and (iii); 45 C.F.R. 99.12(2) and (3)]*

Another intrusiveness danger arises in institutions that have law enforcement or campus security units that engage in investigative activities. FERPA tries to build a wall between the records maintained by such a unit and those maintained by the rest of the educational institution. It does so by exempting the records of a law enforcement unit from the FERPA access and correction requirements, provided the law enforcement unit's records are used and disclosed solely for law enforcement purposes, and the law enforcement unit does not have access to education records. *[20 U.S.C. 1232g(a)(4)(B)(ii); 45 C.F.R. 99.3]* This creates a problem because some of the information a law enforcement unit collects can be useful in maintaining school order and discipline. Yet, if a law enforcement unit shares such information with other school officials, even on a limited basis, *all* of its records must be open to student or parent access and no record maintained by the unit could be shared with local law enforcement agencies without student or parent consent, even though it could be disclosed and used widely within the educational institution. Most importantly, FERPA imposes no requirement that standards of appropriateness, relevance, or accuracy for such information be established and the Commission has found that the current statute in fact encourages a law enforcement unit to share

---

[31] National Committee for Citizens in Education, *op. cit.*.

information surreptitiously with other components of an educational institution.[32]

PROTECTIONS FOR FAIRNESS

Fairness is a major objective of FERPA. The basic tools for achieving it are the right of a parent or student to inspect, review, and challenge the contents of his record; and the obligation levied on the institution to provide a hearing, to correct or delete the challenged portion of a record, or to incorporate into the record a parent or student's explanatory statement. Again, however, these tools are not enough to achieve the Commission's objectives.

Particularly in elementary and secondary schools, the record-keeping practices that lead to unfairness also weaken the effectiveness of access and correction rights as protections against unfairness. Identifying unfair record-keeping practices requires the ability to relate records to decisions. In the educational process, however, parents are often unaware that important decisions are being made about their children. In fact, schooling can be looked upon as a continuous set of decisions, and it is unlikely that an institution could keep parents informed of each and every decision made about their child even if it tried to do so. Moreover, if rights of access and correction are tied to "adverse decisions," as the Commission recommends in other chapters of this report, is difficult to do in education because it is so difficult to define an adverse decision. Is placing a child in a compensatory program, for example, an "adverse" decision?

There are, of course, many decisions about which parents are informed, such as promotion, major disciplinary actions, or placement in particular academic programs. In some of these decisions, the role of records is clear and it is easy to label a certain outcome as negative or positive for the student. There are, however, many more decisions made about students that either parents do not know about, that are not clearly based on easily identified items of information, or whose effect on the child is difficult to assess. Such decisions can be based on so many factors that it is difficult for a parent to assess whether information in a record is inaccurate, misleading, or irrelevant as it relates to the decision. Standing alone, the right to inspect and request correction of a record places the total burden for assuring the reliability of records on the individual who often does not understand the system well enough to use the right effectively.

Particularly at the elementary and secondary level, there are also pressures on a student or his parent not to exercise such rights lest they be stigmatized as troublemakers or malcontents. In any relationship between an individual and an institution that has discretion to grant or deny him a benefit, there is the danger that the individual will be penalized for exercising a record-keeping right, unless the institution has strong incentives, legal or economic, not to retaliate. As far as schools are concerned,

---

[32] Testimony of Los Angeles Unified School District, Education Records Hearings, October 7, 1976, pp. 16-26, 40-45; and Testimony of Juvenile Services Division, Los Angeles Police Department, Education Records Hearings, October 8, 1976, pp. 288-91, 303-07, 309-20.

testimony presented to the Commission confirmed that educational institutions do sometimes retaliate, and that a number of parent and student organizations believe that they do so frequently.[33] Moreover, as pointed out in the discussion of intrusiveness, access and correction rights for individuals are at best remedial, not preventive, and do not readily lead to systemic improvements. An individual can contribute to improving the quality of information about him in records, but only if he knows what the record-keeping standards of an institution are. FERPA does not address the issue; it neither places an obligation upon educational institutions to establish standards nor requires that parents and students be informed about the record-keeping standards of the institution.

Because elementary and secondary schools treat individuals over time, they engage in substantial problem diagnosis. Hence, like any other treatment institution, they have established dual record systems—the official records kept by the institution and the so-called "desk drawer" notes that individual teachers, administrators, or ancillary personnel keep primarily for their own use. The latter type of record usually contains observations, impressions, questions, or even tentative interpretations and diagnoses. FERPA recognized that student or parent access to such information can be a two-edged sword in that it can deter the keeping of records and knowledge of what is in the records can impede an individual's course of treatment. Therefore, FERPA tried to balance the need for this type of record against the equally compelling argument that access to records by their subjects is an essential component of fairness in record keeping. The FERPA solution was to exempt desk drawer notes from student or parent access provided they are not revealed to any person other than a person substituting for the note taker. Educators have argued that this has reduced the value of such notes and thus has discouraged school personnel from keeping them. Educators argue that desk drawer notes work to the overall benefit of the student, but some parent and student groups contend that the notes of administrators with disciplinary responsibilities have in effect become secret record systems used to support disciplinary decisions.

In higher education, access and correction rights to most records are effective tools because institutions have standards for the content of records and their use. Nonetheless, when standards for the content of records are not clearly established, or when students are not clearly informed of those standards, as is the case with departmental records, the inadequacies of these FERPA requirements are the same as in elementary and secondary school systems. The pressures against the exercise of such rights are even stronger in post-secondary institutions than they are in elementary and secondary schools because the emphasis on professionalism and on the autonomy of faculty members is much stronger. The student is so dependent upon the professional judgments of individual faculty members that he is not likely to risk prejudicing them by asserting his rights.

---

[33] Testimony of Parent Education Center, Education Records Hearings, October 7, 1976, pp. 172-84; and Testimony of American Civil Liberties Union's Student Rights Center, Education Records Hearings, October 8, 1976, pp. 360-64.

An equally serious problem in post-secondary education is that FERPA grants no right of access or correction to records regarding admissions. This is the one area in which access and correction rights alone could be important protections. As in admissions, a record is compiled for a single decision of unquestionable importance to the individual. To assure fairness in making admission decisions, an individual needs to be able to challenge the contents of a record and request its correction so that the record will truly reflect facts about himself, his background, and his previous performance. Denying the applicant access to his admissions record and an opportunity to request correction of it leaves a serious breach in his defense against unfairness. This is especially true for a rejected applicant, because a successful applicant can have access to his admission record when he becomes a student, as such records must by law be maintained for 18 months.

The FERPA provision that permits a student to waive his right of access to letters of recommendation is another loophole in the statute that has special import for post-secondary students. While FERPA recognizes the individual's right to inspect such letters, the waiver provision can have the effect of placing a student under substantial pressure to relinquish his right at a time when he is most vulnerable to pressure. Empirical evidence presented to the Commission indicates that waiving one's right of access to a letter of recommendation has no discernible impact on the content and quality of such letters, although the myth persists that a student's refusal to do so inevitably debases the quality and thus the usefulness of the letter.[34] One university proposed barring waivers, but had to withdraw the proposal in the face of student assertions that accepting it would weaken their competitive position for admission to other institutions.[35] This is an even greater problem than it might otherwise appear to be by virtue of the fact that there are no content standards for letters of recommendation.

Another major deficiency of FERPA is that it does not aply to testing and data-assembly service organizations. Hence, an applicant has no legal right to inspect and challenge information in their files. This is significant because, despite their elaborate quality control procedures, the testing and data-assembly organizations have been known to transmit erroneous information about an individual,[36] and to be unable to detect errors that do not occur on a large scale. In addition, these organizations create records

---

[34] Testimony of Ohio State University College of Law, Education Records Hearings, November 11, 1976, pp. 177-78; and Testimony of National Association of State Universities and Land Grant Colleges, Education Records Hearings, November 11, 1976, p. 127.

[35] Testimony of National Association of State Universities and Land Grant Colleges, Educational Records Hearings, November 11, 1976, p. 127.

[36] See, for example, Testimony of Ohio State University College of Law, Education Records Hearings, November 11, 1976, p. 163 and pp. 184-185; Testimony of Ralph Nader, Education Records Hearings, November 11, 1976, pp. 216-217; and Testimony of Educational Testing Service, Education Records Hearings, November 12, 1976, pp. 348-55.

without the knowledge of the individual, such as lists of "unacknowledged repeaters,"[37] or "weighted" scores for individuals based on information supplied by the client institution. Such secret records or special scores may stigmatize an applicant or student (as when "unacknowledged repeaters" are branded as "cheaters") or subject the individual to an adverse decision (as when an applicant is rejected because his "weighted" score is too low).

Finally, FERPA makes no provision for an individual at any level of schooling to have a decision based on erroneous, incomplete, or inappropriate information reconsidered. The Act merely provides that a student or his parent can request correction or amendment of a record. Although there are due process mechanisms in schools that can be used to force reconsideration when the decision is a major one, many decisions do not lend themselves to formal reconsideration, nor is correction or amendment of a record always enough to repair or halt the damage. In decentralized educational organizations, corrections or amendments may not be propagated throughout the systems; and in large systems, where administrative decisions are separated from the process of correcting or amending records, corrections may not come to the attention of decision makers. Moreover, in certain types of selection processes where there are more applicants than available places, as in the case of programs for gifted children or admission to professional schools, the institution may have strong incentives to overlook a correction or amendment made by a rejected applicant. The right to correct an erroneous record may be a hollow remedy if the individual has no way to challenge a decision based on that record.

CONTROL OVER DISCLOSURE OF INFORMATION

Limiting the disclosure of education records is a primary goal of FERPA. The Act firmly establishes the principle that parent or student consent for disclosure of all education records is the rule, rather than the exception. Its restrictions extend even to those records maintained by schools that are not commonly considered education records. For example, law enforcement records maintained by schools may be disclosed only for law enforcement purposes and only to law enforcement agencies of the same jurisdiction *[20 U.S.C. 1232g(a)(4)(B)(ii)]*; medical records may be disclosed only for medical treatment purposes *[20 U.S.C. 1232g(a)(4)(B)(iv)]*; desk drawer notes may be seen only by substitutes *[20 U.S.C. 1232g(a)(4)(B)(i)]*; and letters of recommendation may be used only for the purpose for which they were acquired. *[20 U.S.C. 1232g(a)(1)(C)]* Moreover, exemptions from the requirement of parental or student consent for disclosure are all conditioned on an assurance that records will not be redisclosed. *[20 U.S.C. 1232g(b)(4)(B)]* A school's policy under FERPA must state the criteria by which it decides which school officials may have access to records and for what purposes. *[45 C.F.R. 99.5]* When records are transferred to another

---

[37] "Unacknowledged repeaters" are individuals who have taken an examination, particularly the Law School Admissions Test, previously but fail to indicate on their application form that they have taken such a previous examination; see Kim Masters "ETS's Star Chamber," *The New Republic*, February 5, 1977, pp. 13-14.

school, parents must be notified and given a copy of the record, and must have an opportunity to challenge the contents of the record in a hearing. Auditors, evaluators, or researchers who are allowed to have access to records without parent or student consent must destroy their copies of the records when they are no longer needed. *[20 U.S.C. 1232g(b)(1)(F); 45 C.F.R. 99.31]* Pursuant to FERPA, a student can bar disclosure of any item of directory information in his record. *[20 U.S.C. 1232g(a)(5); 45 C.F.R. 99.37]*

Despite these protections, the extensive exceptions to the basic presumption of confidentiality create problems. Some of the exceptions weaken an educational institution's ability to prevent disclosure when it wishes to do so. This is particularly true with regard to Federal agencies seeking access to student records for evaluation or research purposes. Although Federal and State agencies can receive student records only on the condition that they do not redisclose them, no *written* agreement barring redisclosure is required, and therefore neither the institution nor the individual can hold Federal or State agencies, or their contractors, accountable for failure to abide by the redisclosure prohibition. Moreover, when government agencies request access to information in individually identifiable form, they do not have to show that such access is either required by law or demonstrably necessary to accomplish the purpose for which they are requesting the information. Once such an agency has information about a student, neither FERPA nor the Privacy Act of 1974, in the case of Federal agencies, prevents the information from being passed from agency to agency within Federal or State governments without obtaining the consent of the individual to whom it pertains.

Another weakness in FERPA's confidentiality provisions involves the use of records for research purposes in a decentralized system. FERPA does not require central review of requests for access to education records for research purposes, nor does it require that parents or students be notified that records will be used for such purposes.

A major confidentiality problem arises from FERPA's failure to require student or parent consent to the disclosure of records maintained by school law enforcement units or security forces to law enforcement officials of the same jurisdiction. The main concern in this regard was that school law enforcement units were, or would become, conduits for information about a student's behavior, background, and character. Although this problem affects only a limited number of students—an alleged juvenile delinquent in elementary and secondary school, or a radical activist in higher education— it has great import both for these students and for an educational institution.

The relationship of educational institutions to law enforcement agencies varies according to the social, economic, and cultural environment in which a school or school system operates. FERPA, however, gives an educational institution almost no flexibility in dealing with disclosure to law enforcement agencies.

There are other examples of inflexible disclosure rules in FERPA that work to the disadvantage of the student, the school, or other institutions, or all three. For example, a school's relationship with social services agencies varies from community to community. FERPA, however, does not take account of these different working relationships. The Act dictates one inflexible rule regarding disclosure—that school records may not be disclosed to social services agencies without student or parent consent. FERPA leaves no flexibility for sharing any information about students with any social service agency for any purpose except in connection with a financial-aid program. For example, under a strict interpretation of FERPA, schools cannot assist local services agencies that provide clothing to needy children, by giving those agencies information to identify potential candidates. Nor can schools report cases of possible child neglect to local services agencies without parental consent.

The same lack of flexibility is apparent in the FERPA provision that permits disclosures for research purposes without individual consent *only* if the research is done for, or on behalf of, an educational institution for a specific educational purpose. As Chapter 15 of this report points out, because administrative records are a vital tool in research and statistical activities they should be available for research or statistical purposes provided that stringent precautions are taken to protect the individuals to whom the records pertain from harm.

Finally, it is puzzling that, of all of the exemptions from FERPA's restrictions on disclosure without individual consent, the exemption for the least sensitive information—directory information—is qualified by rigid protections for the individual. FERPA permits an individual to bar the disclosure without his consent of any or all directory information. The requirement is an economic and administrative burden whether many or only a few students exercise the option. In addition, the requirement has frustrated press access to information, made it possible for individuals to claim credentials or honors falsely without fear of being discovered, and will even make it difficult for the Bureau of the Census to get resident student housing information necessary for drawing census sample frames for the 1980 Census. Moreover, the requirement effectively limits the freedom of many States in creating or modifying public-record and freedom of information statutes. If such statutes were to designate as a matter of public record information included under FERPA as directory information, the State would force educational institutions to choose between losing needed Federal funds or being in violation of State law.

THE FERPA ENFORCEMENT MECHANISMS

Statutory protections are seldom effective unless the statute provides strong incentives to comply or credible sanctions for failure to comply, or both. Unfortunately, FERPA provides neither. In this respect, FERPA's "enforced self-regulation strategy" is deficient in that it calls for educational institutions to exercise substantial discretion in formulating procedures while failing to make them locally accountable for doing so. Enforcement of FERPA must begin with a complaint to DHEW, and the only penalty for failure to comply is a financial sanction that lacks credibility because it is so rarely used.

FERPA and its implementing regulations depend on four mechanisms to achieve "enforced self-regulation": (1) educational institutions must provide parents and students with the means to exercise the rights the Act establishes; (2) educational institutions must inform parents and students of their rights and the procedures for exercising those rights; (3) the Department of Health, Education, and Welfare must establish an office to investigate, process, review, and adjudicate violations; and (4) if adjudication fails, termination of Federal funding through the U.S. Office of Education is a last resort.

While these mechanisms may be theoretically sound, in practice they give the individual little protection. Abuses of FERPA requirements normally occur at the operational level, and are perpetrated by individual employees at a specific school. The effectiveness of FERPA currently depends upon more centralized control than most educational institutions have. What should be required instead is local handling of complaints and internal sanctioning systems. The entire burden of enforcement of FERPA currently falls on parents and students, but the only way for an individual to exercise the initiative that will lead to enforcement is to file a formal complaint to DHEW. This process is not only burdensome to the individual, but is unlikely to provide timely relief, and is therefore not likely to be used.

The sanction of total withdrawal of Federal funds is so disproportionate to the nature of most FERPA violations that it lacks credibility and thus serves only as a poor incentive for institutions to prevent or correct systematic violations or unfair practices. In addition, it does nothing to redress injustices to a particular individual. The penalty, if enforced, would in effect punish all students and parents, including those whose rights have been violated, by forcing the curtailment of essential educational programs. Moreover, it would nullify FERPA's protections since it would remove the sanctioned institution from FERPA's jurisdiction.

Thus, the individual who tries to protect his rights has little hope of success, and if he succeeds, he may threaten the survival of the educational institution, thereby diminishing the well-being of other students and parents as well as his own. The net result is that an individual's rights will only be protected, as they were before FERPA, by the initiative and sense of responsibility of the educational institution. FERPA itself, may, however, undermine even that protection. By failing to obligate institutions to monitor their own practices, and by giving students and parents the role of monitoring practices and reporting the institution's misdeeds to the Federal government, FERPA stresses an adversary, not a cooperative, relationship. In so doing, it forces an aggrieved student or parent who has complained to DHEW to assume the risk that the school will retaliate and puts the school in a defensive posture toward its students and their parents.

RECOMMENDATIONS

As a result of its inquiry into educational record-keeping practices and its analysis of the Family Educational Rights and Privacy Act, the Commission has concluded that even with FERPA, the interests of students and parents in education records and record-keeping practices are not well enough protected. Serious gaps in the coverage of FERPA make this situation particularly serious in the admissions processes of post-secondary institutions.

If students and their parents are to be protected properly from intrusive or unfair practices in the collection, use, and dissemination of education records, educational institutions must bear a large part of the burden for protecting them. Relying solely on individuals to protect their own interests simply is not good enough in view of the broad authority that educational institutions must have to carry out their missions. To give an individual all the procedural protections he would need to safeguard his own interests in every decision made about him, could well paralyze the educational system. On the other hand, sole reliance on institutional responsibility for the protection of an individual's interests in record keeping would require prescriptive regulation by Federal or State governments that would have its own paralyzing effect.

While institutions recognize the need to protect the interests of students and parents, the bureaucratic setting that dominates most educational institutions today tends to make institutional interests in record-keeping practices overshadow those of the individual. There is a serious imbalance between an institution's incentive to protect its own interests on the one hand, and its incentive to protect student interests on the other. FERPA does little to correct this imbalance.

Since the quality of education always depends ultimately on human judgment, protections must be designed carefully so that they will not lead to further depersonalization in the relationship between student and institution. An educational institution must make difficult and sensitive decisions regarding such things as the placement of children in special programs, the admission of only a few qualified applicants to a graduate or professional school, and the choice of the proper mix of rewards and punishments to help a child learn social responsibility. There is already great pressure on schools to rely on information about individuals that has been converted into standard measurements of ability or performance, and to use it to make decisions in a way that eliminates the consideration of individual differences. Such processes are often adopted without considering their impact on society and on the individual. Overly restrictive protections for the individual often cause educators to rely even more heavily on decision making based on standard measurements in order to protect themselves against the threat of liability to the individuals affected by the decisions. Until quite recently, education records mattered little in the educational process. They have now become significant. Record keeping has evolved to meet many changes and pressures, but the evolution has occurred at the expense of students' rights. The situation requires not the rapid imposition of untested requirements to restore the balance, but a careful reshaping of the record-keeping practices of educational institutions so that all of the stakeholders will be fairly represented.

In sum, the Commission finds that FERPA is a solid foundation upon which to restore the balance in educational record-keeping practices between the interests of students and parents and the needs of educational institutions. FERPA not only recognizes the individual's interest in education records, and provides the baseline for developing a minimum set of rights and responsibilities, but does so with a sound sense of both the limits of regulation and the proper roles of the various parties in implementing its requirements. Nevertheless, further steps are needed to achieve a proper balance.

The Commission's approach to formulating protections for the individual's interest in education records is not to limit the authority of educational institutions, but to strengthen the accountability of those institutions to the individual and to society. The Commission's approach depends on the tradition of stewardship among educational institutions and seeks ways that will make institutions continually aware of, and responsive to, that tradition.

Educators recognize that they have a stake in protecting and promoting the interests of the individual and in maintaining public confidence in their ability to do so. Not all of them recognize that their record-keeping practices are undermining that confidence among citizens generally, as well as among students and parents. The fear and mistrust of schools may be vague, ill-defined, and sometimes unjustified, but it exists nonetheless. Educators are only beginning to be aware of these attitudes. The Commission places great emphasis on the value of openness, both to dispel unfounded fears and to identify and resolve real problems.

In formulating its recommendations, the Commission had three objectives:

(1) to expand and strengthen FERPA's minimum requirements so as to place additional responsibility for the quality of records and record-keeping practices on educational institutions, and to broaden the spectrum of institutions and records subject to the Act's requirements;

(2) to make educational institutions more accountable for their record-keeping practices than they now are by giving the individual effective remedies for specific abuses; putting record-keeping policy and practice on the agenda of local bodies and groups that hold educational institutions accountable for their actions; limiting Federal enforcement to cases of systemic abuse; and providing more effective Federal sanctions; and

(3) to expand the latitude of each educational institution or agency in meeting its increased responsibilities and adapting the basic requirements of FERPA to local circumstances within the context of strengthened accountability.

EXPANDING AND STRENGTHENING INSTITUTIONAL RESPONSIBILITY

FERPA currently forbids an educational institution or agency to have a policy that denies individuals the rights recognized by the statute, but does not require an affirmative policy to implement the Act's requirements. The

Department of Health, Education and Welfare sought to remedy this deficiency by promulgating regulations that require institutions to formulate and adopt affirmative policies. *[45 C.F.R. 99.5]* The Commission agrees that to create the conditions under which an individual can exercise his rights under FERPA, and to foster an atmosphere of cooperation rather than confrontation, institutions must be required to take affirmative steps to meet their obligations to the individual and to create policies and procedures consistent with FERPA requirements. Therefore, the Commission recommends:

Recommendation (1):

That the Family Educational Rights and Privacy Act be amended to require an educational agency or institution to formulate, adopt, and promulgate an affirmative policy to implement FERPA requirements, as well as the additional requirements recommended by the Commission.

ADDITIONAL INSTITUTIONAL OBLIGATIONS

FERPA and the DHEW regulations oblige educational institutions only to assure that individuals are given the opportunity to inspect and correct their records and to exercise limited control over the use and dissemination of those records. The Commission believes, however, that an educational institution should be obligated to protect the interest of a student or parent in an education record it maintains. The institution's obligation should be threefold: (a) to attend to the content and quality of the records it maintains on individuals; (b) to provide redress for an individual when a decision has been based on a record subsequently found to be erroneous, incomplete, misleading, or otherwise inappropriate; and (c) to protect the rights of students whenever it permits or undertakes survey and other data collection activities.

The problem of standards for the content of records is crucial, both for effective educational service delivery and protection of the individual. The relevance and necessity of each category of information, the reliability of information for certain types of decisions, the accuracy and completeness of information in an anecdotal record, and the appropriateness of sources and reporting standards for records are all significant problems for educational record keepers, especially those in elementary and secondary schools. Many of the complaints that led to FERPA's passage were directed at institutional failures to assure the quality of education records and the resulting unfair treatment of students. The Commission realizes that setting such standards is difficult and is well aware of the lack of consensus about the need for standards and what the standards should be. It does not believe that the government should set standards, except where there is a clear consensus about the need for them and what they should be. It does believe, however, that an institution must assume responsibility, and be accountable, for the content and quality of its records about individuals.

Levying responsibility for the content and quality of records on educational institutions would not totally prevent the inclusion of erroneous, incomplete, or misleading information in them. It would, however, reduce the recording of such information, and would assure that the individual's rights of access and correction are not the only means by which the quality of records is monitored.

Correcting a record does not assure that previous decisions based on it will be reviewed or corrected because there is no assurance that the correction will come to the decision maker's attention, or even if it does, that the decision maker will reconsider his previous decisions. Hence, the Commission believes that an educational institution should be required to take steps to assure that decisions based on inaccurate information are reviewed. The Commission's intent is not to allow a challenge of the substance of a decision if the inaccurate information had no bearing on it, but merely to assure that procedures exist to review decisions once information bearing on the decision has been corrected.

FERPA recognizes the responsibility of educational institutions and agencies to protect the privacy of students when they conduct or authorize data collection activities, but the DHEW regulations fail to specify any minimum requirements for such activities. A decision to conduct, assist, or authorize such activities may be influenced by a variety of factors, including professional interests and pressures on an institution to cooperate with various agencies of the Federal government or with a university that provides much of the continuing education for the school's teachers and administrators. Within large school systems, moreover, individual administrators in units of the system often have both *de facto* autonomy and strong incentives to authorize data collection activities. Chapter 15 recommends specific guidelines for institutional review of research and statistical activities in addition to requirements for notice and consent before research is carried out on captive populations such as students. The Commission feels that an educational institution should assume responsibility for protecting individuals from intrusive data collection whether or not the organization conducting the research does so. Educational institutions and agencies should not only assure that proposals for data gathering are centrally reviewed, but should also assume responsibility for assuring that research about an individual will not be carried out without his informed consent. Accordingly, the Commission recommends:

Recommendation (2):

That the Family Educational Rights and Privacy Act be amended to require an educational agency or institution to include in its institutional policy to implement FERPA reasonable procedures to protect against unwarranted intrusiveness and against unfairness in its education record-keeping practices including:

(a)   reasonable procedures to prevent the collection and maintenance of inaccurate, misleading, or otherwise inappropriate education records;

(b) procedures that provide a student or parent a reasonable opportunity for reconsideration of an administrative decision regarding the student that is based in whole or in part on an education record about the student that has been corrected or amended as a result of rights exercised under FERPA subsequent to the decision; and

(c) procedures to assure that except as specifically required by law, no survey or data collection activity will be conducted, assisted, or authorized by an educational agency or institution unless:

(i) the proposal for such an activity has been reviewed and approved by the educational agency or institution, and not a component thereof, to eliminate unwarranted intrusion on the privacy of students or their families; and

(ii) parents of affected students have been notified of such activity, provided a reasonable opportunity to review the collection materials, and allowed to refuse participation in such activity by their children or families.

EXPANDING THE RECORDS AND INSTITUTIONS COVERED BY FERPA

Several significant areas of educational record keeping are currently beyond the purview of FERPA. The records and record-keeping practices of organizations that perform testing and data-assembly services for educational institutions are not subject to the Act. Nor does the Act protect an applicant for admission who does not subsequently matriculate. In addition, the waiver provision and the regulation that allows an institution to request such a waiver *[20 U.S.C. 1232g(a)(1)(B)* and *(C); 45 C.F.R. 99.12]* have effectively encouraged students to sign away their right of access to letters of recommendation which, although of debatable usefulness, are required in most admissions processes.

While testing and data-assembly services organizations have shown a sense of responsibility to individuals, and have incorporated many of the requirements of FERPA into their policies and practices, the individual has no legally assertible interest in records maintained by such organizations. That is, he has no way of assuring that policies adopted voluntarily will be followed. This is especially a problem where such policies prove costly, or where a testing and data-assembly organization comes under pressure from its clients to compile a record which, if compiled by the client, would be subject to FERPA. As the Commission has observed in other chapters of this report, a service organization that serves a number of clients engaging in the same type of activity (e.g., the Medical Information Bureau, which serves insurers, or the independent authorization services that support credit grantors) will attenuate the relationship between the primary record keeper (the insurer or credit grantor) and the individual unless it is subject to the same fairness and accountability requirements as the primary record keeper. Thus, the Commission recommends:

Recommendation (3):

That the Family Educational Rights and Privacy Act be amended to broaden the definition of an "educational agency or institution" to include organizations that provide testing or data-assembly services under contract to educational agencies or institutions or consortiums thereof, except that such organizations should not be subject to Section (b)(3) of the Act which requires educational institutions to permit access by Federal auditors to educational records without the consent of the student or his parent.

The Commission believes that the applicant who is not admitted to an educational institution has above all others an interest in securing correction or amendment of an education record, as well as reconsideration of a decision based on faulty or inappropriate information. It understands and sympathizes with the difficulties faced by an institution in making admissions decisions, and also realizes the temptation for a disappointed applicant to challenge a rejection on whatever grounds he can muster. The Commission is also aware, however, of the enormous importance of an admissions decision to an individual. It does not seek to eliminate human judgment from the decision process, nor does it believe that providing the FERPA protections to applicants will lead to that result. An admissions decision is necessarily a comparative judgment. While making records about applicants subject to FERPA would not lay bare the selection process, it would assure that an individual was being judged on the basis of accurate, timely, complete, and relevant information. Therefore, the Commission recommends:

Recommendation (4):

That the Family Education Rights and Privacy Act be amended to:

(a)   **broaden the definition of "student" to include an applicant for student status;**

(b)   **make all provisions of FERPA applicable to education records pertaining directly to an applicant; and**

(c)   **require that records created about an unsuccessful applicant be maintained by an educational agency or institution for 18 months from the close of the application process, after which time they must be destroyed.**

FERPA specifically allows only waiver of the right of access to letters of recommendation. The DHEW regulations implementing FERPA provide, however, that any right recognized by FERPA may be waived, although they forbid an educational institution or agency to *require* a parent or student to waive a right. Although the whole concept of waiver is inconsistent with the spirit of FERPA, it was included for letters of recommendation at the urging of educators in post-secondary schools. As noted earlier, the Commission found no consensus about the value of letters of recommendation nor about the impact on their credibility of allowing students access to them. Nevertheless, preventing students from having access to letters of recommendation is somewhat of a *cause celebre* for educators. Many regard such letters as private communications and thus keeping them confidential as a professional prerogative. Many faculty members who write letters of recommendation fear that student access might expose them to liability or retaliation. Many educational institutions fear that openness would make letters less candid. The evidence presented to the Commission does not support these arguments, but it does show that many institutions and faculty members feel strongly about the confidentiality of letters of recommendation.[38]

The Commission believes that evaluations are part of the professional responsibility of any educator, and that candid professional judgment should be sought and expected in letters of recommendation. Furthermore, analysis of case law indicates that evaluations of students communicated without malice in the course of official duties do not make an educator vulnerable to libel or slander.[39] Of course, any evaluation creates some risk of physical reprisal but the risk does not relieve the educator of his duty to render judgments about students.

The Commission believes, moreover, that candor is a professional obligation and should not carry the price of secrecy or potential unfairness. A student can, if he chooses, make an informal agreement with a professor that he will not exercise his right of access as the price for securing a letter of recommendation, but it is difficult to justify the formal blanket waiver of this right which institutions now solicit.

While it is difficult to argue against the individual's right to waive any of his rights, it is also difficult to conceive of ways to maintain the right to waive while assuring that it is exercised on a purely voluntary basis. The Commission does not wish to preclude any individual from choosing not to exercise his right to see a record, but it does wish to prevent him from forfeiting that right. Thus, the Commission recommends:

Recommendation (5):

That the Family Educational Rights and Privacy Act be amended to provide that the right of a student or his parent to inspect and review letters and statements of recommendation not be subject to waiver by the student or his parent, provided further, however, that letters and statements of recommendation solicited with a written assurance of

---

[38] See, for example, Testimony of Ohio State University College of Law, Education Records Hearings, November 11, 1976, pp. 177-78; Testimony of National Association of State Universities and Land Grant Colleges, Education Records Hearings, November 11, 1976, p. 127; Testimony of Yale University, Education Records Hearings, November 11, 1976, p. 51; and Testimony of Franklin and Marshall College, Education Records Hearings, November 11, 1976, pp. 11-13.

[39] See, for example, *Blair v. Union Free School Dist.*, 67 Misc. 2d 248, 324 N.Y.S. 2d 222, (1971); *Everest v. McKenny*, 195 Mich. 649, 162 N.W. 277 (1917); *Morris v. Rousos*, 397 S.W. 2d 504, (Tex. Civ. App., 1965); *cert. denied*, 385 U.S. 868 (1965); *Morris v. Univ. Texas*, 352 S.W. 2d 947 (Tex. 1962), *cert. denied*, 371 U.S. 953 (1963); and *Morris v. Nowotny*, 323 S.W. 2d 301, (Tex. Civ. App. 1959), *cert. denied*, 385 U.S. 868 (1965).

confidentiality, or sent and retained with a documented understanding of confidentiality prior to the effective date of the statutory change not be subject to inspection and review by students or parents.

STRENGTHENING LOCAL ACCOUNTABILITY

The Commission has recommended that substantial responsibilities to protect individuals from unfairness in record keeping be levied on educational institutions. The Commission also believes that steps should be taken to strengthen an institution's incentive to live up to its responsibility, and that to make that happen, problems and abuses must be brought to the institution's attention.

As noted earlier, the size and degree of decentralization of educational institutions and agencies, and the many problems and responsibilities that compete for their time, attention, and resources, have meant that existing mechanisms for assuring accountability (e.g., parent or student involvement in governance, due process, administrative control procedures, and public governance structures) have not focused on record-keeping practices and their impact on the individual. FERPA allows substantial local discretion, but does not attempt to utilize fully existing local accountability mechanisms to enforce institutional responsibilities for fair record keeping.

The record-keeping policies and practices of an educational institution will not be effective unless they take into account the views and experience of students and parents as well as those of teachers and administrators. Protections for the individual depend on the development of good policies and practices because asserting interests on a case-by-case basis in remedy of specific abuses does not always provide the impetus for institutional change that will prevent future abuses. All of the mechanisms mentioned in the Commission's recommendations that appear below are now in place in most educational institutions. The Commission believes that the best way to assure that institutions respond effectively to the challenge of reforming their record-keeping practices is to focus the attention of these existing mechanisms for assuring accountability on record-keeping issues, so that public pressure will encourage the development of procedural standards. Accordingly, the Commission recommends:

Recommendation (6):

That the Family Educational Rights and Privacy Act be amended to require an educational agency or institution that conducts instructional programs to provide for parent or student participation in the establishment and review of its policies and practices implementing FERPA; and further

Recommendation (7):

That the Family Educational Rights and Privacy Act be amended to require an educational agency or institution that conducts instructional programs to have procedures whereby parents or students may challenge its policies or practices implementing FERPA.

The Commission believes that the regulations implementing FERPA as amended pursuant to *Recommendations (6)* and *(7)* should require each agency or institution that conducts instructional programs[40] to establish procedures to hear and resolve complaints about FERPA policies or practices that (a) provide for the participation of parents or students; (b) require the agency or institution to state its reasons if it does not take any action to change its policy or practice in response to a complaint; (c) require the agency or institution to maintain a public record of the complaint and its disposition; and (d) provide for an appeal to the governing body of such agency or institution.

Further, the Commission recommends:

Recommendation (8):

That the Family Educational Rights and Privacy Act be amended to require that an educational agency or institution establish, promulgate, and enforce administrative sanctions for violations of its policy implementing FERPA. Such sanctions should be levied upon chief executive officers of educational agencies and components thereof who are negligent in pursuit of institutional compliance as well as upon employees who violate provisions of such policy.

THE FEDERAL ENFORCEMENT ROLE

Federal administrative agencies, even those with regulatory powers, cannot effectively correct each particular abuse, especially when the area being regulated is as large and decentralized as education. Even if FERPA provided a more effective sanction than the withdrawal of Federal funds, DHEW could not attempt to monitor each institution's performance or pursue each individual complaint. The Federal role should be much as DHEW currently interprets it to be—an instrument for assuring that educational agencies and institutions meet the minimum Federal requirements. The Commission believes that Federal administrative agencies should intervene if an institution's policies fail to comply with FERPA's requirements or when an institution systematically departs from its own policy. It is also convinced that to reserve DHEW as the court of last resort for complaints of systematic institutional failure to comply with FERPA is feasible, reasonable, and preferable to requiring Federal review and approval of each local policy. The Commission strongly approves of DHEW's current system of enforcement which, like compulsory arbitration, seeks to obtain voluntary compliance. It recognizes, however, that the Secretary of Health, Education, and Welfare needs a more credible and

---

[40] The Commission feels that administrative services organizations should be exempt from this requirement.

flexible sanction to make these efforts to secure voluntary compliance effective. Hence, the Commission recommends:

Recommendation (9):

That the Family Educational Rights and Privacy Act be amended to provide that all or any portion of DHEW funds earmarked for education purposes may be withheld from an educational agency or institution when its policy does not comply with FERPA requirements or when evidence of systematic failure on its part to implement its policy is presented to the Department of Health, Education, and Welfare. Such withholding of funds should only be imposed if the Secretary has determined that compliance cannot be secured through voluntary means or that systematic failures to implement policy have previously been brought to the attention of the educational agency or institution and it has not taken sufficient steps to correct such failures. The amount withheld should be appropriate to the nature of the violation, and should provide incentives for future compliance.

An individual needs some further remedy when, because of inertia, inefficiency, recalcitrance, or ignorance on the part of school officials at the operating level, a school or other component of a large and decentralized educational system refuses to permit him to exercise his FERPA rights. None of the Commission's recommendations so far outlined provide, individually or collectively, such a remedy. Civil action can provide timely relief, and the threat of it increases the incentive for institutions to be responsive. Such civil action, however, should be corrective rather than punitive, and thus limited to assuring that institutions accord individuals their FERPA rights. Therefore, the Commission recommends:

Recommendation (10):

That the Family Educational Rights and Privacy Act be amended to permit an individual (in the case of a minor, his parents or guardian) to commence a civil action on his behalf to seek injuctive relief against an educational agency or institution that fails to provide him with a right granted him by FERPA. The district courts should have jurisdiction, without regard to the amount in controversy or the citizenship of the parties, to order an educational agency or institution to perform such act or duty as may be required by FERPA and to grant costs of the litigation, including reasonable attorney's fees.

INCREASING LOCAL DISCRETION

The section of this chapter that describes problems in educational record keeping under FERPA cites a number of examples of where FERPA is prescriptive rather than permissive insofar as the exercise of local discretion is concerned. The examples cited involved the conflicting interests of the individual in the use of desk drawer notes in diagnostic and treatment situations; the conflict between privacy and freedom of information in the matter of directory information; the tension between individual protections and societal benefits in research; and the school's relationship with other societal agencies that share responsibility for the child's welfare and the rights of the individual.

In the Commission's judgment, FERPA's attempts to prescribe the proper balance in these situations have created more problems than they solve. Thus, the final set of Commission recommendations seeks ways of giving educational institutions more responsibility for striking the balance. The Commission believes that the accountability mechanisms called for in *Recommendations (6), (7), (8), (9),* and *(10)* will assure that the responsibility is not abused.

Desk Drawer Notes. FERPA provides that a student or his parents may have access to an educator's desk drawer notes about the student only if the educator shares information from them with someone other than a substitute. This restriction may often be harmful to a student and may reduce the effectiveness of the educational program. The provision tries to resolve two real concerns about the sharing of such information: (1) the possible stigmatization of an individual by information whose nature and quality are not subject to institutional control; and (2) the possibility that desk drawer notes will be hidden from parents and students but used in institutional decision making. The latter problem can be solved by giving an individual access to all the data used in making administrative decisions about him, and recourse if those data are erroneous or incomplete. Since desk drawer notes serve primarily as a memory aid to assist in diagnosing the problems of a child and as such have only a temporary value, the threat of stigmatization can be alleviated by arranging for the destruction of desk drawer notes at the end of each regular academic reporting period, unless they are incorporated into the official record system of the educational institution. Sharing information in desk drawer notes during that period is unlikely to result in stigmatizing an individual. If such information is so difficult for an educator to remember that it must be written down, one might fairly assume that it will be forgotten quickly. If some particular bit of information in a desk drawer note is significant enough to stigmatize an individual, then it will probably be remembered and shared with others whether or not it is recorded. Indeed, desk drawer notes seem to have sufficient educational value to argue for their improvement; not for their abolition. The dangers inherent in maintaining them can be controlled by routinely destroying them or by exposing them to the same access and correction rules to which other education records are subject. Therefore, the Commission recommends:

Recommendation (11):

That the Family Educational Rights and Privacy Act be amended to make it permissible for records of instructional, supervisory, and administrative personnel of an educational agency or institution, and educational personnel ancillary thereto, which records are in the sole

possession of the maker thereof, to be disclosed to any school official who has been determined by the agency or institution to have legitimate educational interests in the records, without being subject to the access provision of FERPA, provided, however:

(a)   that such records are incorporated into education records of the agency or institution or destroyed after each regular academic reporting period;

(b)   that such records are made available for inspection and review by a student or parent if they are used or reviewed in making any administrative decision affecting the student; and

(c)   that all such records of administrative officers with disciplinary responsibilities are made available to parents or students when any disciplinary decision is made by that officer.

Directory Information. The purpose of establishing an exemption for the disclosure of directory information was to let institutions create a category of information about students that is freely available to the public. FERPA requires that categories of directory information be defined in an institution's FERPA policy and that students and parents be informed of what information the categories include. Given the mechanisms to assure accountability recommended by the Commission, it is highly unlikely that an institution would characterize any information as directory information whose disclosure might cause harm or embarrassment to an individual. Because the administrative burden and the cost of permitting students to specify that some or all directory information about them may not be released is substantial, and because the only information normally characterized as directory information that is likely to create problems for the student if disclosed is information that serves to locate him, the Commission recommends:

Recommendation (12):

That the Family Educational Rights and Privacy Act be amended to provide that insofar as directory information is concerned, a student or parent may only require that address and phone number not be published without his consent or that it only be disclosed to persons who have established to the satisfaction of the institution a legitimate need to know.

Disclosures for Research and Statistical Purposes. The Commission believes that its recommendations regarding the disclosure of administrative records for research or statistical purposes in Chapter 15 should apply equally to education records. Adoption of the Commission's recommendations on research and statistics would allow educational institutions to permit the use of administrative records for any legitimate research or statistical purpose, but would, at the same time, make it easier for them to resist requests which they consider unwarranted. It would also give them more control over the conditions of disclosure, because the research organization seeking administrative records would have to sign a written agreement accepting the conditions stipulated by the educational institution. The Commission also believes that the decision to disclose records for research and the stipulation of the conditions under which they will be disclosed should be made by a central authority in an educational institution or agency and not a component thereof. Therefore, the Commission recommends:

Recommendation (13):

That the Family Educational Rights and Privacy Act be amended to permit an educational agency or institution to use or disclose an education record or information contained therein in individually identifiable form for a research or statistical purpose without parent or student consent, provided that the agency or institution:

(a) **determines that such use or disclosure in individually identifiable form does not violate any conditions under which the information was collected;**

(b) **ascertains that such use or disclosure in individually identifiable form is necessary to accomplish the research or statistical purpose for which the use or disclosure is to be made;**

(c) **determines that the research or statistical purpose for which any use or disclosure is to be made warrants the risk to the individual from additional exposure of the record or information;**

(d) **requires that adequate safeguards to protect the record or information from unauthorized disclosure be established and maintained by the user or recipient, including a program for removal or destruction of identifiers;**

(e) **prohibits any further use or redisclosure of the record or information in individually identifiable form without its express authorization;**

(f) **prohibits any individually identifiable information resulting from such research from being used to make any decision or take any action directly affecting the individual to whom it pertains;**

(g) **makes any disclosure pursuant to a written agreement with the proposed recipient which attests to all of the above;**

and provided further, that all such determinations, requirements, and prohibitions are made by the educational agency or institution (and not a component thereof).

Disclosures to Social Services Agencies. While the Commission understands the importance of the free flow of information between educational institutions and agencies and other social services agencies, it is also concerned that education records not become a source of information for purposes that are not acceptable to the individuals to whom they pertain. The achievement of educational goals, however, often depends upon ancillary services provided by other institutions, and the Commission believes that an educational agency should get all the help possible in meeting the needs of its students. The Commission's recommendations stress the need for participation by students, parents, and the public in the development of FERPA policies, vesting responsibility for record keeping in an educational institution's central authority rather than in components of the institution, and using a variety of mechanisms to assure that parent and student rights are protected. Given such protections, the Commission believes that educational institutions should be permitted to make determinations regarding whether certain routine disclosures of information are necessary for the educational agency to accomplish its own mission, and thus what disclosures should be permitted without the consent of students or parents. The burden should be on the educational institution to demonstrate the educational purpose of such disclosures, and the policy should be specific as to the agencies and types of information involved in such disclosure. The Commission, therefore, recommends:

Recommendation (14):

That the Family Educational Rights and Privacy Act be amended so as to permit an educational agency or institution to designate in its policy implementing FERPA that disclosures may be made on a routine basis without the authorization of the parent or student to a particular welfare or social service agency for a specified purpose that directly assists the educational agency or institution in achieving its mission, provided that the categories of information which may be disclosed to such agency are also specified and that further redisclosure by such agency is prohibited.

Disclosure to Law Enforcement Units. Current FERPA requirements make it difficult for an educational institution to deal with both its own law enforcement unit, if it has one, and with local law enforcement agencies. In the first case, if an educational institution discloses student records to its own law enforcement unit, *all* records of that unit become subject to FERPA. In the second case, while restricting disclosures of student records to local law enforcement agencies is laudable in most instances, it creates a problem when the educational institution is a party of interest in a criminal investigation or when disciplinary problems and delinquency problems involving violations of law are difficult to differentiate. The Commission believes this problem demands a three-part resolution: (a) assuring that a parent or student has access to any recorded information used to make any disciplinary decision about the student; (b) holding an educational institution responsible for the quality of the information it uses to make disciplinary decisions about students or discloses to third parties that will make such decisions; and (c) assuring that an educational institution is in a position to get the help it needs from both its own law enforcement unit and local law enforcement units to protect the safety of employees or students and the property of the schools and individuals.

The measures thus far recommended by the Commission, if adopted, would guarantee that students and parents have the right to see and challenge all records of disciplinary officials, including desk drawer notes, when a disciplinary decision is made about a student. They would also require educational institutions to have reasonable procedures to assure the accuracy, timeliness, completeness, and relevance of such records for educational purposes, and mechanisms to force continual review of the adequacy of such procedures. Given these recommended protections, the Commission sees no reason to recommend that an educational institution have less latitude to exchange information with its own security or law enforcement unit than it does to make disclosures to law enforcement units outside the educational institution. Therefore, the Commission believes that a law enforcement unit of an educational institution should be allowed to exchange information with the rest of the educational institution without making its law enforcement records subject to FERPA. At the same time, educational institutions should be able to share education records, including disciplinary records, with their law enforcement unit only to the same extent as they can share such records with other law enforcement agencies.

Current FERPA requirements prohibit disclosure of education records to law enforcement agencies without parent or student consent, except under judicial order with advance notice to the parent, or in an emergency when such disclosure is necessary to protect the health or safety of the student of other persons. In effect, this prevents educational institutions from sharing information legally with law enforcement units in cases where the safety and welfare of students, faculty, and school property are involved. The emergency exception does not permit routine cooperation with law enforcement agencies even when the educational institution may be a party of interest. The DHEW regulations make this clear by including as one criterion of an emergency, that time be of the essence, and by stressing that the emergency clause is to be construed strictly. In many urban and suburban schools, however, there are extortion rings, gang violence, theft rings, hard drug traffic, and other continuing criminal activities. While education records are seldom vital to the conduct of a criminal investigation, they can sometimes be extremely helpful. It is the Commission's judgment that educational institutions should be allowed to make the determination that a disclosure is necessary as long as it is publicly accountable for its decision.

Therefore, the Commission recommends:

Recommendation (15):

That the Family Educational Rights and Privacy Act be amended to provide:

(a) **that records collected or maintained by the security or law enforcement branch of an educational agency or institution solely for a law enforcement purpose—**

(i) **shall not be considered to be education records subject to the provisions of FERPA when the security or law enforcement branch does not have access to education records maintained by the agency or institution; and**

      (ii)   may be disclosed only to law enforcement agencies of the same jurisdication and to school officials responsible for disciplinary matters;

  (b)   that disclosure of information may be made by an educational agency or institution to law enforcement officials without the consent of the student or parent, provided that:

      (i)   an official determination is made by the educational agency or institution (and not by a component thereof) that the information disclosed is necessary to an authorized investigation of ongoing violations of law which threaten the welfare of the educational agency or institution or its students or faculty; and

      (ii)   each determination is publicly reported to the governing board of the agency or institution including the type of information disclosed, the number of individuals involved, and the justification for such disclosure, but not the names of the individuals involved.

*   *   *   *   *   *   *

The Commission believes that its recommendations will strengthen the protections afforded parents and students by the Family Educational Rights and Privacy Act and will give localities greater latitude in formulating FERPA policies that meet their particular needs and circumstances. The Commission also feels that the Department of Health, Education, and Welfare should provide substantial technical assistance to educational institutions to facilitate and expedite the development and implementation of such policies. Federal assistance might take the form of grants to consortiums of schools to develop and promulgate model policies, public information projects to inform schools, parents and students of their rights and responsibilities, and projects to identify and disseminate information about model practices. DHEW's experience with FERPA places it in a unique position to provide or sponsor such assistance.

Chapter 11

The Citizen as Beneficiary
of Government Assistance

Two factors led the Privacy Protection Study Commission to study the record-keeping practices of public assistance and social services[1] agencies.[2] First, the number of Americans who receive government assistance or service in some form is enormous. Second, the process of administering the welfare system[3] depends on the collection and use of personal information. The collaboration between the Federal government and the various States in developing the present welfare system has provided a complex set of eligibility criteria and formulae for determining the level of benefits to which an individual is entitled. Applying them demands a great deal of personal information. No one could deny that the welfare system is "intrusive," if one test of intrusiveness is the volume, detail, and sensitivity of the information collected about clients[4] of the system.

Perhaps because the intrusive nature of the system is so widely acknowledged, Congress has, since the 1930's, recognized the need to provide some protection from unfairness in the use of records about clients of federally assisted welfare programs. Federal law regarding record keeping does not, however, encompass all the basic issues of fairness identified by the Commission. In addition, although the largest federally assisted welfare

---

[1] "Public assistance and social services" include, for the Commission's purposes, cash or in-kind benefits (including, for example, food coupons, medical services, day care, counseling, alcohol and drug abuse treatment, employment training and housing) subsidized by government funding and provided to individuals or families on the basis of financial need. The term does not include benefits provided under an insurance scheme, such as Old-Age, Survivors and Disability Benefits, Medicare, or Unemployment Insurance. This chapter, and the recommendations contained herein, do not apply to any public assistance and social services program that is federally administered (such as Supplemental Security Income) and thus subject to the Privacy Act of 1974.

[2] "Agencies" include, for the Commission's purposes, any public or private organization administering, supervising the administration of, or delivering services to individuals or families pursuant to, a public assistance or social services program. This definition would include, for example, private service organizations providing services to clients under Title XX of the Social Security Act. It does not include medical-care providers rendering medical assistance to Medicaid and Title XX recipients, except insofar as these institutions determine eligibility for the Medicaid and Title XX programs. Recommendations affecting the record-keeping practices of medical-care providers are found in Chapter 7.

[3] "Welfare system" and "welfare," as used in this chapter, refer to the entire complex of public assistance and social services programs.

[4] The term "client" will be used throughout this chapter to refer to both applicants and recipients of the programs under discussion.

programs are required by Federal law to maintain some standards of fairness, many are not required to take into account even minimal considerations of fairness in their record keeping. Moreover, programs funded only by a State or local government are often constrained by no laws or standards for protecting the personal privacy interests of clients.

Two main considerations guided the Commission in its task of analyzing current Federal policy with respect to the practices of agencies providing public assistance and social services. The first consideration was the principle that individuals compelled by necessity to seek assistance and services from programs funded by government agencies should not have to renounce all claim to personal privacy in exchange for the benefits they seek. In the Commission's view, welfare clients have as much right to respect and dignity as other groups and should be as carefully protected from unfairness stemming from record keeping as are consumers of insurance, medical care, and credit.

Second was the need to maximize the strengths and minimize the weaknesses of a welfare system which divides responsibilities—for funding and for administration—among Federal, State, and local government agencies. Although its great spending power gives the Federal government a powerful regulatory tool, when the Federal government lacks sufficient knowledge of, or sensitivity to, local circumstances, some discretion should appropriately be left to the States and localities.

While this report was in preparation, the Department of Health, Education, and Welfare and other government agencies and private organizations were exploring various welfare reform alternatives. Although the shape reform will take is not yet clear, safeguards against unfairness to individuals will always be needed, and thus review of record-keeping policies and practices is timely. The Commission hopes this report will help policy makers both in modifying record-keeping practices under the present welfare system and in formulating policies to protect the privacy rights of clients under whatever system may emerge. In particular, in the event that the administration of certain welfare programs is assumed by the Federal government, this chapter may help concerned parties to determine whether special protections should be provided for records about welfare clients that supplement those provided in the Privacy Act of 1974.

METHOD OF STUDY AND ANALYSIS

There are dozens of federally assisted programs for providing help to the needy, and unnumbered assistance and services programs funded by State and local governments. Since in-depth study of all these programs was impossible, the Commission confined its detailed examination to the record-keeping policies applicable to agencies administering the four largest federally assisted programs in terms of dollars and clients. These programs are Aid to Families with Dependent Children, Medicaid, Title XX Social Services, and Food Stamps. In addition, the Commission examined the Child Support Enforcement Program. This program seemed to merit the

Commission's attention because it has been particularly controversial, some groups seeing it as entailing abrogation of absent parents' privacy interests. The Commission did not study in detail the public assistance and social services programs administered directly by the Federal government rather than by States and localities, and therefore makes no recommendations regarding them. The Privacy Act of 1974 already covers such programs, including Supplemental Security Income (SSI) for the aged, blind, and disabled and cash benefits for veterans with disabilities not related to military service.

The Commission's study of the four specified programs included a review of pertinent Federal statutes and regulations, meetings with Federal, State, and local officials and representatives of private organizations and public interest groups, and the services of an expert consultant with many years of experience in the welfare field. After completing the initial study, the Commission formulated a set of draft recommendations which were published in the *Federal Register*[5] and otherwise made available for public comment. Three days of public hearings on the recommendations were held in January, 1977, and, in addition, the Commission has received more than 90 written comments regarding them. Although the Commission could not make detailed studies of record keeping by the welfare agencies of all fifty States, the written comments and oral and written testimony offered at the hearings yielded rich and valuable information regarding current practice in these agencies.

The Commission's inability to make a detailed study of the record-keeping policies applicable to all of the various federally funded assistance and services programs reflects a central problem: present law provides no clear, consistent set of policies applicable to record keeping in all federally assisted welfare programs. Each of the various statutes establishing a program either prescribes its own policy or is silent on the subject. Anyone who tries to administer public assistance and social services programs established by different Federal statutes may well encounter inconsistent, and perhaps incompatible, statutes and regulations governing record keeping. It is doubtful that anyone has, or, without very substantial resources, could have, a clear picture of how the laws governing this multitude of programs interrelate. In short, the Commission found that the descriptive word for record-keeping policy in this area is "complex." Thus, a primary Commission goal was to find ways of simplifying the complexity.

PROGRAM OVERVIEWS

The public assistance and social services programs studied by the Commission serve specific client populations. Each program operates within organizational and funding structures defined by Federal statute and regulations and, in some cases, by State and local statutes and regulations. Administrative responsibilities are delegated to Federal, State, and local government units as the laws require. The following sections briefly identify the clients served and the basic administrative characteristics of the programs studied.

Aid to Families with Dependent Children

Title IV-A of the Social Security Act authorizes payments to States for the provision of financial assistance to needy families with dependent children. The Act defines dependent children as those children under 18 (or in the case of children attending school, under 21) who have been deprived of parental support or care by reason of the death, continued absence from home, physical or mental incapacity, or, under certain conditions, the unemployment of a parent. Within the broad requirements of the Social Security Act, a State has considerable latitude in defining the categories of the needy who will be served by the program in that State (e.g., whether or not to include families with an unemployed parent), in applying the eligibility criteria, and in determining what level of assistance will be provided to those eligible.

Aid to Families with Dependent Children (AFDC) provides financial assistance to help cover the costs of food, shelter, clothing, and other basic living costs. Emergency assistance and funds to support certain children in foster homes and institutions may also be provided. To supplement this assistance, an AFDC recipient is also eligible for assistance under the Medicaid, Food Stamp, and Title XX Social Services programs, and may also qualify for other forms of public assistance and social services.

Administrative and funding responsibilities for AFDC are shared by the Federal government and State and local governments. Program administration is overseen by the Social Security Administration of the Department of Health, Education, and Welfare (DHEW).[6] A State may either administer the program or supervise its administration by local governments. Federal funds (ranging from 50 percent to 65 percent of the total cost) help to finance assistance payments to recipients and may also be used to help cover administrative costs at the State and local level. States must share in the cost of the program and, in some but not all cases, local governments also contribute.

Medicaid

The Medicaid program authorized by Title XIX of the Social Security Act provides Federal funds to States for use in paying for medical services rendered to both the categorically needy and the medically needy. The categorically needy are those receiving assistance under the AFDC or Supplemental Security Income programs. The medically needy are those who meet all criteria for federally funded cash assistance, except the income criterion, and who lack the income and resources to meet the costs of

---

[6] Prior to the March 1977 reorganization of the Department of Health, Education, and Welfare, administration of the AFDC program was supervised by the Assistance Payments Administration of the Social and Rehabilitation Service.

necessary medical care and services. Their income may not exceed 133-1/3 percent of the State's cash assistance standard.

At minimum, a State must provide categorically needy individuals with:

- inpatient hospital services;
- outpatient hospital services;
- other laboratory and x-ray services;
- skilled nursing facility services for individuals 21 years of age or older;
- early and periodic screening and diagnosis of individuals under 21 to discover and treat mental and physical defects;
- family planning services and supplies; and
- physician's services.

The State may use the Federal funds in providing the medically needy with the above services or with other services which qualify for Federal funding under the Act. The services are rendered to recipients by qualified medical-care providers who are then reimbursed by the State.

The Health Care Financing Administration of the Department of Health, Education, and Welfare[7] oversees the administration of the Medicaid program. A State agency is responsible for either the administration of the program or the supervision of its administration by local government units. The designated State agency may, however, contract with other State agencies for performance of specified functions such as utilization review. States may also contract with private organizations to process claims, to act as the State's fiscal agent, or to develop and operate its Medicaid Management Information System, a mechanized claims-processing system for which special Federal funding is available.

The Federal share of Medicaid program costs is calculated according to a formula based on the State's per capita income in relation to national per capita income. The Federal share ranges from a low of 50 percent in many States to a high of 78 percent in one. States or localities, or both, provide the remaining funds.

Social Services

Title XX of the Social Security Act authorizes Federal grants to States for the provision of social services to recipients of public assistance under the AFDC or Supplemental Security Income programs and to other low-income persons who do not qualify for public assistance but whose income does not exceed 115 percent of the median income of a family of four in the State. The grants provided under Title XX are to be used for five specified purposes:

1. achieving or maintaining economic self-support to prevent, reduce, or eliminate dependency [of eligible clients];

---

[7] The Medical Services Administration of the Social and Rehabilitation Service, DHEW, supervised Medicaid administration prior to the March 1977 DHEW reorganization.

2. achieving or maintaining self-sufficiency, including reduction or prevention of dependency;
3. preventing or remedying neglect, abuse, or exploitation of children and adults unable to protect their own interests, or preserving, rehabilitating, or reuniting families;
4. preventing or reducing inappropriate institutional care by providing for community-based care, home-based care, or other less intensive forms of care; and
5. securing referral or admission for institutional care when other forms of care are not appropriate, or providing services to individuals in institutions.

Among the many services Title XX cites as appropriate to these five purposes are: child care services; services related to the management and maintenance of the home; day care services for adults; employment services; information, referral, and counseling services; health support services; appropriate combinations of services designed to meet the special needs of: (1) children; (2) aged, mentally retarded, blind, emotionally disturbed and physically handicapped individuals; and (3) alcoholics and drug addicts.

A single agency of each State administers or supervises the administration of the services programs of Title XX under the oversight of the Office of Human Development, DHEW.[8] In providing services to those eligible, a State may elect to use State facilities and personnel, to purchase services from private providers, or to use a combination of these alternatives. The State may also delegate certain administrative responsibilities to providers. For example, responsibility for determining an applicant's eligibility for a Title XX service may be delegated to the provider.

Federal funds totaling approximately $2.7 billion a year are available under Title XX. They can be used to reimburse States for 75 percent of the cost of social services, and in the case of family planning services, for 90 percent of the cost.

Food Stamps

The Food Stamp Program permits low-income households to buy coupons for less than the coupons are worth in exchange for food at federally certified food stores. Families receiving cash assistance under the AFDC or SSI programs are eligible for food stamps, as are those whose income falls below levels established by the Federal government.

State or local welfare offices administer the program under the supervision of the Food and Nutrition Service of the Department of Agriculture. The Department of Agriculture pays 100 percent of the cost of the food stamp coupons and 50 percent of the administrative costs incurred by States and localities.

---

[8] Before the March 1977 reorganization of the Department of Health, Education, and Welfare, the administration of Title XX programs was overseen by the Public Services Administration in the Social and Rehabilitation Service.

Programs Not Studied by the Commission

As noted above, the Commission could not make a detailed study of all the public assistance and social services programs funded by Federal, State, and local governments, and it made no attempt to study social services programs administered by private organizations that do not receive any government funding. Examples of the different types of government programs the Commission did not study are cited here to lend perspective on the universe of public assistance and social services programs.

Besides the four major programs studied by the Commission, the Federal government funds a great many categorical grant programs that provide assistance and services to the needy. Illustrative of these are:

- nutrition programs administered under Department of Agriculture supervision, such as the School Breakfast and School Lunch Programs, the Special Supplemental Food Program for Women, Infants and Children, and the Summer Food Service Program;
- health programs administered under the supervision of the Department of Health, Education, and Welfare, such as Family Planning Projects, Maternal and Child Health Services, Drug and Alcohol Abuse Community Services Programs, and Community Mental Health Programs;
- education programs under the auspices of DHEW, including Follow Through and Vocational Education;
- human development programs administered under the supervision of DHEW, including Head Start, Runaway Youth, Vocational Rehabilitation, and Special Programs for the Aging;
- housing programs funded by the Department of Housing and Urban Development, such as public housing and rent supplement programs; and
- employment programs of the Department of Labor, such as the Work Incentive Program, Job Corps, and Comprehensive Employment and Training Programs.

States also fund cash assistance and social services programs, especially to meet needs in areas where Federal financial assistance has not been made available. The most common of these State programs, usually called "general assistance," makes cash available to the needy who are not eligible for Federal cash assistance under AFDC or SSI, such as young, single individuals and young couples with no children. States may also fund special purpose programs to supplement Federal programs. Examples of these in California are the State's Emergency Loan Programs and Special Circumstances Program.

Obviously, the record-keeping issues inherent in administering the AFDC, Medicaid, Social Services, and Food Stamp programs also arise in these other programs. Eligibility for these programs is generally based on financial need. Those seeking assistance under any of the programs must apply for it and submit to the prescribed methods of verifying the information they supply. Inevitably, a record is created to document the relationship between the client and the agency administering the program. Therefore, as explained in more detail below, the Commission believes that the information safeguards recommended for the four major programs which the Commission studied in detail should be required of the other programs as well.

PRINCIPAL FINDINGS AND CONCLUSIONS

The basic philosophy of any system of government is reflected in its welfare system and in the way policy regarding the welfare system evolves. In a federal system, responsibilities for governing are divided between national and state governments. The welfare system of the United States is a product of our federal system of government, and methods of determining welfare policy and the policy itself must reflect this reality.

Historically, "poor relief" was a local responsibility. During the Great Depression of the 1930's, the tidal wave of unemployed quickly overwhelmed community resources, throwing the burden of supporting them on the States. When the States, in turn, found themselves helpless against the floodtide, the Federal government stepped in. Since the 1930's, the funding of welfare has been a shared responsibility of Federal, State, and in some cases local, governments; administrative responsibility for alleviating the plight of the needy, however, has remained with the States, even though the Federal government has assumed an ever larger share of responsibility for financing the benefits and the cost of administering them.

The States are not, however, free to administer welfare programs as they see fit. Acceptance of Federal funds carries with it the obligation to adhere to Federal standards and requirements. The extent of Federal constraint on the States has fluctuated over the years and varies from program to program, in record keeping as in other aspects of administration.

When Federal law is silent on a record-keeping activity, States retain the discretion to establish their own policies and practices within the limits established by the Constitution. To the extent that the Federal government has chosen to regulate the record keeping of agencies administering federally assisted programs, the minimum requirements for acceptable practices are set forth in Federal statute and regulation. These, or more stringent, requirements must be included in State statutes, regulations, or plans. The result is that welfare record keeping reflects a medley of practices prescribed by Federal statutes and regulations in some areas, by State laws in others, by a combination of the two, or, in some cases, by no formal policy at all.

A comprehensive policy to guide all the record-keeping activities of welfare agencies has never been formulated by the Federal government. A few States have recently enacted laws that deal comprehensively with fair information practice, but the laws are general in scope, applicable to all State records. Some federally assisted programs must conform to Federal requirements, such as those regarding client access to records, contents of a case file, and permissible disclosures of records, while others—either through oversight or deliberate omission—need not. For the great bulk of federally assisted programs, Federal law has not yet prescribed fair practice regarding such factors as the accuracy, timeliness, completeness, and relevance of information used, and the ability of a client to contest erroneous information. In the case of programs funded solely by State or local governments, the administrators, however attentive they may be to professional ethics, often receive little direction from State legislatures in setting record-keeping policy.

It is against this background that the Commission's general findings must be understood. The Commission has evaluated the extent to which existing law on record keeping is faithful to the principles of fair information practice described earlier in this report. Specific recommendations (see below) focus on the deficiencies of existing policy; the following general findings help put them into perspective.

First, the Commission could find no general, overall policy on public assistance and social services record keeping. In the few programs that address and attempt to control practices from which unfairness to clients can flow, attention has concentrated on some controls—most notably constraints on disclosures of records—while other sources of unfairness have been largely ignored. Failure to define general policy leaves the way open for unfair record-keeping practices.

Second, the Commision finds that the lack of a general policy creates problems within an agency. Even where law has been developed to regulate the record-keeping practices of the federally assisted programs, the resolutions arrived at are not necessarily consistent from one program to another. For example, the AFDC, Medicaid, Social Services, and Food Stamp programs are each subject to somewhat different restrictions on disclosure of client records to third parties. Nor are the rules regarding client access to a case file the same in the Food Stamp program as in the AFDC program. Such policy inconsistencies often confuse those administering a program, as well as the program's clients, and may create unnecessary administrative costs. The confusion is compounded when a private services agency receives funds under several federally assisted programs. Such a private agency may find it all but impossible to keep its records so that they meet the requirements of the different funding sources.

Third, the Commission finds that lack of a general policy creates great problems in the exchange of information among and within agencies. Federal record-keeping policy fails to take full account of the interrelationship in administration of all of the federally assisted programs. Again, this problem is especially acute in the area of policy that defines and limits the range of permissible disclosures of a program's records. Information about Medicaid and Food Stamp clients, for instance, may not be disclosed for purposes other than the administration of the program for which it was collected. Yet one worker in a State or local welfare agency may have responsibilities for administering not only these two programs, but others, such as AFDC and Social Services, as well. It may be impractical for the agency to segregate records about the client as a Medicaid or Food Stamp

454 PERSONAL PRIVACY IN AN INFORMATION SOCIETY

recipient from those about the same client as an AFDC or Social Services client.

Fourth, the Commission finds uncertainty about the extent to which the Federal government should dictate the record-keeping practices of State and local welfare agencies. Federal law in some areas clearly directs the practices to be followed, while in other equally crucial areas, Federal law is silent, leaving the States with wide discretion in formulating their own policies. Disclosure policy, for example, is clearly specified in Federal law, whereas the States are left to decide what practices are permissible in verifying information.

Fifth, the Commission finds weak oversight of record-keeping practices, even where requirements are quite clear. Federal agencies like the Departments of Agriculture and Health, Education, and Welfare apparently lack the resources to monitor State practices adequately, so that a State which ignores or circumvents their regulations can probably do so with impunity. For example, despite a clear DHEW regulation permitting an AFDC client access to his case file prior to a hearing, the Commission found substantial evidence that some States deny this right.

Sixth, the Commission finds that even when State policy incorporates Federal requirements, the workers at the State and local level sometimes fail to translate policy into practice. Factors which contribute to these failures include the complexity of the laws and frequent changes in requirements, which increase the work load to no purpose and make it difficult for workers to know what is required of them. Complexity and frequent change in requirements are not the exclusive prerogative of Federal legislators; State legislators also contribute.

Finally, the manner in which Federal spending power has been exercised and the inaction of the States have meant that cash assistance and social services programs funded by State and local governments may be subject to record-keeping requirements that are different from those applicable to federally assisted programs or, in some cases, to no requirements at all. This is true even when such programs are administered by the same State agency responsible for administering federally assisted programs. This means that the privacy interests of clients of these programs may be wholly unprotected and that flows of information between federally assisted programs and those financed through other means are subject to no coherent policy.

GENERAL RECOMMENDATIONS

The above findings should make clear the advantages of establishing a comprehensible and generally applicable record-keeping policy to guide public assistance and social services programs at all levels. Such a policy would have to be enacted by the Congress, spelled out in Federal regulations, and overseen by Federal agencies. To the large and growing number of citizens who perceive welfare as a national problem, this is the obvious approach. Since most of the money for welfare comes from the Federal government, it has a strong responsibility for directing how the programs will be carried out. Furthermore, the Federal government, having created a patchwork of uncoordinated public assistance and social services programs and equipping them with inconsistent regulations, can fairly be charged with responsibility for bringing the record keeping of at least the federally assisted programs into alignment, and for assuring the fair use of records about their clients.

On the other hand, standardization always carries a price tag. It is difficult for any national policy to take full account of the particular needs of each of the States and the variety of arrangements the States have devised for providing public assistance and social services. Furthermore, a balance must always be struck between privacy and other goals and values, and the trade-off satisfactory to the citizens of one area may or may not be acceptable to the citizens of another area. The controversy over how private providers report individually identifiable data about Title XX clients to State agencies illustrates this problem.[9] An added cost is that standardization inevitably stifles innovation.

After considering all of these arguments, the Commission concluded that the need for a Federal policy on record keeping by public assistance and social services agencies overwhelmingly outweighs the potential drawbacks. These drawbacks can be minimized by leaving the States significant latitude in formulating the specifics of a record-keeping policy within the guidelines imposed by Federal law.

Accordingly, the Commission recommends:

Recommendation (1):

(a)   That the Congress enact a statute that requires each State, as a condition of the receipt of Federal financial assistance for public assistance and social services programs, to enact a fair information practice statute applicable to records about public assistance and social services clients of any agency administering or supervising the administration of any federally assisted public assistance or social services program (the requirements of the State statute are described below);

(b)   That Congress give a State two full State legislative sessions to enact the required statute before it is considered not to be in compliance with Federal law;

---

[9] A controversy arose when private providers under contract with State agencies to provide Title XX services objected to a requirement that they report individually identifiable client data to State agencies. The information was needed by State agencies to report to DHEW an "unduplicated count" of Title XX recipients. Some provider agencies, especially those providing legal assistance and mental health services, protested that compliance with such a reporting requirement would breach the confidentiality of their relationship with their clients, deter individuals from seeking needed services, and give the State agency the capability to construct a Title XX client "data bank" which could be used to the detriment of clients. Although this controversy reached crisis proportions in some States, it simply never became a significant issue in others. Although DHEW responded by making it possible for States to report an estimated, rather than actual, unduplicated count, some State agencies would like to continue to collect individually identifiable data for their own planning and evaluation purposes.

(c)   That the Congress specify in the statute the general principles
       of the fair information practice policy, leaving to the States
       some discretion to tailor specific means of implementing the
       principles to their own needs, where appropriate;
(d)   That the Congress make the Secretary of Health, Education,
       and Welfare responsible for determining that each State has
       enacted the required State statute and that it has the character-
       istics required by Federal law. The Secretary should consult
       with the heads of other Federal agencies funding public
       assistance and social services programs in carrying out this
       responsibility;
(e)   That every Federal agency responsible for overseeing the
       administration of a public assistance or social services program
       be required by Federal statute to review State compliance with
       the record-keeping requirements set forth in Federal and State
       statute;
(f)   That the process that States use for formulating and enacting
       specific fair information practice requirements provide ample
       opportunity for public participation, including public hearings;
       and
(g)   That appropriate sanctions and remedies, at the Federal and
       State level, be available to deal with violations of the statutorily
       prescribed requirements.

Adoption of this recommendation would achieve several ends. It
would:

•   resolve most of the problems created by inconsistencies in
     Federal policy regarding the records of various programs
     while at the same time allowing the States a measure of
     flexibility in implementing the policy;
•   provide the same protections for all client records maintained
     by agencies that receive Federal financial assistance, includ-
     ing their records about clients of programs that are not
     federally assisted;
•   supersede with a single Federal and a single State statute the
     myriad laws that currently govern record-keeping practices,
     thereby substantially reducing the complexity which renders
     such laws ineffective;
•   remove the temptation for agencies to diversify their record-
     keeping practices in incompatible directions by embodying a
     uniform general policy in statute;
•   strengthen oversight by Federal agencies; and
•   provide legal sanctions and remedies to deal with violations.[10]

Simplicity and comprehensiveness are the goals of these general
recommendations. Comments submitted to the Commission by many public

---

[10] See Chapter 10 for a discussion of the need for Federal sanctions that are proportionate to
the seriousness of State non-compliance.

agencies and private organizations attest that these goals are urgently desired. As the representative of one welfare agency noted in testimony before the Commission:

> We strongly urge the adoption of the same standards for all the programs under consideration. It is sufficiently difficult to administer complex and varied programs, without having to be constrained by different standards for different programs. Not only is it confusing to staff but to recipients who begin to view us as a "schizophrenic" agency.[11]

States will need a reasonable period of time—two legislative sessions—to formulate the recommended statute. Only after that time would a State not be in compliance with Federal law, if the Commission's recommendation were adopted.

Because of the central role of the Department of Health, Education, and Welfare in funding and overseeing the administration of public assistance and social services programs, the Commission considers the HEW Secretary the appropriate person to assume primary responsibility for evaluating State compliance in enacting the recommended statute with, of course, the benefit of consultation with heads of other Federal agencies to assure coordination and understanding.

The Commission further believes that record keeping by government agencies and private providers that do not receive any Federal funding should also be subject to the fairness standards set forth for agencies receiving some Federal assistance, but the Commission acknowledges the fact that the Federal government cannot impose such standards on them. Therefore, the Commission recommends:

Recommendation (2):

That every State enact a statute applying the fair information practices required of agencies receiving Federal public assistance and social services funds to records of cash assistance and social services agencies that do not receive any Federal funding.

SPECIFIC RECOMMENDATIONS

This section discusses the policies underlying the Commission's specific recommendations for a State fair information practice statute. Some of the recommended provisions simply embody present practice. They would serve the purpose of making such practice a statutory requirement. Others broaden the rights already accorded to clients. The remainder prescribe new record-keeping requirements. All of these recommendations are framed to apply to *all* client records maintained by agencies that receive

---

[11] Written statement of the Middlesex County, New Jersey, Welfare Board, *Public Assistance and Social Services Record Keeping,* Hearings before the Privacy Protection Study Commission, January 12, 1977, p. 12, (hereinafter cited as Public Assistance and Social Services Hearings).

any Federal funds, not just to those records of an agency about clients for whom Federal assistance has been secured.

For the Commission's specific recommendations to take effect, two legislative steps would be required: (1) enactment of a Federal statute requiring that a State, as a condition of receiving Federal financial assistance for any public assistance and social services program, adopt a statute mandating certain minimum record keeping requirements; and (2) enactment of such a statute by the State.

Intrusiveness

Only details about the circumstances of a particular applicant can show whether he or she qualifies for help under any public assistance or social services program, and additional data about an eligible applicant inevitably accumulate as long as he or she receives assistance or services. When the eligibility requirements are complex, and verification requirements stringent, as they are in many welfare programs, the information collected about applicants for, and recipients of, welfare becomes very detailed indeed. In some areas of the country, for example, a worker visits clients' homes to verify their statements. These home visits, although made by prior appointment, give the agency an opportunity to collect more detailed personal information than the client might be willing to disclose. Furthermore, a welfare agency striving conscientiously to provide as much help as it can to its clients has a strong incentive to delve deeply into a family's problems in order to make sure all members of the family are getting all the help to which they are entitled.

Such efforts produce detailed records about virtually all aspects of a welfare family's personal life—its finances, possessions, habits, sexual relationships, need for family planning services, physical and mental health problems, education, prior employment, dependence on alcohol and drugs, and utilization of medical services. Welfare agencies are more likely than the other agencies and organizations studied by the Commission to have the makings of a profile covering every aspect of client families' lives.

The ability of a welfare agency to collect such sensitive information imposes the obligation to control its records with exceptional care, as explained below. In addition, the Commission was prompted to consider the need for constraints on the power of a welfare agency to collect and record some kinds of information.

Criticism of welfare agencies often focuses on the kinds of questions asked regarding eligibility and resources. Eligibility criteria, and consequently the questions asked on application forms, differ from State to State. Even when information collected for eligibility determination is clearly relevant to that purpose, some critics nonetheless oppose its collection on the grounds that it is so sensitive that its collection constitutes an unwarranted invasion of personal privacy.

In the welfare area—unlike some of the other areas the Commission studied—a disgruntled client cannot choose among a number of different agencies with different eligibility criteria from which to seek assistance or services. Only one State agency can serve him. Thus, one might conclude that there is no way in which an individual can limit the degree of intrusion to which he must submit in order to get public assistance and social services.

To a certain extent this is true. A client, acting independently, is not likely to be able to exercise much control over a welfare agency's probing into the details of his personal life. But clients who feel the intrusion goes too far are not totally without recourse.

There are now two ways of settling disputes between clients and a welfare agency over the appropriateness of using particular items of information in a determination or redetermination of eligibility. If a client claims that a denial of benefits was based on irrelevant information, he can demand a hearing to contest the basis of the decision. Because eligibility criteria are set out in State statutes, regulations, and plans, they provide some objective standards against which the relevance of the disputed information can be assessed that are independent of the whim of an agency or worker.

Because eligibility criteria are usually determined either by State legislatures or through some sort of rule-making process, there is a second recourse for clients, or alternatively, organizations of clients or others acting in their interests, and that is to seek amendment of the official eligibility criteria. The need to ask certain questions can be removed if the eligibility criteria are changed. Louisiana, for example, now specifies that the value of musical instruments and jewelry of a sentimental value will not be taken into account in its assets tests. Although the exception may not have been prompted by concern about intrusiveness, the example illustrates that this method of limiting the collection of information is feasible.

The question of intrusiveness may also arise when an agency believes that a client is entitled to services other than the ones for which he has applied. After a family is found eligible for AFDC, for example, the AFDC worker may try to help the members of the family determine what other services they need, and then refer them to appropriate service providers. In some instances, referral to another agency is mandatory. An eligible AFDC client must be referred to the Work Incentive Program (WIN), and thus has no choice but to acquiesce in the exploration of factors relevant to WIN status. But where the acceptance of services is voluntary, an agency is hardly justified in demanding more information than the individual client or family is willing to divulge.

The exploration by agencies of factors relating to possible needs of a family that are not being met is wholly laudable. Unless participation in another program is a condition of eligibility under the program for which the client has initially applied, however, the Commission believes that clients of a public assistance or social services program should not be *required*, or *coerced*, to divulge information about either need or potential eligibility for other assistance or services programs. The Commission has therefore concluded in its recommendation on "Notification of Rights" (see below) that a client be told, at the time information is requested of him, whether he must divulge the information as a condition of receiving benefits, or whether its disclosure is voluntary.

Fairness

FAIRNESS IN COLLECTION

In making determinations about a client's initial or continuing entitlement to benefits, an agency may contact third-party sources (e.g., banks, schools, neighbors, State agencies) in order to verify information the client has supplied. The extent to which such collateral verification is sought, and the methods by which it is obtained, vary among States and programs, among agencies, and even among workers responsible for determining a client's eligibility in a single locality.

Federal statutes and regulations currently give agencies little guidance with respect to the collateral verification process. Food Stamp regulations, for example, require verification of income, and also of eligibility factors if the information the applicant has provided is unclear, inconsistent, incomplete, or otherwise raises doubts about eligibility. *[7 C.F.R. 271.4(a)(2)(iii)]* To supplement these directions, the Department of Agriculture prescribes the "prudent person rule" which advises eligibility workers to use reasonable judgment in deciding what information supplied by the applicant should be verified with other sources.

In 1969, the Social and Rehabilitation Service of DHEW promulgated regulations outlining acceptable verification procedures for the AFDC, Medicaid, and pre-Title XX social services programs.[12] The regulations provided that verification be limited to that which is reasonably necessary to ensure the legality of expenditures under a program and required the agency to rely on the client as the primary source of information in determining eligibility. The agency could, however, help the client obtain information or obtain information for a client who could not get it himself without help (e.g., because of mental or physical impairment). If collateral contacts were necessary, the regulations required the agency to explain to the client what information would be needed, why it was needed, and how it would be used. The agency then had to obtain the client's consent to the contact. If the information supplied by the applicant or recipient could not support an eligibility decision, the agency had to explain what else was needed, and try again to get it from the client. If the client could not supply the necessary information and refused permission for the agency to contact a source, assistance could be denied or terminated.

These regulations were repealed in 1973, apparently to give States greater flexibility in developing their own collateral verification processes. The large number of overpayments to clients and payments to ineligibles that had been uncovered made greater flexibility seem desirable.

The Commission recognizes that collateral verification can be necessary, especially when inconsistencies or vagueness in the information received from an applicant or recipient, or inadequate records, raise doubt about eligibility. It also believes that State and local agencies unquestionably need a degree of flexibility in determining when verification is

---

12 Prior to the enactment of Title XX, Federal funding for State administered social services was available under Titles IV, VI, X, XIV, and XVI of the Social Security Act.

necessary and from what sources verification may be secured. Nevertheless, because stigma sometimes attaches to the receipt of public assistance and social services, the Commission believes that there should be some Federal prescription of procedures to be followed by agencies so as to assure that the collateral verification process does not result in more information than necessary about a client being disclosed to third parties. Therefore, the Commission recommends:

Recommendation (3):

That the Congress require the States to provide by statute that public assistance and social services agencies must, to the greatest extent practicable, collect information and documentation directly from the client, unless otherwise requested by the client.

The Commission believes that both agency and client will benefit if the agency's need to contact collateral sources is kept to a minimum. When the client supplies documentation supporting the eligibility decision, the agency saves the time that eligibility workers would otherwise spend contacting collateral sources. At the same time, the client retains some control over the collection, use, and disclosure of information about himself. The client can usually seek records about himself from third parties without explaining why he is asking, whereas the agency would need to disclose the fact that the client is applying for or receiving a benefit and, in some cases, the nature of the benefit.

Current agency practice, according to witnesses and those who submitted written comments to the Commission, is generally for agencies to rely on clients for verification of the information they supply. Clients are usually requested to bring with them documentation of the information on the application form when they come to the welfare agency for an interview. Agencies will usually accept as evidence documents such as rent receipts, wage statements, bank books, report cards, or insurance policies supplied by the client. Client representatives stressed to the Commission that most applicants and recipients are quite able to supply adequate documentation, and that all should therefore have a chance to do so before the agency starts contacting third-party sources. Clients who are not able to obtain the information may, of course, require the agency's help in getting it.

On the other hand, Federal, State, and local agency representatives affirmed the need of agencies to contact collateral sources. They see a positive relationship between an agency's ability to contact third-party sources and its ability to reduce error rates and thus assure the accuracy of eligibility determinations. Even among the client and professional association representatives, most conceded that agencies need to contact third parties, at least under certain circumstances (e.g., where there is uncertainty about the information supplied by the client or reasonable cause to believe that the client is misrepresenting his situation), although there was little consensus among them beyond that point.

The Commission recognizes that there are circumstances that justify an agency's contacting third parties for information on clients. At the same time, the Commission contends that applicants and recipients should have a right, albeit qualified, to determine what sources are contacted. Clients have an undeniable interest in limiting not only the number but also the kinds of sources to be contacted by agencies. Clients have reason to fear unwarranted consequences, such as loss of residence or employment, if people in certain relationships to them (e.g., landlords or employers) learn that they have applied for or are receiving public assistance or social services. Even clients who do not fear such adverse consequences may simply not wish certain individuals to know of their application for or receipt of benefits.

The Social and Rehabilitation Service, DHEW, submitted to the Commission samples of forms and letters used by State and local agencies to secure, for AFDC purposes, client authorization for the release of information from third-party sources. Several of these forms contained authorization statements which the Commission found unduly broad. For example, a South Carolina form provides that the client authorize

> . . . any person, agency, or organization to furnish such information as may be requested by an authorized representative of the County Department of Social Services or the State Department of Social Services, with or without additional consent from me.

As in other areas it has examined, the Commission believes that collateral verification authorizations of that type effectively deprive the individual of any control over inquiries made about him to third parties, and are both unacceptable and unnecessary. Moreover, because of the special problems associated with being identified as a welfare applicant or recipient, the Commission also believes that no collateral contacts should be made by a welfare agency until the client has been informed that his documentation is unacceptable and why, and has had a chance to produce alternative evidence to the agency. Therefore, the Commission recommends:

Recommendation (4):

That the Congress require the States to provide by statute that a public assistance or social services agency must:

(a)   notify a client as to:
    (i)   all types of information which may be collected about him;
    (ii)   the techniques that may be used to collect or verify such types of information;
    (iii)   the types of sources that may be asked to provide each type of information.

(b)   limit its collection practices to those specified in any such notice;

(c)   provide the client an opportunity to indicate particular sources of information which he does not want the agency to contact and to provide alternatives to those sources so indicated;

(d)   provide the client an opportunity to withdraw his application should the agency require that a source be contacted notwithstanding his objections;

provided, however, that such procedures shall not be required when there is a reasonable belief that the client has violated a law relating to the administration of the assistance or services program.

This recommendation, in the Commission's view, outlines an effective mechanism for balancing an agency's need to contact collateral sources against the interest of the client in limiting the collection of information about himself from others. Moreover, it also conforms to present practice in some agencies. The authorization form used by the Oregon Division of Public Welfare, for example, lists the commonly contacted sources, some by category (e.g., employers, financial institutions, schools) and others by name (e.g., agencies or organizations), and invites applicants to check the ones they authorize. The authorization form used by the Tennessee Department of Human Services lists a broader spectrum of sources to be contacted, and adds "any other individual or organization" having knowledge of the client's circumstances. There is, however, a space on the form where clients can list specific sources the Department may not contact.

It has been argued that the protections for client rights recommended by the Commission are meaningless because "everybody knows who's on welfare," and because clients must ultimately choose between bowing to the agency's insistence on contacting a "necessary" source or foregoing benefits. Since a client who needs the assistance can ill afford to forego the benefits, the argument continues, his choice is hollow. The Commission believes, however, that clients should have the opportunity to decide for themselves whether or not such rights are meaningless. Moreover, it believes that the procedural modifications outlined in the Commission's recommendations and compliance in good faith on the part of agencies and clients will offer clients intermediate alternatives to a stark choice between yielding to an agency's demands for information and foregoing assistance.

The Commission recognizes that an exception to the collateral verification practices outlined in the above recommendations may be necessary when a client is suspected of violating laws relating to the administration of the welfare programs. Under those circumstances, the agency could not logically be expected to notify the client of the verification sources it intended to contact or to ask the client to suggest alternative sources, since doing so might well compromise fulfillment of the agency's duty to gather evidence.[13]

The Commission also realizes that some States operate automated verification systems in which lists of clients are matched with records maintained by other State agencies, such as State employment agencies. Although the Commission recognizes the utility of such systems in reducing both overpayments and payments to ineligibles, it believes that each client should be informed that such methods will be used and offered an opportunity to withdraw his application should he object to this means of collateral verification. Withdrawal of an application by an individual who is

---

[13] The agency would, of course, have to comply with the restrictions on disclosure of records imposed by agencies and organizations from which it seeks information for a law enforcement purpose including, in some cases, the production of a subpoena.

not in fact eligible would in effect achieve the desired end—reduction of payments to ineligibles.

The Commission further contends that, just as a client has an interest in limiting the number or kinds of sources contacted, he also has an interest in limiting the amount and kind of information disclosed to third-party contacts in the course of collateral verification. More specifically, while a client may not object to collateral contacts which disclose that he is seeking benefits, he may well object to a contact's learning of the particular kind of benefit sought, and the same applies to any information which does not directly relate to verification. The client's interest may be especially acute when he or she is seeking a service that is widely perceived to be sensitive, such as alcohol and drug abuse treatment or mental health counseling.

Regulations applicable to the Title XX Social Services program already require that a provider agency under a State agency contract to determine eligibility must notify a client if collateral contacts are to be made, so that a client who wishes to keep the nature of the service he is seeking confidential may ask that the State agency make the contact. When notified of the client's request, the State agency must make the necessary contact and relay the information to the provider. *[45 C.F.R. 228.61(f)(1) and (2)]* This regulation implies acknowledgement of the State agency's responsibility to make the contact discreetly without revealing the nature of the service being sought.

The Commission supports this regulation and recommends that it be adopted by all agencies that provide social services to clients. While the Commission understands than an agency may not be able to disguise the fact that an individual has applied for cash assistance, or some type of social service, it does believe that the specific nature of the service sought need not be revealed to a third-party source in order to obtain necessary collateral verification. Accordingly, the Commission recommends:

Recommendation (5):

That Congress require States to provide by statute that public assistance and social services agencies must give clients of social services programs the opportunity to require that collateral contacts, made to secure information about their eligibility in a services program, are made in a manner that, to the maximum extent possible, does not reveal the specific nature of the service sought by the client.

More broadly, the Commission recommends that all public assistance and social services agencies adopt a policy of revealing only the very minimum amount of any kind of information about the client consistent with obtaining verification even in cases in which it is necessary to reveal that the client has applied for cash assistance, as opposed to social services. This issue is further dealt with in the Commission's recommendation on disclosure of records, below.

FAIRNESS IN USE

ACCESS TO RECORDS

DHEW regulations governing the AFDC, Medicaid, and Title XX Social Services programs *[45 C.F.R. 205.10(a)(13)(i)]* specify that an applicant or recipient who has requested a hearing may examine at reasonable times before the date of the hearing, as well as during the hearing, the contents of his case file and all documents and records to be used by the agency at the hearing. A hearing may be requested by a client whose claim for benefits has been denied or not acted upon with reasonable promptness, or who has been aggrieved by any agency action resulting in suspension, reduction, discontinuance, or termination of assistance.

Regulations applicable to the Food Stamp program afford clients who have requested a hearing a more limited right of access: these clients may examine at reasonable times before and during the hearing only those documents and records to be used by the agency at the hearing. *[7 C.F.R. 271.1(o)(5)(i)]* A hearing may be requested by a client whose household has been aggrieved by any action of the State agency, or of a coupon-issuing agency, in the course of its administration of a Food Stamp program, provided the action affects the participation of the household in the program.

Although the DHEW regulations governing hearings in the Medicaid, AFDC, and Social Services programs specify that a client may inspect the contents of his *entire* case file, the Commission has found substantial evidence to suggest that agencies often do not, in fact, make the entire case file available on request. To the extent that this is true, a client is denied the opportunity to decide what information in the case file he feels should be introduced at the hearing. For example, a representative of Community Legal Services, Philadelphia, Pennsylvania, attested that a client's right to full access to his case file before and during the hearing process is not always respected, noting:

> . . . 45 C.F.R. 205.10(a)(13)(i) allows for inspection of case files and documents when there is a hearing, but is written in such a way that most States feel that it only gives the recipient the right to inspect such documents as are actually produced in evidence for the hearing. This leads to significant problems, since a lot more information may prove useful to the person, including any exculpatory evidence that he may want to raise or that the administration may know of. . . .[14]

For another example, a manual for welfare advocates in New York City prepared by Community Action for Legal Services, Inc. noted that New York State and New York City policies regarding access to the case record are more restrictive than Federal policy. For example, New York City regulations provide that, upon request, the client or his authorized representative is entitled to receive copies of only those portions of the

---

[14] Testimony, Public Assistance and Social Services Hearings, January 11, 1977, p. 587.

client's record which would be "beneficial" to the client *[18 New York Code of Rules and Regulations (N.Y.C.R.R.) 357.3(c)]* or which will be introduced at a hearing. *[18 N.Y.C.R.R 358.9(d) and 358.12 (a)]* The manual advises advocates that when access is denied, the denial should be raised as an issue at the hearing.[15]

The Commission also received a written comment from the Land of Lincoln Legal Assistance Foundation, Inc. (Danville, Illinois) citing its attorneys' inability to obtain full access to a client's case record. The Foundation states that even when the client's written authorization has been obtained, the local department of welfare will not permit a client's attorney to examine any portion of the client record unless a notice of appeal to initiate a hearing has been filed with the department. After the notice has been filed, according to this comment, the local department will allow examination only of material relating specifically to the issues raised in that notice.

Even if full access to the case file prior to a hearing were in all cases permitted, the applicant or recipient with no legally acceptable reason to seek a hearing cannot currently be assured an opportunity to inspect his record, and so can neither discover nor request correction of inaccuracies. Moreover, except for these rights of access in connection with the hearing procedure, the four major welfare programs are not required by Federal law to permit a client to inspect records about himself, nor are other public assistance and social services programs. Although in some instances eligibility workers may, upon client request, give a client access to records about himself, this is usually at the sole discretion of the eligibility worker involved with the case.

The Commission believes that without a general right of access a client cannot make informed decisions about the use of information in a record by others than the welfare agency, nor can he discover and request correction of inaccuracies in the record before the information is used to his detriment. The Commission believes that the right of access is an essential component of fairness in record keeping and therefore recommends:

Recommendation (6):

That the Congress require States to provide by statute that a client who is the subject of a record maintained by a public assistance and social services agency shall have a right to see and copy that record upon request.

The Commission recognizes that implementing the general right of access may put additional administrative burdens and cost on the agencies and individuals charged with welfare administration.[16] Data gathered by the Commission indicates, however, that the advantages and protections

---

[15] Community Action for Legal Services, Inc., *Manual for Welfare Advocates in New York,* New York, 1976, p. 125.

[16] The Commission believes that if any fees for copying records are charged clients, they should not exceed the actual cost of copying, and further, that fees should be closely related to the ability of clients to pay them.

afforded the client would far outweigh the additional burden, especially if agencies are allowed to set reasonable limits on the hours during which clients may view their records. The Minnesota Data Privacy Act, for example, gives individuals a right of access, with certain qualifications, to information maintained about them by the State. Representatives of the Minnesota Department of Public Welfare attested to the Commission that:

> We anticipated that far more clients would ask to see their record than we could possibly process. To our surprise, this multitude did not materialize. As we look back on it now, we attribute the lack of interest to the openness by which most of the counseling, therapy, and casework operations are carried out by our local agencies. Our agencies have kept clients reasonably well informed during our involvement with them—how they will use the information, with whom they will share it, et cetera—to the extent that most clients probably don't feel the record would tell them anything they don't already know . . . .[17]

The Commission expects that the openness which its other recommendations should foster will minimize clients' demands for access to their records.

The arguments presented to the Commission in oral testimony and written comments brought out the need to qualify or deny the right of access in certain situations. The Commission identified six kinds of situations meriting special consideration:

1) *Clients' access to medical information.*[18] Agency records on clients may include sensitive information regarding a client's physical or mental health or status (e.g., information regarding the physical or mental incapacity of an AFDC client). Allowing clients access to such information might, in some instances, jeopardize their health or impede their recovery. The Commission heard a number of recommendations that the right of access be qualified when, in the opinion of a qualified medical professional, full access might adversely affect the client. In such cases, an alternative might be to assign the client's right to full access to someone qualified to represent him. When a medical record is the basis of an adverse determination about a client, however, the Commission believes that it should be available to him.[19]

2) *Parents' access to records of minors.* Should a parent or guardian be granted access to the child's record? Should the minor be granted access? Most of the opinions submitted to the Commission held that a minor who seeks treatment on his own initiative (e.g., for family planning services, drug rehabilitation) should have access to that record, especially if State law permits the minor to obtain treatment without the knowledge or consent of

---

[17] Testimony, Public Assistance and Social Services Hearings, January 11, 1977, p. 764.

[18] As noted earlier, the recommendations in this chapter are not intended to apply to records maintained by medical-care providers rendering services to Medicaid and Title XX clients, except insofar as they are used to determine eligibility. Recommendations regarding client access to, and correction of, records maintained by medical-care providers are found in Chapter 7.

[19] See Chapter 7 for additional discussion of this problem.

his parents. Furthermore, it was argued that parents or guardians of such minors be given access in such situations only upon the minor's authorization. These arguments are based on the belief that a minor is likely to be discouraged from seeking necessary treatment by the knowledge that his parents will be notified that he is seeking the treatment and, especially, if he knows that his parents will have access to his records.

3) *Access to adoption records.* The Commission, which unfortunately could not make a study of the special problems involved in access to adoption records, suggests that this matter be addressed in a special inquiry.

4) *Clients' access to information submitted under assurance of confidentiality.* Agency administrators stressed to the Commission their belief that it would be impossible for them to get the information necessary for the detection of fraud if they could not promise the sources of such information confidentiality. This is true primarily in cases in which the source is an individual, rather than a record maintained by another agency or organization. Opinions differed as to whether or not both the source and the information provided should be kept confidential. It was generally agreed, however, that information provided by confidential sources should not be used as the basis of an adverse decision about the client unless it could be revealed to the client prior to, or during, a hearing. Implicit in this argument is the Commission's belief that an agency should adequately inform its sources of information about the agency's policies regarding the release of information to the client. Furthermore, upon soliciting or accepting information about a client from a source seeking an assurance of confidentiality, the agency should determine whether the source would be willing to have the information he supplied revealed to the client during a hearing—that is, whether he is seeking an absolute guarantee of confidentiality that extends not only to his name but to the information he supplies. His decision will influence the uses to which the agency will be able to put such information.

Arguments in favor of protecting the confidentiality of informants indicate that confidential sources may be essential in detecting and investigating cases of child abuse and neglect. Agency representatives are convinced that the very people who are in a position to know of abused or neglected children would be unwilling and often afraid to report the situation if they could not report in confidence. Those who report such cases may have good reason to fear reprisal, especially if the informant is a member or close friend of the child's family.

5) *Access during an investigation of a violation of laws relating to the administration of a program.* The argument for this exception is that allowing clients suspected of fraud access to their records would give guilty clients a chance to evade justice by concealing or destroying evidence or by absconding.

6) *Access to records covering more than one client.* Public assistance and social services records often contain information about more than one individual. AFDC records, for example, deal with individuals as members of an assistance unit; Food Stamp records treat individuals as members of their household; and a services agency may keep a single record on several

individuals who apply as a group. These records raise special access problems. For example, which members of an assistance unit, household, or treatment group have a right of access to the entire record? Does a member have the right to the record's information concerning the other members, or only the information on himself or herself? Has a minor a right of access to information maintained on his parents?

The Commission found merit in the arguments for qualifying or denying access in the situations described above. On the theory that the States rather than the Federal government are best able to find reasonable solutions to the problems they raise, the Commission recommends:

Recommendation (7):

That the Congress permit the States to enact provisions of law that:

(a) **provide that a medical record may be disclosed either directly to the client or through a medical-care professional designated by the client, provided, however, that a client must be given direct access to any medical-record information that is used to make a determination about his eligibility;**

(b) **restrict a parent or guardian's access to a minor's record, or a minor's access to a record that contains information about him;**

(c) **provide that the source of information in a record, or the information itself to the extent that it would reveal the identity of the source, need not be disclosed to the client if the source is an individual who has requested an assurance of confidentiality or, absent such a request, if disclosure can reasonably be expected to result in harm to the source, provided, however, that an adverse determination may not be based on information that is not disclosed to the client;**

(d) **deny a client access to a record that is being used for an ongoing investigation of a suspected violation by the client of a law relating to the administration of the welfare program; and**

(e) **provide for segregation of information in records maintained about multiple subjects so that a client may see only that information in a record that pertains directly to him.**

CORRECTION OF RECORDS

As in the other areas it has studied, the Commission believes that an individual's right to review records about himself is of little value unless a procedure for correcting any erroneous information he may find is available to him as a matter of right. If the client could inspect but not request correction of information in records, inaccurate, outdated, irrelevant, or incomplete information could be used by the welfare agency or others to unfairly deny him a right, benefit, or opportunity. Accordingly, the Commission recommends:

Recommendation (8):

That the Congress require States to provide by statute that public
assistance and social services agencies will permit a client to request
correction or amendment of a record pertaining to him, and that the
agency must:

(a)   promptly correct, amend (including supplement), or delete any
      portion thereof which the individual can show is not accurate,
      timely, relevant, complete, or within the scope of information
      which he was originally told would be collected about him,
      except that in the case of a medical record, the agency shall
      disclose to the client the identity of the medical-care provider
      who was the source of the record, and, if the latter agrees to the
      requested correction, the agency must make the correction;

(b)   assure that any corrections, amendments, or deletions are
      reflected wherever information about the client is maintained
      that is similar to that which has been corrected, amended, or
      deleted; or

(c)   inform the client of its refusal to correct, amend, or delete part
      of the record in accordance with his request and the reason(s)
      for the refusal, permit the client to have the refusal reviewed at
      a hearing, and permit a client who disagrees with the refusal to
      correct, amend, or delete the record to have placed with the
      record a concise statement setting forth his disagreement; and
      further

(d)   provide reasonable procedures to assure that corrections,
      amendments, and deletions made pursuant to (a), or statements
      of disagreement filed pursuant to (c), are made available to
      prior and subsequent recipients of the record.

It should be noted that adoption of this recommendation would
broaden the conditions under which a client may request a hearing.
Currently, a client cannot obtain a hearing to challenge information unless
that information has been used as the basis of an adverse decision against
him. The Commission wishes to emphasize, however, that this proposal to
expand the use of the hearing process should not be interpreted as a license
for clients to contest earlier hearing decisions about the merits of cases,
although the correction of information may, of course, be relevant to a
future decision.

The injustices that may be perpetrated because clients lack a means of
forcing a welfare agency to correct information in their files which they
believe to be inaccurate, or to place in the file a statement of dispute, are
illustrated by the experience of Catherine Tarver. Tarver, an AFDC
recipient, learned that a caseworker's report in the file on her maintained by
the Department of Health and Social Services in the State of Washington
contained detailed allegations accusing her of child neglect. Shortly after the
report was written, Tarver had been exonerated of these charges by a
juvenile court. With this exoneration to back her, she asked the county

Department of Public Assistance for a hearing to request it to correct its file, but the Department refused. The Washington State Supreme Court supported the Department, holding that the hearing provision was not intended as a forum in which to litigate general grievances against the Department's administration of the welfare laws. *[State ex rel. Tarver v. Smith*, 78 Wash. 2d 152, 470 P.2d 192 (1970); *cert. denied*, 402 U.S. 1000 (1971)]

Although adoption of *Recommendation (8)* would not mitigate such past injustices, it would go far toward preventing future ones.

ACCURACY, TIMELINESS, COMPLETENESS, AND RELEVANCE

The Commission recommends:

Recommendation (9):

That the Congress require States to provide by statute that public assistance and social services agencies must have reasonable procedures to assure that all records they use in making any determination about a client are maintained with such accuracy, timeliness, completeness, and relevance as is reasonably necessary to assure that the records themselves are not the cause of an unfair determination.

Those who suffer when benefits are unfairly denied are not the agencies, but people who are already experiencing hardship. Thus, it is clear to the Commission that both the agency and its clients should share the responsibility for assuring the accuracy, relevance, timeliness, and completeness of the agency's files. Clients have an obvious interest in seeing that the responsibility is fulfilled, but the agencies' obligation is nowhere spelled out in Federal law. When benefits are unfairly denied because of carelessly kept records, the affected person has only one formal, assured recourse: to ask for a hearing where he can at least challenge the accuracy of the information used as a basis for the adverse decision.

The Commission's recommendations regarding the general right of access and procedures for requesting correction would provide a second and more comprehensive safeguard. *Recommendation (9)*, above, provides a third. For example, it would encourage agencies to investigate third-party source information before entering it in a record or relying on it to make a judgment, and might prompt agencies to take the obvious step of asking the client to explain or document information that may be inaccurate before incorporating it in the file.

It should be noted that many agencies are consciously attempting to modify the traditional practice of routinely including in a case file not only the worker's professional assessment of the client's circumstances, behavior, and needs, but also notes on almost everything that transpires between worker and client. While that practice may sometimes work to the client's best interest, it often means that irrelevant and extremely subjective judgments become part of the file. Such judgments are useful only to the extent that social workers have been trained to recognize information pertinent to the case, and not all personnel employed by public assistance and social services agencies have such training. This is increasingly true of eligibility workers, many of whom have had no professional training.

Comments received by the Commission indicate that many agencies currently consider fulfilling their responsibility for accuracy, timeliness, completeness, and relevance as fully consistent with sound public assistance and social services delivery practices. For example, the Iowa Department of Social Services noted that acceptance of such responsibility:

> . . . would appear to be the practice in any agency which follows personal and professional, accepted ethical standards, and which complies with an effective administrative procedures act, especially concerning contested cases.[20]

Expectation of Confidentiality

DISCLOSURE OF CLIENT RECORDS

Any comprehensive revision of Federal policy on disclosure must start with an assessment of the adequacy of present restrictions. In considering the matter of confidentiality, the Commission was guided by the principle that records about individuals should not be disclosed for purposes incompatible with those for which they were compiled without the consent of the individual, except as specifically authorized by law.

The Commission was not able to analyze the statutory constraints on the use or disclosure of information about clients in all of the federally assisted programs. A review of some of these laws, however, was enough to show that coverage is distinctly uneven. For example, there are no provisions on confidentiality in the laws regarding the National School Lunch Program, Maternal and Child Health Services, and Services for Crippled Children. By contrast, the regulations governing Juvenile Delinquency Prevention Programs require that records about youths served by these programs "shall be held to be confidential," and the ". . . use of such information and records shall be limited to purposes directly connected with the system . . . ." [45 C.F.R. 1350.61(c)]

There are also variations in the statutes governing the four programs studied in detail. While Federal statutes and regulations require State plans for carrying out AFDC, Medicaid, and Title XX Social Services programs to include certain provisions relating to the confidentiality of program records, the specific requirements are not the same for all three. Thus, a State plan for AFDC must prescribe restrictions on the use or disclosure of information concerning applicants or recipients to purposes directly connected with:

- the administration of the AFDC, Child Welfare, Work Incentive, Medicaid, Social Services, or Supplemental Security Income programs;

---

[20] Submission of Commissioner, Iowa Department of Social Services, Public Assistance and Social Services Hearings, January 11, 1977, p. 5.

- • any investigation, prosecution, or criminal or civil proceeding conducted in connection with the administration of any such plans or programs; and
- • the administration of any other Federal or federally assisted program which provides assistance in cash or in kind, or services, directly to individuals on the basis of need. *[42 U.S.C. 602(a)(9)]*

The AFDC statute also prohibits disclosure of individually identifiable information about clients to any committee or legislative body. Under another provision of Federal law, a State may, notwithstanding the confidentiality provisions cited above, enact a law making the names of AFDC recipients and the amount of assistance they receive available to the public. Finally, DHEW regulations governing the AFDC, Medicaid, and Title XX Social Services programs provide that:

In the event of the issuance of a subpoena for the case record or for any agency representative to testify concerning an applicant or recipient, the court's attention is called, through proper channels, to the statutory provisions and the policies or rules and regulations against disclosure of information. *[45 C.F.R. 205.50(a)(2)(iv)]*

Agency officials are apparently successful in contesting such disclosure in most, but not all, cases.

The Federal statute governing the Medicaid program provides that a State Medicaid plan must:

provide safeguards which restrict the use or disclosure of information concerning applicants and recipients to purposes directly connected with the administration of the plan. *[42 U.S.C. 1396a(a)(7)]*

The Social Security Act also contains restrictions on the use of information concerning Title XX Social Services clients, namely:

the use or disclosure of information obtained in connection with administration of the State's program for the provision of the services [funded under Title XX] concerning applicants for and recipients of those services will be restricted to purposes directly connected with the administration of that program, the plan of the State approved under part A of Title IV [AFDC], the plan of the State developed under part B of that title [Child Welfare Services], the Supplemental Security Income program established by Title XVI, or the plan of the State approved under Title XIX [Medicaid]. *[42 U.S.C. 1397b(d)(1)(B)]*

Finally, the Federal statute establishing the Food Stamp program provides that a State Food Stamp plan must include:

safeguards which restrict the use or disclosure of information obtained from applicant households to persons directly connected with the administration and enforcement of the provision of [the

Food Stamp Act] or the regulations issued pursuant to [the Act]. *[7 U.S.C. 2019(e)(3)]*

The Commission reached several conclusions about the adequacy of current disclosure policy.

1) *Federal disclosure policy for federally assisted programs is neither consistent nor comprehensive.* While the four programs the Commission studied in detail do contain restrictions on disclosure of program records, some of the other federally assisted programs do not, and the policies of still others are inconsistent with those of the major programs.

For example, Federal policies on disclosure of alcohol and drug abuse treatment records *[42 U.S.C. 4582 and 21 U.S.C. 1175]* differ from those applicable to records maintained under the Title XX program, which also funds alcohol and drug abuse treatment services. Thus, there has been confusion about what rules should be applied to a treatment provider who receives funding from Title XX as well as other Federal government sources.[21]

For another example, the statutes and regulations governing the provision of legal assistance under grants made by the Legal Services Corporation contain one provision relating to confidentiality, namely that:

> . . . neither the [Legal Services] Corporation or the Comptroller General shall have access to any reports or records subject to the attorney-client privilege. *[42 U.S.C. 2996h(d)]*

By contrast, the statute governing confidentiality of Title XX legal services records also limits permissible disclosures for non-Title XX purposes but permits the imposition of reporting requirements that would, in the opinion of some groups, violate the attorney-client privilege.

For a third example, family planning assistance is provided under Title X of the Public Health Service Act, and also under Title XX of the Social Security Act. Regulations implementing Title X provide that:

> Each grant award is subject to the condition that all information obtained by the personnel of the project from participants in the project related to their examination, care, and treatment, shall be held confidential, and shall not be divulged without the individual's consent except as may be required by law or as may be necessary to provide service to the individual. *[42 C.F.R. 59.10]*

This provision for confidentiality differs from the one found in the Title XX statute

Finally, regulations governing services to individuals under the Older Americans Act provide that:

> . . . the State agency will take steps to insure that no information

---

[21] Section 2003(f) of the Social Security Act currently provides that "The provisions of Section 333 of the Comprehensive Alcohol and Alcoholism Prevention, Treatment, and Rehabilitation Act of 1970 [pertaining to the confidentiality of records] shall be applicable to services provided by any State pursuant to this title with respect to individuals suffering from drug addiction or alcoholism."

about, or obtained from, an individual, and in possession of an agency providing services to such individual . . . shall be disclosed in a form identifiable with the individual without the individual's informed consent. *[45 C.F.R. 903.139]*

This regulation is significantly stricter than those applicable to records about senior citizens services provided under Title XX.

2) *By applying different disclosure criteria to federally assisted and non-federally assisted programs, Federal disclosure policies erect a statutory barrier that hampers the work of both.* For example, AFDC program records may circulate to other federally assisted programs, however remote in purpose from the AFDC program, but disclosure to a program funded solely by a State is prohibited without client consent, even when the aims of the State program are closely allied with those of AFDC. Similarly, Title XX records may be circulated freely among Title XX providers of quite unrelated services but not to a State-funded social services program without the client's consent.

3) *In all four main programs, the same disclosure restrictions apply to both factual data regarding an individual's eligibility and level of need (e.g., income, assets, resources, number of children), and the record of a client's physical or mental condition.* Thus, sensitive information regarding an AFDC recipient's physical incapacity may be disclosed just as freely as the simple fact that the recipient has three children. Failure to establish different criteria for different categories of information encourages either undue restriction of factual data needed for effective program administration, or inappropriate disclosures of sensitive material which may derive from subjective judgments.

The Commission found a need for a comprehensive policy on client record disclosures that would apply uniformly to all public assistance and social services records maintained by State and local government agencies, if the rights of clients are to be consistently protected and if welfare programs are to be effectively administered. It then addressed the question of how to formulate such a policy, and what it should cover.

The Commission considered recommending that Congress enact a detailed statute regulating disclosures of records maintained by all assistance and services agencies receiving Federal funds. It rejected this solution for several reasons:

- the differences in State programs and their administration made it unlikely that the Commission could formulate a workable single policy;
- a detailed Federal policy would tend to frustrate innovative State records-management practices, such as the development of multi-purpose application forms and integrated management information systems;
- any detailed Federal policy would undoubtedly conflict with State fair information practices statutes that apply to welfare records as well as to other State agency records; and
- a single policy could not reflect the different trade-offs

different States would make between confidentiality and other values.

Instead of a detailed Federal policy, the Commission has chosen to recommend broad Federal guidelines which leave latitude for the States to arrive at their own specific policies. Accordingly, the Commission recommends:

Recommendation (10):

That the Congress provide by statute that no disclosures of records about a public assistance or social services client may be made without the authorization of the client, unless disclosure has been specifically authorized by State statute, which must contain:

(a) **provisions relating to the permissible uses and disclosures of individually identifiable information about clients for purposes related to the administration and enforcement of the specific program for which the information was acquired, as well as for purposes related to the administration and enforcement of other public assistance and social services programs for which the individual has applied, is required to apply, or may be eligible;**

(b) **a prohibition on the disclosure of individually identifiable information about clients to members of the public and to legislative committees;**

(c) **a prohibition on the use or disclosure of individually identifiable information about clients for purposes unrelated to the provision of public assistance and social services without the consent of the client, provided, however, that:**

(i) **disclosure necessary to assure the health or safety of the client or another individual in compelling circumstances may be permitted;**

(ii) **disclosure made pursuant to a court order may be permitted if the agency has contested the order, provided, however, that adequate notice and ability to participate in any action regarding the order has been provided the client if the client is the subject of the investigation or prosecution in furtherance of which the court order is issued; and**

(iii) **disclosure for a research or statistical purpose may be permitted, provided, however, that:**

(A) **the agency maintaining the information ascertains that use or disclosure in individually identifiable form is necessary to accomplish the purpose for which disclosure is made;**

(B) **further use or disclosure of the information or record in individually identifiable form is prohibited without the express authorization of the agency or the client;**

> (C) reasonable procedures to protect the record or information from unauthorized disclosure are established and maintained by the recipient, including a program for removal or destruction of identifiers; and
>
> (D) the agency determines that the research or statistical purpose for which any disclosure is to be made is such as to warrant risk to the individual from additional exposure of the record or information;
>
> (d) provisions stating which redisclosures of individually identifiable information may be made by agencies or persons authorized to obtain such information; and
>
> (e) a requirement that all permissible disclosures be limited to information that is necessary and relevant to the purpose for which disclosure is made, including those disclosures made for collateral verification purposes.

Finally, the Congress should provide that when enacted, the required State statute shall constitute the sole authority for disclosures of client records maintained by public assistance and social services agencies receiving Federal funding except that 42 U.S.C. 4582 and 21 U.S.C. 1175, regarding the confidentiality of alcohol and drug abuse treatment records, will continue to be in force.

The Commission feels that this recommendation outlines a sensible approach to the complex problem of handling the disclosure of client records. These recommendations seek to resolve problems created by inconsistency in Federal confidentiality policies by requiring each State to develop a comprehensive statute tailored to the State's particular needs, regulating disclosure of records about clients of *all* federally assisted programs operating in the State, as well as of other programs operated within the State by agencies that receive Federal funds. The Commission believes that the State, rather than the Federal government, is best able to define specifically the limits of permissible disclosure within broad limits set by Federal law for all the States. The Federal government cannot be expected to appreciate fully the particular needs which guide each of the 50 States in administering its programs, nor can the Federal government respond as effectively as the States to future changes in these particular needs.

On the other hand, the recommended measures do not give the States a license to ignore a client's right to be treated fairly. Three features of the recommendations seek to assure that the policies formulated by the States will be fair to the individual.

First, the recommended process for States to follow in formulating their policies provides for public participation. Specifying that the policies be enacted into statute means that their adoption must follow the legislative process, and that they will not be changed without public involvement. The Commission's general recommendations further require public hearings to precede enactment of such a State statute.

478   PERSONAL PRIVACY IN AN INFORMATION SOCIETY

Second, the recommended measures require State statutes to be faithful to a key principle of fair information practice—that information acquired for one purpose should not be used for an unrelated purpose without the individual's consent, either actual personal consent or consent as collectively arrived at through the legislative process. Thus, the recommended measure requires that a State's statute forbid disclosures of public assistance and social services records without the consent of the individual to whom they pertain, unless such disclosure is specifically authorized by statute. The authorizations in the statute should be sufficiently specific so that clients will either know or can find out the particular purposes for which information about themselves will be used.

Finally, the recommended Federal statute would require States, in enacting their own statutes, to adhere to minimum standards regarding permissible disclosures. As long as a State's statute complies with these recommended standards, State legislators can incorporate into their statute those disclosure policies that reflect their own State's administrative needs and citizen concerns. The Congress could, of course, require that States enact provisions of law that permit Federal auditors to have access to welfare records. In that regard, the Commission urges the Congress to follow the recommendations set forth in Chapter 9 for government access to records.

The recommended measure allows States to enact statutes which permit disclosures without client consent *within* the welfare system. It would, however, prohibit disclosure of individually identifiable records to the general public or to legislative committees, or for purposes unrelated to the provision of public assistance and social services, except under certain narrow conditions. Disclosures of client records without authorization would be permitted under compelling circumstances affecting the health or safety of the client or another individual, and for use in research or statistical activities. In cases in which a court order is issued to an agency for a client record, the recommendation would permit disclosure in response to the court order only if the agency contested the order, and if the client who is the subject of the record were given notice and an opportunity to participate in any proceedings regarding the order. Notice to, and participation by, the client would be required only if he is the subject of the investigation or prosecution for which the court order is issued. Moreover, the Commission understands that the States, in enacting the recommended statute, may well wish to limit the number of record subjects who would receive notice when the record being sought contains information about all the members of an assistance unit or household.

These prohibitions on disclosure are generally consistent with existing Federal and State disclosure policies, except insofar as States are currently free to pass statutes making certain information about AFDC recipients available to the general public. The Commission found no compelling arguments supporting disclosure to the public that outweighed the possible harm or embarrassment that would result if a recipient's name and amount of assistance were publicly available.

Another recommendation—that States be required to apply the same safeguards as in federally assisted programs to client records of programs that are not federally assisted but that are maintained by agencies receiving Federal funding—would assure consistency in all a State agency's public assistance and social services record-keeping activities. It would also facilitate necessary flows of information between federally assisted programs and those in which there is no Federal involvement.

The Commission believes that in enacting the recommended statute, States may wish to apply different—probably more restrictive—disclosure standards to subjective or judgmental information regarding a client's mental or physical health or status than to factual information regarding eligibility. The Commission would approve of an approach that takes into account the relative sensitivity of different types of information.

Another important principal reflected in *Recommendation (10)* is that no more information should ever be disclosed than the minimum necessary to accomplish the purpose for which disclosure is made. As noted earlier, this is crucial when collateral verification of information supplied to the agency by the client is necessary.

Examples of the benefits to be expected from adoption of the recommended measures are not hard to find. California, for example, has a State-funded program for providing cash assistance to intact families with an unemployed father or mother. The eligibility criteria for this State program are more liberal than those of the Federal AFDC-Unemployed program, which California also administers. A single family—whose situation with respect to employment may vary from month to month and thus who may qualify under different programs in successive months—may one month receive a check partially paid for out of Federal funds, and the next month one financed solely by the State treasury. The client may not realize who is footing the bill from month to month. There is only one case record about such a family—that is, there is not one record of the family's eligibility for Federal help and another of its eligibility for the State program. AFDC case records cannot, however, by Federal law, be used in the administration of a solely State-financed assistance program. The recommended measure would eliminate such problems of technical compliance with detailed Federal requirements and few people would argue that an outcome reinforcing present practice in this case would represent an unwarranted invasion of the client's privacy.

Another example concerns the development of multi-purpose application forms. Where there is a common set of data elements used to determine a client's eligibility for several programs, it would clearly be economical to collect such information on only one form. Such simplification would be welcomed by clients as well as by agencies. Some States, in fact, have been trying to develop such a form. Their efforts may be impeded by the fact that, for example, information about Food Stamp eligibility may not be disclosed to persons unrelated to the administration of the Food Stamp program, so that a multi-purpose application might violate the Federal Food Stamp disclosure law.

If the Commission's sampling of Federal confidentiality laws is a fair indication, the minimum protections guaranteed by the recommended measure would not significantly reduce any protections individuals currently enjoy. In one special area, however, it might be argued that the form of the recommended measure might create the *risk* of undermining privacy rights. The argument concerns alcohol and drug abuse treatment records. Because these kinds of records are extremely sensitive, and because individuals with problems relating to use of alcohol and drugs must be encouraged to seek needed treatment, the Federal government has formulated very restrictive policies regarding permissible disclosures of alcohol and drug abuse treatment records. The Commission recommends that these policies not be modified, and further, that they continue to apply to alcohol and drug abuse treatment records maintained by every program receiving *any* Federal funds (including Title XX funds), whatever the provisions of State statutes.[22]

Notification of Rights

The Commission believes that in order for a client to exercise the rights its recommendations would establish, he must be cognizant of those rights, and of agencies' information management practices. Therefore, the Commission recommends:

Recommendation (11):

That the Congress require States to provide by statute that public assistance and social services agencies must inform each client in plain language of:

(a) **the kinds of records that the agency maintains, and the purposes for which the information in those records may be used;**

(b) **the client's right to see, copy, and request correction of a record about himself;**

(c) **whether information requested of the client by the agency *must* be provided as a condition of eligibility for public assistance and social services, or whether providing it is voluntary;**

(d) **of the agency's procedures regarding collateral verification [as required by *Recommendation (4)*], including its use of inter-agency and inter-jurisdictional data exchanges; and**

(e) **the provisions of the State statute governing disclosure.**

Regulations currently applicable to the AFDC and Medicaid programs already provide that agencies must inform applicants about their rights and obligations under the program. They require that applicants be notified, either in written form, or orally when appropriate, of the coverage, eligibility, and scope of the program, of related services available to them, and the rights and responsibilities of applicants for and recipients of assistance. To fulfill this requirement agencies must develop bulletins and pamphlets which explain the rules of eligibility and appeals in simple,

---

[22] The statutory requirements for confidentiality of drug and alcohol patient records are found at 42 U.S.C. 4582 and 21 U.S.C 1175.

understandable language. Such bulletins or pamphlets must be publicized and available in quantity. *[45 C.F.R. 206.10(a)(2)(i)]*

Thus, there is already some precedent for requiring agencies to notify clients of their rights. Comments received by the Commission indicate that giving the recommended notice of an agency's record-keeping policies and practices would not create excessive administrative burdens for agencies. The Commission believes that the recommended notice should be made available to clients in their primary language wherever possible.

Subsection (c) of the above recommendation reflects the Commission's concern that to limit intrusiveness, clients should know whether they are required to disclose information about themselves as a condition of receiving assistance, or whether disclosure is voluntary.

Remedies for Violations of a State Statute

The Commission believes that a State statute regarding fair information practice in welfare record keeping would not be complete if it did not provide remedies and penalties for violation of its requirements. Accordingly, the Commission recommends:

Recommendation (12):

That the Congress require the States to provide by statute that appropriate remedies and penalties will be available in cases in which a public assistance or social services agency violates a provision of the State fair information practice statute.

Although the Commission feels that the States are best able to determine what type of remedies and penalities are appropriate, it believes that its suggested amendments to the civil remedies and criminal penalties sections of the Privacy Act of 1974 represent a model for the kinds of statutory provisions the States would be required to enact.[23]

CHILD SUPPORT ENFORCEMENT

There is one area of public assistance and social services record keeping that seemed to merit the Commission's special attention: record keeping carried out in connection with Child Support Enforcement activities. The Commission promised to address this issue in its June, 1976 report on *Federal Tax Return Confidentiality*.

Although the recommendations thus far made in this chapter are intended to apply to Child Support Enforcement programs, they do not address all of the special record-keeping issues that arise in that particularly controversial area. Therefore, the Commission includes below a brief description of the program and several specific recommendations that apply only to it.

Part D of Title IV of the Social Security Act authorizes Federal grants

---

[23] See Chapter 13 for a discussion of the suggested revisions.

to the States for the purpose of locating absent parents who have defaulted on their child support obligations, for establishing the paternity of children for whom child support may be owed, and for enforcing child support obligations. To be eligible for Federal grants for these purposes, a State must establish a State Child Support Enforcement agency and a State Parent Locator Service within the agency. The agency's functions may be performed either by that agency or by law enforcement officials (e.g., district attorneys, State attorneys general) who have entered into cooperative agreements with the agency. The agency may also contract with private investigatory agencies for assistance in locating absent parents.

In addition to providing Federal financial assistance for State child support enforcement activities, Title IV-D established an Office of Child Support Enforcement within the Department of Health, Education, and Welfare to oversee States' administration of the program, as well as a Federal Parent Locator Service within that Office to aid in the location of absent parents. Although the primary purpose of the Child Support Enforcement program is to find the parents of children who are AFDC recipients and to see that they fulfill their parental obligations, the State Child Support Enforcement agencies and the Federal Parent Locator Service (PLS) may make their services available, for a fee, to individuals who are not AFDC recipients.

Title IV-D of the Social Security Act does not prescribe statutory standards for the safeguarding of information obtained by State Child Support Enforcement agencies. Federal regulations provide that States, pursuant to State statutes which impose legal sanctions, shall apply the same limitations on the use or disclosure of information concerning applicants and recipients of child support enforcement services as are prescribed for AFDC records. *[45C.F.R. 302.18]* Additionally, the regulations require that all requests for information from a State to the Federal Parent Locator Service shall include a statement, signed by the head of the State Child Support Enforcement agency or his designee, affirming both that information obtained from the Federal Parent Locator Service will be treated as confidential and safeguarded pursuant to the requirements of the AFDC confidentiality regulations, and that the State agency will take protective measures to safeguard information transmitted to and received from the Federal Parent Locator Service *[45 C.F.R. 302.70(e)(2) and (3)]*.

The Commission finds that these regulations do not adequately safeguard the information collected by State IV-D agencies about the individuals being sought. The regulations only place limits on the use and disclosure of information about absent parents obtained from the Federal PLS, and do not apply to information regarding absent parents obtained by State agencies from State and local sources.

Information on missing parents is collected by State and local AFDC offices, and by the State Child Support Enforcement agencies. Both ask a client for basic identifying information such as the name, address, and Social Security number of the absent parent. In addition, clients may be asked about the absent parent's work and social life. For example, in Michigan a "support specialist" responsible for locating an absent parent must, as the first step of the location procedure, ask for information including, but not limited to, the absent parent's employment, occupational skills, work shift, date and place of marriage, physical description, names of creditors, names and addresses of friends or relatives, arrest record, and memberships in fraternal organizations. In addition to the information obtained from the client, and from the AFDC office, the record will include any information that can be gathered from other sources contacted in the course of the location effort.[24]

The Commission believes that the standards regarding confidentiality currently contained in regulations should be embodied in statute, so that they can be changed only by the legislative process, and not at the discretion of agencies. Moreover, the Commission believes that information about absent parents, as well as AFDC clients, should be subject to these statutory safeguards, and that the use of information about absent parents obtained from the Federal Parent Locator Service should be confined to the purposes for which the State acquired it.

Consistent with these findings, the Commission recommends:

Recommendation (13):

That the use and disclosure of information obtained on applicants for and recipients of child support services as well as on alleged absent parents should be subject to the same statutory disclosure policy called for by *Recommendation (10)*. Furthermore, Congress should require by statute that information obtained by State agencies from the Federal Parent Locator Service regarding absent parents may not be disclosed for purposes unrelated to the establishment of paternity, the location of the parent, or enforcement of child support obligations, except to the extent that disclosures of such information result from court proceedings.

The Commission also believes that Section 454(8) of the Social Security Act, which mandates that States utilize all sources of information and available records should be qualified to except explicitly the classes of information which may not be disclosed under State or local laws. If, in the judgment of a State legislature, the nature of certain data warrants holding that data confidential, the State Parent Locator Service should be required to respect the legislature's judgment, and should not be held not to be in compliance with Federal law for doing so. For example, the Commission learned during its Tax Return Confidentiality hearings that an Ohio tax statute *[Ohio Revenue Code §5747.18]* holds data maintained by the State Department of Taxation confidential. The Ohio Department testified before the Commission that it refuses requests for information from the State PLS. In written testimony a representative of the Ohio Department of Taxation noted:

. . . some provisions of the Federal welfare laws, specifically the parent-locator service provisions, encourage, if not require, efforts

---

[24] State of Michigan, Office of Standards and Investigation, Item CR-240, September 8, 1976.

to use State tax department files. This latter is a dangerous precedent, because once that first breach of confidentiality is legitimized, the legislative branch of both State and Federal governments will find it easier to create other special cases. Such legislation should not be encouraged.[25]

The Commission concurs with this opinion and therefore recommends:

Recommendation (14):

That the Congress amend Title IV-D of the Social Security Act to provide that the provision requiring States to "utilize all sources of information and available records" [Section 454(8)] not be construed to override State and local laws prohibiting the disclosure of certain types of information unless these laws have made provision for disclosure to the State Parent Locator Service.

The Commission also objects to Section 453(e)(2) of the Social Security Act which provides that, notwithstanding any other provision of law, Federal agencies shall supply information to the Federal Parent Locator Service (PLS). The only exceptions to this provision are for disclosures to the Federal PLS that would contravene national security or the confidentiality of census data.[26] The Commission believes that when other provisions of law dictate that the use or disclosure of certain information be restricted, and when such provisions do not explicitly allow, by exception, for release of information to the Federal PLS, the Federal PLS should not be permitted access to that information. Furthermore, the Commission strongly believes that Federal agency information available to the PLS should be limited to the minimum necessary to aid in the location of absent parents, and should not involve additional information regarding, for example, the individual's income or assets.[27] Accordingly, the Commission recommends:

Recommendation (15):

That the Congress amend Section 453(e)(2) of Title IV-D of the Social Security Act to provide that Federal agencies maintaining information which, by other provisions of law, has been deemed to be confidential, shall not be required to provide that information to the Federal Parent Locator Service (PLS), unless disclosure to the Federal PLS is specifically authorized by a Federal statute that specifies the agency that may disclose information to the PLS; and

---

[25] Written statement, *Federal Tax Return Confidentiality*, Hearings before the Privacy Protection Study Commission, March 12, 1976, p.3.

[26] In testimony before the Commission, Office of Child Support Enforcement officials testified that, although the Federal Parent Locator Service may utilize all Federal sources of information, it currently relies primarily upon the Social Security Administration, the Internal Revenue Service, and the Department of Defense.

[27] See Chapter 14 for a further discussion of this topic.

further, that the Congress limit disclosures of information by Federal agencies to the PLS to the minimum necessary to locate the absent parent (e.g., place of employment and home address).

These two recommendations reflect the Commission's conviction that no law regarding the gathering of information should override all other laws regarding confidentiality. Instead, policy makers formulating laws on the disclosure of the kinds of records that the PLS would find useful should be required to decide explicitly whether the PLS should have access to each type of record. Such a decision would require legislators to weigh all of the considerations involved, including the interests at stake in child support enforcement, and would assure that child support enforcement is not automatically viewed as paramount to all other considerations.

TECHNICAL ASSISTANCE FOR THE STATES

Lacking any comprehensive Federal and State fair information practice policy, Congress and the Federal agencies have been compelled to develop policies in special areas where the absence of record-keeping policies is especially risky, most notably in the areas of alcohol and drug abuse treatment and child abuse and neglect prevention and treatment. In these two areas, Congress has enacted statutes and Federal agencies have developed regulations dealing with permissible uses and disclosure of records about individuals. The Commission's recommended measure on disclosure, *Recommendation (10)*, would supersede other Federal policies on confidentiality, except in the case of alcohol and drug abuse treatment records, and would require States to enact their own comprehensive confidentiality statutes. Although some may contend that this measure would ultimately lessen privacy protection for clients, the Commission expects that States are as sensitive as the Federal government has been to the need to control carefully the dissemination of such information.

Nevertheless, not all of the States have had extensive experience in preparing this kind of legislation. Many Federal agency employees are intimately familiar with the policy issues that arise not only in the two areas cited above, but also in other areas where sensitive records are created with the help of Federal financing. The States, particularly those for which fair information practice is a novel concept, may find this experience most useful.

Therefore, the Commission recommends:

Recommendation (16):

That the Congress require the heads of all Federal agencies funding public assistance and social services programs to provide assistance to the States in developing their fair information practice statutes.

The Commission feels that such assistance could be provided by, for example, a committee made up of representatives of all appropriate Federal agencies which would meet with State legislators and other concerned citizens to advise them in developing the State statutes required by the recommended measures. Assistance might also take the form of grants to consortiums made up of representatives of clients' groups, State and local government agencies, and State legislatures to serve as information clearinghouses, and to draft model statutes for the States.

*   *   *   *   *   *   *

Adoption of the Commission's recommendations with respect to public assistance and social services record keeping would, in the Commission's judgment, simplify the administration of the many programs and provide a reasonable balance between the demands of effective program administration and legitimate rights and interests of clients.

Chapter 12

The State Role in Privacy Protection

Naming the new nation the "United States of America" reflected the founders' commitment to the Federal Principle, the division of power between the States and the national government. From the beginning, each State was, and still is, a sovereign authority, with power to perform within its borders almost all of the activities, legislative, executive, and judicial, that the Federal government performs, except to represent itself in foreign affairs, burden interstate commerce, and provide for the national defense. It can, and does, tax its citizens, provide services, regulate commerce, license professions, and exercise police powers. Indeed, the national government was intended to be the government of limited, delegated powers, with the States exercising domestically, any of the powers one might expect a government to use. That was the theory, though in practice the pendulum has gradually swung so that the Federal government is now the forum where the great domestic policy issues, social as well as economic, are resolved. The States' role is still important, and shows signs of growing, but currently is the more limited one. The State still functions as a basic provider of government services, but in many cases is simply carrying out programs that originate at the national level and are funded, at least in part, by the Federal government. Even in the sectors it controls, for example, police protection, Federal statutory programs carried out by agencies like the Law Enforcement Assistance Administration (LEAA) are beginning to make inroads on its authority. The States are still the governmental vehicle for determining land use and allocation of most of the natural resources within their borders; though, once again, the Federal government has begun to take a prominent role in order to assure environmental quality and effect national resource policies. Population growth, urbanization, mobility, and economic integration have turned many of the social and economic problems that could once be managed at the local level into problems that require national attention. Thus, the Federal government, of necessity, now dominates many areas that were traditionally State preserves.

The role of State governments in protecting personal privacy is, however, still enormously important. The records a State government keeps about the individuals under its jurisdiction are often as extensive as those kept on the same individuals by the Federal government, and in some respects even more so. As a prelude to the following chapters which consider various aspects of the relationship between the individual and agencies of the Federal government, this chapter briefly summarizes how the Federal-

State relationship enters into the Commission's recommended program for protecting personal privacy. Four aspects of that relationship are important to the national policy the Commission proposes:

- How the Federal government constrains State activities;
- How States have tried to protect personal privacy;
- How State record-keeping practices affect personal privacy; and
- How the Commission's recommendations fit into the existing system for implementing national policy at the State level.

FEDERAL CONSTRAINTS ON STATE ACTIVITIES

The Federal government may restrict State action or take action itself affecting apparently intrastate activity on the basis of four Constitutional provisions: the commerce clause, the spending clause, the Fourteenth Amendment, and the welfare clause. The commerce clause enables the Federal government to regulate interstate commerce by precluding certain State regulation. In legislating under the commerce clause, however, the Congress sometimes explicitly leaves existing State regulation intact, or provides that States may also regulate, so long as State regulation does not conflict with existing Federal law. For example, Federal and State Fair Credit Reporting Acts and the existing banking system provide for dual regulatory structures in those areas. In fact, only in limited areas such as trademark and copyright law has the Federal government prohibited the States from acting. Congress has also used the commerce clause, alone or in conjunction with the Fourteenth Amendment, as its authority for enacting some laws that are basically social legislation, for example, the Equal Credit Opportunity Act, the Civil Rights Act of 1964, and the Equal Employment Opportunity Act.

The Fourteenth Amendment, mainly through its equal protection clause, enables the Congress to limit State regulation in areas of social policy, but it is the combination of the welfare and spending clauses that gives the Congress most of its power to affect social issues and limit State action that affects them. Federal programs predicated on the spending power can either restrict or require State action, or both. The Medicaid program, for example, requires the States to maintain certain records about individuals and restricts the disclosure of that information. The constraints of these programs are not mandatory on the States, as commerce clause and Fourteenth Amendment legislation is, but since they require State compliance as a condition of receiving Federal program funds, the effect may be about the same. They are, moreover, the only way that the Federal government can affect the internal management and functioning of a State government where there is no Fourteenth Amendment interest. While the Fourteenth Amendment enables the Federal government to forbid the States to discriminate improperly against individuals, or to deprive them of their Constitutional rights, neither the Fourteenth Amendment nor the commerce clause would seem to enable the Federal government to regulate State activities that are essential to the performance of *internal* governmental functions, such as record keeping. As recently as 1976, the U.S. Supreme Court ruled in *National League of Cities v. Usery*[1] that the Federal government may not legislate in ways that "operate to directly displace the States' freedom to structure integral operations in areas of traditional governmental functions." The national government, in other words, may not use *coercion* to influence, for example, State government record-keeping practices, but the *National League of Cities* decision does not preclude the use of *inducements*, such as making certain record-keeping practices a condition of Federal funding.

STATE PROTECTIONS FOR PERSONAL PRIVACY

Within the strictures the Federal government imposes on public and private-sector record-keeping practices, some States have strengthened the federally prescribed protections. California, for example, includes in its State Constitution a specific protection for the "inalienable right" to personal privacy. The California guarantee goes beyond traditional limitations on government surveillance and government access to information to include protections for the records about individuals maintained by private and public entities. The California legislature has followed court interpretations of the State Constitutional provisions and, in specific areas of record keeping, has enacted statutes that prescribe procedures whereby an individual can exercise his right to participate in a record keeper's decision to disclose information about him.

In response to the invitation in the Federal Fair Credit Reporting Act, a number of States have passed their own credit-reporting laws, and some go considerably beyond the strictures of the Federal law, but there is little consistency among State laws to protect records maintained about individuals, in either the scope or the degree of protection provided, and few States give adequate minimal protection.[2]

The States have been active in privacy protection, and in many cases innovative, but neither they nor the Federal government have taken full advantage of each other's experimentation. Altogether, the Commission's inquiry into State record-keeping practices forces it to conclude that an individual today cannot rely on State government to protect his interests in the records and record-keeping practices of either State agencies or private entities.

This is not true, of course, of all States. Some of them approach the protection of the individual's interests in State records and record keeping in as comprehensive a way as has the Federal government. Seven States have enacted omnibus statutes similar to the Privacy Act of 1974 to regulate the collection, maintenance, use, and disclosure of State agency records. The Constitutions of four States provide a right to privacy that includes a record keeper's corresponding duty to keep certain records confidential. Several

---

[1] *National League of Cities v. Usery* 426 U.S. 833 (1976).
[2] An overview of State efforts and a comprehensive list of State legislation affecting the rights of individuals in records and record-keeping practices will be published separately as an appendix volume to this report.

States regulate the employment and personnel record-keeping practices of their State agencies. Almost every State has some kind of freedom of information or public records law opening State government records to public inspection. The States diverge widely, however, in their determinations of which records belong in the category of public records. Some exempt from disclosure specific categories of records, such as tax and adoption records; others exempt records that are required or permitted by any other statute to be withheld; and still others adopt the Federal standard and prohibit disclosure of information in government records if disclosure would constitute an unwarranted invasion of personal privacy. A few exempt any records if their disclosure would result in a denial of Federal funds, a provision that brings into focus the far-reaching effect of linking privacy protection requirements to the receipt of Federal funding.

Whatever a State may or may not elect to do about its own record-keeping practices, requirements to collect or protect information, or both, flow with Federal money and often supersede whatever State arrangements exist. On another level, the constraints thus placed on State activity frequently require private organizations to alter their record-keeping practices. The information collection criteria established by portions of the Medicaid program, for example, require State agencies to collect and retain information which they gather from private organizations, which, in turn, may very well have to keep certain records, or keep records in certain ways that they would not otherwise do.

State Record-Keeping Practices

The Commission looked at the State's role in protecting personal privacy from two perspectives: the State government as record keeper, and the State as regulator of the record-keeping practices of private organizations. In selecting State public-sector record-keeping relationships to examine, the Commission concentrated on areas in which the Federal government exercises substantial responsibility, and thus looked primarily at the State role as an implementor of national policy. As noted above, the Commission is also aware of the Constitutional limits on the power of the Federal government to regulate the activities of State government that are essential to the performance of internal governmental functions, such as record keeping. For these reasons, most of the recommended measures that directly effect State record-keeping practices can be implemented as a condition of Federal funding under various programs.

The Commission emphatically does not recommend wholesale application by the Federal government of the Privacy Act of 1974 to State and local government record keeping. The Commission believes that the States' creative work in devising privacy protections for the individual in his relationships with State government should continue. Indeed, the Commission believes that the fair information practice statutes or executive orders of the several States that have them constitute one good approach to resolving the privacy protection problems raised by a State's own record-keeping practices. The recommendations advanced in Chapter 9 of this report regarding government access to records about individuals maintained by private organizations, the recommendations in Chapters 10 and 11, on education and on public assistance and social services record keeping, and the analysis of record-keeping practices and requirements associated with various aspects of the citizen-government relationship in Chapters 13 through 15, should help to guide the States in determining the type, degree, and mode of protections they will provide the individual in their own record-keeping operations.

Furthermore, while the Federal government has placed certain privacy protection requirements on States as a condition of receiving Federal funding, the cut-off of funds is an extreme and rarely effective enforcement technique. Hence, implementing such minimum protections by State law can have two advantages. A State can extend its requirements to the State agencies and organizations that do not receive Federal funds or benefits; and, it can use more flexible enforcement mechanisms and incentives for compliance than termination of Federal benefits. Depriving a State agency of Federal funds, for example, does not help an individual whose rights have been violated, and it harms other individuals. It is seldom an effective incentive for compliance since the sanction is so drastic that the threat of it lacks credibility, especially if the program is a large one where cutting off Federal funds would penalize a great many blameless individuals. By contrast, a State statute can create the alternative of allowing aggrieved individuals to seek redress and remedy against States in State courts, and can provide administrative or criminal sanctions for remiss State employees without disrupting the entire program.

THE STATE ROLE IN A NATIONAL POLICY

In formulating its recommendations, the Commission has recognized and encouraged the existing role of the States in providing individuals with the ability to protect their own interests. In areas such as insurance and medical care, for example, the Commission suggests that the States retain their current power to regulate in conjunction with the creation or extension of a Federal role. Indeed, the significant increase in State regulatory efforts to protect the interests of the individual in records kept about him, noted above, has already led a number of States to try out innovative protections, particularly in their regulation of private-sector organizations. Of the four States that extend Constitutional privacy protections to records about individuals, all apply these same restrictions to their local governments, and two apply them to private organizations as well. Eleven States have gone beyond the protection required by the Federal Fair Credit Reporting Act and enacted Fair Credit Reporting statutes to legislate somewhat stricter requirements. A number of States restrict the disclosure of bank records and define the confidentiality an individual has a right to expect, a right not currently recognized in Federal law for either credit or depository relationships. A number of States have enacted statutes regulating the disclosure of medical records about individuals, many using their licensing power to enforce this standard of confidentiality. A number of States recognize a patient's right of access to medical records about him.

The Commission takes no single position on the general role of State governments in regulating record-keeping practices. It suggests a role for State agencies in most of the areas it has examined, but always in the context of the current division of regulatory responsibility between the Federal government and the States. The recommended measures create no new authority to regulate the record keeping of organizations that are not now subject to State regulation, nor do they deprive a State of regulatory authority it now has.

Consider, for example, the recommendations regarding credit and depository institutions. The authority to regulate financial institutions is shared between Federal and State governments, and the Federal government has not preempted State regulation. Nonetheless, the recommended measures recognize the ability to preempt certain State regulation and therefore rely on Federal statutes and enforcement mechanisms. Yet, beyond setting basic protection requirements, the recommendations do not limit existing State authority. The States would remain free to provide additional legal protections for the interest of an individual in the records about him maintained by financial institutions.

Or consider the reverse. Regulation of insurance is traditionally the province of the States where the Federal government does not act. As Chapter 5 points out, however, the States have not provided adequate protection for the interests of the individual in the records insurers maintain about him. Thus, the Commission recommends Federal statutes to establish certain basic rights of access and correction, but these protections depend on the individual to assert the rights the Federal statutes would give him, and on State regulatory agencies as well as Federal agencies where the States do not act to provide oversight of insurance company compliance. The State role is defined in several recommendations. The Commission recommends that States amend their unfair trade practices acts, so that they can establish and enforce the recommended notification requirements. The Commission also recommends that State governmental mechanisms receive complaints regarding the propriety of information collected by insurance companies and bring them before policy-making bodies that have the authority to address them, or if the existing entity already has such authority, to consider such propriety questions itself.

In the record-keeping relationships that directly involve State agencies, the Commission recommends that protections for the individual be required as a condition for the receipt of Federal assistance. These areas are: public assistance and social services, education, research and statistical activities, and the confidentiality and use of Federal tax returns. In each of these areas, the extent to which the Commission's recommendations must be implemented thus will depend upon the degree to which the State's agencies participate in the relevant Federal programs. In two of these five areas, moreover—public assistance and social services, and the confidentiality of Federal income tax data—the Commission recommends that States be required to enact prescribed statutes establishing protections for personal privacy. In both cases, the State agencies themselves are the primary recipients of either money or information from the Federal government, and also, most States have supervisory responsibility for much of the activity conducted by their county and city governments. In public assistance and social services, the Commission further recommends that each State enact a statute that would also apply to public assistance and social service programs in the State that do not receive Federal assistance, although it does not recommend or suggest that the enactment of a statute of that scope be a Federal requirement.

The medical-care area is something of a special case because the State's major role there is to reimburse Medicaid expenses. It is not usually a primary medical-care provider, nor is it involved in the flow of Federal assistance to individuals through the Medicare program where most of the direct Federal requirements on medical-care providers are imposed through the process of qualifying for Medicare participation. Nonetheless, the Commission still recommends that States enact their own statutes incorporating the protections for medical records recommended by the Commission so that individuals will not have to rely on the Federal government to enforce the rights the recommended measures would establish and so that the recommended rights and obligations can be extended to public and private medical-care providers who do not need to qualify for Medicare or Medicaid participation.

In research and statistical activities, Federal assistance usually flows directly to the performing institution through discretionary grants and contracts. The only State agencies that receive an appreciable amount of Federal funding for research and statistical activities are State universities. Chapter 15 presents guidelines for the protection of personal privacy which the Commission recommends as a basis for the research and statistical activities conducted by State agencies or with State assistance.

The Commission's major departure from the general policy of relying on the State to implement Federal requirements is in education. There the Commission does not recommend a State role. Several factors influenced this decision. First, Federal regulation of record-keeping practices under the Family Educational Rights and Privacy Act (FERPA) does not require an implementing State law, mainly because most Federal funds flow directly to local school districts or to universities. The recommended measures strengthen FERPA protections but do not alter that process. Second, the Federal law is comprehensive, and since almost every public and private educational institution currently receives Federal assistance, State law would not extend the law's coverage appreciably. Third, although there are State educational codes for public elementary and secondary schools, those schools have a strong tradition of local autonomy.

Nonetheless, nothing in current FERPA provisions or in the Commission's recommendations prevents a State from enacting its own legislation as long as the Federal requirements are met. Indeed, California, for one, has already done so, and the protections prescribed by California law are stricter than FERPA's. But while State law may be needed to provide civil remedies for individuals whose rights with respect to education records are violated, the Commission prefers to stress local accountability in education as in the other areas. The recommended provisions of recourse to a Federal court which could enjoin the institution to respect the individual's FERPA rights should provide a vehicle for redress of grievances, if and when a governing board fails to see that an educational institution discharges its obligations to an individual.

It should be noted that in all of these areas, in addition to keeping the privacy protections required of State agencies to the minimum, most of the recommended measures leave the primary responsibility for enforcement with the States, seeking to strengthen the accountability of State agencies to their State legislatures and courts rather than making them more accountable to the Federal government. Concomitantly, the recommended measures restrict the Federal role to first reviewing and approving the required State law or policy, and then to receiving complaints about State enforcement efforts. Moreover, the Commission relies wherever possible on existing mechanisms to monitor performance: in medicine, the Joint Commission on Accreditation of Hospitals and State licensing agencies; in research and statistical activities, institutional review boards; in public assistance and social services, appropriate State agencies; and in education, elected boards and institutional governing boards.

In the matter of Federal sanctions, the Commission concluded that a Federal agency should have some alternative sanctions short of cutting off all Federal funds when a State or private agency is in violation. These alternatives might include withholding or asking for the return of a proportion of benefits, graduated according to the seriousness of the violation. In categorical grant programs a percentage of the total grant could be withdrawn as a penalty or withheld as security for specific performance of obligations. In reimbursement programs, monies could be withheld on a similar basis. To give the Federal agency graduated alternatives would make the threat of sanction credible, which in turn would increase the State's incentive to maintain compliance.

Finally, in a sixth area, employment and personnel, five of the Commission's recommendations specifically affect State employment and personnel record-keeping practices. These recommendations (*Recommendations (6), (7), (8), (9)* and *(10)* in Chapter 6), deal with the use of arrest records in employment. *Recommendations (6), (7)* and *(8)* invite State legislatures to restrict State use of arrest records in determining eligibility for employment and licensing. *Recommendation (9)* further expresses the Commission's deep mistrust of the use of arrest records in employment by recommending Federal financial assistance to States to help them devise means of limiting inappropriate arrest disclosures to employers by State and local law enforcement agencies, and to improve the accuracy and timeliness of arrest records.

As noted earlier, the Commission does not recommend that State governments be required to adopt a particular omnibus privacy protection statute to regulate their agencies' record keeping. The Privacy Act, however, recognizes that the Federal government owes the States assistance in developing appropriate legislation. In fact, the Privacy Act authorized the

Commission to provide technical assistance in the preparation and implementation of such legislation. The Commission sees a clear need for continued assistance of this kind, and includes suggestions to this effect in the chapters on medical records, education, and public assistance, and also in the implementation discussion in Chapter 1.

With respect to records maintained or regulated by State agencies, the Commission also makes two quite specific recommendations: (1) that States amend their penal codes to provide criminal penalties for getting information from a medical-care provider through deception or misrepresentation; and (2) that each State review all direct-mail marketing and solicitation uses made of State records about individuals. This is especially important when State agencies prepare mailing lists for the express purpose of publishing, selling, or exchanging them, as motor vehicle departments often do without apprising drivers and owners of registered vehicles that they do so. The Commission recommends that State agencies be directed to develop a procedure whereby an individual can notify the agency and, through the agency, any user of the record for direct mail marketing or solicitation that he does not want his name disclosed for such a purpose.

STATE AGENCY ACCESS TO THIRD-PARTY RECORDS

For many of the record-keeping relationships examined in this report, the Commission recommends constraining the voluntary disclosure of records about an individual by private-sector record keepers. Individually identifiable credit, depository, and insurance records may not be disclosed without the authority of the individual to whom they pertain or the presentation of valid compulsory legal process. This would include disclosures to State and local government agencies. There are exceptions, of course, where valid legal process is served on the record keeper or where the record keeper is subject to statutory reporting requirements. With respect to the use of Federal tax return information, the recommended measures also prohibit any disclosure by one State agency to another for nontax purposes. With respect to federally assisted research or statistical projects, no recorded information may be disclosed in individually identifiable form for any purpose other than a research or statistical purpose or the purpose of auditing a grant or contract.

To the extent that these restrictions affect State agencies, they place few specific limitations on State use of compulsory legal process or even on State reporting requirements. The limitations on Federal compulsory processes and Federal reporting statutes recommended in Chapter 9, however, provide a model for the States. Indeed, as noted at several points in that chapter, the broad public policy and specific recommendations it presents are equally applicable to State and local governments. The recommendations were not explicitly directed to the States because of the difficulties of dealing properly with fine, but often crucial, distinctions in the forms of compulsory legal process in 50 jurisdictions.

Chapter 13

The Relationship Between Citizen and Government: The Privacy Act of 1974

The Privacy Protection Study Commission was given the broad mandate to investigate the personal-data record-keeping practices of governmental, regional, and private organizations and to recommend to the President and the Congress the extent, if any, to which the principles and requirements of the Act should be applied to them.[1] Early in its inquiry, the Commission decided that to fulfill this mandate an assessment of the Privacy Act itself, its underlying philosophy, and the experience of Federal agencies to date in complying with it would be necessary. This chapter reports the results of that assessment. In so doing, it responds to the Commission's mandate directing it to:

> report on such other legislative recommendations as it may determine to be necessary to protect the privacy of individuals while meeting the legitimate needs of government and society for information. *[Section 5(b)(2) of Public Law 93-579]*

As the preceding chapters demonstrate, the Commission has concluded that the Privacy Act should *not* be extended in its present form to organizations outside the Federal government. This conclusion is based on several considerations. First, economic incentives can be used to induce organizations in the private sector to limit their acquisition and retention of information about individuals much more easily than they can be used in government. Private-sector organizations can be moved to protect their customers' privacy interests if their customers know and understand their record-keeping practices and use the competition of the marketplace as an ally in securing compliance with privacy protection safeguards. In addition, a private-sector organization's legal liability for violation of certain individual rights compels attention to fair practices and procedures in carrying out privacy protection safeguards even at the lowest levels. A mistake that costs a company money can cost the responsible employee his job. In government organizations, however, such incentives are much more tenuous, as the discussion later in this chapter will indicate.

A second consideration that argues for distinguishing private organizations from governmental ones is the high degree of uniformity, particular-

---

[1] Section 5(b)(1) of Public Law 93-579.

ly of Federal government administrative processes and practices, in contrast to the diversity of similar practices found at other levels of government and throughout the private sector. The standards of government operation outlined in the Administrative Procedures Act *[5 U.S.C. 551 et seq.]* apply to all but the most limited of Federal agency activities. No parallel exists in the private sector.

The third consideration that led the Commission to reject wholesale, uniform application of the Privacy Act to other than Federal government agencies is related to the second; uniform and specific Federal requirements imposed on all private-sector record keepers and other governmental ones would inevitably require broad-based regulation, giving government an unprecedented role in channeling and monitoring flows of information throughout all of society. While the Commission recognizes that government intervention in some areas of record keeping may not be avoidable, it strongly believes that the safeguards for personal privacy it seeks to establish and preserve require and, in fact, demand that such intervention be limited and controlled.

A fourth reason for concluding that the Privacy Act should not be extended to organizations outside the Federal government is the recognition that some of the requirements imposed by the Privacy Act on Federal agencies simply do not, or cannot, apply to private-sector organizations. For example, the restriction the Privacy Act places on the collection of information on an individual's exercise of his First Amendment rights would be ill-considered, and perhaps unconstitutional, if it were to be applied to all private-sector organizations without limitation.

Finally, the Commission has reached the conclusion that the Privacy Act needs significant modification and change if it is to accomplish its objectives within the Federal government. Much of this chapter supports that conclusion.

All of these arguments persuaded the Commission that it should not recommend omnibus legislation to extend the Privacy Act to other levels of government or to the private sector. The Commission further observes that even within the Federal government different requirements apply to some records about individuals. While the Privacy Act establishes minimum requirements for the keeping of records about individuals, other statutes set out additional ones directed at records maintained by particular agencies or used to perform particular functions.

The prohibitions on the disclosure of individual tax returns in the Tax Reform Act of 1976 are one example of such legislation. The rationale for these additional requirements recognizes that in government information about individuals is often acquired and recorded under different circumstances by different agencies. While every individual has a basic relationship with government that demands a minimum set of protections against abuse of the records government keeps about him, in specific circumstances the individual is entitled to a higher threshold of protection. This is particularly true in relation to standards limiting disclosure. The information a citizen gives to the revenue system, for example, because he is forced to do so under the threat of criminal sanctions, deserves more than minimum protections.

The Commission, as further discussed in Chapter 14, encourages the Congress to enact specifically targeted legislation in areas where the amount of detail in the records, the manner in which they are obtained, or the nature of the agency mission involved, warrant special safeguards.

METHOD OF STUDY AND ANALYSIS

To assess the Privacy Act's requirements and the effectiveness of its implementation, the Commission sought to identify the principles and underlying philosophy that formed the basis for the Act. To do so, a study of the Act's legislative history, the language of the law, and its actual implementation was necessary. The findings and conclusions presented below are based on communications with agency heads and their designated Privacy Act points-of-contact, testimony from various Commission hearings, agency annual reports, some informal workshops, and literally hundreds of personal and telephone interviews by staff. Although the Commission's inquiry was conducted in the early days of the Act's implementation, it believes that this close and continuous staff contact with agency operating personnel has allowed a fair assessment of agency implementation experience.[2]

In conducting its inquiry, however, the Commission encountered both conceptual and drafting problems with the current law. As the subsequent discussion will indicate, drafting details can have important consequences in an area which is both new to regulation and dependent upon changing technology. Thus, the Commission's conclusions concentrate on policy objectives rather than on the specifics of implementation. Its objective in setting out its conclusions and offering suggestions for change in the Act is to allow the policy objectives of the current law to be achieved more successfully without destroying necessary opportunities for flexibility in implementation. The Commission adopted this approach to allow for changing information technology and diversity of agency information needs and uses, as well as to foster the constructive creativity that can arise in the absence of overly restrictive requirements.

In many instances, the difficulty with the current law is not in its objectives nor in the flexibility it allows, but rather that agencies have taken advantage of its flexibility to contravene its spirit. Yet, making the law less flexible is not a desirable solution. Implementation costs would rise dramatically, and new developments in information technology could invite uncontrollable circumvention of rigidities in the statute. Thus, the Commission's approach is to strengthen flexibility and provide incentives for agency compliance while preserving the essential autonomy of each agency to decide how best to comply with each requirement.

If one accepts the view that it is best to tell an agency *what* to do, rather than *how* to do it, there are still issues that each agency cannot, and in some cases should not, resolve singly. The most obvious one is the question of

---

[2] The detailed results of this inquiry will be presented in a separately published appendix volume that will also contain an illustrative statute showing how the Commission's suggestions might appear as legislative requirements.

whether a particular type of record-keeping system should exist at all; another is whether particular transfers of records among agencies are desirable. Such questions require independent policy judgments and thus must be addressed by an entity other than the one directly involved. In Chapter 1, the Commission enumerates the functions it believes such an entity should fulfill.

Finally, it is worth noting at the outset that the concerns expressed by the various agencies at the time of the Act's passage regarding anticipated costs of implementation, numbers of access requests, and burden of administration have generally proved to be unwarranted. For example, the expected controversy over patient access to medical records has not developed. Cost figures recently released by the Office of Management and Budget (OMB) show expenditures to be much lower than originally estimated. In 1974, OMB had estimated that implementing the Act would cost $200-$300 million per year over the first four to five years and require an additional one time start-up cost of $100 million, which would be expended in the first two years. In 1977, however, OMB estimated that start-up costs in the nine months between the Act's passage and the date it took effect were $29,459,000, and that an additional $36,599,000 was spent for first-year operating expenses.[3]

THE PRIVACY ACT PRINCIPLES

The *requirements* of an act, although not always easy to interpret, derive from the words of legislation. *Principles,* on the other hand, are sometimes less readily apparent. The statement of principles in a law's preamble, the law's legislative history, and the conditions or problems that led to its passage must all be read along with the language of its specific provisions.

Although many issues in the 1960's and early 1970's were loosely grouped under the category of invasions of privacy, it is clear that many of the perceived problems had very little in common. Some of the actual or potential invasions of privacy involved physical surveillance or wiretapping; some involved mail openings or burglaries conducted by government agencies; others centered on harassment of individuals for political purposes; and still others concerned the unfair use of records about individuals.

The inquiry into these matters by a number of congressional committees did not share a common analytical framework, nor were the distinctions among different types of privacy invasions sharply drawn. Nonetheless, they succeeded in focusing public attention on privacy issues and in amassing useful information regarding particular aspects of the privacy protection problem.

In 1972, the Secretary's Advisory Committee on Automated Personal Data Systems was appointed by the then Secretary of Health, Education,

---

[3] Letter from Hon. Bert Lance, Director, Office of Management and Budget, to Senator Abraham A. Ribicoff, Chairman, Committee on Governmental Affairs, United States Senate, March, 1977, including a report on Costs of Implementing the Privacy Act of 1974, p. 5.

and Welfare, Elliot L. Richardson, to explore, as its name suggested, the impact of computers on record keeping about individuals and, in addition, to inquire into, and make recommendations regarding, the use of the Social Security number. The Advisory Committee did not examine issues arising from the physical surveillance of individuals or the wiretapping of conversations. Nor did it study mail openings, harassment of political dissidents, or violations of Fourth or Fifth Amendments rights. Instead, the Committee limited its inquiry to the use of records about individuals by government agencies and private organizations, and it focused its recommendations on automated systems while also suggesting their possible applicability to manual systems.

After examining various definitions of privacy, the Secretary's Advisory Committee concluded that the most significant aspect of the way organizations keep and use records about individuals was the extent to which individuals to whom the records pertained were unable to control their use. Accordingly, to strike a better balance between institutional and individual prerogatives, the Committee recommended a "Code of Fair Information Practices" based on the following five principles:

- There must be no personal data record-keeping systems whose very existence is secret.
- There must be a way for an individual to find out what information about him is in a record and how it is used.
- There must be a way for an individual to prevent information about him obtained for one purpose from being used or made available for other purposes without his consent.
- There must be a way for an individual to correct or amend a record of identifiable information about him.
- Any organization creating, maintaining, using, or disseminating records of identifiable personal data must assure the reliability of the data for their intended use and must take reasonable precautions to prevent misuse of the data.[4]

These five principles and the findings of the DHEW Committee, published in July 1973, are generally credited with supplying the intellectual framework for the Privacy Act of 1974, though in drafting the statute the Congress, influenced by its own inquiries, refined the five principles to eight:[5]

(1) There shall be no personal-data record-keeping system whose very existence is secret and there shall be a policy of openness about an organization's personal-data record-keeping policies, practices, and systems. (The Openness Principle)

(2) An individual about whom information is maintained by a record-keeping organization in individually identifiable form

---

[4] DHEW Secretary's Advisory Committee on Automated Personal Data Systems, *Records, Computers and the Rights of Citizens*, (Washington: U.S. Government Printing Office, 1973), p. 41.

[5] This identification of eight principles results from Commission analysis, not a specific Congressional statement.

shall have a right to see and copy that information. (The Individual Access Principle)

(3)   An individual about whom information is maintained by a record-keeping organization shall have a right to correct or amend the substance of that information. (The Individual Participation Principle)

(4)   There shall be limits on the types of information an organization may collect about an individual, as well as certain requirements with respect to the manner in which it collects such information. (The Collection Limitation Principle)

(5)   There shall be limits on the internal uses of information about an individual within a record-keeping organization. (The Use Limitation Principle)

(6)   There shall be limits on the external disclosures of information about an individual a record-keeping organization may make. (The Disclosure Limitation Principle)

(7)   A record-keeping organization shall bear an affirmative responsibility for establishing reasonable and proper information management policies and practices which assure that its collection, maintenance, use, and dissemination of information about an individual is necessary and lawful and the information itself is current and accurate. (The Information Management Principle)

(8)   A record-keeping organization shall be accountable for its personal-data record-keeping policies, practices, and systems. (The Accountability Principle)

Each of these principles is manifest in one or more of the Privacy Act's specific requirements, and in their application they all require a balancing of individual, organizational, and societal interests.

FINDINGS AND CONCLUSIONS

In assessing the Privacy Act of 1974, the Commission sought answers to the following two questions:

•   Does the Act effectively address the issues and problems it was intended to address?

•   Are there important information policy issues and problems the Act might address but does not address, or does not address adequately?

On the whole, the Commission has concluded that:

(1)   **The Privacy Act represents a large step forward, but it has not resulted in the general benefits to the public that either its legislative history or the prevailing opinion as to its accomplishments would lead one to expect;**

(2)   **Agency compliance with the Act is difficult to assess because of**

the ambiguity of some of the Act's requirements, but, on balance, it appears to be neither deplorable nor exemplary;

(3)   The Act ignores or only marginally addresses some personal-data record-keeping policy issues of major importance now and for the future.

The more specific conclusions that follow stem from these three basic conclusions. The Commission believes that if the Congress seeks to remedy these deficiencies by amending the Act, three steps are essential:

First, the ambiguous language in the law should be clarified to minimize variations in interpretation, but not implementation, of the law.

Second, any clarification should incorporate "reasonableness tests" to allow flexibility and thus give the agencies incentives to attend to implementation issues and to take account of the differences between manual and automated record keeping, diverse agency record-keeping requirements, and future technological developments.

Third, the Act's reliance on its system-of-records definition as the sole basis for activating all of its requirements should be abandoned in favor of an approach that activates specific requirements as warranted.

The impact of the first two of these suggestions will become clear when the specifics of the Commission's other, more detailed, conclusions are explained. The third, however, is central to the operation of the Act. From an examination of both the language of the Act and its legislative history, it seems clear that the intent of Congress was to include in the definition of the term "record"[6] every one that contains *any* kind of individually identifiable information about an individual. However, because the Congress was mindful of the burden such a definition could impose on an agency, it limited the Act's coverage to records retrieved from a "system of records" by "name . . . or identifying number, symbol, or other identifying particular . . . ." *[5 U.S.C. 552a(a)(5)]* Thus, unless an agency, in fact, retrieves recorded information by reference to a "name . . . identifying symbol, or other identifying particular . . .," the system in which the information is maintained is not covered by the Act. Whereas the current record definition refers to information about an individual which *contains* his name or identifier, the system-of-records definition refers to information about an individual which is *retrieved* by name, identifier, or identifying particular. The crucial difference is obvious, and the effect has been wholesale exclusion from the Act's scope of records that are not accessed by name,

---

[6] The Act defines a "record" as "any item, collection, or grouping of information about an individual that is maintained by an agency, including, but not limited to, his education, financial transactions, medical history, and criminal or employment history and that contains his name, or the identifying number, symbol, or other identifying particular assigned to the individual, such as a finger or voice print or a photograph." *[5 U.S.C. 552a(a)(4)]*

identifier, or assigned particular. None of the Act's protections accrue to an individual whose record is so treated.

There are many examples of readily accessible individually identifiable agency records that are not retrieved by personal identifier,[7] and current and emerging computer and telecommunications technology will create more. While the language of the Act speaks in terms of retrieval by discrete individual identifiers, most automated record systems facilitate identification of an individual's record based on some combination of the individual's attributes or characteristics, natural or assigned, as well as by reference to individual identifiers in the more conventional sense. Thus, it would be easy to program a computer to locate particular individuals through attribute searches (e.g., "list all blonde, female Executive Directors of Federal Commissions").[8] Retrieval of individually identifiable information by scanning (or searching) large volumes of computer records is not only possible but an ever-increasing agency practice. The Federal Trade Commission, for example, is transcribing all written material in its litigation files for computer retrieval, thereby making it possible to search for all occurrences of a particular name, or any other character pattern for that matter.

In summary, the system-of-records definition has two limitations. First, it undermines the Act's objective of allowing an individual to have access to the records an agency maintains about him, and second, by serving as the activating, or "on/off switch" for the Act's other provisions, it unnecessarily limits the Act's scope. To solve this problem without placing an unreasonable burden on the agencies, the Commission believes *the Act's definition of a system of records should be abandoned and its definition of a record amended.*

The term *record* should include attributes and other personal characteristics assigned to an individual, and a new term, *accessible record,* should be defined to delineate those individually identifiable records that ought to be available to an individual in response to an access request. Accessible records would include those which, while not retrieved by an individual identifier, could be retrieved by an agency without unreasonably burdening it, either through its regular retrieval procedures or because the subject is able to help the agency find the record. If an individual knew he was mentioned in a particular record, for example, he would be entitled to access to it whether or not agency practice is to access the record by reference to him.

The Commission believes that *when an individual asks to see and copy information an agency maintains on him, the agency should be required to*

---

[7] Two examples will illustrate the extremes of agency implementation of the "system of records" provision. A small component of one agency rearranged its personnel records by Civil Service grade, instead of individual identifier, in order to avoid the Act's requirements. The Department of the Navy, on the other hand, elected to bring a file of interview records under the Act even though they were filed (and hence retrieved) by the date of the interview.

[8] An "attribute search," contrary to the more common "name search," or "index search," starts with a collection of data about many individuals and seeks to identify those particular individuals in the system who meet the prescribed conditions or who have the prescribed attributes.

provide that information if it can do so without an unreasonable expenditure of time, money, or other resources or if the individual can provide specific enough locating information to render the record accessible without an unreasonable expenditure. In implementing this provision, however, an agency should not have to establish any new cross-referencing schemes for the purpose of granting access, such as would be required if the agency had to be aware of all references to one individual in other individuals' files or in files indexed in any other manner (e.g., references to agency officers in files indexed by agency name). In this connection, the Commission would also urge deletion of the clause (in Subsection d(1)) of the Act which requires an agency to allow an individual access "to any information pertaining to him which is contained in the system . . . ." This requirement is impossible to satisfy since an agency often does not know how to find "all" such information.

The Commission also believes that the terms *record, individually identifiable record,* and *accessible record* should operate as separate activators, or "on/off switches," for the appropriate provisions of the Act. For example, the Act's civil remedies could apply in all cases in which the misuse of an individually identifiable record through failure to comply with one of the Act's requirements resulted in injury to an individual, while the access to records provision could be subject to the reasonable burden test of the accessible record definition. This would allow more flexibility and broaden the scope of the current Act.

Another provision of the Act that limits its scope is the one dealing with contractors. Recipients of discretionary Federal grants who perform functions similar or identical to functions performed by contractors are not covered. Agency personnel interviewed by Commission staff frequently expressed the view that the implicit distinction in the Act between contractors and grantees is, in many cases, artificial. The Commission agrees. In Chapter 15, moreover, it recommends that a uniform set of requirements and safeguards be applied to records collected or maintained in individually identifiable form for a research or statistical purpose under Federal authority or with Federal funds, and the Privacy Act is suggested as a basic vehicle for implementing these recommendations.

While care must be taken to avoid creating undue burdens on the contractor or grantee, the Commission believes that *the Federal government must assure that the basic protections of the Privacy Act apply to records generated with Federal funds for use by the Federal government.* Specifically, the Commission believes that any contractor or recipient of a discretionary Federal grant, or any subcontractor thereof, who performs any function on behalf of a Federal agency which requires the contractor or grantee to maintain individually identifiable records, should be subject to the provisions of the Act. The Act, however, should not apply to employment, personnel, or administrative records the contractor or grantee maintains as a necessary aspect of supporting the contract or grant, but which bear no other relation to its performance. The Act also should not apply to individually identifiable records to which the following three conditions all apply: (1) records that are neither required nor implied by terms of the contract or grant; (2) records for which no representation of Federal sponsorship or association is made; and (3) records that will not be provided to the Federal agency with which the contract or grant is established, except for authorized audits or investigations. The added specificity in delineating which records fall within the Act's purview represents an attempt to preserve the intent of the Act while removing some of the confusion that could result in undue burden on contractors and grantees.

The remaining analysis of agency implementation of the Privacy Act will be based on the eight Privacy Act principles identified earlier. The extent of their fulfillment will be examined and the Commission's suggestions for change in their implementation will be presented and explained.

IMPLEMENTATION OF THE PRIVACY ACT PRINCIPLES

THE OPENNESS PRINCIPLE

The Privacy Act asserts that an agency of the Federal government must not be secretive about its personal-data record-keeping policies, practices, and systems. No agency may conceal the existence of any personal-data record-keeping system, and each agency that maintains such a system must describe publicly both the kinds of information in it and the manner in which it will be used. This is accomplished in two ways. The first is through the required annual publication of system notices in the *Federal Register*. The second is through the "Privacy Act Statement"[9] given at the time individually identifiable information is collected from an individual.

The requirements implementing the Openness Principle are intended to achieve two general goals:

(1)   facilitate public scrutiny of Federal agency record-keeping policies, practices, and systems by interested and knowledgeable parties; and

(2)   make the citizen aware of systems in which a record on him is likely to exist.

The Commission has found that the Act has made a significant step toward fulfillment of these objectives, especially the first one, but that it has still fallen short of expectations.

The Commission believes that publishing record-system notices once each year in the *Federal Register* is worthwhile. It develops an inventory of agency record-keeping operations that is useful for both public scrutiny of Federal agency record-keeping practices and for internal management control. Unfortunately, however, the annual notices tend to be less informative than they could be, and they are not required to describe the extent to which information is used within the agency. Furthermore, the Act is silent on the distinction between a *system* and a *subsystem*, and there are no criteria for limiting the diversity of information, purposes, or functions that may be incorporated in any one record system, and thus subsumed in

---

[9] The "Privacy Act Statement" contains the authority for the solicitation of the information, the principal purposes for which it will be used, its "routine uses," and the effect on the individual of not providing the information. *[5 U.S.C. 552a(e)(3)]*

one annual *Federal Register* notice. As a result, some annual notices are too encompassing to be informative. Likewise, duplicate, substantially similar, or derivative systems are frequently either unlisted or not cross-referenced. The Commission believes that the primary purpose of the public notice requirement should be to facilitate internal and external oversight of agency activities, including public scrutiny. Thus, it believes that *the annual notices should provide more detail than they now do and should reflect more accurately the context or manner in which an agency maintains records.*

One of the specific shortcomings of the system notices has been the literal interpretation of the requirement to describe the *routine uses.* While limiting these descriptions to *external* uses is consistent with the prevailing interpretation of the Act's routine-use definition, in many cases, the more significant uses are *internal* ones. Therefore, the Commission believes that *the section in the annual notice on routine uses of records maintained in a system, including categories of uses and the purposes of such uses, should include a description of internal uses of information as well as external disclosures.*

Describing the context and manner in which an agency uses the records in a system would at least partially reveal the relationships among systems that are often obscured today. When a large, complex record system is covered by one system notice, the subsystems should be described in detail. The important concern should not be to define the level at which a subsystem must be described, or the way to describe indices, but rather that an agency present a true picture of how it uses information in a system and how the system itself is perceived by the agency. The goal should be to remain faithful to the Openness Principle by assuring that there are no secret systems. The possibility that an agency may comply with the technical requirements of the Act's notice provisions but still maintain systems that are effectively secret must be avoided.

The goal of facilitating public scrutiny is hindered by the fact that the *Federal Register* is at best a limited vehicle for reaching the general public. Every effort should be made to classify, compile, and index the information in notices logically. For example, it would be useful to differentiate between the large group of systems that are solely devoted to record keeping about agency personnel and the much smaller group that contains information on citizens in general. The *Federal Register* compilation should make it easy for a private citizen, a member of a public interest group, or a congressional staff member to pinpoint a particular type of record or system of records.

Given the limited readership of the *Federal Register,* however, the best way of making the citizen aware of systems in which he is included is through the "Privacy Act Statement," which is similar to the annual system notice, except that it also informs the individual of internal agency uses of information about him. Like the annual notices, however, Privacy Act Statements are often too vague or general to inform the individual adequately. They need not explain that supplementary information may be collected from other sources and not every agency or system is subject to the Statement requirement.

There is a problem in finding a balance between the length of a Privacy Act Statement and its clarity; if it is too long, individuals are not likely to read it; if it is too short, it may not convey enough information for the individual to understand fully how the information will be used. The contents of the Privacy Act Statement are discussed in the section on the Collection Limitation Principle.

THE INDIVIDUAL ACCESS PRINCIPLE

The Privacy Act's second principle is that an individual should have a right to see and obtain a copy of a record an agency maintains about him. Prior to the Act's passage, an individual was able to obtain copies of the records a Federal agency might keep about him in several ways. The Armed Services, for example, made many personnel, medical, and performance records available to servicemen. In fact, the subjects of certain personnel records are required to review and sign them once each year. Federal agencies also have procedures that give an individual access to records about him when there is a dispute over his entitlement to benefits.

In addition, the Freedom of Information Act (FOIA) *[5 U.S.C. 552]*, which predates the Privacy Act by seven years, allows any person to see and obtain a copy of any record in the possession of the Federal government without regard to his need for or interest in it. An agency can withhold a record that falls within one of nine FOIA exemptions, but its determination to do so, if appealed by the requestor, must withstand administrative and judicial review.

Individuals could and did use the Freedom of Information Act to gain access to their own files prior to passage of the Privacy Act. There were several drawbacks, however. First, an agency could decline to release information deemed to be part of the internal deliberative processes of government.[10] In certain cases, this resulted in a considerable amount of information about an individual being taken out of a file prior to giving the file to him. Second, in the early days of the Freedom of Information Act, some agencies refused to disclose personnel and medical files to an individual on the grounds that disclosure to the individual would constitute a clearly unwarranted invasion of *his* personal privacy.[11]

The individual access provision of the Privacy Act *[5 U.S.C. 552a(d)]* was enacted in part to clarify these uncertainties with respect to an individual's right to see and obtain a copy of a record about himself. The Privacy Act has its own set of exemptions from its individual access requirement which will be discussed below. For all other systems subject to the Act, however, agencies must now facilitate access by an individual when he so requests and may never keep records about himself from him on the grounds that they constitute communications within or among agencies. Nonetheless, the Commission has found that the number of Privacy Act access requests (i.e., requests specifically citing the Privacy Act) has not been great and that most have come from agency employees or former employees. One reason for this may be that pre-existing law and practice continue to be used. In addition, the public's awareness of the Freedom of

---

[10] 5 U.S.C. 552(b)(5)
[11] 5 U.S.C. 552(b)(6)

Information Act still appears to be much sharper than its awareness of the Privacy Act. Another reason may also be that the Privacy Act's own exemptions from the access requirement are too sweeping. The Central Intelligence Agency and some major law enforcement systems qualify for a blanket exemption from the access requirement. Thus, individuals who want access to records about themselves in those systems must use the Freedom of Information Act as their vehicle.

The Privacy Act exemptions from the individual access requirement are permissive, not mandatory. In addition, unlike the Freedom of Information Act exemptions, they apply to *systems of records* rather than to *specific requests* for access to specific information. To invoke any one of them an agency must publish its intention to do so in advance. As a result, some over-cautious lawyers and administrators have made excessively broad claims of exemption. Once an exemption is published, moreover, agency operating personnel are inclined to use it, thus eliminating exercises of judgment in light of the particular record sought.

On the other hand, some agencies have not claimed exemptions to which they may have been entitled, and others have claimed them but do not use them. The Central Intelligence Agency, for example, processes individual access requests under the Privacy Act despite having claimed the broad exemption the Act provides it. On balance, however, the Act's requirement that exemptions be claimed in advance, and that they cover entire systems rather than types of records or specific requests, has resulted in unnecessary exclusions of records from the scope of the Act's individual access requirement.

Agency rules on individual access, and on the exercise of the other rights the Act establishes, appear, in most instances, to be in compliance with the Act's rule-making requirements. Yet, they too are often difficult to comprehend, and because the principal places to find them are in the *Federal Register* and the *Code of Federal Regulations*, it is doubtful that many people know they exist, let alone how to locate and interpret them. Furthermore, the Act's requirement that an individual specifically name the record system in which the record he desires is located is not realistic. Fortunately, many agencies have gone beyond the letter of the law in assisting individuals whose access requests reasonably describe the records sought, but the requirement to name the system still seems likely to discourage some people from asking to see their records. Finally, the Act's requirement that an agency keep an accounting of each disclosure of a record to the individual to whom it pertains appears to be an added incentive to process access requests under the Freedom of Information Act rather than the Privacy Act when an agency has a choice (i.e., when the individual does not specify that his request is being made under one Act or the other).

It would appear, in sum, that individuals continue to rely on pre-existing laws and practices when they want access to agency records about themselves. From the individual's point of view, one advantage of the Freedom of Information Act is that there are specific limits on how long an agency may take to respond to a request, whereas in the Privacy Act there are none. Furthermore, although the FOIA permits agencies to charge search fees, while the Privacy Act does not, in practice such charges are rarely made when an individual is asking for information about himself.

The Privacy Act has benefitted a current or past Federal employee to the extent that it allows him to circumvent the FOIA exemption for documents pertaining to internal agency deliberations when he wants access to some of the more interesting parts of an evaluation report or inquiry into his background. The Privacy Act has retained a limited exemption for some personnel evaluations, but its net effect has been to increase the accessibility of such material. It could also be concluded that Federal employees, unlike the private citizen, are aware that the Act exists and, being comfortable with bureaucratic procedures, have quickly learned how to use it.

To aid an individual in gaining access to his record, the Commission believes that *the Privacy Act should parallel the approach of the Freedom of Information Act in that an individual should be required to make a request which reasonably describes the record to which he desires access.* In those situations in which an agency believes an individual has made too broad an access request, it should help him refine his request. This is the procedure most agencies are following now, but modification of the language of the Act is important. The likelihood of a private citizen being aware of the name of a system of records published in the *Federal Register* is too remote to be relied on.

In addition, the Commission believes that the Privacy Act should be the exclusive vehicle for individuals requesting access to records about themselves, *provided that the Privacy Act's approach to exemptions from the individual access requirement is modified to parallel that of the Freedom of Information Act* (as discussed below). Making the exemption approaches parallel is necessary to assure that the individual does not receive less information using the Privacy Act as his access vehicle than he would if his request for access were processed under the Freedom of Information Act. Because agencies may currently ignore the time limits suggested in guidelines for implementation of the Privacy Act issued by the Office of Management and Budget,[12] *explicit time limits should also be added to the Privacy Act so that by making the Act the individual's exclusive access vehicle he will not lose the time limit protections now in the Freedom of Information Act.* The fees, appeal rights, and sanctions of the Privacy Act, however, would still apply.

Besides the direct benefits for the individual of such an approach there are certain procedural benefits to the agencies which should be noted. Currently, Freedom of Information Act offices and officers are required to respond to requests for access to both personal information about individuals and information about agency activities (e.g., regarding agency policies). By making the Privacy Act the exclusive access vehicle for any individual requesting information about himself, some stress will be removed. The actual number of requests for information will not be affected, but this approach better divides responsibility in the agencies.

---

[12] Office of Management and Budget, *Privacy Act Guidelines,* issued as a supplement to Circular A-108, *Federal Register,* Volume 40, Number 132, July 9, 1975, pp. 28948 - 28978.

Perhaps some of the confusion surrounding the interrelation between the Freedom of Information Act and the Privacy Act will even be reduced.

In addition to requiring an agency to assist an individual in reasonably describing the records to which he seeks access, it is important for an individual to have access to, and the right to amend, information about which he may not have enough detailed knowledge to formulate a specific request. Thus, the Commission believes that *access to substantially similar or derivative versions of records sought by an individual should be provided automatically in response to his request for the original record to the extent that providing such access does not constitute an unreasonable burden on the agency.*

There are two related situations at issue here. The first is where there may be an exact duplicate of a record maintained in another part of the agency. The second, and more important, is where some portion of a record may have been copied and then subsequently amended, appended, or otherwise altered. Alternatively, two records, or portions thereof, may have been combined. In each of these cases, it can be reasonably inferred that the individual would want to know about all versions of the record were he aware of them. Thus, the burden must be on the agency to take reasonable affirmative steps to describe and, if requested, to make available to the individual the several versions. While the individual may not want to see an exact duplicate of the original record, for example, he may wish to amend it if he amends the original. Moreover, the uses and disclosures of exact duplicates of a record, as well as substantially similar or derivative versions of the record, often will not be the. same as the uses and disclosures of the original, and thus it can be assumed that the individual will want to know about them.

The Commission believes that *the Privacy Act's approach to exemptions from the individual access requirement should be modified to parallel that of the Freedom of Information Act.* Currently, Privacy Act exemptions are claimed in advance and apply to entire systems of records. Pre-claimed exemptions can be waived on a case-by-case basis, and while there is evidence that agencies are not using all of the exemptions claimed, they still seem to be claiming every one possible (including, in some cases, exemptions to which they would not appear to be entitled), but then using them only as needed. This creates uncertainty for the individual which the framers of the Act did not intend.

Abandonment of the system-of-records definition currently in the Privacy Act necessitates a different exemption strategy than the one the Act now has. The natural model to use is the Freedom of Information Act. The FOIA allows exemptions for certain types of information rather than for entire systems of records; exemptions may be invoked only when applicable, not claimed in advance. In addition, any segregable portion of a record which by itself does not qualify for an exemption must be provided to the individual. The FOIA approach appears to be working well, and its presumption that access should be granted to any part of a record for which an agency cannot sustain an exemption claim seems highly desirable.

Using the FOIA approach to exemptions would have the unintended effect, however, of voiding the Privacy Act provision that allows the CIA and law enforcement agencies to maintain unverified information obtained from intelligence or investigative sources.[13] Consequently, if the suggested exemption policy is adopted, it should allow the CIA, or any agency or component thereof which performs as its principal function any activity relating to the enforcement of criminal laws, to maintain information whose accuracy, timeliness, completeness, or relevance is questionable, *provided, however, that such information is clearly identified as such to all users or recipients of it.* This would preserve the Act's current policy. The only new requirement would be that the unverified information be clearly identified as such when it is disclosed to anyone else.

The Commission believes that *certain of the specific exemptions in the Freedom of Information Act should actually be duplicated in the Privacy Act. These include the Freedom of Information Act exemptions dealing with information specifically authorized to be kept secret in the interest of national defense and foreign policy, certain investigative information compiled for law enforcement purposes, and operating reports used by an agency responsible for the supervision of financial institutions.* This, too, would clarify, without altering current policy, and it would have the further advantage of incorporating the existing body of judicial interpretation as to what may or may not be withheld pursuant to the FOIA exemptions. Today, an individual is supposed to be granted access to the larger of the amounts of information to which he would be entitled under the FOIA *or* the Privacy Act, so there seems to be no practical reason for the two Acts to have different exemptions in the same area.

Finally, the Commission believes that *the Act's requirements with respect to a patient's access to a medical record an agency maintains about him should be brought into line with* Recommendation (5) *in Chapter 7 of this report.* The Commission also believes that *the Act should be refined to allow agencies to deny access to a parent or legal guardian in those situations in which another statute authorizes such withholding.*

THE INDIVIDUAL PARTICIPATION PRINCIPLE

The third Privacy Act principle holds that an individual should have the right to challenge the contents of a record on the grounds that it is not accurate, timely, complete, or relevant. The principle specifically recognizes that information can be a source of unfairness to an individual. In theory, the right to participate in the maintenance of a record allows for complaint, involvement, and representation in order to force a balancing of the individual's interests against the record keeper's. If this principle is enforced, the individual is able to keep some measure of control (although not absolute control) over the substance of what he himself reveals to an agency, as well as to check on what the agency collects about him from other sources.

The Act has made significant progress toward fulfillment of this principle through its requirement that agencies establish procedures whereby the individual may request correction or amendment of a record,

---

[13] 5 U.S.C. 552a(j).

appeal any denial of his request, and file a statement of disagreement if the denial and appeal result in a stand-off, either before or after judicial review. In allowing the individual to file a statement of disagreement, even after the agency's denial of his request is upheld by a court, the Act implicitly recognizes that the agency and the individual may have divergent interests in the content of a record, as well as the fact that there may be no clear-cut criteria for assessing accuracy, timeliness, completeness, or relevance.

Despite the Act's sophistication in this area, however, the correction and amendment rights have not been widely exercised. This doubtless reflects the small number of access requests under the Privacy Act; but it may also be due in part to the fact that so many of the agency records an individual might want to correct or amend are exempt from the individual access requirement and therefore not open for correction or amendment. Nevertheless, the right to correct or amend a record, once access has been obtained, is an area in which the Privacy Act represents a significant advance for the individual.

THE COLLECTION LIMITATION PRINCIPLE

The fourth principle of the Privacy Act is that there shall be limits on the type of information a record-keeping institution collects about an individual, as well as certain requirements with respect to the manner in which it may be collected. An agency may not collect whatever information it wishes, nor may it collect information in whatever manner it wishes. The principle is implemented by requiring that agencies (1) collect only information that is relevant and necessary to accomplish a lawful purpose;[14] (2) collect information to the greatest extent practicable directly from the subject individual;[15] (3) give every individual a Privacy Act Statement at the time individually identifiable information is requested of him;[16] and, (4) in certain instances, refrain from collecting an individual's Social Security number[17] and information relating to his exercise of First Amendment rights.[18]

The requirement to limit collection to information that is relevant and necessary to accomplish a lawful purpose of the agency seems to have resulted in a modest amount of revision and reduction of data-collection forms, and consequently a modest reduction in data collection itself. In contrast, the requirement that agencies collect information to the greatest extent practicable from the subject individual does not appear to have changed practices at all.

The required "Privacy Act Statement" seems not to have had much of an effect on the amount of information individuals are asked to provide about themselves or on their willingness to provide it. There appears to have been a slight reduction in the willingness of individuals to answer survey

---

[14] 5 U.S.C. 552a(e)(1).
[15] 5 U.S.C. 552a(e)(2).
[16] 5 U.S.C. 552a(e)(3).
[17] Section 7 of Public Law 93-579.
[18] 5 U.S.C. 552a(e)(7).

questions since passage of the Act, but this cannot be confidently attributed to the Privacy Act Statement.

In addition, there appears to be some troublesome ambiguity in the subsection of the Act that contains the "Privacy Act Statement" requirement. Subsection 3(e)(3) reads in part:

Each agency that maintains a system of records shall—

(3)   inform each individual whom it asks to supply information
. . .

Some agencies have interpreted this to require a statement only when individually identifiable information is collected from the subject individual and not to require it when such information is collected from a third party. The Commission believes that *a Privacy Act Statement should be provided to all individuals from whom individually identifiable information is collected, including third parties.*

On the other hand, the Privacy Act Statement must now be supplied or read each time individually identifiable information is collected, regardless of the frequency of contact between an agency and an individual. This is burdensome to the agency and can cause the Statement to be ignored by the individual. The purpose of the Statement is to provide the individual with enough information to allow him to judge whether or not to provide the information requested. There appears to be no useful purpose in doing this repeatedly if the individual has been provided with a copy of the Statement within a reasonable period of time prior to a follow-up request for information so long as the follow-up request is consistent with the original statement. Thus, the Commission believes that *the burden on agencies could be safely reduced by requiring that the individual be given a Privacy Act Statement only if he had not already been given a retention copy within a reasonable period of time prior to a subsequent request for information from him.*

A second problem with the Privacy Act Statement is that it tends to state the obvious and does not explicitly spell out other possible uses of the information. The Commission, consistent with its recommendations in other areas, believes that *the Statement should describe those uses of information that could reasonably be expected to influence an individual's decision to provide or not to provide the information requested.* Since the individual's decision may be influenced by the techniques used to verify the information he provides, *the Statement should also include a description of the scope, techniques, and sources to be used to verify or collect additional information about him.*

Providing a concise statement on uses and third-party sources may, upon occasion, prove to be more confusing than enlightening. Therefore, the Statement should, in addition, *identify the title, business address, and business telephone number of a responsible agency official who can answer any questions the individual may have about the Privacy Act Statement.*

The proscription on the collection of information about how an individual exercises his First Amendment rights appears to have had no noticeable effect on agency collection practices. The prohibition does not apply when an agency is expressly authorized to collect such information either by statute or by the individual, or where collection is "pertinent to and within the scope of an authorized law enforcement activity." *[5 U.S.C. 552a(e)(7)]* Because virtually all government agencies can be said to be involved in some type of law enforcement, the latter exception, in particular, has tended to negate the prohibition. A more accurate, and hence more effective, way of stating the congressional intent would be to refer to "an authorized investigation of a violation of the law." This change would not prohibit an agency from collecting a specific item of information whose collection is expressly required by statute or expressly authorized by the individual to whom it pertains, or whose collection would be a reasonable and proper library, bibliographic, abstracting, or similar reference function.

Section 7 of the Privacy Act, which attempts to limit collection of the Social Security number from individuals, also appears to have had little effect on agency practice. Its "grandfather clause," which allows agencies to continue to demand the number if they did so under statute or regulation prior to January 1, 1975, has encompassed almost all uses of the Social Security number at the Federal level, as indicated in Chapter 16 below.

THE USE LIMITATION PRINCIPLE

The fifth Privacy Act principle asserts that, once collected, there are limits to the *internal* uses to which an agency may put information about an individual. Once an agency has legitimately obtained information, it still may not use it internally without restriction.

The Act requires an agency to obtain an individual's written consent before disclosing a record about him to any of its employees other than "officers and employees . . . who have a need for the record in the performance of their duties." *[5 U.S.C. 552a(b)(1)]* However, because the terms "need" and "duties" are open to interpretation, the effect of this restriction is limited.

In theory, the requirement speaks to the kind of situation described in Chapter 6, wherein the employee-employer relationship was seen to subsume other record-keeping relationships, such as the medical-care and insurance ones. A problem inherent in the provision is the fact that one agency may have many different types of relationships with an individual but the provision takes no account of the difference between them; for that reason it has no practical effect on limiting certain internal uses of information. This is particularly true in the case of the larger cabinet departments which, for purposes of the Privacy Act, have defined themselves as one "agency."

Where differences in record-keeping relationships have been recognized in other statutes, such as where a component of the Department of Health, Education, and Welfare is subject to a confidentiality statute elsewhere in the U. S. Code, the integrity of the relationship that the statute addresses may be preserved within the framework of Subsection 3(b)(1). Section 1106 of the Social Security Act, for example, limits the disclosure of records maintained by the Social Security Administration, and thus it functions as a limitation on internal agency uses of records, even though the Department of Health, Education, and Welfare has defined itself as one agency for the purposes of the Privacy Act.

It can reasonably be assumed that the Privacy Act was not intended to nullify other statutes which limit the use and dissemination of information. Indeed, while the Act is silent on this issue, the OMB Guidelines advise that: "Agencies shall continue to abide by other constraints on their authority to disclose information to a third party including, where appropriate, the likely effect upon the individual of making that disclosure."[19] One would expect the OMB guidance to be definitive, but the internal use issue is a murky one. The "confidentiality" statutes in the U.S. Code are many and various, and it is not clear how statutes that *authorize* use or disclosure, rather than *prohibit* it, should be treated in relation to Subsection 3(b)(1).

The Commission believes that *the way to resolve this issue is through a revised routine-use provision that would apply to both internal and external agency uses and disclosures of information.* Such a provision would act as a minimum standard against which potential uses and disclosures of information would be measured. It would supersede preexisting statutes that authorize disclosures in a vague or general manner, but not statutes in which the Congress, as a matter of public policy, has called for the use and disclosure of specific types of information in specific situations. Such a provision, moreover, would not be construed as expanding an agency's authority to use or disclose information if the agency was already subject to a preexisting statute that restricted its use and disclosure of information more narrowly than the Privacy Act does.

The only way for the individual to discover the internal agency uses of a record about himself is through the "Privacy Act Statement," which cannot anticipate future uses over which the agency has no control. For example, two days after the Privacy Act was passed, the Congress passed another law creating a Federal Parent Locator Service (PLS) authorized to obtain information from the Social Security Administration upon request, regardless of the strictures of other statutes such as the Privacy Act. As already noted, moreover, the "Privacy Act Statement" need not inform the individual that information about him may be collected from third parties, thereby diluting the effect of the Use Limitation Principle even further.

While the Commission believes that the problem of controlling internal uses of information cannot be solved by levying specific requirements on the agencies, *the "routine use" provision, which forbids disclosures that are not compatible with the purpose for which the information was originally collected, should be applied to internal agency uses.* In addition, by strengthening the individual enforcement mechanism and establishing a central office within each agency for Privacy Act implementation (see below), compliance with the spirit of the internal use requirements will be improved.

---

[19] Office of Management and Budget, Circular A-108, *op. cit.*, p. 28953.

THE DISCLOSURE LIMITATION PRINCIPLE

The sixth Privacy Act principle asserts that there must be limits on the *external* disclosures of information an agency may make. That is, once an agency has legitimately obtained information, it still may not disclose it externally without restriction.

The Privacy Act authorizes ten categories of external disclosures that may be made without the consent of the individual. The most important one is found in Subsection 3(b)(3) which authorizes any disclosure that has been established as a "routine use"; that is, any disclosure for a "purpose which is compatible with the purpose for which [the information] was collected." *[5 U.S.C. 552a(b)(3); 5 U.S.C. 552a(a)(7)]* The key word is "compatible," which some agencies have interpreted quite broadly. As but one example, the United States Marshals Service published a routine-use notice on September 16, 1976, which read in part:

A record may be disseminated to a Federal agency, in response to its request, in connection with . . . the issuance of a license, grant, or other benefit by the requesting agency, *to the extent that the information relates to the requesting agency's decision on the matter.*[20] [emphasis added]

Other agencies, however, have interpreted the routine-use provision narrowly. Prior to passage of the Privacy Act, the Railroad Retirement Board (RRB) obtained benefit and employee name and address information from the Social Security Administration (SSA) to check the accuracy of payments made to claimants under the Railroad Unemployment Insurance Act (RUIA). The statute requires RUIA benefits to be calculated in the light of all other social insurance, employment, or sickness benefits payable to an individual by law. Today, however, the RRB is no longer obtaining information from the SSA, because the SSA has concluded that it cannot legitimately establish the disclosure as a routine use. The RRB estimates that this is costing it more than $85,000 a year in unnecessary payments.

Another problem with the routine-use provision for disclosures in Subsection 3(b)(3) is its relation to Subsection 3(b)(7), which authorizes disclosures of individually identifiable information to agencies for law enforcement purposes if the head of the agency requests the information in writing and specifies the legitimate law enforcement activity for which the information is desired. While treating the routine-use provision narrowly for some purposes, most agencies have employed it in combination with other laws to facilitate the flow of information to and between law enforcement and investigative units.

The combination of the Privacy Act's routine-use provision and Section 534 of Title 28, for example, permits agencies to circumvent the requirements of Subsection 3(b)(7). Under Section 534 of Title 28, the Department of Justice is required to maintain a central law enforcement information bank and to provide a clearinghouse for such information, particularly for agencies of the Federal government. Agencies have

---

[20] *Federal Register*, Volume 41, Number 181, September 16, 1976, p. 40015.

understood this provision to be a congressional endorsement of the routine exchange of law enforcement information, at least under the auspices of the Attorney General.

Currently, agencies of the Federal government seem to be employing the routine-use provision in order to permit the free flow of law enforcement and investigative information without having to comply with the standards of Subsection 3(b)(7). Agency system notices frequently indicate that information will be supplied to appropriate Federal, State, local, and, sometimes, foreign law enforcement agencies of government. In short, the Privacy Act does not place an effective burden on, or barriers to, the free flow of information within the law enforcement and investigative community.

Concurrent with formal endorsement of relatively unrestricted information flow to and between investigative agencies, the agents of investigative units have continued to employ the informal information network that exists within the law enforcement community. An agent of one unit may call his counterpart in a second agency to see if it might have any information on the subject of an investigation or any leads to people who might be appropriate to investigate. As the system currently operates, there would be some impediments to such disclosure—though not insurmountable ones— where the units of government involved only investigative agencies and the information exchanged came exclusively from their files. Today, however, the unfettered ability to exchange information between law enforcement and investigative units amounts to access by such units to virtually any governmental records without the need to comply with the strictures in Subsection 3(b)(7).

Almost all agencies have law enforcement units of one sort or another through which information desired by other units in other agencies may be channeled. Indeed, the law enforcement unit of an agency might seek information on an individual from records maintained by other components of an agency and transmit it to a second agency which could subsequently maintain it in a form (e.g., retrievable by docket number) which leaves it free of Privacy Act restrictions. Law enforcement units and investigation agencies can, and often do, operate in this fashion and thus function as a conduit for the exchange of information with other law enforcement units. The problem is not so much that law enforcement units disclose information about individuals to illegitimate recipients, but rather that the determination of legitimacy is more often than not highly informal, with the decision to disclose being made by anyone from the field agent level to the head of an agency. Such informality presents substantial potential for improper disclosure. This is a problem the Commission has not dealt with extensively, though a structure for effective examination of it is suggested later in this chapter.

Although the effect of the routine-use provision has been limited, due mainly to the fact that it has been interpreted as applying only to external transfers of information, its safety-valve aspects should be preserved. The disclosure provisions of the Privacy Act must allow for a certain amount of agency discretion, since, in an omnibus statute, it is impossible to enumerate all of the necessary conditions of disclosure. Nonetheless, the Commission believes that *the compatible-purpose test of the routine-use provision should be augmented by a test for consistency, with the conditions or reasonable expectations of use and disclosure under which the information was provided, collected, or obtained.* The individual's point of view must be represented in the agency's decision to use or disclose information, and today the compatible-purpose test only takes account of the agency's point of view.

The routine-use definition should also apply to internal, as well as external, agency uses and disclosures of information. This is important, since the majority of uses of information are made by the agency that originally collects it.

Congress may, of course, elect, as it has done in the Tax Reform Act of 1976, to authorize particular uses or disclosures of information that are either incompatible with the purpose for which the information was collected, or inconsistent with the individual's reasonable expectations of use and disclosure. Such additional uses and disclosures of information should be treated as routine uses, provided that the statute authorizing them establishes specific criteria for use or disclosure of specific types of information. Ideally, the Congress should review all the statutes that authorize such incompatible uses and disclosures and determine which ones it wishes to retain. The point, however, is that the Commission, as in other areas, believes that blanket disclosure authorizations or limitations should be actively discouraged.

One might think of incompatible uses and disclosures as "collateral uses." The question of whether a particular use or disclosure qualifies as a "collateral use" would then arise only after it has been established that the proposed use or disclosure was not a "routine use." The "collateral use" concept would also give the Congress a means of relating subsequently enacted disclosure statutes to the Privacy Act so that there will be no question about whether such disclosures are subject to the Act's requirements. As indicated earlier, and as discussed more thoroughly in Chapter 14, the Tax Reform Act of 1976 is a good example of how this would work.

Besides resolving the routine-use issue, there is also a need to take explicit account in the Act of agency disclosures concerning constituents of Members of Congress. In the early days of the Act's implementation, Congress had trouble obtaining information for its own use. Congressional caseworkers found that they were unable to get individually identifiable information from agencies when they called them on behalf of constituents. Agencies refused to give out information to Members of Congress unless they received prior consent from the individual, since Subsection 3(b)(9) only authorizes disclosures to congressional committees or to the House or Senate as a whole. Members of Congress felt this undermined their role as representatives of their constituents, and it was, in fact, an oversight in the drafting of the current law.

To solve this problem, the Office of Management and Budget

suggested to agencies that they establish disclosures to congressional offices as a routine use,[21] and this is now a government-wide practice. The Commission believes this practice should be allowed to continue but that a specific provision should be included in the Act to permit it, since the current solution puts a strain on the interpretation of the compatible-purpose test. Disclosure of a record should be allowed to a Member of Congress, but only in response to an inquiry from the Member made at the request of the individual involved, *provided the individual is a constituent of the Member*. Such a request could also be made by a relative or legal representative of the individual, if the individual is incapacitated or otherwise clearly unable to request the Member's assistance himself, *and the requestor or the individual is a constituent of the Member*.

Finally, some observers are of the view that, because the Privacy Act *limits* disclosures to the public, and the Freedom of Information Act *directs* disclosure to the public, there is an unresolvable conflict between the two laws. This view, however, is overly simplistic and, in the final analysis, an erroneous formulation of the relationship between the two statutes. The Privacy Act and the Freedom of Information Act mesh well. There are no statutory conflicts. Recent court decisions have also better defined the balances that must be struck between the competing interests. Nonetheless, there do appear to be some practical problems in the implementation of these two laws.

The "conditions of disclosure" section of the Privacy Act that establishes the ten categories of permissible external disclosures allows an agency to disclose a record about an individual to a member of the public who requests it, if the disclosure would be *required* under the Freedom of Information Act.[22] On the other hand, Subsection (b)(6) of the Freedom of Information Act allows an agency to refuse to disclose a record to a member of the public (i.e., anyone other than the individual to whom the record pertains) if it is a medical, personnel, or similar record, the disclosure of which would constitute a "clearly unwarranted invasion of personal privacy."[23]

To understand the meshing of these requirements, it is useful to consider first the situation prior to the passage of the Privacy Act. The exemptions on access to information in the Freedom of Information Act are discretionary, not mandatory. Thus, under the FOIA (prior to the passage of the Privacy Act), an agency *could* withhold information, the disclosure of which would, in the agency's opinion, constitute a "clearly unwarranted invasion of personal privacy," but the agency was not *required* to do so. Today, after passage of the Privacy Act, an agency is still *required*, by the Freedom of Information Act, to disclose information that would *not* constitute a "clearly unwarranted invasion of personal privacy," but now an agency no longer has the *discretion* to disclose information it believes would constitute such a clearly unwarranted invasion.

---

[21] Office of Management and Budget, *Implementation of the Privacy Act of 1974, Supplementary Guidance, Federal Register*, Volume 40, Number 234, December 4, 1975, pp. 56741-56743.
[22] 5 U.S.C. 552a(b)(2).
[23] 5 U.S.C. 552(b)(6).

A major problem in this area, however, is that agency operating personnel responsible for the day-to-day implementation of the two Acts have not been clearly enough apprised of how the laws mesh, of the applicable interpretations and court decisions, and of an agency's corresponding responsibilities under them. As a result, confusion, widely differing implementation, and occasional frustration of the intent of both laws have resulted. While determining what constitutes a "clearly unwarranted invasion of personal privacy" will always require a certain amount of interpretation, more can and should be done to assist and guide those who have to make such determinations in the course of their daily work. Indeed, one of the primary functions of the entity recommended by the Commission in Chapter 1 would be to assist agencies in developing policy to assist agency employees in making such determinations.

THE INFORMATION MANAGEMENT PRINCIPLE

The Privacy Act incorporates the principle that there are proper approaches to the management of information and that agencies should take affirmative steps to assure that their information management practices conform to a reasonable set of norms. Subsection 3(e)(1) of the Privacy Act requires an agency to:

> maintain in its records only such information about an individual as is relevant and necessary to accomplish a purpose of the agency required to be accomplished by statute or by executive order of the President; [5 U.S.C. 552a(e)(1)]

In addition, Subsection 3(e)(5) requires that:

> all records which are used by [an] agency in making any determination about an individual [must be maintained] with such accuracy, relevance, timeliness, and completeness as is reasonably necessary to assure fairness to the individual in the determination; [5 U.S.C. 552a(e)(5)]

Further, Subsection 3(e)(10) requires an agency to:

> establish appropriate administrative, technical, and physical safeguards to insure the security and confidentiality of records and to protect against any anticipated threats or hazards to their security or integrity which could result in substantial harm, embarassment, inconvenience or unfairness to any individual on whom information is maintained; [5 U.S.C. 552a(e)(10)]

In theory, these requirements, in combination with the requirements implementing the Individual Participation and Accountability Principles, keep the individual from having to bear the full burden of monitoring the content of records an agency maintains about him, and they also grant him recourse when he can prove damages as a consequence of willful behavior in violation of the Act's requirements.

The Act's several information management provisions have had a positive effect on agency conduct by focusing an agency's attention on its policies and practices relating to the collection, maintenance, use, and dissemination of records about individuals. In addition, the Act's requirement that information must be relevant and necessary to accomplish a mandatory agency purpose seems to have reduced slightly the amount of information agencies maintain.[24] Likewise, the "Privacy Act Statement" requirement[25] and the annual notice requirement[26] have somewhat limited the number of systems of records. But the requirement that information be kept accurate, timely, complete, and relevant[27] appears to have had little effect on reducing or altering the types of information maintained.

Most agencies, to the extent they have a position, stand by their prior record maintenance practices. They contend that they have always attempted to achieve accuracy, and that the terms "timely, complete, and relevant" are meaningful only in the context of a specific record or record-keeping situation—which is true. Nonetheless, interviews with operating personnel suggest that, although some accuracy standards have been tightened and retention periods for documents have been re-examined, agencies continue to maintain a substantial amount of information that is not as accurate, timely, complete, and relevant as it should be. The fact is that there are few if any formal mechanisms to review existing records and there is seldom, if ever, enough time to do so.

Because no specific, consistently applied criteria have been established for determining when an agency is in compliance with the Act's information management principles, they are not being adequately implemented. Within agencies, there has often been little or no compliance monitoring, as well as no office to which agency operating personnel can turn for guidance. Although efforts to train agency personnel are being made, awareness of the Act's requirements is much weaker than it should be—in all areas, not just information management.

Generally speaking, each agency or major agency component has a nucleus of employees who are well versed in matters relating to the Privacy Act, but many middle-level and lower-level operating personnel still do not know enough about the Act to allow them to carry out their responsibilities under it. For example, the Privacy Act is too often cited as the reason for withholding information from the public, when, in fact, such withholding is improper. Yet, without training, it appears that the one thing an agency employee is likely to know about the Act is that it contains criminal penalties for unauthorized disclosures, and thus that he should behave warily, particularly in responding to third-party Freedom of Information Act requests of the sort discussed in the preceding section on the Disclosure Limitation Principle.

The Commission has found that those agencies that have established formal, structured approaches and mechanisms to implement the Privacy Act are the most successful in their implementation of the Act. They have

---

[24] 5 U.S.C. 552a(e)(1).
[25] 5 U.S.C. 552a(e)(3).
[26] 5 U.S.C. 552a(e)(4).
[27] 5 U.S.C. 552a(e)(5).

provided the best training for their personnel, have issued detailed, consistent internal guidelines, and have devised procedures for auditing their own compliance with the Act. In addition, agencies with previous experience with issues relating to information policy have generally adapted more readily to the requirements of the Act than have agencies for which information policy issues can be considered a relatively new experience.

In order to provide for more effective implementation of the Act, the Commission believes that *the head of each agency should designate one official with authority to oversee implementation of the Act.* The official's responsibilities would include issuing instructions, guidelines, and standards, and making such determinations, as are necessary for the implementation of the Act. He would also be responsible for taking reasonable affirmative steps to assure that all agency employees and officials responsible for the collection, maintenance, use and dissemination of individually identifiable records are aware of the requirements of the Act.

The Commission believes that this is the minimum step necessary to ensure effective implementation of the Privacy Act. It parallels, and enhances, the approach taken by the agencies which are currently most successful in their implementation of the Act. Someone other than the individual record subject must be in a position to hold agency record keepers accountable; the Act's individual enforcement model is simply ineffective on a broad scale. Moreover, someone must have the authority to make decisions under the Act (e.g., to interpret the "reasonableness" and "compatible-purpose" tests); someone must be in a position, for example, to review a particular record-keeping practice or computer system design and assert, with authority, that it is reasonable. Obviously, such an approach addresses more than information management, and it can reasonably be expected that the designated agency official's activities would span the gamut of issues relating to the Act's implementation.

The Commission looks with favor on the Act's basic assumption that each agency is in the best position to judge what is best, reasonable, or appropriate for it. As indicated in the implementation in Chapter 1, it favors abandonment of the individual agency autonomy model of the Privacy Act only in instances where a clear societal interest is at stake or where it is necessary to establish an independent check on the agency.

Strengthening the individual agency enforcement mechanisms in the Privacy Act by the appointment of a Privacy Act officer in each agency is not intended to relieve the agency's operating personnel of their responsibilities under the Act. Rather, it is intended to make their jobs easier by providing a mechanism for guidance, instruction, and interpretation. A "reasonableness" test in the law is important for a court, but it does little to provide insight and guidance for those charged with the day-to-day implementation of the law.

By the same token, creation within an agency of an enforcement mechanism will serve to hold agency employees accountable in a way that no external entity or individual record subject can. This is as it should be, for ultimately the record-keeping agency must bear the burden for assuring that its record-keeping practices are fair.

While the Commission found that the Act's requirements regarding the necessity, accuracy, timeliness, completeness, and relevance of information in records *[5 U.S.C. 552a(e)(1); 5 U.S.C. 552a(e)(5)]* appear to have had little effect on agency practices, it suggests no specific changes in those requirements. Rather, it believes that by altering the implementation strategy and incentives for compliance along the lines it suggests, the goals of these requirements will be achieved.

The Commission has also found that the Act's requirements for propagation of corrections does not adequately assure that decisions are made on the basis of accurate, timely, complete and relevant information. Under the Act, for example, corrections do not have to be sent to prior internal agency recipients or to the sources of erroneous information. In addition, corrections of erroneous information initiated by the agency rather than by the individual, no matter how important, do not have to be propagated at all. As in other areas it has examined, the Commission believes that *corrections made by the record-keeping agency, as well as those made by the individual, should be propagated; and that, with some exceptions, corrections should be sent automatically to sources and prior internal and external recipients who provided or received the erroneous information, within a reasonable period of time prior to the making of the correction, as well as to any person (organization or individual) the individual specifically designates.*

The Commission believes that corrections of erroneous information by the agency, in accordance with the Act's requirements to "maintain all records which are used by the agency in making any determination about any individual with such accuracy, timeliness, completeness, and relevance as is reasonably necessary to assure fairness . . ." *[5 U.S.C. 552a(e)(5)]* should be automatically propagated if two conditions exist: first, if the correction could reasonably be expected to affect a determination about the individual by the source or a prior recipient of the erroneous information that provided or received the information, within a reasonable period of time prior to the making of the correction; and second, if the source or prior recipient could not reasonably be expected to otherwise become aware of the error. However, propagation should not be required to prior recipients who received the erroneous information under the Freedom of Information Act or to any source who, acting on his own behalf, rather than in an official capacity, provided the erroneous information to the agency.

This approach provides for propagation of corrections in cases in which they would make an important difference to the individual, while limiting to the greatest extent possible the burden on the agency. Relating the propagation requirement to the Act's fairness-in-decision-making provision is important because doing so excludes certain corrections, such as those made to keep an historical record accurate.

The Commission believes it appropriate to place the basic responsibility for propagating corrections on the agency because there is no other realistic way for the individual to protect himself against the spread of erroneous information about him through the Federal government. Information can flow so freely within and between agencies, and decision points are so diffuse or difficult to isolate, that linking a propagation of correction requirement to an adverse determination, or to an initiative by the individual, destroys its efficacy.

By including the requirement that corrected information be sent to internal agency recipients and to sources, the Commission is also responding to evidence that suggests that more harm or unfairness can result to an individual from inaccurate internal agency uses and disclosure than from external uses and disclosures, since the former are more frequent and less apt to be independently verified. The requirement that an agency notify any person specifically named by the individual to whom the information pertains, of any corrections made by either the individual or the agency, is included to allow for propagations that the individual determines are important to him.

The Privacy Act requirement to maintain an accounting of disclosures of information about an individual is widely regarded as the statute's single most burdensome provision. It also appears to be one which has engendered little interest on the part of the general public. There are three objectives which can be potentially served by this requirement: (1) providing the record subject with a listing of the uses and disclosures of a record about him; (2) facilitating the propagation of corrections; and (3) internal agency auditing and compliance monitoring. Currently, the emphasis is on the first objective. Consequently, the Act, with two exceptions, requires an accounting of disclosures to every recipient of information from a system of records, including the individual himself, and the accounting must include the date, nature, and purpose of the disclosure, as well as information identifying the recipient. This required accounting is frequently burdensome, as well as occasionally unnecessary, and has led a number of Federal agencies to construe it as inapplicable in cases in which the individual is the recipient of the information. Moreover, an accounting does not have to be kept of internal agency uses and disclosures, and these are frequently of the most interest to the individual and the most important insofar as the propagation of corrections is concerned.

The Commission believes that *the primary emphasis of the accounting of disclosure requirement should be on its utility in propagating corrections and that a "reasonableness" test should be established for determining the period of time for which an accounting must be kept, as well as for the amount of detail about each disclosure that must be kept.* In addition, the Commission believes that *when an individual so requests, an agency should make available to him its accounting of disclosures about him to (a) all prior recipients to whom it could reasonably be expected to propagate corrections, and (b) other recipients of which it could reasonably be expected to be aware.* This would allow an individual to see the information an agency must maintain on its disclosures about him for the purpose of propagating corrections automatically, but would not require a log in any greater detail than that. This requirement, coupled with the suggested propagation of corrections requirement, would, however, mean that an individual would be able to obtain an accounting of disclosures to *internal agency recipients* of information, as well as to external ones, since under the new approach all prior internal recipients will now receive corrections when they are propagated.

An agency should be left free to decide how long to keep an accounting of disclosures based on its determination of how long it needs to keep the information for propagating corrections, as well as the amount of detail that needs to be kept about each disclosure. In all accountings disclosed to the individual, however, an agency should take reasonable affirmative steps to inform the individual, in a form comprehensible to him, of the date, nature, and purpose of each disclosure and the name and address of the person or agency to whom the disclosure was made.

One principal difference between this approach and the Act's accounting requirement is that an accounting would not need to be kept for five years, or the life of the record, whichever is longer.[28] The Commission would also preserve the Act's use of the word "accounting" as opposed to "record," in order to allow for any scheme that enables the agency to reconstruct a list of past disclosures; that is, an explicit record or log entry need not be made for each disclosure. This is especially important in the case of frequent bulk transfers of data (when even the nature and purpose may only be generally known.)

The Privacy Act requirement that agencies establish safeguards to assure the security of individually identifiable records[29] has run the gamut from business-as-usual to extreme measures aimed at forestalling any conceivable risk, no matter how small its chance of occurring. On balance, however, the "safeguarding of information" requirement has resulted in minor modifications, and some strengthening, of agency data-security standards.

A recently publicized example of a government information system with inadequate security involved the computer and telecommunications system, SSADARS, which connects private insurance companies acting as Medicare intermediaries for the government with the Social Security Administration (SSA) data file. The Social Security Administration reported at the Commission hearings on Medical Records in July 1976 that its longstanding policy of protecting the confidentiality of individually identifiable information in its files had been adequately carried out in its administrative and technical safeguards. On October 23, 1976, however, SSA announced that it had discovered that it was mistaken in its belief that there was "no way the Medicare intermediaries and carriers can use their telecommunications system to gain access to the files used to administer"[30] other SSA programs. SSA staff found that the SSADARS terminals installed in the offices of two intermediaries could have been altered relatively easily, thereby permitting access to files other than the Medicare eligibility files the intermediaries needed to see. Although no actual access to other SSA program information is believed to have occurred, the technical safeguards to assure the confidentiality of information in the SSADARS system were not as effective as SSA had thought.

---

[28] 5 U.S.C. 552a(c)(2).

[29] 5 U.S.C. 552a(e)(10).

[30] Written statement of the Bureau of Health Insurance, Social Security Administration, *Medical Records*, Hearings before the Privacy Protection Study Commission, July 20, 1976, p. 11.

In spite of the Privacy Act, and assurance by the Social Security Administration that insurance company employees are subject to criminal sanctions as if they were Federal employees, SSA's Data Acquisition and Response System (SSADARS) has created a great deal of concern among the public and press. Inasmuch as the SSADARS system is a forerunner of the type of computer and telecommunications system which would be necessary for the administration of a broad-based Federal health-insurance program, it is imperative that Federal agencies take immediate affirmative measures to prevent information in such a system from becoming a source of unfairness to the individuals to whom it pertains. Therefore, the Commission recommends:

Recommendation (1):

That a Federal agency administering a health-insurance program which employs the services of a private health-insurance intermediary provide to the intermediary only that information necessary for the intermediary to carry out its responsibilities under the program.

Compliance with this recommendation would require that Federal agencies administering health-insurance plans develop administrative, physical, and technical safeguards as required by Section 3(e)(10) of the Privacy Act to assure the integrity of, and to prevent unauthorized access to, federally maintained data bases.

To correct the drafting deficiencies in the current safeguard requirement, as well as to make the obligation imposed by the requirement more realistic, the Commission believes that *an agency should be required to establish* reasonable *administrative, technical, and physical safeguards to assure the integrity, confidentiality, and security of its individually identifiable records so as to minimize the risk of substantial harm, embarrassment, inconvenience, or unfairness to the individual to whom the information pertains.* Such a change would be consistent with the Act's legislative history and should protect against the overreaction occasioned in some agencies by the current language of the Act which requires agencies to establish *appropriate* safeguards against *any anticipated threats or hazards.*

There is another related issue which also must be addressed. The Commission was specifically required by Subsection 5(c)(2)(B)(iv) of Public Law 93-579, to examine the issue of:

whether and how the standards for security and confidentiality of records under section 3(e)(10) of [the Privacy Act] should be applied when a record is disclosed to a person other than an agency.

The use of the word "standards" in this directive raises the question of the type of standards contemplated by the drafters. Within the Federal sector, the term standards has a precise meaning, and there are well defined procedures for establishing Federal Information Processing Standards (FIPS). A standard may be considered as synonymous with a "requirement," and, once established, is binding on Federal agencies. On the other hand, the term "guideline" may be equated with a "suggestion," and is not binding on Federal agencies. It seems clear from a reading of the Act and the legislative history, however, that the drafters did not intend the term standards, as used in Subsection 5(c)(2)(B)(iv), to be interpreted precisely, but rather to be interpreted more broadly as meaning "general criteria" for the establishment of security and confidentiality safeguards. Regardless of the meaning intended, however, the conclusion of the Commission remains the same.

The Commission's inquiry has shown that there are currently no standards, in the strict sense of the word, for security and confidentiality at the Federal level. Guidelines have been issued by the National Bureau of Standards, but their specificity and hence their utility is uneven. FIPS Publication No. 31,[31] which establishes guidelines for automatic data processing physical security and risk management, is much more detailed and specific than FIPS Publication No. 41,[32] which is intended to establish computer security guidelines for implementing the Privacy Act of 1974. As already noted, the Commission's assessment of the Federal experience indicates that agency practice in response to the safeguard requirement in Subsection 3(e)(10) is extremely varied, ranging from no response whatsoever to what could be termed technological overkill. At the Federal level, in other words, there are, at best, limited standards, guidelines, or general criteria for safeguards which are susceptible to extension to any non-Federal agency recipient of information subject to the Privacy Act. Thus, in response to the mandate given it in Subsection 5(c)(2)(B)(iv), the Commission recommends:

Recommendation (2):

That there should be a continued examination of the standards, guidelines, and general criteria for safeguards within the Federal government, but there should not be a general extension of any Federal standards, guidelines, or general criteria for safeguards for security and confidentiality of records when a record is disclosed to a person other than an agency, except as specifically provided in other recommendations of the Commission.

THE ACCOUNTABILITY PRINCIPLE

The eighth principle of the Privacy Act holds that an institution should be accountable for its personal-data record-keeping policies and practices, or, more specifically, for adherence to the other seven information policy principles. Under the Privacy Act, a Federal agency can be held accountable for its record-keeping policies and practices in several ways. The individual can hold the agency accountable through exercise of his rights to see, copy, and challenge the contents of a record about himself, to review an

---

[31] National Bureau of Standards, *Guidelines for Automatic Data Processing Physical Security and Risk Management,* June, 1974.

[32] National Bureau of Standards, *Computer Security Guidelines for Implementing the Privacy Act,* May 30, 1975.

agency's accounting of disclosures made of a record about him, and to sue for any damages he incurs as a consequence of agency misconduct. In addition, agency employees are subject to criminal sanctions for particular violations of the law's requirements.[33]

The access, correction, and amendment procedures have been discussed. They appear to work reasonably well, although they have not been widely used. As previously noted, the agencies regard the Act's accounting of disclosures requirement as the most burdensome of the Act's provisions. It represents 26 percent of the operating costs of the Act[34] and requires extra effort by agency employees on an almost daily basis. The Social Security Administration, which keeps its accounting of disclosures manually, has stated that to perform the accounting effectively it would have to totally redesign its computer system. In addition, few individuals have asked for an accounting of the disclosures made of a record about them, perhaps because they do not know they have a right to do so. Even when an individual does ask, however, he will not learn about internal agency disclosures, as no accounting need be kept of them.

The civil remedies provided by the Act are similarly ineffective from the individual's point of view. The vast number of systems involved,[35] the need to establish willful or intentional behavior on the part of the agency, and the cost and time involved in bringing a law suit, often make enforcement by the individual impractical. Moreover, an individual must show actual injury in all cases except the ones that can be brought to force an agency to allow an individual to see and copy, or correct or amend, a record.

The criminal penalties also require a showing of willfulness and apply only to unauthorized disclosures, failures to publish annual system notices, and obtaining a record from an agency under false pretenses. The circumstances in which an individual can bring suit, his possible reward for doing so, and the instances in which a court can order an agency into compliance with the Act are all too limited to provide an effective accountability mechanism. Consistent with its recommendations in other areas, the Commission believes that *a suit should be permitted to force compliance with the requirements of the Act absent a demonstration of injury to, or adverse effect on, the individual and that a court should be able to order an agency to comply.*

In many cases, it is simply too difficult to show injury or adverse effect as a result of a violation of the Privacy Act. In the case of a violation of the notice requirements, for example, such a showing is most likely impossible. Even in the case of inaccurate information, it can be difficult to demonstrate actual injury. Hence, the Commission believes an individual should be granted standing without the requirement to show injury. While it could be argued that this will encourage frivolous law suits, experience to date indicates that it is not likely to do so. Moreover, this approach should

---

[33] 5 U.S.C. 552a(i).

[34] Letter from Hon. Bert Lance to Senator Ribicoff, *op. cit.*

[35] As of December 21, 1975, there were 6,723 systems of records of varying size containing 3.8 billion records about individuals which had been declared.

increase agency accountability and provide agencies with increased incentives to comply with the Act in order to avoid law suits by individuals.

Under the Privacy Act contractors and grantees are not directly liable for violations (although they are subject to the Act's criminal penalties) and the government may indemnify them for any civil liability resulting from their performance of a contract. This defeats the intent of the Act. If the Act's protections are so important that the government is waiving its sovereign immunity and thus subjecting itself to civil liability, it would seem reasonable for the same standard to apply to contractors and discretionary grantees, as discussed earlier. Therefore, the Commission believes that *contractors and grantees which fall within the scope of the Act should be made civilly liable under the Act in the same manner that the government makes itself civilly liable; and no official or employee of any Federal agency should include or authorize to be included in any contract or grant any provisions indemnifying the contractor or grantee from civil liabilities under the Act.*

In a related area, the Commission's mandate specifically required an examination of "whether the Federal government should be liable for general damages incurred by an individual" when an agency violates his rights under the Act. *[Section 5(c)(2)(B)(iii) of Public Law 93-579]* This required consideration of whether the current liability standard in the statute which limits recovery to "actual damages" should be broadened. To reach a judgment on the appropriate recovery standard, the Commission needed to answer two questions: (1) what the definitions of actual and general damages are or ought to be; and, (2) what the costs and benefits of each would be were it to be the Act's standard for recovery against the government.

Traditionally, damages have been divided into two classifications, general and special. Compensation for *any* injury done to an individual is available under a claim of general damages. An individual can make claims for losses due to pain and suffering, for example, even though it is impossible to fix a precise dollar value to such an injury. Special damages, on the other hand, only compensate for injury that has caused clear economic loss to the individual. The Commission has found that there is no generally accepted definition of "actual damages" in American law, but the Commission has concluded that, within the context of the Act, the term was intended as a synonym for special damages as that term is used in defamation cases. For that reason, the Commission believes the phrase "actual damages" should be discarded in favor of the more traditional and clearer term, special damages.

In addition, special damages in defamation cases are more limited than in other situations; the injuries clearly covered by them are loss of *specific* business, employment, or promotion opportunities, or other tangible pecuniary benefits. Injuries not provided for are those which may be labeled intangible: namely, loss of reputation, chilling of constitutional rights, or mental suffering (where unaccompanied by other secondary consequences).

The legislative history and language of the Act suggest that Congress meant to restrict recovery to specific pecuniary losses until the Commission could weigh the propriety of extending the standard of recovery. It has determined that the arguments in favor of extending recovery to general damages, within dollar limits, appear stronger than the arguments against such extension.

The restriction on recovery articulated in the "actual damage" standard of the Privacy Act reflects the ancient limitation on governmental liability embodied in the principle of sovereign immunity. Arguments in support of this limitation of liability focus primarily on the need to protect the public purse and the problems involved in making the government fully responsible for the vast scope of its operations, which it has no practical means of controlling. One set of counter-arguments to this position derives from notions of fairness, which require both that wrongdoers be responsible for their wrongdoing and that those who benefit from governmental activity be asked to pay the price of their enjoyment, instead of letting that cost fall wholly on the small group of injured parties. Another counter-argument derives from basic notions of social utility. If the costs of government information practices are borne by the government, it is in a better position to decide whether the benefits of the activity outweigh their costs. In other words, restricting liability only restricts the incentive for government to reform its practices.

If the rights and interests established by the Privacy Act are worthy of protection, then recovery for intangible injuries such as pain and suffering, loss of reputation, or the chilling effect on constitutional rights, is a part of that protection. There is evidence for this proposition both in the cases which have already been brought under the Act and in common law privacy cases. Thus, to protect individuals under the Privacy Act more fairly and effectively, while ensuring that recovery does not become too burdensome, and to clarify the meaning of the Act, the Commission recommends:

Recommendation (3):

That the Privacy Act of 1974 permit the recovery of special and general damages sustained by an individual as a result of a violation of the Act, but in no case should a person entitled to recovery receive less than the sum of $1,000 or more than the sum of $10,000 for general damages in excess of the dollar amount of any special damages.

In addition to the individual's enforcement opportunities and the modest oversight role assigned to the Office of Management and Budget (OMB) *[Section 6 of Public Law 93-579]*, the Act also requires that reports on new or materially altered record systems be sent to OMB and both Houses of Congress *[5 U.S.C. 552a(o)]*, and to the Privacy Protection Study Commission. *[Section 5(e)(2)(A) of Public Law 93-579]* None of these bodies, however, has had the staff nor the consolidated expertise necessary to evaluate each report submitted. Furthermore, there is no agreement on how to assess the potential impact of a proposed system change along the lines called for in the Act, that is:

the probable or potential effect . . . on the privacy and other personal or property rights of individuals or the disclosure of information relating to such individuals, and its effect on the preservation of the constitutional principles of federalism and separation of powers. *[5 U.S.C. 552a(o)]*

Currently, although this requirement has had the healthy effect of forcing agencies to examine the need for, and the details of, the particular system, the kind of information needed to evaluate it is not always supplied nor is it always presented in enough detail to permit an in-depth and independent evaluation of the system in question.

Given this weak enforcement framework and the flexibility of interpretation many provisions of the Act allow, there are few incentives for more than minimal compliance with most of its provisions. For example, there is a universal lack of post-award monitoring of contractor performance; and as previously noted, many agencies have not established any effective internal compliance monitoring procedure. This can be partly explained by the fact that Congress appropriated no additional funds for Privacy Act implementation. While many of the requirements of the Act represent procedures or steps that the agencies should have been following anyway, there is still cost associated with them.[36] In addition, attention to information policy issues is not usually a priority concern of agency personnel. While many employees view the Privacy Act and the issues it raises as important, a sizeable number still see the Act as a nuisance and an impediment to the performance of their agency's missions and functions.

OTHER POLICY ISSUES TO BE ADDRESSED

There are some important information policy issues the Act either ignores or does not address adequately. For example, in almost any discussion of the intent of the Privacy Act, mention is made of limiting the amount of information agencies actually collect about individuals. There is a commonly held belief, evident in the Act's legislative history and voiced by numerous agency personnel, that the Act was intended to reduce the amount of information the Federal government collects about individuals. Yet the fact of the matter is that the Act only establishes the outer boundaries of legitimate government inquiry, and it does so in a way that reflects rather closely the boundaries that had grown up prior to the Act's passage. Similarly, as the discussion of the routine-use provision indicated, transfers of information among agencies have only been slightly reduced as a result of the Act's passage.

While the Section 7 proscription against compelling an individual to divulge his Social Security number, unless specifically required by law to do so, has induced minimal change in agency practice, agencies commonly rely on Executive Order 9397,[37] issued in 1943, when they can find no other authority for demanding the Social Security number. Additionally, once the

---

[36] Letter from Hon. Bert Lance to Senator Ribicoff, *op. cit.*

[37] *Federal Register*, Volume 8, Number 237, November 30, 1943. This order provides that whenever a head of a Federal agency "finds it advisable to establish a new system of permanent

Social Security number is collected, its use is regulated only by the other disclosure provisions of the Privacy Act or whatever other confidentiality statutes govern agency disclosures of other types of personal information.

The Privacy Act grew out of nearly a decade of congressional examination of information systems in the Executive branch, and it followed closely on the heels of the record-keeping abuses and invasions of personal privacy associated with the Watergate affair. It was passed partially as a protection against premeditated abuses of Federal agency records but, more importantly, in recognition of the fact that even normal uses of a record about an individual can have harmful consequences for him and that this potential harm can be greatly magnified by the use of emerging computer and telecommunications technology. Despite these antecedents, however, there is little in the Privacy Act to prevent premeditated abuses of power through the misuse of recorded information, particularly where internal agency uses are concerned. Although the individual's position in relation to an agency is much stronger as a result of the Act, the safeguard provisions have not been implemented in a way that adequately deters abuse by agency personnel, especially in view of the lack of internal agency compliance monitoring or auditing.

Moreover, the problems perceived by the Congress at the time of the Act's passage have turned out to be more complex than anticipated, and by and large they are independent of the problem of premeditated abuse. Actual or potential information abuses are much more likely to result from continuing growth in the government's appetite for information about individuals and in the use of that information for growing numbers and types of purposes. *The real danger is the gradual erosion of individual liberties through the automation, integration, and interconnection of many small, separate record-keeping systems, each of which alone may seem innocuous, even benevolent, and wholly justifiable.* Dramatic developments in computer and communications technology, which both facilitate record-keeping functions previously performed manually and provide the impetus and means to devise new ones, can only exacerbate this problem.

The Act's failure to attend to the impact of technological advances on individual liberties and personal privacy is compounded by the manual, or file-cabinet, view of record keeping that underlies it. As indicated early in this chapter, reliance on a traditional view of individual identifiers and their role in retrieving records serves to exclude certain types or forms of individually identifiable records from the Act's coverage. Because a record retrieved by attribute or characteristic, as opposed to identifier, does not fall within the definition of a "record" maintained in a "system of records," the Act's notice access, correction, and accountability requirements do not apply to it.

In addition, there is no compatible-purpose test in the Act for internal agency uses of records; hence, such uses are unregulated. One exception is

account numbers pertaining to individual persons, [he] shall utilize exclusively the Social Security Act account numbers . . ." This was ordered "in the interest of economy and orderly administration." (See Chapter 16 for a more detailed discussion of this topic.)

the case in which there is a confidentiality statute governing the uses or disclosures of certain types of records of a particular component of an agency. Section 1106 of the Social Security Act was cited earlier as one such example. Unfortunately, however, the assortment of such confidentiality statutes is incomplete and uncoordinated.

Furthermore, it is probable, again because of technological advances, growth in government programs, and pressures to reduce paperwork, that the prediction of significant new uses of information will become even more difficult—and, hence, more difficult to deal with as a matter of public policy. A compromise which would achieve a reasonable balance between individual knowledge and agency efficiency concerns would seem to be in order.

The increased demand for information is changing the relationship between the record keeper and the record subject, as well as the character of the record-keeping relationship itself. As the Federal government has become increasingly involved in providing services and financial assistance, there have been increased pressures to ensure that all recipients are, in fact, eligible. This has led agencies into areas normally associated with civil or criminal law enforcement functions. In assessing this phenomenon, it must be remembered that much of what the agencies do in the area of record keeping and investigating is in response to direct or perceived mandates from the Legislative branch; in order to accomplish the tasks set for them, agencies need enforcement units with investigative capabilities. The recent creation of an office to investigate fraud and abuse in the Medicaid program provides an example of a unit which developed as a response to congressional direction.

Parallel to this increasing role for Federal agencies in law enforcement and investigative activities, the Federal government has begun to develop sophisticated criminal justice information systems, and to offer the services of those systems, as well as related technical and financial assistance, to State and local law enforcement agencies. While a number of questions need to be resolved in regard to this use of technologically sophisticated information systems by Federal or State law enforcement and investigative agencies, three problems are particularly pertinent to the protection of personal privacy.

The first emerges from even the briefest consideration of how information enters criminal justice information systems and how it is used. As such systems are currently structured, there is little control over the accuracy and reliability of information when it passes from one investigative agency to another. In particular, there is minimal control over the accuracy of criminal history information—often the most revealing and potentially the most damaging recorded information routinely exchanged by law enforcement agencies. The criminal history files of the FBI's Identification Division illustrate the inability of a central record keeper to control the quality of the information in its records, since by and large the central record keeper has little enforceable authority over other agencies reporting to it. [See *Menard v. Saxbe*, 498 F.2d 1017 (D.C. Cir. 1974)] Further, the information in such systems is ordinarily derivative; in other words, the record maintained in an automated system is often copied from another record which in turn may be a copy of a third. The chances for error in transferring information from one record to another are great, particularly when the first transfer is from a paper record. These vulnerabilities to error create a system with inherent accuracy and reliability problems, but one which nonetheless is used to make decisions that affect individuals powerfully and immediately.

The second problem generated by these new systems grows out of the current pattern of unrestricted information flows between law enforcement and investigative agencies at all levels of government. Those flows, formal and informal, are usually justifiable, but they are also easily amenable to abuse. Easier access to information by agents within a unit, and greater facility to exchange information between units, will increase the potential for abuse and thus for the misapplications of police powers of the sort Americans experienced in the late 1960's and early 1970's. Moreover, the unsupervised information flows that facilitated improper domestic intelligence activities, and the government operations based on them, are still without oversight mechanisms to assure their accountability. As the deployment of technology increases the ease with which current information flows can be abused, the Congress should work rapidly to discover the extent and patterns of such flows and to develop statutorily mandated protections against their abuse.

The final problem that needs resolution results from Federal agencies providing computer-communications services to State and local law enforcement agencies. At one level, it is a classic problem of federalism, of the proper role of the central government in furnishing local services; at another level, however, it is a problem posed by one agency operating the information services on which other agencies depend and thus being able, at least potentially, to control the format of the other agencies' records and to use those records for its own purposes. Some of the consequences of a Federal law enforcement agency controlling the flow of State and local criminal justice information are illustrated in the continuing controversy over whether the Federal Bureau of Investigation should supply a message-switching, or interstate data communications, service through its National Crime Information Center (NCIC).

As the operator of NCIC, the FBI would exercise central control over, and have the ability to reach into, any State or local records that were directly hooked into the system, as well as the ability to monitor the flow of information through the system. While such an ability is only a potential, the transformation of that potential into an actuality has occurred before,[38] and would permit the agency controlling the system to collect and use information to which it might not be legitimately entitled. For example,

---

[38] Between April 1971 and February 1974 the FBI monitored requests for information in the NCIC made by State and local government agencies. The monitoring was conducted on behalf of the Department of Justice and other agencies of the Federal Government. The monitoring involved flagging the names of persons in whom the Federal agencies had some interest, including 4,700 who had no criminal record. In other words, any inquiry by a State or local government agency that included a flagged name was automatically noted and recorded for later examination by Federal agents. See letter of July 18, 1975, from Hon. John V. Tunney,

intelligence might be gathered on individuals whom the Administration in power considered politically undesirable, and be gathered by more sophisticated and comprehensive methods than those employed by the infamous Special Services Staff of the Internal Revenue Service.

Given the particularly damaging character of the information involved and the potential for misuse, any long-range decision to permit Federal agencies to provide such services should be made only if there is no alternative. Further, the Commission believes that the decision to permit Federal agency operation of such services ought to be made through the legislative process, not unilaterally by the Executive branch of government.

Perhaps the most significant finding in the Commission's assessment of the Privacy Act arises from its examination of the vehicles available for evaluating and assessing existing record systems, new systems, and agency practices and procedures. Quite simply, there is no vehicle for answering the question: "Should a particular record-keeping policy, practice, or system exist at all?" While the Act takes an important step in establishing a framework by which an individual may obtain and question the contents of his record, it does not purport to establish ethical standards or set limits to the collection or use of certain types of information. Without such standards, however, the principal threat of proliferating records systems is not addressed. Nowhere, other than in the ineffective section requiring the preparation and review of new system notices, does the Act address the question of who is to decide what and how information should be collected, and how it may be used. To deal with this situation, the Congress and the Executive Branch will have to take action.

U.S. Senator, to Hon. Harold Tyler, Deputy U.S. Attorney General; letter of August 29, 1975, from Hon. Harold Tyler to Hon. John V. Tunney.

Chapter 14

The Relationship Between Citizen and Government: The Citizen as Taxpayer

In 1974, the Congress made all Federal agencies subject to a broad set of restrictions regarding the uses and disclosures that can be made of records they maintain about individuals. Section 3(b) of the Privacy Act of 1974 permits a Federal agency to disclose information about an individual without his consent only if one of eleven conditions is met.[2] As the Commission has pointed out in Chapter 13, however, it believes that no one set of rules applicable to all Federal agencies can suffice in all instances. Effective disclosure policy must make special provision for the confidentiality of the records of particular Federal agencies :hrough enactment of statutes that set disclosure policy for a single agency, or for the records generated in a particular type of relationship an individual may have with one or more agencies. Records that contain a great amount of detail about individuals or that must be held in strict confidence if individuals are to be induced to participate in a government undertaking deserve special attention in this regard.

The Internal Revenue Service and the records it maintains about taxpayers represent such a special case. Although the taxpayer volunteers most of the information the IRS needs, his disclosures to it cannot be considered voluntary because the threat of criminal penalties for failure to disclose always exists. The fact that tax collection is essential to government justifies an extraordinary intrusion on personal privacy by the IRS, but it is also the reason why extraordinary precautions must be taken against misuse of the information the Service collects from and about taxpayers.

In June 1976, the Commission recommended the enactment of a

---

[2] These conditions are met when a disclosure is: (1) to officers and employees of the agency [maintaining the record] on a "need to know" basis; (2) required under the Freedom of Information Act; (3) for a "routine use" [a "use of the record for a purpose compatible with the purpose for which it was collected"]; (4) to the Bureau of the Census, for activities related to censuses and surveys; (5) to recipients who have provided assurance that the record will be used solely as a statistical research or reporting record, and the record is transferred in other than individually identifiable form; (6) to the National Archives; (7) to a Federal, State, or local agency for use in an authorized law enforcement activity; (8) to a person pursuant to a showing of compelling circumstances affecting the health or safety of an individual; (9) to a committee of Congress in connection with matters within its jurisdiction; (10) to the Comptroller General; and (11) pursuant to the order of a court of competent jursidiction.

Federal statute more stringent with respect to disclosures of records made by the IRS than either the Privacy Act of 1974 or the confidentiality provisions of the Internal Revenue Code (IRC) then in force. The recommended statute would constitute the Service's sole authority to disclose its records about individuals to other Federal agencies and to agencies of State government. The Congress enacted a statute similar in many respects to the one recommended by the Commission as Section 1202 of the Tax Reform Act of 1976 [P.L. 94-455].

The Commission believes that its 1976 recommendations for IRS disclosure policy can serve as an example of the kind of particularized disclosure statutes the Congress should enact for certain types of government records that deserve or require special confidentiality protections. The Commission also believes that the rationale for its 1976 IRS recommendations which is articulated here and in an appendix volume on Federal tax return confidentiality, exemplifies the kind of considerations that should be taken into account in enacting any Federal confidentiality statute. Although the Congress, in enacting Section 1202 of the Tax Reform Act, did not reach the same conclusions as the Commission in every detail, the Commission approves without reservation the process by which the disclosure was formulated—enactment of a statute by the Congress with opportunities for public comment and participation in its deliberations.

THE PRIVACY COMMISSION MANDATE

The Privacy Act of 1974 required the Privacy Protection Study Commission to report to the President and the Congress on

> whether the Internal Revenue Service should be prohibited from transferring individually identifiable data to other [Federal] agencies and to agencies of State governments. [Subsection 5(c)(2)(B)(ii) of P.L. 93-579]

After conducting public hearings and a review of policies and practices regarding Federal tax return confidentiality, the Commission, as noted above, made an interim report to the President and to the Congress in June 1976 in which it recommended special constraints on IRS disclosure of individually identifiable data to other Federal agencies and to State and local government agencies.

The Commission believes that to satisfy its statutory obligation to reflect and report on questions of Federal tax return confidentiality it must take account of the 1976 changes in the law governing disclosure of tax returns and related information and consider the need for further recommendations. Accordingly, this chapter compares the Commission's earlier recommendations with the modifications contained in the Tax Reform Act of 1976.

In addition, the Commission has reconsidered two interim recommendations that were not intended to be final. One concerned the Department of Health, Education, and Welfare's Parent Locator Service (PLS), which had begun to operate only a short time before the Commission's interim report was released. The Commission reserved judgment on IRS disclosures to the PLS until it could see how the PLS would perform. The other concerned information about a taxpayer provided to the IRS by "third-party sources" (i.e., persons other than the taxpayer himself). The issue demanding resolution was whether the same disclosure standards should apply to third-party source information as to information provided by a taxpayer about himself. To help answer that question, the IRS agreed to monitor disclosures of both taxpayer-supplied and third-party source data for a three-month period beginning April 1, 1976. The Commission's interim report was completed before the Commission had the results of this monitoring, so a final judgment on the third-party source issue was deferred.

In considering its recommendations for further legislative change, this chapter also takes note of criticisms made by Federal agencies of the 1976 restrictions on the disclosure of taxpayer data for non-tax purposes.

THE IRS DISCLOSURE PROBLEM

The reasons for congressional and public concern about the widespread use of Federal tax information by government agencies other than the IRS, and for purposes unrelated to tax administration, have been well documented.[3] While the Congress long ago recognized the sensitivity of information obtained and retained for purposes of Federal tax administration, it had nonetheless, in 1910, designated tax returns as "public records" and given to the President and the Secretary of the Treasury broad discretion in making them available to other agencies and persons.

The disclosure to other government agencies of information about individual taxpayers has increased steadily since 1910. In most instances, new uses of such information were authorized administratively and without any real opportunity for public debate. Federal and State agency recipients of the information met criticisms of their uses of it by asserting that the information was essential to the performance of their particular government functions. In the face of such pleas, it was difficult for IRS administrators to deny them access, and in a substantial number of cases they did not.

The abuses that inevitably resulted were from time to time brought to the attention of the Congress and the public, sometimes dramatically. The Nixon Administration allegedly used tax returns to harass its political adversaries, and an announcement early in the 1970's that information about individual taxpayers would be made available to the Department of Agriculture to aid in statistical analysis aroused intense controversy. Allegations that special powers of the Internal Revenue Service were being misused to collect information for purposes well beyond tax administration but related to other law enforcement activities eventually led to a series of Congressional hearings on the propriety of various uses of tax information.[4] They led in turn to the mandate in the Privacy Act of 1974 given the

[3] See, e.g., Administrative Conference of the United States, *Report on Administrative Procedures of the Internal Revenue Service,* Senate Document 94-266 (October 1975) at pages 821 et seq.
[4] See, for example, *Federal Tax Return Privacy,* Hearings before the Subcommittee on

Commission and, two years later, to the restrictions embodied in the Tax Reform Act of 1976.

THE RATIONALE FOR THE COMMISSION'S RECOMMENDATIONS

Federal tax administration depends in large measure on the power of government to compel its citizens to disclose information about themselves, and the existence of special investigative authority. The Commission's mandate did not require it to study the administrative structure of tax administration in detail, although in sections of Chapter 9 the Commission has in a general way examined issues of fairness arising in that context.

Some argue that because the IRS uses government resources to collect tax information, such information should be treated as a generalized governmental asset, and that such generalized use does not constitute a material violation of any interest of the taxpayer because the information belongs to the Federal government. The only disclosure constraint needed, say the proponents of this view, is to assure that the information is used only in pursuit of legitimate government objectives.

The Commission emphatically rejects these arguments for two reasons. First, the individual taxpayer is inherently at a disadvantage vis-a-vis a government agency that has access to IRS information about him because the IRS has the threat of serious punishment to compel the disclosure of information the individual would otherwise not divulge. That fact alone, in the Commission's view, argues in general for carefully controlled dissemination of IRS data on individual taxpayers and in most cases for no dissemination. It is understandable that other agencies with important responsibilities want to use information the IRS has authority to collect but they have not, in fact, been vested with the IRS's authority to compel such information from the taxpayer.

Second, the Commission believes that the effectiveness of this country's tax system depends on the confidentiality of tax returns and related information. While no one has tried to measure how the knowledge that other Federal and State agencies can inspect tax returns affects an individual taxpayer, the Commission believes that widespread use of the information a taxpayer provides to the IRS for purposes wholly unrelated to tax administration cannot help but diminish the taxpayer's disposition to cooperate with the IRS voluntarily. This is not to say that the taxpayer will decline to cooperate, but that his incentive to do so may be weakened. Such a tendency in itself creates a potentially serious threat to the effectiveness of the Federal tax system.

The Commission believes that authorizing the IRS to disclose individually identifiable tax information to another agency for a purpose unrelated to the

Administration of the Internal Revenue Code of the Committee on Finance, U.S. Senate, 94th Congress, 1st Session; *Proposals for Change in the Administration of the Internal Revenue Laws,* Hearings before the Oversight Subcommittee of the Ways and Means Committee, U. S. House of Representatives, 94th Congress, 1st Session; *IRS Disclosure,* Hearings before the Subcommittee on Administrative Practice and Procedure of the Committee on the Judiciary, U. S. Senate, 93d Congress, 1st Session.

administration of a Federal tax law is seldom defensible unless the Congress would be willing in principle to compel individuals to disclose the same information directly to the agency requesting it from the IRS. Even then, however, the agency seeking the information should still have to demonstrate a compelling societal need that disclosure of tax information to it by the IRS would fulfill.

SCOPE OF THE COMMISSION'S RECOMMENDATIONS

The Commission restricted the scope of its study to individually identifiable information about individuals. The decision is consistent with the scope of the Privacy Act and its mandate to the Commission. The Commission did not inquire into issues regarding disclosure of IRS information about corporations and other business entities. While the recommendations in this chapter do not apply to disclosure of these other kinds of information, they do apply to the *individually identifiable* data about individuals in the tax returns of business entities.

As prescribed by the Privacy Act, the Commission further restricted its study of IRS disclosure to disclosures to agencies of Federal and State government. It did not inquire into the propriety of IRS disclosures to the President and to the Congress, nor has it formulated standards for determining how much access to tax information the public should have. Nonetheless, the Commission notes with approval that the Tax Reform Act of 1976 creates statutory limitations on the disclosure of individually identifiable tax information to members of the public *[Section 6103(e) of the I.R.C.]*, to Committees of Congress *[Section 6103(f) of the I.R.C.]*, and to the President and White House staff *[Section 6103(g) of the I.R.C.]*.

GENERAL RECOMMENDATIONS

The Commission's interim report proposed general recommendations regarding the manner in which disclosures of tax information without individual consent should be authorized. The general recommendations and the rationale for them are set forth in the Commission's June 1976 interim report. In brief, the Commission recommended:

(1) that no disclosure of individually identifiable data by the Internal Revenue Service be permitted unless the individual to whom the information pertains has consented to such disclosure in writing or unless the disclosure is specifically authorized by Federal statute;

(2) that the Congress itself specify by statute the categories of tax information the IRS can disclose and the purposes for which the information can be used, rather than delegate general discretionary authority in this matter to the Commissioner of Internal Revenue or any other representative of the Executive Branch;

(3) that the IRS be prohibited from disclosing any more individually identifiable taxpayer information than is necessary to

accomplish the purpose for which the disclosure has been authorized, and that the IRS adopt administrative procedures to facilitate public scrutiny of its compliance with this requirement; and

(4)   that recipients of tax information from the Internal Revenue Service be prohibited from redisclosing it without the written consent of the taxpayer, unless the redisclosure is specifically authorized by Federal statute.

The Tax Reform Act of 1976 is consistent in the main with the Commission's general recommendations. Although tax returns were designated as public records prior to the 1976 legislation, Section 6103(a)(1) of the Internal Revenue Code (IRC) provided for inspection of them " . . . only upon order of the President and under rules and regulations prescribed by the Secretary [of the Treasury] or his delegate and approved by the President." While this language suggested that disclosure should be narrowly restricted, in practice tax return data were disseminated widely throughout the Federal government and to State and local government officials.

The Tax Reform Act of 1976 substantially modified this section of the Internal Revenue Code. The general rule, now established by Section 6103(a) of the Code, is that "Returns and return information shall be *confidential*." (emphasis added) While the Internal Revenue Code, as modified by the Tax Reform Act, authorizes certain disclosures that are not consistent with the Commission's specific recommendations, the Commission regards the substitution of the basic rule of confidentiality for the prior assumption that tax records are public records as a major step forward in controlling the disclosure of tax information.

In enacting the 1976 law, Congress also undertook direct responsibility for determining which disclosures should be permissible. Under prior law, authority to determine the propriety of intragovernmental disclosures was delegated to the Executive branch. In practice, IRS officials had found it hard to deny other agencies and departments access to tax information if it was argued forcefully that such information was essential to the fulfillment of statutory responsibilities. The revised Section 6103 makes confidential treatment mandatory unless disclosure is specifically authorized by Federal statute.

Having established the principle of confidentiality, the Congress, in the Tax Reform Act, listed categories of permissible disclosures of tax information. While the Commissioner of Internal Revenue and the Secretary of the Treasury bear major responsibilites for assuring compliance with the law, and for organizing the administration of permissible disclosures, the Executive branch now has no discretion to permit disclosures of individually identifiable tax information in ways not specifically authorized by the Congress in the Internal Revenue Code. The fact that future disclosures must be specifically authorized by statutory directive provides, in the Commission's view, a valuable check on access to tax information for purposes unrelated to the collection of revenue undertakings.

The revised Section 6103 also limits redisclosure, as the Commission had recommended. It now provides that, except as authorized by statute:

(1)   no officer or employee of the United States;
(2)   no officer or employee of any State or of any local child support enforcement agency who has or had access to returns or return information under this section; and
(3)   no other person (or officer or employee thereof) who has or had access to returns or return information . . . shall disclose any returns or return information obtained by him in any manner . . . *[Section 6103(a) of the I.R.C., as amended by the Tax Reform Act of 1976.]*

For the first time, the other government agencies that obtain tax information from the IRS are in all cases expressly prohibited by statute from redisclosing it for purposes unrelated to the purpose for which the information was acquired.

The 1976 legislation also took heed of the Commission's recommendation that the IRS be prohibited from ever disclosing any more individually identifiable tax information than is necessary to advance the government objective for which disclosure has been authorized. Nonetheless, there are instances in which the statutory authorizations for disclosure contained in the Tax Reform Act are overly broad in describing the types of information that may be disclosed and the purposes for which the information may be used. These will be discussed below. The Commission strongly reaffirms its commitment to the principle of "limited disclosure" and urges the Internal Revenue Service to respect that principle in implementing the 1976 law.

SPECIFIC RECOMMENDATIONS

DISCLOSURE FOR PURPOSES RELATED TO FEDERAL TAX ADMINISTRATION

The Commission recognizes that almost every use of tax data in any aspect of tax administration is clearly compatible with the purpose for which the information was collected and with the legitimate expectations of the taxpayer. Accordingly, it recommended in 1976 that the IRS be authorized by statute to disclose tax data " . . . to the Department of Justice for use in investigations and prosecutions of violations of tax laws, provided that the information pertains to a party to the actual or anticipated litigation."

On this point, the Tax Reform Act of 1976 provides that:

A return or return information shall be open to inspection by or disclosure to attorneys of the Department of Justice (including United States attorneys) personally and directly engaged in, and solely for their use in, preparation for any proceeding (or investigation which may result in such a proceeding) before a Federal grand jury or any Federal or State court in a matter involving tax administration, but only if—

(a)   the taxpayer is or may be a party to such proceeding . . . .

[Section 6103(h)(2)(A) of the I.R.C., as amended by the Tax Reform Act of 1976]

Section 6103(h)(4) of the Internal Revenue Code, as amended by the Tax Reform Act, also specifically authorizes the disclosure of a return "in a Federal or State judicial or administrative proceeding pertaining to tax administration . . . if the taxpayer is a party to such proceeding . . . ."

The Commission finds the disclosures authorized in these provisions consistent with its recommendations.

The Commission recommended that some limited disclosure of tax information to the Department of Justice about an individual who is not the object of a tax investigation or prosecution, be authorized but only if " . . . the information disclosed is relevant to issues in an actual or anticipated tax litigation." Moreover, the Commission concluded that "information . . . should be considered relevant only if the treatment of an item on the return of a party to an actual or anticipated tax litigation, or the liability of such a party for

The Tax Reform Act of 1976 authorizes the disclosure to the Justice Department of tax information about individuals not under investigation or prosecution in two situations:

—   if . . . the treatment of an item reflected on such return is or may be related to the resolution of an issue in the proceeding or investigation; or

—   such return or return information relates or may relate to a transactional relationship between a person who is or may be a party to the proceeding and the taxpayer which affects, or may affect, the resolution of an issue in such proceeding or investigation. *[Section 6103(h)(2)(B) and (C) of the I.R.C., as amended by the Tax Reform Act of 1976]*

Section 6103(h)(4)(B) and (C) authorizes the disclosure of such information in Federal and State judicial or administrative proceedings pertaining to tax administration. The Commission finds the disclosures authorized by these provisions consistent with its recommendations.

The Commission specifically recommended in 1976 that the Congress prohibit access to tax information in two situations involving tax administration. In the past, tax information could be used against witnesses in tax litigation solely for the purpose of impeaching their testimony. The Commission found no justification for this use of tax data unless, of course, the testimony impeached is relevant to the issues in litigation in the ways contemplated by the new Section 6103(h)(4)(B) or (C) of the Internal Revenue Code. While the language of those two sections has not yet been interpreted by the judiciary, both of them authorize disclosure only if the data are "directly related" to an issue or a transaction in the lawsuit. The Commission assumes that these two sections will not be construed as authorizing disclosure solely for purposes of impeachment in ways unrelated to the issues in litigation, and thus finds them consistent with its recommendations.

The Commission, in its interim report, also recommended against the continued use of tax information by government attorneys in connection with the selection of jurors. Tax information has been used to determine whether prospective jurors may be biased against the government because of a previous action against them by the IRS. The Commission found this practice highly inappropriate even with respect to litigation involving the tax laws, especially because counsel almost always has substantial opportunities to discover possible prejudice against the government in a prospective juror directly through *voir dire* procedures.

The Tax Reform Act of 1976 authorizes the use of tax data for jury selection. It provides that:

> In connection with any judicial proceeding [involving tax administration] . . . to which the United States is a party, the Secretary [of the Treasury] shall respond to a written inquiry from an attorney of the Department of Justice (including a United States attorney) involved in such proceeding or any person (or his legal representative) who is a party to such proceeding as to whether an individual who is a prospective juror in such proceeding has or has not been the subject of any audit or other tax investigation by the Internal Revenue Service. The Secretary shall limit such response to an affirmative or negative reply to such inquiry. *[Section 6103(h)(5) of the I.R.C., as amended by the Tax Reform Act of 1976]*

By making limited information regarding jurors available to all parties to the litigation, this provision removes one element of unfairness that obtained under prior laws, which permitted only government counsel to have access to tax data. Nevertheless, the Commission still finds no justification for the use of confidential tax data from IRS files in jury selection, particularly because it is so clearly incompatible with the purpose for which the IRS acquires the information. Whatever value tax information may have in jury selection appears to be marginal, and in any case, the same information can be obtained directly from the prospective juror. Therefore, the Commission reiterates the recommendation in its interim report:

Recommendation (1):

That the Congress prohibit the disclosure of any tax information about a prospective juror for use in jury selection.

DISCLOSURE FOR USE IN ADMINISTERING CERTAIN FEDERAL PROGRAMS

The Commission recommended in 1976 that the IRS be authorized to disclose certain individually identifiable tax data to the Social Security Administration for its use in administering the Social Security Act and the Employee Retirement Income Security Act (ERISA). The Tax Reform Act of 1976 authorizes such disclosures *[Section 6103(l)(1) and (5) of the I.R.C., as amended by the Tax Reform Act of 1976]* and limits the type of information that may be disclosed and the purpose for which it may be used, as recommended by the Commission. The Tax Reform Act of 1976 also authorizes the IRS to disclose information to the Department of Labor and Pension Benefit Guaranty Corporation " . . . for the purpose of, but only to the extent necessary in, the administration of titles I and IV" of ERISA *[Section 6103(l)(2) of the I.R.C., as amended by the Tax Reform Act of 1976].* The Commission believes that all of these disclosures are justified by the statutory and administrative relationship between the income tax laws and, respectively, the Social Security Act and the pension laws.

The Commission also recommended in 1976 that the IRS be authorized to disclose certain tax information to the Railroad Retirement Board in furtherance of the latter's responsibility for administering the Railroad Retirement Act, again because of the interrelationship between tax administration and the administration of railroad retirement benefits. The 1976 legislation provides such authorization *[Section 6103(l)(1)(C) of the I.R.C., as amended by the Tax Reform Act of 1976].* The Commission finds this provision consistent with its recommendation.

DISCLOSURE TO STATES AND LOCALITIES FOR PURPOSES OF TAX ADMINISTRATION

The Commission, in its interim report, concluded that IRS disclosure of individually identifiable tax information to State tax administrators for use in connection with the administration of the general revenue laws of the States is compatible with the purposes for which information from and about a taxpayer is collected. Such use is also consistent with the need for cooperation between the different levels of government in a federal system, and serves the interest of effective and fair tax administration. Thus, the Commission recommended that the IRS be authorized to disclose individually identifiable tax data to State tax officials, but with certain limitations.

In particular, the Commission recommended against the disclosure of Federal tax information to help a State administer its regulatory or licensing laws even though a license fee—sometimes called a "tax"—may be required as part of the regulatory scheme. The Commission believes that to justify disclosure of tax information to a State, there should be at least a general correspondence between the State tax law for the administration of which the Federal tax information is sought, and the Federal tax law for the administration of which the information was originally collected. In accord with its general recommendation regarding the principle of limited disclosure, the Commission also recommended that disclosures to the States be limited to specified tax returns, the schedules accompanying them, and summary information regarding adjustments thereto, and that such disclosure be permitted only to the extent necessary to determine a taxpayer's liability under a State's general revenue law.

The Tax Reform Act of 1976 specifically authorizes the IRS to continue its disclosures of Federal tax information to State tax collectors in Section 6103(d) of the Internal Revenue Code, as amended by the Tax Reform Act of 1976. This section provides that

returns and return information . . . shall be open to inspection by or disclosure to any State agency, body, or commission, or its legal representative, which is charged under the laws of such State with responsibility for the administration of State tax laws for the purpose of, and only to the extent necessary in, the administration of such laws, including any procedures with respect to locating any person who may be entitled to a refund.

The Commission is not satisfied that the new law defines the purposes for which it authorizes disclosure to the States carefully enough and regrets that the statute does not specify the particular types of tax information that may be disclosed. The Commission urges the IRS to take care that its disclosures of tax information to the States conform to the principle of limited disclosure.

Although it approves IRS disclosure of Federal tax information to State taxing authorities, the Commission notes that this practice increases the risk of subsequent unauthorized redisclosure of such information. Accordingly, the Commission recommended in 1976 specific statutory requirements calculated to reduce that risk. In particular, it recommended:

(1) that requests for disclosure be submitted in writing by the principal tax official of the State rather than by the governor;

(2) that a State receiving tax data have in effect a statute prohibiting the disclosure of information acquired from the IRS *and* information supplied by the State taxpayer that is a copy of or copied from his Federal return, for purposes other than State tax administration, but that a two year grace period be allowed for enacting such legislation;

(3) that States receiving Federal tax data institute reasonable physical, technical and administrative safeguards satisfactory to the IRS to reduce the likelihood of unauthorized use or disclosure; and

(4) that the IRS be specifically empowered to suspend a State's access to Federal tax information, despite the existence of State legislation, if unauthorized disclosures are made or if adequate safeguards have not been established.

Section 6103(a)(2) of the Internal Revenue Code, as amended by the Tax Reform Act of 1976, requires that officers and employees of a State treat IRS tax information as confidential. The 1976 legislation also provides for disclosure of tax information to State taxing officials

only upon written request by the head of such [taxing] agency, body, or commission, and only to the representatives of such agency, body, or commission designated in such written request as the individuals who are to inspect or to receive the return or return information. *[Section 6103(d) of the I.R.C., as amended by the Tax Reform Act of 1976]*

Another provision contained in Section 6103(d) of the Internal Revenue Code, as amended by the Tax Reform Act of 1976, deters the use of Federal tax data for political purposes by denying access to the chief executive officer of a State.

The Tax Reform Act also requires States to establish safeguards against unauthorized redisclosures that are satisfactory to the IRS and subject to monitoring by Federal tax officials. Section 6103(p)(4) of the Internal Revenue Code, as amended by the Tax Reform Act of 1976, now conditions continued access to Federal tax information on the maintenance of such safeguards. The Commission finds that these provisions of the Code mitigate the risk of unauthorized redisclosure of Federal tax information once it is in the hands of State officials.

The Tax Reform Act of 1976 does not require States to enact statutes prohibiting disclosure of information acquired from the IRS as well as information supplied to the State by a taxpayer that is a copy of information on his Federal return for purposes other than State tax administration. It does, however, require as a condition of receiving IRS tax information that a State law make statutory provision for confidentiality if its own tax law requires its taxpayers to file copies of their Federal tax returns with their State tax returns. The reason for this requirement is that when the State's file on a taxpayer includes a copy of his Federal tax return or information from it, and also information about him that the State received from the IRS, it would be hard to determine if disclosure of information from the file was or was not an unauthorized disclosure of IRS information. The existence of a State penalty for the unauthorized disclosure of copies of Federal returns acquired by the State from its taxpayers would assure that unauthorized disclosures do not go unpunished because of the difficulty in determining the source of the Federal tax information. The Tax Reform Act's provision in this regard differs from that recommended by the Commission in that it does not require an absolute ban on disclosure of such information for purposes unrelated to State tax administration. Instead, it permits disclosure of copies of Federal tax returns "to another officer or employee" of the State for purposes other than State tax administration. *[Section 6103(p)(8)(B) of the I.R.C., as amended by the Tax Reform Act of 1976]*

The Commission concluded in its interim report that the use of tax information by local revenue authorities is also compatible with the government purpose that justifies the collection of tax information by the Federal government. Accordingly, the Commission recommended in 1976 that State taxing authorities be given authority to use Federal tax information in administering local tax laws, and that the IRS be authorized to disclose certain taxpayer identification and location information directly to local taxing authorities. The Tax Reform Act of 1976 does not authorize any disclosure to local taxing officials, nor does it authorize the use of Federal tax data by State officials in administering local tax law.

The main reason for not authorizing the disclosure for the purposes of local tax administration seems to be the risk of unauthorized redisclosure. The Commission believes, however, that requiring IRS approval of local safeguards and the threat of denying access if safeguards are not adequate mitigate this risk. The Commission notes, moreover, that the Congress in the Tax Reform Act gave local government officials authority to obtain certain

Federal tax information for their use in locating absent parents, despite doubts about the ability of a local government to safeguard Federal tax information.

DISCLOSURE FOR STATISTICAL PURPOSES

When the Commission issued its interim report, it knew of only one Federal agency that had clearly demonstrated its need for individually identifiable tax information about individuals for statistical purposes—the Bureau of the Census. Noting the crucial role administrative records play in statistical analysis, and the stringent statutory restrictions on the disclosure of information by the Census Bureau, the Commission recommended that the IRS be authorized to continue to disclose tax information to the Census Bureau.

The Tax Reform Act is consistent with the Commission's recommendation in that it authorizes the IRS to provide tax data to the Bureau of the Census ". . . for the purpose of, but only to the extent necessary in, the structuring of censuses and national activities authorized by law." *[Section 6103(j)(1) of the I.R.C., as amended by the Tax Reform Act of 1976]*

The Commission's interim report did not include a recommendation with respect to the Treasury Department's use of individually identifiable data for statistical studies connected with tax policy analysis. The interim report noted, however, that the Commission would approve such disclosure if the Treasury Department can demonstrate its need for *individually identifiable* data for statistical purposes. Section 6103(j)(3) of the I.R.C., as amended by the Tax Reform Act of 1976 authorizes disclosure:

> to officers and employees of the Department of the Treasury whose official duties require such inspection or disclosure for the purpose of, but only to the extent necessary in, preparing economic or financial forecasts, projections, analyses, and statistical studies and conducting related activities.

The Commission recognizes that the purposes described in this section can be interpreted broadly, but finds the disclosures it generally authorizes to be consistent with the Commission's reasons for recommending continued disclosure to the Bureau of the Census. The Commission also notes with approval that, according to the applicable Internal Revenue Code provisions, such disclosures

> . . . shall be permitted only upon written request which sets forth the specific reason or reasons why such inspection or disclosure is necessary and which is signed by the head of the bureau or office of the Department of the Treasury requesting the inspection or disclosure. *[Section 6103(j)(3) of the I.R.C., as amended by the Tax Reform Act of 1976]*

Dependence upon written requests with articulated objectives should deter unjustified disclosures.

DISCLOSURE OF INFORMATION ABOUT PROSPECTIVE FEDERAL APPOINTEES

In 1976, the Commission recommended termination of the IRS practice of disclosing tax information about prospective Federal appointees to the White House and to heads of Federal agencies without the consent of the individual to whom the information pertains. The Tax Reform Act, however, endorses current practice by authorizing the disclosure of tax information to:

> a duly authorized representative of the Executive Office of the President or to the head of any Federal agency, upon written request by the . . . head of such agency, or to the Federal Bureau of Investigation on behalf of and upon written request by . . . such head, [of] return information with respect to an individual who is designated as being under consideration for appointment to a position in the executive or judicial branch of the Federal Government. *[Section 6103(g)(2) of the I.R.C., as amended by the Tax Reform Act of 1976]*

The Tax Reform Act does, however, limit the information that may be disclosed as follows:

> Such return information [about prospective appointees] shall be limited to whether such individual—
>
> (A) has filed returns . . . for not more than the immediately preceding 3 years;
> (B) has failed to pay any tax within 10 days after notice and demand, or has been assessed any penalty . . . for negligence, in the current year or immediately preceding 3 years;
> (C) has been or is under investigation for possible criminal offenses under the internal revenue laws and the results of any such investigation; or
> (D) has been assessed any civil penalty . . . for fraud. *[Section 6103(g)(2)(A) - (D) of the I.R.C., as amended by the Tax Reform Act of 1976]*

The Commission's reasons for recommending against this practice include: such use is not compatible with the purpose for which the information was originally obtained by the IRS; the same information can be obtained directly from the prospective appointee; an office seeker would be eager to authorize such disclosure if he considered it to be in his interest; and the prospective appointee might have no opportunity to rebut adverse information about himself thus revealed. The 1976 legislation has partially obviated the last of these concerns by requiring that "within 3 days of the receipt of any request . . ., the Secretary [of the Treasury] shall notify such individual in writing that such information has been requested." *[Section 6103(g)(2) of the I.R.C., as amended by the Tax Reform Act of 1976]* While this notification reduces the potential for unfairness somewhat, the Commission still finds the disclosure of tax information without the consent of the prospective appointee neither necessary nor justified.

Accordingly, the Commission reiterates its earlier recommendation:

Recommendation (2):

That the Congress not permit tax information about prospective Federal appointees to be disclosed to the White House and heads of Federal agencies without the consent of the individual to whom the information pertains.

DISCLOSURE TO THE PARENT LOCATOR SERVICE

The Federal Parent Locator Service (PLS) of the Department of Health, Education, and Welfare provides address and place of employment information obtained from Federal agencies to State and local authorities which use this information in locating "absent parents" in order to enforce child-support obligations. The Commission addresses the general issue of the propriety of the policies governing access to various types of information by the Federal and State Parent Locator Services as a separate issue in Chapter 11 of this report.

In its 1976 interim report, the Commission pointed out that despite the obvious propriety of the PLS program, the use of individually identifiable tax information for locating absent parents is obviously not compatible with the purposes for which the IRS was empowered to collect such information. The PLS was then too new for its performance to be assessed, however, and thus the Commission refrained from recommending that tax information be withheld from it. Rather, the Commission recommended:

(1)   that if tax information is to be disclosed for parent location, such disclosure be specifically authorized by Congress;

(2)   that any disclosures so authorized be limited to situations in which residence and employment information may serve to locate individuals against whom outstanding court orders for child support were unsatisfied;

(3)   that there be strict prohibitions against redisclosure of such information by either Federal or State officials; and

(4)   that statutory penalties for unauthorized disclosure be applied in such cases.

The Tax Reform Act of 1976 specifically authorizes the disclosure of tax information in aid of child-support enforcement by providing that:

The Secretary [of the Treasury] may, upon written request, disclose to the appropriate Federal, State, or local child-support enforcement agency—

(i)   available return information from the master files of the Internal Revenue Service relating to the address, filing status, amounts and nature of income, and the number of dependents reported on any return filed by, or with respect to, any individual with respect to whom child-

> support obligations are sought to be established or
> enforced pursuant to the provisions of part D of Title IV
> of the Social Security Act and with respect to any
> individual to whom such support obligations are owing;
> and
>
> (ii)   available return information reflected on any return
> filed by, or with respect to, any individual described in
> clause (i) relating to the amount of such individual's
> gross income . . . or consisting of the names and
> addresses of payors of such income and the names of
> any dependents reported on such return, but only if such
> return information is not reasonably available from any
> other source. *[Section 6103(l)(6)(A) of the I.R.C., as
> amended by the Tax Reform Act of 1976]*

The Internal Revenue Code also provides, however, that such disclosures
are permissible " . . . only for purposes of, and to the extent necessary in,
establishing and collecting child-support obligations from, and locating,
individuals owing such obligations."

The Commission appreciates that the Tax Reform Act of 1976 fulfills
one of its recommendations in that the Congress, after considering the
question, specifically approved disclosure of IRS records to the PLS. The
disclosures authorized by the Tax Reform Act, however, exceed substantially those contemplated by the Commission. Implicit in its 1976 recommendation was the belief that the IRS should be authorized to disclose to the PLS
only residence and place of employment information and only for the
purpose of locating an individual. The Tax Reform Act authorizes the IRS
to disclose to the PLS much more information than necessary to help locate
an absent parent, and the Act permits the PLS to use IRS information in
calculating the individual's support obligation. Moreover, the Tax Reform
Act, in contrast to the Commission's recommendations, authorizes the IRS
to disclose to the PLS information regarding the individual to whom support
is owed by the absent parent, in addition to information about the absent
parent.

The Commission finds a marked qualitative difference between the use
of tax information to locate someone and the use of tax information to prove
the extent of the individual's liability for child support. Moreover, there are
alternative sources of information to prove the extent of liability, including
the individual himself, which do not raise the specter of unfettered and
unwarranted trespass on the confidentiality of information the absent
parent is compelled to give the IRS. In addition, the disclosure of
information about the individual to whom support is owed is, in the
Commission's view, a totally unjustified incursion into IRS files, given that
the individual can be requested to disclose, or authorize the disclosure of,
information about himself or herself to State or local child-support
enforcement officials. Thus, the Commission recommends:

Recommendation (3):

That Federal tax information authorized to be disclosed to the Parent Locator Service be limited to the minimum necessary to locate an alleged absent parent; that such information be used only in aid of location efforts; and that no disclosures of IRS information about an individual to whom support is owed be permitted without the individual's authorization.

The Commission is further concerned that State and local child-support enforcement officials not make unauthorized redisclosure of information received from the IRS. While the penalties for unauthorized disclosure established by the Tax Reform Act would apply to such officials, and while safeguards to avoid unauthorized disclosure would have to be maintained as mandated by the Act, the Commission urges that special care be devoted by the Federal officials responsible for monitoring child-support enforcement activities to assure that the risk of unauthorized disclosure has been effectively diminished by the penalty and safeguard provisions.

DISCLOSURE TO FEDERAL LAW ENFORCEMENT AGENCIES FOR NON-TAX INVESTIGATIONS AND PROSECUTIONS

The Commission pointed out in its interim report that the use of tax information in non-tax civil and criminal investigations is wholly incompatible with the public finance purposes for which the information was collected, and objectionable on intrusiveness grounds in that it takes advantage of the fact that such information is often provided to the IRS under threat of criminal penalties. The Commission also noted, however, that under applicable statutory and constitutional standards, Federal law enforcement authorities can usually get a copy of a taxpayer's return directly from him. The Commission therefore recommended in 1976 that the IRS be forbidden to disclose tax information for non-tax criminal or civil investigations and prosecutions, except in situations in which the Federal investigator or prosecutor could legally obtain a copy of the return directly from the taxpayer. In sum, *the Commission believes that Federal law enforcement officials should not have easier access to information about a taxpayer when it is maintained by the IRS than they would have if the same information were maintained by the taxpayer himself.*

Consistent with this general position, the Commission recommended in its interim report that a taxpayer be notified of a request for tax information for law enforcement purposes unrelated to tax administration and given an opportunity to oppose the disclosure before a United States District Court. Disclosure would then be authorized by the District Court only if it found:

(a) probable cause to believe that a violation of civil or criminal law has occurred;

(b) probable cause to believe that the tax information requested

> from the IRS provides probative evidence that the violation of civil or criminal law has occurred; and

(c)   that no legal impediment to the applicant agency acquiring the information sought directly from the taxpayer exists.

The Commission also recommended that where appropriate, the District Court considering the disclosure request inspect the data *in camera*, and that the District Court be empowered to award litigation costs, including reasonable attorneys fees, to taxpayers who successfully oppose disclosure requests.

The Tax Reform Act of 1976 authorizes disclosures for non-tax criminal (but not civil) investigations. In the case of information provided directly to the IRS by or on behalf of the taxpayer, the Tax Reform Act conditions disclosure upon the issuance of a United States District Court order. Nevertheless, the circumstances outlined in the Tax Reform Act under which the court may order disclosure differ markedly from those the Commission recommended.

The Tax Reform Act provides that:

> A return or taxpayer return information shall, pursuant to, and upon the grant of, an *ex parte* order by a Federal district court judge as provided by this paragraph, be open, but only to the extent necessary as provided in such order, to officers and employees of a Federal agency personally and directly engaged in and solely for their use in, preparation for any administrative or judicial proceeding (or investigation which may result in such a proceeding) pertaining to the enforcement of a specifically designated Federal criminal statute (not involving tax administration) to which the United States or such agency is or may be a party. *[Section 6103(i)(1)(A) of the I.R.C., as amended by the Tax Reform Act of 1976]*

The order can only be sought upon the authorization of the Attorney General, Deputy Attorney General, or an Assistant Attorney General, or if the requesting agency is other than the Department of Justice, by the head of the agency. Tax information acquired by a Federal agency pursuant to a court order may be entered into evidence in any administrative or judicial proceeding pertaining to the enforcement of a Federal criminal statute to which the United States or the agency is a party, but only if the court finds that such return or return information is probative of a matter in issue relevant in establishing the commission of a crime or the guilt of a party. *[Section 6103(i)(4) of the I.R.C., as amended by the Tax Reform Act of 1976]*

The Tax Reform Act of 1976 does not require that the taxpayer be notified of the request; it does not require that the taxpayer be given an opportunity to oppose the disclosure; and all of the proceedings are *ex parte*. The Tax Reform Act further provides for the issuance of the *ex parte* disclosure order by a District Court judge

> . . . if he determines on the basis of the facts submitted by the applicant that—

(i)   there is reasonable cause to believe, based upon information believed to be reliable, that a specific criminal act has been committed;

(ii)   there is reason to believe that such return or return information is probative evidence of a matter in issue related to the commission of such criminal act; and

(iii) the information sought to be disclosed cannot reasonably be obtained from any other source, unless it is determined that, notwithstanding the reasonable availability of the information from another source, the return or return information sought constitutes the most probative evidence of a matter in issue relating to the commission of such criminal act. *[Section 6103 (i)(1)(B) of the I.R.C., as amended by the Tax Reform Act of 1976]*

To find that the first two conditions exist, the judge apparently needs to conclude only that there is some basis to believe that a crime has been committed and that the information sought may be relevant to the investigation of a crime. Any law enforcement authority conducting any legitimate investigation should be able to satisfy both conditions easily. The third subsection might be read to suggest that law enforcement officers must try to get a copy of the tax return from other sources—probably the taxpayer himself—before they can seek a court order for it. It seems unlikely, in most instances, that a determination of nonavailability from alternative sources could reasonably be made without an attempt to secure the information directly from the taxpayer, the person who is most likely to have a copy of it. Nonetheless, the legislative history of this provision offers no basis for inferring that a Federal law enforcement official would be required to try to obtain a copy of a tax return directly from the taxpayer (or another source) before seeking an *ex parte* disclosure order. Federal law enforcement officers have consistently asserted to the relevant Committees of the Congress and to the Commission itself that notification to the taxpayer of a pending investigation might seriously impair the investigation. The Commission must conclude, therefore, that the third condition required to be found by the court does not require a prior direct approach to the taxpayer.

The 1976 legislation also authorizes disclosure of information that has not been provided to the IRS by or on behalf of the taxpayer for non-tax criminal investigations *without* resort to court order. The IRS may disclose such information on receipt of a written request from the Attorney General, Deputy Attorney General, Assistant Attorney General, or head of an investigating agency other than the Department of Justice setting forth:

(A)   the name and address of the taxpayer with respect to whom such return information relates;

(B)   the taxable period or periods to which the return information relates;

(C)   the statutory authority under which the proceeding or investigation is being conducted; and

(D)   the specific reason or reasons why such disclosure is or may be material to the proceeding or investigation. *[Section 6103(i)(2) of the I.R.C., as amended by the Tax Reform Act of 1976]*

Tax information obtained by a Federal agency pursuant to such a written request may be entered into evidence in any administrative or judicial proceeding pertaining to the enforcement of a Federal criminal statute to which the United States or the agency is a party. *[Section 6103(i)(4) of the I.R.C., as amended by the Tax Reform Act of 1976]*

The legislative history of the Tax Reform Act does not reveal the rationale for distinguishing between a disclosure of information that was provided by or on behalf of the taxpayer and a disclosure of information about the taxpayer provided by another source. The Congress appears to have concluded that Fifth Amendment concerns only arise when information submitted by the taxpayer is used against him in a non-tax criminal investigation. When information is supplied to the IRS by another source, use of it in a non-tax investigation apparently poses no problem. Congress, like the Supreme Court, seems to assume that information in the possession of someone besides the taxpayer cannot be the confidential and protectable information of the taxpayer. As the Commission discovered in its broad inquiry into government access to records about individuals held by third-parties, however, the assumption is incorrect.

Information obtained by the IRS from sources other than the taxpayer is often derived from records which the taxpayer has no choice but to have that other party maintain, such as bank and credit-card records. In essence, such third-party source information is not obtained from an independent source, but from a surrogate without whom the taxpayer could not participate in contemporary society. Frequently, the information maintained by such an agent of the taxpayer illuminates those "intimate areas of personal affairs" that the Fourth and Fifth Amendments are intended to protect from unsupervised inquiry by the executive branch of government. It is exactly such revealing record information that other agencies of government are often anxious to acquire.

Since much of the third-party source information held by the IRS is information supplied from the confidential records of the taxpayer, though the records are in the possession of another party, the Commission believes that such information should be protected by the same standards as information obtained directly from the taxpayer. Two further considerations strengthen this conclusion. First, a good deal of third-party source information is available only because the source is required to keep records about the taxpayer open to inspection by the IRS, or to routinely report information to the IRS for purposes of tax administration. Second, even where there is no compelled reporting or record keeping, the expansive reach of the IRS's administrative summons power permits it to acquire information that other agencies cannot acquire through their ordinary investigative processes. Powers to collect information about an individual and intrude on his privacy were granted for the specific purpose of enforcing the tax law, not as a general device by which any government agency can acquire intimate and revealing details of a taxpayer's activities. For all of these reasons, the Commission finds no justification for applying less stringent disclosure standards to third-party information than to information supplied by the taxpayer. Therefore it disagrees with the distinction the Tax Reform Act makes in its provisions governing disclosure of information for use in non-tax criminal investigations, and recommends:

Recommendation (4):

That the Congress subject all information about a taxpayer to the same restrictions on disclosure for non-tax investigations and prosecutions that the Commission recommended in its interim report.

While disagreeing with certain aspects of the 1976 law, as indicated above, the Commission believes that the actions taken by the Congress to limit disclosures for non-tax criminal law enforcement are salutary. The Commission is, however, concerned that information disclosed properly for purposes of tax investigation and litigation will be used by the recipient agencies for non-tax criminal law enforcement in ways not consistent with the new restraints in the Tax Reform Act of 1976.

In January, 1977, the IRS promulgated Temporary Regulations[5] implementing the disclosure provisions of the Tax Reform Act that at best seem ambiguous as to the non-tax uses to which the Justice Department may put tax information they have received from the IRS for purposes relating to tax administration. Section 404.6103(h)(2)-1(a)(1) of the Temporary Regulations provides for the use of tax information originally disclosed to the Department of Justice in connection with "a matter involving tax administration" in " . . . any . . . proceeding . . . also involving the enforcement of a related Federal criminal statute which has been referred by the Secretary [of the Treasury] to the Department of Justice." There is no mention of a court order for such supplementary uses of the tax data, as specified in the Tax Reform Act's amendment to section 6103(i) of the Internal Revenue Code. Other portions of the Temporary Regulations *[Section 404.6103(h)(2)-1(a)(2)]* open the door wider by authorizing the Justice Department to use information conveyed under the provisions of the Tax Reform Act permitting disclosures for tax administration in a non-tax proceeding or investigation that " . . . involves or arises out of the particular facts and circumstances giving rise to the proceeding (or investigation)" relating to tax administration or to a matter involving the enforcement of a Federal criminal statute referred to the Justice Department by the Secretary of the Treasury.

These regulations seem to permit the use of tax information in joint investigations and prosecutions of non-tax as well as tax violations. The language of the regulations is, however, sufficiently vague to allow for the use of tax information for non-tax criminal law enforcement even where there is not a joint investigation or prosecution. It would seem, therefore, that the Temporary Regulations provide an easy way to avoid the Tax Reform Act's restrictions on the disclosure of tax data for non-tax criminal

---

[5] 42 *Federal Register* 16 (January 25, 1977), pp. 4437-40.

law enforcement. The Commission believes that the Temporary Regulations may be inconsistent with the spirit and substance of the 1976 restrictions contained in the Tax Reform Act, and with the Commission's recommendations. Accordingly, the Commission urges that the Temporary Regulations be reevaluated to consider whether these regulations do indeed violate the restrictions imposed by the Tax Reform Act on the use of tax data for non-tax investigations and prosecutions.

SAFEGUARD REQUIREMENTS FOR RECIPIENT FEDERAL AGENCIES

The Commission is concerned that Federal agencies receiving tax information from the IRS are not always fully cognizant of the importance of guarding against unauthorized disclosures of such information. The Commission therefore recommended in 1976 that the IRS, experienced in protection of its records, be empowered to require recipient Federal agencies to institute reasonable administrative, technical, and physical safeguards satisfactory to the IRS to avoid the unauthorized use or disclosure of tax information.

The Tax Reform Act of 1976 prescribes a series of safeguards and vests substantial powers to enforce them in the Federal tax officials. It provides that recipient Federal and State agencies " . . . shall, as a condition of receiving returns or return information [from the IRS]—

(A) establish and maintain, to the satisfaction of the Secretary [of the Treasury], a permanent system of standardized records with respect to any request, the reason for such request, and the data of such request made by or of it and any disclosure of return or return information made by or to it;

(B) establish and maintain, to the satisfaction of the Secretary, a secure area or place in which such returns or return information shall be stored;

(C) restrict, to the satisfaction of the Secretary, access to the returns or return information only to persons whose duties or responsibilities require access and to whom disclosure may be made under the provisions of this title;

(D) provide such other safeguards which the Secretary determines (and which he prescribes in regulations) to be necessary or appropriate to protect the confidentiality of the returns or return information;

(E) furnish a report to the Secretary, at such time and containing such information as the Secretary may prescribe, which describes the procedures established and utilized by such agency, body, or commission or the General Accounting Office for ensuring the confidentiality of returns and return information required [hereunder]." *[Section 6103(p)(4) of the I.R.C., as amended by the Tax Reform Act of 1976]*

The 1976 law also requires that after using IRS data the recipient agency must either return it to the IRS or render it completely undisclosable and so report to the Service.

The 1976 law requires the Secretary of the Treasury to file quarterly reports with the House Committees on Ways and Means, the Senate Committee on Finance, and the Joint Committee on Taxation describing

> . . . the procedures and safeguards established and utilized by [recipient agencies] . . . for ensuring the confidentiality of returns and return information . . . [as well as] deficiencies in, and failure to establish or utilize, such procedures. *[Section 6103 (p)(5) of the I.R.C., as amended by the Tax Reform Act of 1976]*

The 1976 law also authorizes the Comptroller General to audit the implementation of safeguard requirements.

The Commission is satisfied that the confidentiality of IRS information disclosed to other Federal agencies is now well protected by the statutory safeguard requirements, IRS review authority, periodic reporting on safeguards to Congress, and the Comptroller General's audits.

PENALTIES FOR UNAUTHORIZED DISCLOSURE

The Commission recommended in 1976 that the ceiling on the fine for unauthorized disclosure of tax information specified in Section 7213 of the Internal Revenue Code be raised from $1,000 to $5,000, and that penalties be made applicable to former employees of Federal, State, and local governments as well as to present employees and to government agency contractors that have access to Federal tax information. The Commission refrained from recommending that the offense be treated as a felony, rather than a misdemeanor, but only because the change might present practical problems in obtaining convictions.

The Tax Reform Act of 1976 amended Section 7213 to raise the potential fine to $5,000, to provide for possible imprisonment of up to five years, and to make unauthorized disclosure a felony. It applies its penalties specifically to offending present *and* former Federal and State employees who have or have had access to Federal tax information, to agents (including contractors) of Federal and State agencies, and to local child-support officials who receive tax information in connection with their enforcement activities. Offenders who are Federal employees may also be dismissed.

A new section of the Internal Revenue Code, added by the Tax Reform Act of 1976, provides additional deterrence to unauthorized disclosure by permitting taxpayers to bring civil actions to recover actual damages against officials who knowingly or negligently make such an unauthorized disclosure of tax data. *[Section 7217 of the I.R.C.]* Where willful or grossly negligent violations have occurred, it specifies that the taxpayer may be awarded punitive damages as well.

While the Commission did not recommend the enactment of statutory authorization for civil actions in its interim report, it recognizes that the availability of civil remedies for taxpayers is likely to deter departures from the rules of confidentiality prescribed by the Tax Reform Act of 1976. Moreover, the Commission has considered as a general matter the desirability of civil remedies for Federal agency violations of the Privacy Act of 1974, and has recommended that citizens aggrieved by intentional or willful agency violations be able to pursue civil remedies to recover actual and general damages and attorneys' fees.[6] The details of the Tax Reform Act creating civil remedies are not congruent with the Commission's general recommendations, however, in that they make individuals, rather than an agency, liable for wrongful disclosure. The Department of Justice has expressed concern about this aspect of the Tax Reform Act of 1976.

THIRD-PARTY SOURCE INFORMATION

THE PROBLEM

Much of the discussion, analysis, and debate regarding IRS disclosure of tax information to other government agencies has focused on the dissemination of an individual's tax return. In fact, these issues are often characterized collectively as "tax return confidentiality."

In undertaking its examination of IRS policies and practices regarding disclosure, the Commission has also focused primarily on the dissemination of tax returns and information from tax returns for uses other than Federal tax administration. In developing the recommendations, both in its interim report and in this chapter, the Commission has not questioned the basic violation of privacy resulting from the decision by Congress to require extensive disclosure of personal information by individual taxpayers to the IRS. Accepting the congressional determination that such compulsory disclosure is justified by the need to finance government operations, the Commission directed its attention to the propriety of using such data for purposes for which, and in circumstances where, the Congress has never established such extraordinary disclosure requirements.

In examining IRS disclosure policies, however, the Commission realized that a substantial portion of the information maintained and disclosed by the IRS has not been provided to it by the taxpayer. In addition to disclosing tax returns, the IRS discloses many types of individually identifiable information that it has acquired from third-party sources during the course of administering the tax laws. The Commission considered as a separate issue whether the standards of disclosure that apply to such third-party source information should differ materially from those recommended for tax returns.

The Commission recognizes that there are reasons for concluding that lesser standards of confidentiality should be applied to third-party source information; however, the Commission also recognized that there are reasons for applying more stringent safeguards. Accordingly, the Commission solicited the views of witnesses at its hearings and of other interested persons and organizations regarding the treatment of third-party source information. In addition, the Commission requested the IRS to undertake a

---

[6] See Chapter 13 for a discussion of this issue.

special three-month monitoring of its disclosures to identify precisely what types of third-party source information are disclosed regularly by the Service to other government agencies for purposes unrelated to Federal tax administration.

THE CASE FOR BROADER DISCLOSURE

There is an obvious argument for the proposition that information obtained by the IRS about an individual from sources other than the individual himself should be more generally available to other government agencies than the tax return filed by the individual.

A primary concern that permeates the consideration of tax return confidentiality arises from principles and values that are reflected in the Fifth Amendment to the Constitution. When is it appropriate to compel an individual to disclose information that can be used to penalize him? The courts have held that the Fifth Amendment does not prevent prosecutions for violations of the filing requirements of the Internal Revenue Code.[7] While the statutory establishment of appropriate disclosure standards is not limited by Constitutional protections, the fairness of using data disclosed as a result of legal compulsion for purposes unrelated to the purpose for which the information was compelled is an issue of overwhelming importance. When information about an individual has been accumulated by the IRS from sources other than himself, the question of self-incrimination simply does not arise. Accordingly, it can be argued that disclosure of such information need not be limited to the same extent as information acquired by the IRS from the individual under threat of criminal penalties.

This argument can be buttressed by the fact that much of the information acquired by the IRS from third-party sources is a product of the investment of time and other resources by employees of the Federal government. As a result, the conclusion that such data ought properly be characterized as a "generalized governmental asset"—a conclusion specifically rejected by the Commission in this chapter—can more easily be defended with respect to third-party source information than to tax returns, which are largely the product of the taxpayer's efforts and not those of the government.

THE CASE FOR STRICTER STANDARDS

While the absence of Fifth Amendment considerations and the recognition of the cost of collecting the data suggest that restrictions on disclosure of third-party source information need not be as severe as those applicable to tax returns, there are in fact compelling reasons for the imposition of more severe limits on the disclosure of third-party source data than on the disclosure of tax returns.

Although information disclosed to the IRS by a taxpayer is disclosed under compulsion of law and the threat of severe criminal and civil penalties, the taxpayer knows the substance of information that might be

---

[7] *United States v. Sullivan*, 274 U.S. 259 (1927).

used against him and, some argue, he should realize that the information he gives to the IRS will be used for purposes well beyond Federal tax administration. During hearings before the Commission, for example, a representative of the Department of Justice asserted, in defending continued access to tax information by the Department of Justice, that taxpayers know full well that information contained on tax returns might be used by other government agencies for purposes unrelated to Federal tax administration.[8]

When information about a taxpayer is acquired from third-party sources, the taxpayer is very unlikely to know its substance and may not even be aware of its existence. In such circumstances, the opportunity for an individual to protect himself against the use by others than the IRS of erroneous, incomplete, or outdated information is effectively negated. Accordingly, the risk to individuals of arbitrary or unfair treatment at the hands of his government are significantly increased.

It is, moreover, apparent that the IRS has not been designated by the Congress as an agency responsible for routinely collecting information on behalf of other agencies. Just as the Congress has given the IRS extraordinary powers to compel the disclosure of information by an individual about himself, the Congress has established broad powers to enable the Service to gather information from other sources as well. The rationale for both forms of power is the same—effective government depends upon revenue collection. The overwhelming importance of that objective justifies the compulsion of information from a citizen about himself as well as the creation and use of broad investigative authority. The Commission believes, however, that the fact that the Congress has not given such broad investigative authority to other government agencies wishing to acquire tax information from the IRS is itself a clear manifestation of the inappropriateness of disclosure by the Internal Revenue Service. Such inappropriateness, compounded by the increased risks to the subject because he may be unaware that data about him has been collected or what the data collected includes, suggests that third-party source information collected by the Service should be used and disclosed solely for purposes of Federal tax administration.

The Internal Revenue Service Special Study

As noted above, the Commission requested the Commissioner of Internal Revenue to maintain a full accounting for one month of the disclosures that were actually made by Internal Revenue Service offices throughout the nation. Former Commissioner Alexander graciously consented to undertake the accounting, and ordered that detailed disclosure logs be maintained in the field for the month of April 1976. The Commissioner directed all Regional Commissioners, District Directors, and Service Center Directors to furnish a report of all disclosures made to Federal agencies. To assure accuracy, the Commissioner further ordered

---

[8] Testimony of Deputy Attorney General, U. S. Department of Justice, *Federal Tax Return Confidentiality*, Hearings before the Privacy Protection Study Commission, March 11, 1976, pp. 70-71.

that negative reports should be filed if there are no disclosures during this period. In order to diminish the probability of generating results skewed by the pecularities of a single month, the disclosure accounting order was subsequently extended through the end of June 1976 at the Commission's request.

The individual summaries of disclosures prepared in the field were provided by the IRS to the Commission staff. The staff prepared a summary of disclosures recorded for each of the three months, which appears in the appendix volume of this report on tax return confidentiality.

The summaries set forth the number and character of disclosures both of information provided by taxpayers and information provided by third parties. They clearly reflect an interdependence between data accumulated from third parties and data acquired directly from a taxpayer insofar as recipient agencies' needs are concerned. Much third-party information relates to particular tax returns, and in many instances, third-party information has been acquired because of a compulsory reporting requirement on the third party. A taxpayer's own return may, for example, reflect information about other individuals. Information returns, compelled by law, are specifically designed to provide substantial amounts of information about third parties. In other instances, the third-party information disclosures made during this three-month period reflect the value to other agencies of the IRS's special investigative authority. Intelligence files, reports of conversations, and the work product of revenue agents were disclosed on a regular basis.

There are clear indications in the disclosure accounting of the tendency of other agencies to view IRS files as sources of information that could have been easily obtained from other sources. In a number of instances, for example, the IRS disclosed to other agencies information that was clearly taken from generally available public records. Reliance upon the IRS as a source of "newspaper articles" and "auto registrations obtained from State department of motor vehicles" confirms the habitual reliance by other government agencies on the IRS as a rich source of data.

THE COMMISSION RECOMMENDATION

The results of its analysis of the IRS's disclosure accounting confirm the Commission's belief that disclosures of third-party source data cannot be regarded lightly. The Commission does not believe that the absence of Fifth Amendment considerations constitutes a compelling argument in favor of the untrammelled disclosure of third-party source information. Concerns about invasions of personal privacy are not synonomous with Fifth Amendment protections, nor does the Commission believe that statutory measures to protect personal privacy should be limited to the scope of the Constitution's protections.

The Commission has, therefore, concluded that the same standards of disclosure should be applied to third-party source and to taxpayer-supplied data maintained by the IRS. The Commission believes that there are compelling arguments justifying strict disclosure safeguards for both types of information. Moreover, if the standards are not the same, an agency whose access to one type of information is restricted may well be able to circumvent the restriction by seeking the same information acquired by the IRS from a different source. Finally, the Commission is fully aware that the establishment of different disclosure restrictions for information obtained by the IRS from different sources may well impose significant administrative burdens on the IRS. In light of the foregoing considerations, the Commission recommends:

Recommendation (5):

That all of the information about taxpayers in the possession of the IRS, regardless of source, be subject to the same disclosure restrictions recommended by the Commission in this chapter and in its interim report.

Desirability of Further Legislative Change

The Commission believes that the Tax Reform Act of 1976 has effected a number of important and highly desirable changes in furtherance of the protection of taxpayers' rights. The Commission's overriding concern at present is that those agencies whose access to tax data for non-tax purposes was partially or wholly frustrated by the 1976 legislation will prevail upon the Congress to weaken its restrictions before the impact of the 1976 changes can be adequately assessed. The Department of Justice has already requested that the new limitations on disclosure be postponed because of its concern about ambiguous language in the statute and the possibility of a proliferation of civil suits by taxpayers aimed at delaying important non-tax criminal investigations.

Attorney General Bell presented this argument in a letter to the Chairman of the House Committee on Ways and Means, and repeated it in testimony before the Oversight Subcommittee of that Committee.[9] He recommended in particular that civil and criminal sanctions be imposed only where "willful" rather than "knowing" or "grossly negligent" unauthorized disclosures of tax information have been made. Such a modification, if adopted, would increase the standard of proof necessary to sustain an action for wrongful disclosure.

The Commission recognizes that the complexity of the 1976 legislation will require judicial interpretation. Moreover, it fully recognizes that the new disclosure limitations may to some extent impede non-tax law enforcement activities that depended in the past on easy access to tax information. The Commission made its recommendations with a full understanding that denial of access to tax information is likely in some instances to prove burdensome to the agency subject to the restrictions. This is a price that the

---

[9] Letter from Attorney General Griffin Bell to Representative Al Ullman, Chairman of the House Committee on Ways and Means, February 11, 1977; and testimony of Attorney General Griffin Bell, *Administrative Summons and Anti-Disclosure Provisions of the Tax Reform Act of 1976* , Hearings before the Subcommittee on Oversight of the Committee on Ways and Means, U. S. House of Representatives, 95th Congress, 1st Session, pp. 4-47.

Commission would consciously accept in return for the protection of individual rights that will ensue.

The Commission believes that continuous public and congressional scrutiny of IRS disclosures is essential if taxpayers' rights and agencies' needs are to be constantly weighed and balanced. It therefore hopes that disclosure policy will be a matter of continuing concern and public debate. Information regarding the practices and consequences of disclosure should be made available on a regular basis both to the Congress and to the public to assure that the disclosures authorized by law continue to be warranted and to reduce the likelihood that unauthorized disclosures will result from inattention or actions taken in the interest of administrative convenience.

Chapter 15

The Relationship Between Citizen and Government:
The Citizen As Participant in Research and Statistical Studies

The variety of research and statistical studies that require the collection of information in individually identifiable form is limited only by the interests and concerns of society for human wants and needs, and by the assumptions of researchers and statisticians as to the topics that merit exploration. This chapter reports on the Commission's examination of these activities and recommends action by the Congress and agencies of the Federal government to protect the interests of individuals who are the subjects of research and statistical records developed under Federal authority or with Federal funds.

The Commission's examination of the collection, maintenance, use, and dissemination of information and records about individuals for research or statistical purposes was premised on the following observations.

First, research and statistical activities generally do not lead to an immediate or direct benefit for the individual subject as such. The researcher asks for the individual's participation or for information about him, but society as a whole, rather than the individual, is the ultimate beneficiary.

Second, research and statistical activities depend heavily upon the voluntary cooperation of the individual in providing *accurate* and *reliable* information. On the theory that responses will be more candid and complete if individuals are convinced that the information they provide will not come back to haunt them, researchers who directly question subjects usually assure them confidentiality and, when the study design calls mainly for observation, the observer usually promises anonymity.

Third, assuring that information will not be disclosed to third parties in individually identifiable form is especially important in research on deviant behavior, such as drug and alcohol abuse, gambling, and prostitution; in studies of topics such as abortion and institutionalized discrimination; and in probes of public attitudes on controversial social issues, such as busing and welfare.

Fourth, both government agencies and research institutions outside government are undertaking more and more of the kinds of studies that require assurances of confidentiality or anonymity. The vast banks of records on individuals built up by the Federal government in the course of performing its legitimate functions constitute a valuable data resource for research and statistical activities. Some of these records are currently released in anonymous form for general public use. Because careful removal of the elements of individual identification is a complex and expensive process, however, the rich lode of agency data has barely been tapped.

Fifth, different research and statistical projects use widely differing methods of collecting information about individuals. These differences affect the relationship between researcher and subject, which, in turn, affects the individual's ability to comprehend and control the way information about him is used. In a laboratory setting there is likely to be a close working relationship between researcher and subject. Surveys based on personal interviews similarly involve a direct, if somewhat more transient, relationship. Telephone interviewing, of course, weakens the relationship considerably, and mail surveys can be conducted without any personal contact. When information is extracted from program records or data archives, the individual subject is seldom even aware that information about him is being used.

After examining the standards and procedures for the protection of personal privacy in a number of research and statistical activities, the Commission reached three main conclusions:

- Research and statistical activities are becoming more dependent on information originally collected or maintained for administrative purposes, a dependence that attenuates the relationship between researcher and data subject and weakens the individual's ability to control the way information about him is collected and used.
- While an expectation of confidentiality is, and has been, an integral part of research and statistical activities, their growing number raises serious questions about the validity of that expectation.
- The use of individually identifiable research and statistical records for administrative, regulatory, or law enforcement purposes encourages abuse of the expectation that information will be kept confidential.

The Commission's principal objective is to strike a proper balance between the individual's interest in personal privacy and society's need for knowledge. In research and statistical activities, the threat to personal privacy comes mainly from information and records collected and maintained in individually identifiable form. Thus, the Commission believes that the first and fundamental step toward achieving the desired balance is to establish a clear boundary between the use of such information (regardless of source) that is collected, maintained, or disseminated for a research or statistical purpose, and the use of information that is collected, maintained, or disseminated for other purposes. Assuming that such a functional boundary can be established, the Commission proposes policy and rules for the transfer of individually identifiable information or records within and across the boundary, and identifies the role it believes an individual should play in such transfers.

The Commission's public-policy objectives here are, as in other areas of its inquiry, to minimize intrusiveness, to maximize fairness, and to create a legitimate, enforceable expectation of confidentiality. The recommendations in this chapter aim mainly at achieving the third goal; that is, at strengthening and systematizing the confidential status of individually identifiable information used for research and statistical purposes. A clearly marked boundary between the use of information for such a purpose and its use for administrative or other purposes is an essential first step in eliminating the possibility that the information an individual contributes directly or indirectly to a research or statistical activity will be used to his detriment.

Nevertheless, minimizing intrusiveness and maximizing fairness are also of concern to the Commission here. The close dependence of research and statistical activities on public cooperation acts as a natural brake on intrusiveness in the nature of the questions asked of research subjects. The notice and consent requirements specified in *Recommendations (10), (11),* and *(12),* below, would reduce intrusiveness by reinforcing the individual's right to refuse to participate in the data-collection process. They also promote fairness in collection practices by specifying the ground rules for use and disclosure of the data collected. *Recommendation (13)* promotes fairness by assuring the individual an opportunity to see and copy any record about himself that is disclosed unless the record keeper can guarantee that the record itself, or the individually identifiable information it contains, will not be used to his detriment.

The Commission's study focused on federally controlled or assisted research and statistical activities and thus its recommendations are confined to research and statistical activities in that category. This limitation should not be interpreted as a judgment by the Commission that the protection of individually identifiable data is of concern only when there is some Federal involvement. Rather, it recognizes that most of the country's organized research and statistical activities are at least partially dependent on Federal funding, and that where there is Federal involvement, some means of protecting record confidentiality already exist and are being used to at least some degree.[1]

The Commission considers its general principles valid as guidelines for research and statistical activities beyond the reach of Federal involvement. The Commission does not have enough evidence to judge whether these guidelines will need modification to make them generally applicable, or to suggest policy mechanisms for implementing them where research and statistical activities are independent of the Federal government. The Commission does believe, however, that the recommendations in this

---

[1] For example, the Federal Reports Act *[44 U.S.C. 3501-3511]* provides central structure for the disclosure of Federal agency records. Disclosure is also regulated by the Privacy Act *[5 U.S.C. 552a],* the Freedom of Information Act *[5 U.S.C. 552],* and by specific confidentiality statutes regarding alcohol and drug abuse treatment records *[42 U.S.C. 582 and 21 U.S.C. 1175].*

chapter can serve as a paradigm for the guidance of all research and statistical activities.

RESEARCH AND STATISTICAL ACTIVITIES

The term *research* will be used in this chapter to refer to any systematic, objective process designed to obtain new knowledge, regardless of whether it is "pure" (aimed at deriving general principles) or "applied" (aimed at solving a specific problem or at determining policy). *Statistics* refers both to the data obtained through enumeration and measurement and to the use of mathematical methods for dealing with data so obtained. *Statistical methods* can be *descriptive*, that is, any treatment designed to summarize or describe important features of data, or *inferential*, that is, techniques for arriving at generalizations that go beyond the sample being analyzed.

The research and statistical activities that use individually identifiable information draw huge quantities of it from Federal administrative records, both for routine production of statistical reports and for the performance of statistical analysis or other research tasks. Researchers draw other information directly from individuals as part of the research process. As to Federal agencies, some conduct the bulk of their research themselves. For example, the Bureau of the Census not only conducts all its own surveys but also performs data-collection services for other agencies on a reimbursable basis. A great deal of Federal agency research, however, is contracted out to private and semi-public research organizations and Federal grants support numerous research projects at other levels of government and in the private sector.

A typical research project starts with a hypothesis and proceeds through four stages: data collection; data processing; data analysis and interpretation; and finally, publication or dissemination of findings. Before data collection can begin, assumptions must be made about what information is relevant to the hypothesis and what kind of individuals are appropriate data subjects or respondents. Processing may involve anything from simple arranging and manual tabulations to complex coding and sophisticated computer analysis. Data storage and retrieval may rely on anything from handwritten notes and human memory to punched cards, magnetic tapes and discs, films, and computer memory. Data can be analyzed and interpreted in terms of the original hypothesis, or—when the research design less closely approximates the canons of the scientific method—in the light of less clearly articulated assumptions. Statistical manipulation may or may not be required. For some studies, a simple tabulation or descriptive case study may be the result. The final step is a research report to make the findings available to others.

In most studies, the researcher or statistician is interested in the individual primarily as a carrier of attributes or characteristics of groups or distributions. Individual data are often used as major building blocks during the analytical process, but in the final stage both research findings and statistical data are characteristically presented in aggregate form. In research, the purpose is to discover and analyze relationships among variables; in statistics, the purpose is to define average characteristics or discover their distribution or both. Individual data are therefore grouped according to characteristics and reported in the aggregate.

To illustrate, suppose the Department of Labor, for its own policy-making purposes, sponsors a study comparing and contrasting two manpower training programs. The project design requires extensive questioning and observation of two groups of trainees over a two-year period during which at least three series of interviews are conducted. Despite the research team's close, long-term involvement with the research participants, no information supplied by the respondents is released until the final report and then the information is in statistical summary form. If the final report contains quotations from respondents for illustrative purposes, they are presented anonymously, not as individual data with identifiers attached. The bulk of the data are presented in tables according to categories, such as training program A or B, sex, extent of formal education previously received, training, occupation, attitudes toward training programs, and whether participation was mandatory or voluntary.

In most cases, omitting identifiers, such as name, address, telephone number, or subject identification number, is enough to protect the participants' anonymity. In certain cases, however, other information can identify the respondents, as when the study is about people in a relatively unusual occupation such as network TV anchorwomen, or is limited to people in a specific geographic area or income bracket. In such cases, characteristics such as occupation, age, or income may have to be suppressed to preserve the participants' anonymity.

It is often difficult to decide in advance which information beyond the standard items of name, address, or telephone number will or will not constitute identifying information. It must be emphasized, however, that research and statistical activities are undertaken not in the investigative sense of discovering what there is to know about identified individuals, but in pursuit of systematic knowledge about human beings in groups. A distinction should also be drawn between the *use* of information for research and statistical purposes and the *methods* employed for information gathering and analysis. The methods researchers and statisticians use in data collection and analysis may also be useful for purposes wholly unrelated to research and statistics, notably for law enforcement, evaluating compliance with program requirements, assessing performance, and even for commercial exploitation. Thus, the duties and safeguards recommended in this chapter do not apply to all information about individuals collected or used according to what may be considered research or statistical methods.

Definitions

In the discussion of the Commission's recommendations, the following definitions apply:

Individual:
     any citizen or permanent resident of the United States.

Individually Identifiable Form:
   any material that could reasonably be uniquely associated
   with the identity of the individual to whom it pertains.
Research and Statistical Information:
   any information about an individual, obtained from any
   source, used for a research or statistical purpose.
Research and Statistical Record:
   any item, collection or grouping of information maintained in
   any form of record *solely* for a research or statistical purpose.
Research and Statistical Purposes:
   the developing and reporting of aggregate or anonymous
   information not intended to be used, in whole or in part, for
   making a decision about an individual that is not an integral
   part of the particular research project.
Functional Separation:
   separating the use of information about an individual for a
   research or statistical purpose from its use in arriving at an
   administrative or other decision about that individual.

THE PRINCIPLE OF FUNCTIONAL SEPARATION

Federal agency research and statistical activities tend to be reasonably
well defined and performed by organizational components functionally
separated from policy and decision-making units. This is also generally
characteristic of research conducted by academic institutions and by
organizations specializing in research, but less likely to be true of research
and statistical activities conducted by State or local governments. Even
where organizational separation exists, however, individually identifiable
information and records used for research or statistical purposes can be
commingled with information and records used for administrative purposes.
This can occur by design, as well as by chance, as when a continuing study
of a program serves not only as a source of statistical summaries but also as
an element in determining the eligibility of particular individuals for benefits
under the program. Furthermore, in some social experiments the same
individual may be both a beneficiary under the program and a research
subject. Thus the flow of information from researchers to program personnel
who make decisions about the individual may be loosely restricted or not
restricted at all.
   Existing law does not clearly discourage such commingling. Neither
does it clearly restrict the exchange of information between research or
statistical components and administrative units of an organization, nor
necessarily preclude access to individually identifiable data maintained by
researchers for investigative, legislative, or judicial purposes. The Federal
Reports Act *[44 U.S.C. 3501-3511]*, which prescribes the central structure
for Federal agencies' data management practices, was in fact framed to
facilitate data sharing among agencies in order to reduce the reporting
burden on business by eliminating redundant data collection. It does not,
however, license unrestricted flows of information among agencies and there

are laws that extend confidentiality protection to data collected or maintained by certain agencies, or to some particular types of information under the control of any agency.

The Commission believes that existing law and practice do not adequately protect the interests of the individual data subject. It perceives two main deficiencies. First, the individual needs more protection from inadvertent exposure to an administrative action as a consequence of supplying information for a research or statistical purpose. The individual is entitled to protection when he supplies information indirectly by way of applying for benefits under an agency program that uses client information for research or statistical purposes, just as when he volunteers information directly to a researcher. Second, public confidence in the integrity of research and statistical activities and in the collection and use of the data on which they depend needs strengthening. Research and statistical results are too important to the common welfare to risk eroding public trust in the activities and processes that produce them.

The Commission believes both needs will be met if the data collected and maintained for research or statistical use cannot be used or disclosed in individually identifiable form for any other purpose. To erect such a barrier, however, there must be a clear functional separation between research and statistical uses and all other uses. The separation cannot be absolute in practice but the principle must be established that individually identifiable information collected or compiled for research or statistical purposes may enter into administrative and policy decision making only in aggregate or anonymous form. The reverse flow of individually identifiable information from records maintained by administrators and decision makers to researchers or statisticians can be permitted, but only on the basis of demonstrated need and under stringent safeguards.

There are two classes of exceptions to the principle of functional separation. One is when the data subjects directly receive the benefits of the research findings, as in experimental medical treatment or testing, or experimental housing or education projects. The other is when societal imperatives outweigh the individual's claim to protection.

The Commission recognizes that it is not always easy to decide whether a particular investigative purpose can properly be considered research or statistical. Program evaluation, for instance, is considered evaluation research in some cases, but in others it is considered a standard operational component of an agency's mission. For functional separation to protect the individual's interest, the criteria for determining what is a research or statistical activity must be consistently applied.

The threshold policy question is the extent to which innovative administrative and program management practices, including quality control, are to be considered research and statistical activities. The answer lies in what functional separation is meant to achieve. The aim of functional separation is to prevent individually identifiable research or statistical information from affecting or modifying decisions about the individual to whom the information pertains. Consequently, if a given activity can gain nothing from identifying particular individuals—if, for example, its interest

is only in uncovering underlying principles of good management practice—
the investigation can safely be considered research, and respondents
informed accordingly. If, however, the reverse is true, the investigation
cannot be considered a research or statistical activity and the respondents
cannot be promised confidentiality.

The Commission sees the need for a specific set of standards and
guidelines for organizational information practices to limit the exposure to
risk of the individual who contributes information, either directly or
indirectly, to a research or statistical activity. The standards and guidelines
should also strengthen the ability of the individual to protect himself. The
Commission believes that standards and guidelines can do this without
discouraging the rigorous research and statistical activities that society
needs, provided that clear functional separation is accepted as a basic
principle. Accordingly, the Commission recommends:

Recommendation (1):

**That the Congress provide by statute that no record or information
contained therein collected or maintained for a research or statistical
purpose under Federal authority or with Federal funds may be used in
individually identifiable form to make any decision or take any action
directly affecting the individual to whom the record pertains, except
within the context of the research plan or protocol, or with the specific
authorization of such individual.**

ASSURING COMPLIANCE WITH THE SEPARATION PRINCIPLE

Establishing the principle of functional separation within a Federal
agency requires three preliminary steps:

- deciding what uses and disclosures of the individually
  identifiable information an agency collects or maintains for a
  research or statistical purpose are proper;
- establishing procedures for protecting the confidentiality of
  the individually identifiable data an agency gathers or
  maintains; and
- setting forth the conditions under which information an
  agency maintains may be used or disclosed in individually
  identifiable form for a research or statistical purpose.

Because these three steps are interrelated, the measures recommended for
implementing each of them are prescribed below in order of dependence.
Thus, acceptance of each recommendation assumes acceptance of those that
precede it.

DECIDING WHAT USES AND DISCLOSURES ARE PROPER

There would be little chance that the principle of functional separation
would be violated if research and statistical findings could not enter into
decision-making processes in individually identifiable form. Strictly applied,

functional separation would eliminate the disclosure of individually identifiable research and statistical data for any purpose other than a research or statistical one.

Most researchers regard the pledge of confidentiality as the *sine qua non* of voluntary participation in research for the reasons noted earlier. Recognition of its necessity underlies the statutory protections for the confidentiality of data collected by the Bureau of the Census *[13 U.S.C. 8,9]* and the National Center for Health Statistics *[42 U.S.C. 242m]*, as well as the confidentiality protection that special legislation provides to particular research projects using alcohol and drug addiction treatment records. *[42 U.S.C. 4582; 21 U.S.C. 1175]*

Nor is it only protection of information collected directly from individuals for a research or statistical purpose that demands consideration. The confidentiality of research data obtained from other sources, including administrative records, without the immediate knowledge of the research subject is equally significant to both the researcher and the policy maker. Public attitudes are volatile, and the public's willingness to participate, or ultimately to consent to researcher access to administrative records, is dependent on trust in the integrity of the process.

Conversely, there is the public's right to hold public agencies accountable for efficiency and economy in the discharge of their duties. Assuring compliance with laws and regulations in the conduct of government programs, carrying out criminal law enforcement and investigative functions, and assuring fairness in civil and criminal court proceedings can all create demands for access to individually identifiable research and statistical records that are difficult to deny as a matter of public policy. So far such value confrontations have not been common but there are signs that they will grow in number and thus must be taken into account. Because other justifiable goals may impinge on the individual's privacy interest and on the integrity of the relationship between researcher and data subject, the Commission believes that it would be unrealistic to deny *all* claims for disclosure of *all types of research and statistical records* under *all circumstances*. At present, the mechanisms agencies use to resolve confrontations over disclosure are largely *ad hoc* and tend to vary considerably depending on the source of the request and the class of information sought. Judicial demands for individually identifiable research or statistical information, for instance, may be resolved on Constitutional or common law grounds, or by invoking State or Federal protective statutes. In some instances, the newsman's privilege, established by State statute, has been invoked to apply to research information.

Section (3)(b)(1) of the Privacy Act of 1974 allows one component of a Federal agency to ask another component of the same agency for access to research or statistical records for use in administrative decision making. These requests, which the Privacy Act treats as internal need-to-know disclosures, are dealt with administratively, and the result may be governed or influenced by the existence or absence of independent statutory directives. For example, in the Commission's hearings on medical records,[2] the Director of the National Center for Health Statistics (NCHS) described the kind of dilemma that can arise. Another component of the Department of Health, Education, and Welfare (DHEW), NCHS' parent agency, had requested individually identifiable data collected by the Center on family planning procedures for the purpose of checking whether the consent procedures for sterilization, as reported to NCHS, were adequate. NCHS declined to release the information, citing the confidentiality provisions in its own enabling statute. The Secretary of DHEW did not compel NCHS to make the data available to the other DHEW component although he had discretionary authority to do so under the NCHS statute. He might well have done so if the legislative history of the NCHS statute had not made clear that such information should be disclosed without individual consent only for research and statistical purposes.

There are now two basic mechanisms for limiting the use and disclosure of records maintained for research and statistical purposes. One is to protect the confidentiality of such records by statute, a method that can specify the criteria for disclosure with some precision. The other is for the agency maintaining such records to exercise its discretion in responding to requests for disclosure as they arise.

Sole reliance on agency discretion has serious shortcomings. An official with responsibilities for both research and administrative activities is not always the best fulcrum on which to balance competing claims, as the NCHS dilemma suggests. It may be particularly difficult for an administrative official to be entirely objective in weighing the pros and cons of a disclosure when the request is in support of a program within his own agency, and the disclosure is requested by agency personnel on a need-to-know basis. Relying on agency discretion alone may well dilute any pledge of confidentiality for both researcher and data subject.

Objective criteria and orderly determination of the propriety of voluntary disclosures are better safeguards for the integrity of the research process than ad hoc ones, and are easier to define and adhere to uniformly when they are established by statute rather than by administrative action. It is particularly important that the prospective data subject know of, and know that he can rely on, the limitations on use and disclosure as a basis for consenting to participate in any research project. It is equally important that users have no doubt about what uses are permitted and what disclosures they may make.

STATUTORY EXCEPTIONS

Two types of statutory exceptions to the principle of functional separation deserve special consideration: (1) disclosures in response to compulsory process; and (2) disclosures for auditing purposes.

The Commission recognizes that several statutes presently protect

---

[2] Testimony of the National Center for Health Statistics, *Medical Records*, Hearings before the Privacy Protection Study Commission, pp. 54-56.

some specific types of data and all the records of some specific agencies, such as the Bureau of the Census, against compulsory process. No Federal statute, however, protects the confidentiality of individually identifiable research data in general. Consequently, they are subject to no uniform standard of protection.

As explained above, the Commission believes that when an individual is asked to reveal information about himself in confidence—less for his own than for society's benefit—the disadvantages of making the information available for purposes other than those stated to the individual usually outweigh the advantages accruing to other users. This is particularly true when the information is available through compulsory process because the disadvantages of this type of disclosure to researcher and subject far outweigh the advantage to any law enforcement investigation. If research and statistical data remain subject to compulsory process, regulatory agencies can seek access to research data for law enforcement and compliance control purposes, thereby immeasurably increasing the risk to the individual of participating in research. Furthermore, it is confusing for the research subject if some of the information he may provide is protected by law from compulsory disclosure but other information is not. For these reasons, the Commission believes the present legal protections are unacceptably ambiguous and far too limited.

There are at least three ways to give individually identifiable research information better protection from compulsory process: (1) by constitutional interpretation; (2) by statute; and (3) by administrative action. The DHEW regulations regarding research involving human subjects *[45 C.F.R. 46]* and the grant and contract instruments of several Federal sponsors of research illustrate the administrative approach. Better and wider use could certainly be made of this approach, but it is limited in that administrative regulation only governs the conduct of persons bound in one way or another to the agency issuing the rules. Furthermore, administrative regulations by themselves do not take precedence over legislative or judicial demands for information, and the courts are unlikely to recognize an administrative agency's plea that they do so.

A constitutional approach also has practical limitations. The experience of newspeople who have claimed the privilege of confidentiality as a First Amendment right does not encourage the hope that an analogous researcher's privilege would find judicial support. Although in civil litigation, where countervailing Fifth Amendment or other powerful rights are not asserted, the courts may be willing to recognize a privileged status for the researcher,[3] in criminal prosecutions where a researcher privilege might infringe upon the Sixth Amendment right to cross-examine, courts are not likely to heed assertions of Constitutional privilege based on nothing stronger than a generalized concern for the integrity of the research process.

Statutory protections from compulsory process can be provided either

---

[3] See *Richards of Rockford, Inc. v. Pacific Gas & Electric Company* 71 F.R.D. 388 (N.D. Cal. 1976); also, *Branzburg v. Hayes* 408 U.S. 665 (1972) where the Supreme Court held that a Grand Jury, given its unique powers of inquiry and pledge of secrecy could compel a reporter to disclose information that was "relevant and material to a good-faith grand jury investigation."

by general legislation to be interpreted by the courts with or without criteria; or by authority to grant immunity from compulsory process according to specified criteria that is delegated by statute to one or more administrative entities. Each method has its strengths and weaknesses. The former may be simpler but it is less predictable, because it would require the courts to adjudicate on a case-by-case basis. The latter, also subject to judicial review, can provide greater uniformity, but in turn has the disadvantage of interposing an additional level of administrative review.

Current Federal law, as noted above, provides examples of several types of protections of research data from compelled disclosure. The statute regarding disclosure of Bureau of the Census records [13 U.S.C. 8, 9] prohibits the use of individual census records for any purpose other than the statistical purposes for which they are created, and further prohibits anyone other than Bureau personnel from examining them. The National Center for Health Statistics has limited statutory protection [42 U.S.C. 242m] for all the individually identifiable research information it collects. Use for any purpose other than that for which the information was collected is prohibited except as authorized by DHEW regulations, and no publication or disclosure of information in individually identifiable form is permitted except with the consent of the individual to whom it pertains.

Patient records maintained in connection with any drug or alcohol abuse program or research activity conducted, regulated, or directly or indirectly assisted by a Federal agency or department, may only be disclosed for specified purposes, namely, to qualified personnel for specific research or audit provided that patient identities are not disclosed in any resulting reports, or pursuant to a court order issued for good cause. [42 U.S.C. 4582; 21 U.S.C. 1175]

The Secretary of DHEW may also authorize researchers engaged in mental health or alcohol or drug abuse research to withhold names or identifying characteristics of data subjects, and this immunity covers them in any Federal, State or local civil, criminal, administrative, legislative, or other proceeding. [42 U.S.C. 4582] The Law Enforcement Assistance Administration (LEAA) has both statutory immunity from compulsory process and a statutory prohibition against voluntary disclosure. [42 U.S.C. 3371] The LEAA statute prohibits any Federal employee or recipient of assistance under it to use or reveal individually identifiable research or statistical information for any purpose other than the one for which the information was obtained. In addition, copies of any individually identifiable information furnished under the statute are immu•e from legal process, and cannot be admitted as evidence without the individual data subject's consent, or used for any purpose in any action, suit, or other judicial or administrative proceeding.

Such statutory protections demonstrate that there are mechanisms that can effectively protect the subjects of research or statistical data from the hazards of compulsory disclosure and at the same time hold researchers accountable for unauthorized use or voluntary disclosure. Immunity can be provided for the researcher, protecting him from being compelled to disclose information; or to the research relationship, creating privilege for the researcher-subject communication; or to protecting the interests of the data subject. Since researcher immunity would interfere with researcher accountability, the Commission considers it unacceptable. Similarly, a researcher testimonial privilege is deficient in that it expresses paramount concern for the research process, rather than for the individual data subject. It is the Commission's position that the relationship between the *individual* and the record-keeping *organization* is the one that needs to be controlled. The Commission, therefore, strongly favors statutory immunity which protects the rights and interests of the individual and also includes researcher accountability for voluntary disclosure.

The Commission has concluded that the individual's privacy interests as well as his right to refuse to testify against himself demand, albeit indirectly, that research and statistical records be generally immune to disclosure compelled by judicial order. Total immunity, however, is too broad. In part to protect research subjects, and in part to protect society's interest in assuring proper conduct by the researcher, access to research records ought to be permitted (though carefully controlled) when a researcher or research institution is under investigation for possible violation of law and confidential records constitute the only available source of information necessary for the investigation. If a research activity is suspected of having unnecessarily endangered research subjects, as in the infamous Central Intelligence Agency research on LSD, for example, or if a researcher is suspected of fraud, access to confidential research records may well be the only way to establish guilt or innocence.

There are also arguments for a statutory exception to the non-disclosure rule if disclosure is essential for auditing or evaluating Federal and federally funded research and statistical activities. Management and fiscal accountability are, after all, as fundamental to the integrity of the research process as is assuring the confidentiality of information. Nevertheless, the Commission believes that such access should be permitted only if the Congress has made a public-policy determination that audit or evaluation is necessary in the public interest; that is, if audit or evaluation has been authorized by statute. Even then, however, the Commission recommends stringent restrictions on disclosure.

There must also be an exception for transferring research and statistical information in individually identifiable form to archival storage. There are differences of opinion between the Bureau of the Census and the National Archives and Records Service as to how many years should elapse before census records are transferred to the Archives where they would become available to researchers. The Commission regards this as a matter of public policy that the Congress can resolve by redefining the statutory disclosure authority of both agencies.

There is also the researcher's moral and legal obligation to report acts of interpersonal violence he either witnesses or can reasonably anticipate. The Commission also believes that serious threats to the health and safety of an individual may, in some cases, justify violation of record confidentiality. Finally, the Commission believes that one of the surest ways to protect the interests of the individual is to give him a legal remedy when his rights have been violated. The Commission therefore considers it essential for the individual to have the legal capacity to challenge researcher users or record keepers he believes are violating his interest in, or are demanding unwarranted access to, information about him, or to obtain redress after his rights have been violated. Consequently, *for areas in which such minimum protections do not now exist,* the Commission recommends:

Recommendation (2):

That the Congress provide by statute that any record or information contained therein collected or maintained for a research or statistical purpose under Federal authority or with Federal funds may be used or disclosed in individually identifiable form without the authorization of the individual to whom such record or information pertains only for a research or statistical purpose, except:

(a)   where the researcher reasonably believes that the information will forestall continuing or imminent physical injury to an individual, provided that the information disclosed is limited to that information necessary to secure the protection of the individual who may be injured;

(b)   where information is furnished in compliance with a judicial order, including a search warrant or lawfully issued subpoena, and the purpose of the judicial order is to assist inquiry into an alleged violation of law by a researcher or an institution or agency maintaining research and statistical records, provided that:

(i)   any information so disclosed shall not be used as evidence in any administrative, legislative, or judical proceeding against anyone other than the researcher or research entity,

(ii)   any information so disclosed shall not be used as evidence (or otherwise made public) in such a manner that the subject of the research may be identified, unless identification of an individual research subject is necessary to prove the violation of law, and

(iii)   an individual identified in any information to be made public in identifiable form be given notice prior to such publication and be granted standing to contest the necessity of such publication;

(c)   where information is disclosed in individually identifiable form for the purpose of auditing or evaluating a Federal research program and such an audit or evaluation is expressly authorized by Federal statute; or

(d)   where information is disclosed to the National Archives and Records Service pursuant to the Federal Records Act.

And further, that should information be disclosed under any other conditions, an individual research subject identified in the information disclosed shall have a legal right of action against the person, institution, or agency disclosing the information, the person, institution or agency seeking disclosure and, in the case of a court order, the person who applied for such an order.

CONDITIONS FOR STATUTORILY AUTHORIZED AUDITS

The legitimacy of access to individually identifiable research or statistical information for auditing purposes recognized in *Recommendation (2)* leaves some important issues to be resolved. The project manager who monitors an agency research project may have to examine individual data as an integral part of his responsibility, and the agency itself has an internal management obligation to audit. Also, the General Accounting Office (GAO) conducts external audits under its statutory authority to hold agencies and their research contractors accountable. While an audit is primarily financial, the audit team may occasionally need access to raw data about individual data subjects.

It is good information practice to incorporate safeguards for individually identifiable data as early as possible in the collection and processing stages of a research project, since every subsequent stage of research further exposes the data and increases the potential for breaches of confidentiality. The same reasoning applies to the auditing process. There are various ways for the auditing process itself to incorporate safeguards without losing efficiency.

First, the necessity for access to individually identifiable data can be minimized by inserting review mechanisms into the project plan and creating an audit trail. Second, if audit requirements cannot reasonably be met without access to individually identifiable data, the audit team can adopt procedures such as on-site inspection of the data or stripping the data of identifiers before they are removed from the research site. Such matters should be negotiated with the audit team to assure that the record subjects' interests are represented.

When auditors take individually identifiable data away from the research site, other safeguards will be needed. Inadvertent disclosure is obviously a concern in such instances. In addition, auditors may be less responsive to the assurances of confidentiality given when the data were collected than the researcher who collected them. This would be especially true for data open to compulsory process. The researcher would tend to resist access demands for law enforcement or other judicial and legislative purposes on principle, but the auditor might not. Unless the auditor is prohibited by law from disclosing individually identifiable data, some prior agreement between auditor and researcher covering compulsory demands would appear to be necessary. This is the reason the Commission recommends statutory restrictions on the disclosure of individually identifiable data.

Aside from the possibility of inadvertent or compulsory disclosure to third parties, there is the possibility that the auditor will use the information as the basis for a reinterview of the data subject. The issue is particularly sensitive from the research standpoint. If recontact occurs before the research study is completed, the experience may modify the research environment and bias the results. For longitudinal studies, recontact by the auditor may make it more difficult for the researcher to obtain the further cooperation of data subjects, biasing the results in ways difficult to compensate for statistically. If information provided for research purposes may be used by auditors for individual review and perhaps recontact, the data subject should be notified of the possibility in his initial interview with the researcher.

In addressing these issues, it is helpful to keep in mind the distinction made earlier between studies that do not benefit data subjects and those that do. Studies connected with experimental social programs are an example of the latter. In the usual survey situation, respondents cooperate from a simple desire to contribute to the general fund of knowledge or perhaps out of a sense of social duty. There is nothing in such transactions to suggest that the information solicited will go farther than the stated use; indeed, usually the data subject gets assurances, not necessarily legally binding, that the information will be reported anonymously and used only for research purposes. If this is the case, an agency would be hard put to defend any use of the information as a basis for any action—particularly adverse action—with respect to an individual respondent. On the other hand, a person who receives benefits from participating in a pilot or other experimental program has, it can be argued, entered into an implied contract with the agency and assumed the responsibilities concurrent with the benefits. The information so collected can be considered to have administrative as well as research implications.

In dealing with Federal programs of the latter sort, the General Accounting Office has taken the position that its fiscal obligations to Congress require it to audit all aspects of experimental programs. According to the GAO, proper performance of its duties may oblige it to recontact data subjects and, in some circumstances, to reinterview participants as a check on the information collected by the original interviewer. The GAO has a substantial statutory base for its claim to this authority, and the scope of the examination-of-records clause which is mandatory in Federal procurement contracts has been construed broadly for auditors. On the other hand, an audit may uncover fraud or some other actionable breach of conduct on the part of the interviewer or program official. If that happens, and if there are no restrictions on the auditor's access to or use of individually identifiable data, completely innocent data subjects can be drawn into the investigation and have individually identifiable information about them made part of the record. Such disclosure can harm both the data subject and the research process without any corresponding benefit to the audit process or the investigation. Clearly, the data subject in these circumstances deserves complete insulation from disclosures of information about him. Safeguards should be required to minimize any untoward consequences arising from his unfortunate connection with someone else's wrongdoing.

The audit may also uncover some reportable condition or unlawful behavior on the part of the data subject himself. Unless the researcher is legally obliged to report such a condition or offense, the auditor ought not to be permitted to do so. Information about the data subject should not be disclosable for law enforcement or other compliance purposes, nor should audit results be used for such purposes. Auditors who so disclose individually identifiable information should be subject to legal sanctions.

If compliance or law enforcement actions may result from the auditing of an experimental program, anyone asked to participate in the program should be so advised in advance. No data subject should be persuaded to participate in or provide information for a research project under assurances of confidentiality only to discover later that the data he has supplied have been used in ways he was not told in advance to expect.

In sum, the position of the Commission is that auditors should have as little access as possible to individually identifiable information obtained for research purposes, and that when audit access is necessary, there should be safeguards to protect individually identifiable data from inadvertent disclosure. In addition, an auditor should recontact research subjects only as a last resort. Research plans should be designed to include adequate monitoring and audit trails so as to minimize the need for recontact, and alternative methods of validation should be developed. To minimize harm to the individual or to the research results, any recontact should be negotiated, in advance, with the researcher.

Moreover, individually identifiable information obtained by the auditor should not be open to administrative use or compulsory process. Disclosure of individually identifiable data by the auditor should be governed by the restrictions applicable to the researcher. There should be sanctions for unauthorized use or disclosure of the information. The data subject should also be protected from disclosure of individually identifiable information about him when an audit involves the researcher in a civil suit or criminal proceeding. Finally, the prospective data subject should be adequately informed, in advance of participation, of the possibility of recontact for audit, if any, and of any compliance or law enforcement use of the information which could reasonably be expected to result from an audit. The Commission, therefore, recommends:

Recommendation (3):

That when a Federal statute expressly authorizes disclosure in individually identifiable form of a research or statistical record for the purpose of auditing or evaluating a Federal or federally funded program, such statute should prohibit the use or disclosure of such information to make any decision or take any action affecting the individual to whom it pertains, except as authorized by that individual, or as the Congress specifically permits by statute.

PROCEDURES TO PROTECT CONFIDENTIALITY

Given the basic principle of functional separation and the recommended standards of confidentiality, there remains the question of responsibility and procedures for maintaining those standards. The basic arguments for functional separation apply here as well: the public's trust in the confidentiality of research and statistical records needs strengthening, as do the legal safeguards protecting them.

Guidelines for analyzing the risk and establishing appropriate safeguards for individually identifiable information are essentially the same whether the information is used for research or for administrative purposes. Confidentiality safeguards for research and statistical data do not differ appreciably from those for other information about individuals, except that additional safeguards are needed in organizations which do more than conduct research and statistical activities. In those organizations, intramural transfers of information need monitoring in order to maintain functional separation and to prevent internal administrative or management uses of new information about individuals generated by a research or statistical activity.

The Commission believes that the single most important procedure for maintaining the confidentiality of research and statistical data is the prompt removal and destruction of identifiers. This procedure is already practiced in many research organizations. Ideally, identifiers should be removed or destroyed as soon as the data are collected and verified.

The Commission recognizes that identifiers must be retained in some kinds of research, most notably longitudinal and panel-survey studies which refer to the same respondents from time to time, but retention should be the exception, not the rule. The decision to retain identifiers should not be left solely to the discretion of researchers; it should be a matter of public policy, or a decision of agency administrators. Furthermore, the retention of identifiers should trigger special precautions, such as maintaining face-sheet information separate from the survey instrument, or recording personal identifiers in a separate file that is cross referenced to the rest of the data.

Accordingly, the Commission recommends:

Recommendation (4):

That any Federal agency that collects or maintains any record or information contained therein in individually identifiable form for a research or statistical purpose should be permitted to maintain such records or information in individually identifiable form only so long as it is necessary to fulfill the research or statistical purpose for which the record or information was collected, unless retention of the ability to identify the individual to whom the record or information pertains is required by Federal statute or agency regulation.

The Commission believes that the legal requirements for confidentiality should extend to all the research and statistical activities conducted under Federal sponsorship, the only question being whether Federal agencies should require them as a condition of funding. Federal agencies contract out much of their research and statistical work, and through grants support much private and academic research on human subjects. The relationship of contractors and grantees to their funding agency varies widely, especially in the degree of Federal control. In theory, the contractor works to the agency's specifications and is required to deliver a defined product, whereas the grantee is funded to study a stated question as it sees fit and report its findings, whatever they may be. In actuality, however, these differences are more differences in form than substance, since the grantee is often required to develop and follow a detailed, exacting protocol. If the agency influences a grantee's data collection methods, the Office of Management and Budget (OMB) must approve the reporting form used by the grantee just as it does those of contractors.

From the standpoint of fair information practice, there is no compelling reason to differentiate between grantees and contractors, or between different classes of contractors if they all collect essentially the same sort of data and perform similar activities for similar research purposes. The important question is: does the Federal agency have the responsibility for the confidentiality of information disclosed to and collected by its contractors and grantees, or is the researcher solely responsible? The Commission's answer is that agencies have *de facto* responsibility for monitoring the performance of their contractors and grantees and that it makes them responsible for record confidentiality as well. To fix responsibility explicitly, however, the Commission recommends:

Recommendation (5):

That whenever a Federal agency provides, by contract or research grant, for the performance of any activity that results in the collection or maintenance of any record or information contained therein in individually identifiable form for a research or statistical purpose, the terms of such contract or research grant should:

(a) **require the contractor or grantee to establish and maintain reasonable procedures to protect such record or information from unauthorized disclosure, including provision for removal or destruction of identifiers;**

(b) **include rules for the disposition of such information or record upon termination of the contract or grant that provide appropriate protection against future unauthorized disclosure; and**

(c) **make the contractor or grantee subject to the requirements of the most stringent applicable Federal and State statutes.**

Federal agencies have several alternative mechanisms for implementing *Recommendation (5)*. Contracts can specify safeguards or require agency approval of the contractor's safeguard procedures. An agency could simply require applicants to certify that they would protect the confidentiality of individually identifiable data and be liable if their performance fell below the agency's statutory standards. These alternatives obviously entail different levels of responsibility that the Commission is not prepared to assess. The Commission's concern is that Federal agencies take care to see that proper procedures are established and that grantees and contractors, in turn, are given clear responsibility for safeguarding the data under their control. The Commission is also concerned that research organizations not be overburdened with a multiplicity of different implementation requirements, and urges that agencies standardize the safeguard procedures they require. The Office of Management and Budget should take the lead in seeing that this is done.

In addition to procedural safeguards, individually identifiable data need technical and administrative safeguards. When an agency publishes research and statistical data as anonymous microdata (that is, data in the form of individual records stripped of identification), it publishes detailed information about the characteristics of individuals and must take care to avoid publishing details that can identify individuals on the basis of unique characteristics or as members of an identifiable group.

There are various techniques for avoiding this which an agency can further develop and apply. Scholars in the field and professional associations, like the American Statistical Association, are paying considerable attention to the problem, as are agency task forces. An OMB task force, for example, is currently working on methodologies for protecting the identity of individuals in statistical reports.[4]

Techniques for minimizing identifiers or separating identifiers from responses include collecting the responses without names or under aliases; randomizing responses;[5] or using face-sheets to be detached by a third party. After they are collected, information and records can be protected during maintenance and retrieval by techniques such as deleting identifiers; random error injection;[6] and microaggregation.[7] When data sets are interlinked, link-file brokerage[8] can be used and direct linkage reestablished under statistical safeguards such as error injection or microaggregation; or by statistical matching; or file linkages can be mutually insulated. These techniques can be particularly useful in longitudinal studies,[9] where the data must include identifiers.

Suppression and contamination techniques include eliminating small cells, collapsing classifications, and injecting random error. Many statistical agencies routinely use these techniques in screening data for publication.

---

[4] Federal Committee on Statistical Methodology.

[5] "Randomizing responses" is a process whereby the respondent is given two questions of which he selects one to answer on a random basis without revealing which question he answered. The researcher can estimate proportions through statistical methods that reflect the incidence of the response to the sensitive question in the population.

[6] "Random error injection" is the innoculation of error into a report on a random basis but where the general character of the error is controlled by the researcher so that it is possible to estimate statistical parameters from a large sample even though it is not possible to tell if any given response is accurate.

[7] "Microaggregation" is the process of creating many synthetic average persons and releasing data on those rather than on real individuals.

[8] A "link-file system" is a system that maintains subject identifications in a file separate from the individual data file and which allows the linkage of subject identities and data about the individual in one or more files through codes that carry no individual identification. Brokerage refers to the maintenance of the link file by an unrelated third party whose sole function is to keep the identity of the record subject anonymous to the record collector and user.

[9] A "longitudinal study" involves tracking a group of individuals over time to establish how the state of that group varies and the average relation between an individual's state in one point of time and his state at another point in time.

When the Bureau of the Census, for example, prepares tabulations and tapes for public use, it employs elaborate screening procedures, including the suppression of geographical identifiers and limiting the detail of small samples, to prevent disclosure of individual identities by way of cross-classifications.

All agencies and organizations that collect individually identifiable data for research and statistical purposes should continually strive to improve their techniques for minimizing the amount of identifiable information collected, removing identifiers as soon as possible after the data have been processed, and protecting the links between personal identifiers and the data in their files. To assist them, the Commission recommends:

Recommendation (6):

That the National Academy of Sciences, in conjunction with the relevant Federal agencies and scientific and professional organizations, be asked to develop and promote the use of statistical and procedural techniques to protect the anonymity of an individual who is the subject of any information or record collected or maintained for a research or statistical purpose.

CONDITIONS FOR USE OF INDIVIDUALLY IDENTIFIABLE RECORDS

The growing practice of making individually identifiable information available to the research community increases the risk of unauthorized use or inadvertent disclosure. To block this flow of information would paralyze a great many socially valuable research and statistical activities and increase the cost of the others. It would quickly increase the reporting burden on the public to intolerable proportions. The Commission's concern is neither to augment nor hinder the flow of individually identifiable information, but to establish safe limits to it.

Given the basic principle of functional separation and the recommended standards and procedural safeguards, the next issue is how to protect the individually identifiable information that was collected for other purposes when it is used for research and statistical purposes. When administrative records are made available for research and statistical uses, the principle of functional separation is as basic as in other flows of individually identifiable information and adequate safeguards and mechanisms for assuring accountability for the maintenance of confidentiality are equally essential.

Researchers and statisticians often request access to administrative records, and less often request access to previously collected or compiled research and statistical data. The two types of access requests must be considered separately because of the difference in the assumptions about confidentiality under which each is collected. The recommendations in this section are for modification in Federal agency disclosure practice with respect to these two kinds of requests, and for making contractors and grantees more accountable for data security in disclosures both to and by them.

Use of Administrative Records

Researchers and statisticians use administrative records in a variety of ways. One of the Bureau of the Census' duties is to study revenue sharing and voting rights, and for this it draws information from sources such as records of automobile registrations and births and deaths. Because administrative or program records cover all the individuals in a defined population, another important use of them is for drawing statistical samples from groups such as participants in a manpower training program, military personnel, hospital patients, veterans, Medicaid recipients, retired persons, taxpayers, or students. The Bureau of the Census, for example, draws from Internal Revenue Service (IRS) records the names and addresses of all taxpayers who report farm income. It uses this list to conduct its Census of Agriculture, mailing survey forms to everyone on the list, thus creating a new sampling frame.[10] The Department of Defense draws samples from its own personnel records for surveys of military personnel characteristics and Armed Forces manpower potential.[11]

Researchers also use the records of other programs to enrich the information in their own records. Different programs record different kinds of information about clients, so that matching records of different programs about a given sample made up of individuals who participate in all or some of them gives a more complete picture of the sample. The Department of Labor, for example, may give the Social Security Administration (SSA) its records on a sample of individuals who have completed manpower training programs to help the Department find out how manpower training affects the individuals' earning capacity.

A third research use of administrative records is in secondary analysis of research data. For example, the Bureau of the Census bases its studies of population migration on research records produced by its own surveys and censuses. If it decides to study commuting patterns of persons living in particular metropolitan areas, it would reanalyze its own research records to extract the necessary information for a new sample of individuals, but would need to update some particular items of information, such as residence or employer ZIP codes, from the more current records of some other agency. It might, therefore, request access to the administrative records on the individuals in its sample held by perhaps the IRS or the SSA.

Reuse of Research and Statistical Records

The arguments in favor of reusing research and statistical information and records in individually identifiable form for research and statistical

---

[10] This exchange of information is described in detail in Appendix B to a U.S. Department of Commerce report entitled "The Use of Tax Data in the Structuring of Basic Economic Tools," November 4, 1974.

[11] Submission of Department of Defense, *Research and Statistics*, Hearings before the Privacy Protection Study Commission, January 5, 1971.

purposes are analogous to those for the use of administrative records for the same purposes. Secondary analysis of data sets can not only reduce the reporting burden on the public, but also can add new knowledge about social processes. It is also cumbersome, expensive, and in many cases impossible to replicate an already existing body of data. Moreover, secondary analysis of data can be a valuable verifier of findings originally derived from them. Finally, research and statistical information in individually identifiable form can be reused to match two or more data sets to gain more information than each singly provides, to draw samples, and to recontact individuals in the original sample for a longitudinal study of physical, social, or attitudinal change over time.

Nevertheless, the Commission urges caution. Here, as elsewhere, the flow of individually identifiable information can erode the public's willingness to cooperate voluntarily in data collection, and here, more than elsewhere, it is easy for researchers to forget the promises of confidentiality made to data subjects at the time information was collected.

The Commission believes that unless it is essential to recontact the individuals who took part in an earlier study, disclosure of information in individually identifiable form should be strictly limited to cases where public need clearly overrides private rights and then only after careful policy review of each case. This constraint need not unduly hamper research and statistical activities because, for the great bulk of them, anonymous microdata are as useful as individually identifiable data.

Conditions for Use and Disclosure

A mosaic of statutory rules governs access to and disclosure of Federal agency records at present. The Federal Reports Act, designed primarily to minimize respondent burden, permits an agency to share information collected by other agencies, subject to certain constraints. It also minimizes duplication of effort by requiring the Office of Management and Budget (OMB) to review and approve the forms used in collecting information from individuals, whether the information is for program administration purposes or for research and statistical purposes. The OMB is also authorized to designate one agency as the sole collection agent for some types of information. The OMB has seldom exercised this authority, but recently used it to designate the Bureau of the Census as the sole collector of the population statistics needed for allocating some benefits such as revenue sharing.

Release of an agency's records is also governed by its own confidentiality statutes, if any, and by general statutes, such as the Privacy Act and the Freedom of Information Act. As noted above, however, a Federal agency can have substantial freedom to set its own threshold conditions for disclosing individually identifiable data from its records. Subsection 3(b)(1) of the Privacy Act permits disclosures within an agency on a need-to-know basis without reference to the original purpose of collection, and more than one executive department has arbitrarily broadened the resulting potential for circulation of data by defining itself as a single entity. Subsection 3(b) allows disclosures for "routine uses" outside even those organizational boundaries. In general, an agency may not disclose records outside the agency except ". . . for a purpose which is compatible with the purpose for which . . . [they were] originally collected." *[5 U.S.C. 552a(a)(7)]* However, since the Act does not define "compatible," the office, bureau, center, or institute within the agency which actually maintains the records has a substantial latitude in deciding what purposes meet the test. In addition, the Freedom of Information Act may require an agency to comply with requests to disclose that it would refuse if it could.

In practice, agencies do not generally allow researchers and statisticians unrestricted access to their records. Some are tightly restrained from doing so by statute. The Bureau of the Census confidentiality statute, for example, permits only Bureau officials and employees to examine individual records. Other agencies interpret the Privacy Act compatibility test narrowly, while still others that have statutory discretion to do so often release data to their own contractors under the "routine use" provision of the Privacy Act. Only one agency appears to release individually identifiable data not only to its own grantees, but also to other researchers. Thus, the pool of researchers and statisticians who have in fact received individually identifiable information from Federal agencies is composed almost entirely of Federal agency employees, contractors, some grantees, and a relatively small number of people who have neither contracts nor grants. Even these groups do not ordinarily get full access to records. The typical disclosure is a sample list of names and addresses. An agency's disclosure problems are complicated by the fact that it can sponsor research by contract or by grant.[12] Most agencies follow different disclosure policies depending upon whether the request for information comes from a contractor or a grantee but, as noted above, that simple distinction is not always valid as far as fair information practices are concerned.

Whenever an agency discloses individually identifiable information under the Privacy Act's "routine use" provision to a researcher whose procedures it controls, the funding instrument should contain safeguards for the released information, and these should be the same whether the request is from a contractor or a grantee. In practice, agencies differ in the safeguards they require in these cases. At the completion of the research project, for example, some contracts explicitly require that all identifiers be expunged from the records retained, others require that all data be returned to the agency, and some remain silent on this point. There are, in short, numerous ambiguities in the way disclosures of individually identifiable information are now regulated. If the research community is to have access to already existing individually identifiable information without endangering the privacy of data subjects, these ambiguities will have to be cleared up, and the conditions of disclosure made more explicit.

The Commission is well aware that opinions vary widely on how important given research endeavors are to society, and hence, how much

---

[12] It must be noted that the grants discussed here are Federal discretionary grants, not formula or block grants, which involve Federal-State issues beyond the scope of these recommendations.

disclosure is warranted in any instance. Nonetheless, there are minimum conditions that should be met before any disclosure or use of individually identifiable records for research and statistical purposes is permitted, and these conditions should be set by statute. First, the applicant must demonstrate a vital need for individually identifiable data to achieve its proposed research or statistical purpose. Second, in assuring responsibility for maintaining proper safeguards, a responsibility obviously shared by both the applicant for and the provider of information, the Commission believes that the provider of information has the prime obligation for assuring that the conditions of disclosure are met by the receiving body. The provider can meet this obligation by stipulating the conditions for releasing the information and requiring the receiver to agree in writing to honor them, subject to criminal or other sanctions. In all cases, the user should be accountable to the agency responsible for the collection of the data. In addition, if the research purposes include recontact of data subjects, protection of the expectation of confidentiality under which the information was originally collected should be made a condition of disclosure.

The Commission recommends:

Recommendation (7):

That unless prohibited by Federal statute, a Federal agency may be permitted to use or disclose in individually identifiable form for a research or statistical purpose any record or information it collects or maintains without the authorization of the individual to whom such record or information pertains only when the agency:

(a) **determines that such use or disclosure does not violate any limitations under which the record or information was collected;**

(b) **ascertains that use or disclosure in individually identifiable form is necessary to accomplish the research or statistical purpose for which use or disclosure is to be made;**

(c) **determines that the research or statistical purpose for which any disclosure is to be made is such as to warrant risk to the individual from additional exposure of the record or information;**

(d) **requires that reasonable procedures to protect the record or information from unauthorized disclosure be established and maintained by the user or recipient, including a program for removal or destruction of identifiers;**

(e) **prohibits any further use or redisclosure of the record or information in individually identifiable form without its express authorization; and**

(f) **makes any disclosure pursuant to a written agreement with the proposed recipient which attests to all the above, and which makes the recipient subject to any sanctions applicable to agency employees.**

The above recommendation holds the disclosing agency accountable for assuring that the individually identifiable information it releases for research and statistical purposes is used responsibly. This presents no problem when an agency discloses information to a contractor or grantee supported by the agency itself. The situation is more complex when a contractor or grantee funded by one agency needs access to information maintained by another agency. To clarify the chain of accountability in these instances, disclosure should be contingent on an agreement by the agency funding the research or statistical activity to take prime responsibility for assuring that the user satisfies the conditions under which the information is released. Therefore, the Commission recommends:

Recommendation (8):

That when disclosure pursuant to *Recommendation (7)* is made to a Federal contractor or grantee, the written agreement should be between the disclosing agency and funding agency, with the latter responsible for assuring that the terms of the agreement are met.

Recommendations (7) and *(8)* are designed to regulate disclosure by Federal agencies, but can be applied as well to Federal contractors and grantees when they are asked to disclose individually identifiable information. Under existing law, individually identifiable information collected by grantees is not subject to the provisions of the Privacy Act. The granting agency may require safeguards for such information, but any obligation to do so is a matter of administrative policy or regulation.

Individually identifiable information collected by contractors in performance of their work for an agency is also not necessarily subject to the Privacy Act. The Privacy Act states:

> When an agency provides by a contract for the operation by or on behalf of the agency of a system of records to accomplish an agency function, the agency shall, consistent with its authority, cause the requirements of this section to be applied to such system . . . . *[5 U.S.C. 552a(m)]*

Some agencies interpret this clause to mean that contractors may not collect information about individuals under conditions that are less confidential than the conditions applying to records maintained by the agency itself. In a May 1976 memorandum, however, the General Counsel of DHEW interpreted it to mean that, in performing this kind of work, contractors are comparable to grantees, and that

> . . . the requirements of the Privacy Act of 1974 are not applicable to HEW research and other contracts which call for the contractor merely to furnish to the HEW contracting agency statistical or

other reports, even though it is necessary for the contractor to establish a system of records to perform the contract.[13]

Although contractor records compiled under these conditions are not thought to be subject to the Privacy Act, the memo advises DHEW contracting officers to incorporate into contracts, where appropriate, " . . . the provisions designed to protect the confidentiality of the records and the privacy of individual identifiers in the records."

These differences in agency interpretation of obligations under the Privacy Act, and the lack of any explicit policy concerning the protection of individually identifiable data collected under a grant, make for a less than satisfactory disclosure situation. This is especially true since, as noted before, the agencies' existing disclosure policies are complicated by differing confidentiality provisions in statutes and the several methods of procuring research. Yet, where individually identifiable information is collected and maintained as a consequence of Federal funding, there is a corresponding obligation on the part of the Federal government to maintain accountability to the individual. Individually identifiable information held by a contractor or grantee should be disclosed only when the recipient can be held accountable for any violation of the individual's right to have identifiable data about him shielded from improper use or disclosure. For this, an additional accountability mechanism is necessary and the Commission, therefore, recommends:

Recommendation (9):

That any person, who under Federal contract or grant collects or maintains any record or information contained therein for a research or statistical purpose, be prohibited from disclosing such record or information in individually identifiable form for another research or statistical purpose, except pursuant to a written agreement that meets the specifications of *Recommendations (7)* and *(8)* above, and has been approved by the Federal funding agency.

PROTECTIONS TO BE INVOKED BY THE INDIVIDUAL

Once individually identifiable research and statistical data are insulated from all other types of use by adequate safeguards and standards of accountability, there remains only the question of what the individual can do for his own protection, or have done on his behalf. Specifically, the following questions about the role of the individual need to be answered.

- When should the individual's authorization to gather or disclose information about him be necessary?
- What constitutes adequate notice to the individual of the level

---

[13] Memorandum from General Counsel William H. Taft III to John Ottina, Assistant Secretary for Administration and Management, Department of Health, Education, and Welfare, regarding the application of the Privacy Act to DHEW contractors, May 14, 1976.

of confidentiality an agency or organization expects to maintain?

• What constitutes adequate notice to the individual that the information he supplies for administrative purposes may also be used for a research or statistical purpose?

• Under what conditions should the individual be allowed access to research and statistical records pertaining to himself?

These questions reveal important differences between information collected directly from the individual for a research or statistical purpose and information extracted from administrative records for the same purpose. It may be useful to begin by examining the individual's role as prescribed by the Privacy Act of 1974, and then to consider whether the same role for the individual will suffice when the information is for research or statistical use.

A goal of the Privacy Act is to permit an individual to monitor an agency's collection, use, and dissemination practices with respect to information about him in its possession by giving him access to the information about him in agency files, and an opportunity to challenge errors. In addition, the Privacy Act specifies that the individual has the right to learn of disclosures to others, with a few significant exceptions (i.e., internal agency uses, disclosures made pursuant to the requirements of the Freedom of Information Act, and disclosures to law enforcement agencies). The Privacy Act's main mechanisms for giving the individual some control over government *use* of the information it collects about him are notice and authorization. At the time information is collected from an individual he must be notified of the authority under which it is being collected and whether his response is mandatory or voluntary, and also of the purposes for collecting the information and the uses to which it will be put. He must also be told the consequences of not supplying the information. *[5 U.S.C. 552a(e)(3)]* The agencies must give public notice annually of their existing record systems, *[5 U.S.C. 552a(e)(4)]* although the OMB guidelines have modified this requirement so that after an agency has published its initial list of record systems it need only report any new ones or any changes in existing systems. An agency must advise an individual, on request, if it maintains any records on him and, on request, allow him to examine the records on him and challenge their accuracy. *[5 U.S.C. 552a(d)]* The record of an individual may not be used for purposes other than those for which it was collected without the individual's consent except as expressly authorized by any one of the 11 exceptions in the Privacy Act. *[5 U.S.C. 552a(b)]* One such exception, as noted earlier, is for a "routine use," which, being open to interpretation, diminishes the efficacy of the Act's authorization requirements.

Notice and authorization work together, but not in the same way. Generally speaking, the intent of the Privacy Act notice requirements is to assure that the individual, knowing in advance the purpose for which the information is collected and what uses may be made of it, can refuse to cooperate if his participation is voluntary, or challenge the questioner's authority if it is not. The Privacy Act assumes that any reasonable individual will expect that the information he contributes may be disclosed for auditing use, or in response to court order or legislative inquiry, or for tax and other law enforcement purposes. The assumption, however, is seldom justified when information is collected for a research or statistical purpose. It is not reasonable to expect the subject to know that the data he supplies for a research or statistical purpose may be disclosed in response to compulsory process or may enter into an administrative decision pertaining to him. Thus, unless there is functional separation of research and statistical uses of information from administrative uses, the notice requirements of the Privacy Act are clearly inadequate.

Assuming that functional separation can be established as recommended by the Commission, the question of how much control the individual should have over how information pertaining to him is used in research or statistical activities remains, as well as the question of how that control should be exercised.

INFORMATION COLLECTED FOR RESEARCH AND STATISTICAL PURPOSES

Individually identifiable data about individuals flow into research and statistical record systems, as into other record systems, from several sources. Some is obtained directly from individuals by means of questionnaires, interviews, and other methods of systematic inquiry, such as controlled experiments, sometimes with the individual's full knowledge and sometimes without it. For example, data are sometimes collected from persons not fully competent to understand the collection process, while other information is extracted from administrative or program records, or supplied by third parties.

In considering an individual's control over information about him when it is used for research and statistical purposes, the important distinction is between the information researchers and statisticians get from him directly and that which they get from him indirectly by culling it from administrative files. The distinction is important because of the difference in the individual's expectation of confidentiality. When asked to contribute information for administrative purposes, he can reasonably expect that his contribution will enter into administrative decisions about him and act accordingly, but when asked to contribute it for research or statistical purposes, he is not likely to anticipate any uses other than the ones stated by the questioner.

When an individual is asked to provide information for a research or statistical purpose, he should, in all fairness, have a reasonable idea of the consequences to him of agreeing or of refusing to answer. Minimally, this means he must be told that he can refuse if he chooses, and informed of the purpose and nature of the data collection, and the extent to which the information he supplies will be disclosed further in individually identifiable form. Accordingly, as a supplement to notice requirements already embodied in the Privacy Act[14] the Commission recommends:

Recommendation (10):

That absent an explicit statutory requirement to the contrary, any Federal agency that collects or supports the collection of individually identifiable information from an individual for a research or statistical purpose be required by Federal statute to notify such individual:

(a)   of the possibility, if any, that the information may be used or disclosed in individually identifiable form for additional research or statistical purposes;

(b)   of any requirements for disclosure in individually identifiable form for purposes other than research and statistical use; and

(c)   that if any such required disclosure is made for other than a research or statistical purpose, he will be promptly notified.

Some research involves children or people of diminished mental competence; other research involves population groups, such as prisoners, whose circumstances compromise their freedom to choose whether or not to participate. There are also research experiments so designed that the validity of the findings depends on the participants' ignorance of some aspects of the research, and sometimes even of the fact that they are participating in research. To create special protection for such data subjects, the Commission recommends an institutional review process. The Commission recognizes the difficulty of creating institutional review boards where they do not now exist, and holding a Federal agency accountable for the actions of those collecting information for research or statistical activities on its behalf as well as for its own actions. The Commission's intent is not to specify how institutional review is to be established, but rather to make the point that the safeguards that enable an individual to protect himself must be applied to the individual who, for one reason or another, cannot take advantage of them on his own initiative. Accordingly, the Commission recommends:

Recommendation (11):

That Congress provide by statute that when information about an individual is to be collected in individually identifiable form for a research or statistical purpose by a Federal agency or with Federal funding, an institutional review process be required to apply the principles enunciated in *Recommendation (10)* in order to protect the individual:

(a)   who is not competent to give informed consent to provide information about himself (e.g., a minor or mentally incompetent individual);

---

[14] The Privacy Act already requires that an individual be told whether his participation is mandatory or voluntary and the purposes and nature of the data collection. *[5 U.S.C. 552a(e)(3)]*

(b)   whose consent may be seriously compromised by fear of some loss of benefit or imposition of sanction (e.g., "captive populations," such as students, welfare recipients, employees, prison inmates, or hospital patients);

(c)   when the ability to conduct statistical or research activity is predicated on the individual being unaware of its existence, purpose, or specific nature.

In this context, the Commission observes that although its mandate is confined to protecting the interests of research subjects with respect to information and records about them generated by research and statistical methods, its broad concern is with protecting the more general rights and welfare of human research subjects. The Department of Health, Education, and Welfare, as the Federal agency sponsoring the bulk of such research, has, since 1966, taken the lead in this area by issuing guidelines and regulations setting conditions designed to control research on human subjects. Recent action by the Congress, furthermore, portends even wider ramifications. For example, the National Research Act of 1974 *[P.L. 93-348]* establishes a National Commission for the Protection of Human Subjects in Biomedical and Behavioral Science Research (NCPHS) with a mandate to define the ethical principles of such research and recommend policies for assuring that the research does not violate ethical principles in practice. Among other things, the National Research Act provides for making the NCPHS recommendations applicable to all Federal agencies, and for establishing a National Advisory Council to monitor the protection of human subjects after the NCPHS completes its task.

The DHEW regulatory activities to protect human research subjects have focused on the institutional responsibility of the organization that actually conducts the research. Under current policy, no DHEW extramural research involving human subjects may be undertaken unless a committee known as an institutional ethical review board has assured DHEW that it has reviewed the proposed research design and determined whether human subjects will be placed at risk, and if so, that: the risks are outweighed by the sum of the benefits to the individual and the importance of the knowledge to be gained; the rights and welfare of the subjects will be adequately protected; legally effective informed consent will be obtained from each participant; and the conduct of the research will be reviewed at timely intervals.

The NCPHS does not expect to issue its final recommendations until the end of 1977. It is already clear, however, that institutional review committees will continue to have the prime responsibility for protecting human subjects. Consequently, where institutional ethical review boards do not already exist pursuant to DHEW regulations, there is every likelihood that they will soon be established pursuant to recommendations of the NCPHS. When this happens, the existing boards and the newly created ones will provide a suitable vehicle for carrying out *Recommendation (11)*.

INFORMATION COLLECTED FROM ADMINISTRATIVE RECORDS

From the standpoint of protecting the individual, the two most pertinent questions about the use for a research or statistical purpose of individually identifiable information drawn from administrative or other records are: whether information ostensibly collected for administrative purposes is actually being collected for research and statistical purposes without the individual's authorization; and whether delivery of program or other benefits should be contingent on the individual's willingness to have administrative information about him also used for a research or statistical purpose?

With respect to the first question, the Commission believes that while research and statistical "piggy-backing" on administrative data collections does perhaps occur more often than necessary, the measures recommended by the Commission will protect the individual from having additional information generated by research activities used to his detriment. The first question will then be less important than it is now.

The second question presents a more difficult problem, since the answer depends on balancing the individual's right to control the collection and use of information pertaining to him against the society's need for knowledge. The preceding recommendations recognize the societal utility of information generated by research and statistical activities, and the extent to which the continuing productivity of these activities depends on access to administrative records by allowing individually identifiable data in administrative records to be disclosed for research or statistical purposes under appropriate safeguards.

Additional protections for the individual about whom information in administrative records is used for a research or statistical purpose are not necessary because the measures in the preceding recommendations will be adequate. Research and statistical activities can safely be spared the costly burden of obtaining the authorization of each individual if adequate notice is given when the information is collected for administrative records in the first place. The individual will then realize that the information he supplies for administrative purposes may also be used for research or statistical purposes, and that he may be contacted by a researcher. Accordingly, the Commission recommends:

Recommendation (12):

That Congress provide by statute that when individually identifiable information is collected from an individual by a Federal agency or with Federal funding for a purpose other than a research or statistical one, the individual be informed that:

    (a)   such information may be used or disclosed in individually identifiable form for a research or statistical purpose, with appropriate safeguards;

    (b)   that he may be recontacted as a result of such use or disclosure.

INDIVIDUAL ACCESS TO RESEARCH AND STATISTICAL RECORDS

The right given an individual by the Privacy Act to see and copy a record maintained about him and to challenge the information in the record recognizes that the individual has a role to play in decision-making processes that affect him. Records that are dedicated by statute solely to research or statistical use may be exempted from the general right of access and challenge because, unlike administrative records, they are not used for making decisions about individuals. If information in research or statistical records cannot be disclosed in individually identifiable form for any other purpose, the individual need have no great concern about it. Unless such records can be totally protected against the possibility that individually identifiable information in them will be disclosed for any other purpose, the individual's concern is obvious and his access right highly relevant.

Two points are important. First, it is important for the individual to retain a measure of control over individually identifiable research or statistical information pertaining to him because he needs some way of finding out who else gets the information. Second, whether an individual needs to have access to records maintained about him for research or statistical purposes depends on how well these records can be kept separate from other uses. If separation is not maintained, and the information is in fact disclosed in individually identifiable form for other than a research or statistical use without a guarantee that the disclosure will not affect the individual, fairness demands that the individual be informed of the disclosure and to whom it was made, and be given a right of access to the record. Accordingly, the Commission recommends:

Recommendation (13):

That Congress provide by statute that if any record or information contained therein collected or maintained by a Federal agency or with Federal funding for a research or statistical purpose is disclosed in individually identifiable form without an assurance that such record or information will not be used to make any decision or take an action directly affecting the individual to whom it pertains (e.g., to a court or an audit agency), or without a prohibition on further use or disclosure, the individual should be notified of the disclosure and of his right of access both to his record and to any accounting of its disclosure.[15]

IMPLEMENTATION STRATEGY

No single vehicle is adequate to carry out all of the Commission's recommendations in this chapter. Thus, the Commission has chosen a strategy which encompasses amendments to the Privacy Act of 1974, other legislative action, and voluntary compliance on the part of national study organizations.

---

[15] The Privacy Act already requires an accounting of such disclosures. *[5 U.S.C. 552a(c)]*

The Commission feels that the principle of functional separation (*Recommendation (1)*) can be established by amending the Privacy Act.[16] The first set of steps necessary to apply that principle to Federal and federally assisted research, namely, establishing appropriate uses and disclosures for research and statistical records (*Recommendations (2) and (3)*) can best be implemented through a new Federal statute to provide a common line of minimum protection for the confidentiality of Federal or federally assisted research and statistical records.

The second set of steps necessary to apply the principle of functional separation—namely, establishing procedures for protecting the confidentiality of individually identifiable data—seeks to establish a consistent set of safeguards among Federal agencies and their contractors and grantees. *Recommendations (4)* and *(5)*, which would achieve this objective, can be implemented through amendment of the Privacy Act. In addition, the Commission believes that new techniques for collecting, maintaining, and using records about individuals in ways that avoid personal identification ought to be developed and promulgated, and, therefore, recommends that the National Academy of Sciences voluntarily take the lead in doing so.

The third set of recommended steps, establishing the conditions of disclosure for individually identifiable information to be used for a research or statistical purpose, seeks to assure that a common set of conditions are met in a consistent and accountable way by Federal agencies and their contractors and grantees (*Recommendations (7), (8), and (9)*). These recommendations can be implemented through amendments to the Privacy Act of 1974 which currently sets minimum conditions for the use and disclosure of Federal records.

Recommendations (10) through *(13)* address the role of the individual in protecting himself and focus on notice and access. *Recommendations (10), (11), and (12)* which deal with notice, and *Recommendation (13)*, which deals with access, can best be implemented through amendment to the Privacy Act. As pointed out in the earlier discussion of *Recommendation (11)*, however, the Commission did not specify how the institutional review the recommendation would require should be established or what the required steps in the review process should be. The Commission urges that the National Commission for the Protection of Human Subjects in Biomedical and Behavioral Research incorporate *Recommendation (11)* into the mandate of the institutional review process it will recommend for all Federal agencies and also that Federal agency regulations implementing the Privacy Act incorporate the National Commission's recommendations.

POLICY GUIDELINES

The 13 recommendations in this chapter collectively provide a means of protecting personal privacy in research and statistical activities conducted or sponsored by the Federal government. The Commission's findings lead it to present for consideration to other research communities the following nine policy guidelines which it hopes will be voluntarily adopted by all those

---

[16] See Note 2, Chapter 13.

who conduct research and statistical activities. The Commission also believes that they could help to shape any State legislation in the field. The fundamental principle for the guidelines, as for the recommendations in the previous sections of this chapter, is that of functional separation—insulating the use of individually identifiable information for research and statistical purposes from all other uses. These guidelines follow the precepts in the Commission's recommendations.

Guideline (1):

Any record or information contained therein collected or maintained for a research or statistical purpose should not be used in individually identifiable form to make any decision or take any action directly affecting the individual to whom the record pertains, except within the context of the research plan or protocol, or with the specific authorization of such individual; and

That based on the foregoing principle, a special set of information practice requirements should be established for records and information contained therein collected or maintained in individually identifiable form for a research or statistical purpose.

Great care is needed to protect individually identifiable information from unauthorized or inadvertent disclosure. The Commission is persuaded not only that full technical, administrative, and physical safeguards must be established to protect confidentiality, but also that information should be rendered anonymous by being stripped of identifiers as soon after collection as possible.

Guideline (2):

Any entity that, for a research or statistical purpose, collects or maintains in individually identifiable form any record or information contained therein should be required:

(a)   to establish and maintain adequate safeguards to protect such record or information from unauthorized disclosure; and

(b)   to maintain such record or information in individually identifiable form only so long as is necessary to fulfill the research or statistical purpose for which it was collected, unless the entity can demonstrate that there are reasons for retaining the ability to identify the individual to whom the record or information pertains which outweigh the increase in the risks to the individual of exposure of the record.

Once the principle of functional separation is accepted, and adequate mechanisms for implementing it are in place, individually identifiable information can safely be disclosed for research and statistical purposes provided certain minimal conditions are met.

Guideline (3):

Except where specifically prohibited by law, an entity that collects or maintains a record or information may use or disclose in individually identifiable form either the record or the information contained therein for a research or statistical purpose without the consent of the individual to whom the record pertains, provided that the entity:

(a) determines that such use or disclosure does not violate any limitations under which the record or information was collected;

(b) ascertains that use or disclosure in individually identifiable form is necessary to accomplish the research or statistical purpose for which use or disclosure is to be made;

(c) determines that the research or statistical purpose for which any disclosure is to be made is of sufficient social benefit to warrant the increase in the risk to the individual of exposure of the record or information;

(d) requires that adequate safeguards to protect the record or information from unauthorized disclosure be established and maintained by the user or recipient, including a program for removal or destruction of identifiers; and

(e) prohibits any further use or redisclosure of the record or information in individually identifiable form without its express authorization.

The remaining six guidelines are for the further protection of individual data subjects from unfair collection practices, and to assure individual access whenever the principle of functional separation cannot be upheld.

The Commission believes it advisable that the fair information practice principles established by the Privacy Act of 1974, and supplemented by *Recommendation (10)* above, be extended to include individuals who supply information for research and statistical activities that are independent of the Federal government.

Guideline (4):

Absent an explicit statutory requirement to the contrary, no individual should be required to divulge information about himself for a research or statistical purpose. To assure that there is no coercion or deception, the individual should be informed:

(a) that his participation is at all times voluntary;

(b) of the purposes and nature of the data collection;

(c) of the possibility, if any, that the information may be used or disclosed in individually identifiable form for additional research or statistical purposes;

(d) of any requirements for disclosure in individually identifiable form required for purposes other than research and statistical use; and

(e)   that if any such required disclosure is made for other than a research or statistical purpose, he will be promptly notified.

Individuals whose consent to participate in a research or statistical project cannot be given because of youth or disability or because the research design precludes it, and individuals whose circumstances coerce their participation need extra protection.

Guideline (5):

When information about an individual is to be collected in individually identifiable form for a research or statistical purpose, an institutional review process or responsible representative should be required to apply the principles enunciated in *Guideline (4)* in order to protect the individual:

(a)   **who is not competent to give informed consent to provide information about himself (e.g., a minor or mentally incompetent individual);**

(b)   **whose consent may be seriously compromised by fear of some loss of benefit or imposition of sanction (e.g., "captive populations" such as students, welfare recipients, employees, prison inmates, or hospital patients); or**

(c)   **when the ability to conduct statistical or research activity is predicated on the individual being unaware of its existence, purpose, or specific nature.**

When individually identifiable information collected in the first instance for some other purpose is used for research and statistical purposes, it needs special attention.

Guideline (6):

When individually identifiable information is collected for a purpose other than a research or statistical purpose the individual should be informed:

(a)   **that such information may be used or disclosed in individually identifiable form for a research or statistical purpose, with appropriate safeguards; and**

(b)   **that he may be recontacted as a result of such use or disclosure.**

So long as all individually identifiable information used for research and statistical purposes is kept separate from use for any other purpose, the individual data subject does not need access to the record. When the information cannot be protected from use for other purposes, the individual should have a right of access.

Guideline (7):

When research or statistical records or information are collected and

maintained in conformity with all the foregoing policy recommendations, an individual should have a right of access to a record or
information which pertains to him if such record or information is
used or disclosed in individually identifiable form for any purpose
other than a research or statistical one (e.g., an inadvertent
unauthorized disclosure).

Fairness demands that individuals have a way of finding out, if they
wish, what disclosures of individually identifiable information about them
have been made.

Guideline (8):

Any entity that collects or maintains a record or information for a
research or statistical purpose should be required to keep an accurate
accounting of all disclosures in individually identifiable form of such
record or information contained therein such that an individual who is
the subject of such record or information can find out that the
disclosure has been made and to whom.

The importance to an individual of access to information used for
research and statistical purposes depends on the extent to which the
information can be kept separate from use for other purposes.

Guideline (9):

If any record or information contained therein collected or maintained for a research or statistical purpose is disclosed in individually
identifiable form without an assurance that such record or information will not be used to make any decision or take an action directly
affecting the individual to whom it pertains, or without a prohibition
on further use or disclosure (e.g., to a court or an audit agency), the
individual should be notified of the disclosure, and of his right of
access to the record and to the accounting for its disclosure, as
provided by *Guidelines (7)* and *(8)* above.

Chapter 16

The Social Security Number

The Commission's mandate suggests that the Privacy Protection Study Commission make a study of:

> the use of social security numbers, license plate numbers, universal identifiers and other symbols to identify individuals in data banks and to gain access to, integrate, or centralize information systems and files. *[Section 5(c)(1)(C) of P.L. 93-579]*

In accordance with this suggestion, the Commission undertook such a study, but decided to limit its empirical study to the use of the Social Security number (SSN). There is more public concern about the SSN than any other identifier and second only to names, the SSN appears to be the most widely used label[1] in America. The Commission's findings, however, apply to any widely used system of labelling individuals; its SSN study is a case study of the advantages and disadvantages of any commonly used label.

There are essentially three basic ways to identify a person—by his physical attributes (e.g., color of hair and eyes, voiceprints, fingerprints); by a possession (e.g., passport with a photograph); and by a label (e.g., name, SSN, address). This study covers only the third because the Privacy Act, the Commission's mandate, focuses primarily on the use of labels to identify individuals.

IDENTIFICATION AND AUTHENTICATION

Before the issues surrounding the use of the SSN are described, it is necessary to understand precisely what identification and authentication mean; their role in record keeping; and the way the SSN is used in identifying and authenticating individuals and records.

Identification is the process by which an individual asserts who he is or by which an organization initially determines that a record pertains to a particular individual. Although the first process can be achieved by visual recognition, people usually identify themselves by stating or showing a label; typically an individual introduces himself to an organization by stating his name. For a record-keeping organization a label is essential to select a record that pertains to a particular individual from a set of records.

---

[1] "Label," as used in this chapter, is a general term that includes other identifiers and authenticators in addition to the SSN.

Authentication is the process of confirming that a person is who he claims to be, or that a particular record does indeed pertain to a particular individual. Typically, an individual authenticates his identity by providing a fact about himself, or another label in addition to his identifier, that is known both to the individual and to the organization. An organization authenticates that it has correctly associated a record with an individual by comparing what it learns about the individual with information already in the record.

An example of how these processes work may be helpful. When Arthur Klein goes to his bank to make a withdrawal from his savings account, the bank first asks him for his name and then for his account number. His name is used in this instance as an identifier; the account number is used as an authenticator. The bank maintains a list of all customer names with cross-references to account numbers and when Arthur recites his number, the bank employee locates it on the list to ascertain that Arthur is who he purports to be. Before Arthur's withdrawal is processed, his account record must be located. The records clerk goes to the file containing records about customers with last names beginning with "K." There are, however, three records identified by the name "Arthur Klein." Thus, the records clerk must use Arthur's account number to discriminate among the three records identified by the label "Arthur Klein" and to authenticate the fact that a particular record pertains to *the* Arthur Klein in question.

After Arthur makes his withdrawal, he asks the bank to use some of the money he has withdrawn to make a payment on his mortgage. Because mortgages are handled by another bank employee, information about the mortgage payment must be transferred from one part of the bank to another. When the information is transferred, it is labelled with Arthur's name and account number. When the mortgage section receives the information about the payment, it includes it in another previously compiled record about Arthur. In the process of doing so, it locates records about three Arthur Klein's and uses Arthur's account number to assure itself that the record finally selected does indeed pertain to the Arthur Klein in question.

Finally, when the bank reports information about the interest on Arthur's account to the Internal Revenue Service each year, it labels the information with Arthur's name and Taxpayer Identification Number. When the IRS receives the information and wishes to add it to a record it already maintains about Arthur, it will use his Taxpayer Identification Number to discriminate among the 100 Arthur Klein's on whom it maintains records.

As this example illustrates, identification and authentication processes are essential in almost any transaction that involves an individual and an organization, an organization's employees and its record systems, and the record system of one organization and that of another. For ease of reference, the process will be called *personal identification* and *personal authentication* in the first instance, and *record identification* and *record authentication* in the latter two instances. Record identification and authentication can be intra-organizational or inter-organizational; that is, they can take place between two record systems maintained by the same organization, or by separate organizations.

In some cases, notably where there is an automated record system involved, a label normally used as an authenticator can serve also as a record identifier and so either eliminate the authentication step altogether or require yet another label for authentication. In the above illustration, if the bank's savings and mortgage records were automated, the right Arthur Klein's record could be located by using his account number alone without reference to his name, so that the account number would be the record identifier, not the authenticator. Another label, Arthur's address, for example, could be used for record authentication purposes, or an authenticator may not be needed, especially if the identifier is known to be unique and accurate. The point here is that the same label can serve as an identifier in some instances, and as an authenticator in others. The development of automated record systems has, to a large extent, provided the impetus for widespread use of numerical labels such as the SSN for identification purposes.

As long as individuals have established relationships with organizations, personal identification and authentication have been important processes. For organizations which maintain records in order to facilitate their relationships with individuals, a record identification and authentication procedure within the organization is essential. As organizations and the populations served by them increase in size, the importance of identifying and authenticating the records which document and mediate interactions between organizations and individuals grows correspondingly. And, whenever organizations exchange records about an individual, inter-organizational identification and authentication become crucial. In such cases, the identifiers and authenticators used by the organizations between which exchanges of records take place must be common to both. This is one important reason why the use of a few widely available labels, such as the SSN, has become pervasive.

The genesis of the Social Security number offers a good example of the compelling need of organizations for accurate identification and authentication. Shortly after the Social Security Act of 1935 became effective, the Bureau of Internal Revenue issued a regulation requiring the issuance of an account number to each employee covered by the Social Security program, called a "Social Security account number." The need for the regulation is obvious. In order to carry out its program, the Social Security Administration would have to keep records about millions of workers for the rest of their lives. A worker's career could span more than half a century and could include many different employers in different locations. A separate account of the wages paid to, and the taxes withheld from, each worker had to be kept so that his eligibility for benefits, and the amount of those benefits, could be correctly established at retirement and paid thereafter.

Because the information in a single record might come from many different sources, because many workers share the same name, and because an individual may assume more than one name in the course of a lifetime, there had to be some way of uniquely labelling each worker. The solution adopted was to issue each worker a different number, and require a worker to report his number to his employers. Employers, in turn, were required to report to the Social Security Administration (SSA) certain information regarding the wages paid to, and the taxes withheld from, every worker. This information had to be labelled with the worker's Social Security number, which would enable the Social Security Administration to keep accurate accounts of each worker's earnings over the years. Then when a worker applied for benefits, the SSN would help SSA to match worker to record, and confirm that the worker was, in fact, the person he claimed to be.

A great many other organizations with large numbers of customers, beneficiaries, or employees also found it necessary to use labels other than names. Credit-card issuers, for example, assign unique numbers to individuals when they extend credit. When an individual uses his card to charge purchases at a wide variety of organizations in many different geographical locations, each charge on an account is reported to a central location so that the client can be billed at one time for all of his purchases. Like the Social Security Administration, credit-card issuers must consolidate information about individuals received from many different sources. It is important to know which of two John J. Smiths charged $1,000 to his account and which charged $50. This kind of discrimination is more easily and accurately made if each John J. Smith has a unique credit-card account number.

There are also exchanges of personal information about individuals between organizations. Here, accurate identification and authentication is especially important. If, for example, an individual is incorrectly billed for a credit-card purchase because of name confusion, he can probably identify the source of the error easily and attempt to get it corrected. If, however, the credit-card issuer has reported information about the wrong individual to a credit bureau, and the credit bureau then reports it to still another credit grantor, it can take much time and effort even to locate the source of the error.

As long as organizations have relationships with individuals, most of whom are not known personally by someone within the organization, effective personal identification and authentication is an essential social mechanism. As long as organizations make decisions about individuals on the basis of recorded information, some means of assuring that the information being used does indeed pertain to the individual affected by the decision is necessary. It should also be clear that while accurate identification and authentication facilitates the work of organizations, it also benefits individuals who seek fair and prompt decisions from them. If individuals and records are not correctly identified and authenticated, an individual may be unfairly denied a right, benefit, or opportunity as a result. Society as a whole also suffers when a benefit is given to an undeserving individual. In sum, accurate identification and authentication are an essential component of fairness in record keeping.

THE SOCIAL SECURITY NUMBER AS AN IDENTIFIER AND AUTHENTICATOR

Because names are sometimes inadequate as identifiers—many

individuals may possess the same name, a single individual may change his name—and because a different label must be used as an authenticator when a name is used as an identifier, alternative labels had to be developed. There are essentially two processes that can be used to develop these alternative labels. First, a government body can decree a system of labelling and registering citizens and either mandate the use of the new labels or make them available to organizations on a voluntary basis. Some European countries have used this method and, during World War II, the United States considered adopting it to facilitate draft registration and commodities rationing.[2] Second, without such government action, the needed labelling systems grow up on an *ad hoc* basis to serve the special needs of particular private organizations and government agencies.

The United States did not choose the first alternative and thus, by default, has many systems of unique individual identification and authentication. Thus, today's typical American adult has a wide array of labels in addition to his or her name—a credit-card number, bank account number, driver's license number, license plate number, health insurance number, utilities account number, employee identification number, library card number, as well as a Social Security number.

Although the SSN is only one of many labels used for identification and authentication in America, it is relied on for these purposes more widely than any other kind of label except name; but the SSN is, at best, an imperfect identifier and authenticator. One reason is that until 1972, an applicant for an SSN was not asked if he had already been issued a number, nor was he asked to produce proof of identity. The result is that several million individuals now have more than one SSN—clearly a source of confusion. Another reason is that one SSN is sometimes used by more than one individual—as when a son, confused about how the system operates, uses his father's number when he goes to work. These problems are gradually being resolved in part because a Federal law *[Section 205(c)(2)(B)(ii) of the Social Security Act]* now gives the Department of Health, Education, and Welfare (DHEW) the authority to require verification of the identity of SSN applicants and to determine whether an applicant has previously been issued an SSN. Experience is slowly clearing up confusion about the system's operation.

An individual's SSN may be used for personal *identification*, although the instances in which an individual identifies himself with his SSN appear to be rare. The SSN is more often used for personal *authentication*, as when an individual wants to cash a check. The use of the SSN in *record identification and authentication*, both within and between organizations, however, is common. Most of these uses of the SSN have nothing at all to do

---

[2] See, for example, *Measures Relating to Vital Records and Vital Statistics*, U.S. House of Representatives, Document No. 242, 78th Congress, 1st Session.

with the purpose for which the SSN was originally created—the administration of the Social Security Act.[3]

CONCERN ABOUT THE USE OF THE SOCIAL SECURITY NUMBER

The clear need of organizations to identify and authenticate individuals and records accurately, both internally and in the course of exchanging personal information with other organizations, is seldom questioned. The propriety of certain widely used systems of labelling individuals and records, however, is hotly debated in this country. Much of this debate today centers on what uses of the Social Security number are appropriate. To understand the Commission's recommendations in this area, the arguments advanced against the use of the SSN as a widely used identifier and authenticator must be explored.

Some individuals simply resent being identified by a number rather than a name, and of these, most seem uncomfortable with the use of the SSN across the board for both personal and record identification and authentication. The case was stated by one of the Commission's correspondents, who implored the Commission to "prevent us from becoming our Social Security numbers." This concern seems to reflect the feeling that to label a person by a number rather than by a name is dehumanizing. It is probably safe to assume that these people do not object specifically to the Social Security number, but to any widely used numerical label. After all, the telephone companies incurred much wrath when they changed from name to number labels for exchanges.

In most cases, however, opposition to the use of the SSN appears to arise from a fear that if several organizations possess an individual's SSN, the ability with which these organizations can exchange information about the individual will be greatly facilitated. This kind of opposition is directed primarily to the use of the SSN for record, as opposed to personal, identification and authentication. Some individuals feel that information exchanges will not always be beneficial to them—particularly because some kinds of information should not be available to certain decision makers—and thus these exchanges should not be encouraged. Such concern is also related to a more general feeling that if the SSN is used to facilitate unconstrained exchanges of information about people, dossiers about individuals may be created that will follow them throughout life. Thus, an individual's capacity to "make a fresh start" in life would be hampered, and the processes of social control of individuals would become increasingly threatening.

Several of the Commission's correspondents expressed this general fear. For example, one asserted that "the extensive use of this single number by all government agencies allows unscrupulous individuals within the government to easily obtain all the information in a file concerning an individual." Another objected to the collection of SSNs by credit grantors

---

[3] See DHEW Secretary's Advisory Committee on Automated Personal Data Systems, *Records, Computers, and the Rights of Citizens* (Washington: U.S. Government Printing Office, 1973), Chapter VII.

and life insurance companies because he opposed the ease with which ". . . one computer can 'interface' with another guy's computer and swap information."

Again, there is no evidence to suggest that any unique aspect of the Social Security number is peculiarly objectionable. Presumably, any other label—except a name—that is used as widely would arouse the same opposition and, if each individual had a unique name for life, used by him alone, it is conceivable that names also would become a target of concern.

RESTRICTIONS ON THE USE OF THE SSN

The Privacy Protection Study Commission is not the first government organization to study the use of the SSN and other identifiers and make recommendations regarding them. The Social Security Administration's Social Security Number Task Force,[4] the DHEW Secretary's Advisory Committee on Automated Personal Data Systems,[5] and the Federal Advisory Committee on False Identification,[6] have all reported on the use of the Social Security number and other means of labelling individuals. In addition, the Congress has enacted legislation regarding the conditions under which disclosure of an individual's Social Security number can be compelled.

The enactment by the Congress of Section 7 of the Privacy Act of 1974 was the first step in establishing a Federal policy limiting compulsory divulgence of the SSN.[7] Section 7 provides that:

(a) —
   (1) It shall be unlawful for any Federal, State or local government agency to deny to any individual any right, benefit, or privilege provided by law because of such individual's refusal to disclose his social security account number.
   (2) the provisions of paragraph (1) of this subsection shall not apply with respect to—
      (A) any disclosure which is required by Federal statute, or
      (B) the disclosure of a social security number to any Federal, State, or local agency maintaining a system of records in existence and operating before January 1, 1975, if such disclosure was required under statute or regulation adopted prior to such date to verify the identity of an individual.
(b) Any Federal, State, or local government agency which

---

[4] See Social Security Number Task Force, *Report to the Commissioner*, Social Security Administration, May 1971.

[5] DHEW Secretary's Advisory Committee on Automated Personal Data Systems, *op. cit.*

[6] See Federal Advisory Committee on False Identification, *The Criminal Use of False Identification* (Washington: U.S. Government Printing Office, 1976).

[7] At least three States—Oklahoma, Arkansas, and Virginia—have also enacted statutes restricting compulsory disclosure of the SSN.

requests an individual to disclose his social security account number shall inform that individual whether that disclosure is mandatory or voluntary, by what statutory or other authority such number is solicited, and what uses will be made of it.

This statute implicitly endorses two proposals of the DHEW Secretary's Advisory Committee on Automated Personal Data Systems: (1) that an individual whose SSN is requested should be informed as to whether or not divulging his number is legally required; and (2) that no individual should be denied a benefit because of his refusal to divulge his SSN for purposes other those required by Federal law.

The Privacy Act's Section 7 exempts from its restrictions demands for an individual's SSN that are mandated by statute or regulation adopted prior to January 1, 1975 for systems of records in operation prior to that time, and, of course, does not apply at all to private organizations. Section 7 was not, however, intended to do more than impose a moratorium on demands for an individual's Social Security number by government agencies under circumstances where the individual has no choice but to comply.

In 1976, for the first time since passage of the Privacy Act, the Congress exercised its authority to authorize compulsory divulgence of the SSN. Section 1211 of the Tax Reform Act of 1976 provides that:

(i)   It is the policy of the United States that any State (or political subdivision thereof) may, in the administration of any tax, general public assistance, driver's license, or motor vehicle registration law within its jurisdiction, utilize the social security account numbers issued by the [HEW] Secretary for the purpose of establishing the identification of individuals affected by such law, and may require any individual who is or appears to be so affected to furnish to such State (or political subdivision thereof) or any agency thereof having administrative responsibility for the law involved, the social security account number (or numbers, if he has more than one such number) issued to him by the Secretary.

(ii)   If and to the extent that any provision of Federal law heretofore enacted is inconsistent with the policy set forth in clause (i) of this subparagraph, such provision shall, on or after the date of the enactment of this subparagraph, be null, void, and of no effect.

(iii) For purposes of clause (i) of this subparagraph, an agency of a State (or political subdivision thereof) charged with the administration of any general public assistance, driver's license, or motor vehicle registration law which did not use the social security account number for identification under a law or regulation adopted before January 1, 1975, may require an individual to disclose his or her social security number to such agency solely for the purpose of administering the laws referred to in clause (i) above and for the purpose of responding to requests for information from an agency

> operating pursuant to the provisions of part A or D of title IV of the Social Security Act [AFDC and Child Support Enforcement programs].

This provision was designed primarily to help State Child Support Enforcement units locate parents who have defaulted on their child support obligations, and to facilitate the matching of information on Federal and State tax returns by State taxing authorities.

The Privacy Act's Section 7 appears to have had little impact on Federal, State, and local government agencies. Most Federal agencies have been able to cite some legal authority in effect before January 1, 1975 that lets them continue to demand disclosure of the SSN. Although a few State and local agencies have abandoned the use of the SSN because they lack such legal authority, the Tax Reform Act grants most State and local government agencies that found its continued use necessary the authority to demand it. In short, the Privacy Act and the Tax Reform Act essentially preserved the status quo with respect to the SSN: namely, widespread collection and use of the number.

To make Section 7 of the Privacy Act truly effective—that is, to severely restrict the circumstances under which an individual can be required to divulge his SSN to a government agency—could easily entail costly changes for agencies that rely on the SSN for identification and authentication. If even a few persons asserted their right to refuse to divulge the SSN to a government agency, it would be required to develop and administer a new labelling system, and to revise its automated record-keeping processes. Because of the character of such revisions—which involve creating the capacity for an automated record system to deal with identifiers and authenticators other than the SSN—the cost involved would be essentially the same whether only a few individuals refused to divulge the SSN or all subjects of the system's records declined to disclose the number.

CONCLUSIONS

As noted above, the Commission believes that most concern over the use of the SSN as identifier and authenticator can be traced to two sources: (1) the belief that the SSN may facilitate the exchange, consolidation, and linkage of records or information about individuals for purposes which may be unfair to them; and (2) resentment at being labelled with a number. Revisions in Federal policy on the use of the SSN must recognize these concerns.

As to the first point, the Commission agrees with many students of the issue[8] that the SSN is a surrogate for the problem of record linkage, exchange, and consolidation. Much of the Commission's work in other areas has focused on finding solutions to this problem. Although the SSN is often used to facilitate record exchanges, it is only one of many possible ways that

---

[8] See, for example, Social Security Number Task Force, *Report to the Commissioner*, and DHEW Secretary's Advisory Committee on Automated Personal Data Systems, *Records, Computers, and the Rights of Citizens*.

records and information can be, and currently are being, linked, exchanged, and consolidated. Technical studies[9] indicate that record-matching techniques using a combination of attributes and labels other than numerical labels (e.g., name, address, birth date, sex) are entirely adequate in many situations and record-keeping organizations do use such means of identification and authentication instead of the SSN. The U.S. Department of Transportation's National Driver Register office, and TRW Credit Data, provide two examples of organizations with large record systems that rely largely on labels other than numerical labels for identification and authentication purposes. The National Driver Register keeps records of license suspensions and revocations throughout the United States and supplies information to States upon request. TRW Credit Data is a large, automated credit bureau described in detail in Chapter 2.

The National Driver Register (NDR) contains about 5.7 million records. It receives 94,000 inquiries daily, produces 3,500 *possible* matches every day, and mails 900 *probable* matches to the States. Yet the SSN (or another unique identifier) is not the primary identifier used in this system. Instead, NDR first uses name and date of birth as primary identifiers and then uses sex, height, weight, and eye color to discriminate among records of people with similar or identical names and birth dates. The SSN is, in some cases, used to facilitate this discrimination process, but it is not available for all drivers listed in the system.

Similarly, TRW Credit Data, which has approximately 50 million records in its system, does not use the SSN or another unique identifier as its primary identifier. Like the NDR, it relies on data elements such as name, address, zip code, and age to facilitate its matching processes.[10]

It is true that if organizations other than the Social Security Administration were forbidden to collect and use the SSN, their exchange of records might be inhibited for a time. Such a prohibition or restriction would, however, be extraordinarily costly and cumbersome, and it would also inhibit record exchanges everyone perceives as wholly desirable along with those perceived to be threatening. Furthermore, organizations which now rely on the SSN would devise alternative methods of identification and authentication that are equally effective for record exchanges.

In any case, the question of the appropriate limitations on exchange of records would remain even if the SSN were done away with altogether. *The Commission finds that restrictions on the collection and use of the SSN to inhibit exchange beyond those already contained in law would be costly and cumbersome in the short run, ineffectual in the long run, and would also distract public attention from the need to formulate general policies on record exchanges.*

The Commission is sensitive to the second point—the belief that being labelled with the SSN is dehumanizing. Clearly, a society in which each of us is called upon at every turn to state "name, rank, and serial number" is not

---

[9] See, for example, *Accessing Individual Records from Personal Data Fields Using Non-Unique Identifiers*, National Bureau of Standards, Special Publication 500-2.

[10] Testimony of TRW Credit Data, *Credit Reporting and Payment Authorization Services*, Hearings before the Privacy Protection Study Commission, August 4, 1976, p. 468.

pleasing to contemplate. The Commission fails to see, however, how drastically restricting the use of the Social Security number would make much difference in this respect, since any other widely used numerical label would, as pointed out earlier, be likely to engender the same feeling. Nonetheless, the Commission believes that some of the concern about dehumanization could be diminished if government agencies and private organizations would examine the circumstances under which they request an individual's SSN, and continue only those in which the SSN furthers a legitimate and valid record-keeping purpose.

RECOMMENDATIONS

Although the Commission's mandate merely states that it may "research, examine, and analyze" the use of the Social Security number and other identifiers, its inquiry led it to conclude that some minor revisions to existing Federal policy on the use of the Social Security number are desirable. The Commission's recommendations and underlying rationale are set forth below.

SECTION 7 OF THE PRIVACY ACT

The Commission considered—and rejected—the idea of recommending repeal of Section 7 as it currently applies to Federal, State, and local government agencies. Although it does believe that, like any restrictions on the collection and use of the SSN, Section 7 does not address the complex problem of permissible exchanges and disclosures of records, the Commission recognizes that Section 7 may be somewhat successful in alleviating citizens' concerns about the "dossier-building" capacity of government. Accordingly, the Commission recommends:

Recommendation (1):

That Section 7 of the Privacy Act be retained for government agencies.

Although the Commission does not believe that legal restrictions on the collection or use of the SSN should be made to apply to private organizations, it recognizes that private organizations are in many cases willing to respond to inquiries by customers and employees regarding whether the organization requires the disclosure of the SSN, and how it will be used and disclosed. To the extent that private organizations respond to such specific inquiries, such information may permit a concerned individual to determine whether the drawbacks he perceives in giving the SSN outweigh the potential benefits, and thus whether he wishes to continue to do business with a company or to take his business elsewhere.

Individuals cannot exercise a similar option with respect to government agencies—there is generally only one government agency with which an individual can "do business"—and thus limitations on the collection of the SSN by government agencies are appropriate even though the Commission considers them to be inappropriate for the private sector.

EXECUTIVE ORDER 9397

The Commission also recommends:

Recommendation (2):

That the President amend Executive Order 9397 *(November 30, 1943, 8 Federal Register 237, an order directing Federal agencies to use the Social Security account number when establishing a new system of permanent account numbers)* so that Federal agencies may not, as of January 1, 1977, rely on it as legal authority by which to create new demands for the disclosure of an individual's SSN.

Executive Order 9397, issued in 1943 by President Roosevelt, provides in part as follows:

> Whereas certain Federal agencies from time to time require in the administration of their activities a system of numerical identification of accounts of individual persons; and . . .
> Whereas it is desirable in the interest of economy and orderly administration that the Federal Government move towards the use of a single, unduplicated numerical identification system of accounts and avoid the unnecessary establishment of additional systems;
> Now, therefore, . . . it is hereby ordered as follows:
> 1. Hereafter any Federal department, establishment, or agency shall, whenever the head thereof finds it advisable to establish a new system of permanent account numbers pertaining to individual persons, utilize exclusively the Social Security account numbers . . . .

This order has been cited by some Federal agencies as the legal authority permitting them to compel an individual to disclose his SSN to them, especially in cases in which no more specific legal authority for compelling SSN disclosure exists. Section 7 of the Privacy Act appears to suggest that government agencies need specific legal authority to support a request for SSN disclosure, rather than authority of general applicability such as that contained in E.O. 9397. Thus, to the extent that Federal agencies interpret E.O. 9397 as sufficient authority to establish requirements for collection of the SSN, the intent of Section 7 is undermined.

The Commission believes that Federal agencies should no longer be able to rely on E.O. 9397 as authority for new requests for SSN divulgence. In order to minimize the disruption that outright repeal of the order would cause, however, the Commission believes that agencies that cited it as the basis for their requests for the SSN prior to January 1, 1977 should be able to continue to do so. If the Commission's recommendation were adopted, any Federal agency that wishes to support a demand for the SSN after that date would have to seek specific legal authority from the Congress unless some other specific authority is otherwise available to them.

This means that if an agency had cited E.O. 9397 as authority to require disclosure of the SSN for one purpose prior to January 1, 1977—such as personnel record keeping—it could not cite the executive order as authority for collecting the SSN for a new purpose—such as indexing records about individual contractors—after January 1, 1977. Because Section 7 of the Privacy Act currently requires Federal agencies to tell individuals under what legal authority they are soliciting the SSN, a record of the agencies citing E.O. 9397 as authority, and the purposes for which they requested the SSN pursuant to it, already exists and could be used in enforcing this recommendation.

MONITORING AND FURTHER STUDY

The Commission recommends:

Recommendation (3):

That the independent entity recommended by the Privacy Commission monitor the use of the SSN and other labels by private organizations and consider the desirability and feasibility of future restrictions on the use of the SSN and other labels for identification and authentication purposes.

Although the Commission does not believe that legal restrictions on the collection or use of the SSN by private organizations are appropriate at this time, it realizes that the use of the SSN may be a source of continuing public concern. The Commission hopes that as legislatures, public agencies, and private organizations take steps to apply its recommendations regarding the proper uses of records about individuals, this concern will diminish. If the independent entity recommended by the Commission[11] is created by the Congress, it could, however, continue to monitor the use of the SSN by private organizations and recommend legislation if at any point it seemed to be warranted.

STANDARD UNIVERSAL LABEL

Finally, the Commission recommends:

Recommendation (4):

That the Federal government not consider taking any action that would foster the development of a standard, universal label for individuals, or a central population register, until such time as significant steps have been taken to implement safeguards and policies regarding permissible uses and disclosures of records about individuals in the spirit of those recommended by the Commission

---

[11] See Chapter 1 for a discussion of this recommendation.

**and these safeguards and policies have been demonstrated to be
effective.**

Here as elsewhere, the Commission stresses the need to adopt policies
regarding the permissible uses and disclosures of records about individuals,
and in other chapters of this report the Commission has made recommendations regarding what the permissible uses and disclosures should be in a
number of record-keeping areas. These recommendations address the
substantive issues of record use and exchange and their adoption would
more effectively deal with these issues than would restrictions on the use of
the SSN.

At the same time, however, there is currently much debate about the
need to develop foolproof methods of identification in order to deter
fraudulent uses of standard documents widely used for identification and
authentication purposes, such as drivers' licenses and Social Security cards.
The Commission recognizes that such use of identification documents
imposes a heavy cost on industry, government, and society as a whole, but
also recognizes that the development of improved identity documents is
often viewed as inconsistent with America's tradition of civil liberties. The
conflict would become especially acute if a standard universal label were
linked to a central population register that maintained records of not only
the name and label of each individual, but also his current address, and
much more so if such location data were freely available to government
agencies and private organizations. Such a central population register could
be created anew, or an existing record system—such as one maintained by
the Social Security Administration—could serve as such a register.

Because of this potential conflict, the Commission believes that any
consideration of a standard universal label and of a record system
approximating a central population register, should be postponed until
society, through its legislatures, has made significant progress in establishing
policies to regulate the use and disclosure of information about individuals
collected by both private organizations and government agencies, and until
such policies are shown to be effective.

The Commission sees a clear danger that a government record system,
such as that maintained by the Social Security Administration or the
Internal Revenue Service, will become a *de facto* central population register
unless prevented by conscious policy decisions. Therefore, *Recommendation
(4)*, above, means also that the Federal government should act positively to
halt the incremental drift toward creation of a standard universal label and
central population register until laws and policies regarding the use of
records about individuals are developed and shown to be effective.

Epilogue

This report has called for a national policy to guide the way public and private organizations make, use, and disclose records about individuals. It looks toward a national policy on personal-data record keeping that minimizes intrusiveness, maximizes fairness, and defines obligations with respect to the uses and disclosures that will be made of recorded information about an individual. It does not address many privacy protection problems that have been the focus of legal controversy during the last decade. It is not concerned with wiretapping, abortion, or the advertising and sale of contraceptives. Nor does it specifically address misleading publication and defamation, actions that form the heart of the torts of privacy and libel. While the constitutional questions raised by specific court cases helped to direct the Commission's inquiry, the study and deliberations culminating in this report had a broader context.

The Commission has not been concerned simply with limiting *government* actions that impinge on personal privacy. Recognizing that private institutions have also become big enough and powerful enough to diminish personal privacy, many of the problems the Commission has addressed stem from actions of private organizations. Throughout the report, the Commission has tried to fashion a structure within which privacy protection problems of a nongovernmental nature can be considered and balances between the interests of the individual and the needs of social and economic organizations can be achieved. Although the framework the Commission offers provides for continuing attention to privacy issues from a broad public-policy perspective, it relies at its base on strengthening the social relationships between individuals and record-keeping organizations by articulating enforceable rights and responsibilities. This reliance grows from the realization that the intrusiveness, unfairness, and unrestricted disclosure characteristic of so much organizational record keeping today is largely the result of weaknesses in the relationship between the individual and those who need to know intimate details of his life.

The Commission recognizes the delicate nature of the balance of interests it has sought to achieve. It is aware that information is emerging as a basic currency of social, political, and economic relationships in American society. Thus, as information continues to become more valuable, public and private organizations may increasingly argue that the impact of allowing individuals to participate in deciding what organizations do with personal information are greater than society can bear. Rather than expecting organizations to justify their activities, the individual may have to bear the burden of justifying any restrictions on the collection, use, or disclosure of the information they keep about him.

The Commission's studies made it quite clear that developments in computer and telecommunications technology provide both the means and the impetus for the creation of information services that challenge assumptions implicit in existing law and regulation. In many of the chapters of this report, there is evidence that the lines that historically have separated record-keeping relationships can be blurred—easily, rapidly, and unobtrusively. The advent of compliance monitoring in public assistance programs and the merging of that function with more traditional law enforcement roles is one example. The expansion of the employee-employer relationship to include insurance and medical-care relationships is another. As the lines demarcating the record-keeping relationships individuals have with organizations blur, new balances between the individual's interest and the organization's must be forged.

To understand the focus and direction of the Commission's work, one must appreciate the moment in time at which this report is written. Portions of the area of public-policy concern labeled "privacy" have been charted; fundamental questions, such as the individual's relationship with government, have been recast. The Commission took this earlier work into account in framing its recommendations, but believes it has also presented a structure within which protections for personal privacy can be greatly strengthened.

Nonetheless, the Commission's resolution of particular issues should not be taken as answers for all time. Though the structure proposed for resolving problems is designed to survive, changes in technology and social organization may by-pass particular solutions recommended in this report. As long as America believes, as more than a matter of rhetoric, in the worth of the individual citizen, it must constantly reaffirm and reinforce its protections for the privacy, and ultimately the autonomy, of the individual.

Appendix

Hearings of the Privacy Protection Study Commission

Mailing Lists

NOVEMBER 12, 1975

- Robert DeLay, President; Gilbert Weil, Counsel; Celia Wallace, Vice President; *Direct Mail/Marketing Association, Inc.*
- Gary Beller, General Counsel; J. M. Stetler, Vice President, Card Division; *American Express Company*
- Louis Kislik, President, Publishers Clearing House, on behalf of *Associated Third-Class Mailers*
- Julian W. Haydon, Vice President, General Manager, Marketing Services Division; John M. O'Hara, Vice President, General Counsel; *R.L. Polk Company*
- Herbert E. Gertz, Data Base Director, Marketing Division; William M. Buchanan, Jr., Vice President, Secretary, and General Counsel; *Reuben H. Donnelley Company*
- Leo Gans, President, *National Business Lists, Inc.*
- Richard Krieger, Chairman, Mail Order and Book Club Division, *Association of American Publishers, Inc.*
- Henry Turner, Vice President and Circulation Director, The McCall Publishing Company, and Chairman, Circulation Committee, MPA, on behalf of *Magazine Publishers Association*
- Louis Haugh, Senior Editor, *Advertising Age Magazine*

DECEMBER 10, 1975

- Robert Ellis Smith, Editor, *Privacy Journal*
- David Cohen, President; Jack Fieldhouse, Director of Membership for Field Organization; David Dawson, Treasurer and Director of Mail Operations; Robert Myer, Budget Control Director; *Common Cause*
- Dennis Bates, Director, *Minnesota Privacy Commission*
- Richard A. Viguerie, President, *Richard A. Viguerie Company, Inc.*

- Richard Spring, Driver Services Administrator, *Virginia Department of Motor Vehicles*
- John G. Lancione, Attorney, Spangenberg, Shibley, Traci, Lancione, and Markus, Cleveland, Ohio
- Roger M. Craver, President, *Craver Company*
- William B. Walsh, Director, *Project HOPE*

DECEMBER 11, 1975

- Robert Jordan, Director, Product Management; George C. Davis, Assistant General Counsel for Consumer Protection; John Ventresco, Law Department; Stanley Mires, Law Department; *U.S. Postal Service*
- Meade Emory, Assistant to the Commissioner; James Owens, Deputy Commissioner, Accounts Collection and Taxpayer Service; *U.S. Internal Revenue Service*
- Joan Manley, Group Vice President, Publisher, Book Division; Kelso Sutton, Vice President, Magazine Circulation; John Diamond, Law Department; *Time, Inc.*
- Edward J. Bride, Vice President, *ComputerWorld Magazine*
- Harold Oram, Consultant on Fundraising, *Oram International*

Credit Cards and Reservation Systems

FEBRUARY 11, 1976

- Dee W. Hock, Jr., President, *National BankAmericard, Inc.*
- John W. Reynolds, President, *Interbank Card Association*
- J. M. Stetler, Vice President; Gary Beller, Counsel; *American Express Company*
- Kenneth Larkin, Senior Vice President; Susan L. Hedemann, Counsel; *Bank of America*
- Jeremiah S. Gutman, on behalf of *American Civil Liberties Union*
- Richard W. Selberg, Vice President, The Bank of California; Harold Bachrach, Chase Manhattan Bank; Howard E. Weston, Vice President, Washington Trust Company; Thomas J. McClaine, Vice President, National Bank of Greenwood; John Hines, Vice President, United Bank and Trust Company; Drew Tidwell, Legislative Representative; all on behalf of *Consumer Bankers Association*
- Roland Brandel, Counsel, *Western States Bankcard Association*
- Anthony P. Nicholas, Vice President; Robert Malley, Counsel; *Citibank*
- H. Randolf Lively, Director of Public Affairs, General Credit Office, *Sears, Roebuck Company*

FEBRUARY 12, 1976

- The Honorable Bella Abzug, *U.S. Representative, New York*
- William Caming, Counsel, *American Telephone and Telegraph Corporation*
- Frederick Soloman, Director, Office of Saver and Consumer Affairs, *Federal Reserve Board*
- Christian S. White, Assistant Director, Division of Special Statutes, *U.S. Federal Trade Commission*
- Rudolph J. Megaro, Manager, Retail Credit System; Herbert Birenbaum, Counsel; *Atlantic Richfield*
- Sumpter T. Priddy, Jr., President, Virginia Retail Merchants Association; Milton Schafer, Counsel, ARF; James Burke, Vice President, Credit Division, Aldens, Inc.; all on behalf of *American Retail Federation (ARF)*
- J. Keith Brooker, Assistant Credit Manager; George Gordon, Jr., Counsel; *J.C. Penney Company, Inc.*
- Charles H. Reynolds, Jr., President, Reynolds Brothers, Inc.; Jack Reid, Director, Credit Operations, J.L. Hudson Company; Sheldon Feldman; all on behalf of *National Retail Merchants Association*

FEBRUARY 13, 1976

- Max Hooper, Assistant Vice President, Data Processing and Communications Services; Jeffrey Denay, Corporate Legal Staff; *American Airlines*
- Theodore R. Trentler, Director of Reservation and Ticket Offices; Audrey Goldberg, Assistant Counsel; *Pan American World Airways, Inc.*
- Bruce G. Curry, Division Vice President; Charles A. Bovino, Counsel; *Hertz Corporation*
- Marco Armani, President; Lee Thornton, Assistant Vice President in Charge of Operations, Field Office; *Hilton Service Club Corporation*
- Edward Pritchard, Director, Reservations and Communications; Richard Braverman; *Sheraton Hotels (ITT)*

Federal Tax Return Confidentiality

MARCH 11, 1976

- The Honorable Donald C. Alexander, Commissioner; David E. Dickinson, Technical Advisor to Chief Counsel; James J. Keightley, Assistant Director for Disclosure Division, Chief Counsel; Charles A. Gibb, Chief, Disclosure Staff; Frank Malanga, Research and Operations Analysis Division, Planning and Research; Meade Emory, Assistant to the Commissioner; *U.S. Internal Revenue Service*

- The Honorable Harold Tyler, Deputy Attorney General, *U.S. Department of Justice*
- Vincent Barabba, Director; Daniel B. Levine, Associate Director for Demographic Fields; Theodore Clemence, Planning and Programs Officer; *U.S. Bureau of the Census*
- Stanley Sporkin, Director, Division of Enforcement; Paul Gonson, Associate General Counsel; Ira Pearce, Special Counsel; David Romanski, Assistant General Counsel; Charles Learner, Branch Chief, Division of Enforcement; *Securities and Exchange Commission*
- Sheldon Cohen, former Commissioner, Internal Revenue Service
- Robert Lewis, General Counsel; Jay C. Shaffer, Attorney; *U.S. Federal Trade Commission*
- Aryeh Neier, Executive Director, *American Civil Liberties Union*
- Sherwin P. Simmons, Trenam, Simmons, Kemker, Scharf and Barkin, Tampa, Florida, and Chairman, Section of Taxation, ABA; Mac Asbill, Jr., Sutherland and Asbill; both on behalf of *American Bar Association (ABA)*
- David B.H. Martin, Research Director, *Administrative Conference of the United States*

MARCH 12, 1976

- The Honorable Lowell Weicker, *U.S. Senator, Connecticut*
- William Penick, Chairman, Division of Federal Taxation; Gene Holloway, Chairman, Special Task Force on Privacy Disclosure; John Gilbert, Chairman, Committee on Tax Administration; Joel Forester, Director, Tax Division; all on behalf of *American Institute of Certified Public Accountants*
- Thomas McFee, Deputy Assistant Secretary for Management Planning and Technology; Louis Hays, Deputy Director, Office of Child Support Enforcement, Social and Rehabilitation Service; A. Robert Trazzi, Privacy Coordinator, Social Security Administration; *U. S. Department of Health, Education, and Welfare*
- Edgar Lindley, Commissioner, *Ohio Department of Taxation*; Richard E. O'Brien, Chairman, Tax Committee, *Ohio Municipal League* and Commissioner of Taxation, *City of Toledo*; John R. Urban, Administrator, *Regional Income Tax Agency*; Oscar Q. Kniceley, Income Tax Administrator, *City of Cleveland*
- James H. Tully, Jr., Commissioner, *Department of Taxation, New York*
- Owen L. Clarke, Chairman, Board of Trustees, Federation of Tax Administrators, and Commissioner of Corporate Taxation, Commonwealth of Massachusetts; Leon Rothenberg,

Executive Secretary, NATA; both on behalf of the *National Association of Tax Administrators (NATA)*
- Marion Lawless, Assistant Bureau Chief, *Florida Department of Revenue*
- Daniel Smith, Administrator, *Income, Sales, Insurance, and Excise Taxes, State of Wisconsin*
- Louise Brown, *Tax Reform Research Group*
- James D. Smith, Professor of Economics, Pennsylvania State University

Depository and Lending Institutions

APRIL 21, 1976

- Raymond R. Nelson, Vice President; John J. Higgins, General Counsel's Staff; *General Motors Acceptance Corporation*
- James Browne, President; Ralph Fenza, General Counsel; Dominick Sensa; Regional Director; *FinanceAmerica Corporation*
- Robert Walker, Vice President and Associate Corporate Counsel; Joseph P. Coriaci, Vice President and Cashier; Joseph W. Saunders, Personal Banking Officer; James A. Matthews, Vice President; *Continental Illinois National Bank and Trust Company*
- William Evenson, Vice President and Staff Counsel, *Bank of Virginia Company*
- Roger Jewett, Director; Sheri Cole, Associate; *TRW-Validata Systems*
- Lucille M. Creamer, Senior Vice President, Bayview Federal Savings and Loan Association; John C. Rasmus, Legislative Research Counsel, U. S. League of Savings Associations; both on behalf of *U.S. League of Savings Associations*
- June Majors, Manager, Western Electric Employees Credit Union; Arthur Samson, General Manager, Defense Mapping Federal Credit Union; Sharon Campbell, Counsel, Credit Union National Association; all on behalf of *Credit Union National Association*
- Michael Savage, Director, Office Management Systems, Office of the Assistant Secretary for Housing Production, Mortgage Credit, and Federal Housing Administration; Burton Bloomberg, Assistant General Counsel for Administrative Law and Financial Affairs; Harold Rosenthal, Departmental Privacy Act Officer; Thomas Weaver, Director, Single Family Mortgage Credit Division, Office of Underwriting Standards, HPMC; *U. S. Department of Housing and Urban Development*

APRIL 22, 1976

- Stephen Ege, Attorney; Franklin Wright, Advisor; Robert Thompson, Special Assistant; Management Systems and Administration; *Federal Home Loan Bank Board*
- Robert Haydock, Bingham, Dana, and Gould, Boston, Massachusetts
- Frederick Soloman, Assistant to the Board, and Director, Office of Saver and Consumer Affairs; Board of Governors; Warren Swaney, Legal Division; Elliot McEntee, Division of Federal Reserve Bank Operations; *U.S. Federal Reserve System*
- Charles E. Marson, Legal Director, *Civil Liberties Union of Northern California*
- Singleton Wolfe, Assistant Commissioner, *U. S. Internal Revenue Service*
- The Honorable James J. Featherstone, Deputy Secretary; Mr. Robert Stanky; Mr. Robert MacBrian; *U. S. Department of the Treasury*
- Harold R. Arthur, Vice President and Cashier, Wells Fargo Bank of North America; Robert Fabian, Sullivan, Roche, Johnson, San Francisco, California; both on behalf of *American Bankers Association*

MAY 20, 1976

- Donald L. Boudreau, Senior Vice President, *Chase Manhattan Bank, N.A.*

Insurance Institutions

MAY 19, 1976

- Robert S. Seiler, Vice President and General Attorney, Allstate Life Insurance Company; Charles N. Walker, Vice President, New England Mutual Life Insurance Company; Robert W. Blevins, Senior Vice President, Southland Life Insurance Company; A. Douglas Murch, Senior Vice President, Prudential Life Insurance Company; William H. Creamer, III, Vice President New York Life Insurance Company; Thomas F. McDermott, Vice President, Metropolitan Life Insurance Company; Jack M. Bernard, Vice President, Colonial-Penn Life Insurance Company; all on behalf of *American Life Insurance Association*
- David J. Blackwell, Vice President; A. Peter Quinn, Executive Vice President and General Counsel; Adolph Jakobek, Underwriting Secretary; *Massachusetts Mutual Life Insurance Company*
- John Petraglia, Director of Underwriting; Myles R. Tashman,

Assistant Vice President; *New York Savings Bank Life Insurance Company*
- Charles G. Katibian, Executive Vice President, *Connecticut Savings Bank Life Insurance Company*
- Jerome E. Bolin, President, *Abraham Lincoln Insurance Company*
- Neil M. Day, Executive Director and General Counsel, *Medical Information Bureau*

MAY 20, 1976

- Jerome S. Beigler, M.D., on behalf of *American Psychiatric Association Committee on Confidentiality*
- Benjamin Lipson, President, *The Benjamin Lipson Insurance Agency*
- Sheila M. Smythe, Senior Vice President, Operations, New York Blue Cross Plan; Gerald J. Duffy, Vice President, EDP and Telecommunications Services, Blue Cross Association; Daniel Lewis, Senior Vice President, Florida Blue Shield Plan; Marshall Crawford, Legal Division, National Association of Blue Shield; all on behalf of *Blue Cross - Blue Shield*
- Angele Khachadour, Chief Counsel, *Department of Insurance, State of California*
- David G. Taylor, Deputy Director, *Department of Insurance, State of Illinois*
- J. Robert Hunter, Acting Federal Insurance Administrator, Federal Insurance Administration; Howard Clark, Special Assistant to the Administrator; *U.S. Department of Housing and Urban Development*

MAY 21, 1976

- Russell G. Press, Jr., Secretary, Property/Casualty, Government Affairs, and Law Division; Hale C. Reed, Vice President, Casualty/Property Personal Lines Department; George R. Cretney, Second Vice President, Casualty/Property Claim Department, The Travelers Insurance Companies; Jules H. Marckmann, Vice President; Richard M. Sargent, Jr., Vice President, The Chubb Group of Insurance Companies; all on behalf of *American Insurance Association*
- Richard E. Dunkley, *H. L. Rust Company*
- William E. Cassidy, Vice President, *A. H. Baker and Company*
- Frank Patterson, President, *Patterson and Associates*
- James McTurnan, Vice President, *MFA Mutual Insurance Company*
- James M. Tulloch, President; Walter Bjork, General Counsel; *Dairyland Insurance Company*

- Bradley D. Kirk, Vice President, Systems and Data Processing, *Nationwide Mutual Insurance Company*
- Robert V. McGowan, President, R.V. McGowan Insurance Agency, and former President of the National Association of Mutual Insurance Agents; Wayne Naugle, President, Naugle Insurance Agency, Inc., Vice President, National Association of Mutual Insurance Agents, and Chairman, Federal Legislation Committee, on behalf of *National Association of Mutual Insurance Agents*
- Bernard L. Hines, Jr., Vice President, *American Insurance Association*
- James F. Ahearn, Director, *Insurance Crime Prevention Institute*

Medical Records

JUNE 10, 1976

- Marian Mlay, Acting Director, Office of Policy Development and Planning, Office of the Assistant Secretary for Health; Dorothy P. Rice, Director, National Center for Health Statistics; *U.S. Department of Health, Education, and Welfare*
- Dr. John Dooley, on behalf of *California Medical Association*
- Dr. E. Martin Egelson, Manager, Division of Medical Services; Mary Converse, Senior Staff Specialist; *American Hospital Association*
- Andrew Bailey, Director, Medical Record Department, Stanford University Hospital
- Mary-J Waterstraat, Executive Director, *American Medical Record Association*
- Dr. John D. Porterfield, Director, *Joint Commission on Accreditation of Hospitals*
- Dr. Joseph F. Boyle, member, Board of Trustees; John A. Krichbaum, Assistant Director, Legislative Department; on behalf of *American Medical Association*
- Dr. Sidney M. Wolfe, Director, *Public Citizen Health Research Group*
- Dr. Charles Lewis, Director, Health Services Research Center, *University of California at Los Angeles*
- Dr. Lester Breslow, Dean, School of Public Health (UCLA), on behalf of the *American Public Health Association*

JUNE 11, 1976

- Frances Hornstein, Co-Director, *Feminist Women's Health Center*
- Dr. Maurice Grossman, Department of Psychiatry, Stanford University School of Medicine
- C. Donald Hankin, Senior Vice President, Occidental Life of

California, Chairman, CMA Joint Committee on Confidentiality of Medical Information, on behalf of *California Medical Association (CMA)*

- Dr. Catherine E. Rosen, Director, Research and Evaluation, *Northeast Georgia Community Mental Health Center*
- Dale Tooley, *District Attorney*; Peter Bornstein, *Deputy District Attorney*; Denver, Colorado
- Patrick Lynch, Attorney, Department of Preventive Medicine and Public Health, *Creighton University School of Medicine*
- Dr. Richard E. Sedlack, Chairman, Coordinating Committee; Robert Moore, Jr., General Counsel; Dr. Leonard Kurland, Chairman, Department of Epidemiology and Medical Statistics; *Mayo Clinic*
- Charles G. Collins, President; Alexander Ratco; *Micro Reproduction Services, Inc.*

JULY 20, 1976

- The Honorable Marjorie Lynch, Under Secretary; Thomas McFee, Deputy Assistant Secretary for Management Planning and Technology; Edward Gleiman, Director, Fair Information Practice Staff; *U.S. Department of Health, Education, and Welfare*
- Donald S. Fredrickson, Director, National Institutes of Health; Dr. Francis Neil Waldrop, Deputy Administrator, Alcohol, Drug Abuse and Mental Health Administration; Dr. Robert Dormer, Office of Director, National Institute of Drug Abuse; Dr. H. Bruce Dull, Director, Center for Disease Control; Dr. Faye Abdellah, Director, Office of Long-Term Care; Dr. Robert E. Streicher, Director, Center of Medical Services; Dr. Emery A. Johnson, Director, Indian Health Service; Dr. Michael J. Goran, Director, Bureau of Quality Assurance; *U.S. Department of Health, Education, and Welfare*
- Dr. Harold Margulies, Deputy Administrator, Health Resources Administration; Dr. Melvin Blumenthal, Deputy Director, Program Policy, Bureau of Health Insurance; Jean Harris, Bureau of Health Insurance; Dr. Herbert L. Blumenfeld, Acting Chief Medical Officer, Bureau of Disability Insurance, Office of Program Operations; *Social Security Administration, U.S. Department of Health, Education, and Welfare*
- Paul Willging, Deputy Commissioner, Medical Services Administration, *Social and Rehabilitative Services, U.S. Department of Health, Education, and Welfare*
- Douglas Besherov, Director, National Center on Child Abuse and Neglect, *Office of Human Development, U.S. Department of Health, Education, and Welfare*

- Dr. E. Cuyler Hammond, Vice President for Epidemiology and Statistics, *American Cancer Society*

JULY 21, 1976

- David O. Cooke, Deputy Assistant Secretary of Defense for Administration; William T. Cavaney, Executive Secretary, Defense Privacy Board; Herbert Hainer, Office of Assistant Secretary of Defense for Health Affairs; Captain L.T. Schaffner, Medical Service Corps, U.S. Navy; Major W.L. Augsburger, Medical Service Corps, U.S. Army; Lt. Col. James W. Johnson, Office of Judge Advocate, U.S. Air Force; Major Stuart S. Myers, Biomedical Sciences Corps, U.S. Air Force; Robert D. Seaman, Assistant Legal Counsel, Office of Civil Health and Medical Program for Uniformed Services; *U.S. Department of Defense*
- Dr. Lawrence B. Hobson, Deputy Assistant Chief Medical Director for Research and Development, Department of Medicine and Surgery; R.L. Carpenter, Director, Administrative Services, Department of Veterans Benefits; Joseph L. Erwin, Chief, Policies and Procedures, Medical Administration Services, Department of Medicine and Surgery; Ralph Smith, Director, Systems Development Services, Department of Veterans Benefits; John DeLeo, Assistant General Counsel; William F. Lelfrick, Attorney; Eugene O'Neill, Assistant Deputy Director, Policy and Planning; David Van Hooper, Hardware Manager, Target Systems, Department of Veterans Benefits; *U.S. Veterans Administration*
- Dr. Vergil Slee, President, CPHA; Roland J. Loup, Data Quality Control Manager, CPHA; Edward B. Codd, Director, Research and Development, CPHA; George I. Tebbel, Partner, Ernst and Ernst; all on behalf of the *Commission on Professional and Hospital Activities (CPHA)*

Credit Reporting and Payment Authorization Services

AUGUST 3, 1976

- The Honorable William Proxmire, Chairman; Ralph Rohner, Staff Counsel; *Committee on Banking, Housing and Urban Affairs, United States Senate*
- James C. Millstone, Assistant Managing Editor, *St. Louis Post Dispatch*
- Howard A. Slayback, President; David Slayback, Vice President, *O'Hanlon Reports, Inc.*
- W. Lee Burge, President and Chief Executive Officer, *Equifax Services, Inc.*; R. N. Jones, President, *Equifax Services, Inc.*; and Jeffrey V. White, President, *Credit Bureau Incorporated of Georgia*

AUGUST 4, 1976

- The Honorable Jake Garn, *U.S. Senator, Utah*
- Jeremiah S. Gutman, on behalf of *American Civil Liberties Union*
- John L. Spafford, President; D. Barry Connelly, Vice President, Public Affairs/Public Relations, Associated Credit Bureaus, Inc.; Clarke Newlin, President, ACB Services, Inc.; Don Ogden, Credit Bureau of Monroe, Wisconsin; Glen Uffman, Credit Bureau of Baton Rouge, Louisiana; all on behalf of *Associated Credit Bureaus*
- Edward J. Brennan, Jr., Vice President and General Manager; Sheri L. Cole; Government Relations Staff; *TRW Information Services Division, TRW Credit Data*
- J. E. R. Chilton, III, Chairman of the Board; Van Smith, President; James Sutton, Counsel; *Chilton Corporation*
- Richard P. Erichson, President; Rene P. Daussin, Jr., Vice President; *Credit Bureau Reports, Inc.*

AUGUST 5, 1976

- Hamilton B. Mitchell, Chairman of the Executive Committee; Harold T. Redding, Senior Vice President; *Dun and Bradstreet*
- Stephen S. J. Hall, Chief Executive Officer; Joshua Kalkstein, Corporate Counsel; *Hooper-Holmes Bureau, Incorporated*
- Mr. Michael Goldgar, Atlanta, Georgia
- Floyd Denee, Executive Vice President, *Telecredit, Inc.*
- Christian S. White, Assistant Director; Lee Peeler, Assistant to the Assistant Director, Division of Special Statutes; *U.S. Federal Trade Commission*

Educational Institutions

OCTOBER 7, 1976

- Dr. James Taylor, Deputy Superintendent; Merle Tracy, Director, Pupil Services and Attendance Branch; Richard W. Green, Chief Security Agent; David Bower, Director, Counselling and Psychological Services; Walker Brown, Principal, Van Nuys Senior High School; Owen Cornell, Principal, Utah Street High School; William Zazueta, Principal, Edison Junior High School; Dr. Dorothy Lyons, Director, Health Services; Dr. Everett Waxman, Legal Advisor; *Los Angeles Unified School District*
- Ms. Roberta Fiedler, *Citizens Advisory Committee on Integration*
- Gigi Ray, Los Angeles, California
- Robert Feran, Los Angeles, California
- Stefan Jovanovich, J.D., *Urban Policy Research Institute*

- Rosa Lopez, Executive Director, *Parent Education Center, Parents Involved in Community Action*
- Dr. Scott Gray, Assistant Superintendent; John Griffith, Director of Research; Daniel Nasman; *San Diego Unified School District*

OCTOBER 8, 1976

- Captain W. J. Riddle, Commander, Juvenile Services; Lt. Alfred R. Bongard; Investigator William Johnston, Juvenile Services Division; *Los Angeles Police Department*
- Lt. Raymond Gott, Youth Services Bureau, *Los Angeles Sheriff's Office*
- Carole Thurston; Barbara Simons; Students Rights Center; *American Civil Liberties Union*
- Marilyn Kizziah, Los Angeles, California
- Ronald Vera, *California Rural Legal Assistant*
- Martin Flam, *El Monte Legal Office*
- Ernest Gutierrez, Los Angeles County, California
- Betty Lindsay, President, *31st District, Parent-Teachers Association*, Los Angeles Unified School District
- Alan F. Charles, Assistant Chancellor-Legal Coordinator, *University of California, Los Angeles*
- Mayer Chapman, General Counsel; William Knight, Counsel; *The California State University and Colleges*
- Dr. Catherine Fink, Assistant Dean for Student Affairs and Member, Admissions Committee, Medical School, *University of California, Los Angeles*
- Judy Samuelson, Co-Director, *University of California Student Lobby, University of California, Sacramento*

NOVEMBER 11, 1976

- Keith Spalding, President, *Franklin and Marshall College*
- Richard H. Francis, Staff Assistant, on behalf of *National Association of Independent Colleges and Universities*
- Martin I. J. Griffin, Jr., Associate Dean, Yale College and Dean of Undergraduate Studies; James A. Mau, Associate Dean, Graduate School; and John B. Latella, Assistant Legal Advisor; *Yale University*
- Gerald K. Bogen, Vice President for Student Affairs, University of Oregon, representing the *National Association of State Universities and Land Grant Colleges*
- L. Orin Slagle, Dean; Thomas White, Director of Law Programs; *Ohio State University College of Law*
- Ralph Nader; Allan Nairn, Administrative Associate; *Center for the Study of Responsive Law*
- Ms. Evelyn Schroedl, Assistant Registrar, *Goucher College*

- William C. Spann, Associate Director of Registration and Records, *University of Maryland*

NOVEMBER 12, 1976

- Robert Solomon, Executive Vice President; Ernest Anastasio, Director for Research Administration; Dwight H. Horch, Program Director of Financial Aid Program; Robert E. Smith, Acting Vice President; Thomas O. White, Director of Law Programs; John A. Winterbottom, Special Assistant, Office of the President; John Kramer, General Counsel; *Educational Testing Service*
- John R. Dilworth, Director, *College Entrance Examination Board Systems*
- Frank Till, Director of Information Services, *National Student Association*
- Jo Ann Weinberger, Special Assistant to the Director, Research for Better Schools, on behalf of *American Educational Research Association*
- Dr. Henry Shetterly, Director, Division of Public Services; William Riley; Special Assistant to the Superintendent; *Montgomery County Schools*
- Dr. Stuart Sandow, Associate, *National Committee for Citizens in Education*
- Thomas McFee, Deputy Assistant Secretary for Management Planning and Technology; Edward J. Gleiman; Director, Fair Information Practice Staff; and Steven N. Schatken, Chief of Special Services Branch, Education Division, Office of General Counsel; *U.S. Department of Health, Education, and Welfare*

Employment and Personnel Records

DECEMBER 9, 1976

- Richard B. Stoner, Vice President; Ted L. Marston, Vice President of Personnel; F. J. Loughrey, Manager, Research Information Systems; *Cummins Engine Company*
- James Mazzi, District Two; John Morgan, Special Assistant to the President; Sharon Gorka; *Communications Workers of America, AFL-CIO*
- Edward A. Robie, Senior Vice President; Joseph J. DeGennaro, Executive Assistant; Edward S. Cabot, Assistant General Counsel; *The Equitable Life Assurance Society of the United States*
- Helen S. Lessin, Attorney-Advisor, Office of General Counsel, *Law Enforcement Assistance Administration, U. S. Department of Justice*

- Aryeh Neier, Executive Director, *American Civil Liberties Union*
- John Morris, Consultant, Payroll Practices and Insurance Benefits; Christopher Barreka; Office of the General Counsel; *General Electric Company*

DECEMBER 10, 1976

- Walton E. Burdick, Vice President, Personnel Plans and Programs, *International Business Machines Corporation*
- John R. Lanahan, Assistant Comptroller-Systems; David D. Byrne, Assistant Director of Personnel; David Birch; Gene Nichols Simons; Clark L. Wagner; George L. Yoxall; *Inland Steel Company*
- Robert J. Drummond, Jr., Director; Llewellyn M. Fischer, Associate General Counsel; *Bureau of Personnel Investigations, U. S. Civil Service Commission*
- Franklin A. Owens, Jr., Director, *Maryland State Employment Service*
- Charles B. Farr, Manager of Personnel Relations; Charles R. Lotter; *J.C. Penney Company, Inc.*

DECEMBER 16, 1976

- C. Hoyt Anderson, Director, Personnel Relations and Research Office; W. H. Corrigan, Manager, Security Department; A. W. Hanlon, Manager, Employment Practices and Programs Department and Labor Relations Staff; N. C. Kiefer, Supervisor, Administrative Analysis and Services; Dr. D. C. Laderach, Associate Medical Director, Medical Services; Donald S. Martin, Personnel Relations Manager; *Ford Motor Company*
- David Addleston, Deputy Director for Litigation, *National Military Discharge Review Project*; Barton Stichman, Litigation Counsel, *Georgetown University Law Center*
- Frederick W. Oswald, Vice President, Personnel; Robert W. Keith; Vice President; *Manufacturers Hanover Trust Company*
- John Fillion, General Counsel; Doris Siegner, Research Associate; *United Auto Workers*

DECEMBER 17, 1976

- Norbert Roberts, M.D., Medical Director, *Exxon Corporation*
- Bruce W. Karrh, M.D., Assistant Medical Director, Medical Division, *E. I. Dupont de Nemours and Company*
- Anthony Mazzocchi, Legislative Director, *Oil, Chemical and Atomic Workers International Union*
- Daniel Steiner, General Counsel; Daniel Cantor, Director of Personnel; *Harvard University*

- Robert E. Olsen, Director of Central Payroll, Personnel Operations; Edwin C. McManus, Staff Vice President, Employee Benefit Programs; Robert H. Murphy, Staff Vice President, Executive and Management Development; John W. Dale, Director of Industrial Security; Robert V. Underwood, Director, Personnel Practices for West Coast Operations; Marilyn P. Maledon, Assistant General Counsel; *Rockwell International*
- Constance L. Dupre, Associate General Counsel, *U. S. Equal Employment Opportunity Commission*
- Walter Davis, Special Assistant to the President, *Retail Clerk's International Union*

Research and Statistics

JANUARY 5, 1977

- Wray Smith, Director, Office of Technical Support and Statistics; Dr. Robert S. Slevin, Privacy Act Coordinator, N.F.H. Public Health Service; Thomas Jabine, Chief Mathematical Statistician, Social Security Administration; Dr. Robert S. Gordon, Jr., Special Assistant to the Director, National Institutes of Health; Robert Muggee, Assistant to the Director, National Center for Health Statistics; Darwin Stolzenbach, Manager, National Center for Education Statistics; Dr. John Michael, National Center for Education Statistics; *U.S. Department of Health, Education and Welfare*
- Vito Natrella, Director, Statistics Division; James Keightley, Office of Chief Counsel, Disclosure Division; Walter E. Bergman, Director, Research and Operations Analysis Division; *U.S. Internal Revenue Service*
- Dr. Lawrence B. Hobson, Deputy Assistant Chief Medical Division; Rufus Carpenter, Director, Administrative Services; Eugene O'Neil, Legal Consultant, Compensation and Pension Division; *U. S. Veterans Administration*
- Thomas Madden, General Counsel; Helen Lessin, Attorney, Advisor and Privacy Officer; Carol Kaplan, Director, Security and Privacy Staff; *Law Enforcement Assistance Administration; U.S. Department of Justice*
- David O. Cooke, Deputy Assistant Secretary of Defense for Administration; Kenneth Scheflen, Office of Manpower; Col. Aurelio Nepa, Jr., Defense Privacy Board; Col. Gary Johnson, Office of Manpower and Reserve Affairs; Col. James Johnson, N.S.A.F. JAG.; Commander Paul Nelson, Naval Research Development Command; *U.S. Department of Defense*
- Donald Keuch, Associate Commissioner, *U.S. Department of Labor*

- Joseph Duncan, Deputy Associate Director, *U. S. Office of Management and Budget*

JANUARY 6, 1977

- Geraldine Brubar, Senior Attorney; Robert Gellman, Attorney-Advisor, Office of the General Counsel; *General Accounting Office*
- Joseph L. Gastwirth, Chairman, *American Statistical Association*
- Robert F. Boruch, *American Psychological Association*
- N. J. Demerath, III, *American Sociological Association*
- David Flaherty, *The Ford Foundation Study*
- David M. Levy, Associate Director, *National Legal Aid and Defender Association*
- Eliot Friedson, Chairman, Department of Sociology, New York University
- Arthur R. Miller, Professor of Law, Harvard University
- Stanley Seashore, Professor of Psychology, University of Michigan
- James D. Carroll, Professor, Syracuse University
- Charles Knerr, Professor, University of Texas at Arlington
- Paul Nejelski, Assistant Executive Secretary, *Connecticut Judicial Department*
- Irving Crespi, Vice President, *Mathematica Policy Research*
- Edward Bryant, President, *Westat Corporation*
- Kenneth Prewitt, Director, *National Opinion Research Center*
- Marshall Greenburg, Senior Vice President, *National Analyst*

Public Assistance and Social Services

JANUARY 11, 1977

- David Levy, Associate Director, *National Legal Aid and Defender Association*
- Richard Weishaupt, Attorney, *Philadelphia Community Legal Services*
- Gary Yoh, Acting Executive Director, *Pennsylvania Legal Services Center*
- Barry Powell, Acting Deputy Assistant Bureau Director for Operations, Supplemental Security Income; Robert Trazzi, Director, Division of General Policy, Office of Policy and Regulations; Bruce Dailey, Office of Operations Systems and Coordination, Office of Program Operations; Dale Anderson, Bureau of Supplemental Security Income; Paul Gasparotti, State Systems and Procedures Branch; *Social Security Administration, U.S. Department of Health, Education, and Welfare*
- Nancy M. Snyder, Director, Food Stamp Division, Food and Nutrition Service, *U.S. Department of Agriculture*

- Jeffrey Kirsch, Staff Member, *Food Research Action Center*
- Ronald Lang, Director of Special Services; Dennis Erickson, Assistant Director of Special Services; *Minnesota Department of Public Welfare*
- Dennis Maher, Assistant County Attorney, *Henepin County, Minnesota, Department of Welfare*
- James Bryan, Counsel to the *Special State Prosecutor for Health and Social Services, New York State*

JANUARY 12, 1977

- Gloria Chevers, Director, Standards Department, *Child Welfare League of America*
- Max Waldgear, Deputy Commissioner, *Department of Social Services, New York City*
- Bernard Henault, Second Vice President; George Moore, Member of the Board; *National Clients Council*
- Paul Allen, Chief Deputy Director, *Michigan Department of Social Services*
- John Townsend, Assistant Commissioner for Coordination; Alton W. Ashworth, Jr., Director, Special Projects Bureau; Sherron L. Eberle, Planner, Advanced Technology and Systems Evaluation Division; Clifton Martin, Chief Administrator of Social Services; Howard Smith, Director of Investigations; Frederick J. Biel, General Counsel; Ray Barron, Director, Parent Locator Service; *Texas State Department of Public Welfare*
- Maudine Cooper, Deputy Director, Washington Bureau, *National Urban League, Inc.*
- Delores Delahanty, Co-Chairman, *Kentucky Commission on Computer-Stored Information and Personal Privacy*
- Robert Cohen, Staff, *National Association of Social Workers*
- Dorothy Forney, Co-Founder and Member of the Board, *National Welfare Fraud Association*
- Carol Puleio, Deputy Director, *Board of Welfare, Middlesex County, New Jersey*

JANUARY 13, 1977

- Steven Cole, Deputy Director, *Center on Social Welfare Policy and Law*
- Larry Bolton, Attorney, *State Department of Benefits Payments, Legal Affairs Division, California*
- Peter Pennington, Acting Executive Director; William Atkinson, General Counsel, *Governor's Council on Drug and Alcohol Abuse, Pennsylvania*
- Nicholas Norton, Commissioner, Assistance Payments Administration; Dr. M. Keith Weikel, Commissioner, Medical

Services Administration; Michio Suzuki, Deputy Commissioner, Public Services Administration; Louis B. Hays, Deputy Director, Office of Child Support Enforcement; *U. S. Department of Health, Education, and Welfare*

• Jerry Shroder, Director of Information Services, *Community Council of Greater New York*

Investigative Reporting Agencies

JANUARY 26, 1977

• John S. Ammarell, Executive Vice President; James E. Hastings, Vice President, General Counsel; Warren W. Altmann, Director of Investigations; *Wackenhut Corporation*

• Eugene Fey, Executive Vice President, Pinkerton's, Inc.; Ralph McAfee, Counsel, Crevath, Swaine and Moore, New York, New York; both on behalf of *Pinkerton's, Inc.*

• John Duffy, President; Garris Distlehorst, Executive Director, *National Council of Investigations and Security Services, Inc.*

• Sorrel Wildhorn, Senior Staff Member, *Rand Corporation*

Index

Access by individuals to records
    authorization service records 80-81
    credit bureau records 80-81
    credit grantor records 77-78
    depository records 109
    education records 420, 423-25
    employment records 253-261
    generally 17, 18, 34
    insurance records 199-204
    medical records 288-289, 291, 293, 295-300, 512
    public assistance and social services records 465-469
    research and statistical records 599
    See also Privacy Act of 1974
Access by parents or guardians to records 512
Actual Damages. *See* Damages, special
Adams, John 345
Administrative summons 53, 367-373, 376, 379, 556
    See also Government access to personal records, Subpoena
Admissions records 406-407, 424, 434-435
Adoption records 468
Adverse decisions
    credit 11, 78-80
    depository 109-111
    FCRA 79-80
    generally 18, 28, 35, 67, 68-71
    insurance 18, 208-212
Age Discrimination and Employment Act 227
Aid to Families with Dependent Children .. 446, 448, 449, 450, 451, 453,
    454, 459, 460, 462, 465, 467, 469, 472, 473, 475, 478, 479, 480, 482,
    483
Alexander, Donald 370, 390, 562
American Civil Liberties Union 349
American College Testing Program 410
American Express Co. 44, 45, 49, 350
American Hospital Association 290, 305, 311
American Insurance Association
    Burglary and Theft Loss Index 166

Fine Arts Loss Index 166
Fire Marshall Reporting Service 166
generally 165-167
loss indexes 167-169
American Medical Association 305
American Medical Record Association 282
American Psychiatric Association 286, 314
American Statistical Association 586
American Telephone & Telegraph Co. 33, 356
Arrest records 16, 242-247, 534-535
Associated Credit Bureaus, Inc. 47
Atlantic Richfield Co. 49
Authentication, generally 605-608
Authorization of disclosure
  credit records 85-87
  depository records 113
  education records 414
  generally 17, 19, 21, 22, 33, 38
  insurance records 196-198
  medical records 289, 314-316
Automated Clearinghouse
  description 113-115
  impact on financial records 116-119
  See also Electronic funds transfer, U.S. Federal Reserve System
Automation. See Computers and telecommunications

BankAmericard 44
Bank records 8, 9, 10, 20, 34, 35, 347, 350, 356, 357, 383
  See also Bank Secrecy Act, Checking account records, Savings account
  records
Banks, commercial 38, 101-105, 114-115, 117, 119
Bank Secrecy Act of 1970 .... 103-105, 347-348, 386, 388
Barz Lag List 333
Bay View Federal Savings & Loan Assn. of California 49
Bell, Griffin 564
Billing
  country club 46
  descriptive 46
  disputes 17
  generally 17
Black, Hugo L. 383
Blue Cross-Blue Shield 156, 195, 286
Boston Tea Party 390
Buckley Amendments. See Family Educational Rights and Privacy Act
Buckley, James L. 412
Burrows v. Superior Ct. 362

California
  constitutional right to privacy 351, 352, 357, 361-362

court of appeals 362
generally 32, 405
insurance department 182, 186, 187, 189
labor code 227
Special Circumstances Program 451
State Emergency Loan Program 451
Supreme Court 351, 362
Carlson v. Superior Ct. 362
Checking account records 20, 101-103, 347-348
Child Support Enforcement Program 447, 451, 482
Chilton Corp. 56
Church League of America 333
Citibank 47
Civil Rights Act of 1964 488
Collection agencies 60, 62
College Entrance Examination Board 410
Commercial-credit relationship 88-100
Commercial reporting services 11, 38, 88-96
Commercial Speech Doctrine. *See* Constitution, U.S., First Amendment
Commission on Professional and Hospital Activities 387
Commission on Uniform State Laws 198
Community Action for Legal Services, Inc. 465
Community Mental Health Programs 451
Compliance monitoring 522-524, 532, 533
Comprehensive Employment and Training Program 451
Compulsory legal process. *See* Administrative summons, Government
   access to personal records, Subpoena
Computer service bureau 127, 132
Computers and telecommunications
   automating records
      credit records 11, 61, 63
      medical records 289-290
   generally 11, 12, 13
   government uses of 105, 122-124, 526-527, 532-536
Conference on Ethical and Legal Aspects of School Record Keeping ... 412
Confidentiality, legitimate expectation of
   assertible interest 352, 360-362
   breach of 358
   consumer-investigative reports 343
   credit records 85-87
   definition of 19-21, 360-363
   depository records 112-113
   education records 402-403, 409-410, 425-427
   generally 13, 15, 26, 27, 35, 42, 71
   insurance records 156, 179, 183, 185, 214
   medical records 305-316
   need for 347-348, 352, 360-361, 384-385
   research and statistical records 587-595

See also Government access to personal records

Congress, U.S.

generally 189, 362, 370, 379, 382, 385-386, 387-388, 519, 531,
538, 539, 542, 552, 556, 559, 562, 564-565

House of Representatives

Committee on Government Operations 239

Committee on Ways and Means 559

Committee on the Judiciary 349

Joint Committee on Taxation 555

Senate

Committee on Finance 559

Committee on the Judiciary, Subcommittee on Constitutional
Rights 239

Select Committee on Intelligence Activites 365, 390

Constitution, U.S.

Bill of Rights 345, 346, 374

commerce clause 488

generally 382

First Amendment 21-24, 513, 514-515, 577

Fourth Amendment . 7, 20, 345, 349, 352, 353, 354, 356, 363-364,
367, 382, 391, 556

Fifth Amendment . 20, 345, 349, 353, 364, 374, 375, 379, 382-383,
556, 577

Sixth Amendment 577

Tenth Amendment 29

Fourteenth Amendment 22, 488

privacy in 355, 391

spending clause 488

welfare clause 488

Consumer Investigative Reports. *See* Investigative reporting agencies

Continental Illinois National Bank & Trust Company of Chicago . 49, 349-350

Conviction Records 245, 246, 534-535

Correction and amendment of records

credit 69-71, 98-99

education 423-424

electronic funds transfer 122

employment 260-264

generally 11, 13, 14, 18, 30

insurance 204-208

medical 299-303

public assistance and social services 469-471

Cost of protecting privacy 12, 21, 27, 31, 35, 531

Credit, definition of

closed end 41

open end 41

Credit Bureau of Greater Houston 55-56

Credit bureaus

confidentiality of records 86-87
generally 9, 10, 12, 42, 55-65
inaccuracies in records 80-82
operations 59
Credit Bureau, Inc. 55-56
Credit Card Authorization Service 11, 44-46
Credit Card Issuer Survey 54-55, 357
Credit grantors
confidentiality of records 85
credit-card issuer 5, 20, 41, 45, 46
disclosure of records to government 52-55
disclosure of records to support organizations 47-52, 83-84
generally 9, 10, 11, 16, 17, 21, 38, 42-55, 66
quality control in record keeping 60-62
See also Access by individuals to records, Adverse decisions, Authorization of disclosure, Confidentiality, legitimate expectation of, Fairness in record keeping, Investigative reporting agencies
Credit guide, definition of 58
Credit reports. *See* Credit bureaus, Investigative reporting agencies
Credit unions 101-105
Criminal Justice Information Systems 534-536
Cummins Engine Company 235

Damages
general 530-532
generally 35
special 530-532
Day, Neil M. 160, 161
Defamation 22, 28, 30, 530
Denver, Colorado Grand Jury 285
Depository and Lending Institutions Hearings 349
Depository Institutions 18, 20, 38
See also Banks, commercial, Savings and loan associations
Depository institution records. *See* Bank records, Bank Secrecy Act, Checking account records, Savings account records
Direct-mail advertising 125
Direct-mail marketing. *See* Mailing lists
Direct-Mail Marketing Association (DMMA) 141, 145-146
Directory information 26, 270, 272, 440
Donaldson v. United States 360
Douglas, William O. 101, 383
Drug and Alcohol Abuse Community Services Programs (HEW) .. 27, 451
Drug and alcohol abuse legislation 292, 314
Drug Enforcement Administration 131
Dun & Bradstreet 89-93, 335

Eagleton, Thomas 294
Education records
desk-drawer notes 423, 439

disclosure to law enforcement 409-410, 421-422, 442-443
disclosure to social service agencies 441-442
elementary and secondary 5, 399-401
generally 11, 26, 34, 39
post-secondary 406-408
use for research and statistics 402-403, 440-441
    See also Access by individuals to records, Authorization of disclosure,
    Confidentiality, legitimate expectation of, Fairness in record
    keeping, Family Educational Rights and Privacy Act
Educational Testing Service 410
Electronic funds transfer
    description 113-116
    generally 9, 38
    government operation 122-124, 349
    impact on financial record keeping 116-119
Ellsberg, Daniel 294
Employer-employee relationship 5, 6, 16, 19, 32, 223-275, 515
Employment records
    constitutional protection of 357, 361
    employer duty of confidentiality 270-273
    generally 16, 17, 34
    payroll 263
    See also Access by individuals to records, Fairness in record keeping,
    Investigative reporting agencies, Polygraph
Employee Retirement Income Security Act 227, 545
Epidemiological research 280, 309-310
Equal Credit Opportunity Act 66, 67, 93-94, 107, 108, 110, 111, 112,
                                                    187, 227, 233,488
Equal Employment Opportunity Act 488
Equifax Inc. 89, 93, 95, 320, 321, 332, 336
Executive Order 9397 616-617
Expectation of confidentiality. See Confidentiality, legitimate expectation of

Factual Service Bureau 174, 190, 191, 285-287, 294, 303, 304, 334
Fair Credit Billing Act 47, 67, 69, 108, 113, 122
Fair Credit Reporting Act ... 10, 13, 32, 34, 57, 61, 65, 68, 69, 72, 107,
    110, 111, 112, 159, 161, 162, 175, 177, 182, 185, 190, 194, 198, 199,
    200, 203, 204, 207, 208, 209, 210, 227, 231, 240, 241, 249, 250, 251,
                        252, 256, 257, 261, 272, 326, 337-343, 489, 491
Fairness in record keeping
    generally 17-19, 42
    credit records 75-84, 97-99
    depository records 108-112
    education records 422-425, 432-437
    employment records 235-238
    insurance records 156, 175, 183, 191
    medical records 242-268, 295-304
    propagation of corrections 12, 18, 81-92
    public assistance and social services records 470-472

Family Educational Rights and Privacy Act of 1974
    experience under 416-418
    generally 17, 251, 394-395, 411-413, 493
    origins 411-413
    DHEW regulations 415-416
    requirements of 413-415
    See also Education records
Family Planning Projects 451
Federal Information Processing Standards 527
Federal Insurance Administrator 189
Federal preemption 32
Federal Privacy Board 37
Federal Register 447
Federal Reports Act 573, 589
Federal Reserve System. *See* U.S. Federal Reserve System
Federal Tax Return Confidentiality 481
Finance America Corporation 50
Follow Through Program 451
Food Stamps Program 447, 448, 450, 451, 466, 468, 473, 479
Ford Motor Company 274
Freedom of Information 21, 24, 25
Freedom of Information Act ... 22, 25, 130, 131, 293, 368, 520-521, 522,
                                          524, 590, 594

Functional Separation
    principle of, ... 572-574, 575
    compliance with, ... 574-587

Gate-keeping function, definition of 291
Getman v. N.L.R.B. 131
General Electric Corporation 246
Goldgar, Michael 95-96
Government, ability to violate individual privacy increasing . 346, 380-381,
                                        384-387

Government access to personal records
    compulsory reporting requirements 27-28, 32, 353, 380-390
    generally 5, 8, 20, 24, 27, 52-55, 63, 356, 391
    informal 348, 357, 364-365
    voluntary disclosure by record keeper
        generally 349-350, 351-352, 356-359
        where legitimate 358-359
    through unreviewed executive discretion 366, 370, 372, 388, 391
    See also Law enforcement and investigative agencies, U.S. Depart-
        ment of Justice, U.S. Department of Treasury, Internal Revenue
        Service
Grand jury
    history 375-376
    indictment or presentment 374, 379
    standard of secrecy 374, 376-77
    See also Subpoena

Great Depression of 1930's 452

Harlan, John M. 382
Harvard Community Health Plan 313
Haydon, Julian 127
Head Start Program 451
Hippocratic Oath 283
"Hit list" 136

IBM 235, 246
Identification 605-608
Immunity of research and statistical records 579-581
Impairment Bureau, National Insurance Association .. 162, 164, 170, 175,
179, 206, 208, 213
Independent authorization service. *See* Credit card authorization services,
Independent check guarantee services
Independent check guarantee services 111-112
Information policy issues 532-536
Inner-Facts, Inc. *See* Factual Service Bureau
Insurance institution
definition of 221
Federal regulation 185-186, 203
generally 5, 9, 11, 17, 18, 19, 21, 26, 32, 35, 38, 155-223
life and health insurers 157-164
moral hazard 173, 187
property and liability insurers 164-165
self-insurer 169
State regulation 32, 185-186, 191, 203
Insurance records
confidentiality of 179-180, 183, 185
claims 26
disclosure within the industry 169-173, 213
generally 27, 31, 35, 347, 356
index system 166-170
maintained by an employer . 259, 260, 261, 262, 263, 264, 267, 268
underwriting 28, 31, 208-210
See also Access by individuals to records, Adverse decisions, American Insurance Association, Authorization of disclosure, Confidentiality, legitimate expectation of, Fairness in record keeping
Insurance support organizatons
definition of 221
generally 170-173, 190, 213, 299
inspection bureaus 165, 319-330
Insurance Crime Prevention Institute 170, 171, 172, 194, 219
See also Investigative reporting agencies
Internal Revenue Code 542, 544, 546-547
Internal Revenue Service. *See* U.S. Department of Treasury, Internal
Revenue Service
Intrusiveness

credit 42, 73-75, 96-97
depository 106-107
education 419-422, 432-433
employment 238-241
generally 14-17, 30
governmental mechanisms to assess relevance of information .. 73-74,
106-107, 186
insurance 156, 173-174, 183, 186-191
medical care 282
minimization of 14, 15-17
public assistance and social services 458-459, 514
See also Government access to personal records
Investigative reporting agencies
adverse information quotas 327-328
compliance with FCRA 337-340
consumer investigative reports 11, 34, 33, 257-258
generally 11, 18, 38, 196, 319-344
role of 319-328
in adversary situations 335
investigative interviews 16, 190, 198, 240
information collection practices 322, 325
See also Credit Bureaus, Private investigative agencies
Iowa Department of Social Services 472

J. C. Penney Company 43, 236, 245
Joint Commission on the Accreditation of Hospitals 287, 293, 310, 494
Jordan, Robert 149
Juvenile Delinquency Prevention Programs 472

Katz v. United States 361
Kislik, Louis 135
Krieger, Richard 135

Lamont v. Postmaster General 23, 24
Land of Lincoln Legal Assistance Foundation, Inc. 466
Larkin, Kenneth 139
Law enforcement and investigative agencies
collection of information 513, 519
disclosure of tax information to 553-558, 563
federal ... 364-366, 372, 376-378, 381, 386, 390, 391, 534-536, 555,
557
generally 21, 26, 27, 346, 353-355, 384, 393
records maintained by 355, 511, 534-536
sharing of information 354, 385-386, 534-536
unrestricted flow of information between 517-518, 563
See also Government access to personal records
Law School Admissions Council 410
Lender's Exchange, the 50-51
Licensing, professional 36, 243, 245

Limited disclosure, principle of. *See* Confidentiality, legitimate expectation of
Los Angeles Unified School District 398
Mail Preference Service 141, 144-146
Mailing Lists
    direct-mail marketing 141, 145-146, 156, 495
    exchange 132-133
    generally 11, 33, 34, 38, 126
    government agency maintainers 130-132
    negative check-off option 141-144
    multiple response compiler 137-138
    private record compilers 129-130
    public record compilers 127-129
    rental 132-133
    selectivity in 135-141
McCarren-Ferguson Act 31
Manley, Joan 135
Marchetti v. United States 382-383
Marine Index Bureau 170, 171
Master Charge 44, 47
Maternal and Child Health Services 451, 472
Medicaid
    generally 31, 387, 446, 447, 448-449, 451, 453, 460, 465
    fraud and abuse office 387
    operation of 488, 490, 483
    Medicaid management information system 387, 449
Medical-care institution
    definition of 277n
Medical-care provider
    definition of 277n
    generally 18, 21, 31, 38
Medical Information Bureau
    generally 10, 159, 160, 161, 162, 164, 169, 170, 175, 177, 178,
                    179, 200, 204, 206, 208, 213, 302, 319, 433
    company visit program 162, 163
Medical professional, definition of 277n
Medical record
    definition 278n
    generally 10, 11, 22, 26, 37, 38, 356, 383, 387
    information reporting requirements 310-311
    maintained by an employer . 258, 259, 261, 262, 263, 264, 266, 267
    problem-oriented 289
    third-party payment of claims 278
    safeguards against unauthorized disclosure 303-305
    third-party requests for 280-281, 290
    See also Access by individuals to records, Authorization of disclosure, Confidentiality, legitimate expectation of, Intrusiveness
Medicare 31

Military discharge records 10, 247-249
Miller, Mitchell 6
Millstone v. O'Hanlon Reports 337-340
Minor v. U.S. 380
Minnesota Data Privacy Act 467
Minnesota Department of Public Welfare 467
Model Unfair Trade Practices Act 181, 182
Mutual Savings Banks.. 101-105

National Association of Credit Management 89, 93
National Association of Insurance Commissioners 198
National Automobile Theft Bureau 167
National Center for Health Statistics 287
National Commission for the Protection of Human Subjects in Biomedical
   and Behavioral Science Research 597, 600
National Commission on Uniform State Laws 293
National Council of Citizens in Education 412
National Crime Information Center 535
National Driver Registry 614
National health insurance 316-17
National League of Cities v. Usery 489
National Research Act 597
National Technical Information Services 131
Negative check-off option. *See* Mailing lists
New York
   Code of Rules and Regulations 466
   drug reporting statute 381-382, 383, 384, 388
   New York City 465
Nicholas, Anthony 44

Occupational Safety and Health Act 227, 228, 273, 274
O'Hanlon Reports, Inc. 325
Ohio Department of Taxation 483
Older Americans Act 474-475
Omnibus Crime Control and Safe Streets Act 244
Oregon Division of Public Welfare 463
Organization, definition of 32-33

Parent Locator Service 482, 483, 484, 485, 516, 538-539, 551-553
Pension Benefit Guaranty Corporation 546
Per-Mar Security 331, 334
Personal Identification Number 114
Personnel. *See* Employer-employee relationship, Employment records
Pinkerton's, Inc. 331, 332, 334
Pittsburgh Press v. Human Relations Commission 23
Point-of-sale services. *See* Electronic funds transfer
Point scoring 11, 43, 44
Polygraph 238-240
Powell, Lewis F. 374

Pre-screening 48, 56, 139-141
Pretext Interviews 16, 190, 240
Privacy Act of 1974
    access by individual to record 508-512
    annual notice 522
    contractors and grantees 530
    correction and amendment 512-513, 524-525, 526
    generally 15, 17, 25, 32-33, 35, 36, 37, 39, 186, 187, 191, 195,
        204, 223, 225, 447, 481, 489, 490, 497-536, 538, 541, 576, 590,
               592-594, 595, 600, 611, 612, 613, 615
    Privacy Act Statement 513-514, 516, 522
    "routine-use" provision 516, 517-521
    system notices 518, 529, 536
    system of records 514, 525, 531
    unauthorized disclosures, criminal penalties for 522
Privacy Board, Federal 37
Privacy, legitimate expectation of 7, 351-352
    See also Confidentiality, legitimate expectation of
Private investigative agencies
    generally 163, 238, 239, 326
    preemployment investigations 330-331
    types, methods of information collection 332
    See also Investigative reporting agencies
Professional Standards Review Organization 279, 310
Psychological Stress Evaluator 239-240
Psychiatric Records. See Medical records
Public assistance and social services
    confidentiality of records 469-470, 472-480
    generally 34, 39, 445-486
    See also Access by individuals to records, Correction and amendment
        of records, Authorization of disclosure, Fairness in record keeping,
        Parent Locator Service
Public Health Service Act 474
Public records 9

R.L. Polk and Co. 128, 129, 130, 133
Railroad Reform Act 123
Railroad Retirement Board 517, 546
Regulatory and enforcement mechanisms 29, 30
Rehabilitation Act 228
Research and statistical records 39, 567-604
    See also Access by individuals to records, Confidentiality, legitimate
        expectation of, Education records, Epidemiological research, Fair-
        ness in record keeping
Retail Clerks Association 239
Reuben H. Donnelley Corporation 128, 129, 135
Richard A. Vigurie Co. 137, 138
Robert Morris Associates 98
Runaway Youth Program 451

Russell Sage Foundation 412, 419

Saint Elizabeths Hospital 289
Savings account records 101-103
Savings and Loan Associations 38, 101-105, 115, 117, 119
School Breakfast Program 451
School Lunch Program 451, 472
Secretary's Advisory Committee on Automated Personal Data Systems
    (DHEW) 611, 612
Search warrant 360, 363-364, 376, 391
Sears, Roebuck, and Co. 44
Security of records 526-528
Self-insurers. See Insurance institutions
Services for Crippled Children 472
Social Security Act
    generally 292-293, 515, 545, 609
    Title IV 448, 482, 484
    Title XIX, Social Services 448
    Title XX, Social Services 446, 447, 448, 449-450, 453, 454, 455,
                                   460, 464, 465, 472, 473, 474, 475, 480
Social Security Number
    as authenticator 609-610
    as identifier 609
    generally 39, 103, 105, 513, 515, 532, 605-618
    task force on 611
South Carolina Department of Social Services 462
Sovereign immunity 530-531
Special Program for the Aged 451
Special Supplement Food Program for Women, Infants, and Children . 451
SSADARS 526-527
    See also Computers and telecommunications
Standard Universal Identifier 614-615, 617-618
    See also Social Security Number
State and local government
    disclosure of tax information to 546-547, 558
    federal funding 380, 389
    generally 487-496
    government access 356, 380, 385, 387, 389
    insurance regulation 180
    relationship with Federal government ... 21, 29, 36, 37, 39, 487-489
Stewart, Potter 368, 370, 382
Study on Student Records in Higher Education 412
Subpoena
    duces tecum 368, 379
    generally 27, 312, 357, 359-379
    grand jury 373-379
    how issued 366-367
    in course of litigation 373, 379

See also Administrative summons, Government access to personal records
Supplemental Security Income 447-473

Tarver v. Smith 471
Tarver, Catherine 6, 470, 471
Tax Reform Act of 1976 .... 39, 360, 390, 542, 543-545, 612-613
Tax returns. *See* U.S. Department of the Treasury, Internal Revenue Service
Tax Return Confidentiality Hearings 483
Telephone
    providers of long-distance service 21, 27
    toll records 356
Tennessee Department of Human Services 463
Testimonial privilege 284-285, 358, 365
Testing and Data Assembly Service Organizations .. 410-411, 424-425, 433
Trade Verification Service 47n
Trans Union 55
Truth in Lending Act 30, 108, 113
Truth verification devices. *See* Polygraph
TRW
    Credit Data 48, 55, 65, 614
    Business Credit Services 89
    National Credit Information Services 93, 95

Unfair Claims Practices Act 181
United States v. Mandujano 374
United States v. Miller 20, 27, 34, 101, 106, 350, 351, 361, 377
U.S. Atomic Energy Commission 123
U.S. Attorney 366, 367, 376-377, 378
U.S. Bureau of the Census 25, 27, 128, 549, 570, 575, 577, 578, 579, 588, 589, 590
U.S. Central Intelligence Agency 54, 579
U.S. Civil Service Commission 25, 286
U.S. Courts
    Court of Appeals 7, 131, 359, 370
    district court 553-554
    Supreme Court   6, 7, 22, 23, 24, 29, 357, 361, 370, 374, 381, 382, 383-384, 385, 489, 556
U.S. Department of Agriculture
    Food and Nutrition Service 450
    generally 454, 460, 539
U.S. Department of Commerce, National Bureau of Standards ... 224, 290, 528
U.S. Department of Defense
    Form DD-214 247-250
    generally 297, 588
    industrial security regulations 229
    Separation Program Number 247-250
U.S. Department of Health, Education and Welfare

Food and Drug Administration 370
General Counsel of 593
generally 36, 293, 297, 307, 316, 454, 457, 465, 515-516, 551,
576, 577, 597, 609
National Center for Health Statistics 575, 576, 578
National Institute of Mental Health 286
Office of Education 33
Public Health Service 33, 288, 289
Secretary of 32-33, 456, 457, 576, 578
Social and Rehabilitation Services 460, 462
Social Security Administration 33, 448, 515, 516, 517, 526, 529,
545, 607, 608, 618
U.S. Department of Housing and Urban Development 369, 451
U.S. Department of the Interior 131
U.S. Department of Labor 274, 451, 546, 571, 588
U.S. Department of Justice
Attorney General 386, 554, 555, 564
Federal Bureau of Investigation 54, 245, 368, 377-378, 534-535
generally 54, 122, 377, 391, 517, 543, 544, 554, 555, 557, 560,
562, 564
Law Enforcement Assistance Administration 244, 488, 578
Marshal's Service 517
U.S. Department of Transportation 245, 614
U.S. Department of Treasury
Bureau of Alcohol, Tobacco and Firearms 6
Customs Service 103
generally 7, 103
Internal Revenue Service
Commissioner 370, 390, 542, 562
disclosure of taxpayer information to law enforcement agencies .
553-558
disclosure of third party source data 558-562
generally 21, 39, 54, 103, 122, 588, 606, 618
Special Service Staff 390
special study by 562-563
summons 349, 360, 361, 369-370
tax returns 25, 27, 549, 550-551
See also Internal Revenue Code, Tax Reform Act
Secretary of 542, 557, 559
U.S. Federal Deposit Insurance Corporation 245
U.S. Federal Home Loan Bank Board 105, 106
U.S. Federal Reserve System
Board of Governors 46, 76, 86, 113, 122, 123, 124
District Banks 105, 116, 119, 123
EFT 116, 117, 119, 122-124
generally 30, 36, 37
Regulation Z 30, 37

U.S. Federal Trade Commission .. 32, 36, 75, 78, 99, 107, 131, 139, 190, 191, 203, 210, 211, 241
U.S. General Accounting Office 559, 581, 582
U.S. Interstate Commerce Commission 123
U.S. National Academy of Sciences 587, 600
U.S. National Archives and Records Service 579, 580
U.S. National Labor Relations Board 25
U.S. Office of Management and Budget 296, 516, 519, 531, 585, 586, 589, 594
U.S. Postal Service 23, 125, 134, 146-147
U.S. Securities and Exchange Commission 103
U.S. Small Business Administration 88
U.S. Veterans Administration 131-132, 247-249, 297, 408

Virginia State Board of Pharmacy v. Virginia Citizens Consumer Council .. 23
Vocational Education Program 451
Voluntary compliance 34, 36

Wackenhut Corporation 333, 334, 336
Walsh, Dr. William B. 147
Washington, State of
    Department of Health and Social Services 470
    Department of Public Assistance 6
    Supreme Court 471
Watergate 391, 533
Welfare applications 26
Western Electric Employees Federal Credit Union 50
Westin, Alan F. 224, 281, 284, 290
White House, tax return disclosure to 550
Wildhorn, Sorrell 333
Willful interest 30
Wine Hobby U.S.A. Inc. v. Internal Revenue Service 131
Work Incentive Program 451, 459, 472

☆ U.S. Government Printing Office: 1977—237-994